# Pride of Smoketown:

## THE 1935 PITTSBURGH CRAWFORDS

*Edited By* FREDERICK C. BUSH & BILL NOWLIN
*Associate Editors* LEN LEVIN & CARL RIECHERS

Society for American Baseball Research, Inc.
Phoenix, AZ

*Pride of Smoketown: The 1935 Pittsburgh Crawfords*

Edited by Frederick C. Bush and Bill Nowlin

Associate editors Len Levin and Carl Riechers

Copyright © 2020 Society for American Baseball Research, Inc.

All rights reserved. Reproduction in whole or in part without permission is prohibited.

Front cover photograph courtesy of National Baseball Hall of Fame. Artistic treatment and colorization thanks to Ron A. Bolton and Don Stokes.

Rear cover photography courtesy of Noir-Tech Research Inc.

ISBN 978-1-970159-25-7

(Ebook ISBN 978-1-970159-24-0)

Book design: Rachael Sullivan

Society for American Baseball Research

Cronkite School at ASU

555 N. Central Ave. #416

Phoenix, AZ 85004

Phone: (602) 496-1460

Web: www.sabr.org

Facebook: Society for American Baseball Research

Twitter: @SABR

# CONTENTS

PREFACE AND ACKNOWLEDGMENTS.....5

1. **SAM BANKHEAD**
   *Dave Wilkie*..................7

2. **JAMES (COOL PAPA) BELL**
   *Dave Wilkie*..................14

3. **WILLIAM BELL**
   *Kevin Larkin and
   Frederick C. Bush*..................26

4. **TED BOND**
   *Richard Bogovich*..................34

5. **ERNEST "SPOON" CARTER**
   *Frederick C. Bush*..................41

6. **OSCAR CHARLESTON, PLAYER-MANAGER**
   *Tim Odzer*..................54

7. **JIMMIE CRUTCHFIELD**
   *William H. Johnson*..................64

8. **ROOSEVELT DAVIS**
   *Jay Hurd*..................69

9. **JOSH GIBSON**
   *William H. Johnson*..................75

10. **CURTIS "POPEYE" HARRIS**
    *Wes Singletary*..................82

11. **DAVID WILLIAM "BILL" HARVEY**
    *Matthew Clever*..................95

12. **CARL HOWARD**
    *Richard Bogovich*..................102

13. **HOW WE HAPPENED UPON HOWARD:** UNEXPECTED COLLABORATION LEADS TO INFORMATION ABOUT LITTLE-KNOWN NEGRO LEAGUE PITCHER
    *F.B., R.B., B.N.*..................108

14. **BERTRUM HUNTER**
    *Paul Hofmann*..................111

15. **WILLIAM "JUDY" JOHNSON**
    *Thomas Kern*..................117

16. **HARRY KINCANNON**
    *Margaret M. Gripshover*..................131

17. **LEROY MATLOCK**
    *Richard Bogovich*..................144

18. **CLARENCE "SPOONY" PALM**
    *Jon Henson*..................163

19. **ANDREW "PAT" PATTERSON**
    *William H. Johnson*..................179

20. **BILL PERKINS**
    *Bob LeMoine*..................184

21. **SAM STREETER**
    *Alan Cohen*..................190

22. **CHESTER WILLIAMS**
    *David Wilkie*..................199

23. **GUS GREENLEE, OWNER**
    *Brian McKenna* .................................. 206

24. **ROY SPARROW, PUBLICITY MAN**
    *Margaret M. Gripshover* .................. 211

25. **GREENLEE FIELD**
    *Jeb Stewart* ....................................... 222

26. **A NOTE ON ADDITIONAL PLAYERS WHO SOMETIMES APPEAR ON PITTSBURGH'S 1935 ROSTER**
    *Frederick C. Bush* ............................ 233

27. **SPRING TRAINING FOR THE 1935 PITTSBURGH CRAWFORDS**
    *Mark Blaeuer* .................................... 236

28. **1935 PITTSBURGH CRAWFORDS SEASON TIMELINE**
    *Bill Nowlin* ......................................... 241

29. **AUGUST 11, 1935:** THE EAST-WEST ALL-STAR GAME, COMISKEY PARK
    *Frederick C. Bush* ............................ 283

30. **SEPTEMBER 22, 1935:** PAIGE TAKES THE MONEY BUT NOT THE MOUND IN 12-2 WIN OVER PHILADELPHIA STARS, YANKEE STADIUM
    *Mark S. Sternman* ............................ 287

31. **THE 1935 NEGRO NATIONAL LEAGUE CHAMPIONSHIP SERIES:** PITTSBURGH CRAWFORDS V. NEW YORK CUBANS
    *Rich Puerzer* ..................................... 290

32. **GUS GREENLEE AND THE CRAWFORD GRILLS**
    *Leslie Heaphy* ................................... 296

33. **GUS GREENLEE AND THE EAST-WEST ALL-STAR GAME:** ORIGINS AND CONFLICT (1932-1944)
    *Duke Goldman* ................................. 300

34. **WHERE WAS SATCHEL IN 1935? PAIGE AND GREENLEE FEUDED AS CRAWFORDS RULED THE NNL**
    *Frederick C. Bush* ............................ 319

35. **KINGS OF THE HILL:** THE STORY OF THE PITTSBURGH CRAWFORDS
    *Jeremy Beer* ..................................... 328

**CONTRIBUTORS** .................................. 340

# PREFACE AND ACKNOWLEDGEMENTS

The 1935 Pittsburgh Crawfords team has become legendary and is often compared to the 1927 "Murderer's Row" New York Yankees. The squad from Smoketown – a nickname that the *Pittsburgh Courier* often applied to the metropolis better-known as "Steel City" – boasted four Hall of Fame players in outfielder James "Cool Papa" Bell, first baseman/manager Oscar Charleston, catcher Josh Gibson, and third baseman William "Judy" Johnson. Two other stalwarts, outfielder Sam Bankhead and pitcher William Bell, both were on the Hall of Fame ballot for the 2006 Special Committee on the Negro Leagues, though they fell short of induction. Add in stars like outfielder Jimmie Crutchfield, second baseman Andrew "Pat" Patterson, as well as pitchers Leroy Matlock and Sam Streeter, and it is easy to see why the Crawfords were dominant.

The "Murderer's Row" assertion may lend itself to argument among Negro League historians and aficionados. Certainly there were other teams in the history of the Negro Leagues that had better winning percentages and that dominated their respective leagues. The 1943 Homestead Grays, for instance, ruled the Negro National League with a 53-14-1 league mark and 78-23-1 record against all competitors. The Grays' .791 winning percentage in NNL play outdid the .662 percentage that the 1935 Crawfords posted via a 51-26-3 record. Perhaps the primary difference between these two squads lies in the era in which they played. The 1943 Grays' roster included five future Hall of Famers and had plenty of other stars, but many of their opponents did not have the same roster depth due to the loss of players to military service during World War II. Additionally, several of the 1943 Grays' stars had been members of the 1935 Crawfords – Bankhead, Cool Papa Bell, Gibson, and pitcher Ernest "Spoon" Carter – and contributed to the greatness of both teams. Fans of the Chicago American Giants and Kansas City Monarchs are also likely to prefer one of the dominant squads from each franchise's history. We say, "Let the debates commence."

It is true that, while the Crawfords won the NNL's first-half championship in 1935 and finished 10 games ahead of the Columbus Elite Giants, New York Cubans, and Philadelphia Stars in the composite standings, they were stretched to the limit by the Cubans in the NNL championship series. Nonetheless, the Crawfords prevailed in a tight seven-game affair to lay claim to the title of 1935 Negro National League champions.

The Crawfords might have dispatched the Cubans more easily had they had the services of Satchel Paige, who had been a member of the 1934 squad and who returned to Pittsburgh in 1936. As it was, Paige and Crawfords owner Gus Greenlee spent the 1935 season at odds with one another, and Paige pitched in various other locales. Since Paige was not a member of the 1935 Pittsburgh Crawfords, his biography is not included in the present volume. However, because Paige's shadow loomed large over the franchise, a feature article about the hurler's accomplishments in 1935 and a game article about Paige's failure to appear for a Crawfords game at Yankee Stadium in September of that year have been included here.

It bears mention that researching Negro League players and teams is an endeavor that often results in almost equal parts of exciting discoveries and frustrating disappointments. Press coverage of the leagues was inconsistent at best, and historical records are often incomplete or, in the case of certain items, impossible to find. Two brief articles address this challenge: one about players who only briefly appeared with the Crawfords in 1935 and another about the serendipitous circumstances that led to the inclusion of a biography about pitcher Carl Howard in this book.

Gratitude is due to our fact-checker Carl Riechers, who did an outstanding job with a daunting task. Thanks also go out to final copy editor Len Levin, whose deft touch improved every article in this book. We are grateful for all of the SABR members who have contributed their time, research, and writing to this book. This is the third SABR book about Negro League teams, and none of them would have come to fruition without the participation of so many dedicated members.

Additionally, our thanks go out to numerous individuals who have contributed in other ways, be it by providing information, photographs, or simply encouragement: SABR Negro League Committee Chair Larry Lester and his company Noir-Tech Research, Inc.; Jay-Dell Mah, who maintains the Western Canada Baseball website; Dr. Layton Revel and Larry Wilhelm at the Center for Negro League Baseball Research; Gary Ashwill at Seamheads.com (be sure also to visit his Agate Type website for information about Negro League and Latin American baseball); Robert D. Retort, author and publisher of *Pictorial Negro League Legends Album* for the use of several photographs; Shannon Crabtree of the *El Campo* (Texas) *Leader-News*; Chester Lee Moses and Monique Jeffers, the daughter and granddaughter of shortstop Chester Williams.

Thanks as well to several of the authors of various articles in the book for help and assistance on other portions of the book as well.

If we have neglected to mention anyone who provided assistance, please accept our apologies here.

We look forward to working with many of the same individuals, as well as new participants, on the next volume, which will feature the 1942 Kansas City Monarchs.

Frederick C. Bush
Bill Nowlin
March 2020

# SAM BANKHEAD

## By Dave Wilkie

*Sam Bankhead, here in a Homestead Grays uniform, played left field for the Crawfords. The longtime Negro League stalwart batted .338 in NNL games in 1935, which was his fourth professional season.*

(National Baseball Hall of Fame)

Hall of Famer and Negro League legend Judy Johnson called Sam Bankhead "one of the greatest outfielders we had."[1] Wilmer "Red" Fields, ace pitcher and 1948 World Series-winning Homestead Grays teammate, said, "He was the greatest team player I ever saw."[2] Blessed with a cannon for an arm, a penchant for clutch hitting, and the ability to play every position on the field, Sam enjoyed a 20-year-plus career playing with some of the most storied teams in baseball history. Left-handed slugger and All-Star Bob Harvey had this to say about Sam's throwing prowess: "He had a beautiful arm. Nobody tagged up at third and scored on a fly. He'd throw you out from the warning track."[3]

Samuel Howard Bankhead was most likely born on September 18, 1910, in Sulligent, Alabama.[4] His father, Garnett Bankhead Sr., labored in the coal mines and played first base in the Cotton Belt League, while his mother, Arie Armstrong, gave birth to five boys and two girls. Sam worked alongside his father loading coal until baseball led him to a better life.

# Pride of Smoketown

All four of Bankhead's younger brothers played in the Negro Leagues. Fred was a slick-fielding second baseman from 1936 to 1948, making an All-Star appearance in 1942. Garnett played for three seasons from 1947 to 1949, including a short stint on the 1948 champion Homestead Grays with his brother Sam as manager. Joe had the shortest career, taking the mound a few times with the 1948 Birmingham Black Barons, and Dan became the first black pitcher in major-league history when he took the mound on August 26, 1947. for the Brooklyn Dodgers. Dan also hit a home run in his first major-league at-bat, but his success was short-lived; he was out of the majors by 1951.

Sam Bankhead punched his ticket out of the coal mines and into his Negro League career in 1929 with the Birmingham Black Barons, but he did not get much playing time as an 18-year-old rookie. From 1930 to 1932 he bounced around with Birmingham and the Louisville Black Caps until he finally found a home and a starting position with the Nashville Elite Giants.

In 1933 Negro League baseball introduced its inaugural East-West All-Star Game, which has been called "the pinnacle of any Negro League season," and described as "an All-Star game and a World Series all wrapped in one spectacle."[5] The annual games were so popular and star-studded that many observers, including Negro League historian Larry Lester, have credited them with helping to integrate Organized Baseball. Bankhead, as he often did in high-pressure situations, shined in these contests. A nine-time all-star at five different positions, Sam had 12 hits in 31 at-bats with 7 runs, 4 RBIs, and 2 stolen bases. He is also credited with scoring the first run in an East-West All-Star Game. Coincidentally, the National and American Leagues also debuted the major-league All-Star Game in 1933, but by the early 1940s it was often being outdrawn by its Negro League counterpart.[6]

After a solid season in 1934, his last with the Nashville Elite Giants, Bankhead moved on to one of the greatest teams in Negro League history, the Pittsburgh Crawfords. The 1935 Crawfords squad included future Hall of Famers Josh Gibson, Oscar Charleston, Judy Johnson, and Cool Papa Bell. Mark Koenig, shortstop for the 1927 New York Yankees, compared the '35 Crawfords favorably to his legendary World Series-winning team.[7] Bankhead made a seamless transition into this team of superstars, hitting .298 and playing a starring role as one of the Raindrop Rangers, a trio of speedy outfielders with Sam playing alongside Bell and Jimmie Crutchfield. Fanciful legend had it that the three players were so fast that they could keep a field dry by catching the raindrops before they hit the ground.[8] The Crawfords capped off their magical season with a hard-fought seven-game victory over the New York Cubans in the Negro League World Series. Bankhead had a solid Series with seven hits, including a clutch single, stolen base, and run scored that gave Pittsburgh the lead in the seventh inning of the seventh game.[9]

The Crawfords began a steady decline in 1936. Bankhead had an off-year, hitting just .204. Though the Crawfords still ended up winning the Negro National League championship, no agreement could be reached with the Negro American League to play a World Series that year. After the season Gus Greenlee, owner of the Crawfords and creator of the East-West All-Star Game, was forced to cut payroll and players due to his involvement in racketeering. The Crawfords hung on through the 1938 season, but they were a mere shell of the team that dominated Negro League baseball from 1932 to 1936.

In 1937 Greenlee's misfortunes turned into a boon for Crawfords players Bankhead, Bell, Gibson, and Satchel Paige, as they were all recruited to play in the Dominican Republic for dictator Rafael Trujillo's Dragones team. Trujillo, a corrupt and violent leader, paid exorbitant salaries to these players in order to field a winning team to gain favor in the coming election. His two political opponents also fielded highly competitive teams made up largely of players raided from Negro League squads. The pressure on the

# THE 1935 PITTSBURGH CRAWFORDS

Trujillo players was such that they felt that winning the championship was a life-or-death endeavor. The team would often be locked up at night to ensure that they would be in tip-top shape for the next day's game.[10]

Bankhead posted a .309 batting average with 21 hits in 68 at-bats, but it was Gibson's .453 average and Paige's 8-2 record that led the Dragones to the championship game against San Pedro de Macoris. In that game Bankhead had the most dramatic at-bat of his career. The Dragones were trailing 5-4 in the seventh inning against Negro League All-Star pitcher Chet Brewer when Bankhead strode to the plate with Bell on first base. Bell recalled:

> Brewer knew Bankhead was a great clutch hitter and tried to be careful with him. Too careful. The count went to three and one. Brewer came in with some smoke, but he got it high. I thought Bankhead would drive the pitch, but he had a big cut and fouled it back. Then he connected on the three-two pitch. He was a line-drive hitter, and this one went way over the left field fence. We were pretty happy.[11]

Paige retired the final six batters, five on strikeouts, to ensure the victory. "I guess we helped Trujillo stay in office," claimed Bell,[12] but the players could not get out of the Dominican Republic fast enough.

Bankhead, like many other Negro League players, treated baseball like a year-round job, and the winter of 1937 found him playing for the Santa Clara Leopards in Cuba. This turned out to be one of his finest seasons as he led the league in several categories, including a .366 batting average, 89 hits, 5 triples, and 47 runs scored.[13] The Leopards finished with a 44-18 record and stood in first place in the final league standings.[14]

The year 1937 proved to be a busy one for Bankhead as he also married Helen M. Hall on February 25. The two had a daughter, Brenda, in 1939, and a son, Anthony, in 1941. Anthony

(Courtesy of Jay-Dell Mah/Western Canada Baseball)

*In addition to his 15-year Negro League career, Sam Bankhead also played in Cuba, Mexico, Puerto Rico, and Venezuela, and he was a member of Dominican dictator Rafael Trujillo's Santo Domingo team in 1937.*

was diagnosed with colon cancer in 1970 and died at the age of 29. Brenda's fate is unknown, and Helen died on October 10, 1985 in Pittsburgh.

Bankhead was known as Hall of Famer Josh Gibson's best friend and confidant.[15] Josh Gibson Jr. had this to say about their friendship: "I know that as far back as I can remember, Sammy was a constant. I don't think they were inseparable, 'cause my father didn't get that close to nobody. But they clicked out of mutual respect."[16] Unfortunately the two were also known for their legendary drinking prowess. Stories of drinking contests that lasted long into the night, drinking on buses, between doubleheaders, and sometimes even during games, can be found in every Gibson biography and article where Bankhead is mentioned. In 1947 Bankhead was managing in Caracas, Venezuela, when he received a telegram announcing Gibson's death. All-Star catcher,

Bill "Ready" Cash was there and had this to say: "Bankhead went out that night, got drunk, came in and tore up everything in his room. They had to send him home."[17]

Bankhead mended fences with Gus Greenlee in time to join the Pittsburgh Crawfords for the 1938 season. Greenlee had been upset that many of his star players had been lured to the Dominican Republic and had chosen money over loyalty. The Crawfords lacked star power that year as Gibson headed to the Homestead Grays while Bell and Paige played in the Mexican League. The Crawfords finished in fourth place with a 24-16 league record that placed them 4½ games behind Gibson's first-place Grays.

The year 1939 marked the end of the great Pittsburgh Crawfords franchise, as Greenlee Field was demolished and replaced with housing projects.[18] Bankhead started the season with the relocated but short-lived Toledo Crawfords; however, he quickly jumped to the Homestead Grays to play second base with his old friend Josh Gibson. Bankhead hit a solid .292, as the Grays won the Negro National League pennant, but lost the Negro League World Series to future Hall of Fame catcher Roy Campanella and his Baltimore Elite Giants. Bankhead went 7-for-23 in the series for a .304 batting average.

Throughout the 1930s and 1940s, the integration of black players into Organized Baseball was a hot topic for both black and white sportswriters. Bankhead's name often came up in such discussions. In 1936 William G. Nunn, city editor for the *Pittsburgh Courier*, wrote, "We don't believe the majors can produce three outfielders with the all-around ability of 'Cool Papa,' Bill Wright or Bankhead."[19] Two years later white sportswriter Jimmy Powers of the *New York Daily News* wrote about seven Negro League players who would guarantee the New York Giants a pennant and included Bankhead as his starting center fielder.[20] Even white superstar players like Honus Wagner, Dizzy Dean, and Paul Waner went to bat for integration, but their cries fell on the deaf ears of antiquated thinkers like Washington Senators owner Calvin Griffith, Philadelphia Athletics owner Connie Mack, and Commissioner Kenesaw Mountain Landis.[21] Sadly, the window of time closed on Negro baseball legends like Gibson, Leonard, Bell, Bankhead, and many others.

In the decade preceding Jackie Robinson's arrival in the major leagues, more than 100 players from the Negro Leagues played in Mexico.[22] Mexican business mogul and multimillionaire Jorge Pasquel was a big reason why. Pasquel, a strong and fearless leader,[23] wanted to turn the Mexican League into baseball's third major league. He lured dozens of black players south of the border by offering them salaries that were two to four times greater than what they were making in the States.

In 1940 Bankhead signed with the Monterrey Carta Blanco, playing shortstop and leading the league in stolen bases with 32. He had 122 hits in 384 at-bats for a .315 average, but his team finished the year nine games behind Pasquel's championship club, the Vera Cruz Azules.[24] The Azules fielded one of the most impressive line-ups in baseball history with Bell, Gibson, Ray Dandridge, Leon Day, Martin Dihigo, and Willie Wells, each of whom eventually received enshrinement in Cooperstown.

Bankhead signed with Monterrey again in 1941, which turned out to be career year for him as he tore up the league with 142 hits in 405 at-bats for a stellar .351 average. He hit 8 home runs, scored 74 times, stole 19 bases, and drove home 85 runs.[25] In spite of Bankhead's batting prowess, the Monterrey team finished in last place with a 43-59 record, 24 games behind the repeating champion Azules.[26]

At the conclusion of the 1941 Mexican League season, All-Star catcher Quincy Trouppe formed a barnstorming team that played throughout the United States. The team was called the Mexican League All Stars and included the familiar names of Bell, Dandridge, Wells, Gibson, and Bankhead. The team won all 10 of its games before disbanding for lack of financial support.[27] The well-traveled Bankhead then finished off the year by playing for the Ponce Leones in Puerto Rico.

Bankhead returned to the Negro Leagues with the Homestead Grays in 1942. Garnett Blair, pitcher for the Grays, said:

> Sam Bankhead to me was an outstanding player. He played shortstop and he would go behind third to get it and throw you out waist high across the diamond. He could not only play short, he could play second, third, he could play outfield, he could pitch, and he could catch. He was all around, so anytime I was pitching I said if that ball goes to Sam Bankhead, fine. There's nothing wrong with that, let it go there because if he got his glove on it, he was going to throw you out.[28]

Bankhead batted .283 while playing shortstop for the first-place Grays. On July 21, 1942, the *Mansfield* (Ohio) *News Journal* credited the Grays with a 79-4 record that included exhibition games.[29] The team reached the Negro League World Series but was quickly dismantled by Paige and the Kansas City Monarchs in five games.[30]

All the stars aligned for the Homestead Grays and Sam Bankhead in 1943, as the Grays finished the year with a 44-15 league record. Bankhead was second in the batting title race with an otherworldly .483 average.[31] The Grays won a hard-fought eight-game Negro League World Series against the Birmingham Black Barons.[32] With the Grays trailing 4-2 and two outs in the eighth inning, Bankhead delivered a clutch single to drive in what turned out to be the Series-winning runs.[33]

In what must have seemed like a foregone conclusion to the rest of the league, the Homestead Grays easily finished in first place in 1944 and 1945. Bankhead hit .345 in 1944 but slumped to .262 in 1945. The 1944 team once again met the Black Barons in the World Series and easily dispatched them in five games this time. Bankhead went 7-for-18 (.388) in the Series. The 1945 Series was a different story for the Grays as they were swept by future major leaguer Sam Jethroe and the Cleveland Buckeyes. In keeping with his subpar 1945 season, Bankhead had an uncharacteristically bad Series: 1-for-16 (.063).

The 1946 and 1947 seasons were both disappointments for the proud Homestead Grays. The 1946 team fell to third place with a losing record of 27-28, with Bankhead hitting .265. The 1947 squad finished in second place with a more respectable 38-27 record but Bankhead's average dipped to an anemic .246. A Grays team composed of aging veterans, Jackie Robinson's integration of major-league baseball, and the tragic death of Josh Gibson on January 20, 1947, seemed to spell the beginning of the end for the Homestead Grays.

The 1948 season turned out to be a last hurrah for both the Homestead Grays and the NNL. The press was paying far less attention to the Negro Leagues by this point, but it is known that the Grays defeated the Baltimore Elite Giants in the NNL playoffs and met the Birmingham Black Barons in the Negro League World Series for the third time in six years. The Black Barons had knocked off a strong Kansas City Monarchs team in the NAL playoffs and featured a 17-year-old legend in the making, Willie Mays.

Bankhead helped lead the Grays to a five-game championship victory. After the series ended, the NNL disbanded, which meant that the 1948 Negro League World Series had been the last of its kind.

The Homestead Grays still fielded teams for the 1949 and 1950 seasons, with Bankhead staying on as player-manager. By all accounts these teams were highly competitive, with newspapers reporting records of 97-15 and 64-8 for the 1949 and 1950 seasons respectively.[34] In 11 box scores found from the 1950 season, an aging Bankhead banged out 18 hits in 45 at-bats.[35] The decline of the Negro Leagues continued apace, however, and the Grays folded after the 1950 season.

# Pride of Smoketown

After Josh Gibson's death in 1947, Sam became a surrogate father for 16-year-old Josh Gibson Jr., who played second base and third base for Bankhead's 1949 and 1950 Grays teams; however, Josh Jr. could not escape his father's enormous shadow. In 1951 Sam took Josh Jr. with him north of the border to play in the Class-C Canadian Provincial League for the Pittsburgh Pirates-affiliated Farnham Pirates. Canada was where Bankhead attained one of baseball's most underappreciated milestones by becoming the first black manager for a mostly white professional baseball team. Josh Jr. did not fare as well: While playing for Farnham, he broke his ankle sliding into second base, effectively ending his baseball career.

After spending the 1951 season in Canada, Sam and Josh Jr. returned home to the Hill District in Pittsburgh and took jobs working side by side for the Pittsburgh Sanitation Department. Josh Jr. had this to say about their experience together: "I worked with him. I listened to him still, like playin' baseball. He was one of the smartest guys 'cause he read all the time."[36]

Bankhead's post-baseball life has led to speculation, most notably by Negro League historian John Holway,[37] that the character Troy Maxson, from August Wilson's Pulitzer Prize-winning play *Fences* was based on Sam. Like Bankhead, Maxson was a bitter ex-Negro League star who worked on a garbage truck in Pittsburgh's Hill District. Bankhead was bitter that he never got the chance to play in baseball's major leagues,[38] and he refused to go to baseball games in his later years, even missing the chance to see his younger brother, Dan, pitch for the Brooklyn Dodgers. In a 1971 interview, Bankhead had this to say about major-league baseball: "After I quit, I never went to see a game again. I am not jealous, but I cannot be a fan."[39] Sam preferred to stay close to home, playing cards with his buddies, endlessly talking about the old days, and – most of all – drinking. Bankhead's brother Fred died in 1972, and his youngest brother, Dan, died in 1976, events that made Sam lean on the bottle even more heavily than before. While the exact circumstances of Sam Bankhead's death are not known, it is known that he was shot in the head and killed on the night of July 24, 1976.[40] Whether he was shot by a friend after an argument in a downtown hotel, or shot in self-defense by a co-worker at the William Penn Hotel in downtown Pittsburgh, one thing is certain: Negro League legend Sam Bankhead's life came to an unceremonious end at the age of 65.

In 2005 the *Washington Post* honored Negro League legend Ted "Double Duty" Radcliffe upon the occasion of his 102nd birthday and asked him, "What player do you think of when you think of the Negro Leagues?" Radcliffe responded, "Bankhead. He was a great player."[41] Indeed, Bankhead had been picked as the first-team utility player as early as 1952 in a *Pittsburgh Courier* poll that named the all-time Negro League All-Stars.[42] He was universally respected as a player and manager and continually rose to the occasion when playing with and against the greatest players in Negro League history.

Bankhead would have made a tremendous major-leaguer. By all accounts he was an exceptional fielder, a speed demon on the basepaths, and a skilled batsman, as his lifetime .289 batting average attests.[43] If nonleague statistics are included, then his average shoots up to well above .300. Bankhead is also credited with a .301 average against white major leaguers in barnstorming games.[44]

As of January 2017, there have been 220 major-league players elected to baseball's Hall of Fame. Negro League players have been grossly underrepresented, with only 35 players honored with plaques thus far. When examining the scope of his entire career, it is not hard to envision a place for Sam Bankhead in the hallowed halls of Cooperstown.

# THE 1935 PITTSBURGH CRAWFORDS

## *All Statistics* (UNLESS OTHERWISE NOTED)

Holway, John B. *The Complete Book of Baseball's Negro Leagues: The Other Half of Baseball History* (Fern Park, Florida: Hastings House Publishers, 2001).

## *Notes*

1. John B. Holway, *Black Giants* (Springfield, Virginia: Lord Fairfax Press, 2010), 92.
2. John B. Holway, *Black Giants*, 92.
3. John B. Holway, *Black Giants*, 92.
4. Conflicting sources have Bankhead being born on September 18, 1905, in Empire, Alabama, but the 1910 birthdate shows up on both the US Social Security Death Index and on his gravestone in Sharpsburg, Pennsylvania.
5. Larry Lester, *Black Baseball's National Showcase* (Lincoln: University of Nebraska Press, 2001), 1.
6. Lester, 1.
7. Jim Bankes, *The Pittsburgh Crawfords* (Jefferson, North Carolina: McFarland & Company, Inc., Publishers, 2001), 148.
8. Lester, 88.
9. John B. Holway, *The Complete Book of Baseball's Negro Leagues: The Other Half of Baseball History* (Fern Park, Florida: Hastings House Publishers, 2001), 321.
10. Holway, John B., *Josh and Satch: The Life and Times of Josh Gibson and Satchel Paige* (New York: Meckler Publishing, 1991), 90.
11. Bankes, 110.
12. Bankes, 110.
13. Dr. Layton Revel and Luis Munoz, *Forgotten Heroes: Samuel "Sam" Bankhead* (Carrollton, Texas: Center for Negro League Research, 2011), 23.
14. Dr. Layton Revel and Luis Munoz, 23.
15. Brad Snyder, *Beyond the Shadow of the Senators* (New York: McGraw-Hill, 2003), 171, 274.
16. Mark Ribowsky, *The Power and the Darkness: The Life of Josh Gibson in the Shadows of the Game* (New York: Simon and Schuster, 1996), 164.
17. Brent Kelley, *Voices From the Negro Leagues: Conversations With 52 Baseball Standouts* (Jefferson, North Carolina: McFarland & Company, Inc., Publishers, 1998), 145.
18. Holway, *The Complete Book of Baseball's Negro Leagues*, 356.
19. Lester, 89.
20. Lester, 109-110.
21. Holway, *Josh and Satch*, 151-155.
22. John Virtue, *South of the Color Barrier* (Jefferson, North Carolina: McFarland & Company, Inc., Publishers, 2008), 11.
23. Virtue, 12.
24. Virtue, 85.
25. Revel and Munoz, 11.
26. Ibid.
27. Revel and Munoz, 12.
28. Larry Lester and Sammy J. Miller, *Black Baseball in Pittsburgh* (Charleston, South Carolina: Arcadia Publishing, 2001), 75.
29. Revel and Munoz, 12.
30. Holway, *The Complete Book of Baseball's Negro Leagues*, 398-399.
31. Tetelo Vargas of the New York Cubans hit .484.
32. Game Two ended in a tie.
33. Holway, *Josh and Satch*, 171.
34. Revel and Munoz, 19.
35. Ibid. 19.
36. Brent Kelley, *The Negro Leagues Revisited: Conversations With 66 More Baseball Heroes* (Jefferson, North Carolina: McFarland & Company, Inc., Publishers, 2000), 258.
37. Holway, *Black Giants*, 92.
38. August Wilson, *Fences* (New York: Plume, 1986).
39. Holway, *Black Giants*, 97.
40. Ibid.
41. "Ex-Washington Player Goes Back a Few Years," *Washington Post*, April 12, 2005. washingtonpost.com/archive/sports/2005/04/12/ex-washington-player-goes-back-a-few-years/4a2faf00-9223-4718-b46c-e1b8e0213a6b/?utm_term=.66be349249e0. Accessed December 31, 2016.
42. James A. Riley, *The Biographical Encyclopedia of the Negro Baseball Leagues* (New York: Carroll & Graff Publishers, Inc., 1994), 52.
43. Holway, *Black Giants*, 99.
44. Holway, *Black Giants*, 101.

# COOL PAPA BELL

## By Dave Wilkie

"He was a beautiful person. Yes he was. Cool Papa Bell. He was a loveable person. And still is. And always has been. I love him. My goodness, that's one beautiful man."

- Dave Barnhill
(hard-throwing ace pitcher and all-star of the New York Cubans.)[1]

"He had time for everybody. Never hurried. Signed autographs, talked to the people, gave advice on baseball, anything they wanted. All the time showing his big beautiful smile. He was so kind. If everybody was like Cool, this would be a better world."

– Judy Johnson
(Hall of Fame third baseman)[2]

He was often described as regal, noble, gentle, and soft-spoken, and a person would be hard pressed to find an ill word uttered about Negro League legend Cool Papa Bell. Just the mention of his name conjures up a seemingly endless line of

*James "Cool Papa" Bell is best-known for his blazing speed, but he was no slouch at the plate either. In 21 seasons of Negro League play, he batted .324 and had a .392 OBP.*

mythical stories, some true and some no doubt exaggerated. Bell played for three of the greatest teams in Negro League history, the St. Louis Stars of 1928-1931, the Pittsburgh Crawfords of 1932-1936, and the Homestead Grays of 1943-1945. He played in eight East-West All-Star games, was enshrined in the National Baseball Hall of Fame in Cooperstown in 1974, and is often mentioned as the fastest baseball player ever to lace up a pair of spikes.

James Thomas Nichols was born just outside of Starkville, Mississippi, on May 17, 1903. His mother, Mary Nichols, was widowed before his birth when Samuel Nichols died just a month after they were married. Bell had six brothers and two sisters.[3] He claimed that his grandfather was three-quarters Indian and his great-grandfather was full-blooded Indian, although he didn't know which tribe they were from.[4] Mary was remarried some time after James was born to a man named Jonas Bell. James didn't take on his stepfather's name until he was forced to do so after his move to St. Louis in 1920. As he recalled, "They said you got to have your father's name. Just changed my name to Bell."[5]

James spent the majority of his childhood helping out on his grandfather's farm, on which the family raised cotton, corn, fruit, vegetables, and just about anything else that people had a use for.[6] He also began to play baseball on those hot summer days in rural Mississippi and later recalled playing ball at the age of 10 as one of his fondest memories:

> I was just a little boy, but I could throw hard. One day there was a picnic in a little town called Blackjack. After we ate under the cool shade trees, they asked me to pitch in the men's game. I was scared, but I went out and did my best. I pitched three innings and struck out eight of the nine men I faced. The only guy who hit the ball was Joe Minor. He was the best hitter around, a big guy with thick wrists and real strong forearms. But all he could do was hit a little grounder back to me.
>
> When it was my turn to hit, a big woman came running to the plate, picked me up, and put me on her shoulder. She yelled at the pitcher, 'You're throwing too fast, and this little boy's going to get hurt.' But they convinced her to let me bat, and, on the first pitch, I hit a line drive into the outfield for a single. I stole second base and wound up scoring the winning run in the game. Was I happy!
>
> After I left the field the girls came running up to me and gave me a big piece of chocolate cake. I remember that game better than any I played as a professional.[7]

Bell moved north to St. Louis at the age of 17 to live with his brothers and (perhaps) stepbrothers, Robert, Fred, L.Q., and Sammy.[8] It is not known which siblings were fathered by Samuel Nichols and which by Jonas Bell, although James claimed that he was raised without a father. He got a job at a packing house and had hoped to go to night school, but the lure of baseball was just too strong.[9] He started playing sandlot ball on the weekends with the Compton Hill Cubs. Bell's first known appearance in a game was mentioned in a short write-up in the October 15, 1920, edition of the *St. Louis Argus*. The game took place on October 10, against the East St. Louis Cubs, and Bell was listed as the pitcher – with his older brother Robert catching – in a 15-4 victory for the Cubs.[10]

In the spring of 1922 those same East St. Louis Cubs were looking for a pitcher to go up against the Negro National League's St. Louis Stars. Bell jumped at the chance. Although he lost that contest, 9-1, on Sunday, April 30, he struck out eight and impressed the Stars so much that they immediately signed the 19-year-old for $90 a month and headed out on a long road trip with Bell in tow.[11]

Bell's first Negro League appearance most likely took place on May 9, 1922, against the

# Pride of Smoketown

*Crawfords center-fielder James "Cool Papa" Bell, the fastest man in Negro League baseball, showed off his speed in other countries as well. He is pictured here in the uniform of the Mexican League's Tampico Alijadores.*

Indianapolis ABCs as a lanky knuckleball pitcher.[12] In regard to his pitching, Bell said, "I used to throw the knuckle ball. If I got two strikes on you, I could throw my knuckle ball and it would just do this dart-down. I bet you I could strike anybody out with that knuckle ball. My brother couldn't catch me. But you know who could catch me with that knuckle ball? My sister."[13]

It was around this time that Bell received his legendary moniker. Big Bill Gatewood, manager of the Stars in 1922, who had twirled the Negro Leagues' first no-hitter during the previous season, is most often credited with bestowing the fabled "Cool Papa" nickname upon Bell.[14] Supposedly, Bell fanned Oscar Charleston during a tight spot in an early-season game and Gatewood commented about how cool under pressure he was. Papa was added later to make it sound better.[15] Gatewood's influence on Cool Papa's career didn't stop there. He also had the foresight to move Bell to the outfield to get his bat in the lineup more often, and persuaded him to bat left-handed to take advantage of his speed heading to first.[16] Bell switch-hit for the remainder of his career.

Negro Leagues pioneer Rube Foster was so impressed with Bell's speed that he issued him a challenge. Wanting to see how fast Cool Papa truly was, he pitted Bell against Jimmy Lyon, the league's fastest player at the time. Bell won the race easily. Afterward, Foster remarked on Bell's cheap shoes:

> If you can run that well in those shoes, just think what you might do in a good pair. Tell you what, go down to the Spalding Sporting Goods Store here in Chicago and tell the man you want the best pair of spikes he has in stock. Charge them to me.' I thanked him and told him I'd get the shoes, but I was going to pay him back. I was raised to pay my debts. The man at the store gave me a pair of kangaroo-hide shoes. They cost $21, but by the end of the season, I had saved enough to pay Mr. Foster back.[17]

Bell continued to pitch for the Stars in 1922 and posted a 7-7 record as he completed nine of his 12 starts and spun one shutout. He fared better in 1923, going 11-7 and completing nine of 14 games started in a total of 25 appearances. However, the team ranked near the bottom of the league in both seasons.[18]

The California Winter League was the first professional circuit to pit Negro League teams against squads of white professionals. The league began play at the turn of the twentieth century and its season ran between October and February until the league disbanded after the 1947 campaign. Cool Papa was a fixture in the league and played 12 seasons out West. His first go-around in California came after his rookie season with the Stars in 1922-1923. According to Bell:

> I went to California that winter on the pitching staff to play in the winter league. We got rooms in a little hotel down by the station,

# THE 1935 PITTSBURGH CRAWFORDS

a big room, had two beds. My brother Fred Bell and I slept in one. Turkey Stearnes slept in the other. … (Stearnes) went to Cuba and they needed an outfielder, so they put me out there. One Saturday we were playing in Pasadena and a lot of balls were hit over the center fielder's head. I'd run over behind him and catch them. So from then on I played center field. I wasn't a pitcher anymore.[19]

Bell split his time between playing center field and pitching for the Stars in 1924. He batted .289 in 246 at-bats and went 3-1 on the mound, but Bell and the St. Louis Stars did not really hit their stride until 1925.[20]

Between 1925 and 1927 Bell's batting average never dipped below .316, including a stellar 1925 campaign in which he batted .342 in 409 at-bats with 99 runs scored. Of course, these are only the partial numbers that historians have been able to unearth so far; his actual statistics were likely much higher. The St. Louis Stars were 180-103 during this period for a .636 winning percentage, and, with the addition of Hall of Famer and powerhouse slugger Mule Suttles in 1927, the best was yet to come.

Bell met his wife, Clara, at some point in the late 1920s, but there initially was a slight roadblock to their union. Bell's best friend and roommate, future Hall of Fame shortstop Willie Wells, was courting Clara at the time, but Wells's mother disapproved of the relationship, which gave Bell the opportunity to swoop in. This turn of events did not affect the two players' friendship; Bell and Wells remained close for the remainder of their lives.[21] Willie Wells summed up the situation and their relationship when he said:

Cool Papa Bell was my best friend in St. Louis. He was the most beautiful ballplayer and a great base runner. And Bell was a clean liver, he wouldn't dissipate at all. He was like me. We'd sit in the room and play cards, he and I. We were roommates. He married a girl who was my sweetheart. But he and I were just like this-friends-you know? It never came between us. A good relationship. A wonderful fellow. Bell, he was a beaut.[22]

Cool Papa and Clara were married in 1928 and they went on their honeymoon to Cuba, where Bell got his first taste of life and baseball in Latin America.[23]

Bell enjoyed tremendous success in the Cuban Winter League. In the 1928-29 season he led the league with 44 runs scored, 5 home runs, and 17 stolen bases. He hit a robust .325 while playing for the Cienfuegos Elefantes.[24] The following season saw more of the same as Bell once again led the league with 52 runs and became the first player in Cuban League history to hit three home runs in game when he stroked three inside-the-park four-baggers in a game played on New Year's Day in 1929.[25]

The St. Louis Stars started firing on all cylinders in 1928 as Bell, along with Mule Suttles and Willie Wells, led their team to a 65-26 record and a nine-game championship series victory over the Chicago American Giants, including wins in Games Eight and Nine as they faced elimination. Bell hit a solid .336 during the season and turned it up a notch for the championship series, in which he rapped out 11 hits in 27 at-bats (.407).[26]

The Stars continued their successful run into the early 1930s. The team captured the Negro National League championship in 1930, with a seven-game win over Turkey Stearnes and his Detroit Stars, and repeated as uncontested champions in 1931, a season in which the squad won both the first- and second-half NNL titles. Bell was outstanding during the 1930 campaign: He hit .350 and scored 109 runs in only 366 at-bats and led his team to a sparkling 73-28 record, 13½ games ahead of the second-place Kansas City Monarchs.

The Negro National League fell victim to the Great Depression and disbanded after the 1931 season. The demise of the first NNL also marked the downfall of one of the greatest teams in Negro League history, the St. Louis Stars. Bell spent 1932 bouncing around between the Independent League Kansas City Monarchs and the Detroit Wolves and Homestead Grays of the East-West League before finally settling in with the storied Pittsburgh Crawfords amid the return of the Negro National League in 1933.[27]

Bell was often called the black Ty Cobb and was also compared to other players, like Wee Willie Keeler, who chopped down at the ball and relied on their speed to beat opponents. Bell said as much as he explained, "I'd stand back from the plate and chop down on the ball. That's something I learned from the old players. By the time the ball comes down, they can't throw me out. They'd bring in their infield, as if there was a man on third and no out; they couldn't get me if they played back in their normal position. I'd just hit the ball to short, and if he has to move over for it, he can't throw me out."[28] Hall of Fame third baseman Judy Johnson put it this way: "He was so fast, that if he hit a ground ball to the left side of the infield that took more than one hop, you just couldn't throw him out. Might just as well hold the ball."[29]

Gus Greenlee, racketeer and owner of the Pittsburgh Crawfords, began to load up on talent for the 1933 season. He had already signed Josh Gibson and Satchel Paige, the best hitter and pitcher available, and soon set his sights on Cool Papa Bell, the fastest player in the Negro Leagues. "Greenlee told me that I had the chance to be part of the best team in the history of black baseball and that I was the key," Bell remembered.[30] Greenlee's boast may not have been exaggeration as the 1933 Pittsburgh Crawfords featured five future Hall of Famers in Bell, Gibson, Oscar Charleston, Paige, and Judy Johnson. Bell appreciated what Greenlee was trying to do with the Crawfords: "Gus really did his best to run a class organization. We had a fine bus, nice uniforms, good equipment, everything."[31]

One of Bell's signature achievements is said to have taken place during the 1933 season. Although the claim cannot be supported by currently available statistics, it is something that Bell consistently claimed to be true throughout his lifetime. He asserted, "The best year I ever had on the bases was 1933. I stole one hundred and seventy-five in about one hundred and eighty to two hundred ball games, all of them against other Negro League teams."[32] Bell also kept track of Gibson's mammoth blasts during his stint with the Crawfords: "People ask me how many homers Josh Gibson hit and I can't tell them for sure. I did count 72 in 1933. Josh and I played on the Crawfords from 1933 to 1936, and I can tell you that during those seasons he never hit less than 60 home runs and maybe as many as 80 or 85."[33] Such assertions may appear to be tall tales, but, unlike Satchel Paige's legendary hyperbole, Bell was a thoughtful, straightforward man, whose intelligence and honesty make these legends more likely.

The East-West All-Star Game, which became the centerpiece of every Negro League season, took place for the first time in 1933. The creation of sportswriters Roy Sparrow of the *Pittsburgh Sun-Telegraph* and Bill Nunn of the *Pittsburgh Courier*, they took their idea for the game to the man who could make it happen: Gus Greenlee. This annual contest was even more popular than the Negro League World Series and was an event the players excitedly looked forward to each year.[34] Players were selected by the fans through the prominent black newspapers of the day. Bell had already logged 11 seasons before the inaugural game was played, but he still managed to play in eight East-West games. While he did not have much success in these contests, with only six hits in 30 at-bats, he produced a defining moment in the 1934 game.[35] Bell walked in the eighth, stole second, and then scored the only run of the game when he sprinted home from second on a bloop single to give the East a 1-0 victory.[36]

The 1935 Pittsburgh Crawfords were a juggernaut, and the team is often compared to the 1927

# THE 1935 PITTSBURGH CRAWFORDS

*James "Cool Papa" Bell, in Grays uniform, slides safely into third base. Satchel Paige claimed, "Bell was so fast he could flip the switch and then jump in bed before the light went out"*

New York Yankees. The Crawfords were a force of nature and rank among the greatest teams to ever take the field.[37] Sporting a 50-23-3 record, the Crawfords ran away with the first half of the Negro National League season and featured a star player at almost every position. In 49 recorded games, Bell scored an amazing 68 runs and batted .345 in the process. The Crawfords faced Hall of Famer Martin Dihigo and his New York Cubans in the NNL Championship Series in which Bell celebrated another career-defining moment. A back-and-forth series led to a Game Seven that the Cubans led 8-5 in the eighth inning. The Craws mounted a comeback against Luis Tiant Sr. as homers by Gibson and Charleston tied it up before Bell worked his magic. He singled off Dihigo, who had replaced Tiant on the mound, stole second, and then raced home with the winning run on a bobbled infield grounder.[38] For the second time in three years – the team had also won the title in 1933 – the Pittsburgh Crawfords were champions of the Negro National League.

The Crawfords remained a formidable team in 1936 and again captured the NNL championship, but cracks were beginning to show. By the spring of 1937, Gibson had been traded to the Homestead Grays and Bell, Paige, and Sam Bankhead had all left to play in the Dominican Republic and had cited low pay in the Negro Leagues as the reason for jumping their contracts.[39] The mighty Pittsburgh Crawfords hung it up for good after the 1938 season, with the remnants of the team moving to Toledo in 1939 and then Indianapolis in 1940 before finally disbanding. A wistful Cool Papa Bell looked back on his four years with the team. "We had such a great team, a team that could win in every way possible. I was sorry I had to leave the Crawfords."[40]

Instead of playing in the Negro Leagues in 1937, many Negro League stars made the jump to the Dominican Republic in search of a better payday. Satchel Paige helped lure teammates Bell, Josh Gibson, Sam Bankhead, and Chester Williams south of the border to play for dictator

Rafael Trujillo's team in Ciudad Trujillo to help boost his chance for re-election.[41] The players quickly realized the predicament they'd gotten themselves into. Bell asked a local resident, "They don't kill people over baseball, do they?" The man responded. "Down here they do."[42] Luckily for Bell and company, they won the championship game, albeit under very tense circumstances. In the bottom of the seventh, with his team trailing 3-2 and two out, Bell singled and Sam Bankhead homered to give Trujillo a 4-3 lead. Paige retired the final six batters in a row and they escaped with the win. They couldn't get out of town fast enough.[43]

The most improbable of the Cool Papa Bell yarns turns out to be the one that's verifiably true. For over 40 years, Satchel Paige claimed that "Bell was so fast he could flip the switch and then jump in bed before the light went out."[44] At a 1981 Negro League reunion in Ashland, Kentucky, Bell came clean about this story:

> During one winter season in the late 1930's, Satchel and I roomed together out in California. One night, before he got back, I turned off the light, but it didn't go out right away. There was a delay of about three seconds between the time I flipped the switch and the time the light went out. There must have been a short or something. I thought to myself, here's a chance to fool ol' Satch. He was always playing tricks on everybody else, you know. Anyway, when he came back, I said, 'Hey, Satch, I'm pretty fast, right?' 'You're the fastest,' he said. 'Well,' I said, 'you haven't seen anything yet. Why, I'm so fast, I can turn out the light and be in bed before the room gets dark.' 'Sure, Cool. Sure you can,' he said. I told him to sit down and watch. I turned off the light, jumped in bed, and pulled the covers up to my chin. Then the lights went out. I howled and Satchel was speechless for once. Anyway, he's been telling the truth all these years.[45]

Barnstorming against teams made up of white major leaguers was common during the offseason, and Bell was a staple in these contests as well. He is credited with a .311 lifetime batting average in 52 of these exhibitions, with 57 hits and 21 stolen bases, and, like the teams he played for, often dominated squads made up of his white counterparts.[46] In a 1931 game in St. Louis, against a team that included future Hall of Famers Max Carey, Paul Waner, Lloyd Waner, and Charlie Gehringer, the Negro Leaguers embarrassed the white team, 18-3. Bell ran wild in the game as he bunted for a hit his first time up, then stole second, third, and home against New York Giants pitcher Bill Walker. The display of daring and speed prompted Detroit Tigers great Charlie Gehringer to remark, "I saw Ty Cobb many times, even as a young man before I joined the Tigers. But I never saw him do anything like Bell did in St. Louis that night."[47]

The Negro League players played a different style of baseball than the white major leaguers of the time, which is what often gave them the advantage. Bell called it tricky baseball and explained:

> When I came up, we didn't play baseball like they play in the major leagues. We played tricky baseball. When we played the big leaguers after the regular season, our pitchers would curve the ball on 3-2. They'd say, what, are you trying to make us look bad? We'd bunt and run and they'd say, why are you trying to do that in the first inning? When we were supposed to bunt, they'd come in and we'd hit away. We'd go into third standing up so the third baseman couldn't see the throw coming and it might go through him. The major leaguers would play for one big inning. I think we had a better system than the majors. Whatever it takes to win, we did.[48]

In addition to the offseason barnstorming tours, Bell continued to play ball in the Latin winter leagues. Bell and many other Negro League players loved life so much in Latin America that they did not want to leave. Bell said of his time in Latin America, "Everybody was the same down there. We could go in any restaurant, stay in hotels, and oh, the fans? They loved us."[49] Life in Latin America provided a stark contrast to the way Negro League players were treated under Jim Crow laws in the States. Bell played exclusively in the Mexican League from 1938 to 1941, and put his Negro Leagues career on hiatus.

As a former knuckleball pitcher, Bell was able to help his good friend Satchel Paige learn a new pitch while the two were in Mexico. Bell recounted, "In 1938 his arm got sore and I told him, see Satchel, you've got to learn to pitch. I showed him how to throw the knuckle ball, and he was throwing it better than I was. That's what I liked about him, he didn't want anybody to beat him doing anything."[50]

Bell was a superstar in the Mexican League, where he had some of his finest seasons. Perhaps no season was finer than his 1940 campaign with Vera Cruz during which he captured the league's triple crown and led the team to a championship. Bell hit an astounding .437 with 12 home runs and 79 RBIs in 89 games. He also showed off his speed with 15 triples and a remarkable 119 runs scored. Bell's four years in Mexico saw him hit .367 overall, and he scored 310 runs in 287 games.[51]

Bell is obviously most famous for his speed. When Negro League legend, manager, and historian Buck O'Neil was asked, "Just how fast was Cool Papa Bell?," he would always answer the same. "Faster than that."[52] One of Bell's most famous quotes about circling the bases in 12 seconds flat cannot be verified, but a recorded time of 13.60 was reported by the *Los Angeles Times* in 1933, and Bell claims he did it on a wet field. A time of 13.60 puts him slightly behind Maury Wills and ahead of Ty Cobb in recorded times circling the bases.[53] Jesse Owens famously dodged Bell when Owens traveled with different teams and took on all comers.[54] In 1933 Hall of Fame Pittsburgh Pirate great Paul Waner complimented Bell: "The fastest man I have ever seen on the baseball diamond was Cool Papa."[55]

Former Negro League and major-league star and Hall of Famer Monte Irvin also extolled Bell's ability:

He might've been the fastest baseball player who ever lived. They used to tell stories about Bell's running. He was known to score from second base on a bunt. That's right. Now, suppose he'd played under good conditions, you know, get a massage after every game, not have to drive five hundred miles to play a doubleheader, this kind of thing. There's no telling how many bases he would've stolen. It's just a shame that more people didn't get to see him. The only comparison I can give is, suppose Willie Mays had never had a chance to play big league. Then I were to come to you and try to tell you about Willie Mays. Now this is the way it is with Cool Papa Bell.[56]

Although Bell is best known for his feats on the basepaths, he was no slouch in the field, a fact to which Satchel Paige attested in his autobiography: "Why, he was the best fielder you ever saw. He could grab that ball no matter where it was hit. He was just like a suction cup."[57] Paul Waner agreed when he called Bell "the smoothest center fielder I've seen."[58] Trailblazing owner Bill Veeck compared him to center fielders Willie Mays, Joe DiMaggio, and Tris Speaker and called Bell "one of the most magical players I've ever seen." And Hall of Famer Pie Traynor once remarked, "It doesn't matter where he plays. He can go a country mile for a ball."[59]

Bell returned from Mexico to the Negro Leagues for a short stint with the Chicago American Giants in 1942 before he signed on with the Homestead Grays the following year. Bell had a knack for playing on great teams, and the 1943 Grays were an overwhelming force that finished the year with a 78-23-1 record and captured their fourth straight NNL title. The 40-year-old Bell led off, played left field, and had a hand in helping the Grays win their first Negro League World Series title by beating the Birmingham Black Barons in a nailbiter, four games to three.[60] Bell hit a game-winning single in the bottom of the 11th inning to take Game Three, 4-3, and had a solid Series in which he went 8-for-26 for a .308 average.[61]

Bell found a kindred spirit on the Grays for the 1944 season in aging veteran and fellow Hall of Famer Buck Leonard. The two intelligent, soft-spoken men were perfect roommates, who both preferred to forgo the nightlife and retire early every evening; however, they were not above taking a couple swigs of gin before bedtime to help with their arthritis. *Pittsburgh Courier* columnist Wendell Smith said of the duo, "These men weren't big drinkers; they were aging ballplayers trying to stall Father Time."[62]

The Homestead Grays once again met the Birmingham Black Barons in the 1944 Negro League World Series and this time dismantled them, four games to one. The 41-year-old Bell stroked .322 for the season and chipped in with a respectable .260 in the Series.

The 1944-1945 offseason marked Bell's last campaign in the California Winter League. His success in this league rivaled that of his Mexican League accomplishments as he finished with a .368 batting average in 159 games, including 219 hits in 596 at-bats, with 16 homers, 12 triples, and 31 doubles in 12 years of action. He won two batting titles and his teams consistently dominated the league in each season that he played.[63]

Bell began to feel all of his 42 years in 1945 with the Homestead Grays. He recalled, "In '45 I was sick. I had arthritis, I was stiff, I couldn't run."[64] He still managed to hit .299 and helped the Grays to a 47-25-3 record and yet another NNL title, their sixth in a row. The Grays ran into a buzz saw in the World Series, though, and were swept by the Sam Jethroe-led Cleveland Buckeyes in four games. The aging Grays managed only three runs in the Series and hit a paltry .165.

The 1946 Homestead Grays failed to win the title, but Bell amazed everyone by leading the batting race near the end of the season. Soon, he performed one of his most selfless acts as he ceded the title to Monte Irvin. Bell explained his motives thusly: "For the first time the Major Leagues were serious about taking in blacks. I was too old, but Monte was young and had a chance for a future. It was important he be noticed, important he get that chance." Bell removed himself from the lineup and ended up not having enough at-bats to qualify for the title.[65] He still ended up hitting .393 in his final season in the Negro Leagues.

Soon after Bell's retirement, he signed on to manage the Monarch Travelers, an independent team that played west of Kansas City in search of major-league talent. Bell managed this team through 1949 and turned out to be adept at recognizing future stars.[66] He is credited with first spotting Cubs Hall of Fame shortstop Ernie Banks and recommending him to Buck O'Neil and the Kansas City Monarchs.[67]

With major-league integration just around the corner, it was difficult for players like Bell not to wonder what might have been. Had integration come sooner, fans could have witnessed the greatness of players like Bell, Gibson, Charleston, Leonard, Johnson, and Suttles in their primes. They would be household names like Babe Ruth, Lou Gehrig, and Ty Cobb. For more than a decade before Jackie Robinson was signed, the hope that the color barrier might be broken seemed tantalizingly close. Bell had the final word on this false hope: "They used to say, if we find a good black player, we'll sign him. They was lying."[68]

Cool Papa Bell played a role in Jackie Robinson's success at integrating the major leagues. News that Robinson was about to sign with the Dodgers had many veterans worried that he might not make it. Bell told of the players' outlook and his role:

# THE 1935 PITTSBURGH CRAWFORDS

All us old fellas didn't think he could make it at short. He couldn't go to his right too good. We was worried. He miss this chance, and who knows when we'd get another chance. So I made up my mind to show him he should try for another spot in the infield. One night I must've knocked a couple hundred ground balls to his right, and I beat the throw to first every time. Jackie smiled. He got the message. He played a lot of games in the majors, only one of 'em at short.[69]

Bell produced another highlight in 1948 when Satchel Paige got him to suit up against a team led by future Hall of Famer Bob Lemon and, ironically, Jackie Robinson.[70]

Bell also described his iconic moment:

So this time I was hitting eighth and I got on base, and Satchel came up and sacrificed me to second. Well, Bob Lemon came off the mound to field it and I saw that third base was open, because the third baseman had also charged in to field it. Roy Partee, the catcher, saw me going to third, so he went down the line to cover third and I just came on home past him. Partee called 'Time, time!' But the umpire said, 'I can't call time, the ball's still in play,' so I scored.[71]

Cool Papa Bell finally hung up his spikes for good in 1950 and moved back to St. Louis with his wife, Clara, where he took a job working for the city, first as a custodian and later as a night watchman.[72] Bell sometimes took in Cardinals games and on a couple of occasions shared his wisdom and experience with the stars of the day. The Dodgers asked him to help out young speedster Maury Wills. Bell did, and advised Wills, "When you're on base get those hitters of yours to stand deep in the box. That way the catcher, he got to back up. That way you goin' to get an extra step all the time."[73] Wills went on to steal 104 bases not long after that. Cardinals speed demon Lou Brock also listened and learned when Bell was around. Brock recalled, "He was a nice man, a good teacher, and he just instinctively knew more about stealing a base than anyone else I've ever met."[74]

St. Louis Browns owner Bill Veeck made an attempt to sign both Bell and Buck Leonard in 1951, but both players were well past their primes. A 48-year-old Bell explained his decision not to play: "People told me I should have tried for the job just for the money, but I couldn't do it just for a paycheck. I never had any money, so I never worried about it. I just didn't want fans to boo me, and if I had played at that age they sure would have. Sometimes pride is more important than money."[75]

Bell and Clara continued to live in their small St. Louis apartment, which was surrounded by abandoned stores and vacant lots. Bell worked for nine years as a city hall custodian and spent another 13 years as the night watchman on the midnight-to-8 shift. His 22 years with the city earned him a paltry $130-a-month pension.[76]

In the meantime, Bell had to wait until 1974 to finally get the call every ballplayer dreams of. Cool Papa Bell was unanimously voted into baseball's Hall of Fame in Cooperstown and was inducted on August 12, 1974. He was the fifth Negro Leaguer to be elected and joined Paige, Leonard, Gibson, and Irvin in baseball's hallowed shrine. Bell remained cool when he was given the news. He said, "It's the highest honor, but I don't jump up and down and holler and rush to the telephone to call my friends. They'll learn about it sometime."[77] Ed Stack, former president of the Hall of Fame, said of Bell in 1991, "Cool Papa was the dean of the living Hall of Famers. What he said had a tremendous amount of meaning. It was the sermon of the evening, the inspiration and mood-setting for the whole weekend."[78]

Bell made the trip from St. Louis to Cooperstown every year until his health finally prevented him from traveling toward the end of his life. He signed autographs, took pictures, and talked with fans for hours until no one remained. When asked about the dangers of the long journey at his advancing age he responded, "So what if I died on the way to Cooperstown. Besides Clara, baseball has been my whole life."[79]

Cool Papa Bell's beloved wife of 62 years, Clara, died on January 20, 1991. Bell suffered a heart attack shortly thereafter, on February 27, and died at St. Louis University Hospital on March 7.[80] The couple was survived by their only daughter, Connie Brooks. Lou Brock was one of Bell's pallbearers and had this to say after the funeral: "To his grave goes a whole chapter in the black history of baseball, in black history, period. His dream got deferred. I just hope somewhere in history that his performance gets accurately recorded."[81]

Bell wasn't bitter about his exclusion from the major leagues. In 1988, at his home in St. Louis, he reflected on his life.[82] In summary of all he had experienced, he said, "Because of baseball, I smelled the rose of life. I wanted to meet interesting people, to travel, and to have nice clothes. Baseball allowed me to do all those things, and most important … it allowed me to become a member of a brotherhood of friendship which will last forever."[83]

## Sources

All statistics, unless otherwise noted, are from seamheads.com or baseballreference.com.

## Notes

1. Jim Bankes, *The Pittsburgh Crawfords* (Jefferson, North Carolina: McFarland & Company Inc., 2001), 84.
2. Bankes, 43.
3. Rod Roberts, Cool Papa Bell interview, September 26, 1981, 1. Hall of Fame archives.
4. John Holway, *Voices from the Great Black Baseball Leagues* (New York: First Da Capo Press Inc., 1992), 112.
5. Rod Roberts interview, 2.
6. Rod Roberts interview, 4.
7. Bankes, 45.
8. Without access to more information, it proved very difficult to determine all family relationships.
9. Mississippi History Now online publication, 1-2008. mshistorynow.mdah.ms.gov/articles/277/cool-papa-bell.
10. Gary Ashwill, "Cool Papa's Rookie Season," Agate Type, July 15, 2016. agatetype.typepad.com/agate_type/cool-papa-bell/.
11. Gary Ashwill, "Cool Papa's Rookie Season."
12. Gary Ashwill, "How Cool Papa Got His Name," Agate Type, July 27, 2006. agatetype.typepad.com/agate_type/2006/07/how_cool_papa_g.html.
13. Holway, *Voices from the Great Black Baseball Leagues*, 113.
14. Leslie A. Heaphy, *Black Baseball and Chicago* (Jefferson, North Carolina: McFarland & Company Inc., 2006), 79.
15. Gary Ashwill, "How Cool Papa Got His Name."
16. Heaphy, *Black Baseball and Chicago*, 79.
17. Bankes, 47.
18. Seamheads.com seamheads.com/NegroLgs/player.php?playerID=bell-01coo.
19. William F. McNeil, *The California Winter League* (Jefferson, North Carolina: McFarland & Company Inc., 2002), 88.
20. Seamheads.com. seamheads.com/NegroLgs/player.php?playerID=bell-01coo. All statistics are from Seamheads unless otherwise noted.
21. James A. Riley, *Dandy, Day, and the Devil* (Cocoa, Florida: TK Publishers, 1987), 121.
22. Holway, *Voices from the Great Black Baseball Leagues*, 225.
23. Phil Dixon and Patrick J. Hannigan, *The Negro Baseball Leagues: A Photographic History* (Mattituck, New York: Amereon House, 1992), 125.
24. Jorge S. Figueredo, *Who's Who in Cuban Baseball: 1878-1961* (Jefferson, North Carolina: McFarland & Company Inc., 2003), 348.
25. William F. McNeil, *Black Baseball Out of Season: Pay for Play Outside of the Negro Leagues* (Jefferson, North Carolina: McFarland & Company Inc., 2007), 42.
26. John Holway, *The Complete Book of Baseball's Negro Leagues: The Other Half of Baseball History* (Fern Park, Florida: Hastings House Publishers, 2001), 237.
27. Baseballreference.com, baseball-reference.com/register/player.fcgi?id=bell--001coo.
28. Holway, *Voices from the Great Black Baseball Leagues*, 118.
29. Bankes, 44.
30. Mark Whitaker, *The Untold Story of Smoketown: The Other Great Black Renaissance* (New York: Simon & Schuster Inc., 2018), 109.
31. Larry Lester and Sammy J. Miller, *Black Baseball in Pittsburgh* (Charleston, South Carolina: Arcadia Publishing, 2001), 35.

# THE 1935 PITTSBURGH CRAWFORDS

32. John Holway, "How to Score from First on a Sacrifice," *American Heritage*, August 1970. americanheritage.com/how-score-first-sacrifice.
33. Bankes, 42.
34. Larry Lester, *Black Baseball's National Showcase: The East-West All-Star Game, 1933-1953* (Lincoln: University of Nebraska Press, 2001), 21-22.
35. Lester, *Black Baseball's National Showcase*, 412-413.
36. Whitaker, *The Untold Story of Smoketown*, 115.
37. Bankes, 148.
38. Mark Ribowsky, *The Power and the Darkness* (New York: Simon & Shuster, 1996), 148.
39. Averell "Ace" Smith, *The Pitcher and the Dictator* (Lincoln: University of Nebraska Press, 2018), 62.
40. Bankes, 51.
41. Anthony J. Connor, *Baseball for the Love of It: Hall of Famers Tell It Like It Was* (New York: Macmillan Publishing Co. Inc., 1982), 240-241.
42. McNeil, *Black Baseball Out of Season*, 144.
43. William F. McNeil, *Baseball's Other All-Stars* (Jefferson, North Carolina: McFarland & Company Inc., 2000), 172.
44. Bankes, 43.
45. Bankes, 43-44.
46. Todd Peterson, *The Negro Leagues Were Major Leagues: Historians Reappraise Black Baseball* (Jefferson, North Carolina: McFarland & Company Inc., 2020), 228.
47. Bankes, 47-48.
48. McNeil, *The California Winter League*, 111.
49. Patricia C. McKissack and Fredrick McKissack Jr., *Black Diamond: The Story of the Negro Baseball Leagues* (New York: Scholastic Inc., 1994), 110.
50. Holway, *Voices from the Great Black Baseball Leagues*, 132.
51. Pedro Treto Cisneros, *The Mexican League: Comprehensive Player Statistics, 1937-2001* (Jefferson, North Carolina: McFarland & Company Inc., 2002), 93.
52. "No. 99: Cool Papa Bell," Medium.com, medium.com/joe-blogs/99-cool-papa-bell-ef4d0c4d8bf5.
53. Scott Simkus, *Outsider Baseball: The Weird World of Hardball on the Fringe, 1876-1950* (Chicago: Chicago Review Press Inc., 2014), 232-234.
54. Dixon and Hannigan, 214.
55. Dixon and Hannigan, 160.
56. Connor, *Baseball for the Love of It*, 212.
57. Leroy "Satchel" Paige and David Lipman, *Maybe I'll Pitch Forever* (South Orange, New Jersey: Summer Game Books, 2018), 38.
58. William A. Young, *J.L. Wilkinson and the Kansas City Monarchs: Trailblazers in Black Baseball* (Jefferson, North Carolina: McFarland & Company Inc., 2016), 167.
59. Mark Kram, "No Place in the Shade," *Sports Illustrated*, June 20, 1994: 66.
60. Brad Snyder, *Beyond the Shadow of the Senators: The Untold Story of the Homestead Grays and the Integration of Baseball* (New York: McGraw-Hill, 2003), 162.
61. Holway, *The Complete Book of Baseball's Negro Leagues*, 410-411.
62. Snyder, *Beyond the Shadow of the Senators*, 212.
63. McNeil, *The California Winter League*, 250.
64. Holway, *Voices from the Great Black Baseball Leagues*, 127.
65. Bill Kirwin, *Out of the Shadows: African American Baseball from the Cuban Giants to Jackie Robinson* (Lincoln: University of Nebraska, 2005), 31.
66. Janet Bruce, *The Kansas City Monarchs: Champions of Black Baseball* (Lawrence: The University Press of Kansas, 1985); 120.
67. Young, *J.L. Wilkinson and the Kansas City Monarchs*, 178.
68. Connor, *Baseball for the Love of It*, 210.
69. Kram.
70. Timothy M. Gay, *Satch, Dizzy & Rapid Robert: The Wild Saga of Interracial Baseball Before Jackie Robinson* (New York: Simon & Shuster, 2010), 272.
71. Holway, *Voices from the Great Black Baseball Leagues*, 109.
72. Holway, *Voices from the Great Black Baseball Leagues*, 130.
73. Kram.
74. "No. 99: Cool Papa Bell."
75. Snyder, *Beyond the Shadow of the Senators*, 292.
76. William Brashler, *Josh Gibson: A Life in the Negro Leagues* (Chicago: Ivan R. Dee, 2000), 158. See also "Cool Papa Steams Up for Hall of Fame Induction," *St. Louis Post Dispatch*, August 9, 1974.
77. "Cool Papa Bell in Hall of Fame," *New York Post*, February 13, 1974: 76.
78. "Belated Respect," *St. Louis Post Dispatch*, March 17, 1991.
79. Bankes, 139-140.
80. "Cool Papa Dies After Brief Illness," *Sports Collectors Digest*, March 29, 1991.
81. "Belated Respect."
82. Bankes, 83.
83. Shaun McCormack, *Cool Papa Bell: Baseball Hall of Famers of the Negro Leagues* (New York: Rosen Publishing Group Inc., 2002), 87.

# WILLIAM BELL

## By Kevin Larkin and Frederick C. Bush

The 1935 Pittsburgh Crawfords are often considered to be the Negro Leagues' equivalent of the 1927 New York Yankees. That Yankees team had six future Hall of Fame players: Lou Gehrig, Tony Lazzeri, Babe Ruth, Earle Combs, Waite Hoyt, and Herb Pennock, along with manager Miller Huggins, general manager Ed Barrow, and owner Jacob Ruppert. The 1935 Crawfords had four Hall of Famers, player-manager Oscar Charleston, Josh Gibson, Judy Johnson, and James "Cool Papa" Bell (no relation to William Bell). Both teams also had well-known players who were not selected for induction into Cooperstown's hallowed halls, including Bob Meusel and Bob Shawkey of the Yankees and Jimmie Crutchfield and Sam Streeter of the Crawfords.

Another Negro League star who was a member of the 1935 Pittsburgh squad for a time, but who has garnered less mention is William Bell. Over the course of a 12-year career between 1923 and 1937, Bell posted an excellent Negro League pitching record of 93-47 that included an 84-44 ledger in league play, a 6-2 record against Latin League teams, and a 3-1 mark against

*Crawfords pitcher William Bell, pictured here in a Habana Leones cap, has long had his Cuban League statistics misattributed to Cliff Bell. William's nickname in Cuba was "Campanita," which translates to "Little Bell."*

*(Courtesy of Center for Negro League Baseball Research)*

# THE 1935 PITTSBURGH CRAWFORDS

major-league squads; when he was not pitching, Bell sometimes played the outfield. Later he became a manager. Bell also played four seasons in Cuba, where he pitched to a 25-17 record that brings his combined career mark to 118-64. Bell was a finalist on a special committee's Hall of Fame ballot in 2006, but fell short of being one of the former Negro League players to be selected for induction.

William Bell was born on August 31, 1897, in Hallettsville, Texas, to Otto and Viney (Williams) Bell.[1] Hallettsville is the county seat of Lavaca County, so named for the Lavaca River which runs through it, and is about 120 miles east of San Antonio. As was the case with many black residents of Texas in the late nineteenth century, the Bells were poor, minimally-educated farmers; census information indicates that Viney Bell completed school only through the fifth grade. At the time of William's birth, the family already included older brother David; two sisters, Louisa and Estell, came along later.

Otto Bell died at some point before 1910 while William was still a child. The exact year and cause of Otto's death have been lost to history, but the 1910 census lists Viney and her children as boarders in the home of Anthony and Ida Harold of Lavaca County. By the time of the 1920 census, the widowed Viney Bell had moved with her daughter Estell and grandchild Arthur Stewart to El Campo, Texas, where she worked as a cook in a private household. Viney Bell remarried and became Mrs. Viney Mayberry; though she was soon widowed again, she remained in El Campo until her death on March 29, 1949.

In light of the hardscrabble conditions of his youth, Bell was determined to improve his lot in life by attending Paul Quinn College in Waco, Texas, where he also played college baseball.[2] He soon became noticed by the professional Negro League circuits in Texas and was signed by the Galveston Black Sand Crabs of the Texas Colored League in 1921. The league had been founded in 1916 as the Colored Texas League and had franchises in Cleburne, Dallas, Waco, Houston, San Antonio, Beaumont, and Galveston.

After debuting with Galveston, Bell joined the barnstorming All-Nations team the following year. The squad was recognized for imitating the House of David team by having its players wear beards. John Donaldson, a Hall of Fame-worthy Negro League pitcher himself, managed the team during Bell's tenure with the squad.[3]

Bell started the 1923 season with the All-Nations contingent, but in midsummer he began to pitch for the Kansas City Monarchs, for whom the All-Nations team served as a sort of farm club. Bell had made it to the "big-league" club under the best of possible circumstances as the Monarchs were a Negro League powerhouse from 1923 to 1925. The 1923 Monarchs featured two future Hall of Famers, Jose "The Black Diamond" Mendez and Wilbur "Bullet Joe" Rogan, along with a third star pitcher, Reuben "Rube" Curry. Bell acquitted himself well once he joined the team, posting a 3-1 record and a 3.32 ERA with three complete games and one shutout in five starts. The pitching staff had ample offensive support from a lineup including Oscar "Heavy" Johnson, Walter "Dobie" Moore, and Rogan, who was an exceptional all-around player and manned every position except catcher at some point in his career.

The 1924 Monarchs returned most of the same players and Bell had a record of 9-2 in 16 appearances (13 starts) during the regular season. At the end of the season the Monarchs, who at the time were members of the Negro National League, played in the first Negro League World Series against the Eastern Colored League's Philadelphia Hilldales (sometimes also known as the Hilldale Giants). The Hilldale team had its own bevy of stars, including future Hall of Famers Louis Santop, Biz Mackey, and William "Judy" Johnson.

Game Three of the series, which was played at the Maryland Baseball Park in Baltimore because Pennsylvania's Blue Laws did not allow games on

## Pride of Smoketown

Sunday, had Bell on the mound for the Monarchs and Red Ryan on the mound for Hilldale. Bell went 12 innings, allowed 10 hits, and gave up six runs (four earned); he walked nine batters, struck out four, and hit one batsman while going 0-for-3 at the plate himself. Fielding errors by the Monarchs in the fifth and ninth innings allowed Hilldale to stay in the game. In the 13th inning, Bell moved to right field and Bullet Joe Rogan came on to pitch. The game, still tied, was called on account of darkness after the 13th.

Bell started two more contests over the course of the 10-game series. In Game Six he was the winning pitcher as he logged eight solid innings on the mound and hit an RBI double to help his own cause. Kansas City won, 6-5, and now trailed in the series by three games to two. The Monarchs won the next two games, and then Bell started Game Nine hoping to win the clincher for his team. He got a no-decision, lasting only four innings and surrendering two runs (one earned), as Hilldale prevailed, 5-3, to even the series at four games apiece. In Game Ten the Monarchs won the series when Mendez pitched a three-hit shutout.

Bell returned to the Monarchs in 1925 and went 11-5 with a 2.80 ERA over 144⅔ innings in 22 appearances (15 starts) in the regular season and World Series. Mendez managed again, and the team included pitching stalwarts Rogan (15-2) and Nelson Dean (11-3) alongside Bell. The offense continued to be stout as four players hit .300 or better: Rogan (.360), center fielder Hurly McNair (.332), third baseman Newt Joseph (.323), and shortstop Dobie Moore (.312).

The 1925 Monarchs won the first half of the Negro National League season and finished the year with a record of 62-23. They played against the second-half winner, the St. Louis Stars, for the league championship. The St. Louis lineup included such luminaries as shortstop Willie Wells, center fielder James "Cool Papa" Bell, and the veteran Candy Jim Taylor, who also managed the team. William Bell took the mound in the third game of the seven-game series, losing to the Stars, 3-2. He also started Game Six, facing the Stars' Roosevelt Davis – another future Pittsburgh Crawfords teammate – and came away with a 9-3 victory that tied the series at three games apiece. Rogan started Game Seven, which the Monarchs won, 4-0, to capture the NNL title.

With the victory over the Stars, the Monarchs advanced to the Negro League World Series for a repeat matchup against the Hilldale team. This time Kansas City lost to Hilldale in six games. Bell pitched in the sixth and final game, losing a 5-2 decision to Phil Cockrell. He flied out with the bases loaded to end the game.[4]

At the beginning of the 1926 season the Monarchs added Cuban star Cristobal Torriente, another strong hitter. Bell's 15-6 record put him in a tie for the team lead in wins with Rogan, who was 15-5, and the veteran pair had the help of 19-year-old Chet Brewer, who went 13-2. Pitching carried the Monarchs in 1926; the batting fell off from the past few seasons. Torriente (.348) and Rogan (.306) were the only Monarchs batters to hit over .300. Kansas City won the first half of the NNL season with a record of 57-21 and faced the second-half winner, the Chicago American Giants, to determine the league championship. Kansas City won four of the first five games, but Chicago roared back to win the final four games and claimed the pennant.[5]

Rogan took over as the Monarchs' manager in 1927, and Bell returned to the hill as well, his fifth straight year with the team, owned by James Leslie "J.L." Wilkinson. In addition to his 13-3 record (second on the team to Rogan's 16-6 mark), Bell had an excellent 2.99 ERA that year. He batted .280 as the Monarchs (54-29) finished in second place behind the Chicago American Giants. In addition to the games played in their league slate, the Monarchs posted a 26-12 record in exhibition games. Fans turned out in great numbers wherever they played so that they could see Kansas City's great players and winning brand of baseball.[6]

# THE 1935 PITTSBURGH CRAWFORDS

After the Negro League season ended, Bell traveled to the Caribbean to play for the Habana Leones in the Cuban Winter League's 1927-28 season. According to Cuba baseball historian Jorge S. Figueredo, "This edition of Habana was probably the best they ever had in their illustrious history. Not only did the Reds run away with the pennant by 8 games, they had a team batting average of .310 and scored 208 runs in 33 games – over 6 tallies per outing."[7] Habana finished with a 24-13 record as Bell posted a 6-2 record, second best on the team behind Oscar Levis's 7-2 mark. Habana was so dominant that the Almendares team withdrew from the league after suffering an 18-4 thrashing as the hands of the Leones on January 21, and the remainder of the season was terminated shortly thereafter.[8]

On the heels of his success in Cuba, Bell again pitched for the Monarchs in 1928. In spite of an excellent 2.64 ERA, he managed only a 9-7 record for Kansas City as the Monarchs again finished second in the NNL with a 50-29-1 record, well off the 61-26 pace of the St. Louis Stars.

In the winter Bell returned to the Habana Leones and won as many games during the Winter League season – he finished with a 9-3 record – as he had during the much longer Negro League season. This time the full season was played, though Habana again thoroughly dominated the league and finished 10½ games ahead of second-place Almendares. Bell's nine victories tied for the league lead with Adolfo Luque, who went 9-2 for Cuba (8-2) and Habana (1-0).

After helping Habana to another title, Bell was able to accomplish the same feat with Kansas City as the Monarchs in 1929 won both halves of the Negro National League season. The Monarchs finished with a 63-17 record in NNL play and a 66-17 overall mark. Bell contributed to the team's success with a 14-4 record and 3.29 ERA in 26 games (17 starts) and by batting .299. There was neither an NNL playoff series nor a Negro League World Series that year, but the Monarchs did play a championship series against the Houston Black Buffaloes, the champions of the Texas-Oklahoma-Louisiana League who had finished the season with an awe-inspiring 67-8 record. The Monarchs, coming out of the more competitive NNL, bullied the Black Buffs and swept the four-game series, after which the Texas press declared the Kansas City squad to be the "Colored Champions of the World."[9]

When Bell returned for a third season in Cuba's Winter League, he likely expected more of the same results, but Havana ended the 1929-30 season in last place. Although Figueredo attributed Habana's collapse "mainly to poor pitching," Bell managed a 9-8 record for a team that finished at 20-30 in league play.[10] Bell's eight losses were the most in the league, but the fact that he finished with a winning record was a tribute to his remarkable pitching acumen.

Similarly, the Kansas City Monarchs regressed in 1930 and finished at 39-26 in NNL play, which put them third behind the St. Louis Stars (66-22) and the Detroit Stars (50-33). Two highlights of this season involved the Monarchs playing night games under owner J.L. Wilkinson's portable lighting system, and engaging in a 16-game barnstorming tour through Pennsylvania against the Homestead Grays.[11] Bell was the ace of the Kansas City staff in 1930, with a 10-4 record and a 2.96 ERA.[12] In a doubleheader against the San Luis Cubans, Bell pitched the first game, winning 5-3. Game Two saw the Monarchs win 4-3 for a sweep.[13]

Bell made a final trip to Cuba for the 1930 season, which ended up being played under unique circumstances. The actual Cuban Winter League season "was short-lived as only 5 games were played due to a contract dispute between the teams and the management of La Tropical Stadium."[14] Bell, playing for Habana once more, lost his only start, and Habana had a 1-2 record when the season was canceled.

After the regular Cuban season fell by the wayside, a special season – called "Unico" – took place at Almendares Park in November 1930.

## Pride of Smoketown

Three of the four Cuban teams – Almendares, Cienfuegos, and Habana – took part in Unico, with Marianao taking the fourth spot in place of the regular league's Santa Clara squad.[15] Bell finished the special season with a 1-3 record for Habana, which finished in third place with a 5-9 ledger. Perhaps because of the unusual circumstances surrounding the 1930 season, Bell never returned to Cuba.

Bell also failed to return to the Kansas City Monarchs in 1931. Before the season, legendary shortstop John Henry "Pop" Lloyd had been named manager of the newly formed New York Harlem Stars, and he was able to talk Bell, Frank Duncan, and Lee Livingston into leaving the Monarchs and joining his team. The Stars were an independent team that played a limited schedule, and Bell posted a 2-2 ledger with a 2.53 ERA for a squad that had only a 6-12 record.

Bell toiled for three different teams in 1932, including the Detroit Wolves and Homestead Grays in the East-West League and, later in the season, the Pittsburgh Crawfords. He was successful everywhere he went and compiled an 8-3 overall ledger that included a 5-2 mark with the Crawfords, third on the team in wins behind Satchel Paige (7-6) and Ted "Double Duty" Radcliffe (6-4). At the end of the 1932 season, the talent-laden Crawfords played a seven-game series against the Casey Stengel All-Stars. According to the *York* (Pennsylvania) *Dispatch*, Bell "'toyed' with the Stengels" as the Crawfords routed the All Stars, 11-2, in the first game of the series; Bell also won Games Three and Seven for a 3-0 record that paced all hurlers on both sides.[16]

In 1932 the Crawfords had been an independent team, but they joined the Negro National League for the 1933 campaign. The team finished the NNL slate with a 37-21-2 record (47-35-2 against all competition), in second place behind the Chicago American Giants. In Bell's first start of the the season, against the Nashville Elite Giants, he spun a four-hit, 7-0 shutout. But he finished with a 7-6 record in 17 games (13 starts) and had an unusually inflated 5.44 ERA; his win total was only fourth-best on the team.

Although Bell was 36 years old when the 1934 season started, the Crawfords were counting on him to be one of their starters. Bell responded with a fine season and posted an 11-4 record in league play that was second on the team only to Paige's 13-3 mark. The Crawfords finished with a 47-27-3 record and the second-best winning percentage in the NNL, but the team won neither half of the league season: the Philadelphia Stars were the first-half champions and the Chicago American Giants captured the second-half flag.

Bell started the 1935 season with the Crawfords, for whom he pitched to a 1-3 record. His most notable game of the year was the one-hitter he threw against the New York Cubans on May 23. The last game we know him to have pitched for the Crawfords was on May 28.[17] After that, Bell moved to the NNL's Newark Dodgers, where he took over as manager from Dick Lundy. Newark played its home games at Ollemar Stadium in Irvington, New Jersey. The team finished dead last in the league with an 18-43-1 record. (The team's record under Bell was 12-24-1.) Bell inserted himself into six games (two starts) for the Dodgers, going 2-1 with a 4.15 ERA.

In 1936 Brooklyn Eagles owners Abe Manley and Effa Manley purchased the Newark Dodgers and combined the two squads to form the Newark Eagles. They retained Bell as their new team's manager, and he piloted the Eagles to a 14-20 record before an impatient Abe Manley took the reins and led the team to a 13-11-1 finish; the combined 27-31-1 record was good enough for only a fourth-place finish in the NNL. On the mound, Bell finished the season at 4-4 with a 4.50 ERA.

Bell remained with the Eagles for a brief time in 1937. Now 39, he seldom called on himself to pitch (2-2, 3.77), and he retired as a player at the end of the season. He returned for one last stint as manager of the Newark team in 1948. The integration of Organized Baseball, begun in 1946, had depleted the Negro Leagues of much of their young talent and had brought about a dramatic decline in attendance. The Manleys asked Bell to come back for the 1948 campaign, and he led the Eagles to a 29-28-1 record and a third-place finish in NNL play. The home attendance was so dismal that when the Negro National League disbanded after the season, the Manleys sold the franchise and the new owners moved the team to Houston, Texas. Although Bell's adopted hometown of El Campo is only 64 miles southwest of Houston, he was now retired from professional baseball for good.

Bell was held in high esteem by his fellow Negro League players, both during and after his playing days. Crawfords outfielder Jimmie Crutchfield noted, "William Bell pitched a lot like a major-league pitcher, had good control, would mix up his pitches and would just outsmart you at the plate."[18] As to Bell's personal side, star Negro League pitcher Chet Brewer simply said, "[He was] a fine gentleman and a scholar."[19]

Once Bell permanently retired from baseball, he and his wife, Betty, became pillars of the El Campo community. Bell became a successful businessman "on the west side of El Campo at a time when stores separated their clients by color," and he devoted all of his spare time to community service.[20] Among his many activities, he "helped build a new church and organized a local NAACP chapter, making sure all blacks were registered to vote. He organized an 'old-timers' baseball club and a youth baseball league that played at a cow pasture called the Bull-Patch."[21] Betty Bell was a school principal in the nearby town of Louise and later taught special- education courses at El Campo High School. The couple adopted a daughter, Mary, and also raised four nieces and nephews. Mary Bell followed in her adoptive mother's footsteps and worked as a teacher and counselor in El Campo from 1973 until her death in 2009.

Bell died in an automobile accident at the age of 71 on March 16, 1969, when the pickup truck he was driving collided with another vehicle in El

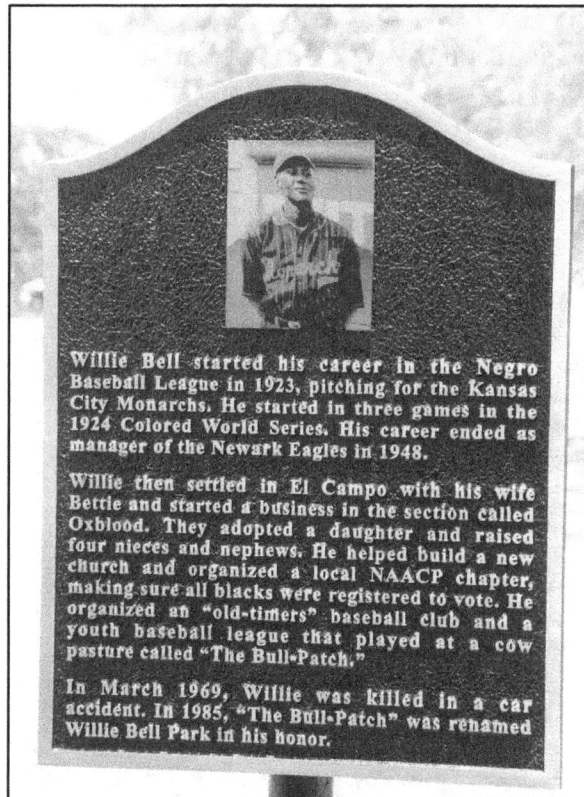

*Marker that commemorates the life and career of pitcher Willie Bell at the park that bears his name in El Campo, Texas, where Bell lived most of his life.*

Campo. Although Bell's truck was struck on the driver's side and both vehicles were thrown more than 30 feet by the impact, police noted that his injuries were slight and "expressed the opinion that Bell died of a heart attack."[22] Bell is buried in the El Campo Community Cemetery, along with Betty and Mary. Also buried there are his mother, Viney, and his older brother, David, a World War I veteran who spent his life in El Campo until his death in 1975.

Bell remained such a popular figure in El Campo that the city named a park after him in 2009. According to the *El Campo Leader-News*, the park is "set on the grounds he once rented so that colored children would have a place to play baseball."[23]

At the park's dedication ceremony, Bell's surviving family members fondly reminisced about their uncle. Paul Bell, a nephew, recalled, "He raised us all up like we was his kids" and asserted that he had "always wanted to help people."[24]

Paula Bell Cole, a great-niece, who was a young child at the time of William's death, best summed up William Bell's influence on the people he came in contact with by stating simply that "more 'Uncle Bills' are needed."[25]

## Author Notes

1. William Bell is often listed as William Bell Sr., but, as this article indicates, Bell had no sons and was not a "Sr." The confusion comes from the fact that some sources have erroneously listed another Negro League pitcher, William Bell Jr., as his son. However, William "Lefty" Bell Jr. was born in 1930 in Des Moines, Iowa, and was obviously no relation to William Bell of El Campo, Texas.

2. Although William Bell managed the Newark Eagles in 1948, a *Chicago Defender* article dated August 6, 1948, reported that "Willie Bell [would be one of] the starting [Homestead] Grays twirlers" in a doubleheader against the New York Black Yankees that day.[26] According to the Center for Negro League Baseball Research's article about William Bell, all other newspaper articles point to his having been with Newark for the entire season.[27] Frederick C. Bush wrote in the book *Bittersweet Goodbye*, "There is the possibility, though, that the 'Willie Bell' listed in the paper as the starting pitcher against the Black Yankees was actually Willie Pope," who was a pitcher for the Grays in 1948.[28]

3. In regard to William Bell's time in Cuba, it has been established that Cliff Bell, another former Kansas City Monarchs pitcher, has erroneously received credit for the seasons that William played in the country's winter league. Dr. Layton Revel and Luis Munoz, co-authors of the Forgotten Heroes article cited in the Notes cite a *Chicago Defender* article among other items to support their conclusion; their most irrefutable proof is a photo of William Bell in a Habana Leones uniform.[29] Negro League researcher Gary Ashwill also provides documentation in the form of ships' logs that list William Bell as a passenger traveling from Cuba to the United States, and he has a different photo of William Bell and two teammates in Habana uniforms posted on his website, which is dedicated to the history of the Negro and Latin leagues.[30] Additionally, Bush's research turned up William Bell's World War II draft card, which lists his height as 5-feet-6. (Most sources inaccurately list a height of 5-feet-11.) William Bell's nickname in Cuba – also erroneously attributed to Cliff Bell – was Campanita, which means Little Bell. The moniker was obviously applied to William Bell due to his short physical stature.

## Sources

All Negro League statistics are taken from the Seamheads.com website unless otherwise indicated. It must be kept in mind that there is great discrepancy among sources regarding Negro League statistics, but Seamheads is becoming the definitive source and continues to conduct research and add new statistics.

All Cuban League statistics are taken from Jorge S. Figueredo, *Cuban Baseball: A Statistical History, 1878-1961* (Jefferson, North Carolina: McFarland & Company, Inc., 2003). Figueredo is one of many authors who has erroneously attributed William Bell's Cuban League career to Cliff Bell, but his book is otherwise accurate in regard to the league's history and statistics; see author note 3 (above) for more information about how this error has recently come to light and been corrected.

Unless otherwise indicated, all information about the 1924 Negro League World Series was taken from Larry Lester, *Baseball's First Colored World Series: The 1924 Meeting of the Hilldale Giants and Kansas City Monarchs* (Jefferson, North Carolina: McFarland & Co., 2006).

## Notes

1. William Bell 1942 World War II draft registration card, ancestry.com, accessed September 14, 2019. Many sources list either Galveston or Lavaca County, Texas, as Bell's birthplace. Bell listed Hallettsville on his draft registration card, confirming that Lavaca County is correct.

2. The college moved to its current location in Dallas in 1990.

3. Dr. Layton Revel and Luis Munoz, "Forgotten Heroes: William Bell," 2. cnlbr.org/Portals/0/Hero/William-Bell.pdf, accessed October 4, 2019.

4. Kyle McNary, *Black Baseball: A History of African-Americans & the National Game* (New York: PRC Publishing, 2003), 110.

5. All statistics and records for the 1926 season were taken from Revel and Munoz: 7.

6. Revel and Munoz, 7-8.

7. Figueredo, *Cuban Baseball: A Statistical History, 1878-1961* (Jefferson, North Carolina: McFarland & Company, Inc., 2003), 174.

8. Figueredo, 174.

9. Revel and Munoz, 9-11.

10. Figueredo, 182.

11. Revel and Munoz, 11-12.

12. Revel and Munoz, 12.

13. "Monarchs Take Two," *Chicago Defender*, April 26, 1930: 8.

14. Figueredo, 189.

15. Figueredo, 192-193.

16. John Holway, *The Complete Book of Baseball's Negro Leagues: The Other Half of Baseball History* (Fern Park, Florida: Hastings House Publishers, 2001), 296-297.

17. This information is contained in Bill Nowlin's timeline for the 1935 Pittsburgh Crawfords season in the present volume.

18. Lester, *Baseball's First Colored World Series* (Jefferson, North Carolina: McFarland & Co., 2006), 52.

## THE 1935 PITTSBURGH CRAWFORDS

19   Lester.

20   Shannon Crabtree, "City Honors Willie Bell Park Namesake," *El Campo* (Texas) *Leader-News*, June 24, 2009.

21   Plaque at Willie Bell Park.

22   "Fatal Accident," *El Campo Leader-News*, March 19, 1969: 1.

23   Shannon Crabtree, "Go Green at City Parks," *El Campo Leader-News* Routine Special Section: Experience El Campo, issuu.com/ecleader-news/docs/eln_routinespecialsection, accessed September 14, 2019.

24   Crabtree, "City Honors Willie Bell Park Namesake."

25   Crabtree, "City Honors Willie Bell Park Namesake."

26   "Grays Oppose Yanks Today," *Chicago Defender*, August 6, 1948: C3.

27   Revel and Munoz, 28.

28   Frederick C. Bush and Bill Nowlin, eds., *Bittersweet Goodbye: The Black Barons, the Grays, and the 1948 Negro League World Series* (Phoenix: Society for American Baseball Research, 2017), 361.

29   Revel and Munoz, 28; also see "Manleys Hire Bill Bell to Pilot Newark," *Chicago Defender*, March 27, 1948: 11.

30   Gary Ashwill, "Which Bell in Cuba?", October 18, 2014, agate-type.typepad.com/agate_type/2014/10/which-bell-in-cuba.html, accessed October 10, 2019.

# THEODORE BOND

## By Richard Bogovich

"What did I do to deserve this?" If Theodore Bond had asked that question a few weeks into the 1935 Negro National League season, nobody would have blamed him. During spring training with the powerhouse Pittsburgh Crawfords, he rose from obscurity to become the starting shortstop. Though his batting average in those first weeks was low, the Crawfords had won nine of their first 12 NNL games.[1] Then, less than a month into the regular season, he was involved in one of the rarest transactions in the history of professional sports: He wasn't simply cut, traded, or demoted to some minor-league team; rather, he was *donated* to the NNL team with the most losses, despite the *Pittsburgh Courier's* calling him "the best first-year prospect in the League" at that point.[2]

Theodore Hubbard Bond was born in Kimball, West Virginia, on January 25, 1904,[3] to William and Louise (Robinson) Bond. His parents were on the same page of the 1880 census, living with their respective parents in Bedford County, Virginia. Theodore's paternal grandparents were farmers Ann and Stephen Bond, and his maternal grandparents were Mary and William Robinson, the

*Shortstop Ted Bond played in 12 NNL games for the Crawfords in 1935 before he was dealt to the Newark Dodgers; he batted .302 in an additional 25 NNL games with Newark.*

(Courtesy Noir-Tech Research, Inc.)

latter a blacksmith. Virginia marriage records indicate that Louise and William had been wed on December 28, 1892, in their home county. The 1910 census indicates that Theodore's three oldest siblings, brother Landon and sisters Nora and Mabel, were born in Virginia between 1894 and 1901. His sister Berta was born in West Virginia around 1902, and their youngest brother, Vernon, was born in 1917.[4]

The Bonds lived in Kimball until at least 1912, because that was identified as Landon's home community in June of that year when he was a student at Storer College in Harpers Ferry, West Virginia. Landon reportedly graduated the following year from Storer, a historically black college that produced mostly teachers.[5] Within a few years, Landon and his family moved to Bluefield, about 30 miles to the southeast. He and his parents had separate entries in Bluefield's 1915 city directory, though with their surname misspelled as "Barnes." William was identified as a brakeman for the Norfolk and Western Railway. Theodore's parents lived on the 100 block of Vine Street for the rest of their lives, very close to the John Stewart Memorial Methodist Episcopal Church, which was built in 1921. At some point, William Bond began to serve as a minister in addition to his railroad job.[6]

By 1920, Bluefield's African-Americans were doing relatively well collectively, and they were served by two hotels, at least four grocery stores, several eateries, four doctors, two hospitals, and two drugstores.[7] Nevertheless, racism had intensified after the World War, and in 1924 the Ku Klux Klan opened an office in Bluefield. It soon held a rally in a theater, and Bluefield's mayor made welcoming remarks to a full house.[8]

According to Chester Washington of the *Courier*, Theodore Bond was a product of the Bluefield Colored Institute,[9] which had been renamed Bluefield State Teachers College by the time he joined the Crawfords. In fact, in Bluefield's 1925 city directory, his occupation was specified as a teacher. Not surprisingly, the *Courier* also reported that he had played on the college's baseball team.[10]

Bond's time as a teacher was apparently short-lived because, by the publication of the next city directory, for 1927, he was listed as an employee of the Norfolk and Western Railway, like his father.[11] By mid-1924 the African-American employees of the railroad's machine shop had formed a baseball team, and it received "strong support" from the company's local management, "both morally and financially," according to the *Bluefield Daily Telegraph*.[12] By May of 1926 this team had taken on the name the "Smart Set" when it defeated the Pittsburgh Keystones and Bond's alma mater.[13] Box scores for Smart Set games are almost nonexistent, but in September of that year Baltimore's *Afro-American* newspaper printed a letter signed by four of the team's leaders, including "T. Bonds," in which they claimed a record of 34 wins to only eight losses.[14]

According to the Center for Negro League Baseball Research, Bond played on "numerous" baseball teams in Cleveland from 1927 through 1934.[15] For the 1931 season, the Cleveland Giants had signed infielder "T. Bond" by mid-February, and he starred in a shutout against the Paducah Black Hawks in mid-June.[16] However, by the end of July, Theodore Bond was playing the first of several seasons in Grand Rapids, Michigan.[17]

He played on teams led by third baseman John Shackelford, who played four seasons in the top Negro Leagues from 1924 to 1930. Shackelford later graduated from the University of Michigan Law School, practiced as an attorney, and was president of the United States Baseball League during its two seasons, 1945 and 1946.[18] The first team onto which Shackelford recruited Bond was the Fineis Oil Giants, and one of its stars was Juan Padrón, a Cuban who pitched in the NNL from 1922 through 1926. Bond soon had the opportunity to watch Padrón and Shackelford play on Grand Rapids all-star teams that faced the previous year's American and National League pennant winners about two weeks apart. The locals defeated the Philadelphia Athletics, 4-3, and the St. Louis Cardinals, 2-1.[19] In between those exhibitions, the Fineis team ran a winning streak to at least 18 games.[20] In a regional tournament semifinal game in late September, Bond faced Jack Wisner, a four-year National League pitcher, and his second-inning single off him led to the decisive run in a victory that guaranteed the Giants at least $500. (Despite having Padrón starting, Shackelford's nine lost the finale, 6-5.)[21] Bond presumably found his experience in 1931 to be rewarding, because in Bluefield's city directory for 1932 his occupation was listed as "ball player."

In 1932 the Fineis Oil Giants began a 10-game winning streak in May, and Bond helped to add one more victory with four hits on June 5. Later that month, he was called "one of the greatest shortstops in western Michigan," though by that point he'd been given a questionable nickname, "Midget."[22] Over the course of about four weeks, starting in late August, Bond and the Giants faced several nationally known teams. They split a pair of games against the Nashville Elite Giants, the Negro Southern League's second-half champions. Nashville won, 7-6, on August 27, but the next day's game was tied, 1-1, until the sixth inning, when Bond scored the final run on a perfect squeeze bunt by Shackelford.[23] The Giants played a series against the Kansas City Monarchs during the first half of September and battled the Indianapolis ABCs later in the month.[24] In one game vs. the ABCs, Bond batted in the sixth inning against reliever Candy Jim Taylor, the Indianapolis manager, with a runner on base and the Giants trailing, 6-4. Bond homered over the right-field fence to tie the score, but his team ultimately lost, 9-8.[25]

For 1933, the team's name changed to the Dixie Gas Stars and it had many newcomers. The *Grand Rapids Press* stated that several of them hailed "from West Virginia and were handpicked by Midget Bond, who is generally regarded as one of the greatest shortstops ever seen here in semipro circles."[26] In June Bond was sent home to Bluefield in search of two additional pitchers. The Stars needed help because they had scheduled 18 games across a span of 13 consecutive days into early July.[27] Apparently one of his recruits was Carl Howard, who in 1935 pitched briefly for the NNL's Brooklyn Eagles.[28]

Bond likely did more recruiting early in the 1934 season, because two additional Dixie newcomers also were from West Virginia.[29] In any event, not long after Independence Day a high point for Bond was being named to a local mixed-race all-star team that faced the American League's eventual pennant winners, the Detroit Tigers. He was the leadoff batter in the game, which was played on July 11 before 2,200 fans. Vic Frazier, in his fourth American League season, pitched a complete game. Shackelford was the hitting star for the locals, with a double among his three hits, to offset two errors. Bond went hitless but his four assists without an error helped keep the game close, and it was tied, 2-2, after eight innings. In the top of the ninth, the Tigers scored the final run when Jo-Jo White smacked what was scored a double, but he continued to home plate when the Grand Rapids right fielder misplayed the ball.[30] Still, 1934 was a very successful season for Bond, Shackelford, and the Stars as they won 84 games and lost only 25.[31]

During the first half of March 1935, the Pittsburgh Crawfords franchise included Theodore Bond on its list of players "submitted to the National Association of Negro baseball clubs in convention in Philadelphia."[32] He had been recommended to them by "Attorney Shackelford."[33] Bond made a good early impression with three singles in one of the first spring-training exhibition games, a 5-4 win over the Memphis Red Sox in New Orleans.[34] Bond received a nice writeup in the *New York Amsterdam News* later in April: "Although Manager [Oscar] Charleston has continually expressed a preference for big men, one little man at least has changed Charley's mind. This man is Bond, peppery little shortstop who hails from Grand Rapids, Mich., and is playing ball like a house afire," the African-American weekly wrote. It added, "Bond may not win the first-string shortstop's job this season, but if he doesn't he will give the regular short a hot race."[35]

Theodore Bond, at the age of 31, remained on the roster as the regular season began on May 11. That day, Chester Washington of the *Pittsburgh Courier* correctly anticipated that the Craws' starting lineup at home against the New York Cubans would include "Timothy Bond, a promising young newcomer from Grand Rapids, Mich., at short."[36] (Bond was then called Timothy repeatedly, but it seems more like an error than a nickname.) From a preview of the game in the *Pittsburgh Press*, it seems that Bond was assigned 6 as his uniform number.[37] Bond, who batted eighth, went hitless in the Craws' 6-5 win, but he was credited with two putouts and three assists. He also participated in the game's only double play, which the *Chicago Defender* specified as "Charleston to Bond to Charleston."[38]

Bond's first NNL hit came the next day in his team's second game, which was the first game of a doubleheader. He had two singles in that game, and what was presumably the second of them was well timed: The Cubans had tied the score, 1-1, in the top of the seventh inning, and Bond singled to right in the bottom half of the frame. He then scored the final run of the game on a triple by Cool Papa Bell. Bond also helped with six assists.[39] The *Courier* called him a "sterling young star who made a fine impression by his fielding in the Cubans-Crawfords series."[40]

The Crawfords won nine of their first 12 regular-season games, though Bond had a batting average of just .194. Over the same span, the Newark Dodgers had won just three games and lost 11.[41] One of those losses was at home to Charleston's nine, and Crawfords owner Gus Greenlee was impressed that 4,000 fans had come to watch their weak local team. He decided to make a gift of two players to the Dodgers, namely Bond and pitcher William Bell, who was immediately named Newark's player-manager.[42] In the Dodgers' 7-6 loss at home to the Crawfords on June 3, Bell put Bond into the second slot in his batting order, and the rookie responded with a double, single, sacrifice, and a run scored, while handling five chances without an error.[43] He put his name into a headline later that month when his three-run double against the Homestead Grays was the key blow in an 8-5 victory at home.[44]

Bond did well enough during his first two months with Newark to finish third among Eastern shortstops in East-West All-Star Game balloting with a respectable total of 11,369 votes. Jake Stephens of Philadelphia edged Bill Yancey of Brooklyn by just 52 votes, 14,028 to 13,976.[45] Bond did quite well overall with Newark; his batting average was .302 in 25 NNL games.[46]

In April 1936 it was reported that Bond would play his baseball back in Grand Rapids, where John Shackelford continued to lead the Chicky Colored Giants. In two preseason articles, it was clear Bond had picked up a new nickname, "Dad." He was again asked to find new talent back home in Bluefield.[47] In an early loss, he batted cleanup, right behind Shackelford, but in a July doubleheader he was back in his more familiar leadoff spot.[48]

In 1937 Bond was with the Chicago American Giants of the Negro American League. It was possible that he had become interested in playing in Chicago because his brother Landon (and his wife, Essie) had been living there since at least the time of the 1930 census. In fact, ample evidence points to Theodore living the rest of his very long life in Chicago. Bond played third base for the American Giants. One highpoint for him came early during the season's second half, in a loss to the Atlanta Black Crackers. He batted second, smacked two doubles and a single, and scored both of his team's runs.[49] In early August Bond batted leadoff in both games of a doubleheader against the Detroit Stars and combined for four runs, three hits including a triple, and two stolen bases.[50] Bond finished third in NAL all-star voting at both third base and shortstop; as a result, he was put on the roster of the East-West All-Star Game, played on August 8, though he did not get into the game.[51] The American Giants won the NAL's second half and faced the first-half champions, the Kansas City Monarchs, in a playoff series. One game ended in a tie, but the Monarchs won five of the other six. In statistics for four of the games, Bond batted just .167, about 100 points lower than his average for the regular season.[52]

In 1940 Bond played a second season with the American Giants. Box scores consistently showed him batting second, such as in a 12-7 loss to the Monarchs in which he led the hitting attack with three hits in four at-bats and two runs scored.[53] Bond was second among Western third basemen in East-West voting but did not make the roster as a reserve.[54] Statistics are currently available for only about half as many of his games as in his 1935 and 1937 seasons, but they show him with a very good average of .304 for his final pro season. The American Giants finished the season in the bottom half of the standings.[55] According to the Center for Negro League Baseball Research, Bond attempted a comeback in 1943 with the Cleveland Buckeyes of the Negro American League in spring training.[56] Apparently, though, his professional baseball career now came to an end.

Bond's father died in Bluefield on December 10, 1940, and his brother Landon died in Chicago three weeks later, on January 1.[57] In early 1942, a few weeks after Theodore had turned 38, he completed a military registration card which indicated that his employer was a printing business called the Cuneo Press. His height was identified as 5-feet-5 and his weight as 142 pounds, which explained the "Midget" nickname that had been applied to him early in his career. He may have made annual trips to visit his mother and sister Mabel in Bluefield.[58] His mother died in early 1953, and Mabel died in November 1963.[59] At some point after Mabel's death, the youngest of the Bond family, Vernon, moved to Chicago. Cook County death records indicate that when Vernon died in 1986, he had been living at the same address as Theodore for many years, 4638 South Prairie Avenue. It may be no coincidence that this dwelling was located near South Side Park, the home of the Chicago American Giants until it was destroyed by fire on Christmas Day in 1940.

Cook County death records indicate Theodore Bond died on December 18, 1997, at the age of 93. The location of his burial (assuming that he was not cremated) was not noted.

## Source

Unless otherwise indicated, all Negro League statistics and team records have been taken from Seamheads.com.

## Notes

1. "Nat'l Association," *Afro-American* (Baltimore), June 1, 1935: 20. In 12 regular-season games with the Crawfords, Bond's batting average was .194, according to seamheads.com/NegroLgs/player.php?playerID=bond-01ted.

2. "Loyalty of Newark Fans Praised; Add W. Bell, Bond to Strengthen Club," *Pittsburgh Courier*, June 8, 1935: Section 2, 4.

3. The location and date of Theodore's birth are from the draft registration card he completed in 1942, and his middle name was used in his father's will, which is also accessible online. As of this writing, Theodore's entries at baseball-reference.com and seamheads.com identify his birthplace as Grand Rapids, Michigan, but there is ample evidence that he lived in West Virginia from his birth through his teens.

4. Vernon's date of birth was identified on the draft registration card he completed just after his 23rd birthday and in death records for Cook County, Illinois (though those two sources differed by a few days). Their mother was often called Louisa instead of Louise, and in the 1880 census as well as her marital record, her surname was entered as Robertson, not Robinson. However, twentieth-century records consistently used Robinson (including as her brother James's surname).

5. "Storer Has 25 Graduates," *Advocate* (Charleston, West Virginia), June 13, 1912: 1, 6. The Jefferson County Black History Preservation Society identifies Landon Bond as a 1913 alumnus in a list available at jcblackhistory.org/wp-content/uploads/2014/10/StorerCollegeStudents.pdf.

6. S.R. Anderson, "Among the Colored People," *Bluefield* (West Virginia) *Daily Telegraph*, August 11, 1921: 5. C.W. Tiffany, "News of the Colored People," *Bluefield Daily Telegraph*, December 13, 1940: 9. An early reference to him as a reverend was in "Funeral Rites Today for Matthew Preston," *Bluefield*

# THE 1935 PITTSBURGH CRAWFORDS

*Daily Telegraph*, March 12, 1930: 8. He may also have been the "Bro. W.M. Bond" who was scheduled to give an invocation at the Scott Street Baptist Church in early 1925; see "News of Colored Folk," *Bluefield Daily Telegraph*, January 9, 1925: 6. Theodore's sister Mabel and her husband, John Hairston, were also longtime residents on the same block of Vine Street.

7   Joe William Trotter Jr., *Coal, Class, and Color: Blacks in Southern West Virginia, 1915-32* (Urbana, Illinois: University of Illinois Press, 1990), 145-146. Trotter quoted from the *Bluefield Daily Telegraph*.

8   Trotter, 127-128.

9   Chester Washington, "Sez Ches," *Pittsburgh Courier*, May 25, 1935: Section 2, 5. The 1940 census indicated that his sister Mabel completed a year of college.

10  "Bond, New Craw Shortstop Find, Is W.Va. Product," *Pittsburgh Courier*, May 18, 1935: Section 2, 5.

11  He may also have worked for the Norfolk and Western railroad prior to being a teacher, based on "News of the Colored People," *Bluefield Daily Telegraph*, August 31, 1924: 30. "Theodore Bonds" served on the Entertainment Committee for what the "First Annual Picnic of Colored Employees of Pocahontas Division N&W."

12  "News of the Colored People," *Bluefield Daily Telegraph*, July 6, 1924: 24.

13  "Local Colored Team Wins Third Straight," *Bluefield Daily Telegraph*, May 13, 1926: 8. "Colored Institute Loses to Railroaders," *Bluefield Daily Telegraph*, May 16, 1926: 11. On May 21 the team took out an ad in the *Telegraph* (page 15) advertising two home games against the Winston Salem White Sox.

14  "Sports Mirror," *Afro-American* (Baltimore), September 4, 1926: 8. The Smart Set continued at least through 1930.

15  See cnlbr.org/Portals/0/Players%20Register/A-B%202018-04.pdf, specifically the entry for "Bond, Theo. H. (Timothy)."

16  "Cleveland Giants Form Company," *Chicago Defender*, February 21, 1931: 9. "Black Hawks Beaten," *Chicago Defender*, June 27, 1931: 8.

17  "Hopkins, Lansing to Visit Ramona," *Grand Rapids Press*, July 31, 1931: 21. In this article Bond's team was called "the Fineis Oils Colored Giants, of Lowell and Grand Rapids." Lowell is less than 20 miles east of Grand Rapids.

18  See SABR member Caleb Hardwick's biography of Shackelford at arkbaseball.com/tiki-index.php?page=-John+Shackelford. For more about his league presidency in 1945-1946, see seamheads.com/blog/2010/01/08/the-united-states-baseball-league/.

19  John J. McGinnis, "Grand Rapids Boys Beat Champion A's," *Grand Rapids Press*, August 18, 1931: 15. Roscoe D. Bennett, "Grand Rapids Team Defeats Cardinals," *Grand Rapids Press*, September 3, 1931: 21. Two of the hits off the Cardinals were made by Neil Robinson of the Fineis nine, according to "Padron to Pitch in Tourney Sunday," *Grand Rapids Press*, September 3, 1931: 23. This is almost certainly the Neil Robinson who later played in multiple East-West All-Star Games. Neil also played on the Fineis team in 1932, with a brother.

20  "Oils Hope to Beat Old Elster Record," *Grand Rapids Press*, August 27, 1931: 20.

21  "Fineis Oils Win Tourney Struggle," *Grand Rapids Press*, September 28, 1931: 13. "Ramonas Victors in Tourney Final," *Grand Rapids Press*, October 5, 1931: 15.

22  "Fineis Giants Win Two More Games," *Grand Rapids Press*, June 6, 1932: 12. "Mariners to Play State's Leading Independents in Twilight Game Friday," *Ludington* (Michigan) *Daily News*, June 22, 1932: 6. This article noted that Bond teammate and longtime local ballplayer Walt "Big Six" Coe, was "a member of the Grand Rapids detective force."

23  "Fineis Giants Split Two with Nashville," *Grand Rapids Press*, August 29, 1932: 10.

24  "Monarchs Arrive for Fineis Series," *Grand Rapids Press*, September 9, 1932: 21. "Monarchs Victors over Oils Friday," *Grand Rapids Press*, September 10, 1932: 15. "Extra Innings in Oil-Monarch Series," *Grand Rapids Press*, September 12, 1932: 15. "Indianapolis Nine Booked for Series," *Grand Rapids Press*, September 16, 1932: 20. "Fineis Oils Lose to Visiting Nine," *Grand Rapids Press*, September 17, 1932: 13.

25  "Jim Taylor's Nine in Easy Victory, 9-8," *Chicago Defender*, September 24, 1932: 8.

26  "Shackelford's Giants Starting Play Sunday," *Grand Rapids Press*, May 26, 1933: 22.

27  "Dixie Stars Face Eighteen Contests in Thirteen Days," *Grand Rapids Press*, June 22, 1933: 26.

28  By mid-August the Stars had pitchers from West Virginia named Sailor Howard and Still, according to "Second Giant-Dixie Game on Saturday," *Grand Rapids Press*, August 18, 1933: 16. This article indicated that at some point Juan Padrón had switched to the Pere Marquette Colored Giants. Sailor Howard's time with the Brooklyn Eagles was noted in "Chicky Presents Star Negro Nine," *Grand Rapids Press*, April 20, 1936: 13. According to seamheads.com/NegroLgs/player.php?playerID=howar01ed-, a pitcher for the Chicago American Giants in 1946, Ed Howard, was also nicknamed Sailor.

29  "Dixie Stars Face David Nine First," *Grand Rapids Press*, May 9, 1934: 20. The two new players from West Virginia were Watkins, a catcher, and Palmer, a first baseman and pitcher.

30  "Tigers Defeat Rapids Nine," *Detroit Evening Times*, July 11, 1934: 15. The box score was printed on page 17. See also John J. McGinnis, "Tigers Beat Locals in Ninth Inning, 3-2," *Grand Rapids Press*, July 11, 1934: 16. The Detroit paper's box score didn't credit Bond with any putouts, and credited his team with only 25, but the Grand Rapids paper's box score credited Bond with one putout and the team with 27. McGinnis noted that the

crowd was roughly half the size of the Tigers' recent exhibition in Traverse City, about 140 miles to the north. "Many diamond devotees undoubtedly were kept away by the prices, which ranged up to $1.65 for adults," he wrote. "This, by the way, is just what you will pay for a box seat at Navin field at any regularly scheduled American league game. An ordinary reserved grandstand seat, even for doubleheaders, costs only $1.40 in Detroit."

31. This record is according to the Kent Base Ball Club, a founding team of the Vintage Base Ball Association, as reported at kentbaseball.wordpress.com/history/timeline-of-baseball-in-grand-rapids/.

32. "Craws' Roster," *Pittsburgh Courier*, March 16, 1935: Section 2, 4.

33. "Bond, New Craw Shortstop Find, Is W.Va. Product."

34. "Craws Top Memphis, to Play in New Orleans," *Pittsburgh Courier*, April 20, 1935: Section 2, 5.

35. "'Craws' Take Clarksdale," *New York Amsterdam News*, April 27, 1935: 11.

36. Chester Washington, "Sez Ches," *Pittsburgh Courier*, May 11, 1935: Section 2, 4.

37. Paul Kurtz, "Negro Nine Opens Here with Cubans," *Pittsburgh Press*, May 11, 1935: 8.

38. "Crawfords Win 2, Tie Pair in Series with N.Y.," *Pittsburgh Courier*, May 18, 1935: Section 2, 4. "League Scores," *Chicago Defender*, May 18, 1935: 14. Though he was hitless, at least Bond wasn't listed among the batters who struck out.

39. "Craws-Cubans," *Pittsburgh Courier*, May 18, 1935: Section 2, 5.

40. "Bond, New Craw Shortstop Find, Is W.Va. Product."

41. "Nat'l Association," *Afro-American* (Baltimore), June 1, 1935: 20. The Cubans kept Newark out of last place with a record of 2-8 for a .200 winning percentage, versus .214 for the Dodgers.

42. "Loyalty of Newark Fans Praised." The full quote, excerpted in the first paragraph, was, "Bond is the Grand Rapids flash. A sure fielder, steady hitter, and looms as the best first-year prospect in the League."

43. "Gibson's Prodigious Homer Paves Way for Crawfords Victory Over Dodgers," *Central New Jersey Home News* (New Brunswick), June 4, 1935: 12.

44. "Bond's Double Cleans Bases and Gives Newark Dodgers Win Over Homestead Grays, *Central New Jersey Home News,* June 25, 1935: 12. The first paragraph noted that the game was "a non-league tussle."

45. "The East," *Pittsburgh Courier*, August 10, 1935: Section 2, 5.

46. seamheads.com/NegroLgs/player.php?playerID=bond-01ted.

47. "Chicky Presents Star Negro Nine," *Grand Rapids Press*, April 20, 1936: 13. "Postums Will Open with Chicky Giants," *Grand Rapids Press*, April 30, 1936: 25. Bond's trip home from Grand Rapids was confirmed in "News of the Colored People," *Bluefield Daily Telegraph*, May 13, 1936: 9.

48. "Postum Wins 6-1 at Grand Rapids," *Battle Creek* (Michigan) *Enquirer and Evening News*, May 11, 1936: 13. "Postums Divide at Grand Rapids," *Battle Creek Enquirer and Evening News*, July 13, 1936: 9. In the July doubleheader, Howard was the winning pitcher for Bond's team, but Juan Padrón was the losing pitcher for them in the nightcap.

49. Ric Roberts, "Crax Crash Chicago American Giants, 8 to 2," *Atlanta Daily World*, July 21, 1937: 5.

50. "Giants Make It 3 Over Detroit to Sweep Set," *Chicago Defender*, August 7, 2937: 21. In the first game of the doubleheader he had the pleasure of watching the other three infielders turn a triple play.

51. "Chicago Ready for Big Baseball Classic," *Chicago Defender*, August 7, 1937: 19. "Colored Nines Meet Today in All-Star Game," *Chicago Tribune*, August 8, 1937: Part 2, 2.

52. seamheads.com/NegroLgs/player.php?playerID=bond-01ted; seamheads.com/NegroLgs/year.php?yearID=1937&lgID=All&tab=standings.

53. "Twin Bill Split on Sunday," *Chicago Defender*, August 3, 1940: 24.

54. "Hilton Smith Tops East vs West Voting," *Chicago Defender*, August 10, 1940: 24. "East and West Negro All-Star Lineups Named," *Chicago Tribune*, August 16, 1940: 27.

55. seamheads.com/NegroLgs/player.php?playerID=bond-01ted; seamheads.com/NegroLgs/year.php?yearID=1940.

56. cnlbr.org/Portals/0/Players%20Register/A-B%202018-04.pdf.

57. C.W. Tiffany, "News of the Colored People," *Bluefield Daily Telegraph*, December 13, 1940: 9. "Burials From Metropolitan Funeral Parlors," *Chicago Defender*, January 11, 1941: 4. All evidence points to Theodore's sister Nora having died before their father; she seems to have disappeared from the public record after the 1910 census.

58. Examples of reports on his visits to his mother and sister Mabel: C.W. Tiffany, "News of the Colored People," *Bluefield Daily Telegraph,* December 28, 1944: 7. "Personals," *Bluefield Daily Telegraph*, January 6, 1946: 15. "News of the Colored People," *Bluefield Daily Telegraph*, December 30, 1947: 9.

59. West Virginia death records indicate that Louise Violet Bond died on February 6, 1953, and was buried in Bedford County, Virginia, as was her husband. Toward the end of 1963, Berta "Bertie" Matthews became Theodore's only surviving sister, according to "Deaths and Funerals," *Bluefield Daily Telegraph*, November 13, 1963: 3. Family obituaries and trips back to Bluefield never mention Theodore having a wife.

# ERNEST "SPOON" CARTER

### By Frederick C. Bush

*Pitcher Ernest "Spoon" Carter was 4-1 with the 1935 Crawfords. He is pictured here with the 1950 Winnipeg Buffaloes, the inaugural Manitoba-Dakota League champions, for whom he went 4-2 at the age of 47.*

(Courtesy of Jay-Dell Mah/Western Canada Baseball)

Although Ernest "Spoon" Carter was never in the top tier of Negro League aces, he had enough pitching acumen to remain in great demand over the course of a 17-year career that also included stints in the Dominican Republic, Cuba, Mexico, and Canada. In fact, teams' desires for Carter's services placed him at the center of numerous disputes, from a 1934 quarrel between the Negro Southern League and Negro National League, to an international squabble between Pittsburgh Crawfords owner Gus Greenlee and the government of Dominican Republic dictator Rafael Trujillo in 1937, to another interleague clash – this time between the NNL and Negro American League – in 1940. Along the way, Carter's career constantly intersected with that of the legendary Satchel Paige, and he played on some of the greatest squads in Negro League history, including the 1935 Pittsburgh Crawfords and the 1943-44 Homestead Grays.

Ernest C. Carter was born on December 8, 1902, in Harpersville, Alabama, to Elick C. and Jennetta (Williamson) Carter. He was the oldest of the Carter children and was followed by a sister, Bera, and a brother, Weldon. Three cousins – Mary, Mattie, and Fred Carter – also grew up on the family farm. Young Ernest completed school through the eighth grade and then worked in Birmingham, 28 miles northwest of Harpersville. He began to play baseball in Birmingham's Industrial League, though it is not known for which team; perhaps it was already for the Tennessee Coal, Iron, and Railroad Company, where he worked in later years. It took time for Carter's pitching to be noticed, and he did not embark upon his career in professional baseball until the ripe old age of 29.

As Negro League baseball struggled amid the depression, Carter signed with the NSL's Birmingham Black Barons for the 1932 season. His rookie season turned out to be brief, because "it was the shortest season ever for a Birmingham team. They played for a little over a month before apparently folding without warning or acknowledgment in the local press."[1] Carter earned the distinction of being Birmingham's Opening Day starter and was the winning pitcher of record in a 7-3 road victory over the Memphis Red Sox.[2] He garnered another win in a 3-2 triumph over the Montgomery Grey Sox in the first game of a May 15 doubleheader.[3] However, the 1932 season "also was one of the poorest covered in the team's long history" and little else is known about the Black Barons' play before the team folded for the year.[4]

Birmingham fielded an independent team in 1933, but Carter moved to the Black Barons' former NSL rival in Memphis. The Red Sox were rolling in the first half of the NSL season, and the *Pittsburgh Courier* reported, "Spoon Carter, Lefty Harvey and Peterson have pitched wonderful ball to help the Sox along."[5] The national black press continued to remark on Memphis's strong showing as the *Chicago Defender* noted, toward the end of June, "It is noticeable that the Memphis bunch has not lost a series in seven weeks, some record for playing."[6] The Red Sox swept a three-game series from the Little Rock Stars at the end of June, with Carter winning the finale, on their way to the NSL's first-half title.[7] However, an event occurred that derailed Memphis's fine season, and they lost the NSL championship to the second-half titlist, the New Orleans Crescent Stars. What happened was that the Pittsburgh Crawfords, members of the second incarnation of the NNL that began play in 1933, gave tryouts to Carter, fellow Memphis hurler Bill Harvey, and pitcher Jim "Speed King" Lewis. According to the *Pittsburgh Courier*, "[t]hese men were later sent to the Akron Grays and ended the season with the Cleveland Club."[8]

The Crawfords' crosstown league rivals, the Homestead Grays, had moved to Akron, Ohio, for the second half of the NNL season and made their debut in that city in a Sunday doubleheader against the Nashville Elite Giants on July 23. Carter turned in a complete-game effort in the first tilt but was saddled with an 8-4 defeat as Nashville swept the twin bill.[9] Akron finished 3-7 in NNL play, and Carter struggled to a 0-3 record with an inflated 7.59 ERA. He then made his lone start for the Cleveland Giants, in which he surrendered seven runs – all earned – in $3\frac{1}{3}$ innings and took the loss. Contrary to the *Courier's* report, Carter finished the year with the Crawfords rather than the Giants. Now pitching for a stronger team, Carter responded accordingly and put up a 2.82 ERA over $22\frac{1}{3}$ innings with the Crawfords. In a late September game, the Crawfords lost to the Philadelphia Stars, 3-2, "despite the airtight pitching of Carter in the initial contest, in which he conceded but two hits to the Quaker City club."[10] Carter continued to be a victim of hard luck and had a 0-2 record with Pittsburgh to finish a winless season.

Carter's move to the Grays and, later, the Crawfords caused understandable displeasure in the Southern circuit and created friction between the NSL and NNL. Dr. J.B. Martin, the NSL's new president and co-owner of the Memphis Red Sox, wrote to NNL Chairman (and Crawfords owner) Gus Greenlee "[in] an effort to prevent club owners from raiding teams in the Southern league" and informed him "that the practice of the major circuit members must be brought to an end." Greenlee agreed to the demand, stating that he did "not want these players [Carter, Harvey, and Lewis] unless they are secured according to the rules and regulations of organized colored baseball."[11]

Although Greenlee's acquiescence meant that Memphis should have had claim to Carter's services once more, it is unclear where he began the 1934 season. What is known is that toward the end of May, Carter and Irving "Lefty" Vincent, another Pittsburgh Crawfords hurler, traveled to Bismarck, North Dakota, to play for car dealer Neil Churchill's integrated semipro team. Satchel Paige had plied his trade for Bismarck the previous year and had been contracted to return for a repeat engagement. When, in typical Paige fashion, he failed to show in Bismarck in 1934, Churchill lured Carter and Vincent to the Dakotas as replacements. A *Bismarck Tribune* account of the two pitchers' arrival reported that "Carter is in midseason form having won five out of seven starts this spring playing with Cleveland in the colored league. In the east he engaged Satchel Paige ... in two pitching duels and broke even."[12] The claim about Carter's pitching prowess that year appears to have been pure propaganda – most likely generated by Churchill – as there is no evidence that Carter pitched for Cleveland in 1934. In all likelihood, Churchill wanted to convince Bismarck fans that he had found a replacement who was the equal of Paige, and there was no better way to make that claim than to assert that Carter had split two duels with Satchel.

While Vincent found success in Bismarck, Carter continued to be plagued by the same bad luck he had experienced with the Crawfords in 1933. He started Bismarck's game against Jamestown "before a record-breaking Fourth of July crowd" and suffered a 4-2 defeat.[13] The *Bismarck Tribune* reported, "In the celebration day attraction, Carter held the Jimmie heavy hitters to six safeties but the combination of four errors and two homeruns paved the way for the Jamestown victory in a game which took only 1 hour and 32 minutes."[14] When Churchill decided he no longer needed Carter, Spoon found employment with Valley City, where he fared no better. On August 16 Bismarck and Valley City engaged in "a nip and tuck battle featuring Frank Stewart and Spoon Carter in a superb pitching duel. The Valley City hurler held his former Bismarck teammates to five hits in the first nine innings and allowed only one man to see third base."[15] Carter's good fortune ran out in the 10th inning and he took the loss in a 1-0 game.

After having traveled from the East to the Midwest to play in one integrated league, Carter journeyed to the West Coast to play in another, the California Winter League. As a member of Tom Wilson's Nashville Elite Giants, Carter teamed with a veritable "Who's Who in the Negro Leagues" – a group that included Satchel Paige, James "Cool Papa" Bell, Willie Wells, Turkey Stearnes, Mule Suttles, Andy "Pullman" Porter, and Larry Brown – to form as formidable a team as the league had ever seen. Satchel Paige was late to the show because he had just married Janet Howard in Pittsburgh on October 26, but he still dominated the league to the tune of an 8-0 record. Pullman Porter led the Elite Giants with 12 wins (to only three losses), but the Opening Day start once again went to Carter.[16]

The Elite Giants opened the 1934-35 season by winning two games of a three-game series against the Pirrone's All-Stars team at White Sox Park in Los Angeles. The first game was played on October 20 and numerous festivities marked the beginning of the new season. The press raved about the event:

> A mammoth street parade formed at 12th and Central Avenue, marched south on Central to Vernon Avenue, then to the park. One hundred and fifty cars and three bands were in the line of march. This was the greatest winter league opening ever staged here. Supervisor Gordon L. McDonough

pitched the first ball and Congressman William Treagur was the umpire.[17]

The Elite Giants romped to a 14-5 victory, and the "[f]eatures of the game were the pitching of Carter, the hitting of Stearns,[sic] Snow, Wells, Williams, Suttler [sic] and Carter, the all around playing of the Giants."[18]

Exactly one week later, Carter again went the distance in a much closer 9-8 triumph over the Pirrone's All-Stars in which Stearnes' second homer, in the bottom of the eighth, provided the game's decisive run.[19] In spite of Carter's 2-0 start, his role diminished once Paige arrived on the scene. Carter started (and completed) only one more game, which he also won, and finished the winter league season with a spotless 3-0 record. It also marked the first of many times that he was a member of a championship team.

Carter's success in California led to renewed interest by the Pittsburgh Crawfords, and he rejoined the team for the 1935 season. In a season preview, the *New York Age* predicted, "With their pitching staff strengthened by the addition of Ernest Carter, a brilliant right hander who was unbeaten in the California Winter League; Harvey, a sterling left hander and "Lefty" Schofield, another promising young portsider, the Pittsburgh Crawfords of 1935 are out to make a determined bid for the championship of the National Negro Baseball Association [which soon became known as the Negro National League]."[20] The *Age's* forecast turned out to be a classic example of understatement as the 1935 Crawfords have become labeled as the Negro Leagues' version of the 1927 Murderers' Row New York Yankees. The Crawfords finished the season with a 50-23-3 record, won the first-half NNL championship, and defeated the second-half champion New York Cubans to win the league title. The team's accomplishments were all the more impressive because they were achieved without expected ace Satchel Paige. In an ironic twist, Paige spurned the Crawfords in 1935 and spent most of the season with Churchill's Bismarck squad, the very team he had abandoned the previous year in order to pitch for Greenlee's Pittsburgh team.

Carter contributed as much as possible to the Crawfords' 1935 championship run. Negro League statistics are notoriously incomplete due to inconsistent press coverage, but available statistics show that Carter appeared in 11 league games and pitched to a 4-1 record with a 3.07 ERA in 55⅔ innings. His lone loss occurred early in the season, on May 21, when, "[i]n the first Negro game of the season [in Harrisburg, Pennsylvania,] the Chicago Americans walloped the Pittsburgh Crawfords 8 to 1 on the island."[21] Carter was erratic, walking three, hitting a batter, and unleashing a wild pitch while allowing seven runs in six innings of relief work. As Carter's statistics show, this game was not representative of his performance over the entire season. One regular-season highlight for Carter was his six-hit victory over the Crawfords' intrastate and NNL rival, the Philadelphia Stars, on May 25 at Greenlee Field in Pittsburgh.[22]

Although Carter pitched effectively in 1935, when the Crawfords faced the Cubans in the NNL championship series, he found himself relegated to bullpen duty. He appeared in Games Two and Four and allowed no runs in 7⅓ innings. In spite of Carter's efficiency, the damage had already been done in those contests, and the Crawfords lost both games, 6-3 and 3-2. Nonetheless, the Crawfords prevailed, 8-7, in Game Seven to capture the title. Carter was a champion once more, but the season was not yet over.

On September 22, the day after Pittsburgh's pennant-clinching victory, the Crawfords took part in a four-team doubleheader at Yankee Stadium. The Nashville Elite Giants defeated the Cubans 4-3 in the first game. The nightcap featured the Crawfords and the Philadelphia Stars and was a highly anticipated matchup because Paige was scheduled to pitch for the Crawfords. Even though Greenlee and Paige had been at odds all year, the former was all too aware of the lanky hurler's drawing power and had paid Paige $350 to appear in New York on this day. In a move that

# THE 1935 PITTSBURGH CRAWFORDS

should have surprised no one, but which certainly dismayed many, Paige failed to appear. Greenlee later informed the press that Paige had gone through Chicago while making his way to New Yotk and had been offered $500 to pitch there for the Kansas City Monarchs on September 22. Apparently, the Monarchs' offer "caused him to forget all about his agreement to appear in New York."[23] Carter stepped into the void created by Paige's absence and scattered 10 hits as he went the distance in the Crawfords' 12-2 throttling of the Stars.

Carter returned to the Crawfords in 1936, as did Paige. The team again captured the NNL title, this time by virtue of having the best record (48-33-2) rather than via a championship series against the second-half champion Washington Elite Giants, but was not as dominant as the previous year's squad had been. Carter was used sparingly, likely because – as his 6.94 ERA demonstrates – he was often ineffective, though he finished on the positive side of the ledger with a 3-2 record. One of Carter's more notable outings was a 3⅓-inning relief stint in an exhibition game against the semipro Belmar Braves on July 24. In that game, Josh Gibson lived up to his billing as the "Black Babe Ruth," clouting three home runs to lead Pittsburgh to victory. Gibson's third homer was a leadoff shot in the ninth inning which sparked the four-run rally that made winners of Carter and the Crawfords.[24] With his 34th birthday right around the corner and a poor individual season in his rear-view mirror, Carter may have wondered what the future held for him.

Initially, it looked as though the 1937 season would spell the end of Carter's career. He started out the year in Pittsburgh but performed worse than he had in 1936. In two appearances, one of them a start, he surrendered 11 earned runs in three innings. In spite of his bloated 33.00 ERA at the time, Carter was still in demand. In fact, the latest bid for his services was the final straw that sparked an international incident.

Rafael Trujillo, the dictator who ruled the Dominican Republic, had changed the name of the country's capital city from Santo Domingo to Ciudad Trujillo, and he wanted a baseball team that would win the Dominican League championship for him and the city that bore his name. Trujillo's pockets were not deep enough to lure white major leaguers, but he had ample money to entice prime Negro League talent. In mid-May, the *Pittsburgh Courier* reported:

> First intimation that the Negro National League was being 'raided' came three weeks ago, when Satchell Paige, the Peck's 'bad boy' of the baseball world; Catcher Perkins and Outfielder Christopher boarded a plane in New Orleans and hustled off to the Island Republic and its diamond 'gold field' breaking contracts with the Crawfords, last year's league leaders.[25]

Soon, players from the New York Cubans and New York Black Yankees also jumped their contracts to play in the Dominican Republic. Then, on May 8, Luis Mendez, an employee of the Dominican consulate in New York City, and Frederico Nina, a "wealthy lawyer and sportsman, representing a syndicate," were spotted scouting players at a game between the Crawfords and the Homestead Grays at Greenlee Field. The two men were arrested and "placed in jail on a charge of 'conspiracy' after they had made an attempt to sign Ernest Carter, wild speedball pitcher with the Pittsburgh Crawfords."[26]

A hearing was held on May 10, and Mendez and Nina were released on bonds of $500 each. Details of their attempt to sign Carter were revealed at this time. The two men testified that they had met with Carter at Greenlee's Crawford Grill and then had accompanied him to his hotel room, where they had made their offer. Crawfords manager Oscar Charleston was informed about the meeting and, according to the two Dominicans, stormed into the room and threatened them: "'I came in here to whip you,' Charleston is alleged to have said, 'but since you're so little, I won't do it. Why don't you go into the white leagues and get your players.'"[27]

Carter also testified at the hearing and admitted that "he had agreed to play for Nina for $775 for eight weeks. In addition to this, he was to receive two round-trip tickets for himself and his wife, plus expenses. To substantiate his claim, he produced a railroad ticket to Miami, which he claimed the representatives had purchased."[28] Carter ended up going to the Dominican Republic, where he played for Santiago, a team that belonged to one of Trujillo's political rivals.

On May 24, the NNL filed the names of all players who had defected from its league's teams with the US State Department and requested "return of the fleeing players and damages for the clubs formerly owning them."[29] By June, Greenlee was headed to Washington to plead the NNL's case with the US government. The *Pittsburgh Press* wrote that Greenlee planned to "create a diplomatic rumble that will shake the crease out of every frock coat and trouser leg from the State Department to Tanganyika" and reported that he already had "enlisted the support of 10 U. S. Senators and 28 Congressmen behind his charge that the Republic of San Domingo has 'dealt with, induced and lured away' ... the brightest stars in the Negro baseball firmament."[30] Greenlee, who had raided other teams for their top talent in the past, now saw the Dominican Republic's raids as an existential threat to all of Negro League baseball.

Meanwhile, the majority of "the brightest stars" of the Negro League belonged to the Ciudad Trujillo team, which, as expected, won the league championship. Little information is available about Carter's stint with the Santiago squad, but ship's logs show that he and the other Negro League defectors returned en masse to the United States in July. Upon arrival, they found out that they had been banned by the NNL, so Satchel Paige formed the Trujillo All-Stars (later renamed Satchel Paige's All-Stars) with his fellow "outlaws," and they sojourned first to Colorado to take part in the Denver Post Tournament.

Carter was a member of the All-Stars, managed by shortstop George Scales, who dominated the field and won the tournament. Paige, the biggest star of them all, was customarily late. He claimed that he had stayed in Cleveland to await a final payment from Trujillo and then had left in such a rush that he forgot his uniform; thus, he had waited in Chicago until his wife arrived there with both his uniform and glove.[31] It was a tale that only Paige could spin and what happened next was, according to Negro League historian Donn Rogosin, an example of "the ambiguity with which the Negro League regulars viewed Satchel Paige."[32] The tournament promoters pressured the team into letting Paige pitch in the championship of the double-elimination tournament, and Paige could smell the $1,000 in bonus money that was to be awarded to the winning pitcher of the final game. However, Paige did not win the prize because the All-Stars did all they could to throw the game.

The Duncan (Oklahoma) Halliburtons handed the All-Stars a 6-4 defeat, their first of the tournament, as "errors played havoc with the Stars in the first game."[33] The team made five errors – more than they had made in their other six tournament games combined – and catcher Clarence "Spoony" Palm was charged with three passed balls that allowed two unearned runs to score in the first inning.[34] Paige struck out 14 batters and allowed only five hits, but he trailed 5-4 after eight innings. Carter pitched the ninth inning and struck out the side, though he also allowed two hits and the Halliburtons' final run. When Leroy Matlock took the mound for the second game, he got the support that Paige had wanted as the All-Stars romped to an 11-1 victory over the Halliburtons to secure the tournament championship. Matlock received the $1,000 bonus and was named the tourney's most valuable player.

The entire All-Star team profited from its members' baseball prowess. In addition to the hefty sums the players had received for playing in the Dominican Republic, their tournament victory earned them another windfall: $5,179.15, to be split evenly among all team members."[35] The team was lauded throughout the tournament and afterward, with one press account stating, "At Denver major league scouts heralded the All Stars as one of the greatest clubs in the country. Special praise was heaped on the pitching staff. ..."[36] The All-Stars continued to barnstorm throughout the country in 1937 and made mincemeat of their opponents. Carter started a game in Grand Island, Nebraska, in which "[t]he all-stars never extended themselves" as they won 11-6.[37] The team was feted wherever it played, so much so that East Chicago, Indiana, declared "Pat Patterson Day" when the team played a semipro aggregation in that city. Patterson had grown up in East Chicago and had starred in football, basketball, and baseball at Washington High School. Once the Trujillo All-Stars' triumphal tour ended, Carter sought baseball employment in yet another country, Cuba.

On the heels of playing for as great a squad as the All-Stars, Carter joined one of the worst teams he played for in his career. The 1937-38 Cuban Winter League's Habana Leones suffered a fate similar to that of his first professional team, the 1932 Birmingham Black Barons. "Habana had the most woeful season of its history," a historian of Cuban baseball wrote. "After only 8 wins in 46 encounters, management withdrew the team" on January 25, 1938.[38] Carter appeared in four games in which he had a 1-2 record.[39]

When the 1938 NNL season rolled around, "the Negro League bosses did an about-face – lifting their ban, lowering their fines, and bringing back into the fold any who would come."[40] Carter came back but to the Philadelphia Stars rather than the Crawfords. He was the Stars' Opening Day starter on May 7 in an exhibition game against the South Phillies and pitched a four-hitter in a 5-1 victory. He also pitched a two-hitter in a 4-3 triumph over his former team from Pittsburgh. The fact that Carter had allowed those three runs in such a low-hit game made this game a microcosm of his entire season. Although he led the Stars' pitching staff with a 7-3 record and 109⅓ innings pitched, he had a hefty 6.01 ERA as Philadelphia finished the season with a 37-31-3 record, good enough only for third place in the NNL.[41]

Carter returned to the Stars for the beginning of the 1939 campaign, but he did not last long. The Stars were touted to challenge the Homestead Grays in the NNL, but the Pittsburgh-area nine asserted their superiority as they pounded the offerings of Carter and his reliever, Henry McHenry, in a 12-5 rout on May 27 in the first game of a key series.[42] It was likely the final game Carter pitched in a Stars uniform. For the season, he made three appearances (all starts) for Philadelphia in which he had a 6.19 ERA in 16 innings.

Shortly thereafter, Carter was back with the Crawfords, albeit in new surroundings. Greenlee had sold the team after the 1938 season, and new owner Hank Rigney had relocated the franchise to Toledo, Ohio; the team had also switched from the NNL to membership in the Negro American League in midseason. To promote his team, Rigney hired Olympic track champion Jesse Owens to run races or simply give exhibitions of his speed prior to the Crawfords' games; as a result, the team was as well-known for Owens' feats as for its play on the field. On June 4 Carter struck out 13 batters as the Crawfords "handed an all-star team made up of Frigidaire and Pure Oil players a 6 to 0 defeat."[43] He continued to pitch well in exhibition games against semipro teams, but in NAL play he was 1-1 with a 5.65 ERA. The team fared poorly, as it finished at 8-11-1, in spite of several notable players: Charleston, who still managed the team, Jimmie Crutchfield, and a young Johnny Wright, who became the second black player to be signed by the Brooklyn Dodgers organization in January 1946.

Although Carter's 1939 season had hardly been a stellar one, he was back with the Crawfords in 1940. The moribund franchise struggled financially and split the 1940 season between Toledo and Indianapolis. The team opened its spring exhibition season against the Miami Ethiopian Clowns at Miami's Dorsey Park on March 31. Carter pitched the final two innings and took the loss when he surrendered the game's lone run in the bottom of the ninth.[44] Carter, whom the *Chicago Defender* referred to as "Satchel Paige's old sidekick," did not spend much time with the Crawfords during the NAL season; he was 1-0 as he won his only start for the team, a 10-inning 2-1 triumph over the St. Louis Stars on June 2.[45] Two weeks later, he ended up embroiled in the third dispute between teams that laid claim to him as their property.

On June 16 Carter pitched for Abe and Effa Manley's Newark Eagles team in a game against the Homestead Grays. Both of these squads were members of the NNL, while Carter was a member of the NAL's Toledo/Indianapolis team. Abe Manley had used Carter and a teammate, shortstop Bus Clarkson, to spite the NAL. The origins of the dispute went back to the end of 1938. At that time, the Manleys had purchased Paige's contract from Greenlee for $5,000; however, Paige never reported to Newark in 1939. Abe Manley believed that "Paige had not reported because one of the members of the Negro American League had influenced him not to play with Newark but to play with an independent club in the west bearing his name."[46] The club in question was another barnstorming squad named Satchel Paige's All-Stars and was affiliated with Kansas City Monarchs owner J.L. Wilkinson. Since Manley held the NAL responsible for Paige's failure to report, he decided he would use any NAL players he could convince to play for his NNL squad until Paige reported to the Eagles.

The matter was finally settled at a joint meeting between NAL and NNL leadership at Harlem's Woodside Hotel on June 18. As had been the case in 1934, team owners – this time in the NAL rather than the NSL – were angry about their NNL counterparts raiding their franchises' players and "the fur flew" as both sides presented their arguments.[47] It was finally decided that Paige would become property of the NAL and that Carter and Clarkson would remain members of the Newark Eagles; subsequently, Paige signed with Wilkinson's Kansas City Monarchs, an NAL team, in 1941. The agreement was described as "a concession by the N.A. league for the sake of inter-league harmony."[48]

The Eagles were an average squad in 1940 and finished the NNL season in third place with a 26-21-1 record. Carter pitched in six league games (two starts) and ended his stint with Newark with a 1-0 record and a 3.86 ERA.[49] At season's end, he returned home to Birmingham, where he resided with his wife, Eloise, and his daughter, Jennetta, whom he had named after his mother.[50] When Negro League legend Candy Jim Taylor brought his "baseball carnival" to Birmingham's Rickwood Field in early October, he enlisted Carter to play on his team of Negro League stars that faced off against "the best players in the city and county industrial league teams."[51]

For reasons unknown, Carter did not play in the Negro Leagues in 1941. He had pitched well enough with Newark to merit consideration for a return engagement, but perhaps the fiasco created by the previous season's dispute between the leagues had left a bad taste in his mouth. As far as can be determined, Carter's only professional baseball activity involved an extremely brief stint with the Mexican League's team in Torreón. Carter made four appearances (one start) and put up a 1-1 record with a 10.13 ERA.[52] Bus Clarkson, the second player who had become Newark Eagles property in the 1940 dispute, also played in Mexico in 1941, though he spent the entire season with Tampico.

In February 1942, as World War II raged, Carter registered for the military draft. He listed the Tennessee Coal, Iron, and Railroad Company as his employer on his draft registration card, but he once again found employment in the Negro Leagues that year. Now 39, he returned to Pittsburgh, this time to join the powerhouse

## THE 1935 PITTSBURGH CRAWFORDS

Homestead Grays. Carter was the elder statesman on the pitching staff and was used sparingly. In eight appearances (five starts) he managed only a 1-4 record with a 7.55 ERA. The Grays were in the middle of a stretch in which the team won nine NNL pennants in 11 seasons, and they dominated the league in 1942. Homestead finished 47-19-3 in league play and 64-23-3 against all competition, but the team ended up being swept by the Kansas City Monarchs in the Negro World Series. Carter's postseason action consisted of one appearance in which he faced two batters and allowed no runs.

In spite of his relative ineffectiveness in 1942, Carter was welcomed back to the Grays again the following season. The 1943 season turned out to be magical for both Carter and the Grays. The team finished the NNL campaign with an amazing 53-14-1 league record and was 78-23-1 against all teams. Johnny Wright, Carter's old Toledo teammate, was the undisputed ace of the Grays' staff that year with an 18-3 record and a 2.54 ERA in NNL games, but Carter was right behind him at 14-2 and had lowered his own ERA to 3.83. Edsall Walker (9-4) and future Hall of Famer Ray Brown gave the Grays the most formidable pitching staff in the Negro Leagues. The Grays won the Negro World Series as they defeated the Birmingham Black Barons in eight games, with one game ending in a tie. Carter made one start but received no decision as Brown earned the win for the Grays in relief.

After the World Series, newspapers reported that Carter would be a member of the Negro Leagues' entry for the 1943-44 California Winter League season. One account said, "Baseball fans will have an opportunity to look over Spoon Carter, one of today's greatest colored players and ace pitcher for the Pittsburgh Homestead Grays when the winter league opens its season at Hollywood baseball park on Sunday, October 24."[53] This report was clearly in error as Satchel Paige made that opening-game start, and Carter did not participate in winter league play at all.

*Ernest "Spoon" Carter, pictured here in a Homestead Grays uniform, pitched for a number of different championship teams and graced the cover of the 1945 Negro League Baseball Pictorial Yearbook.*

Carter would not have been in California for a long time anyway because the season was cut short. In mid-November, Commissioner Kenesaw Mountain Landis refused to allow major leaguers to continue to participate in the winter league by invoking a rule that forbade players to participate in exhibition games 10 days after the major-league season closed.[54] The *Pittsburgh Courier* noted that "[m]ost of the games in which these players have played have been against Negro teams" and lamented that Landis's crackdown "will wipe out the sole means of measuring the abilities of Negro players with major leaguers."[55]

In 1944 Carter returned to a depleted Grays team that was nonetheless still the class of the NNL. Wright was one of the many players who had been lost to military service, but Brown stepped up as the ace with an 11-1 league record. Carter and Walker tied for second on the staff in league wins with identical 6-4 records. After breezing through the NNL with a 47-24-3 record, the Grays again clashed with the Black Barons in the Negro World Series. Carter got the starting assignment at Pittsburgh's Forbes Field in Game Four and took the loss in a 6-0 setback to Birmingham. It was the only defeat for Homestead, which made quick work of the Black Barons in five games to capture its second consecutive championship.

An aging Carter played a reduced role on the 1945 Grays who, due in part to wartime travel restrictions, played so many home games at Griffith Stadium that they were now called the Washington-Homestead Grays. Roy Welmaker (10-2) was the new pitching ace, and Carter appeared in only six league games (three starts) in which he compiled a 1-1 record and a 3.69 ERA. The Grays won the NNL pennant by nine games over the Baltimore Elite Giants and played in their fourth consecutive Negro World Series. Carter saw no postseason action as the Grays suffered a shocking sweep at the hands of the Cleveland Buckeyes, an event that *Pittsburgh Courier* columnist Wendell Smith deemed "one of the biggest surprises in baseball history."[56]

In April 1946, it was reported that "Carter was purchased from the Washington Homestead Grays" by the new Montgomery Dodgers of the Negro Southern League, and Montgomery owner Jake Whatley installed Carter as the team's manager.[57] News reports of the Dodgers' games are scarce, but a June 11 article in the *Montgomery Advertiser* indicated that the team had changed its name to the Red Sox.[58] It is quite likely that the Brooklyn Dodgers organization put legal pressure on Montgomery's owner to make the name change. Carter also made a transition – from one Red Sox squad to another – as he rejoined one of his earliest teams, the NAL's Memphis franchise. He pitched in only three league games for Memphis and had no decisions, though he did have a fine 2.89 ERA.

Although Carter had departed Montgomery in midseason in 1946, the NSL's new Jacksonville Eagles franchise gave him a second opportunity to manage a team at the outset of the 1947 season. Jacksonville opened its season on the road, and Carter debuted with his new squad in a May 4 doubleheader against the Chattanooga Choo Choos.[59] By July 7, prior to a game against the Harbor House of David team in St. Joseph, Michigan, it was reported that "[l]eading pitcher for the Eagles is none other than the manager, Spoon Carter, who made a great name for himself while hurling for the Homestead Grays of the Negro National League."[60]

By mid-July, however, Carter had rejoined the Memphis Red Sox. On July 29 he was part of the West All-Star team in that season's second East-West All-Star game, which was played at the Polo Grounds in New York. Carter pitched the final three innings, allowing only two hits and no runs, as the West sewed up an 8-2 victory.[61] Memphis also played the Harbor House of David squad in Michigan, and this time the local paper reported that Red Sox manager Larry Brown had available among his pitching staff "Ernest (Spoon) Carter" who was "regarded the best relief hurler in the league" and who "often plays third base."[62] Box scores for Negro League games had become scarce by this time, and Carter's statistics for the fourth-place Memphis team are unknown.

In 1948 Carter chose simply to begin the season with Memphis. Many games went unreported and only line scores are available for most others, but the available statistics show Carter with a 1-1 record and a 5.68 ERA in five appearances (two starts). Nevertheless, he was again chosen as a member of the West team for the second All-Star game at Yankee Stadium on August 24. Carter did not pitch in the game, but the 45-year old entered the contest as a pinch-runner for Kansas City Monarchs third baseman Herb Souell. He did not steal a base, nor did he score, in a game that the East team won, 6-1.[63] As for the Red Sox, they finished last in the NAL that year.

The seemingly ageless Carter went to spring training with Memphis in 1949, though it is unknown whether he made the cut. His Negro

League career came full circle when he signed with Birmingham in mid-June. The Black Barons had lost ace hurler Jimmie Newberry to a broken right arm and signed three pitchers – Carter, Felix "Chin" Evans, and Ted Alexander – to fill the void created by Newberry's absence.[64] As a Black Baron, Carter was a teammate of 18-year-old Willie Mays, who already amazed scouts, players, and fans alike with his all-around talent. On September 3 the old man and the young phenom led the way in a 7-1 triumph over the Cleveland Buckeyes. Carter went the distance, allowed only one run, and struck out nine hitters while "Willie Mays paced the victors at bat with a 350-foot homer and a double."[65] It was a highlight in an otherwise down season that saw Birmingham finish in fourth place.

Carter's Negro League career was at an end, but he had one last season left in him. In 1950 he sojourned to Canada, where he played for the Winnipeg Buffaloes of the new Manitoba-Dakota (ManDak) League. The Buffaloes' roster was made up entirely of former Negro League players and included two future Hall of Famers, pitcher Leon Day and manager Willie Wells. Although Winnipeg finished the regular season in second place, seven games behind the Brandon Greys, the team made it to the playoff tournament and advanced to the finals against first-place Brandon. In the fifth and final game of the championship series, both Day and Greys pitcher Manuel Godinez pitched all 17 innings before the Buffaloes emerged with a 1-0 victory and the ManDak League's inaugural championship.[66] Carter, for his part, contributed a 4-2 record in 12 appearances and finished his baseball career as a champion.[67]

Carter retired to his native Birmingham, where he and Eloise raised their two daughters, Janice and Rhonda, and their son Roderick. He owned the Community Barber Shop in the Ensley neighborhood and was active as a deacon with the Macedonia Missionary Baptist Church.[68] Ernest Carter died on January 23, 1974, and was buried in Shadowlawn Memorial Park in Birmingham.

## Author Note and Acknowledgment

Much to the author's chagrin, no information was found to explain how Carter came to have his nickname, "Spoon." Since the moniker was applied to him almost from the outset of his career, it may well have been given to him by his family.

Thanks to Rosalind B. Brooks, an assistant at the Birmingham Public Library, for her thoroughness in fulfilling my request for information about Carter's death.

## Sources

Ancestry.com was consulted for US Census, draft registration, marriage, and death records as well as ships' passenger logs.

Unless otherwise indicated, Seamheads.com was the source for all Negro League statistics.

## Notes

1. William J. Plott, *Black Baseball's Last Team Standing: The Birmingham Black Barons, 1919-1962* (Jefferson, North Carolina: McFarland & Company, Inc., 2019), 87.
2. "Memphis and Birmingham Divide/Teams Own Two Games Each at End of Fourth," *Chicago Defender*, April 30, 1932: 9.
3. Holsey Drake, "Black Barons Take 3 Games Out of 4 From Montgomery," *Atlanta Daily World*, May 18, 1932: 5.
4. Plott, 87-88. Due to the sparse press coverage, there are discrepancies as to the Black Barons' 1932 record. Plott has the team at 11-7-1 in NSL play and 15-15-1 against all teams (page 272) while the Negro Southern League Museum Research Center lists an 8-11 record for the team in NSL play (see negro-southernleaguemuseumresearchcenter.org/Portals/0/Negro%20 Southern%20League/Negro%20Southern%20League%20%20 (1920-1951)STANDINGS.pdf ).
5. "Memphis Reds Have Hope for Pennant," *Pittsburgh Courier*, June 10, 1933: 14.
6. Dr. R.B. Martin, "Southern Flag Is in Memphis' Bag," *Chicago Defender*, June 24, 1933: 9.
7. L.S.N. Cobb, "Memphis Wins Three in Arkansas/Sox Increase Lead in Southern Loop," *Chicago Defender*, July 1, 1933: 9.
8. "Heed Protest of Dixie League Head on 'Raiding,'" *Pittsburgh Courier*, April 14, 1934: 12.
9. "Nashville Giants Defeat Grays in Both Ends of Doubleheader, "*Akron Beacon-Journal*, July 24, 1933: 20.
10. "Craws Lose 3-2 Thriller to Philly," *Pittsburgh Courier*, September 23, 1933: 15.
11. "Heed Protest of Dixie League Head on 'Raiding.'"

12  "Colored Club Has All-Star Players in Every Position," *Bismarck Tribune*, June 15, 1934: 8. This author was unable to locate any game reports or box scores that named Carter as a member of the Cleveland team, let alone that he had twice dueled against Paige. Additionally, Seamheads.com does not list Carter as a member of the 1934 Cleveland Red Sox.

13  "Two Homers Pave Way for Jimmies' 4-2 Victory Over Locals," *Bismarck Tribune*, July 5, 1934: 6.

14  "Two Homers Pave Way."

15  "Bismarck Scores 1-0 Victory Over Valley City in 10 Innings," *Bismarck Tribune*, August 17, 1934: 8.

16  William F. McNeil, *The California Winter League: America's First Integrated Professional Baseball League* (Jefferson, North Carolina: McFarland & Company, Inc., 2002), 171.

17  James Newton, "Suttles' Two Homers Beat All Stars/Stearns Then Uses Bat for a Second Win/Porter and Carter in Rare Form," *Chicago Defender*, October 27, 1934: 16.

18  Newton.

19  "Royal Giants Annex, 9 to 8," *Los Angeles Times*, October 28, 1934: 28.

20  "Crawfords Set to Make Strong Bid for League Championship," *New York Age*, April 27, 1935: 3.

21  "Chicago Americans Win Night Game," *Harrisburg Telegraph*, May 22, 1935: 12.

22  "Crawfords Win Philly Series; Hold Lead in League Race," *Pittsburgh Courier*, June 1, 1935: 15.

23  William E. Clark, "15,000 Fans See 4-Team Series at Yankee Stadium Sunday; Crawford and Elite Gts Win," *New York Age*, September 28, 1935: 8.

24  "Gibson Hits Three Homers as Pittsburgh Crawfords Trounce Belmar Braves by 6 to 2," *Asbury Park* (New Jersey) *Press*, July 25, 1936: 16.

25  "Two Jailed in Baseball War/League Acts to Check 'Raids,'" *Pittsburgh Courier*, May 15, 1937: 1.

26  "Two Jailed in Baseball War."

27  "Two Men Jailed in Big Baseball Scandal": 4. (Continuation of "Two Jailed in Baseball War").

28  "Two Men Jailed in Big Baseball Scandal."

29  "Players Who Fled League Face Return/Morton Files Names with Government for Damages," *New York Amsterdam News*, May 29, 1937: 17. The list of players submitted to the State Department on May 24 included Pittsburgh Crawfords players Leroy Matlock, Ernest Carter, Chet Brewer, Satchel Paige, Bill Perkins, Cool Papa Bell, Thad Christopher, Sam Bankhead, Harry Williams, and Pat Patterson; New York Black Yankees Clarence Palm and George Scales; Newark Eagle Clyde Spearman; and the Philadelphia Stars' Showboat Thomas and Red Parnell.

30  Richard J. Lamb, "Gus 'Whereas-es' Diplomats into Action over Foreign 'Raid' on Negro Ball Team," *Pittsburgh Press*, June 20, 1937: 2.

31  John Bentley, "I May Be Wrong," *Lincoln* (Nebraska) *Journal Star*, August 12, 1937: 13.

32  Donn Rogosin, *Invisible Men: Life in Baseball's Negro Leagues* (Lincoln: University of Nebraska Press, 1983), 140.

33  "Paige's All-Stars Win Denver Tourney/Matlock Hero in $5,000 Win," *Chicago Defender*, August 21, 1937: 21.

34  "Paige's All-Stars Win Denver Tourney"; Jay Sanford, *The Denver Post Tournament: A Chronicle of America's First Integrated Professional Baseball Event* (Cleveland: Society for American Baseball Research, 2003), 64.

35  "Paige's All-Stars Win Denver Tourney."

36  "Satchel Paige and His Denver Champions Play Powers Here Tonight/Famous Negro Team Captures Title in Post's Tournament," *Lincoln* (Nebraska) *Journal Star*, August 12, 1937: 13.

37  "Win at Grand Island," *Lincoln* (Nebraska) *Journal Star*, August 12, 1937: 13.

38  Jorge Figueredo, *Cuban Baseball: A Statistical History, 1878-1961* (Jefferson, North Carolina: McFarland & Company, Inc., 2003), 218.

39  Figueredo, 221.

40  Larry Tye, *Satchel: The Life and Times of an American Legend* (New York: Random House, 2009), 117.

41  Since Seamheads.com has been used as the primary source for Negro League statistics, it should be noted that the site lists Carter as having made (and lost) one start for the Birmingham Black Barons in 1938. Carter made his home in Birmingham, so it is possible that he could have played for the Birmingham team late in the year.

42  "Grays Wallop Philly in Opener, 12-5/Leonard Leads Hitting Assault, *Pittsburgh Courier*, June 3, 1939: 16.

43  "Crawfords Win Over All-Stars," *Dayton* (Ohio) *Herald*, June 5, 1939: 11.

44  "Clowns Edge Toledo, 1-0," *Miami News*, April 1, 1940: 13.

45  "Crawfords Have 6 Ace Hurlers; Star Outfield," *Chicago Defender*, May 11, 1940: 24; "Crawfords Split with St. Louis," *Chicago Defender*, June 8, 1940: 22.

46  "Satchel Paige to American League/All-Star Game is Aug. 18," *Chicago Defender*, June 29, 1940: 22.

47  "Satchel Paige to American League."

48  "Satchel Paige to American League."

49  Seamheads.com shows Carter to have made one appearance for the NNL's New York Cubans in 1940 that covered 1⅔ innings and for which he received no decision. It is possible that he may have been "on loan" to the Cubans for one game

50. or that he pitched one game for the team after Newark's season had ended.

50. Jennetta was Carter's daughter by a woman named Annie Lee Matthews; the author has relied on census information and marriage records for Jennetta Carter to establish this fact. However, no documentation has come to light to determine whether Carter and Matthews were married or, if they were, how their marriage ended (whether by divorce or Matthews' death). The year of Carter's marriage to Eloise Underwood is also undetermined, but the two had a long union and were still married at the time of Carter's death in 1974.

51. "Array of Stars to Compete in Candy Jim Taylor's All Star Carnival Sunday," *Weekly Review* (Birmingham, Alabama), October 4, 1940: 7.

52. All major sources show Carter to have pitched briefly in Mexico in 1941. Pedro Treto Cisneros' book of Mexican League statistics, from which Seamheads.com most likely took its information, lists "Hammis Carter" as the player with a 1-1 record for Torreón in 1941. There was no player, black or white, by that name, and no other pitcher with the last name Carter is reported to have played south of the border at any time. Thus, "Hammis" must be a misprint that may already have occurred in a primary news source. See Pedro Treto Cisneros, *The Mexican League: Comprehensive Player Statistics, 1937-2001* (Jefferson, North Carolina: McFarland & Company, Inc., 2002), 468.

53. "Great Negro Hurler Pitches at Hollywood," *Long Beach (California) Independent*, October 15, 1943: 18.

54. "Landis Clamps Down on Winter Leaguers," *Pittsburgh Courier*, November 27, 1943: 16.

55. "Landis Cracking Down on Players in Winter Loop," *Pittsburgh Courier*, December 4, 1943: 16.

56. Wendell Smith, "The Sports Beat," *Pittsburgh Courier*, September 29, 1945: 12.

57. Leon B. Beauchman, "Birmingham's Sepia Dodgers," *Pittsburgh Courier*, April 20, 1946: 17.

58. "Red Sox Meet Black Barons Here Wednesday," *Montgomery Advertiser*, June 11, 1946: 6.

59. "Largest Negro Crowd May See Opening Pair," *Chattanooga Daily Times*, May 4, 1947: 51.

60. "Davids Meet Eagles Nine," *Herald Press* (St. Joseph, Michigan), July 7, 1948: 7.

61. Larry Lester, *Black Baseball's National Showcase: The East-West All-Star Game, 1933-1953* (Lincoln: University of Nebraska Press, 2001), 299, 301-302.

62. "Memphis Red Sox at Colony Park Tonight," *Herald Press* (St. Joseph, Michigan), August 27, 1947: 12.

63. Lester, 321.

64. "Black Barons Edge New York Cubans," *Pittsburgh Courier*, June 18, 1949: 24.

65. "Black Barons Beat Buckeyes Easily, 7-1," *Birmingham News*, September 24, 1949: 9.

66. Barry Swanton, *The Mandak League: Haven for Former Negro League Ballplayers, 1950-57* (Jefferson, North Carolina: McFarland & Company, Inc., 2006), 20.

67. Barry Swanton and Jay-Dell Mah, *Black Baseball Players in Canada: A Biographical Dictionary, 1881-1960* (Jefferson, North Carolina: McFarland & Company, Inc., 2009), 47.

68. "Deaths: Ernest C. Carter," *Birmingham News*, January 27, 1974: 23.

# OSCAR CHARLESTON

### By Tim Odzer

*"Charleston not only has the speed of a Carey, the arm of a Meusel, the brains of a McGraw and the hitting ability of a Hornsby, but he is a singer of rare ability, a writer of parts, a billiard player of more than ordinary skill and a happily married man. Charleston is a rare specimen of one upon whom the gods have smiled in affable mood. Oh, he's a bird of a boy, is Oscar, and his personality – mysterious, inexplicable, indescribable, has won for him a warm spot in the hearts of each and every one of his players."*[1]

A scout for the St. Louis Cardinals, Bennie Borgmann, once said, "In my opinion, the greatest ballplayer I've ever seen was Oscar Charleston. When I say this, I'm not overlooking Ruth, Cobb, Gehrig, and all of them."[2] Buck O'Neil said that Charleston "was like Ty Cobb, Babe Ruth, and Tris Speaker rolled into one."[3] Honus Wagner said, "I've seen all the great players in the many years I've been around and have yet to see one any greater than Charleston."[4] And, in 2001, Bill James ranked Charleston as the fourth-best player of all time, behind only Ruth, Wagner, and Willie Mays.

*As a player, Oscar Charleston batted .350 over the course of 1,394 official Negro League games. As a manager, he piloted the Pittsburgh Crawfords to NNL championships in 1933, 1935, and 1936*

(National Baseball Hall of Fame)

Charleston was a baseball lifer who served as a player, manager, umpire, and scout. Though he worked an assortment of other jobs to supplement his income, baseball was his life. It was on the ball field that Charleston developed a reputation as a hothead and performed apocryphal deeds such as yanking the hood off a Ku Klux Klansman and throwing a professional wrestler off a train. Off the field, Charleston married twice but divorced one wife and separated from the other; he left behind no children. He neither drank nor smoked and was a stern yet charming man who gained the respect of his peers through his no-nonsense attitude.

Oscar McKinley Charleston was born in Indianapolis on October 14, 1896. He was the seventh of 11 children born to Tom and Mary (Thomas) Charleston. His middle name came about because his parents were Republicans, and William McKinley was the Republican nominee for president in 1896. Oscar's father was a construction worker and, according to one report, a former jockey. As a child, Oscar moved constantly, but always to some place within the greater Indianapolis area. His family was poor, and Oscar finished school only through the eighth grade. During his childhood, Oscar allegedly worked as a batboy for the Indianapolis ABCs, the most prominent local black team.[5]

Rather than continue in school, Charleston lied about his age so that he could enlist in the US Army at 15. Shortly thereafter, he was shipped out to the Philippines and assigned to Company B of the 24th Infantry Regiment. Playing for the regimental team, Charleston starred as a pitcher and was selected for an all-star game in which he pitched a one-hit shutout and hit a triple. When his hitch was over, he was honorably discharged in 1915.

Charleston, who was between 5-feet-8 inches and 5-feet-9 inches, returned stateside and began to play for the Indianapolis ABCs.[6] He pitched a shutout in his first game, striking out nine, walking none, and giving up only three hits. He also displayed impressive hitting prowess throughout the season. At the conclusion of the 1915 season, the ABCs played a series of exhibition games against white teams composed of major leaguers. During one of these games – on October 24, 1915 – a scuffle broke out between an ABCs player and a white umpire. Amid the scuffle, Oscar Charleston ran in from center field and punched the umpire. The sight of a black man punching a white man caused chaos, as players, fans, and police poured onto the field. Before there could be any trouble, Charleston ran away. He was later arrested but was released on bond and allowed to go to Cuba with the ABCs.[7]

After the incident, ABCs owner C.L. Taylor issued a statement apologizing for the actions of his hotheaded center fielder. Charleston also published a statement saying he could not control his temper and that "[he] cannot find words in the vocabulary that will express his regret."[8] After the 1915 season, Charleston played in Cuba with his ABCs teammates. But, perhaps still having trouble controlling his temper, he was at one point dismissed from the team for disobeying club rules.[9]

Charleston played the first part of the 1916 season for the Lincoln Stars in New York before returning to the ABCs in August. In October the ABCs played Rube Foster's American Giants in a seven-game series billed as black baseball's championship. The ABCs won the series, with Charleston going 7-for-18. During the offseason, he worked as a grocery clerk.

On January 9, 1917, Charleston married Hazel M. Grubbs, a young woman in her late teens who was the daughter of a public-school principal. Their marriage did not last long and, by early 1918, the couple had separated; they were divorced in 1921.

Charleston continued playing for the ABCs in 1917. As the United States became involved in World War I, Charleston registered for the draft on June 5, 1917; in order to maintain consistency with his previous lie, he listed his birth date as October 14, 1893.[10] The ABCs posted a sub-.500

record against elite opponents this season, but Charleston continued his ascent. In games against elite opponents, Charleston posted a batting line 50 percent above league average.[11] Because he was registered for the draft, he was unable to play in Cuba during the offseason.

Charleston continued his strong play in 1918. In a game on August 18, he made what was described as one of the greatest catches ever at Washington Park.[12] In the field, Charleston's incredible speed (he clocked in at 23 seconds in the 220-yard dash with the Army) allowed him to play shallow, just behind second base.[13] Later in August Charleston was assigned to Camp Dodge in Johnston, Iowa, and was selected to attend the Colored Students Infantry Officers Training School in Arkansas. The war ended before he could become an officer and, on December 3, he was again honorably discharged.

Charleston emerged as a star in the postwar years. In 1919 he played for Rube Foster's Chicago American Giants and started the year in center field. Charleston showed his talents at bat, in the field, and on the bases. In the majors in 1919, Babe Ruth hit one home run every 19 plate appearances, while Charleston hit one home run every 26 plate appearances.[14] Charleston's defense was frequently written about, with the press describing him as making "hair-raising [catches]" and the "fielding feature[s] of the game."[15] Charleston was also a superb baserunner, and Foster pushed Charleston on the basepaths. In one game, Charleston had what was described as one of the speediest exhibitions of running ever seen on the diamond when he hit a single, stole second, advanced to third as the ball trickled into center field, and came home on a throw down to second.[16] At the season's conclusion, the *Chicago Defender* wrote that Charleston was the best player in the world, even better than Ty Cobb.[17] The paper further credited Foster for developing Charleston's natural abilities and cooling his temper.[18] In fact, Charleston seemed preoccupied with the comparison to Cobb, repeatedly clipping articles for his personal scrapbook that compared him to the Georgia Peach. When the season ended, Oscar took a job as a chauffeur.[19]

With the creation of the Negro National League in 1920, Charleston re-signed with the ABCs, a move Foster allowed in the interest of league-wide competitive balance.[20] His 1920 season was another star turn as he stole 20 bases and posted an OPS that was 76 percent better than the league average. In the inaugural NNL doubleheader, Charleston went 1-for-4 in the first game and laced a two-run triple in the second game.[21] The press also continued to make note of his defensive ability. In a game one week later, the ABCs were leading 4-2 in the top of the ninth with two men on and two men out when Jose LeBlanc hit a rocket to center field. Charleston, who had already made two good catches, saved the game with a dazzling catch made with his back to the plate. The fans jumped onto the field and showered Charleston with money.[22]

Now in demand, Charleston was sold to the St. Louis Giants for the 1921 season. He took pride in his purchase price, clipping a newspaper article that stated he was worth more than Rogers Hornsby or Babe Ruth.[23] He had another strong campaign during which he led the Negro National League in home runs, hitting 15 in 339 plate appearances.[24] In fact, there were three occasions during the season on which Charleston hit two home runs in one game. Because of his surge in power, newspapers started to call him the colored Babe Ruth; this is the major-league player to whom Charleston was most frequently compared during the 1920s.[25] Charleston also stole 32 bases and hit .433. After the 1921 season, Charleston spent the winter in Los Angeles and played in the California Winter League. He hit .405 as the Colored All-Stars went 25-15-1 and posted a winning record in games against teams that included both major- and minor-league players. By the end of the California Winter League season, the Los Angeles press proclaimed Charleston to be the second greatest living player, behind only Babe Ruth.[26]

In 1922, thanks to St. Louis's financial difficulties, Charleston once again returned to the ABCs.[27] C.I. Taylor had died between the 1921 and the 1922 seasons, and ownership of the ABCs transferred to his wife, Olivia. (Charleston later spoke very positively of Taylor, crediting him with teaching him how to manage a team.)[28] In 1922 the ABCs were led by three outstanding hitters – Biz Mackey, Ben Taylor, and Charleston. In the league's opening doubleheader, Charleston went 6-for-8 with a home run and a double. That set the tone for his season: Of the 98 games for which box scores exist, Charleston failed to get a hit in only 16. Bill James has rated Charleston as the best player in the Negro Leagues for the 1921 and 1922 seasons.[29]

After the 1922 season, Charleston married for the second time. The bride was a 27-year-old schoolteacher named Jane Howard. It was also Jane's second marriage; her first husband had died in 1918. She often traveled with Charleston to Cuba during the winter, and several photos of them in Cuba appear in Charleston's scrapbook. In fact, Charleston and Jane traveled to Cuba for their honeymoon, where Charleston played in the 1922-23 Cuban winter league.[30] He and Jane had a rocky marriage, it seems, in part because Jane did not like baseball. It is possible that Oscar was unfaithful, too, as multiple contemporary newspaper articles reported that he was seen in public with women other than Jane.[31] In fact, after a car accident in which Charleston escaped without injury, the *Pittsburgh Courier* wrote that Charleston "wiggled out of some love tangles the same, same way."[32] The couple separated in 1940, though they never divorced. Charleston filed for divorce in 1941, but the case was dismissed in 1942. Jane did not believe in divorce.[33]

In December 1922, Olivia Taylor traded Charleston to Rube Foster's American Giants. Taylor was facing financial difficulties, and Biz Mackey and Ben Taylor also left the team. But Charleston returned to the ABCs prior to the season: Foster realized it was better for the league if Charleston played for the ABCs, and he worked out a deal with Taylor whereby Taylor would receive a subsidy for 1923 and let Charleston go to the American Giants in 1924.[34] Charleston spent the 1923 season with the ABCs and was the leader of a depleted team that struggled to a fourth-place finish. In fact, the team needed Charleston to pitch on multiple occasions.

After the Indianapolis team disbanded, rather than heading to Chicago Charleston played for and managed the Harrisburg Giants, where he remained from 1924 to 1927. Charleston, who seemed to be preoccupied with the press coverage he received, clipped an article for his scrapbook that described him as a big loss for Foster's league.[35] In 1924 Charleston had another strong year at bat; though his team endured a .500 campaign, he reportedly hit 36 home runs by August 24. Charleston even had a stretch in early August where he hit seven home runs in three games.[36] That October, the Harrisburg Giants played a postseason series against the crosstown (and white) Harrisburg Senators. There, in the middle of a competitive game, Charleston erupted when he attempted to punch an umpire after a bad call. The umpire evaded the punch, punched Charleston, and then ejected him from the game.[37] Charleston returned to manage the Giants for the 1925 season. At age 28, he was in the prime of his career and had a magnificent season in which he batted .427/.523/.776 with 20 home runs.[38] Once again, Bill James has rated him as the best player in the Negro Leagues that season.[39] From 1919 to 1925, Charleston posted an OPS+ above 200 four times and compiled a 1.143 OPS. Combined with his superb defense and great baserunning speed, this seven-year stretch ranks among the most dominant in baseball history.

After the 1925 regular season, Charleston played in an exhibition contest against a white "Bronx Giants" team that featured a young Lou Gehrig. Gehrig went 1-for-2 with two walks, while Charleston went 4-for-6 with a home run.⁴⁰ During his career, we have box scores for 53 games in which Charleston played against major-league players, hitting .318 with 11 home runs. He got hits against Walter Johnson, Bob Feller, and Lefty Grove.⁴¹

In addition to his domestic play, Charleston burnished his reputation as a baseball star through his play in Cuba. He was known as "El Terror de los Clubs," with one newspaper describing him as a man capable of fighting alone against other teams.⁴² During the time Charleston played in Cuba, it was a *beisbol paradiso*, as both major-league and Negro League stars spent their winters on the island. He had several superb seasons there and left quite an impression on Cuba's baseball fans. In 1922–23, Charleston hit .446 in league games but was unable to qualify for the batting title when his Santa Clara team withdrew from the league because of a league decision that took away a win.⁴³ In 1925 Charleston was part of a Cuban All-Star team that played against an All-Yankee team in front of Commissioner Kenesaw Mountain Landis.⁴⁴ In 1926-27 Charleston was one of four players (along with Pablo "Champion" Mesa, Tank Carr, and Dick Lundy) to hit over .400.⁴⁵ Over 996 at-bats in Cuba, Charleston hit .361 with 19 home runs and 58 stolen bases.⁴⁶ His team also won three championships.

The best team Charleston played on was the 1923-24 Leopardos de Santa Clara, a team whose reputation in Cuba is much like that of the 1927 Yankees in the United States. That team was so dominant that the other teams in the league decided to award Santa Clara the league title based solely on the first half of the season.⁴⁷ The team had the best Cuban outfield ever, with Charleston, Champion Mesa, and Alejandro Oms giving Santa Clara outstanding offensive performances.⁴⁸ During this season, Cuban newspapers referred to Charleston as the best player in the league and as a perfect star who combined intelligence, baserunning, slugging, fielding, and clutch play in a way never before seen. Charleston led the league in runs scored and stolen bases.⁴⁹

The 1923-24 season also saw Charleston get into a famous fight with a Cuban soldier. The fight started on January 19 after Charleston spiked an opposing player as he slid into third base. The player's brother, a soldier, came onto the field and charged Charleston, sparking other soldiers to come onto the field as well. The fight was broken up and Charleston's scrapbook shows him standing peacefully next to a soldier.⁵⁰ Charleston was initially criticized and mocked in the press, but he was defended by his friends, who described him as a perfect gentleman who had become involved in an unfortunate accident.⁵¹ Charleston met with the Cuban military and explained that he had only been acting in self-defense. The military accepted the explanation, and Charleston received no punishment.

Charleston played the 1928 and 1929 seasons with the Hilldale club of Darby, Pennsylvania. (Darby is a Philadelphia suburb.) As he embarked upon his age-31 season in 1928, Charleston appeared more rotund than in prior years, but his batting performance remained strong, and he posted a .348/.453/.618 line. For the first time, Charleston played first base in addition to the outfield. Hilldale added Martin Dihigo for the 1929 season, which gave the team a powerful duo and led one newspaper to call Hilldale "[the] greatest ball team."⁵² The press's praise for Charleston remained especially effusive, and he was referred to as being "without fault" and "as near perfect as ball players come."⁵³ However, the press has always been fickle, and when Hilldale got off to a slow start in 1929, a newspaper account claimed that Charleston was not performing up to his usual standards.⁵⁴ He still ended up with a 152 OPS+ for the season. Charleston then joined the Homestead Grays for a fall barnstorming tour, after which he stayed in Philadelphia and worked as a baggage handler.⁵⁵

Charleston must have enjoyed playing with the Homestead Grays because he joined the team

# THE 1935 PITTSBURGH CRAWFORDS

for the 1930 and 1931 seasons. Charleston was a leader on the team and during preseason training in Hot Springs, he led the players on daily five-mile runs.[56] This training helped Charleston slim down prior to the 1930 season. In the home opener, Charleston had three hits, including a home run and a triple.[57] The Grays were buoyed by the addition of Josh Gibson and played the Lincoln Giants in a 10-game series to determine who would claim the 1930 championship. In the first contest, Charleston hit a two-run homer as the Grays won, 9-1. In the seventh game, Charleston injured his leg and as a result was unable to play in the series' final game. The Grays still won, and Charleston had his second Negro League championship.

In 1931 Charleston, now playing first base regularly, drew rave reviews for his defensive ability as the Grays won a second consecutive championship with six Hall of Fame players on their roster: Charleston, Gibson, Jud Wilson, Smokey Joe Williams, Willie Foster, and Satchel Paige (though he played in only one game). Newspaper writers continued to praise Charleston, with one columnist asserting that he was a better player than Rogers Hornsby because Charleston not only had a great bat but also was a superb baserunner and exceptional fielder.[58] Batting leadoff, Charleston had a good season. In a mid-July game against Hilldale, he hit a go-ahead two-run homer to give Homestead a 5-4 victory.[59] In a September doubleheader against Kansas City, Charleston hit four doubles and a single in the first game and got two walks and a single in the nightcap.[60]

On January 28, 1932, Charleston was named player-manager of the Pittsburgh Crawfords after Gus Greenlee outbid Cumberland Posey, the Grays' owner, for Charleston's services. The 1932 Crawfords possessed some transcendent baseball talent, as Charleston helped recruit Satchel Paige and Josh Gibson to join the team.[61] Even with so many talented players, Charleston remained the team's main attraction.[62] After the major-league season, the Crawfords played seven games against a team of major-leaguers and won five of the seven contests.

In 1933 the Crawfords added Cool Papa Bell and Judy Johnson, both future Hall of Famers, to the team. Charleston remained an extremely popular player, as was demonstrated by his leading vote total for the inaugural Negro League All-Star Game that year. He also remained extremely competitive: After an umpire made what Charleston deemed an incorrect call, he became so angry that he inserted himself as a relief pitcher and walked six straight men – his way of showing that he considered the game a farce.[63]

The following year, 1934, Charleston ranked as the Crawfords' second-best hitter by OPS+ after Gibson, but the team failed to win either the first- or second-half title. Charleston often continued to be the Crawfords' headliner, although Paige now challenged him for the title as he received more votes than Charleston for the 1934 All-Star Game. Nonetheless, for a game on June 10, the *Washington Post* gave Charleston top billing and referred to him as the highest paid black player in the game.[64] After the season, the Crawfords played a barnstorming white team that featured Paul and Dizzy Dean. In a game that Dizzy Dean pitched, Charleston singled in the only run Dean allowed the Craws.

Going into the 1935 season, Charleston expected his club to be a "hustling, wide-awake ball club and one of the best teams he ever had the privilege of managing."[65] Even though Satchel Paige did not return to the team, Charleston refused to lower his expectations for the 1935 season. He got off to a hot start, hitting a home run in the home opener to lead the Crawfords to a victory and hitting a home run at Greenlee Field that went over 500 feet.[66] Charleston also remained a threat on the basepaths and even made a straight steal of home in a game on August 5.[67] By early June, Charleston believed that his team was the cream of the crop.[68] According to Jeremy Beer, the club posted a 24-6 first-half record but did not play as well in the second half. Charleston was still popular with

# Pride of Smoketown

*Hall of Famer Oscar Charleston manned first base while also managing the 1935 Crawfords to victory in the Negro National League championship series against the New York Cubans.*

(National Baseball Hall of Fame)

the fans and won the All-Star Game voting for first base by one vote over Buck Leonard. At the end of the season, the Crawfords played the New York Cubans in the NNL Championship Series. Charleston hit two home runs in the series and managed the Crawfords to the 1935 championship in a thrilling seven-game series. At the end of the season, even Grays owner Cum Posey praised Charleston's managerial ability, crediting him with a good managerial job in leading the Crawfords to the championship.[69]

In 1936 Satchel Paige rejoined the Crawfords, and Charleston was credited with "taming the temperamental" hurler.[70] Manager Charleston put himself into a first-base platoon with a young player named Johnny Washington and batted himself fifth in the order. Now known as the "Old Maestro of Swat," a well-rested Charleston remained a strong hitter and posted a 152 OPS+.[71]

As a business, the Crawfords struggled in 1936, leaving Greenlee short on funds as the team headed into the 1937 season. The team traded Josh Gibson and Judy Johnson to Homestead for Pepper Bassett, Henry Spearman, and $2,500.

Greenlee was dismayed when Satchel Paige took a lucrative offer to play in the Dominican Republic, leading to the Crawfords losing nine additional members from their roster.[72] Charleston managed a decimated team and sat himself regularly while he gave most of the playing time at first base to Johnny Washington. However, he remained capable of big moments, such as the one he had on Opening Day, when he won the game with a two-run homer in the eighth inning. It was a sign of the changing times and Charleston's gradual decline that he failed to make the All-Star team, losing the first-base voting to Leonard that year. The Crawfords finished with a 21-38-1 final record, but Charleston's reputation remained intact; in December, he was selected as the center fielder on Cum Posey's all-time Negro League squad.[73]

The Crawfords did not fare much better in 1938. Although Charleston attempted to put together a quality team, the squad finished in fourth place. After the season Greenlee sold the Crawfords to Hank Rigney, who moved the team to Toledo, Ohio. The Crawfords lost many of their star players prior to the sale as Greenlee could no longer afford their salaries. Greenlee also sold Paige's contract to the Newark Eagles for $5,000 in an attempt to make one last bit of profit from his franchise. Rigney kept Charleston as manager and part-time player for the Toledo Crawfords in 1939, but the team posted a sub-.500 record and switched leagues – from the NNL to the NAL – in midseason. By this time, Charleston's playing days had effectively ended, though he still played in games on rare occasions. Yet his involvement with baseball continued, as he became the manager of the Philadelphia Stars in 1941 and played for and managed the semipro Quartermaster Depot team, where he worked, in Philadelphia in 1942 and 1943. At the ripe old baseball age of 46, Charleston still managed to garner a player-of-the-week award.

Soon thereafter, Brooklyn Dodgers general manager Branch Rickey sought Charleston's help in identifying black players who could play major-league baseball. In 1945 a new black baseball circuit, the United States League, had been launched by Gus Greenlee. Rickey hired Charleston to manage the Brooklyn Brown Dodgers, the league entry that played at Ebbets Field. Charleston provided information on players that helped Rickey learn about their backgrounds and characters. One of the players Charleston advised Rickey about was future Hall of Fame catcher Roy Campanella, who played for the Baltimore Elite Giants at that time. The USL folded in its second season and, after his work for Rickey, Charleston was unable to find a managerial job, so he decided to become an umpire for the 1946 and 1947 seasons.

In 1948 Ed Bolden hired Charleston to manage the Philadelphia Stars.[74] By this time, the Negro Leagues were losing their best players to Organized Baseball, thanks to the integration of the game that had been initiated by Rickey and Jackie Robinson. Charleston managed the Stars from 1948 through 1952, but the team never finished better than fourth. Still, he was reported to have done a great job with the team.[75] In an era when black baseball players had a reputation for rowdiness, Charleston's team followed the straight and narrow path, earning themselves the nickname "the Saints."[76] Charleston had mellowed with age, and his players referred to him as being "relaxed," "very mild," and "friendly."[77]

The Stars disbanded after the 1952 season, and Charleston was not involved in baseball in 1953. He returned to manage the barnstorming Indianapolis Clowns to an NAL championship in 1954. In October of that same year, Charleston fell down a flight of stairs at his home, an accident that left him paralyzed from the stomach down. Charleston initially thought he would recover, but he died due to the injury on October 5, 1954, at the age of 57. He left behind no spouse or children. Thousands of fans attended Charleston's viewing in South Philadelphia.[78]

In the early 1970s, the National Baseball Hall of Fame formed a committee to remedy the lack of Negro League players in Cooperstown. Charleston was elected in 1976, following the elections of Satchel Paige, Josh Gibson, Buck Leonard, Monte Irvin, Cool Papa Bell, and Judy Johnson. Oscar's sister Katherine delivered his induction speech, which she said was the greatest delight of her life.

Today, Oscar Charleston rests in an unadorned grave in Floral Park Cemetery in Indianapolis. His headstone consists of a simple gray slab – standard issue for United States military veterans. No mention is made of the great American athlete – considered by many the greatest Negro Leagues player of all time – who lies underneath.

## Sources

In addition to the sources cited in the Notes, the author consulted Charleston's player file from the National Baseball Hall of Fame, contemporary newspaper articles about Charleston, and his personal scrapbook.

## Notes

1. William G. Nunn, "Diamond Dope," *Pittsburgh Courier*, June 20, 1925: 12.
2. Grant Brisbee, "Baseball Time Machine: 20 Individual Seasons Worth Going Back in Time For," *The Athletic*, July 19, 2019.
3. Brisbee.
4. Jeremy Beer, *Oscar Charleston: The Life and Legend of Baseball's Greatest Forgotten Player* (Lincoln: University of Nebraska Press, 2019), 328.
5. Beer, 44. Charleston's job as a batboy for the Indianapolis ABCs is typically included in his biography, though no definitive proof exists to show this is true.
6. In the Hall of Fame press release announcing his induction, Charleston's height and weight are listed as 5-feet-11 and 210 pounds. But on his World War II draft card, Charleston listed his height as 5-feet-8.
7. My account of this game is taken from "Race Riot Is Balked by Police," *Indianapolis Star*, October 25, 1915.
8. "Charleston's Unclean Act – He Is Very Sorry," *Indianapolis Freedman*, November 13, 1915.
9. "Charleston Dropped by the A.B.C. Club," *Indianapolis Star*, November 26, 1915.

10. Oscar Charleston, 1917 Draft Card Registration.
11. Beer, 89.
12. "A.B.C.'s wallop New York Red Caps," *Chicago Defender*, August 24, 1918.
13. "Oscar McKinley Charleston," in David L. Porter, ed., *Biographical Dictionary of American Sports* (Westport, Connecticut: Greenwood Press, 2000).
14. Beer, 110.
15. Beer, 109.
16. Beer, 109.
17. "Oscar Charleston, Giants' Crack Center Fielder," *Chicago Defender*, in Oscar Charleston's Personal Scrapbook, available at the Negro Leagues Museum in Kansas City.
18. "Oscar Charleston, Giants' Crack Center Fielder."
19. Beer, 111.
20. Beer, 116.
21. Beer, 117-18.
22. "Great Playing Beats Cubans," *Indianapolis Star*, May 10, 1920.
23. "How Much for This One?" in Oscar Charleston's pPersonal Scrapbook.
24. Beer, 124. This figure differs from the data on Seamheads, which is 17 in 362 PAs.
25. Beer, 124.
26. Beer, 130.
27. Beer, 132.
28. Beer, 132.
29. Bill James, *The New Bill James Historical Baseball Abstract* (New York: The Free Press, 2001), 175.
30. Beer, 145.
31. Beer, 272-73.
32. "Talk 'O Town," *Pittsburgh Courier,* March 12, 1938.
33. Beer, 274.
34. Beer, 149.
35. "Migration Hits Foster League," in Oscar Charleston's Personal Scrapbook.
36. Beer, 160-61.
37. Beer, 163.
38. When sources differ on statistics, SABR uses the statistics from Seamheads.com.
39. James.
40. William E. Clark, "Little World Series for Bronx Title," *New York Age*, October 24, 1925.
41. Phil Richards, "Retro Indy: Oscar Charleston," *Indianapolis Star*, February 28, 2011, available in Charleston's Hall of Fame player file.
42. "El Terror de los Clubs," in Oscar Charleston's Personal Scrapbook.
43. Jorge Figueredo, *Cuban Baseball: A Statistical History, 1878-1961* (Jefferson, North Carolina: McFarland & Company, Inc., 2003), 143.
44. Figueredo, 162.
45. Figueredo, 171.
46. Oscar Charleston record in Cuba, available in Charleston's Hall of Fame player file.
47. *Harrisburg Courier*, February 3, 1924.
48. Figueredo, 150.
49. Figueredo, 149
50. Beer, 155.
51. Beer, 155.
52. W. Rollo Wilson, "Hilldale Is Greatest Ball Team: Aggregation Credit to National Pastime," *Baltimore Afro-American*, March 16, 1929.
53. Wilson.
54. "Cuban Stars Twice Wallop Hilldale," *Baltimore Afro-American*, June 15, 1929.
55. "Johnson, Charleston, Stevens, Thomas play for Posey," *Philadelphia Tribune*, September 19, 1929.
56. Beer, 206.
57. Beer, 209.
58. C.E. Pendleton, "Charleston's Fielding Makes Him Greater Than Hornsby, Opinion," *Pittsburgh Courier*, May 30, 1931.
59. "Homestead Grays Defeat Hilldale 5 to 4, and Takes [sic] Lead in the Series," *New York Age*, July 18, 1931.
60. "Has Big Day," *Pittsburgh Courier*, September 5, 1931.
61. Beer, 229.
62. Beer, 230-31.
63. Beer, 237.
64. "Negro Nines Clash at Stadium Today," *Washington Post*, June 10, 1934.
65. Chester L. Washington, "Sez 'Ches," *Pittsburgh Courier*, May 11, 1935.
66. Al Abrams, "Sidelights on Sports," *Pittsburgh Post-Gazette*, May 29, 1935: 20.
67. "Chester Loses," *Delaware County Times* (Chester, Pennsylvania), August 6, 1935.
68. "Crawford Out to Win from Farmer Nine," *Times Union* (Brooklyn, New York), June 6, 1935: 14.

## THE 1935 PITTSBURGH CRAWFORDS

69 "Cum Posey's Pointed Paragraphs," *Pittsburgh Courier*, December 21, 1935: 13.

70 Beer, 257.

71 "Adding Color to Baseball," *Pittsburgh Courier*, March 7, 1936.

72 "Players Who Fled League Face Return/Morton Files Names with Government for Damages," *New York Amsterdam News*, May 29, 1937: 17. The list of players submitted to the State Department on May 24 included Pittsburgh Crawfords players Leroy Matlock, Ernest Carter, Chet Brewer, Satchel Paige, Bill Perkins, Cool Papa Bell, Thad Christopher, Sam Bankhead, Harry Williams, and Pat Patterson.

73 "Meet Cum's All-Time All-Americans," *Pittsburgh Courier*, December 18, 1937. The final record of the team is as presented by Beer.

74 "Phila. Stars to Begin Spring Training April 1," *Philadelphia Tribune*, March 27, 1948.

75 "Bushwicks Host to Philly Stars at Dexter Tonight," *Brooklyn Daily Eagle*, July 16, 1948.

76 Richards.

77 Beer, 21.

78 Beer, 327.

# JIMMIE CRUTCHFIELD

## By William H. Johnson

The 1935 East-West All-Star Game at Comiskey Park in Chicago, the third consecutive year of the Negro League version of the midsummer classic, ended on a Mule Suttles three-run homer to drive in Cool Papa Bell and Josh Gibson. *Pittsburgh Courier* writer Chester L. Washington, in recounting the contest, made special note of a critical defensive play earlier in the game that made the dramatic home run possible: "Next in the parade of stars," wrote Washington about an earlier inning, "came young Crutchfield, fleet-footed outfielder of the Pittsburgh Crawfords, who made a sensational bare-handed running catch of Bizz [sic] Mackey's mighty smash into center field. Sox park fans say that it was a greater catch than any big outfielder ever made in the Comiskey ball orchard."[1]

Jimmie Crutchfield, the fielding star, would eventually play in four East-West Games, his all-around baseball prowess distinguishing him among his peers despite his relatively small stature at 5-feet-7 and 150 pounds. He was labeled the "black Lloyd Waner," a white analog who was slightly taller, at 5-feet-9 but won a spot in

*Right fielder Jimmie Crutchfield, pictured here in the uniform of the Chicago American Giants, was one of six Crawfords selected to play for the West team in the 1935 East-West All-Star Classic at Chicago's Comiskey Park.*

(Courtesy of Noir Tech Research Inc.)

# THE 1935 PITTSBURGH CRAWFORDS

the National Baseball Hall of Fame on the basis of his well-rounded excellence on the diamond. A left-handed batter and right-handed thrower, Crutchfield was, according to James Riley, a "gusty hustler … a fine all-around ballplayer … a proficient bunter, excellent hit-and-run man, fast base runner, good fielder, and consistent … line drive hitter."[2] He was also, by reputation, one of the true gentlemen of the game. None other than James "Cool Papa" Bell referred to Crutchfield as "the best team player in baseball," adding, "If he never played in a game he would still have been an important part of any baseball team. You always knew you could count on Jimmie to be on the bright side of everything."[3]

John William Crutchfield was born on March 25, 1910, in the vicinity of the tiny community of Ardmore, Missouri, to John H. Crutchfield, a coal miner from Virginia, and his 15-year-old wife, Carrie. The elder John and Carrie would have four daughters as well: Fannie, Agnes, Maggie, and Pauline. By the time the 1930 US Census was taken, Carrie was a coal-mining widow and was listed as "Head of Household," working as a hotel maid.

The young Crutchfield attended elementary school in Ardmore, but the only eligible high school was in nearby Moberly. "My mother said that, even before I could walk, my father used to sit and roll baseballs to me," he said. And when the coal miners would come by, they would say, "Hey come in and look at the baseball player."[4] Crutchfield loved baseball from an early age, and graduated from playing on the local sandlots to playing with an organized team managed by former Negro League star pitcher Bill Gatewood. Crutchfield evidently showed Gatewood a glimpse of the possible, and the latter was encouraged the former's professional ambitions. "He told me I had a good chance, even as small as I was," said Crutchfield. "With the love I had for baseball and, as small as I was, I thought I could play baseball. I believed I could play any place."[5] His career may have begun as early as 1928, playing on a Moberly team called the Gatewood Browns.[6]

In 1930, after less than two years of college at Lincoln University, at the time a historically black institution 66 miles south, in Jefferson City, Crutchfield packed up his dreams and a few meager possessions and left home to try out with the Birmingham Black Barons, a tryout that was arranged through Gatewood's connections with league officials. "When my friends among the people around my hometown … heard that I was leaving, they said, 'Hey Crutch, you got your bus fare back?' and things like that," Crutchfield said. "Because the rumors were about 100-1 that I couldn't make it. But they didn't know the love I had for baseball."[7] After spring training at Fort Benning, Georgia, the Black Barons named Crutchfield their starting center fielder for the season. Playing for a $90-a-month salary, he batted .288 with nine triples. "It wasn't the money, because the money wasn't there," he said. "It was just the recognition that came with being a regular baseball player on a big-time colored baseball team. Just to walk down the street and know you had made it."[8]

After spending 1931 with the Indianapolis ABCs, teaming with his future Chicago manager Candy Jim Taylor, Crutchfield joined Gus Greenlee's Pittsburgh Crawfords. The team, until 1932 more of a semipro team, had almost overnight become a juggernaut in professional baseball, and the young outfielder now played with teammates like Josh Gibson, Cool Papa Bell, Judy Johnson, Satchel Paige, Jud Wilson, Smokey Joe Williams, and manager-first baseman Oscar Charleston. It took Crutchfield some time to worm into Charleston's good graces, but he finally did. In one particular game, "The bases were full and two outs, and I was playing this particular hitter to hit to right-center," Crutchfield remembered. "Charleston came out in front of the whole crowd and moved me over to left-center. And the guy hit a long line drive where he had just moved me from. I was young then and I caught the ball running away from home plate to retire the side. Everybody rushed off the field and into the clubhouse. Charleston came in the dressing room and he didn't even look at me. He just looked straight ahead and said, 'Crutch, you are a fielding ass,' From that time on I had it made. From then on I played outfield for the Crawfords."[9]

During this period, Crutchfield enjoyed opportunities to play against Dizzy Dean's All Stars, toured Puerto Rico with another all-star squad, and played in three consecutive East-West All Star games (1934-1936). While the baseball was often outstanding, the conditions were always challenging. The team often stayed in poor accommodations and traveled via seemingly endless bus and car rides. The few months in which winter weather made baseball impossible found Crutchfield working at whatever jobs he could find. As he recalled, he was a "hotel bellhop, shoe-shine boy in a barber shop – that was about it. We just took whatever we could find. You had to take something because you came home every winter with very little, and even though you knew that the results would be the same, you couldn't wait for March to start again. I love the game so much I would have paid to play."[10]

Crutchfield left the Crawfords after the 1936 season and moved to Abe and Effa Manley's Newark Eagles for the 1937 and 1938 campaigns. Once again teamed with some of the game's immortals – including Leon Day, Ray Dandridge, Mule Suttles, Willie Wells, and, later, Monte Irvin – the speedy outfielder helped the Eagles to finish in second place behind the Homestead Grays in 1937. After a disappointing 1938 season, Crutchfield played for San Juan in the Puerto Rican League's inaugural season. He remembered, "I first came down to Puerto in 1936. At that time, we played six weeks with Paige and Gibson. It was a success, and [Puerto Rico] decided to start a league, and in 1938 I was the first center fielder to play for San Juan."[11] Crutchfield loved the island and returned there for an old-timers game in 1979. He said of his time in Puerto Rico, "If you were nice to the nice people, the sun would shine in your face all the time. It was a fun time."[12]

For the moment, Crutchfield returned to the Crawfords, now based in Toledo, Ohio, for 1939. The next season, Crutchfield, for reasons that remain unclear but that historian James Riley termed "personal,"[13] played very briefly for Indianapolis, and then nowhere else. The 1940 US Census recorded that Crutchfield listed his employer as the Merchants Hotel, and his residence as Moberly, Missouri.

Crutchfield made an abrupt return to the diamond in 1941. At the behest of Candy Jim Taylor, a former teammate of mentor Bill Gatewood and an outstanding manager in his own right, Crutchfield signed with the Chicago American Giants. There, teamed with popular players like Pepper Bassett and Alex Radcliffe, and with a position from which to mentor a young Art Pennington, Crutchfield played well enough to earn his fourth selection to the East-West All Star game. Although the East defeated Crutchfield and the West team, the outfielder managed a hit, his only one in 10 East-West Game at-bats. The outfielder returned to Chicago for the 1942 season, but his performance declined precipitously.

On November 30, 1942, Crutchfield enlisted in the US Army, and he served nearly a year before being discharged on October 20, 1943. "I had a chance to beat the army rap if I wanted to, but I just felt I had to serve," he said. "And when two [draft board] people asked when I wanted to go, I said, 'Well, in the next batch.'"[14] After being discharged with the rank of staff sergeant, Crutchfield returned to the American Giants in 1944, and then ended the year in a Cleveland Buckeyes uniform. He closed out his playing career in 1945, returning to his new home in Chicago to once again play for Taylor and the American Giants.

Crutchfield knew when it was time to hang 'em up and retire. He observed, "I was 35 years of age and I was worn out from the traveling, and all the worst of conditions. … I had made a name for myself."[15] Once he was out of baseball, Crutchfield worked for the Post Office. In 1947 he wed, marrying Julia R. Day, a Chicago elementary-school teacher eight years Crutchfield's senior.[16] While they had no children of their own, they remained happily married until his death in 1993. They split their golden years between their Southside Chicago apartment, a seventh-floor unit in an area called Lake Meadows,[17] which is less than a mile from Comiskey Park, and their vacation home in South Haven, Michigan.[18]

Crutchfield retired from the Post Office in 1970, but he worked for the Continental Illinois Bank for three more years, retiring for good in 1973.[19] The relative explosion of interest in the history of the Negro baseball leagues and teams finally afforded Crutchfield some national recognition, albeit late in his life. The governor of Kentucky named him an honorary Kentucky Colonel.[20] The designation is conferred in "recognition of … noteworthy accomplishments and outstanding service to our community, state, and nation."[21] It was a lifetime honor, and from that point on, Crutchfield almost always signed autographs as "Col. Jimmie Crutchfield." In February 1992 President George H.W. Bush invited Crutchfield and some other former players to participate in a celebration of Black History Month at the White House, and two years later Crutchfield was among the players honored on a poster created by the Metropolitan Museum of Art.[22]

That last acknowledgment came just a year too late. On March 31, 1993, Crutchfield died of cancer. He was survived for three more years by his wife, Julia, and is buried at the Burr Oak Cemetery in Alsip, Illinois.[23] His grave went unmarked until 2003, when members of the Society for American Baseball Research corrected that with a formal marker commemorating Crutchfield's life and final resting place.[24]

John William "Jimmie" Crutchfield was widely acknowledged as a terrific, All-Star-level outfielder, and an even better human being. His gentility and class suffused and influenced much of his thinking. As with so many of the players of his era, those talented athletes who preceded Jackie Robinson's assault on baseball's racial barrier in 1947, and who could be forgiven a degree of bitterness or resentment at the world-as-it-was, he was often asked if he regretted not having had the opportunity to play in an integrated, major league. Lawrence Hogan recounted Crutchfield's thoughts on the subject:

> I have no ill feeling about never having had the opportunity to play in the big leagues. There have been times – you know, they used to call me the black Lloyd Waner. I used to think about that a lot. He was on the other side of town in Pittsburgh, making $12,000 a year and I didn't have enough money to go home. I had to borrow bus fare to come home.
>
> It seemed like there was something wrong there. But that was yesterday. There's no use in me having bitterness in my heart this late in life about what's gone by. That's just the way I feel about it. Once in a while I get a kick out of thinking that my name was mentioned as one of the stars of the East-West game and little things like that. I don't know whether I'd feel better if I had a million dollars.
>
> I can say I contributed something.[25]

## Notes

1. Chester Washington, "Hes' Sez," *Pittsburgh Courier*, August 17, 1935: 14.
2. James A. Riley, *The Biographical Encyclopedia of the Negro Baseball Leagues* (New York: Carroll & Graf, 1994), 201.
3. Tony McClean, "The Negro Leagues: Gone but Not Forgotten: Remembering Jimmie Crutchfield," 2005. blackathlete.net/2005/03/the-negro-leagues-gone-but-not-forgottenremembering-jimmie-crutchfield/, accessed January 11, 2019.
4. James A. Riley, *Of Monarchs and Black Barons: Essays on Baseball's Negro Leagues* (Jefferson, North Carolina: McFarland & Company, Inc., 2012), 120.
5. Riley, 121.

6. This information comes from the Center For Negro League Baseball Research (cnlbr.org) and was specifically located online: cnlbr.org/Portals/0/Players%20Register/C-E%202018-04.pdf Accessed March 21, 2019.

7. Riley, *Of Monarchs and Black Barons*, 120.

8. Riley, *Of Monarchs and Black Barons*, 122.

9. Riley, *Of Monarchs and Black Barons*, 123.

10. J.G. Keenan and S. Cohen, "Jimmie Crutchfield's Baseball Life," *Loyola Magazine* 22(1), 199: 28-34.

11. Thomas E. Van Hyning, *Puerto Rico's Winter League: A History of Major League Baseball's Launching Pad* (Jefferson, North Carolina: McFarland & Company, Inc., 1995), 83.

12. Van Hyning, 83.

13. Riley, *Biographical Encyclopedia of the Negro Baseball Leagues*, 202.

14. Keenan and Cohen, 6.

15. Riley, Crutchfield essay.

16. Julia Crutchfield obituary, *Chicago Tribune*, December 9, 1996: 143.

17. William Brashler, *Josh Gibson: A Life in the Negro Leagues* (Chicago: Ivan R. Dee Publishing, 1978), 166-170.

18. Keenan and Cohen, 8.

19. Keenan and Cohen, 8.

20. Leslie Heaphy, ed., *Black Baseball and Chicago* (Jefferson, North Carolina: McFarland and Co., 2006), 62.

21. For the general criteria regarding selection for this honor, see kycolonels.org/, accessed January 2, 2019.

22. McLean.

23. findagrave.com/memorial/9517611/jimmie-crutchfield, accessed January 4, 2019.

24. Joe Paladino, "In Death, Baseball Pioneer Receives His Due," larrylester42.com/uploads/1/9/5/4/19545937/sol_white_by_joe_palladino.pdf, accessed January 9, 2019.

25. Lawrence Hogan, *Shades of Glory: The Negro Leagues and the Story of African-American Baseball* (Washington: National Geographic, 2006), 377.

# ROOSEVELT DAVIS

## By Jay Hurd

The June 6, 1945, headline in *The Dispatch* (Moline, Illinois) read, "Cincinnati Clowns to Play at Davenport Friday Night." The piece to follow reported, "Some of the greatest names in Negro baseball appear in the Clowns' lineup, among them being Roosevelt 'Duro' Davis, second only to 'Satchel' Paige in Negro pitching circles." Hyperbole or not, Davis, 41 years old at the time of this article, had played baseball for nearly 30 years – a veteran of the Negro National League (I and II), the Negro American League, the Mexican League, and multiple independent leagues.

While records of Roosevelt Davis and his family are, at best, minimal and inconsistent, it appears certain that he was born in Bartlesville, Oklahoma, on November 19, 1904. His father, Will, was born on April 10, 1880, possibly in Bartlesville. Roosevelt's mother has been identified as Anna; however, records indicate that Will did not wed until 1909 when he married, in nearby Arkansas, Octavia Campbell of the Cherokee Tribe, Foreman, Sequoyah, Oklahoma. It is unclear when Octavia died, but by 1935 Will

*By the time his career ended, pitcher Roosevelt Davis was a veteran of 20 seasons in the Negro Leagues, who had won two championships with the St. Louis Stars and one with the Pittsburgh Crawfords.*

(Courtesy of Center for Negro League Baseball Research)

lived in Peoria, Illinois, where he remained until his death in 1960. A brief obituary states that Will had been widowed for a number of years and left a son, Roosevelt; a daughter, Oleander; and a sister, Bertha.[1] While his earlier employments may have varied (including California vineyard worker[2]), during the final 26 years of his life in Illinois Will Davis had been employed as a janitor by the U.S. Barge Lines.

Roosevelt may have attended the Douglass School, which was founded in 1907 for Bartlesville's black students.[3] The 1920 US Census shows Roosevelt, age 15, living in Bartlesville, not with his father and/or mother, but with his aunt Bertha Mackey and her two sons, Eddie and Robert.

There is also uncertainty in regard to exactly when Roosevelt began to play, but his name appears in Bartlesville newspapers in the early 1920s, including one game summary in which he is identified as a pitcher for the Coffeyville, Kansas, baseball team.[4] At this time, and perhaps already in years prior, his baseball talent became evident and he played on other teams including the Wichita (Kansas) Monrovians[5] and an integrated team in Tekamah, Nebraska.[6] The St. Louis Stars, members of the newly organized Negro National League, added him to their roster as a starting pitcher in 1924. He was listed as 5-feet-9 and 168 pounds, and he batted and threw right-handed. He appeared in 25 games that season, compiled a 7-4 record, pitched 121⅔ innings, and held a 4.29 ERA. The Stars' squad, managed by 40-year-old James Allen "Candy Jim" Taylor, included James "Cool Papa" Bell and Willie "El Diablo" Wells. After the season Davis married Lillian Turner of Omaha, Nebraska, on December 5, 1924. How long they remained married is unknown, and it appears that they had no children.

Davis again was a starting pitcher for the 1925 Stars, and his 17-7 record helped the team to reach the Negro National League Championship Series against the Kansas City Monarchs. Although the Stars lost the series, Davis had secured his spot in the starting rotation. For the season, he started 21 games, completed nine, and struck out 54 batters.

In 1926 Candy Jim Taylor left the St. Louis Stars to manage the Detroit Stars; St. Louis's new manager, Dizzy Dismukes, led his team to a third-place finish, and Davis compiled a 8-5 record, with only one complete game, in 18 starts. In 1927 Taylor managed St. Louis to a 62-37 record and a second-place finish. Davis pitched to an 11-8 record that year. Davis appeared in 23 games during the 1928 NNL season, although he made only eight starts, and achieved a perfect 8-0 record; however, he made only a brief one-inning appearance in one game of the championship series. The team, again managed by Taylor, did very well, posting a 61-26 record in league play, and won the Negro National League pennant in the championship series against the Chicago American Giants.

In 1929 Davis split the season between the St. Louis Stars, with Taylor in his final season as the manager, and the Chicago American Giants, managed by Jim Brown. Davis compiled a 6-7 record for St. Louis, but he was with Chicago by the time the team played a seven-game series versus a team of American Leaguers that included Wally Schang, Charlie Gehringer, and Harry Heilmann. The American Giants won the series, five games to two. Davis pitched in two games, one complete-game start and one relief appearance, and struck out six while pitching to a 1.69 ERA in 10⅔ innings.

By then Davis resided in St. Louis. The 1930 US Census listed him as a single lodger who was employed in "League" industry as a ballplayer. The 1930 season again saw Davis play with two teams: theStars, now managed by John Reese, and the Kansas City Monarchs, managed by Charles Wilber "Bullet Joe" Rogan. He was 1-0 in two appearances for the Monarchs but posted a stellar 10-3 regular-season mark for the Stars and won his only start against the Detroit Stars in the NNL Championship Series, which St. Louis won in seven games.

## THE 1935 PITTSBURGH CRAWFORDS

Davis led a peripatetic existence in 1931 as he pitched for three teams. He was 1-0 with the St. Louis Stars before he joined the Indianapolis ABCs, also of the Negro National League, and played again for manager Candy Jim Taylor; Davis won only one of five decisions for the ABCs. He moved on to the Pittsburgh Crawford Giants, a member team of the Independent Clubs League that was managed by Bobby Williams. In Pittsburgh, he posted a 2-2 record that included a shutout and 20 strikeouts in 27⅓ innings pitched.

With the 1932 season came yet more change for Davis. With the Cuban Stars West, also known as [Syd] Pollock's Cuban Stars of the East-West League, he pitched in two games. He also pitched in four games with the Cleveland Stars, another squad that was part of the East-West League. His composite record was 1-3 and he had a cumulative 3.61 ERA.

Davis again played a minor role in the 1933 season, this time for the Columbus (Ohio) Blue Birds of the Negro National League, who were managed by another familiar name, Dizzy Dismukes. Davis had a 2-2 record in eight appearances (four starts), but he had a sparkling 2.66 ERA in 44 innings pitched. The 1933 campaign was also when Davis taught Bill Byrd how to throw the spitball. Once Byrd became known for the spitball, he often faked throwing that pitch "for psychological reasons" to confuse batters.[7] Indeed, Davis himself was a master of the spitball and, "legal or not, he was deemed one of the best spitball and emery-ball pitchers in black baseball."[8] Davis's prowess in applying "slippery elm juice" to the ball would create interesting moments later in his career.

The most notable event for Davis in 1933 occurred when Neil Churchill, who owned an integrated team in Bismarck, North Dakota, recruited him after consulting with Chicago's Abe Saperstein.[9] The *Bismarck Tribune*'s account of Davis's debut noted, "Davis caught the fancy of local diamond enthusiasts in his first game here Sunday when he blanked Fort Lincoln 16-0, allowing only three hits, striking out 16 (four in one inning), getting three hits and driving in five runs."[10] He was later joined in Bismarck by other Negro Leaguers who included, most notably, Satchel Paige.[11]

In 1934 Davis joined forces with Paige, Josh Gibson, James "Cool Papa" Bell, and player-manager Oscar Charleston on the NNL's Pittsburgh Crawfords. He pitched in only five games, starting two and compiling a 1-0 record. He soon made a return trip to North Dakota, along with Quincy Trouppe and Satchel Paige. This time, Davis played for the New Rockford club while Paige and Trouppe again provided Bismarck with a formidable battery. The *Bismarck Tribune* remained complimentary to Davis even as he pitched for a rival team, and wrote about his loss to Bismarck, "Roosevelt Davis, a former teammate … turned in a good pitching exhibition but his erratic support gave him little chance against the Capital City team."[12]

At 30 years old, Davis returned to the Crawfords for their 1935 championship season. After finishing the first half of the season with a record of 26-6, the Crawfords defeated the winners of the second-half pennant, the New York Cubans, in a hotly contested seven-game series. Davis fashioned a 5-1 record in 13 appearances (eight starts) during the regular season, but he was a key cog for the team in the championship series. He made two complete-game starts and one relief appearance against the Cubans and put up a 2-1 record pitching 23⅔ innings against the Cubans. Had it not been for Davis's tough-as-nails pitching efforts, the New Yorkers might have prevailed against the team that many consider to be the finest Negro League squad in history, the 1935 Pittsburgh Crawfords.

On the heels of his great performance in the 1935 championship, Davis moved to New York, where he joined the Black Yankees for the 1936 season. Manager Bob Clarke led the team to a 21-16-1 record in NNL play; Davis put up a 2-4 record. The following season, Davis made one ap-

# Pride of Smoketown

*Roosevelt "Rosey" Davis was the winning pitcher in two of the Crawfords' four victories over the New York Cubans in the 1935 NNL championship series.*

pearance for the Black Yankees before he rejoined the Crawfords, who were still being managed by Oscar Charleston. Davis pitched to the same 2-4 record (all for the Crawfords) he had accumulated the previous season and saw his ERA balloon to 5.04 over 44⅔ innings with the Steel City team.

By 1938 it appeared as though Davis's career might be nearing its end. He once again split time between two teams, playing for the Black Yankees, managed by Walter Cannady, and the Newark Eagles of Abe Manley and Dick Lundy. His cumulative statistics included a 0-1 record in three appearances (one start) and a 6.75 ERA in only eight innings of work.

Perhaps in the hope that a change of scenery might help, Davis moved south to join the Memphis Red Sox of the Negro American League in 1939. On this team, managed by Ted "Double Duty" Radcliffe, Davis started four games, completed three and, while striking out 16, compiled a 1-3 record and brought his ERA down to 3.82.

That same year, Davis made his only venture outside the United States to play for the Monterrey team in the Mexican League. He was one of "the stars of the first year" of the Monterrey Sultanes, who were later renamed the Industriales.[13] During his stint south of the border, Davis was 3-6 in 11 starts, struck out 49 batters, and had a 3.76 ERA in 67 innings.[14]

While baseball had become Davis's main source of income, he still needed to supplement his finances with employment in the winter months. His October 16, 1940, draft registration form indicates that he lived in Chicago and that he was employed by the Palmer House hotel (likely as a waiter).[15] Keenly aware of the limitations of baseball income, Davis noted that "off season employment should have been 'tackled and solved long ago. Baseball players have to eat and sleep and see the laundry man in December as well as June.'"[16]

It also happened that, during the 1939 season, Satchel Paige's ailing arm miraculously healed, and Paige returned to J.L. Wilkinson's "B" team in Kansas City.[17] To prove that Paige could indeed pitch again, Wilkinson and Abe Saperstein scheduled a game with the Palmer House Stars. Paige later recounted, "Abe says, 'If Satch is great again let's let his arm speak for us. The hottest arm in Negro baseball is Roosevelt Davis: How about putting Satch up against him?'" However, Paige knew Davis and he said "Now wait. That Roosevelt Davis throws a cut ball. I don't like to throw no cut ball. ... Davis scratches the ball with his nails and his belt buckle. That makes the ball sail and Davis knows how to control it."[18] Paige continued, "So Abe books a game in late September with the Palmer House Indians, the team Roosevelt Davis was pitchin' for. ... They got three hits and we win, 1-0."[19] Lost in Paige's account is whether he actually faced off against Davis that day, or whether a different pitcher took the mound for the Palmer House team.

Davis returned to the Memphis Red Sox in 1940 as a pitcher and occasional left fielder, but he mostly pitched for the Palmer House Stars in independent baseball. As the Stars traveled north from spring training in Texas, they stopped to play the Kansas City Monarchs in a seven-game series: "[T]he Palmer House team was credited with downing the Monarchs six times before finally losing, 2-1, to Satchel Paige. Roosevelt Davis took the loss in that game even though he struck out 10 Monarchs (besting Paige's eight strikeouts). Davis was accused of scuffing the ball, though nothing came of the accusation."[20] He continued to pitch for the Palmer House nine, with success and controversy. "In 1940 they came in fifth in the Wichita National Semi-Pro Tournament, relying on the solid pitching of Roosevelt Davis."[21] His reputation as a creative pitcher preceded him: "Roosevelt Davis 38 year old Palmer House pitcher, who was ejected from the game in the ninth inning by Umpire Virgil Blueitt [sic] when he refused to surrender what Kansas City players charged was a tampered ball, struck out ten, yielded seven hits, and gave two walks. ... Umpire Bluett chased Davis from the field amusing the crowd by putting on a wrestling act with the Palmer House coaches."[22]

Davis now settled in Chicago and, in addition to playing for the Palmer House squad, also anchored the Chicago Brown Bombers' pitching staff in 1942. In 1943, at the age of 38, Davis pitched in nine games for the Cincinnati Clowns of the Negro American League. He made six starts and completed them all, hurled one shutout, and posted a 2.35 ERA over 61⅓ innings. Davis had brief stints with the same team – now known as the Cincinnati-Indianapolis Clowns – in 1944 and 1945 before his professional pitching career came to an end. In 1944 he finished the year at 3-1, and in 1945 he had no wins and no losses in one start.

Roosevelt Davis played 20 seasons in the Negro Leagues. During that time, he played for 12 teams in four leagues while also competing in multiple independent leagues, where he played alongside many of baseball's greatest players, both black and white. He compiled a 98-63 record, with a .609 winning percentage, and a 4.11 ERA in Negro League play. Despite a well-founded reputation for using the spitball, cut ball, and emery ball, he had remarkable control of his pitches.

On January 22, 1950, the Chicago Chapter of the Baseball Writers Association of America held its annual meeting at the Palmer House. During the occasion, "Some observant sports writers … spotted vaguely familiar faces" among the waiters. Five waiters in starched shirts and ties turned out to be veterans of the Negro Leagues and among them Roosevelt Davis, the first black player brought to Bismarck by Neil Churchill in 1933, the scuffed-ball maestro … in his Mid-forties (and balding), he carried serving trays for a living."[23]

Roosevelt Davis died on December 28, 1968, in Chicago at the age of 64. He was buried in the Burr Oak Cemetery in Alsip, Illinois. Through the efforts of the SABR Negro Leagues Committee and its Grave Marker Project, a marker noting his career in Negro League baseball was dedicated and placed at his gravesite in 2005.

### Sources

Unless otherwise indicated, all Negro League statistics were taken from Seamheads.com. Additional sources of content include Baseball-Reference.com, Ancestry.com, Newspapers.com, the Oklahoma and Kansas Historical Societies, and a statistical bio prepared by SABR member Kevin Larkin.

### Notes

1. Find a Grave, Will Davis, April 10, 1880-November 11, 1960, findagrave.com/memorial/187482031.

2. Alan J. Pollock, *Barnstorming to Heaven: Syd Pollock and His Great Black Teams* (Tuscaloosa, Alabama: University of Alabama Press, 2006), 125-126.

3. Bartlesville, Oklahoma, segregated black students from the rest of the student population until 1956. Bartlesville, Oklahoma Public School site, bps-ok.org/home/district/history/douglass.

4. "Black Oilers Down Hotshots, Score 4-3," *Bartlesville (Oklahoma) Morning Examiner*, June 30, 1922.

5. "Panthers Open with Wichita Monrovians," *Daily Oklahoman* (Oklahoma City), April 29, 1923.

6. Pollock, 125.

7   Negro Leagues Baseball Museum, *"William Byrd,"* nlbemuseum.com/history/players/byrd.html.

8   Mark Schremmer, "Negro League Greats Started in Topeka," *Topeka* (Kansas) *Capital-Journal,* August 6, 2011. cjonline.com/article/20110806/SPORTS/308069876.

9   Donald Spivey, *If You Were Only White: The Life of Leroy "Satchel" Paige* (Columbia, Missouri: University of Missouri Press, 2012), 102.

10  "Bismarck Nine Will Play Gray Ghosts of St. Louis Here Tonight; Expect Roosevelt and Mates Will 'Pack 'Em In,'" *Bismarck* (North Dakota) *Tribune,* June 28, 1933.

11  Spivey, 102-103.

12  "Bismarck Hammers Roosevelt Davis; Wins from Rockford, 13-3," *Bismarck Tribune,* June 18, 1934.

13  Martha Cedillo, "Sultanes de Monterrey, el Iceberg de Beisbol," milenio.com/especiales/sultanes-el-iceberg-del-beisbol

14  Pedro Treto Cisneros, *The Mexican League: Comprehensive Player Statistics, 1937-2001* (Jefferson, North Carolina: McFarland & Company, Inc., 2002), 469.

15  Of note: Roosevelt identifies his father, Will, as next of kin on his draft registration form. Will Davis, at the age of 61, registered for the draft on April 27, 1942.

16  Neil Lanctot, *Negro League Baseball: The Rise and Ruin of a Black Institution* (Philadelphia: University of Pennsylvania Press, 2004), 163.

17  "Satchel Paige," Baseball Hall of Fame, baseballhall.org/hall-of-famers/paige-satchel.

18  Satchel Paige, as told to Hal Lebovitz, *Pitchin' Man: Satchel Paige's Own Story* (New York: Ishi Press International, 2015), 60.

19  *Pitchin' Man*, 61.

20  Leslie Heaphy, "Palmer House Stars," *The National Pastime*, 2015, sabr.org/research/palmer-house-stars.

21  Leslie Heaphy, ed. "Chicago Teams in the Negro League Era," *Black Baseball and Chicago: Essays on the Players and Teams* (Jefferson, North Carolina: McFarland & Company, Inc. 2006), 34.

22  James Segreti, "Satchel Paige Pitches, Grins, and Conquers," *Chicago Tribune*, September 23, 1940.

23  Tom Dunkel, *Color Blind: The Forgotten Team That Broke Baseball's Color Lines* (New York: Grove Press, 2004), 267. According to the Center for Negro League Baseball Research, Davis also pitched in 1945 for the Philadelphia Stars and the Cleveland Buckeyes. He may also have played at one point during his career for the Brooklyn Royal Giants.

# JOSH GIBSON

## By William H. Johnson.

*There is a catcher that any big league club would like to buy for $200,000. His name is Gibson. He can do everything. He hits the ball a mile. He catches so easy he might as well be in a rocking chair. Throws like a rifle. Too bad this Gibson is a colored fellow.*

— Walter Johnson

He was referred to as the black Babe Ruth, but some – then and now – believe it might be just as accurate to call the Bambino the white Josh Gibson.[1] In June 1967 a column in *The Sporting News* credited Gibson with a drive in a Negro League game that hit just two feet from the top of the wall circling the bleachers at Yankee stadium, approximately 580 feet from home plate in the original park. Had the ball been just two feet higher, the article mused, the ball might have carried 700 feet.[2] Jack Marshall, of the Chicago American Giants, swore that he saw Gibson hit a ball completely out of Yankee Stadium,[3] and some accounts credit Gibson with between 800 and 1,000 homeruns in a career that lasted only 16 years.

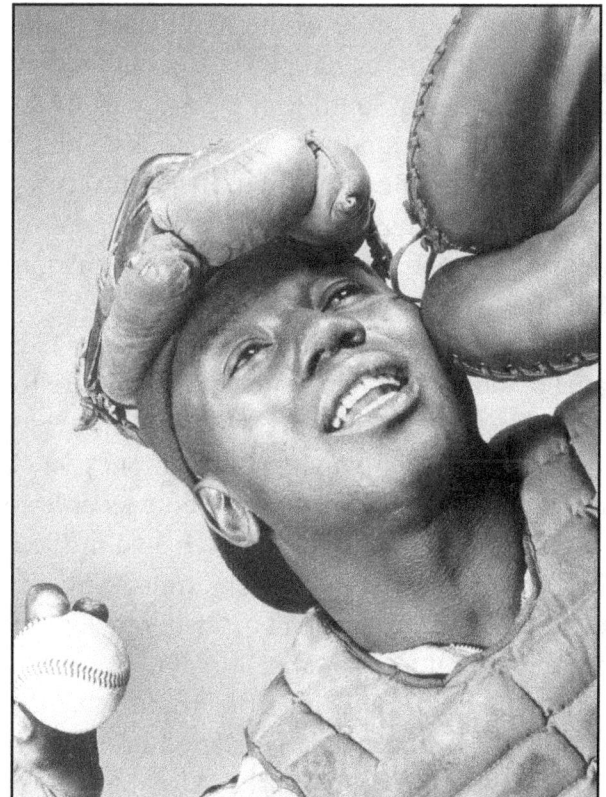

*Josh Gibson, best-known for his prolific slugging – his Hall of Fame plaque credits him with "almost 800 homers" – here strikes a pose in his catcher's gear.*

(National Baseball Hall of Fame)

"There exists no official source of statistics… no compilations of scorecards. … Many gaps exist in the historical record," an authority on the Negro Leagues points out.[4] The record-keeping was incomplete and nonstandardized, so the actual total is unclear and probably unknowable. That reality, that statistics cannot be usefully compared between the Negro Leagues and the pre-integration major leagues, is an unfortunate one, yet it is also largely irrelevant. Josh Gibson was, by so many accounts as to make the claim indisputable, one of the greatest sluggers who ever stepped into a batter's box.

Gibson was born to Mark and Nancy (Woodlock) Gibson in Buena Vista, Georgia, on or about December 21, 1911, named Joshua after one of Mark's grandfathers.[5] As Leigh Montville observed about such specific facts in his biography of Babe Ruth, "Details are important but do not seem to be available. There is so much we want to know. There is so much we never will."[6] That is especially true of the histories of many of the old Negro League players, certainly ones born in the Deep South in the early part of the 20th century. But it is close to certain that Gibson was the eldest of three children. His brother Jerry, who pitched briefly for the Cincinnati Tigers, was three years younger, and sister Annie (Gibson) Mahaffey was six years his junior.[7]

Mark Gibson was a sharecropper who in 1923 traveled to Pittsburgh in search of a better life for his family. He found work with the Carnegie-Illinois Steel Company and sent money back to Georgia for three years until he was able to bring the whole family to Pennsylvania in 1926. The Gibsons bought a house on Strauss Street in the Pleasant Valley section of Pittsburgh, and set about turning it into a home.

Josh had finished the fifth grade while in Georgia. In Pennsylvania he started in the electrical studies program at the Allegheny Pre-Vocational School, and at 13 was placed in a similar program at Conroy Pre-Vocational, in Pleasant Valley.[8] By the time he turned 15 he dropped out of school in order to take a job at an airbrake manufacturing plant to help support the family. At 6-feet-1 and 200 pounds, he was already capable of working with the adult men doing heavy labor. He went to work after school with Carnegie-Illinois Steel, which left his evenings free for recreation.

Despite his combination of size and an easy, natural athleticism, Gibson did not embrace football or basketball, instead preferring swimming and, of course, baseball, the sport at which he excelled. His first formal, uniformed baseball team, at age 16, was an all-Negro team sponsored by Gimbels Department Store.[9] After a stint as a catcher, Gibson finally settled in at third base. Mark Ribowsky summarized it neatly: The firm "thought enough of his ability that (they) gave him a job as an elevator operator so it could keep him in uniform."[10]

The baseball team, along with other amateur black teams, became organized into the Negro Greater Pittsburgh Industrial League. The entity included teams from various steel companies, Pittsburgh Railways, and Pittsburgh Screw and Bolt,[11] and the contests drew quite a few fans (and some gamblers) to the ballyards. One newer team, Pittsburgh Bath House, was able to recruit several additional sponsors and renamed itself the Pittsburgh Crawfords. One of those partial sponsors was Honus Wagner, who, retired as a player and the owner of a sporting-goods store, donated uniforms to the team. Even so, the team might have folded due to lack of funds had it not been for the intervention of Gus Greenlee, who took control in 1926. With the infusion of money, and commensurate talent, the Crawfords dominated both the Negro Industrial league and Pittsburgh's recreational league that year.

In 1927 Greenlee installed Harold "Hooks" Tinker as manager. Tinker happened to watch an Industrial League all-star game at Ammon Field in 1928, and Josh Gibson's life changed forever. "I had two of my Crawford players on that all-star team. … Otherwise I wouldn't have been there.

# THE 1935 PITTSBURGH CRAWFORDS

And that's when I saw Josh. He was playin' third base, and he was very mature in his actions; you wouldn't think he was only 16 years old."[12] "He was built like sheet metal. If you ran into him it was like you ran into a wall."[13] Tinker later recounted: "I signed (him). I brought Josh Gibson into the semipro picture."[14]

Gibson, for all his size and notoriety, was a decent human being. "Now with Josh," Ted Page, a fellow Negro Leaguer, observed, "Nobody could criticize his personality. Next to hitting, I think he liked eating ice cream more than anything else in the world."[15]

In 1928 Gibson met Helen Mason, a year his junior, and by 1929 the two had fallen deeply in love. That February Helen announced that she was pregnant with their first child, and a month later, on March 7, 1929, the two were married at Macedonia Baptist Church in Pittsburgh. The pregnancy did not endure, but Helen became pregnant again in 1930, this time with twins.

On August 11, 1930, Helen went into premature labor. Her pregnancy had evidently "aggravated an undiagnosed kidney condition and by the time she reached the hospital, one of her kidneys had ruptured."[16] Josh arrived at the hospital minutes before Helen died. The babies, at least, were delivered safely. The first was a son, Josh Jr., and a sister, Helen, followed him. Josh Sr., however, was inconsolable at the loss of his wife. Deciding that he was neither ready nor fit to be a single parent, he prevailed on his in-laws, James and Margaret Mason, to take the infants into their home. Gibson was emotionally devastated, and some argue that he never recovered from the tragedy.

On the baseball diamond, though, there was no difference in Josh's performance. Gibson played for the semipro Crawford Colored Giants in 1929 and 1930, earning a few dollars a game while often playing in front of 5,000 or more spectators, and word of his power inevitably reached Judy Johnson and the Homestead Grays. "I had never seen him play," said Johnson, "but we had heard so much about him. Every time you'd look at the paper you'd see where he hit a ball 400 feet, 500 feet."[17] The Grays already had two catchers, Buck Ewing and Vic Harris, so they didn't immediately pursue Gibson, but he was certainly on their figurative radar.

On July 25, 1930, the 1929 Negro League Champion Kansas City Monarchs came to Pittsburgh to play an exhibition. Monarchs' owner J.L. Wilkinson had developed a portable lighting system that the team towed around the country so that they could play at night and maximize the local attendance, but the lights were far dimmer than those used in the modern day. According to legend, Joe Williams was catching for the Grays that night and lost the ball in the low visibility, breaking a finger in the process. Vic Harris was in the outfield that evening, the story goes, so Grays owner Cum Posey called Josh out of the stands and asked him if he would like to catch the rest of the game.[18]

It is, perhaps, an apocryphal story, myth mixed with memory and laced together with a few facts, but there is no other more definitive account of how Gibson became a member of the Homestead Grays. He went hitless that night, but recorded no errors, either, and he remained with the team for the rest of 1930. Johnson had Gibson catch batting practice every day, eventually working him into a few games if only to get his bat into the lineup.

Over his career, there would form several opinions about Gibson's ability as a catcher. Some who saw him said he was passable, even good, but not as talented as Biz Mackey or Bruce Petway. Roy Campanella, though, averred that Gibson was "not only the greatest catcher but the greatest ballplayer I ever saw."[19] Regardless of his ability as a backstop, the man could hit and hit with power. Any team he played for would have found a uniform for Josh. On September 27, 1930, Gibson smote the first of his most legendary homers, a shot that flew an estimated 430 to 460 feet into the left-field bleachers at Yankee Stadium during a playoff game between the Grays and the New York Lincoln Giants.[20]

In 1931 the Homestead Grays affiliated with the American Negro League, a short-lived precursor to the Negro National and American Leagues that would emerge in 1932. The Grays played on a circuit with the Cuban Stars East, the Baltimore Black Sox, and the Philadelphia Hilldale Giants, and 19-year-old Josh had the opportunity to play alongside legends like Oscar Charleston, Bill Foster, Smokey Joe Williams, Jud Wilson, Ted Page, and Ted "Double Duty" Radcliffe. Within league play, Gibson was credited with 132 at-bats, hitting 10 home runs and slugging at a .545 clip.

The next year, 1932, Gus Greenlee enticed Gibson back to the still-independent Crawfords to catch for a pitcher named Satchel Paige, the first time the two were paired. As independents, the Crawfords played exhibitions against a wide array of teams, and some have credited Josh with as many as 72 homers during the long season, although only five are recognized by baseball-reference.com. Again, with incomplete records, unregulated ballparks and fence distances, and a wide span of exhibition pitching talent, the number is less important than the reality that Gibson was already an elite power hitter.

In order to make a few more dollars, and to play in an environment where racial segregation was not an issue, Gibson traveled to Puerto Rico that year to play part of an exhibition season with the new Santurce Cangrejeros for a reported $250 per month. In 1933 he returned to Pittsburgh and played for the Crawfords in the new Negro National League through 1936. The 1934 season saw another epic blast at Yankee Stadium, this time one that Jack Marshall of the Chicago American Giants swore flew completely out of the ballpark.[21] Whether or not it actually departed the friendly confines is, again, largely irrelevant. Even if the blast only made it to the bleachers, it was still one of the longest blows ever in the history of the stadium, and only added to the growing legend. Sam Jethroe later noted: "If someone had told me that Josh hit the ball a mile, I would have believed them."[22] Gibson himself "always pooh-poohed the notion that he'd actually hit a ball out of the House That Ruth Built, maintaining that he'd only reached the center-field bullpen. He was a modest man and a powerful one."[23]

"In the hotel, in the restaurant, or at a bar everybody wanted to meet Josh Gibson," said Monte Irvin. "He could handle the attention that came with his celebrity status. Josh never did get a swelled head. He had that kind of quiet confidence. Naturally the ladies were all crazy about him because he looked so boyish."[24]

After a 1936 season in which he was credited with as many as 84 homers (albeit only six in Negro National League play), Gibson headed back to the Caribbean and the Cuban Winter League for the 1936-37 season. When he returned to the United States, the Crawfords' cash-strapped owner, Gus Greenlee, was forced to sell Gibson back to the Grays for $2,500 and two players (Pepper Bassett and Harry Spearman).Gibson spent part of the season with Homestead, hitting .392 with 12 home runs in just 97 at-bats, and part of the year playing in the Dominican Republic. Working for Dominican dictator Rafael Trujillo, Josh batted .453 and led the Dominican League in RBIs and triples.

Gibson moved back and forth between Pittsburgh and Cuba throughout the period 1937-1940. In 1937 he hit another mythical home run, later credited as 580 feet in *The Sporting News*.[25] In a report filed three decades after the fact, the paper noted that "Gibson hit one in a National Negro League game that hit the escarpments in front of the 161st Street elevated railway, about 580 feet from home plate. It has been estimated that if the drive would have been two feet higher, it would have sailed out of the park and travelled some 700 feet." The various uncorroborated distances reported for some of Gibson's longer home runs have been the source of much of the doubt about the facts of his career.[26]

Regarding Gibson's power and the lore of his tape-measure homers, Sam Jethroe noted: "If someone had told me that Josh hit the ball a mile, I would have believed them."[27] "Gibson himself always pooh-poohed the notion that he'd actually hit a ball out of the House That Ruth Built, maintaining that he'd only reached the center-field bullpen."[28] Jethroe's comment, especially in the context of some of Gibson's reported home-run distances, is laden with implication. Author, historian, and analyst Mark Armour, among others,[29] has noted that over the last 15 years or so, home-run distances are measured with greater precision over earlier times. The new system relies on dozens of measurements taken at every major-league park, and when fused with observed ball velocity and height data for each homer yields a much more accurate estimate of the actual distance. As might be expected, reported home-run distances have dropped considerably under the new protocol.[30]

Perhaps Gibson did not hit baseballs 600 or 700 feet. Perhaps his longest blows were only 450 or 500 feet. Perhaps they were even shorter than that. It remains indisputable that Gibson was hitting the ball farther than any of his contemporaries in the Negro Leagues, and it is quite plausible that he was hitting them as far as, or farther than, his white contemporaries as well. *Pittsburgh Courier* writer Wendell Smith interviewed Dizzy Dean in 1937 and asked his opinion of some of the more prominent Negro League stars. When pressed about Josh, Dean was unusually articulate: "Gibson is one of the best catchers that ever caught a ball. Watch him work this pitcher. He's top at that. And boy-oh-boy, can he hit that ball!"[31]

In 1937-38 Gibson batted .342 for Havana, in the Cuban League, while back with Homestead in 1938 he hit .365 with 10 homers in fewer than 100 at-bats before hitting .380 that winter in Puerto Rico. In 1940 Gibson accepted a pay raise to join the Veracruz Azules in the Mexican League. Despite playing only about one-quarter of the season he tied for second in the league with 11

*Catcher Josh Gibson, the "Black Babe Ruth," posted a .369/.448/.661 slash line (1.109 OPS) for the 1935 Pittsburgh Crawfords. He also batted .355 against the New York Cubans in the NNL championship series.*

(National Baseball Hall of Fame)

home runs. After the Mexican League season he returned to the Puerto Rican Winter League where he not only batted .480, but hit a home run that was estimated at 600 feet.[32]

Back in Mexico for 1941, alongside fellow Negro Leaguers Cool Papa Bell, Martin Dihigo, Leon Day, Willie Wells, and Ray Dandridge, Gibson continued to terrorize pitchers. Josh batted .374 and slugged at a .754 clip with 100 runs, 33 homers, and 124 RBI in 94 games, drawing 75 walks while striking out only 25 times. Burnis "Wild Bill" Wright led the league that year with a .390 batting average, beating Gibson by only .016 for the crown. Of note, Gibson's 1941 RBI total remained, as of 2001, the 19th best single-season total ever in Mexican League history.[33] Josh's slugging percentage topped Wright by 121 points and third-place Bus Clarkson by 156, and he also finished fifth in runs scored, driving in 29 more than runner-up Santos Amaro, third with

31 doubles, and second in walks to Leslie Green. His 33 homers were 14 more than Clarkson as the runner-up, and Gibson nearly outhomered the second- and third-ranked hitters combined.[34]

Gibson returned to Cum Posey's Homestead Grays for the 1942 season. On January 1, 1943, he suffered a seizure and lost consciousness at home. He recuperated at St. Francis Hospital in Lawrenceville, near Pittsburgh, for 10 days, and was ultimately diagnosed with a brain tumor.[35] The newspapers reported that Gibson had suffered a nervous breakdown; he was unwilling to share his true condition with the public. That year Mark Gibson, Josh's father, died, adding tragedy to turmoil, but Josh enjoyed one of the finest seasons of his baseball career in 1943.

Although he was reportedly becoming increasingly reliant on alcohol and marijuana,[36] the 1943 version of Josh Gibson was as lethal as ever. At the age of 31, Josh batted .486 with 12 home runs and 22 two doubles. Posey had crafted a unique arrangement in which some of the Grays' home games were played in Pittsburgh and the rest at Griffith Stadium in Washington, D.C. According to author Brad Snyder, "In front of record crowds, Gibson wrested center stage away from (Satchel) Paige by hitting a home run once every four games."[37] Josh hit more homers over Griffith Stadium's left- and center-field walls in 1943 than did the entire American League that year, Snyder wrote.[38]

Gibson's headaches and the erratic behavior, along with his weight, continued to increase, while his on-field production began to move in the other direction. Josh led Homestead to another Negro National League crown in 1945, batting .323, and in 1946, according to baseball-reference.com, reportedly bashed a 440-foot home run at Yankee Stadium, a 457-foot blow in Pittsburgh, a 500-foot shot at Sportsman's Park in St. Louis, and a ball that cleared the roof at Shibe Park in Philadelphia. Even until the end, he was the best hitter in the universe of black baseball.

On January 20, 1947, at 1:20 in the morning, Gibson collapsed in an unconscious heap. At 1:30 he awoke briefly in a moment of apparent lucidity, then lay back down and died. For three days after his death, Gibson lay in state at the funeral home, then for three more days at the home of Margaret Mason, his mother-in-law. The funeral was held at the same church, Macedonia Baptist, in which he and Helen had been wed 20 years earlier, and according to some accounts, people lined up for more than a half-mile to pay final respects.

For his "official" career, Josh Gibson hit 107 home runs and batted .350. His Grays teams won nine consecutive league titles at one point, and he played on too many all-star teams to count. Unofficially, he may have homered close to 900 times in various settings. Some in the media, and historians since, have occasionally tried to portray Gibson as a martyr of segregated baseball, a big man who died of a broken heart at not getting to play in the integrated major leagues, but that would seem to diminish the contributions of the entire cadre of Negro League players. Gibson's son, Josh Jr., said, "When I hear that stuff about how my father died of a broken heart, that pisses me off. Cause that wasn't my father. He was the last guy to brood about something he couldn't do nothing' about."[39]

Gibson's National Baseball Hall of Fame plaque credits him with "almost 800 homers" in a 17-year career, but it is the testimony of his peers that truly underscores Josh Gibson's prowess. "I played with Willie Mays and against Hank Aaron," said Monte Irvin. "They were tremendous players but they were no Josh Gibson."[40] Josh Gibson was elected to the Baseball Hall of Fame in 1972, part of the inaugural induction of former Negro League stars. He was, truly, worthy of the honor.

## Notes

1. Ken Burns, volume 5 of the documentary series *Baseball* ("Shadow Ball"), 1994. Quote online at hardboiledcinema.blogspot.com/2010/05/ken-burns-baseball-5th-inning-1930-1940.html.

# THE 1935 PITTSBURGH CRAWFORDS

2  Dick Kaegel, "Gibson's HR Blast Was Indeed Majestic," *The Sporting News,* June 3, 1967, quoted in Robert Peterson, *Only the Ball Was White* (New York: Oxford University Press, 1970), 160.

3  Peterson.

4  Lawrence Hogan, *Shades of Glory* (New York: National Baseball Hall of Fame and Museum, 2006): 380.

5  Peterson.

6  Leigh Montville, *The Big Bam: The Life and Times of Babe Ruth* (New York: Doubleday, 2006).

7  Mark Ribowsky, *Josh Gibson: The Power and the Darkness* (Urbana: University of Illinois Press, 2004), 23.

8  Ribowsky, 25.

9  Ribowsky, 26.

10  Ribowsky, 27.

11  Ribowsky, 11.

12  Ribowsky, 29-30.

13  Ribowsky, 30.

14  Hooks Tinker, quoted in Brent Kelley, ed., *Voices From the Negro Leagues: Conversations With 52 Baseball Standouts of the Period 1924-1960* (Jefferson, North Carolina: McFarland and Company, Inc., 1998), 13-14.

15  James Banks, *The Pittsburgh Crawfords: The Lives and Times of Black Baseball's Most Exciting Team* (Dubuque, Iowa: William C. Brown, Publishers, 1991), 48.

16  Ribowsky, 49.

17  Judy Johnson, cited in Peterson, 158-170.

18  Peterson, 160.

19  Peterson, 160.

20  sports.espn.go.com/mlb/columns/story?columnist=neyer_rob&id=3403111.

21  John Holway, *Josh and Satch* (New York: Carroll & Graf Publishing, 1992).

22  baseballhall.org/hof/gibson-josh.

23  mlb.mlb.com/mlb/history/mlb_negro_leagues_profile.jsp?player=gibson_josh.

24  Monte Irvin and James Riley, *Nice Guys Finish First: The Autobiography of Monte Irvin* (New York: Carroll & Graf, 1996), 55.

25  *The Sporting News*, June 3, 1967: 4.

26  In 2004 George Manning, a mechanical engineer with Battelle Memorial Institute and the True Temper Corporation before becoming the vice president of technical services for Hillerich & Bradsby Company in Louisville (home of the Louisville Slugger), commented on the feasibility of such prodigious home runs. There are, according to Manning, an array of factors that impact distance of flight, including speed and mass of the bat, the mass of the ball, weather conditions, direction of bat and ball at impact, the spin on the ball, and perhaps a dozen more. Gibson swung a heavy, 41-ounce bat and held it at the knob, increasing the potential for maximum distance of a perfectly struck fastball, and he was certainly a strong, athletic man. Extrapolating from Manning's remarks, however, there is absolutely no reason to assume that Gibson hit a 700-foot fly ball, a blow that would have flown more than 20 percent farther than Mickey Mantle's shot out of Griffith Stadium in 1953 estimated by a Yankees PR man at 565 feet. The only evidence for the reported distances is the collection of eyewitness accounts from game participants, but such evidence is rife with problems and error (among many, see Laura Englehardt, in a 1999 article in the *Stanford Journal of Legal Studies* (agora.stanford.edu/sjls/Issue%20One/fisher&tversky.htm) in which she clearly impeaches the value of much eyewitness reporting. None of that is to diminish Gibson in the slightest, but only to caution against absolute reliance on that which was reported but which remains unproven. Full contents of the Manning interview available online atsluggermuseum.com/workspace/uploads/hitting-a-baseball.

27  baseballhall.org/hof/gibson-josh.

28  mlb.mlb.com/mlb/history/mlb_negro_leagues_profile.jsp?player=gibson_josh.

29  hittrackeronline.com/howitworks.php.

30  Mark Armour, email dated June 5, 2015.

31  Lester, 110.

32  mlb.mlb.com/mlb/history/mlb_negro_leagues_profile.jsp?player=gibson_josh.

33  Pedro Treto Cisneros, *The Mexican League: Comprehensive Player Statistics 1937-2001* (Jefferson, North Carolina: McFarland, 2002), 40.

34  Cisneros.

35  Ribowsky, 215.

36  Ribowsky, 215.

37  Brad Snyder, *Beyond the Shadow of the Senators* (Chicago: Contemporary Books, 2003), 156.

38  Snyder, 157.

39  Ribowsky, 300.

40  sfgate.com/sports/kroichick/article/NEGRO-LEAGUE-LEGEND-THE-BLACK-BABE-Josh-2519027.php.

# CURTIS HARRIS

## By Wes Singletary

During the Great Depression of the 1930s, a time when black baseball was wide open and strapped for cash, Curtis Harris was in his element. Arriving in Kansas City as a 29-year-old rookie out of Texas in 1931, the good-looking Harris hacked his way from one end of the circuit to the other, leaving opponents, team owners, multiple wives, and at least two children in his wake. In a career that spanned just over a decade, Harris played and barnstormed with some of the game's greatest players, including Satchel Paige, Josh Gibson, Cool Papa Bell, and Judy Johnson. Known alternatively as Popeye, Popsicle, or Muchie, Harris was a utility player of the highest order. Cool Papa Bell remembered Harris as a versatile "underrated hitter" with speed to burn, once gathering a pair of inside-the-park homers in one game when both played for the Kansas City Monarchs in 1932.[1] Today Harris would be considered a "super utility" player and major-league clubs would wager millions on his services. As it was, however, he scratched a dusty, road-weary, segregated existence, playing baseball wherever the money was, and passing well before his time.

Curtis Harris was born to Willie and Vinia (Vinah) Lewis Taplin on February 14, 1902, near Indian Creek in Burton, Texas, a small agricultural and railroad community in western Washington County.[2] Both Willie and Vinia were born in Washington County, as were Vinia's parents, Steve and Jennie Lewis. Willie Harris, a farm laborer, died sometime before 1910, and Vinia married Sandy Taplin. Her son Stephen assumed the Taplin name while Curtis and Henry remained Harris, though the 1920 census taker struck a line through an "H" for their last name and inserted Taplin instead. Vinia, a widow in 1910, was working as a farm laborer to support her boys. By 1920 she had moved inside as a hotel cook in Washington County. Later documents indicate that Henry continued to go by Harris and so did Curtis. Curtis is shown as living with his mother through at least 1920.[3] Vinia died of a cerebral hemorrhage in April 1948 while living in Somerville, Texas.

While there is little information on Curtis Harris's childhood, or what turned him to baseball, it is known that by 1926 he was playing with

## THE 1935 PITTSBURGH CRAWFORDS

the Birmingham Black Barons of the Southern National League – as a pitcher, infielder, and catcher – and that he was a teammate of a fellow Texan, left-handed pitcher Charles Beverly. Beverly had played for the Black Barons the previous year and perhaps persuaded Harris to join him on the 1926 pennant-winning squad. Harris and Beverly ended up having a lengthy partnership as teammates throughout their professional baseball careers.[4]

There was excitement in Birmingham during the spring of 1926, much of it centering on the Black Barons and their entry into the revived Negro Southern League (NSL). The *Birmingham Reporter* noted that veteran Clarence Smith would manage the club and play outfield, with R.T. Jackson serving as club secretary. The NSL was an eight-team loop that year with clubs in Birmingham, Montgomery, Nashville, Memphis, Chattanooga, New Orleans, Atlanta, and Albany, Georgia. With the season opener slated for May 1, Smith had the Black Barons on the road throughout April playing exhibitions to round into shape. In mid-April they played three games at the Meridian Giants, taking "Um All" by scores of 17-1, 5-1, and 10-0. Harris caught the second game, Eli Juran pitching, and then moved to shortstop for game three and belting a homer. Beverly was the winner in game three. A week later, the Black Barons took three games from a competitive squad stationed at Fort Benning, Georgia. While playing left field, Harris made a "pretty shoestring catch in the seventh," checking the soldiers' late rally.[5]

Harris's play earned him a spot on the Black Barons when the regular season began, though he saw little action early on. As the Black Barons set a torrid early pace, claiming series wins at Chattanooga, Memphis, Albany, and Nashville, neither Harris nor Beverly made much noise in the weekly box scores. After a sweep of Nashville in early June, however, Harris began to appear, but more often than not as a pitcher. By the second week of June, with Birmingham having won 28

*Curtis "Popeye" Harris, shown here in a Kansas City Monarchs uniform, played right field and batted .375 in 31 official Negro National League games as Pittsburgh's right fielder in 1935.*

(Courtesy of Ruth Wilson Bayard Collection, Kenneth Spencer Research Library, University of Kansas, Lawrence, Kansas) consecutive games, 21 league and 7 exhibitions, and sitting two up in first place, Harris was listed in the *Reporter* as part of the pitching staff.[6]

The Black Barons faced Memphis in the SNBL championship series, a 10-game set that drew large crowds in both cities and lasted over three weeks. Birmingham jumped to an early series lead, winning three and tying two, the draws coming because of darkness, before winning 2-0 at Rickwood Field. The series then shifted to Memphis, where after the home team took two games and tied another. Jim Jeffries, acquired before the series from Albany, was dominant and scattered four hits in a "decisive" 9-3 victory to claim the 1926 SNBL pennant. As the *Pittsburgh Courier* explained, it was the Barons' effective pitching "in the pinches" that was the deciding factor, "coupled with timely hitting and stellar fielding." While Harris and Beverly, for that matter, had been vital contributors to the team at certain points in the season, neither proved consequential down the stretch. While there was some talk of the Black Barons possibly playing a "Dixie Series" against Dallas of the Texas, Oklahoma and Louisiana League, or maybe the winner of the Negro National Baseball League, it "failed to materialize."[7]

Where Curtis Harris was during the 1927 and 1928 campaigns continues to be a matter of speculation. There was a Harris who played shortstop and pitched for the Evansville Reichert Giants and another who pitched for the Atlanta Black Crackers, both member teams of the black Negro Southern League. The Black Crackers disbanded by mid-June that year and perhaps that is why so little information on Harris exists. Charles Beverly, who up to this point had played with or in the same league as Harris, was with the Nashville Elites in 1927 and 1928, so Harris may have played in the South as well, but it is not certain. What is known is that by 1929, both Harris and Beverly were in the Texas, Oklahoma and Louisiana League, where they played for the San Antonio Black Indians, a club managed in 1929 by W.P. Patterson, who had been Beverly's manager in Birmingham in 1925.[8]

The league itself served as a minor-league circuit of sorts for better-known and well-traveled teams like the Kansas City Monarchs and Homestead Grays, which would occasionally drop in for a weekend series while scouting prospective players.[9] Curtis Harris, along with Charles Beverly, reportedly "came to San Antonio from Houston" to play for Patterson and the Black Indians in 1929 and stayed with the club through late June 1931.[10] It is possible that Harris played for Patterson in Houston in 1927 and/or 1928, though there are no records found to support it other than the reference that they arrived together in San Antonio from Houston.[11]

During the 1929 season, Harris was 13-for-45 at the plate, batting .288, while finishing 2-1 on the mound in six appearances.[12] Against the Dallas Black Giants near the end of April, he began the game on the mound, but was chased after allowing Dallas to knot the score, 3-3, in the third on eight hits, giving way to Charles Beverly, who allowed only a single run the rest of the way. Going behind the plate to catch Beverly, Harris finished the game with two hits, and a run scored as the Black Indians won, 8-4. Harris's best offensive outing of the season came two days later when against the same Dallas squad, he was 3-for-5 with a sacrifice and two runs scored in a 15-6 win. Dallas committed 14 errors in the affair, and was swept in the three-game set.[13] Perhaps Harris's strongest showing of the season as a pitcher came in late July when he tossed a complete-game 12-inning contest, allowing three runs on 11 scattered hits in getting a 4-3 win over Shreveport.[14]

Many of the Texas, Oklahoma and Louisiana League's 1929 games, as well as the entire 1930 season, were covered only scantly in the local press. Three articles early in the 1930 season focused more on the lights brought by the Kansas City Monarchs for an exhibition set with the Black Indians than on the games themselves. As a bankrupt nation struggled during the early

# THE 1935 PITTSBURGH CRAWFORDS

1930s, baseball entrepreneurs did whatever they could to draw attendance, and for the Monarchs it was night baseball on a barnstorming circuit. It was also evident that playing night baseball was something the citizens of San Antonio desired, and a good deal of coverage was afforded to these games.[15]

The Monarchs, "traveling like a circus," trucked a light plant built on special order by team owner J.L. Wilkinson, "one of the most respected and influential figures in the history of black baseball," to San Antonio rivaling "anything ever built in the way of electrical equipment." The "unique plant," weighing five tons, consisted of a generator connected to a 250-horsepower, six-cylinder gas engine. The 100 kilowatts of power generated was transferred to a series of floodlights installed atop 45- to 50-foot high light poles around the field in such a manner that the entire field was "as light as day." It was said that the entire system could be made ready within two hours with no holes dug, no bracing attached to the grandstand or other buildings, the system working off tripods. The plant was put on display in downtown San Antonio for two days prior to the night games, its popularity paying off for Wilkinson, who correctly surmised that just as "talkies saved the movies, lights would save baseball."[16]

The excitement over night baseball, however, did not preclude the local press from salacious race baiting when discussing it. In one postgame report, W.R. Beaumier, sports editor of the *Express*, wrote that he had "overheard" a Negro talking about the lights. The man in question allegedly commented, "I don't like the idea of that night baseball. When one of those boys starts for second base his shadow's gonna follow him right down the baseline and the umpire's not gonna know who's who."[17] In spite of such a hateful mischaracterization, San Antonio was clearly impressed with the operation, and its Texas League Indians were playing under lights the next season.

Harris batted .333 in 1930, catching a majority of the Black Indians games through the summer, yet by the second week in August, he was no longer in San Antonio's lineup. Perhaps he was injured or jumped his contract, though there is no record of either. In any event, Harris was back for his third turn with the club in 1931.[18] During the offseason, Harris had remained in San Antonio, where he resided in a boarding house at 572 Dawson Street with his wife, Roselea. Curtis was five years his wife's senior, the two having wed when they were in their teens. On the population census taken that fall, Curtis listed himself as a "professional baseball player," noting no other income; his wife did not hold a job. He also listed himself as a World War I veteran, though he would have been too young at the time. Roselea was from Louisiana, as were her parents, and she lived until the day after Christmas 1980, when she died at Houston's Memorial Hospital. Harris had long separated from Roselea by this time, marrying Ruth Wilson in 1936, Olice Martin in 1940, and Rebecca Harris sometime before 1947.[19]

In 1931 the Black Indians went through an organizational change at the end of May that portended big things for Harris and Beverly, the two players the new management could most likely sell off as it restructured the club. Cullen E. Taylor was the organization's new president, with George Holley coming in to take over as manager. Holley was quick to assure the community that the Black Indians would be a "well-disciplined team," and one that would do everything it could to win. Beverly, "the fork-handed black hurler," had won his way, not only in the hearts of the colored baseball fans of the city, but also the white patrons, who "flocked to see the locals." Whenever Beverly was on the mound, Harris was behind the plate, the battery becoming a tandem of certain merit.[20]

In early June the Black Indians announced that a set against the New Orleans Pelicans would be the last played by Beverly and Harris, both sold to the Kansas City Monarchs for "a reported sale price" of $750. In their last game with San Antonio, the pair did not disappoint as Beverly scattered six hits and struck out five for the win while Harris doubled in a run and scored another in a 3-2 triumph that pushed San Antonio to the top of the Texas, Oklahoma and Louisiana League standings. In besting New Orleans, they also beat the battery that would take their place with the Indians a few days later, Pelican left-hander Foster, said to be a nephew and protégé of Rube Foster, and Willie Dilworth, a catcher. For Beverly and Harris, it was the kind of swan song every player hopes for.[21]

Within the week, Harris was playing third base for the Monarchs as they took the measure of the Racine Seft's Belles, 5-0. At the plate, he came through early when with a 1-0 lead in the top of the second, he turned on the first pitch offered, a fastball, belting the longest homer "ever seen … in Athletic park in the past nine seasons of baseball."[22] One observer noted that it was "way in the air, looking like an easy out – but that ball kept traveling, and when it landed half way from the hedge to the tennis courts the fielder was nowhere near it."[23]

In mid-August the Monarchs headed to Pittsburgh to take on Cum Posey's mighty Homestead Grays. The Grays were widely considered the best black team on the planet that season. Posey's squad featured five future Hall of Famers, Oscar Charleston, Josh Gibson, Joe Williams, Jud Wilson, and Willie Foster, as well as others deserving of consideration, such as George Scales and Ted "Double-Duty" Radcliffe. For their part, the Monarchs had scuffled somewhat, at least considering the standards set the previous year, because certain regulars – Chester Brewer and others – had been playing in Minnesota. With their return as well as the addition of newcomers like Harris and Beverly, the Monarchs were believed a tough team to beat.[24]

Having made the trip with the Monarchs, Curtis Harris inexplicably finished the season in Pittsburgh with the Crawford Giants. His lone recorded plate appearance came in the first game of a doubleheader at Baltimore against the Black Sox, a 4-2 victory in which he went 1-for-4 while playing left field.[25] Harris's combined 1931 offensive numbers with Kansas City and Pittsburgh were comparable to those he had put up in Texas as he hit .283, with a .333 on-base percentage, in 53 at-bats (17 games). With Harris, however, his offense was negligible when compared to the value he brought as a utilityman. In 1931 Harris played first base most of the time, but also played third base, left field, and shortstop. His league fielding percentage was remarkable, reflecting only a single error, that coming at first base where he was known to flash some classy leather. Harris was carving a multifaceted role for himself as a player, one that stayed with him throughout his playing career.

In 1932 Harris remained in the East with a number of his teammates, at least for a time, as he began the season with William "Pimp" Young's Cleveland Stars in the East-West League. The idea was that the players would play for the Stars through the fall and then regroup with the Monarchs in the winter for a tour of Mexico and the West Coast. Regarding the Stars, Pimp Young was said to be the "prized optimist of the world," an owner who would do whatever it took to establish a strong team in Cleveland.[26] Harris was joined in Cleveland by his Texas batterymate, Charley Beverly; Dink Mothell; veteran right-hander Nelson Dean; and Branch Russell, longtime member of the St. Louis Stars. The East-West League's ambitious first-half schedule called for each of its eight teams to play 56 games by July 3, with the second half beginning on the July 4 holiday weekend.[27]

In spite of Young's optimism, Cleveland stumbled out of the gate, winning just two of its first 10 games, including being swept in an early-season three-game set by Homestead. They went on a brief run in early June, posting four wins against a single loss, improving to 6-13, before dropping two more to stand 7-15 by the middle of the month. The team was hurt by the defection of Charley Beverly, who had jumped to the

# THE 1935 PITTSBURGH CRAWFORDS

Pittsburgh Crawfords as Gus Greenlee sought to field a team of game changers for his splendid new ballpark.

Scheduling 56 first-half games and getting them played were two different things, especially during the Great Depression. The year 1932 proved to be the bottom of what had been a three-year death march for the nation's economy, one that saw a quarter of American breadwinners out of work. The depressed conditions and a lack of publicity manifested themselves at the East-West League turnstiles, and by midseason a majority of the team owners ceased paying monthly salaries to players, canceled the remainder of first-half games, and consolidated the league to six teams. In return, these same owners witnessed many of their players jumping contracts. Pimp Young was quoted in the press as having spent years saving money, only to see it burn now in a matter of days. For their part, the players, many of them with families to think of, could not afford the lack of security the league now offered.[28]

Not all team owners were making cutbacks. J.L. Wilkinson with the independent Kansas City Monarchs had planned to begin organizing his team in December, after the Eastern Colored League and other circuits had finished their respective seasons. This made sense as many of his returning players were currently in the ECL. Once organized, he planned to take his Monarchs on a tour of Mexico and the West Coast, playing all who would pay to face his "traveling circus." Upon hearing of the salary stoppage, however, Wilkinson moved to gather his flock, sending out word that the time to begin was now. In short order, George Giles, Charlie Beverly, Newt Allen, Tom Young, and Willie Wells left the Crawfords for Kansas City, with Curtis Harris, Dink Mothell, Chester Brewer, and others joining them. W. Rollo Wilson, sports editor of the *Pittsburgh Courier*, praised Wilkinson for the concern shown his players. His actions, unlike those of certain ECL owners, elicited the "loyalty of players" rather than disdain. Kansas City opened its 1932 campaign on the road in Chicago on July 10, with Harris listed on the roster as a utility player.[29]

In late July the Monarchs traveled to Winnipeg for an exhibition. The team was well announced as a "Colorful Club," one that was spoken of highly by sportswriters for their "sportsmanship and the fast ball this great club" was capable of playing. A local wag also marveled as the wizardry of the team's preliminary practice, in which they dazzled the crowd with an uproarious game of "shadow ball in which they solemnly went through all the motions of throwing, catching and hitting a purely imaginary baseball." The laughing stopped the next day as the Monarchs, one of the "classiest outfits ever seen in Winnipeg," breezed to a 14-1 victory over the Winnipeg All-Stars. Bert Hunter was the story, mixing a "dazzling speed ball with a fast-breaking curve" to stymie the locals, allowing a scant six hits, while striking out 14. At the plate, Willie Wells blasted a homer to center; Bell and Dink Mothell added three hits each, and Harris, playing right field, had two hits and scored two runs.[30]

With summer nearing an end, it was reported that the Monarchs, as well as the Black Lookouts and the Fort Worth Black Cats, would go to Mexico City to play a series with the Mexico City Aztecs. The Monarchs, "advertised as the colored champions of the world," were to perform in the city from October 22 to November 8.[31] Besides the Mexico City Aztecs, the Monarchs also played against a top Mexican baseball club named the Galos. Kansas City acquitted itself quite well on the road swing, winning 19 games against a single loss. As for Harris, he was just entering the prime of his career. He finished 1932 in Kansas City with a combined .242 batting average and .318 on-base percentage, while playing first base, catcher, and outfield. Over the next year, Harris began to play for Gus Greenlee on the Pittsburgh Crawfords, a team loaded with Hall of Fame skill and on the cusp of becoming one of the great teams in the game's history.

## Pride of Smoketown

In *The Forgotten Players*, Robert Gardner and Dennis Shortelle note that by 1933, Gus Greenlee had spent way too much time and money on the road and that the team's barnstorming schedule was "playing havoc" with his investment. Greenlee concluded that if the black game were to become a "paying proposition and regain the credibility lost" in the post-Rube Foster years, it required "reorganization and resolute leadership." He determined to bring back the old Negro National League, only with Depression-era prices to attract struggling fans. By the start of the 1933 season, Greenlee's Crawfords were joined by Cum Posey's Homestead Grays, the Detroit Stars, Columbus Blue Birds, Indianapolis ABCs, and Chicago American Giants to form a second Negro National League. Although many of the new club owners were "numbers men" and local racketeers, they represented a new breed of Negro baseball men with shrewd business instincts, who brought more financial stability to the enterprise. The league lasted until 1948, two full years after Jackie Robinson's debut with the Brooklyn Dodgers initiated the major leagues' "Great Experiment" to integrate baseball. In the league's first year, Greenlee's Crawfords went 40-21-2 in league play and won the championship.[32]

Where Curtis Harris may have played in 1933 – if he played – is unknown; however, by 1934 he was with the Crawfords. As the club's principal utilityman, he played everywhere – catcher, first base, second, shortstop, right and left field – and posted a combined fielding percentage in excess of .967. Harris's primary position that season was catcher, where he backed up the young Josh Gibson, who was coming into his own as the game's finest catcher and wielded a prodigious bat. When not spelling Gibson, Harris filled in for Oscar Charleston at first base. The 1934 lineup also featured the inimitable Satchel Paige. Cool Papa Bell and Judy Johnson were there as well, along with Vic Harris, Ted Page, Chester Williams, Leroy Matlock, William Bell, and Sam Streeter. With five future Hall of Famers, a barn full of arms, and a jack-of-all-trades, the 1934 Pittsburgh Crawfords proved to be a formidable club.

The Crawfords began the season by taking two out of three from the American Giants in Chicago in mid-May. A week later, they opened their home season, taking two of three from the Philadelphia Stars. With Pittsburgh Mayor William McNair tossing out the first pitch, a slow bender, Charleston led the way for the Crawfords, poling two long homers in the wins. The Crawfords finished the month by sweeping the Bacharach Giants in four games.

On July 4 in front of a great holiday crowd at Greenlee Field, the Crawfords took the measure of their crosstown rivals, the Homestead Grays, 4-0. Satchel Paige allowed just two baserunners while no-hitting the vaunted Grays offense and striking out 17. When later asked the secret of his success, a "smiling Satchel" confessed that he had not realized it was a no-hitter until the final frame. He said it was his first no-hitter with Pittsburgh, but that he had thrown a couple in Chicago. It was reported as being the first time the Grays had been held hitless, "something unheard of before." The Grays fought back in game two, saving the holiday dip, 4-3. An announced crowd of 11,608 witnessed the two games at Greenlee Field, surpassing the previous park record by 5,000.[33]

The league announced that the second annual East-West All-Star Game would be held on August 26. As the early ballots were posted, Curtis Harris was listed on it as a catcher, yet a few weeks before the game, he was in second place in the voting for a utility spot, 142 votes behind the Black Yankees' Rev Cannady. This came in spite of the fact that he had been a nonentity at the plate, batting a scant .192 to that point in just nine games. The lack of playing time could have come from his having been suspended "indefinitely" by Gus Greenlee, along with Chester Williams, for "conduct unbecoming ball players and gentlemen." The suspension cost him because he ultimately fell to fourth in the voting

## THE 1935 PITTSBURGH CRAWFORDS

and missed out on the East-West game, which was played in front of 30,000 people at Comiskey Park and was won by the East, 1-0.[34]

While Chester Williams was back in the lineup quickly, Harris played little after an early-August dip against the Bacharach Giants, one the Crawfords dropped and in which Harris went hitless. He was hitless again in a game at Hightstown, New Jersey, an 11-10 win over the local nine.[35] As the Crawfords marched toward a league championship, Harris was a nonfactor. Box scores in the *Pittsburgh Courier* do not list him again after the series with the Bacharachs. Harris pinch-hit in a game against the Black Yankees in mid-September, but was hitless in in Pittsburgh's 10-8 win.[36] What other playing time he received may have come via weekday games against nonleague opponents. Harris is recorded as playing in 34 games that season and hitting .248 in 101 at-bats. It was his best season to that point, suspension or not, and set the stage for the following year in Pittsburgh.

The 1935 Pittsburgh Crawfords were down a Hall of Famer from the year prior as Satchel Paige opted to pitch in Bismarck, North Dakota, before joining the Kansas City Monarchs, a team for which he ultimately pitched parts of eight seasons. Even without him, the Crawfords were a formidable squad that boasted future Hall of Famers Bell, Johnson, Gibson, and Charleston, the veteran warhorse who as player-manager was still a presence. The roster also included position players Harris, outfielder Sammy Bankhead, Pat Patterson (a 23-year-old switch-hitting second baseman), Jimmie Crutchfield, Chester Williams, catcher Bill Perkins, and rookie infielder Ted Bond. Pitchers Leroy Matlock, Roosevelt Davis, Bert Hunter, Sam Streeter, Bill Harvey, and Ernest "Spoon" Carter, each of whom pitched in at least nine games and hurled more than 50 innings, fronted the staff. Harry Kincannon pitched over 30 innings, and the veteran William Bell and even Josh Gibson toed the rubber. Matlock, the veteran lefty, led the staff with an 8-0 record and a 1.52 ERA.

At season's outset, it was clear that the Crawfords would be a team to reckon with, along with the Philadelphia Stars and Chicago Giants.[37] A club not listed in this prediction was Alex Pompez's New York Cubans. Led by Martin Dihigo, the finest Cuban player of all, the Cubans had an outstanding roster. Having been nudged out in a 3-2 thriller the weekend before, the Cubans came to Pittsburgh "with blood in their eyes," ready to play ball.[38] Amid the "fanfare of martial music," local dignitaries and the "social firmament," 6,000 fans witnessed baseball at its "unadulterated best." The two evenly-matched clubs fought it out in close games throughout the set, the Crawfords winning games one and two, 6-5 and 2-1, while tying games three and four, 4-4 and 3-3. The series left Pittsburgh with a 6-0-2 record in the young season.[39]

Later that week the Crawfords took the measure of the Chicago Giants, winning game one 10-2 at Eagle Park in York, Pennsylvania, before taking two out of three in a weekend set at Greenlee Field. In the first game, Sam Streeter "hurled great ball," fanning 12 batters, while Harris had a double and single, Bell a triple and double, and Gibson a home run. Curtis Harris, on for Charleston at first base, was making his first recorded appearance of the season.

As the Crawfords streaked to the 1935 league crown, besting the New York Cubans in the championship set by four games to three, Harris contributed career highs in games played (36), batting (.359), RBIs (27), slugging (.530), OBP (.414), and OPS (.944). He played everywhere for the Crawfords that season, even pitching, as he did in June when he was called from the bullpen against the Bushwicks in a 7-0 loss. He came back in the following game at first base, going 1-for-3 in an 8-1 win. In the second game of a July doubleheader against the Brooklyn Black Eagles, Harris went 3-for-4 with a homer while playing first and second in a 12-11 loss. (The Crawfords won the opener, 5-3.) With Gibson, Charleston, and Chester Williams entrenched starters, Harris generally came on during the second game of twin bills, or as a pinch-hitter, as he did in a Labor Day split with the Grays, when he entered the game late to belt an RBI double in a 15-11 win. It was Curtis Harris's last season with the Crawfords. His performance opened opportunities for more playing time and in 1936 Harris and Crawfords teammate Andrew "Pat" Patterson both signed to play with the Kansas City Monarchs.⁴⁰

In 1936 Harris traveled on more than one occasion with the Monarchs to Manhattan, Kansas, just over 100 miles away, to play various area clubs. Such was the case when in mid-May they faced the Chastains at Manhattan's Griffith Field. Scoring in every inning except the second and ninth, the Monarchs strung together 16 hits, six for extra bases, along with nine Chastain errors, to win 15-3. Harris, who was playing first base for the Monarchs, was 2-for-5 with two stolen bases. Throughout the contest, a group of "colored folk" cheered for the Monarchs, chanting, "Gee they're sweet. Gee they're sweet. Those Kansas City Monarchs can't be beat."⁴¹

It was in also Manhattan that Curtis Harris met his future wife, Ruth Wilson, born on April 14, 1917, to Harry and Etta (Pitts) Wilson in Manhattan. She frequented ballgames with friends, especially if the Monarchs were in town. While nothing is known about how they met, the two were married on October 5, 1936, in Jackson County, Missouri following Curtis's final season with the Monarchs.⁴² Curtis was 34 at the time and Ruth 19. They eventually had one child, Curtis E. Harris Jr. According to Ruth, while Harris and the other Monarchs had it "pretty rough" traveling all of the time, and often through the segregated South, "they could sure play ball." She opined that had the big leagues been taking blacks at that time, Curtis Harris and the others would have been there.⁴³

The Monarchs set the tone that season, turning out large crowds at every stop and entertaining fans with their skill and gamesmanship. Whether in big cities like Chicago or small burgs like Pampa, Texas, the Monarchs were there both to win and to please. They had been on the road since March and so it is little wonder that they toyed with the crowd when they had a chance. Newt Allen, "the Eddie Collins of colored ball," was a "fast fielding second sacker," who enlivened games with his "uncanny" throws made from any position. Curtis Harris was "the comedian and the noisy player of the club." While at first base, Harris was snatch-happy, "giving the fans many a thrill with one-handed stops and trick plays." One of the Monarchs' "pet stunts" was to get men on first and third and work a double steal. Some of their opponents that season could only scratch their heads, thinking it was all done "with mirrors."⁴⁴

In late August the Monarchs returned from the Pacific Northwest, where they had pasted a pair of Spokane teams of the Idaho-Washington League by scores of 11-3 and 12-3, to prepare for the East-West All-Star Game at the end of the month at Chicago's Comiskey Field. As a tuneup, they took on the Blues of Madison, Wisconsin. The Blues were a white semipro squad, and while the Monarchs managed to beat them in the opener, the Blues fought back in the second game, winning 7-5. It was a rare Kansas City misstep, but they had been ambushed by a special competitor, one who the year before had led golf's US Open before fading to sixth. Alvin "Butch" Krueger was a 29-year-old professional golfer, and one of the most sought-after endorsements on the professional golf tour. He also played baseball. Krueger had pitched in the American Association with the Milwaukee Brewers and with his newfound golf cachet enjoyed a large following in the area. In the game Butch struck out five Monarchs, holding them scoreless after the first inning for seven frames, before the Monarchs struck for three in the ninth, though falling a tally short. The crowd was ecstatic, carrying Krueger from the field.

Harris, batting second rather than his customary fifth or sixth, went 1-for-4.[45]

A probable lineup for the East-West Game was released in August, naming Harris as a first baseman for the West. It was the first time that Popeye, as he was increasingly being called, had earned such an honor. The game, played in front of 30,000 fans, was a mismatch as the East put it on the West, 10-2. While many of the players performed at "Big League Calibre," Satchel Paige was "the Magnet," who drew thousands of fans to watch him play. "Long, tall, dark," and with an aura that "sets him apart," Paige had proven his worth over hundreds of ball fields and the big leagues were well aware of him. "Everywhere baseball is talked," wrote William Nunn in the *Courier*, "they speak of Satchel Paige." By the time Paige entered the game in the seventh inning, however, things were decided, with the East up 8-1.[46]

The Monarchs were billed as the top independent team in the country in 1936. It was a ballclub with five future Hall of Famers: Bullet Joe Rogan, Willard Brown, Hilton Smith, player-manager Andy Cooper, and owner J.L. Wilkinson. The Monarchs changed the way franchises of their merit did things. Rather than grapple with the politics and league issues in the East that plagued organized black baseball year after year, they stayed on the road and played all comers. Harris finished the year batting .294, with a .308 OBP and a .700 OPS. Although he married Ruth that autumn, he chose not to settle in Kansas City and headed east to play with the Philadelphia Stars of the National Negro League. He had some of the best seasons of his career in Philly, batting .309 and .305 in consecutive seasons and playing in more games than he had played since arriving out of Texas, before quickly fading out after the 1939 season.

With Ed Bolden's Philadelphia Stars, Harris was playing with a cast of characters that, while familiar to him, were new as teammates. Future Hall of Famer Jud Wilson manned first base while other veterans including Dewey Creacy, Ted Page, Paul Dixon, and Larry Brown were at third, in the outfield and behind the plate respectively. Youth came in the form of center fielder Gene Benson and Slim Jones, a 24-year-old pitcher who also played first base. Jones would lead the Stars in hitting that season with a .333 mark, but as young as he was, his career was already declining. Just three years earlier, after going 21-6 with a 1.24 ERA and 185 strikeouts, Jones was considered by some to be as good as Satchel Paige, but drinking ruined him.[47]

Harris played wherever he was needed, though early on he mainly spelled Wilson at first. In a May doubleheader loss to the Newark Eagles, 8-6 and 11-2, Harris played first, garnering three hits in game one. A week later, he had three hits against the Crawfords. It was a close affair in which each team had 16 hits, but the Crawfords rallied for two runs in the ninth to take it, 11-9. The Pittsburgh squad was not the team it had been in previous years, as many of its star players had gone south to play in the Dominican Republic. The Stars, having lost Turkey Stearnes and others to Santo Domingo as well, were able to generate some offense and flash enough leather to see their fortunes uptick. In an early July 6-2 victory over the West York Firemen, Harris shined in the field even though he went hitless.[48]

With the first half ending, the Grays, behind the league-leading hitting of Buck Leonard, were winning it going away. Pops Harris, as the *Pittsburgh Courier* called him, was fourth on the Stars in batting, and near the top of the league at .336, just behind his old teammate Vic Harris. Coming out of the turn, the Grays traveled to Philadelphia to face the Stars, winning both ends of a league doubleheader, 10-6 and 12-4. With the score tied 6-6 in game one, the Grays scored four runs in the 10th. The Stars pushed on. By mid-August, Harris was increasingly playing second base, as he did in a nonleague game against Allentown, the Eastern Pennsylvania League's league-leading club. Still playing second, Harris garnered three more hits in a sweep of the Bushwicks, 10-0 and 2-0, before 6,000 fans at Dexter Park in Queens.[49]

The Stars finished the season by defeating the Washington Elite Giants, 4-2 and 9-3, to clinch third place. A few days later, the Stars took on the New York Black Yankees in Asbury Park, New Jersey, losing 4-2. The Black Yankees' Johnny Stanley held the Stars to three hits, striking out 12. Harris, playing first base, had one of the three hits. It was a fitting end to what was perhaps the most complete season of Curtis Harris's career. He had again shown improvement across the board, from games played (36) to batting average (.309) to OPS (.801), though his home run total fell to a single tally, and he was set to do even more the following year.[50]

Ed Bolden flipped his All-Star roster to an extent in 1938, but the Stars were still considered contenders. In May they squared up against a tough semipro club, the Strand Billiards, in Vineland, New Jersey. In front of a "fairly large" and festive crowd, one that saw Mayor John C. Gittone toss out the first pitch, the Stars romped to an 11-1 victory. The Billiards had a good team that season, but in the face of "21 hits for 29 bases," the Stars left little doubt as to who was the better squad. In a rare outing for Harris that season, he went hitless in four at-bats while playing second. The Stars, however, stumbled against another semipro team the following week, the Red Bank Pirates, who behind the 10 strikeouts of local ace Al Caruso topped the Stars 3-1. Harris had one of the Stars' seven hits.[51] In spite of an up-and-down season, the Stars were still in second place before they stumbled against the Newark Eagles and split a pair with the Grays. Inconsistent performances in important moments led to Philadelphia's downfall, and rather than closing the gap they drifted to another pedestrian third-place finish at 37-31-3.[52]

Harris finished the campaign having played a career-high 55 games and batted .305 with 37 RBIs and a career-high .815 OPS. Harris played one more season in Philly, primarily in a reserve role, but his numbers dropped to .282 and .590 OPS. He left the Stars in the middle of 1940, joining Cool Papa Bell and over 200 other former Negro Leaguers in Mexico. Harris and Bell signed with La Unión Laguna de Torreón. In a mere eight games in Mexico, Harris batted .281 with nine hits and five RBIs in 32 at-bats, scored 10 runs and had a .324 on-base percentage.[53]

Upon his return from Mexico, Curtis Harris married again, this time to Olice Martin. The two were wed in Washington County, Texas, on July 8, 1940. There is no record to indicate when Harris would have divorced his second wife, Ruth, if he divorced her, but his Texas marriage license indicates that he was authorized to be married in that state. In that same year, Olice gave birth to a son, Curtis Kenneth Harris. Where the family lived is unknown, but after he batted .154 in 41 plate appearances with the Stars in 1940, Harris's career ended. His draft registration card for World War II, dated June 24, 1942, has him living initially in Houston, Texas, but the address was later amended to Los Angeles. The registration certificate also listed his mother, Vinia Taplin, who was still living in Burton, Texas, as the person who would always know his address. Curtis listed his employer as the C.A.A. Municipal Airport in Houston. Perhaps most importantly, Harris asserted in this document that he was 40 years old, having been born in Washington County, Texas, on February 14, 1902.[54]

By 1947 Harris was residing in the Watts section of Los Angeles, where he was working in construction as a concrete laborer. He was living with Rebecca Harris, who identified herself as his wife, though no official marriage certificate is found. On August 3, 1947, at 8:00 A.M. on a Sunday morning, Curtis Harris was brutally murdered. According to the Los Angeles County medical examiner, he suffered a hemorrhage after being "stabbed with a knife" in the neck at a residence in Willowbrook, Los Angeles County. While his death was recorded as a homicide, there was no report of it in the Los Angeles newspapers, which was common for the deaths of murdered minorities. His body was initially taken to a local funeral parlor before being sent for burial to an

# THE 1935 PITTSBURGH CRAWFORDS

African-American Cemetery in Cameron, Texas. After years on the road, Curtis was finally home.[55]

Curtis Harris lived a life that was no doubt difficult at times, but had its moments. He was the "comedian" on a number of his teams, and his marriage record indicates that he was perhaps difficult to hold down. Like ballplayers of any generation, he was a traveling man, and no doubt that led to certain indiscretions and behaviors that would be difficult for any wife to accommodate. In the end, Curtis Harris was an instrumental player on some of the great baseball teams in blackball history, playing a utility role that his good nature was perhaps better suited for than others might have been. When afforded the chance for more playing time, as in Philadelphia, he came through at an exceptional level, at least as long as his legs could carry him. If Curtis Harris was indeed 45 years-old in 1947, then he had given life and the game quite a run.

## Sources

Unless otherwise noted, Seamheads.com was used for all Negro League player statistics and team records.

## Notes

1. Phil S. Dixon. *The Dizzy and Daffy Dean Barnstorming Tour: Race, Media, and America's National Pastime* (Lanham, Maryland: Rowan & Littlefield, 2019), 194.

2. His birthdate remains a matter of contention. Seamheads and Baseball-Reference.com recognize the date provided on his 1936 marriage license and that in the 1910 Federal Census, 1905. On his World War II draft card, however, perhaps the last official document signed by Harris, he gave his birthdate as 1902. It was also the date provided in the Los Angeles coroner's office death certificate. His headstone in Cameron, Texas, shows 1907. For purposes of this essay, 1902 is the accepted date, again, because it is the last date he personally provided on a federal document, as well as the one provided on his death certificate.

3. 1900, 1910 and 1920 US Census, Washington County, Texas, population schedule; Ancestry (ancestry.com); Certificate of Death, Texas Department of Health, Bureau of Vital Statistics, #15648, Vinah Taplin, filed April 6, 1948.

4. "Black Barons Take Um' All From Meridian Giants," *Birmingham Reporter*, April 24, 1926.

5. *Birmingham Reporter*, April 3, 24, and May 1, 1926.

6. *Birmingham Reporter*, May 8, 15, 22, and 29, and June 12, 1926.

7. *Birmingham Reporter*, September 18 and 25 and October 2, 1926; *Pittsburgh Courier*, October 9, 1926; William J. Plott, *Black Baseball's Last Team Standing: The Birmingham Black Barons, 1919-1962* (Jefferson, North Carolina: McFarland, 2019), 62-64.

8. See *Atlanta Constitution*, May 3 and 4 and June 14, 1927; *Nashville Tennessean*, May 22 and 23, 1927; *Chattanooga Daily Times*, May 15, 1927; *Mount Carmel* (Illinois) *Daily Republican Register*, August 29, 1927.

9. "Grays Win Final Game of Series," *San Antonio Express*, July 8, 1930.

10. The "Black Indians" as opposed to San Antonio's "White" Indians of Organized Baseball's Texas League. There is also no evidence to support Curtis Harris having been in Houston with Patterson prior to the 1929 season.

11. "Black Indians Get Three New Players for Galveston Series," *San Antonio Express*, June 26, 1931; 1930 US Census, Bexar County, Texas, population schedule, Ancestry.com.

12. Harris may have made more than five appearances as a pitcher in 1929, but available box scores cannot prove it. *San Antonio Express*, April 21, May 1, June 25, July 8, and July 29, 1929.

13. "Black Indians Rally to Beat Black Giants," *San Antonio Express*, April 21, 1929; "Black Indians Clean Up on Dallas Giants," *San Antonio Express*, April 23, 1929.

14. "Black Indians Go Twelve Innings to Beat Black Sports," *San Antonio Express*, July 29, 1929.

15. "Negro Clubs Will Play Baseball Here by Electric Light," *San Antonio Express*, April 29, 1930; Charles F. Faber, "J.L. Wilkinson," SABR Baseball Biography Project, sabr.org.

16. "Night Baseball in Debut Here: Huge Portable Plan Attraction Itself," *San Antonio Express*, May 2, 1930.

17. See reports in *San Antonio Express*, April 30 and May 2, 6, and 19, 1930.

18. *San Antonio Express*, August 10 and 19, 1930.

19. 1930 US Census, San Antonio, Bexar County, Texas, population schedule; Ancestry.com; Missouri, Jackson County Marriage Records, Application No. 64566, October 5, 1936, Curtis Harris and Ruth Wilson; Ancestry.com; Texas, Washington County Marriage Records, license filed July 10, 1940, Curtis Harris and Olice Martin; Ancestry.com. Texas divorce records for the time period before 1968 are not readily accessible.

20. "Ebony Tribe Wins from Black Bison," *San Antonio Express*, May 31, 1931; "Black Indians in Winning Stride," *San Antonio Express*, June 2, 1931.

21. "Black Indians Meet Black Pels Tonight," *San Antonio Express*, June 24, 1931; "Black Indians Beat Pels, 3-2," *San Antonio Express*, June 25, 1931; "Black Indians Get Three

New Players for Galveston Series," *San Antonio Express*, June 28, 1931.

22  "Colored Boys Win from Racine Team," *Racine News Journal*, July 10, 1931.

23  "Colored Boys Win from Racine Team."

24  *Pittsburgh Courier*, August 15, 1931.

25  *Pittsburgh Courier*, September 19, 1931.

26  *Pittsburgh Courier*, June 4, 1932.

27  *Pittsburgh Courier*, April 30, 1932.

28  *Pittsburgh Courier*, June 4 and July 2, 1932.

29  "'Kay See' Monarchs Back in Harness," *Pittsburgh Courier*, July 16, 1932. *Courier* sportswriter W. Rollo Wilson exuberantly promised that "Full Accounts" of Monarch games would be published in that paper each week, yet after July 16 the Monarchs were not mentioned in the *Courier* for the rest of the year.

30  *Winnipeg Tribune*, July 21 and 23, 1932.

31  A flyer was posted in various newspapers advertising the series. See *Chillicothe* (Missouri) *Constitution-Tribune*, September 15, 1932; *Ruston* (Louisiana) *Daily Leader*, September 13, 1932; *Macon Chronicle-Herald*, September 26, 1932; and *El Paso Herald-Post*, August 19, 1932.

32  Robert Gardner and Dennis Shortelle, *The Forgotten Players: The Story of Black Baseball in America* (New York: Walker and Co., 1993), 34-35; Jules Tygiel, *Baseball's Great Experiment: Jackie Robinson and His Legacy* (New York: Oxford University Press, 2008).

33  *Pittsburgh Courier*, July 7 and 14, 1934

34  *Pittsburgh Courier*, August 4, 11, and 25 and September 1, 1934; Ryan Whirty, "Lake Charles' Link to Negro Leagues History," americanpress.com/news (Lake Charles, Louisiana), August 8, 2013. Ryan Whirty explains how Williams was shot to death on Christmas night 1952 in his own Lake Charles night club. Williams was reported to have been shot five times, twice in the left arm, twice in the neck, and once in the foot. Police arrested a Tom Scott, who was taken to the local hospital with icepick wounds inflicted by Williams in a brawl.

35  *Pittsburgh Courier*, August 11, 1934; "Hightstown Nine Loses Thriller, 11-10," *Asbury Park* (New Jersey) *Press*, August 2, 1934.

36  "Pittsburgh Crawfords Top Black Yankees, 10-8." *Asbury Park Press*, September 22, 1934.

37  *Brooklyn Daily Eagle*, March 12, 1935.

38  "Cubans, Crawfords Opener Here Holds Spotlight," *Pittsburgh Courier*, May 11, 1935.

39  *Pittsburgh Courier*, May 18, 1935.

40  *Brooklyn Daily Eagle*, June 17, 1935; *Brooklyn Times Union*, July 15, 1935; *New York Age*, September 7, 1935; *Pittsburgh Courier*, September 7, 1935.

41  "Monarchs Win in Easy Manner," *Morning Chronicle* (Manhattan, Kansas), May 20, 1936.

42  Divorce records involving Curtis Harris and his first wife, Roselea Harris, have not been found.

43  Missouri, Jackson County Marriage Records, Application No. 64566, October 5, 1936, Curtis Harris and Ruth Wilson; Ancestry.com; Ruth Wilson Bayard interview, *Manhattan* (Kansas) *Mercury*, February 12, 1984. Ruth Wilson Bayard Collection, Kenneth Spencer Research Library, University of Kansas, Lawrence, Kansas.

44  *Appleton* (Wisconsin) *Post-Crescent*, June 11, 1936.

45  *Salt Lake Tribune*, July 7, 1936; *Capital Times* (Madison, Wisconsin), August 22, 1936; Paul Dickson, *Bill Veeck: Baseball's Greatest Maverick* (New York: Walker & Company, 2012), 71.

46  "Satchell Paige is Magnet at E-W Game; Players of Big League Calibre Perform," William G. Nunn, *Pittsburgh Courier*, August 29, 1936.

47  "Slim Jones," baseball-reference.com.

48  *Philadelphia Inquirer*, May 23, 1937; *Morning News* (Wilmington, Delaware), June 2, 1937; *York* (Pennsylvania) *Daily Record*, July 2, 1937.

49  *Pittsburgh Courier*, July 10 and 17, 1937; *Daily Record* (Long Branch, New Jersey), August 7, 1937; *Morning Call* (Allentown, Pennsylvania), August 11, 1937; *Brooklyn Daily Eagle*, September 13, 1937.

50  *Philadelphia Inquirer*, September 12, 1937; *Asbury Park Press*, September 14, 1937.

51  *Daily Journal* (Vineland, New Jersey), May 14, 1938; *Daily Record* (Long Branch, New Jersey), June 4, 1938; *Pittsburgh Courier*, July 16, 1938.

52  *Philadelphia Inquirer*, August 15 and 28, 1938; *Delaware County Daily Times* (Chester, Pennsylvania), August 25, 1938.

53  Twitter.com, "Algodoneros UniónLaguna Verified," March 30, 2019; Baseball-reference.com

54  Draft Registration Card, #1933, Order #11,509, D.S.S. Form 1, June 24, 1942.

55  Certificate of Death, State of California, County of Los Angeles, date filed: August 13, 1947.

# DAVID WILLIAM "BILL" HARVEY

## By Matt Clever

Bill Harvey was a left-handed pitcher and outfielder who played parts of up to 21 years in the Negro Leagues, Mexico, and Puerto Rico. Though unimposing both physically (5-feet-8, 175 pounds) and statistically (31-52, 5.68 ERA in 140 official Negro League games), Harvey had a long and colorful career that was not without its share of memorable moments. Known as "a dapper dresser and an acknowledged ladies' man who was frequently fined for violating curfew,"[1] he was also a pretty fair hitter, and once hit three home runs in a game at Yankee Stadium.[2]

David William Harvey was born on March 23, 1908, in Clarksdale, Mississippi. At the time of the 1910 census, his parents, Lewis and Sarah Harvey, were living in the home of her parents, Price and Jennie Donaldson. The Donaldsons were farmers; Lewis Harvey was listed as a laborer who did street work. Two of Sarah's sisters, both laundresses for private families, lived there as well.

After "learning baseball on the sandlots of Mississippi and Memphis, Harvey had his first taste of professional ball with the Memphis Red Sox ... when they were in the Negro Southern

*Southpaw Bill Harvey started Game Seven of the NNL championship series against the New York Cubans but was not the Crawfords' pitcher of record in the team's pennant-clinching victory. He is depicted here with the 1939 Baltimore Elite Giants.*

(Courtesy of Robert D. Retort Enterprises)

League."³ Though some sources claim he may have debuted as early as 1926, no reliable records exist for the NSL prior to 1932. On April 16 of that year, in Memphis, Harvey pitched a six-hit, 3-0 shutout for the Red Sox against Rube Foster's Chicago American Giants that completed a sweep of a three-game exhibition series between the two teams.⁴ In May Harvey garnered two more wins, a 14-6 triumph over the Cleveland Cubs and a 5-4 victory over the Nashville Elite Giants in which "he won his own game ... when he clouted a home run with two runners on bases in the seventh inning."⁵ By the end of the season Harvey had posted a 3-2 record with Memphis and also was 0-1 in two appearances for the Monroe Monarchs, another member team of the NSL.

Harvey opened the 1933 season with Memphis and developed into a frontline hurler as the Red Sox captured the first-half championship in the NSL.⁶ Harvey had already become so well-known that he received a nickname. The July 1, 1933, *Chicago Defender* reported that "Son Harvey showed Howard from across the river that it is very hard to secure enough hits while in the Red Sox park to take a victory from him" as it gave an account of Memphis's three-game sweep of Little Rock; Harvey won the middle game by a 4-1 score.⁷ In mid-July Harvey pitched a no-hitter in the abbreviated (six-inning) second game of a doubleheader against Nashville. Not only did he baffle the opposition hitters, but it was his bat that drove in the only run in the 1-0 triumph. According to a news account of the game, in the bottom of the sixth and final inning, Memphis second baseman Marlin Carter "beat out a hit to the infield, [left fielder Harvey] Peterson laced a two-bagger to right field, Carter going to third; on the first ball pitched, Harvey laid down a perfect bunt and Carter crossed the plate with the only run needed for victory."⁸

Harvey's pitching gained notice and, later in the season, he debuted in the much stronger and more prominent Negro National League (NNL)– first, briefly, with Bingo DeMoss's Cleveland Giants, and then with the soon-to-be legendary Pittsburgh Crawfords. Early in his career Harvey developed a reputation both for wildness and for his willingness to knock a batter down. Among his repertoire of pitches was one that he called a "needleball." The needleball created what he called an "overload" which only Harvey could sense, and which he could somehow use to his advantage.⁹ That advantage was not yet apparent in his short stint in the NNL in 1933, as he posted a 23.63 ERA in 2 2/3 innings with Cleveland and a 9.63 ERA in 5 2/3 innings with Pittsburgh.

Fortunately for the 1933 Crawfords, they did not require any contribution from Harvey to win the second half of the NNL's split-season format. The club featured five future Hall of Famers: catcher Josh Gibson, center fielder Cool Papa Bell, third baseman Judy Johnson, ace right-hander Satchel Paige, and manager-infielder Oscar Charleston. With a roster like that, it is no wonder that Harvey played sporadically for two years, unable to establish a full-time spot for himself until 1935. Charleston did whatever he could to help his young southpaw survive against some of the best hitters in the world. "Charleston could take a ball in his hands and loosen the cover. If you wanted to throw a cut ball, you just gave it to him," said Harvey years later.¹⁰

Harvey began the 1934 season back in Memphis; however, neither he nor the team fared as well as in the previous season. This is not to say that there were no highlights. On May 26, Harvey's arm and bat again served him well in a 5-3 victory over the Birmingham Black Barons. It was reported that "Bill Harvey, durable Red Sox hurler, had a swell day Saturday afternoon. ... On the mound he limited the invaders to six hits and at bat the lefthander got four hits out of four times up, knocked in a couple of runs and crossed the plate twice himself."¹¹ The very next day wasn't too shabby either: Harvey entered the nightcap of a doubleheader in relief and earned another win. Once more Harvey helped his own cause as he went 1-for-2 at the plate and scored a run in Memphis's seven-inning, 5-4 triumph.[12]

On June 3 Harvey struck out 12 Monroe Monarchs but his effort was not enough in a tough 8-7 loss in the first game of a doubleheader; Monroe also captured the second game, 4-2, as the Red Sox hit a rough patch in their season. Harvey was also inconsistent, as is evidenced by the report of a series that Memphis played against the 24th Infantry team from Fort Benning, Georgia. The press noted, "Bill Harvey fanned eight of the infantry boys in the nightcap [a 5-1 Memphis victory] even though he was somewhat careless in his mound work."[13]

Inconsistent or not, Harvey was a lefty, and southpaws have always been in demand in baseball. Thus, Harvey made his return to Pittsburgh for the 1935 season. The 1935 Crawfords are considered by many to be the greatest Negro League team ever assembled. Harvey's role was as a spot starter and long reliever, and he posted a 2-3 record with a 4.18 ERA in 51⅔ innings over 12 appearances (5 starts). He collected two hits as a relief pitcher in a 6-2 win over the Philadelphia Stars on May 27, then did so again as the starting pitcher on June 29 when he defeated the Newark Dodgers.

Harvey contributed less to the team's incredible victory on August 24 at Cole's Park in Chicago. He was hit hard by the Chicago American Giants and was no longer in the game when the Crawfords rallied from a 7-4 deficit in the ninth inning to tie the score. Pittsburgh went on to win the game in the 19th inning.

Four weeks later, on September 23, manager Charleston chose Harvey to start the seventh game of the NNL championship series against the New York Cubans, at Parkside Park in Philadelphia. The clincher was truly a team effort as Harvey pitched effectively, Charleston and Gibson each homered, right-hander Roosevelt Davis extinguished a New York rally in the ninth, and the Crawfords became the champions of the Negro National League.

However, the luster of that 1935 championship quickly wore off. The Crawfords' owner, influential black businessman/racketeer/philanthropist Gus Greenlee, found himself in need of cash in 1936 to pay off a hit on a heavily played number in his gambling racket.[14] The ballpark he had built, Greenlee Field, was badly in need of maintenance (and ultimately was seized by the City of Pittsburgh to make way for a housing project).[15] Harvey stuck with the Crawfords through all this turmoil, and posted a 3-4 record in 1936 for a Crawfords team that won a second consecutive NNL championship, though this time by virtue of having the league's best record rather than via a championship series.

Harvey stuck with the Crawfords, though he continued to be used sparingly. Even after Greenlee saw a mass defection of his players to the Dominican Republic in 1937, Harvey's role on the team still did not expand. In fact, an early May news article stated, "(Pitcher Ernest 'Spoon' Carter) and Harvey, serving their third year in Crawfords' uniforms, will be forced to give better performances if they expect to remain in fast company."[16] Harvey struggled to a 1-3 record and 6.00 ERA in 1937, and went 3-3 with a 5.40 ERA in 1938; he pitched slightly more than 40 innings for the Crawfords in both campaigns. By 1938, the club was struggling both on the field and at the gate, with Charleston as its only remaining future Hall of Famer, and Greenlee's financial situation had become so bad that he had no choice but to sell the team. Under a new ownership team led by Hank Rigney, the Crawfords moved west to Toledo, Ohio, for the 1939 season.

Initially, Harvey did not rejoin the Crawfords in their new city. Instead, he began the early part of the year with the Baltimore Elite Giants. He earned the save for Baltimore on April 10 when he tossed three scoreless innings to finish off a wild 11-10 win. After Harvey took over, the Atlanta Black Crackers batters, who "had been murdering the ball, were looking very silly at the plate, driving weak rollers back at (Harvey), producing lazy infield popups, or actually cutting arcs into just so much gentle air as third strikes breezed past," according to "Melancholy" Jones of the *Atlanta Daily World*.[17]

Soon, Harvey sojourned to Toledo, where he rejoined the Crawfords. He made only five starts for the team, which moved from the NNL to the Negro American League (NAL) in midseason, and put up a 0-1 record, and he also started a few games in left field. The Crawfords played to a 4-5-1 record in the NNL and an 8-11-1 mark in the NAL in what can best be described as a lost season.

In the winter of 1939 Harvey signed on to pitch in the California Winter League, the only organized league in which teams of Negro Leaguers could compete against teams composed of white major leaguers and minor leaguers. At Hollywood Stadium, Harvey started a game opposite Cleveland Indians fireballer Bob Feller, the American League's top pitcher that year. Harvey hit a triple and dueled Feller to a 2-2 tie into the late innings. Harvey's teammates broke through against Feller's relievers, and Harvey was credited with the win.[18]

In the spring of 1940 Harvey's best offer came from Los Industriales de Monterrey, so the 32-year-old headed south of the border to the Mexican League. Battling a sore arm for much of 1940, he went 7-9 with a 4.64 ERA between Monterrey, for which team he received all of his pitching decisions, and Los Alijadores de Tampico. The hot, dry air and high elevations made the league a notoriously tough one for pitchers. When Harvey registered for the World War II draft in October that year, he listed his occupation as "Unemployed Baseball Player Tampico [*sic*] Mex Team," perhaps indicating that his prospects of returning to the Mexican League seemed dim after his performance in 1940.

Return he did, however. Harvey pitched for Tampico in 1941, but with his arm still ailing, he posted a 2-7 record with a 7.60 ERA, and issued 44 walks in 58 innings. Nevertheless, Harvey, like many other veteran Negro Leaguers of the era, enjoyed playing in Mexico. Not only did they earn more money than they could in the States but, even more importantly, they did not have to live like second-class citizens because of their color. Quite the contrary, the players were treated like kings. "We live in the best hotels, we eat in the best restaurants, and go anyplace we care to. We are heroes here," observed Hall of Famer Willie Wells, who faced Harvey as a member of Los Azules de Veracruz.[19]

Harvey's struggles in Mexico did not deter the Elite Giants from bringing him back to Baltimore for the 1942 season. The Elites also lured pitcher Tom Glover and hard-hitting outfielder Burnis "Wild Bill" Wright out of the Mexican League that year, and they were poised to contend for the pennant after having finished second to the Homestead Grays the year before. On April 12, during the spring exhibition season, Harvey took part in his second career no-hitter, though this one was a combined effort rather than a solo job. The *New York Amsterdam News* reported on the no-no:

> A seven-inning, no hit, no run performance highlighted the twin victory the Baltimore Elite Giants scored over the Cuban stars at Pelican Stadium [in New Orleans], April 12. The scores were 4-0 and 4-3.
>
> Two lefthanders, Jonas Gaines and Bill Harvey, shared the 4-0 triumph. Gaines went four innings, Harvey three ...[20]

Harvey pitched well enough that he made the Elite Giants' regular-season roster, and he entered Baltimore's Opening Day game in relief in the top of the 10th inning. On May 10, in front of a crowd of 5,500, the Elite Giants defeated the Philadelphia Stars, 9-8, in their home opener at Bugle Field. Catcher Roy Campanella, the future Brooklyn Dodgers Hall of Famer, hit a bases-loaded single in the 10th inning that "produced the winning tally for Tom Wilson's hirelings" as "Bill Harvey hurled the final inning for the Elites and was rewarded with the winning pitcher honors."[21]

## THE 1935 PITTSBURGH CRAWFORDS

The Elite Giants caught fire in the second half of the season, but the Grays, who had already won the first half, kept pace with them. Going into their Labor Day doubleheader at Philadelphia, the Elite Giants needed a sweep of the Stars and a loss by the Grays in order to win the second half and the right to play the Grays for the championship. Harvey started the first game of that doubleheader and rose to the occasion as he tossed a masterful one-hit shutout. But the Grays outslugged the Newark Eagles, 14-12, to clinch their third straight Negro National League championship.[22]

In 1943 Harvey's ERA+ of 109 showed him to be a roughly league-average pitcher in spite of his dismal 2-11 record for a Baltimore team that finished in fifth place in the NNL with an 18-26-3 league record (25-42-3 overall). As usual, Harvey also managed to get a few starts in the outfield and at first base, and he batted .231 with one home run. The reason for the Elite Giants' rapid decline was attrition. In late April, it was reported that "[t]he Baltimore Elite Giants began preparations for the coming Negro National League camping here at Bugle field, with a war-time squad of six players, and a new manager in the person of George 'Tubby' Scales."[23] Campanella, shortstop Pee Wee Butts, and outfielder Bill Wright had defected to the Mexican League while second baseman Sammy Hughes and pitcher Bill Barnes had been lost to military service. In a down season, one highlight for Harvey was his seven-inning, one-hit, 2-0 shutout of the Grays on June 4 at Bugle Field.[24] On August 1 Harvey made his only appearance in the annual East-West All-Star Game at Comiskey Park in Chicago. He entered in the sixth inning, tossed a scoreless frame for the East team in a 2-1 loss, and then was relieved by Hall of Famer Leon Day, who remained a close friend of Harvey's into old age.[25]

In 1944 Baltimore improved its record to 34-36 in the NNL (41-39 overall), but that was still only good enough for a fourth-place finish. Harvey had a 1-4 record with an inflated 7.24 ERA. On September 2, 1944, it was reported that Harvey was among the list of players who had been signed by Gus Greenlee for his second incarnation of the Pittsburgh Crawfords. This new Crawfords team competed in the United States League in 1945 and 1946. Greenlee helped to found the league to compete against the established NNL and NAL, and he was up to his old tricks of raiding other teams for talent. According to the news article, "Greenlee, who figures this winter to take his team to Cuba or South America for a full season of Winter League competition, will be one up on his competitors since he is giving his men year-round employment at high salary."[26]

Greenlee apparently took his new Crawfords to Mexico for Winter League play – rather than to Cuba as had been anticipated – because that is where the FBI eventually tracked Harvey down after he had been drafted into the Army and had not reported for service. The FBI escorted him back to the United States, and Harvey fulfilled his duty to his country.[27] He joined the Army on December 1, 1944, and served through August 13, 1945, when he was given a medical discharge. Since Harvey was stationed at Fort George G. Meade in the Baltimore area, he was still able to play for the Elite Giants at times during his enlistment, and he pitched to a 2-0 record with a 2.55 ERA in 17$\frac{2}{3}$ innings in three appearances.

By this time, Harvey had settled down enough to marry. His wife, Charlotte Cager, was a 1930 graduate of Frederick Douglass High School in Baltimore, the only high school in the city open to black students at that time.[28] She recalled the experience of attending Negro League ballgames in Baltimore to watch her husband: "It was a nice crowd. That is, there were very few arguments among the fans. I would get a ride with someone, or take the old number 27 bus line. Vernon Green [owner of the Elite Giants] always had my ticket, which I think cost 25 cents, in an envelope, for a box seat right behind home plate."[29]

When Harvey attended spring training with the Elite Giants in 1946, it was noted that he had "established himself as something of a Peck's

Bad Boy" – an early twentieth-century term for a prankster or rule-breaker – "and will have to mend his ways greatly if he hopes to stick."[30] For whatever reason, he failed to stick with Baltimore that spring. A brief appearance with the New York Black Yankees later in 1946 was Harvey's last hurrah as a professional ballplayer. His reputation for wildness and willingness to knock a batter down had not diminished over the decades.

At a Negro Leagues reunion in Kentucky in 1981, Harvey was kidded by Ted Page, whose arm Harvey had broken with a pitched ball in 1935. It was the first time the two men had seen each other in more than 40 years. It was also remembered that Harvey had broken two of Vic Harris's ribs in a game against the Crawfords' crosstown rivals, the Grays.[31]

Bill and Charlotte Harvey lived the rest of their lives in a predominantly black neighborhood in West Baltimore, not far from Leon Day's house. "Harvey is older than a New Guinea coconut tree," said Day in 1987. "And they have to be a hundred years old before they bear coconuts!"[32]

Bill Harvey died in his adopted hometown of Baltimore on March 3, 1989, a few weeks shy of his 81st birthday, and was buried in Maryland National Memorial Park in Laurel.

## Acknowledgment

Thanks to Frederick C. Bush, co-editor of this volume, for providing genealogical research as well as numerous articles about Bill Harvey's early years with Memphis, his later years with Baltimore, and his extremely brief stint with the second iteration of Gus Greenlee's Pittsburgh Crawfords.

## Sources

In addition to the sources cited in the Notes, the author also consulted the following:

Holway, John. *The Complete Book of Baseball's Negro Leagues: The Other Half of Baseball History* (Fern Park, Florida: Hastings House, 2001).

Ancestry.com, used to determine Harvey's genealogy and for his military draft and enlistment records.

Unless otherwise indicated, all statistical data and team records were taken from the Seamheads Negro League Player Database:

seamheads.com/NegroLgs/player.php?playerID=harve01bil

## Notes

1. James A. Riley, *The Biographical Encyclopedia of the Negro Baseball League* (New York: Carroll & Graf, 1994), 367. The question of how many years Harvey played revolves around the 1926-31 seasons. Riley states that he played those seasons, but there has been no confirmation of that in other sources.
2. Riley, *Biographical Encyclopedia*, 366.
3. Riley, *Biographical Encyclopedia*, 366.
4. "Memphis Tops Jim Brown's Team, 5 to 0," *Chicago Defender*, April 23, 1932: 8; "Memphis Red Sox and Birmingham Barons Open Today," *Atlanta Daily World*, April 21, 1932: 5.
5. "Memphis Takes 3 Straight from Cleveland," *Chicago Defender*, May 21, 1932: 9; "Memphis Drops Nashville from League Lead; Wins Three Games," *Chicago Defender*, May 28, 1932: 9.
6. For 1933 NSL standings, see negrosouthernleaguemuseumresearchcenter.org/Portals/0/Negro%20Southern%20League/Negro%20Southern%20League%20%20(1920-1951)STANDINGS.pdf.
7. "Memphis Wins Three in Arkansas/Sox Increase Lead in Southern Loop," *Chicago Defender*, July 1, 1933: 9.
8. "Harvey in No-Hit No-Run Win," *Pittsburgh Courier*, July 15, 1933: 15.
9. Riley, *Biographical Encyclopedia*, 367.
10. Bruce Anderson, "Time Worth Remembering," *Sports Illustrated*, July 6, 1981: 51-52.
11. "Memphis Cops Birmingham Series/Harvey Stars for Victorious Nine," *Chicago Defender*, June 2, 1934: 15.
12. "Memphis Cops Birmingham Series."
13. "Memphis Red Sox Whip the Ft. Benning 9," *Chicago Defender*, June 16, 1934: 17.
14. Riley, *Biographical Encyclopedia*, 339.
15. See Jeb Stewart, "Greenlee Field," in the present volume.
16. "Crawfords Send Out SOS and Get Brewer," *Chicago Defender*, May 1, 1937: 14.
17. "Melancholy" Jones, "Black Crax Again Nosed Out by Baltimore, 11-10," *Atlanta Daily World*, April 11, 1939: 5.
18. William F. McNeil, *The California Winter League: America's First Integrated Professional Baseball League* (Jefferson, North Carolina: McFarland & Company, 2002), 181.
19. James A. Riley, *Dandy, Day, and the Devil* (Cocoa, Florida: TK Publishers, 1987), 109.
20. "Elites Score No Hit-Run Win/Cubans Lose Exhibitions, 4-0 and 4-3," *New York Amsterdam News*, April 25, 1942: 12.
21. "Campanella's Homer Beats Phillies, 9 to 8," *Chicago Defender*, May 16, 1942: 20.

# THE 1935 PITTSBURGH CRAWFORDS

22  David E. Hubler and Joshua H. Drazen, *The Nats and the Grays: How Baseball in the Nation's Capital Survived WWII and Changed the Game Forever* (Lanham, Maryland: Rowman & Littlefield, 2015), 82.

23  Dick Powell, "Baltimore Gets Ready/Loss of Snow, Butts, and Campanella Hurts," *Chicago Defender*, April 24, 1943: 21.

24  "Baltimore Wins Couple from Grays," *Chicago Defender,* June 5, 1943: 20.

25  Riley, *Dandy, Day, and the Devil,* 109.

26  "Greenlee Raids Black Yanks in War on NNL/Takes Players from Grays, Elites, Chicago for Crawfords; Will Play in Cuba Winter Loop," *New York Amsterdam News*, September 2, 1944: 6.

27  Riley, *Biographical Encyclopedia,* 367.

28  "National Register Information System," *National Register of Historic Places,* National Park Service, March 13, 2009.

29  Bob Luke, *The Baltimore Elite Giants: Sport and Society in the Age of Negro League Baseball* (Baltimore: Johns Hopkins University Press, 2009), 31.

30  "Elite Pitching Is No Problem; 11 Seek Berths," *New York Amsterdam News,* April 13, 1946: 12.

31  Anderson, 51.

32  Riley, *Dandy, Day, and the Devil,* 57.

# CARL HOWARD

## By Richard Bogovich

Among potentially awkward encounters between semipro baseball teammates off the field, one player having to arrest another must rank very high. Carl "Sailor" Howard, who participated in spring training with the Pittsburgh Crawfords in 1935 and pitched in a couple of midseason exhibition games for the team, was on the receiving end of such an arrest in 1940, a few years after his brief career in the Negro National League had ended. Fortunately for Howard, the matter was settled in less than a week and may have cost him only $15.[1]

Carl Edgar Howard was born on September 21, 1904, near Simmons Creek in Mercer County, West Virginia.[2] His parents were John Howard and the former Pearlie Mae Campbell. By the 1910 census the two had separated. At that time, Pearlie, Carl, and his two brothers were living with the large family of her uncle John in the East River district of Princeton, about 15 miles east of his birthplace.[3] Carl's brothers, Roscoe and John, were two and three years younger respectively. Pearlie worked as a laundress. On October 12, 1910, Pearlie married George Edward Baxter, and

*Carl "Sailor" Howard participated in spring training with the Crawfords and pitched a few mid-season exhibition games for the team, but he spent much of the 1935 season with the Cincinnati Tigers.*

(Courtesy of Robert D. Retort Enterprises)

by the time of the 1920 census, they had two children, daughter Ogilva and son Ira.

A travesty of justice traumatized Mercer County's African Americans in 1912, shortly before Carl's eighth birthday. A 14-year-old white girl reported that she had been assaulted in Bluefield, 10 miles southwest of Princeton, and an African-American named Walter Johnson was taken into custody as a result. The sheriff's office took him to Princeton for better protection, but a mob still managed to lynch him. It was soon announced that Johnson did not come close to meeting the girl's description of her attacker, and Governor William Glasscock vowed that "all the money necessary to be used in apprehending and prosecuting the guilty parties will be placed at the command of the Mercer County authorities." No such prosecutions ever occurred.[4]

Nevertheless, by 1920 the African-American residents of Mercer County were overcoming such embedded racism and serving themselves quite well. In Bluefield they had established two hotels, at least four grocery stores, several eateries, four doctors, two hospitals, and two drugstores.[5]

In the 1920 census the three Howard brothers were part of the Baxter household, and all with the surname Baxter themselves. Carl, at the age of 16, was no longer in school, but Roscoe, John, and Ogilva had been enrolled during the year. Pearlie's husband was a railroad worker.

In early 1921, "Carl Baxter" was one of four young African-American men accused of assault in Princeton by a 20-year-old woman of the same race. A warrant was issued for the four but a few days later, police reported that they all had vanished.[6] It's unclear whether there was any prosecution of the accused men in the following months, but an African-American named Carl Baxter was listed in the Princeton section of the Bluefield city directory for 1923 and was living on the same short street as Edward and Pearl Baxter (neither with a house number identified, but there were no other entries for that surname).

Carl's stepfather apparently died prior to mid-1925,[7] after which Carl reverted to using Howard as his surname. In early 1926 Carl married 22-year-old Rosa Callendar.[8] In the 1923 city directory for Princeton, a Rosa "Calendar" was listed as a waitress at Memorial Hospital. The couple wasn't listed in the 1932 directory, and it's quite possible the marriage had ended by then.

Later in 1926, Pearlie married Jacob "Jake" Eaves, and her sons John and Ira were living with the couple at the time of the 1930 census. Carl Howard does not appear to be anywhere in that census, which might be explained by international shipping records for April through July of that year. The 26-year-old Howard was an assistant ship steward on a United Fruit Company vessel, the Carrillo, which made monthly round trips between New York City and Santiago, Cuba. This also explains why he was nicknamed Sailor during his semipro baseball career in Michigan a few years later.

Little is known about Howard's baseball experience prior to his leaving West Virginia. In May 1929 a brief news item mentioned that Carl and Roscoe were playing on a team in Kimball, 25 miles west of Princeton. By 1932, Princeton had an African-American team called the Grays, and in the middle of that year a pitcher named Howard hurled a shutout for them.[9]

Carl Howard's life changed dramatically in 1933. A semipro African-American team in Grand Rapids, Michigan, the Dixie Gas Stars, was being led by third baseman John Shackelford, who had played four seasons in the top Negro Leagues from 1924 to 1930. Shackelford later graduated from the University of Michigan Law School, practiced as an attorney, and was president of the United States Baseball League during its two seasons, 1945 and 1946.[10] Shackelford's trusted shortstop was Ted Bond, who hailed from Mercer County. Early that season Bond had "hand-picked" new players from his home state, and one of them was pitcher "Sailor Howard from Bluefield, W.Va."[11]

Census data and Grand Rapids city directories indicate that there was already an older African American named Carl Howard in the city (middle initial R. and a wife named Jennie), so the nickname Sailor was most often used in newspaper coverage to distinguish between the two men. At a minimum, star outfielder Walter Coe of the Dixie Gas Stars knew the elder Howard, who was a local singer.[12] Sailor Howard won the team's opener in late May, 2-0, surrendering only five hits to the visiting House of David team from Benton Harbor, Michigan.[13] Two months later, one newspaper assessed Sailor Howard as being "of league caliber," which implied his readiness for promotion to the NNL.[14]

Howard and Bond continued with the Dixie Gas Stars in 1934,[15] but during the first half of March 1935, the Pittsburgh Crawfords included both in a list of its players "submitted to the National Association of Negro Baseball Clubs in convention in Philadelphia."[16] Bond had been recommended to the Craws by "Attorney Shackelford,"[17] and presumably Howard had been as well. Howard was one of four pitchers who saw action in a spring-training game against the Memphis Red Sox in New Orleans on April 12.[18] However, a week later Howard was listed among six new players with the Cincinnati Tigers, a team that eventually joined the Negro American League in 1937.[19] One of the other new Tigers was Cornelius "Neil" Robinson, a Grand Rapids native who had played for Shackelford there[20] and who in mid-1933 was with a newly formed Grand Rapids team, the Pere Marquette Colored Giants.[21] Robinson (whose first name was often spelled "Neal" in news articles) already had some NNL experience and went on to play in multiple East-West All-Star Games.

The Tigers opened their 1935 season at home on April 21 against the Louisville Black Caps. The game was played at Crosley Field, home of the National League's Cincinnati Reds. The Tigers got off to a fantastic start by scoring nine runs in the first inning after two outs. They led 16-0 after three innings and ultimately won by 22-3. The *Cincinnati Enquirer*'s box score shows Howard as his team's third pitcher, and the Tigers trio combined to limit Louisville to five hits. Howard singled in one at-bat, had an assist in the field, struck out one of the Black Caps, and walked none.[22]

It is unclear when Howard concluded his time with the Tigers, but he was mentioned in previews of their games until at least late May.[23] He resurfaced in July with the Crawfords, and he hurled a complete game in Steubenville, Ohio, against the Electrical Department team of the Weirton Steel League on July 23. A crowd of 3,500 watched the Craws take a 9-0 lead after two innings and cruise to an 18-7 victory. Howard yielded 12 hits and a pair of walks but was undercut by four Pittsburgh errors.[24] Three days later he was the first of the Crawfords' three pitchers in Anderson, Indiana. The hometown Indians never scored more than once in any inning and the Craws won, 9-5.[25]

In August Howard spent some time with the NNL's Brooklyn Eagles (though there were mysterious reports in June that the team had acquired a "first-string" right-handed pitcher named Holland from the Crawfords, despite the latter having no player by that name; Howard was the only surname that came close).[26] In the first game of a doubleheader on August 4, an 8-5 loss to Ted Bond's new team, the NNL's Newark Dodgers, Howard entered the game in the ninth inning as a pinch-hitter and made an out.[27] On August 20 he played a full game for the Eagles, though in right field and not against another NNL team; he batted cleanup against the semipro Farmers of Glendale, Queens, and went hitless in five at-bats in a 4-3 loss.[28] Though there has been some question as to whether this was the same player who had been with the Tigers and Crawfords, newspaper articles in 1936 and 1937 noted that Carl "Sailor" Howard had played for the Eagles in 1935.[29]

On August 30 Howard returned to Grand Rapids for a game, but now he was the starting pitcher for the Crawfords against his former semipro team, which now was named the Chicky Bar

Giants. He did not pitch a complete game, but the Craws still prevailed, 5-3. A week later it was reported that "Sailor Howard" had rejoined the Chicky club.[30]

Howard's ballplaying outside of Michigan during 1936 and 1937 is somewhat murky. A couple of sources identify Carl Howard as an outfielder with the Birmingham Black Barons in 1936, and the Atlanta Black Crackers may have had three different Howards on their roster that year, including a left fielder with the first initial of C. In fact, Negro Southern League expert William J. Plott devoted a paragraph of his 2019 book on the Black Barons to the confusion surrounding men named Howard on Birmingham's roster in 1936.[31] However, coverage in the *Grand Rapids Press* during 1936 put Howard on the Chicky club from April well into July.[32] Also, Michigan marriage records reveal that, in June of that year, he married a local waitress named Wilhelmina Rypkema. Just 13 months later she filed for divorce on the grounds of some unspecified cruelty that Howard did not contest.

By mid-April of 1937, Howard and Ted Bond were reportedly reunited in Jackson, Mississippi, during spring training with the Chicago American Giants of the Negro American League.[33] Howard was named as a member of Chicago's pitching staff in at least two previews of subsequent exhibition games in late May and mid-July.[34] In late July and four weeks later, Howard (no first name) was mentioned as the possible starting pitcher for two Chicky Giants games, but in neither instance did he actually pitch.[35] The Chicky team continued to play at least into 1938, but it is unclear whether Howard played with them that season. He might not have played semipro baseball ever again.

In May 1938 Howard and six other residents of his apartment building were arrested during a raid. He was charged with disorderly conduct, for which he was fined $5 and court costs. Two years later, he was arrested for taking $10 from the wallet of a coworker at the Standard Auto Company. In this instance, the arresting officer was Detective Walter Coe, his longtime semipro teammate. Coe had moved to Grand Rapids from Nashville in 1916 specifically to play baseball, but he had become the city's first African-American police officer in 1922. Though he rose through the ranks with promotions to sergeant in 1924 and lieutenant in 1932, he had continued to play baseball and started with Shackelford in 1928.[36] Howard pleaded guilty to simple larceny, and was given the choice of a $15 fine or 20 days in jail.[37] Then late in the following month, he was arrested in another raid for violating state liquor laws by selling without a license; this time he was sentenced to 60 days in jail.[38]

In the 1942 Grand Rapids city directory, Howard's job and employer were specified for the first time: He was a furnace tender for the Liberman & Gittlen metal company, though he was unemployed by October 16, when World War II enlistment records show that he joined the US Army. Military records show that his height was entered as 5-feet-7 and weight as 175 pounds. His enlistment record also indicates that he was divorced at the time, had no dependents, and had completed only a grammar-school education. On March 10, 1943, he was discharged.[39]

In 1948, the city directory listed Carl with a wife named Mildred. Records indicate that Howard's third wife was born Laura Mildred Lett, and the couple had a daughter named Joyce Marie (who was mentioned in his obituary many years later).[40]

Apparently Howard was divorced once again because in mid-1950 he married Christine Simmons, née Burger, and that represented the second major shift in his life as he soon left Michigan to return to his home state. By the time his mother died in the following year, Carl and Christine had moved to Kimball, West Virginia, which is one county west of where he had grown up.[41] The first of their children together, Carl Jr., was born in 1953. By the time Howard's brother John died in early 1962, they were living in Princeton.⁴²

Howard's fourth wife, Christine, may have provided the positive influence he needed to make the remainder of his life a period in which he no longer had periodic scrapes with the law. He eventually retired as an employee of the West Virginia Department of Highways and also served Princeton's Mount Calvary Baptist Church as a trustee for many years. Carl Howard died on February 12, 1980, after "a short illness," as his obituary read, though the cause was lung cancer. He was survived by seven children and stepchildren, plus 21 grandchildren. That same month, Princeton's city council approved a resolution in his honor.⁴³

In sum, because Howard was used so little during his short stints with the Crawfords and other top pro teams, he did not have one particular experience that stood out as a career highlight. Nevertheless, he provided value during the summer of 1935 by eating up innings in exhibition games for the Crawfords as they progressed toward that year's NNL championship series. Despite the team's impressive success during the season's first half, their home attendance was not sustaining them financially in the midst of the Great Depression, so road games against random opponents helped meet payroll, and the presence of a player like Howard allowed the team to keep its stars fresh for the more important league games.⁴⁴ As legendary broadcaster Vin Scully was fond of saying about pitchers stuck in bullpens, quoting the poet John Milton, "They also serve who only stand and wait."⁴⁵

## Sources

Unless otherwise indicated, all Negro League statistics and team records have been taken from Seamheads.com.

Special thanks to Frederick C. Bush for providing considerable early research, especially in regard to Howard's nautical nickname and to his stint with the Cincinnati Tigers.

## Notes

1. "Petty Thefts Reported Here," *Grand Rapids* (Michigan) *Press*, August 10, 1940: 2. "Admits $10 Theft," *Grand Rapids Press*, August 12, 1940: 17.

2. West Virginia Vital Research Records, wvculture.org/vrr/va_view2.aspx?FilmNumber=804468&ImageNumber=219.

3. For genealogical information about John Perry (sometimes "Peery" instead) and Carl Howard's mother, see their respective entries at findagrave.com/memorial/50044583/john-perry and findagrave.com/memorial/92849586/pearlie-mae-eaves. Pearlie's mother, Luella Perry was a sister to John Perry in the 1880 census, living in Jeffersonville (now Tazewell), Virginia.

4. "Sure of Negro's Innocence," *New York Times*, September 8, 1912: 2. For more details, see "Walter Johnson Lynched in Princeton, West Virginia" on the Equal Justice Initiative website at calendar.eji.org/racial-injustice/sep/5. This horror was news halfway around the globe. For examples, see "Wrong Man Lynched," *The Argus* (Melbourne, Australia), September 9, 1912: 13, and "Wrong Man Lynched," *Ashburton* (New Zealand) *Guardian*, September 9, 1912: 5.

5. Joe William Trotter Jr., *Coal, Class, and Color: Blacks in Southern West Virginia, 1915-32* (Urbana, Illinois: University of Illinois Press, 1990), 145-146. Trotter quoted from the *Bluefield Daily Telegraph*.

6. "Princeton – County Seat News," *Bluefield* (West Virginia) *Daily Telegraph*, January 23, 1921: 10. "Princeton –County Seat News," *Bluefield Daily Telegraph*, January 26, 1921: 8.

7. "News of Colored Folk," *Bluefield Daily Telegraph*, June 6, 1925: 13. One "personal" item in the column noted that Mrs. Pearl Baxter had attended a recent "Widows' and Widowers' Club" meeting in Bluefield.

8. "Princeton Paragraphs," *Bluefield Daily Telegraph*, January 5, 1926: 7. A county register of marriages indicates that the ceremony was performed by the Rev. P. J. Dickerson, and there was an African-American minister in Princeton named Peter J. Dickerson around that time.

9. J.A. Creasey, "Princeton, W.Va.," *Bluefield Daily Telegraph*, May 12, 1929: 8. This item named "James Wilson, Roscoe Howard, and Carol Howard," but that surely was supposed to be "Carl." Only the pitcher's surname was mentioned in "Princeton Team Wins," *Bluefield Daily Telegraph*, June 16, 1932: 2.

10. See SABR member Caleb Hardwick's biography of Shackelford at arkbaseball.com/tiki-index.php?page=-John+Shackelford. For more about his league presidency in 1945-1946, see seamheads.com/blog/2010/01/08/the-united-states-baseball-league/.

11. "Shackelford's Giants Starting Play Sunday," *Grand Rapids Press*, May 26, 1933: 22.

# THE 1935 PITTSBURGH CRAWFORDS

12 The elder Carl Howard and Coe's wife were both well-known singers locally and performed on the same occasion at least once. See "Imperial Chorus Choir Gives Concert Tonight," *Grand Rapids Press*, March 17, 1932: 16.

13 "Shackelford Team Wins Its Opener," *Grand Rapids Press*, May 29, 1933: 9. Sailor Howard was a "highly touted right-hander," according to "Dixie Gas Stars Blank Davidites," *Lowell* (Michigan) *Ledger*, June 1, 1933: 1. He was also known as a "curve ball artist," according to "Second Giant-Dixie Game on Saturday," *Grand Rapids Press*, August 18, 1933: 16.

14 "Dixie Gas Stars to Play Sunocos," *Lansing* (Michigan) *State Journal*, July 28, 1933: 18.

15 For examples, see "Shack Gathers His Best Team to meet H. of D.," *Lowell Ledger*, May 10, 1934: 1, and "Tatum's Divide Week-End Tilts," *Battle Creek* (Michigan) *Enquirer*, July 9, 1934: 11. He later won both games of a doubleheader against the Kent-Ottawa League All Stars, according to "Baseball," *Grand Rapids Press*, August 27, 1934: 12.

16 "Craws' Roster," *Pittsburgh Courier*, March 16, 1935: Section 2, 4.

17 "Bond, New Craw Shortstop Find, Is W.Va. Product," *Pittsburgh Courier*, May 18, 1935: Section 2, 5.

18 "Craws Top Memphis, to Play in New Orleans," *Pittsburgh Courier*, April 20, 1935: Section 2, 5.

19 "New Players to Show," *Cincinnati Enquirer*, April 19, 1935: 18.

20 "Hopkins, Lansing to Visit Ramona," *Grand Rapids Press*, July 31, 1931: 21. At that time, the full name of Shackelford's team was "the Fineis Oils Colored Giants, of Lowell and Grand Rapids." One of its outfielders was Johnny Robinson, and he was Neil's brother, according to "Mariners to Play State's Leading Independents In Twilight Game Friday," *Ludington* (Michigan) *Daily News*, June 22, 1932: 6. In addition to Carl Howard and Neil Robinson, another new Cincinnati Tiger in April 1935 was "John Robsinson [sic], third base."

21 "Mariners Meet Whitehall Today, G.R. Boys Monday," *Ludington Daily News*, June 18, 1933: 6. "Postum Wins from Pere Marquette Colored Giants, 6 to 3," *Battle Creek Enquirer*, August 17, 1933: 11. Robinson played for the Homestead Grays in 1934, and he was indeed "the outfielder secured from Grand Rapids," according to Cum Posey, "Cum Posey's Pointed Paragraphs," *Pittsburgh Courier*, April 28, 1934: Section 2, 5.

22 "Amateur Baseball," *Cincinnati Enquirer*, April 22, 1935: 14.

23 "Chevrolets Will Meet Negro Nine," *Wilmington* (Ohio) *News-Journal*, May 25, 1935: 6. "Memphis Sox Here," *Cincinnati Enquirer*, May 30, 1935: 33. It so happened that Memphis had a pitcher named Howard, and he pitched a complete-game loss against the Tigers on May 30. See "Tigers Break Even," *Cincinnati Enquirer*, May 31, 1935: 18. According to the Negro Southern League Museum Research Center, that was right-hander William "Bill" Howard, who was also on the team in 1934. That source also lists lefty Herman "Red" Howard as a pitcher on the Memphis Red Sox in 1934 and 1936, though not in 1935. See pages 68, 73, and 78 of negrosouthernleague-museumresearchcenter.org/Portals/0/Negro%20Southern%20League/Negro%20Southern%20League%20-%20Rosters.pdf.

24 "Electrics Lose to Crawfords," *Steubenville* (Ohio) *Herald-Star*, July 24, 1935: 11.

25 "Pittsburgh Nine Wins at Anderson," *Indianapolis Times*, July 27, 1935: 10.

26 "Holland to Pitch against Columbus," *Brooklyn Times Union*, June 8, 1935: 12. "Brooklyn Eagles Take to the Road," *Afro-American*, June 15, 1935: 12. Both articles said Holland's first name was Jim, but the only regular pro player named Holland within a decade was Bill, a right-handed pitcher with the New York Black Yankees from 1932 through 1941.

27 "Eagles Subdued in Double Header," *Brooklyn Times Union*, August 5, 1935: 3A.

28 "Farmers Click under Francis, Beat Eagles," *Brooklyn Times Union*, August 5, 1935: 3A. Seamheads' 1935 fielding stats (which also list pinch-hitting and pinch-running appearances) show Howard as having played in three NNL games, two as a pinch-runner and one as a pinch-hitter and pinch-runner, hitless in one at-bat but with a run scored.

29 "Chicky Presents Star Negro Nine," *Grand Rapids Press*, April 20, 1936: 13. "Chicago American Giants Arrive Tomorrow," *Atlanta Daily World*, July 18, 1937: 5. The latter also reported his height as 5-feet-9 and weight as 168 pounds; he also batted right-handed.

30 "Baseball," *Grand Rapids Press*, August 31, 1935: 12. "Pro League Ending Season Saturday," *Grand Rapids Press*, September 6, 1935: 22.

31 William J. Plott, *Black Baseball's Last Team Standing: The Birmingham Black Barons, 1919-1962* (Jefferson, North Carolina: McFarland & Company Inc., 2019), 107. See also Dick Clark, and Larry Lester, eds., *The Negro Leagues Book* (Cleveland: Society for American Baseball Research, 1994), 117, 196. At a minimum, Carl Howard was being confused with Herman "Red" Howard. For Atlanta's 1936 roster, see negro-southernleaguemuseumresearchcenter.org/Portals/0/Negro%20Southern%20League/Negro%20Southern%20League%20-%20Rosters.pdf, which draws from Plott's research. In a doubleheader between Atlanta and Birmingham, Atlanta's left fielder was C. Howard and Birmingham's was A. Howard. However, three days later Atlanta's left fielder was identified as J.D. Howard. See "Birmingham Barons, Crackers Split Two," *Atlanta Daily World*, May 26, 1936: 5, and Ric Roberts, "Wellmaker Fans 14 Barons, Gives But 1 Hit," *Atlanta Daily World*, May 29, 1936: 5.

32 For example, Sailor Howard won a game against a team called the Detroit Collegians right after Independence Day, according to "Baseball," *Grand Rapids Press*, July 6, 1936: 12. See also "Postums Divide at Grand Rapids," *Battle Creek*

*Enquirer*, July 13, 1936: 9. On the latter date, Chicky Bar Athletic Association, the owner of Shackelford's team, hosted a concert by Louis Armstrong and his orchestra, according to "Louis Armstrong Next Big Number," *Chicago Defender*, July 11, 1936: 9.

33 J.T. Hardy, "Jim Taylor, Giant Boss Talks of His 9 and East," *Chicago Defender*, April 17, 1937: 13. Howard's first name wasn't mentioned, nor any other identifying information except that he was a pitcher, but his first name was included in "Svoboda Will Toss Ball in Semipro Tilt," *Chicago Daily News*, April 29, 1937: 21.

34 "Hank Casserly, "Blues Victory String in Peril; American Giants Here for 2 Game Series," *Capital Times* (Madison, Wisconsin), May 25, 1937: 17. "Chicago American Giants Arrive Tomorrow," *Atlanta Daily World*, July 18, 1937: 5.

35 "Seater Nine and Metalcraft Win," *Grand Rapids Press*, July 30, 1937: 15. "Y League Pennant Game Ends in Tie," *Grand Rapids Press*, August 27, 1937: 18.

36 Roscoe D. Bennett, "Death Takes Walter Coe, One of Baseball's Best," *Grand Rapids Press*, January 25, 1937: 37. See also Grand Rapids Police Department, February 25, 2019, facebook.com/GrandRapidsPD/posts/in-our-final-week-of-celebrating-black-history-month-we-look-closer-to-home-for-/2425904394109155/.

37 See Note 1.

38 "44 Arrested in Raids Here," *Grand Rapids Press*, September 30, 1940: 15. "Gets 60-Day Term for Sale of Liquor," *Grand Rapids Press,* October 19, 1940: 19.

39 Howard's service was uncommonly short, though his age, 38, could have been a factor. One possibility is that he was discharged for a medical reason. Another possibility is a dishonorable discharge, but his service in the Army was mentioned in his obituary, so he didn't hide that from the family he built long after the war ended. See "Deaths and Funerals," *Bluefield Daily Telegraph*, February 15, 1980: 2. See also "Board 7 Lists 98 for Army," *Grand Rapids Press*, October 23, 1942: 19.

40 "Deaths and Funerals," *Bluefield Daily Telegraph*, February 15, 1980: 2.

41 "Colored News," *Bluefield Daily Telegraph*, May 5, 1951: 3.

42 "Deaths and Funerals," *Bluefield Daily Telegraph*, January 14, 1962: 2. Besides Carl and Roscoe, this obituary mentions a brother named Fred Howard and a sister named Bell Howard, who were half-siblings fathered by Carl's father after his parents split up.

43 "Deaths and Funerals," *Bluefield Daily Telegraph*, February 15, 1980: 2. Jim Gilreath, "Downtown Beer Ban Passes Princeton City Council Tuesday," *Bluefield Daily Telegraph*, February 20, 1980: 3. On page 6D of that paper's March 2 edition, his family placed a classified ad thanking many people connected to the church, plus staffs at two hospitals in the county.

44 "Joe Sephus' Cullings," *Cumberland* (Maryland) *Evening Times*, July 22, 1935: 4. The situation remained dire a month later, according to "Double, Double, Toil and Troubles – Baseball Association Kettle Bubbles," *Philadelphia Tribune*, August 29, 1935: 9.

45 Eric Neel, "Alone in the Booth," espn.com/espnmag/story?id=3717497, October 10, 2005. The line concluded Milton's sonnet, "When I Consider How My Light Is Spent." For other recollections of Scully's fondness for this quotation, see Curt Smith, *Pull Up a Chair: The Vin Scully Story* (Washington: Potomac Books Inc., 2009), 214, and Paul Haddad, *High Fives, Pennant Drives, and Fernandomania* (Solana Beach, California: Santa Monica Press LLC, 2012), 24.

# HOW WE HAPPENED UPON HOWARD:
## UNEXPECTED COLLABORATION LEADS TO INFORMATION ABOUT LITTLE-KNOWN NEGRO LEAGUE PITCHER

Robert Peterson, one of the pioneers of Negro League research, wrote in *Only the Ball Was White*, "Tracing the course of organized Negro leagues is rather like trying to follow a single black strand through a ton of spaghetti. The footing is infirm, and the strand has a tendency to break off in one's hand and slither back into the amorphous mass."[1] Anyone who has researched the Negro Leagues and its players can attest to the veracity of Peterson's statement.

The story of Carl Howard, a little-known pitcher who spent several years in the Negro Leagues and semipro circuits, provides a perfect example of a player who appeared, disappeared, and reappeared, and about whom almost nothing was known to this point. The sources that provide the starting point for many researchers – such as James A. Riley's *Biographical Encyclopedia* and Dick Clark and Larry Lester's *The Negro Leagues Book* – list no date or place of birth for Howard and include him only on the rosters of the 1935 Pittsburgh Crawfords and 1936 Birmingham Black Barons. The Seamheads.com website lists him only with one appearance as a pinch-runner for the 1935 Brooklyn Eagles.

Frederick C. Bush, co-editor of the present volume, put together a brief article about players who are often listed as members of the 1935 Pittsburgh Crawfords but who spent little or no time with the team. Carl Howard was one such player. He appeared in a Crawfords team photo that was taken during spring training in Hot Springs, Arkansas, but Bush found news articles that reported Howard as a new member of the Cincinnati Tigers in April of that year. It appeared as though Carl Howard had jumped from Cincinnati to the Memphis Red Sox in late May. However, this erroneous assumption was made because news articles failed to report the first names of many players; as it turns out, author Richard Bogovich uncovered information that indicates that the Howard who pitched for Memphis in 1935 was likely William "Bill" Howard, who had also been a member of the Memphis team in 1934. There remains the possibility that the pitcher in question could have been Herman "Red" Howard, a lefty who pitched for the Red Sox in 1934 and 1936; however, Red is not listed as a member of the 1935 Memphis team in any sources. It is also more likely that Bill or Red, rather than Carl, was the player with the name Howard on the 1936 Birmingham squad. Later in the 1935 season, a player with the surname Howard also appeared in box scores as an outfielder for the Brooklyn Eagles. Whether or not this was Carl Howard was immaterial for the purposes of this volume; although co-editor Bill Nowlin also had uncovered articles about Howard pitching in a few exhibition games for the Crawfords in midseason, there was still insufficient information for a standard SABR biography about the pitcher. It appeared that Howard would be relegated to the article about other players listed as members of the 1935 Crawfords.

In the meantime, Bogovich was working on a biography of Ted Bond, a shortstop who was seated next to Carl Howard in the spring-training photo and who had played for the 1935 Crawfords during the first half of the season. Bogovich discovered that Bond had recruited Carl Howard from their native state of West Virginia in 1933 to play for the Dixie Gas Stars, a semipro outfit in Michigan. At the time, he included this information merely as an interesting trivia tidbit about the relationship between players in the Negro Leagues. However, when Bush read this, he knew he now had a starting point to try to find out more about Carl Howard in the form of a home state and an approximate age. Bush and Bogovich now combined their efforts, and they found sufficient information for a biography about Howard.

The excitement about all the new finds, each of which was analogous to adding another piece to a jigsaw puzzle, was palpable. Bogovich found articles about a player named Sailor Howard who he thought was Carl Howard, although he was not certain. Given that piece of information, Bush found that in 1930, Howard had been an assistant ship's steward aboard the Carrillo, a cargo ship owned by the United Fruit Company that sailed between New York City and Santiago, Cuba. Suddenly, the nickname "Sailor" made perfect sense for someone from the hills of West Virginia who had not served in the Navy.

Also of interest was the fact that Bond and Howard were obviously friends and that Bond often tried to help Howard find employment with different teams. Since Bond recruited Howard for the Dixie Gas Stars in 1933, it is entirely possible that he also helped Howard get a tryout with the Pittsburgh Crawfords in 1935. Shortly after Bond became a member of the Newark Dodgers in 1935, Howard moved from Cincinnati to Brooklyn, where he became a member of the Eagles. (In 1936 Abe and Effa Manley purchased the Newark Dodgers and combined the team with their Brooklyn Eagles to form the Newark Eagles.) When Bond joined the Chicago American Giants in 1937, Howard became a member of that team as well.

Neither player had a lengthy professional career, but Bond seems to have done his utmost to help Howard find employment on the baseball diamond for as long as he could do so. Bond's efforts also helped Bogovich and Bush to identify Howard and present as full a picture of him as is currently possible in this book.

– F.B., R.B., B.N.

## Sources

Clark, Dick. and Larry Lester. *The Negro Leagues Book* (Cleveland: Society for American Baseball Research, 1994).

Riley, James A. *The Biographical Encyclopedia of the Negro Baseball Leagues* (New York: Carroll & Graf, 1994).

Seamheads.com

## Notes

1. Robert Peterson, *Only the Ball Was White* (New York: Oxford University Press, 1970), 80.

# BERTRUM HUNTER

## By Paul Hofmann

Often referred to as the Pittsburgh Crawfords' "normal fall back man" to Satchel Paige,[1] Bertrum Hunter was among the many supporting stars who helped make the 1935 Crawfords the greatest Negro League baseball team of all time. For five years, from 1932 to 1936, the Crawfords were considered the "Yankees of the Negro Leagues" as owner Gus Greenlee aggressively acquired talent and assembled the best team money could buy.[2] Hunter and other stars such as pitcher Leroy Matlock and outfielders Jimmie Crutchfield and Ted Page played, in relative obscurity, in the tall shadows of their five future Hall of Fame teammates (Satchel Paige, Josh Gibson, Oscar Charleston, Cool Papa Bell, and Judy Johnson).

A two-time George Stovey Award winner,[3] the right-handed-hitting and -throwing Hunter was a stocky 5-feet-9 and 175 pounds. An argument could be made that in the 1932 and 1933 seasons he may have been the best pitcher in the Negro Leagues. He featured a good fastball and an outstanding curve, but was also prone to losing his concentration.[4]

*Bert Hunter, who remains largely a mystery outside of his baseball career, pitched to a 7-4 record in league games for the 1935 Pittsburgh Crawfords' NNL championship team.*

(Courtesy Noir-Tech Research, Inc.)

Bertrum Hunter was born on October 20, 1910,[5] in Phoenix, Arizona.[6] He was the oldest child of at least five children born to Ellis and Gussie (Clemons) Hunter. Ellis was a laborer and Gussie worked as a domestic servant. The family spent much of Bertrum's childhood in a multicultural neighborhood in the Phoenix area. Beyond that, relatively little is known about his childhood or family. However, given the fact that he grew up in a Latino-populated area and spent much of his adult life in Latin America and the Caribbean, Hunter was probably bilingual, speaking both English and Spanish.

One mystery surrounding Hunter involves the spelling of his first name. While most secondary sources examining his baseball career refer to Hunter as Bertrum or Bertram, there is no primary source that spells his name as either. He appears in primary sources with varying spellings of his name, including Berthon, Berthum, Birthum, and Birthuna (presumably a Spanish adaptation).[7]

Hunter, who was interchangeably referred to as Betrum, Bertram, Bert, Nate, Nat, Willie, or "Buffalo" in newspaper articles and accounts of games in the 1930s, came to the Negro Leagues highly recommended. He started his professional career with the Phoenix Giants and in the summer of 1928 was with the Milwaukee Giants, for whom he was credited with winning 24 games.[8] He also played with Los Angeles' Philadelphia Royal Giants in the winter of 1930-31[9] before he broke into the Negro National League with the St. Louis Stars in 1931.[10] He had an impressive rookie year, going 5-2 with a 3.70 ERA. While no official standings were kept, the Stars finished 37-10-1 and were declared NNL champions.[11]

In 1932 Hunter played for both the Detroit Wolves and Homestead Grays of the East-West League (EWL). The two teams were both owned by Negro League legend and league founder Cum Posey. Hunter was among the players who were shuttled back and forth between the two teams.[12] When the EWL began to financially falter, the Grays were unable to pay their players their full salaries. Quincy Trouppe, one of Hunter's teammates on Grays, recalled a conversation he had with the pitcher that illustrated the uncertainty of life in the Negro Leagues. Trouppe told the story as follows:

> One day an older player who had been with the Kansas City Monarchs asked Hunter and [me] if we would like to join that team.
>
> 'Should we do it?' I asked Hunter.
>
> 'No, I think we might as well stay here. Half the season is gone now and if we stay we have a better chance of getting our money,' judged Hunter.
>
> We stayed with the Grays for another two weeks and then I decide to go with the Monarchs. I was so short on cash I had to borrow from Hunter to wire Chicago when we both left to join the Monarchs.[13]

Hunter went 5-2 with one save and a 3.06 ERA with the Wolves, leading the team in virtually every pitching category, including games pitched, wins, complete games, innings pitched, and strikeouts. He went 4-0 with a 2.84 ERA with the Grays and was 1-0 with the Monarchs. Combined, he went 10-2 with a 2.90 ERA[14] and earned his first George Stovey Award.[15] And for the second straight year he played for a first-place team as the Wolves went 25-5 before the EWL collapsed in June. The Grays, his other EWL team, finished second with a record of 24-15-1.

Greenlee, who launched a new Negro National League for 1933, was in the process of building the Pittsburgh Crawfords into a championship-caliber team and acquired many of the stars off Posey's Detroit Wolves and Homestead Grays rosters. Hunter was among the treasure trove of talent secured by Greenlee that included Cool Papa Bell, William Bell, and Matlock. These newly acquired stars joined an already star-studded Crawfords lineup for the 1933 season. Despite all of the talent, the Crawfords were unable to run away with the NNL pennant.

Hunter and his Crawfords teammates were locked in a tight battle for the first-half NNL championship. With the American Giants leading by one game, the first-half championship came down to a two-game series.

The first game was played at McKeesport, Pennsylvania, on July 7, and in a bit of daring, Crawfords player-manager Oscar Charleston elected to start Hunter against the seemingly unbeatable Willie Foster, hoping to set up a winner-take-all matchup with Paige on the mound.[16] The first half of the plan worked out as Charleston had hoped. Hunter scattered 10 hits and held the American Giants to two runs as the Crawfords won 3-2 to pull even in the standings.[17] But Paige gave up three runs in the first inning of the second game and the Crawfords were defeated, 5-3, losing the first-half championship.

Later that summer, Hunter, along with six other teammates and an AWOL Paige, was elected to the play for the East squad in the inaugural East-West Classic held at Comiskey Park in Chicago on September 11.[18] Fan votes were tallied by two of the major African-American weekly newspapers of the day, the *Chicago Defender* and the *Pittsburgh Courier*. Hunter received 22,965 votes, fifth among pitchers, just behind Paige, who received 23,089.[19]

With 19,568 fans in attendance, the East All-Stars were leading 5-4 after five innings. The West took the lead in the top of the sixth when Willie Wells singled and scored on a double by Alex Radcliffe. With the game now tied and a steady rain falling, Hunter was brought in to relieve Sam Streeter. Mule Suttles drove Hunter's first offering for a double to right to drive in Radcliffe, giving the West a lead it never relinquished.[20] Cleveland Giants second baseman Leroy Morney followed with a single to score Suttles, increasing increase the West's lead to 7-5. The inning ended when one out later Larry Brown singled to right but Morney was called out on an appeal play for failing to touch second base.[21]

Hunter gave up a leadoff single to Willie Foster in the bottom of the seventh and was quickly lifted in favor of George Britt of the Homestead Grays. After Turkey Stearnes doubled to right, Foster scored on a fly out by Wells, closing the book on Hunter. In two-thirds of an inning pitched, Hunter gave up three hits and was charged with two earned runs. The West went on to defeat the East by a score of 11-7. Hunter never appeared in the East-West Classic again. While some published box scores listed him as the losing pitcher, it was actually the spitball specialist Streeter who was tagged for the loss.

The second half of the 1933 NNL season ended in a deadlock between the Crawfords and the Nashville Elite Giants, setting up a best-of-three playoff series played at Cleveland's League Park.[22] The series opened with a doubleheader on October 1. The Crawfords captured Game One 5-4 on the strength of Cool Papa Bell's 12th-inning inside-the-park home run. Hunter earned the victory in Game Two when a dusky fog rolled in off Lake Erie, forcing the game to be called after seven innings with the Crawfords leading 3-1. The Crawfords won the series two games to none.

This should have set up a championship series between the Crawfords and the first-half champion American Giants,[23] "but Gus Greenlee – having seen fan interest wane after the East-West Game and not eager to risk all against the potent Giants– unilaterally ended the season right there."[24] Two months later, Greenlee announced in the *Pittsburgh Courier* that the Crawfords were 1933 NNL Champions.

Hunter finished the season with a record of 8-2 and a 4.72 ERA for the Crawfords (40-21-2). Despite not having the opportunity to prove it on the field, for the third consecutive year Hunter had played for a "pennant-winning" team. He also went 3-1 with a 2.01 ERA with the Akron Grays.[25] For the second consecutive year, Hunter won the George Stovey Award.[26]

With Paige, who had rebounded from a mediocre 1933 season, and William Bell leading the Crawfords' pitching staff with 13 and 11 victories, respectively, Hunter was relegated to the back end of the rotation in 1934. He finished the year with a record of 4-5 and 3.42 ERA as the Crawfords compiled the second-best record in the NNL (47-27-3). Despite having only the second-best winning percentage, the Crawfords actually finished one game ahead of the first-half champion Philadelphia Stars and six games ahead of the second-half champion Chicago American Giants on the strength of the number of games they played. The Stars won the NNL championship.²⁷

Late in the 1934 season the Crawfords found themselves without Paige. The star pitcher informed Greenlee that the cost of keeping his new wife in style had created a "powerful lightness in his pocket."²⁸ It wasn't long before an opportunity presented itself: an auto salesman from Bismarck, North Dakota, offered Paige $400 a month and a new car to jump to his integrated semipro team for the rest of the season.²⁹ With Paige otherwise occupied in Bismarck, the Crawfords' pitching staff was led by Matlock, Roosevelt Davis, Streeter, and Hunter.

Hunter was 7-4 with an inflated 4.97 ERA, while Matlock, Davis, and Streeter were 8-0, 5-1, and 6-1 respectively.³⁰ The Crawfords finished with a record of 50-23-3 and were crowned the first-half champions of the NNL. The New York Cubans, who finished with the league's third best record (30-25-5) captured the second-half championship. This set up an epic seven-game playoff series that went down as one of the best in Negro League history.

The Cubans won three of the first four games to take what appeared to be a commanding lead in the series. The Crawfords started to claw their way back with a 3-2 victory in Game Five in which Cool Papa Bell's aggressive baserunning led to an errant throw that allowed him to score the winning run in the bottom of the ninth.

Hunter made his only appearance in the series on September 22 when he was given the start in Game Six, a night game in Philadelphia. The Cubans touched him for a run in the first, one in the fourth, and one in the sixth before finally chasing him in the top of the seventh. Hunter went 6⅓ innings, giving up five runs on seven hits and three walks, before being relieved by left-hander Bill Harvey. The Crawfords found themselves down 6-3 headed into the bottom of the ninth when Cubans manager Martin Dihigo removed rookie pitcher Schoolboy Johnny Taylor and took the mound himself.³¹ The move backfired and the Crawfords rallied for four runs in the bottom of the ninth to send the series to a seventh game. The next day, the Crawfords won the NNL title with a third consecutive one-run victory, 8-7.

By 1936, Hunter, who did not enjoy a cordial relationship with Oscar Charleston, had worn out his welcome in Pittsburgh. In fact, Philadelphia Stars manager Webster McDonald was able to sign Hunter without compensating the Crawfords.³² For the first time in his career, Hunter found himself with a team at the bottom of the standings. He went 5-4 with a 4.26 ERA for the last-place Philadelphia Stars (32-42-1).³³ He also went 0-1 with a 15.43 ERA in a single appearance with the New York Cubans, who finished next to last with a 22-16-1 record.

For Negro League players in Depression era America, a winter season in Cuba, Puerto Rico, Mexico, Panama, Venezuela, or in a special situation, like the Dominican Republic, meant economic survival.³⁴ Hunter was one of the first Negro League players to discover that Latin America provided a reliable source of income. Ship passenger logs and port-of-entry information suggest that Hunter played baseball the Caribbean and south of the border at least as early as the winter of 1934.

In 1937 he was lured to the Dominican Republic to pitch for the Águilas of Santiago. Averell Smith detailed the significance of Hunter's influence on other Negro League stars coming to the island in his book *The Pitcher and the Dictator: Satchel Paige's Unlikely Season in the Dominican Republic*.

> Capital-city fans returned the next day at 3:00 p.m. to cheer on their Dragones in the first game against the newly formed Águilas of Santiago. That day they would be facing American Bert Hunter – at this point the only Negro Leaguer on any of the three teams.
>
> Hunter – the locals called him "King Kong" – dished up his nasty curveball to shut down

the Dragones. He started by striking out the side in the first. The Águilas scored five runs in the second to put the game out of reach, piling up fourteen hits to win 10 to 3.

It was now clear to the little dentist [Dr. José Enrique Aybar]. For the Dragones to win the Campeonato por Reelección de Presidente Trujillo, he must improve his team's talent. Losing no time[,] Aybar called a meeting of the club's executive committee. It was decided that he should fly off to the United States to hire baseball players from the Negro Leagues – talent like "King Kong" Hunter.[35]

Within days, Aybar packed his bags and caught a plane to Miami. From there he drove more than 800 miles to New Orleans to entice Negro League superstars like Gibson, Paige, Bell, and others to come to the come to the Dominican Republic. In this respect, Hunter was a trailblazer who opened doors for his contemporaries.

For Hunter, his foray into Dominican baseball was life-changing. While playing for the Águilas during the Campeonato he fell in love with and married a Dominican woman. When the Campeonato ended, Hunter "stayed on the island, using it as a base to play in the Mexican leagues during the early 1940s."[36] He never again pitched in the United States and it is unknown if he and his wife had any children.

Hunter played in the Puerto Rican Winter League in the 1938-39 season. He began the year with the Ponce Pirates and was allowed to be signed by Guayama Venerables for the playoffs. Hunter was signed to replace another Negro League import on the Guayama roster prior to the finals against the San Juan Senators.[37] He was the winning pitcher in three of team's four victories.

Hunter's Mexican League career was a vagabond type of existence that spanned from 1940 to 1944. In 1940 he pitched for the last-place Chihuahua Dorados of the Mexican League. He went 3-2 with a 5.40 ERA for a team that finished with a record of 14-67, 42 games behind the champion Azules de Veracruz. In 1941 he was 9-11 with a 5.18 ERA for the Veracruz Aguila. He joined the Puebla Angeles in 1942 and finished with a record of 8-13 and a 4.22 ERA. Hunter played for three teams in 1943, the Tampico Alijadores, Veracruz Azules, and Puebla. He had a combined record of 3-4 with a 4.63 ERA for the three clubs. He finished his Mexican League career with a single appearance, in which he was the losing pitcher, for the Mexico City Reds in 1944. In five seasons in the Mexican League, Hunter had a record of 22-32.[38]

Hunter married again while living in Mexico and after his playing career opened a restaurant near Delta Park, home of the Azules.[39] Hunter died on April 25, 1948, in Villahermosa, the capital of the Mexican state of Tabasco. The cause of death and disposition of his remains are unknown.

## Sources and Acknowledgment

In addition to the sources cited in the Notes, the author relied on Baseball-reference.com, Seamheads.com, and Ancestry.com. All statistics quoted in this biography are from Seamheads.com.

The author would like to acknowledge the contributions of Fredrick Bush, whose research contributed to this piece.

## Notes

1. Mark Ribowsky, *Don't Look Back: Satchel Paige in the Shadows of Baseball* (New York: Simon & Schuster, 1994), 93.

2. Pittsburgh Crawfords. Retrieved from negroleaguestore.com/Pitt_Crawfords.htm.

3. The George Stovey Award was named in honor of nineteenth-century left-hander George Stovey. It was the Negro League equivalent of the Cy Young Award. Stovey is considered the first great African-American pitcher.

4. James Bankes, *The Pittsburgh Crawfords: The Lives and Times of Black Baseball's Most Exciting Team* (Dubuque, Iowa: Wm. C. Brown Publishers, 1991), 158.

5. Larry Lester in *Black Baseball's National Showcase* and Baseball-Reference.com identify Hunter's year of birth as 1906. (No date is given.) Other sources, including John Holway's *The Complete Book of Baseball's Negro Leagues: The Other Half of Baseball History* and Seamheads.com, cite his date of birth as October 20, 1910. Primary sources corroborate the later date and/or year. Arizona school records, Hunter's 1943 World War II draft card, and passenger logs list his birth-

date as October 20, 1910, and US Census Records from 1930 and 1940 list Hunter's year of birth as 1910.

6. While all secondary sources are in agreement that Hunter was born in Phoenix, some primary sources identify his place of birth as Nevada or Georgia. One source lists St. George, Nevada, as his place of birth, but there is no St. George, Nevada. There is a St. George, Utah, located near the tri-state junction of Utah, Arizona, and Nevada.

7. Bertrum, the most commonly used form of his name in baseball research, is used throughout this article.

8. "Stars New Moundsman," *St. Louis Argus,* April 10, 1931: 7.

9. Phil Dixon, *Wilber "Bullet" Rogan and the Kansas City Monarchs* (Jefferson, North Carolina: McFarland & Company, 2010), 108.

10. In 1931 the Negro National League was the first iteration of the circuit. It is noted as NNL on Seamheads.com. The second Negro National League commenced in 1933 and is differentiated on Seamheads.com as NN2. For the purpose of this essay and ease of reading, both are referred to as the Negro National League.

11. John Holway, *The Complete Book of Baseball's Negro Leagues: The Other Half of Baseball History* (Fern Park, Florida: Hastings House Publishers, 2001), 272.

12. Holway, 290.

13. Dixon, 108.

14. Holway credits Hunter with a record of 18-4 in 1932.

15. Holway, 289.

16. Mark Ribowsky, *Josh Gibson: The Power and the Darkness* (Urbana, Illinois: University of Illinois Press, 2004), 113.

17. Mark Ribowsky, *A Complete History of the Negro Leagues 1884-1955* (New York: Carol Publishing Group, 1995), 176.

18. Oscar Charleston, Josh Gibson, Cool Papa Bell, Judy Johnson, John Henry Russell, and fellow pitcher Sam Streeter were all elected to the East All-Star Team. Satchel Paige, who did not return for the game, was also elected.

19. Willie Foster received the most votes among pitchers (40,637). First baseman Oscar Charleston was the top votegetter overall with 43,973.

20. Bankes, 117.

21. Bob LeMoine, "The 'Game of Games': The First Negro League All-Star Game," in Gregory Wolf, ed., *The Base Ball Palace of the World: Comiskey Park* (Phoenix: Society for American Baseball Research, 2019), 90.

22. Ribowsky, *Don't Look Back,* 96.

23. The Chicago American Giants went 40-21-1.

24. Ribowsky, *Don't Look Back,* 97.

25. Holway credits Hunter with a record of 17-5 in 1933.

26. Holway, 300.

27. The Stars won the eight-game series over the American Giants, 4-3-1.

28. Mark Whitaker, *Smoketown: The Untold Story of the Other Great Black Renaissance* (New York: Simon & Schuster, 2018), 116.

29. Whitaker.

30. Holway credits Hunter with a 7-6 record in 1935 and Matlock, Davis, and Streeter with records of 17-0, 12-4, and 3-0, respectively.

31. Jeremy Beer, *Oscar Charleston: The Life and Legend of Baseball's Greatest Forgotten Player* (Lincoln: University of Nebraska Press, 2019), 253.

32. James Riley, *The Biographical Encyclopedia of the Negro Leagues* (Boston: DaCapo Press, 2002), 403.

33. Holway credits Hunter with a record of 7-3 with the Philadelphia Stars in 1936.

34. Bankes, 158.

35. Averell Smith, *The Pitcher and the Dictator: Satchel Paige's Unlikely Season in the Dominican Republic* (Lincoln: University of Nebraska Press, 2018), 52.

36. Smith, 112.

37. Thomas Van Hyning, *Puerto Rico's Winter League: A History of Major League Baseball's Launching Pad* (Jefferson, North Carolina: McFarland & Company, 2004), 76.

38. Pedro Treto Cisneros, *The Mexican League: Comprehensive Player Statistics, 1937-2001* (Jefferson, North Carolina: McFarland & Company, 2002), 370.

39. John Virtue, *South of the Color Barrier: How Jorge Pasquel and the Mexican League Pushed Baseball Toward Racial Integration* (Jefferson, North Carolina: McFarland & Company, 2008), 92.

# JUDY JOHNSON

## By Thomas Kern

"Judy Johnson was the smartest baseball player I ever came across."

—Ted Page[1]

Despite his father's aspirations for William "Judy" Johnson to become a boxer, Judy never entered the ring. Instead, Johnson took his game to the diamond. For that, baseball owes him a debt of gratitude. In the Negro Leagues, if Satchel Paige's game was flamboyant, Johnson's was quietly exuberant. If Josh Gibson was sheer power, Judy was pure finesse. Negro League historian Leslie Heaphy noted, "Johnson was well respected by his fellow players for his quiet, unassuming leadership and his intellectual grasp of the intricacies of the game. He was quiet, shy, but mentally tough."[2] And Judy excelled on the only baseball fields on which African-Americans could play until 1947.

William Julius Johnson was born on October 26, 1899, in Snow Hill, Maryland, on the Eastern Shore. He was the third child of William and Annie Johnson, born after siblings John Jr. and Mary Emma.[3] Official records and Johnson

*Hall of Fame third baseman William Julius "Judy" Johnson manned the hot corner for the 1935 Pittsburgh Crawfords. The 35-year old Johnson was in his 16th season, but still batted .281 for the NNL champions.*

(Courtesy National Baseball Hall of Fame)

himself cite different months and either 1899 or 1900 as his actual year of birth. A firm date has never been substantiated. When Judy was still a child, the family relocated to Wilmington, Delaware, where his father worked as a seaman.[4]

Biographers of Johnson are benefited by the oral history to which he himself contributed, which includes several interviews in his later years that shaped our understanding of Judy and gave us his perspective on the game, his teammates, and opponents. To appreciate Johnson's legacy as one of the all-time great Negro League players, statistics and the words of those who watched him play are important. But without Johnson's own insights, the story would be incomplete. Judy Johnson's words highlighted the important events of his childhood: a father's expectations, an emerging love for baseball, and a comfort for the surroundings of his youth – northern Delaware – that would stay with him into adulthood and shape his career.

William Johnson Sr. revered and apparently knew Jack Johnson, and named both of his sons in some form after the pugilist. In fact, the elder Johnson "had a license to train boxers and wanted his son to be a prize fighter."[5] Johnson's career did not take that path, as he rejected his father's advice to box:

> Daddy kept telling me to be a prize fighter, but I couldn't fight a lick. ... My dad made my sister my sparring partner. She was twelve and I was about eight or nine. ... She would bang me and bang me. ... [eventually my daddy] said I wasn't for fighting.[6]

Johnson's interests lay elsewhere. As he recalled, "I was more interested in playing baseball. ... My father was the athletic director of the Negro Settlement House in our neighborhood and so I always had bats and balls. I think that was the only reason the other kids let me play, because I really wasn't very good at the time."[7]

In his later years, Johnson reflected on his baseball beginnings in Wilmington.

> Baseball was my first love. ... One thing I worked hardest at was playing ball. When I became good sized, I joined a Wilmington team called Rosedale. We played on Saturdays against other white and Negro teams from around town. All of us, whites and blacks, played every chance we got at the ballpark at 2nd and Dupont. ... we walked to all the games.[8]

At the same time, as his interest in baseball grew, he dropped out of high school. Johnson explained, "I never finished at Howard High. Since my father couldn't afford clothes I would have liked, I got a job [as a stevedore at Deep Water Point, New Jersey] for $3 a week."[9]

Johnson's player file in the Baseball Hall of Fame includes a fascinating document – a kind of "this is your life" script that his friends used in his later years to celebrate his retirement from Negro League ball. In the script, those honoring him shared:

> And then you were thirteen and showing an interest in organized sandlot ball. You and several other fellows met at the home of Anita Irons, who was later to become Mrs. William J. Johnson. There, her brother Randolph Irons organized a team. ... You played baseball and courted her. She went to Normal School to become an elementary teacher. It was in 1923 Judy that you decided that two could live as cheaply as one and Anita Irons became Mrs. William J. Johnson.[10]

Judy and Anita were married for 62 years. After her death in 1985, Johnson was never the same. "She was the most important thing in my life. Even baseball was second to Anita," he said.[11]

Johnson continued to work at Deep Water Point through World War I, playing ball with the nearby Chester (Pennsylvania) team:[12]

> I thought I was pretty good. I figured I was the best around. I wanted to move up.

## THE 1935 PITTSBURGH CRAWFORDS

Now Chester had a pretty good ballpark, just above the team I was on in Wilmington [Rosedale]. They'd pay me a couple of dollars and trolley fare – there weren't any buses then. They were my first professional club.[13]

Johnson got wider exposure playing for Chester and, according to John Holway, "got his first break when World War I called many of the stars of the top black teams into service."[14] Johnson reminisced, "I must have impressed the manager of the Philadelphia Hilldale club, because he asked me to play with them on Thursdays and Saturdays at their field in Darby. Sundays they'd go to Atlantic City as the Bacharach Giants. "Same club, just different suits on. Like the Globetrotters. [Bacharach was nonetheless a separate team relocated in Atlantic City in 1916 from Florida. The practice Johnson experienced was one of player-sharing during the war when rosters were depleted by call-up or volunteering for the war effort.] I got five dollars a day."[15]

It is around this time that William Johnson gained the nickname Judy. According to Johnson, "[W]hen I left home in 1920 to play in Philadelphia, they had a fellow named Judy Gans, a first baseman, never much of a hitter but a good fielder and they said I looked so much like him they called me Judy too."[16] A closer look at Gans's career shows his years during World War I split between the Chicago American Giants and the Lincoln (New York) Giants. Coupled with his military service overseas toward the end of that time, it is likely that Gans played occasionally for Hilldale or Madison after returning from France.[17]

At the end of the war, as players completed their military service and returned to Hilldale, Johnson was assigned to the Madison Stars, a Hilldale farm club.[18] Over the next two years, Johnson played for Madison with the goal to return to Hilldale. In 1920 he was told by Hilldale owner-manager Ed Bolden, "[Y]ou work hard this winter, come back in the spring, and we will sign you on as a regular."[19] Johnson did just that and Bolden signed him for $100 per month.

Ribowsky noted in his history of the Negro Leagues, "For $100, which was all that Ed Bolden had to pay the Madison club for the boy named Judy, he got a ballplayer with a psychotic passion for getting on base. Judy would meticulously let out the seams of his left uniform sleeve, the one facing the pitcher [Johnson batted right-handed] so he could be hit with the pitch."[20]

Hilldale already had an accomplished third baseman in Bill "Brodie" Francis, but Francis knew that Johnson would be a strong addition to the team. Johnson explained, "Brodie was very good to me. He taught me a lot about playing third base even though he knew I was eventually going to take his job." Francis's teaching stood Judy well. On the topic of bunting, "Francis worked with me on it for hours. I was trying to field a bunt, stand up, and throw. Of course, that didn't work very well. Francis taught me to come in, grab the ball with my bare hand, and throw all in one motion. He also taught me to throw underhand or across my body according to the situation."[21]

Johnson was a raw talent and had a slight build (5-feet-11, 150 pounds). He showed promise but was not an instant success. Monte Irvin, in *Few and Chosen*, noted, "He batted only .227 in his first year, but Pop Lloyd took a liking to Judy and worked with him, helping Johnson to polish his skills at bat and in the field. … Pop taught me more baseball than anybody else."[22] According to Johnson, "Lloyd was a great teacher, he'd make you play your head off, and he was always full of encouragement."[23]

The economics for a Negro League ballplayer in the 1920s were noteworthy, historian Robert Peterson wrote:

Johnson … was signed by the Hilldale Club in 1922 for $135 a month [up from his 1921 salary of $100], an average salary for a young player at that time. … Although this was paid only during the playing season of about six months, it put the ball player on an elite economic plane in the Negro community, especially since he could augment his earnings by playing ball all winter long in Florida, California, or Latin America.[24]

Thanks to Francis and Lloyd, two established players on the Hilldale team, Johnson learned quickly and transitioned into Hilldale's third baseman of the 1920s.

Johnson's lengthy sojourn at Hilldale in the 1920s was unusual. Player movement among teams was common depending on the stability of franchises, the level of pay, personality clashes between players and managers and owners, and frequent dealing of players by owners from one team to another. As one of the relatively stable teams in that time under a strong owner, Hilldale became Johnson's home. Coupled with his local roots and the mutual regard he and Bolden had for one another, Johnson played for Hilldale from 1921 through 1929.

Ed Bolden, a black entrepreneur in Philadelphia and owner of the Hilldale Daisies, was a significant presence in the world of Negro League baseball. Hilldale was not a member of Rube Foster's 1920 formation of the first Negro National League, but instead stayed outside the fold and focused on "the transformation of the Hilldale Athletic Club into a full-time business enterprise."[25] This involved, according to Bolden, total control of scheduling games and a strong competitive schedule, high moral standards of players and of fans in the stands, decent pay for players, and good grounds.[26] All of this offered an attractive environment for players and a reason for Johnson to make it his home.

Hilldale began in Darby, Pennsylvania, originally as a team for youth. Bolden, business manager and part-owner of the Hilldales, "incorporated the club, and with the proceeds of a stock sale, he bought a field and built a wooden grandstand seating about 5,000." According to Johnson, "we usually filled it. … [W]e had the best infield that big league players ever played on … and if it rained for an hour like everything and you sat around for [a] half hour you couldn't see a bit of water anyplace. A ball would very seldom take a bad hop unless someone dug a hole with his spikes."[27]

Although Johnson became best known for his play with the Grays and the Crawfords – the Negro League powerhouses of the 1930s – he made his name with Hilldale in the 1920s.

According to Rendle, "Judy was fortunate to play for one of the best teams in all of the Negro Leagues if a young man wanted to balance a career with a family. The reason was simple. In and around Philadelphia the Hilldales found ample competition, taking on both white and black teams. … [T]hat was the one thing I liked about Hilldale [Johnson said], you were home almost every night.'"[28]

The 1921 season marked Johnson's first full year with Hilldale and his stats were not stellar (.268 BA, .771 OPS in 97 at-bats), but consistent play helped him get his footing. Hilldale finished first among the collection of Eastern Independent clubs, besting its rival the Atlantic City Bacharach Giants. In 1922 Johnson batted .280 with an OPS of .658 in 125 at-bats.[29] The formation of the Eastern Colored League in 1923, intended to counter the Negro National League and its Midwest teams, created a haven for Hilldale and its competitors on the East Coast, the Bacharachs, Brooklyn Royal Giants, Baltimore Black Sox, Cubans, and the Lincoln Giants. Hilldale won the pennant going away, but no postseason competition could be arranged, given Foster's animus for the ECL and its player raids on Midwest teams.

Johnson's batting continued to improve in what was now his full-time role as the team's third baseman. Hilldale played six games against two different squads of major leaguers, many from the Philadelphia Athletics team that had finished sixth that year. In Lanctot's history of Hilldale, he noted, "Hilldale's five victories against two barnstorming clubs provided a stunning climax to an amazing season and placed the club at the forefront of black baseball."[30]

This would not be the only time that Johnson played against major leaguers:

> The white ball players at that time were always glad to play against our Negro ballplayers, because there weren't salaries like there are today. They made almost as much money playing us after the World Series was over as they would make almost the whole season. I played against every big leaguer, from Babe Ruth on down.[31]

Johnson's barnstorming play against white players was too extensive to document here, but one other series is worth noting. After the 1926 World Series, Hilldale played an American League all-star team that included Heinie Manush, George Burns, Jimmy Dykes, and Lefty Grove. The records for the series are incomplete but indicate at least three Hilldale wins to one loss over the all-stars, including two losses by Lefty Grove and a .374 batting average by Johnson.[32]

The year 1924 "pitted the champions from the Negro National League against the champions of the Eastern Colored League in the inaugural Colored World Series between the Kansas City Monarchs and the Hilldale Club."[33] Hilldale had easily won the inaugural ECL season, besting the Baltimore Black Sox by three games; they "were steady throughout the season, never losing more than two games in a row. … Their toughest league opponent was the Lincoln Giants, splitting the series at five games each. And they beat the league's runner-up Black Sox seven games out of ten games and won six of ten from the tough Bacharach Giants."[34] Johnson batted .337 with an .895 OPS in 300 at-bats for the season.

The 10-game World Series began in Philadelphia on October 3. By prior agreement, this first World Series would be played in four cities rather than just at the Kansas City and Hilldale ballparks. The first two games were in Philadelphia, with the Monarchs winning Game One, 6-2, as Johnson went 2-for-3 with a double and a walk, and Hilldale taking Game Two, 11-0. Johnson was 3-for-5 with an RBI in the second game. The Series then moved to Baltimore's Black Sox Park for Game Three, which ended in a 6-6 tie, called because of darkness after 13 innings. Johnson continued his torrid hitting, going 3-for-7 with two doubles.

Game Four in Baltimore was a Hilldale win, 4-3, and Johnson went hitless in three at-bats. Rube Currie's 6⅔ scoreless innings saved the day for the Daisies. The series shifted to Kansas City for Game Five and Hilldale won again, 5-2, to take a 3-1 Series lead. Johnson was 3-for-5 with three RBIs and his ninth-inning "wallop over [George] Sweatt's head in deep center with [Clint] Thomas on 3rd and [Joseph 'Sleepy'] Lewis on first base broke up a hurling duel between ['Bullet'] Rogan … and one 'Nip' Winters" won the game for Hilldale."[35]

All looked promising for Hilldale, but Game Six went to the Monarchs, 6-5. Johnson extended his hot hitting, going 2-for-4 and driving in three of the five Hilldale runs; his Series batting average now stood at .481. Game Seven in Kansas City was another win for the Monarchs, 4-3. Johnson went 2-for-5 and scored both Hilldale runs. The remaining three games took place at Chicago's South Side park with the Series tied at three apiece with one tie. Kansas City won, 3-2, and, for the second time in the Series, Judy Johnson went hitless. Hilldale was ahead 2-0 in the bottom of the ninth when, with two outs and one on, the Monarchs rallied to win the game against Hilldale's starting pitcher, Rube Currie.

Hilldale won Game Nine to tie the Series at four games each when, knotted at 3-3 in the top of the ninth, Johnson led off with a double and then scored the winning run on an unassisted groundout to first. Game Ten was a pitching gem by Jose Mendez as the Monarchs' ageless wonder hurled a three-hit shutout. Johnson went hitless in the finale but ended the Series with a .341 batting average to lead all batters on both teams.[36]

The following year Hilldale found redemption by winning the second World Series, this time defeating the Monarchs in a rematch, five games to one. The first four games were in Kansas City while Games Five and Six took place in Philadelphia. Johnson went only 6-for-24 but was still instrumental in several of Hilldale's wins. In Game One he tripled in two runs in the top of the 12th to spur Hilldale to victory, 5-2. The Monarchs won Game Two, 5-3, but Johnson led off the 10th in Game Three with a single and later scored on a double by Pete Washington to defeat the Monarchs. Hilldale did not lose again, winning Game Four, 7-3, and then winning 2-1 and 5-2 in Philadelphia, both thanks to big hits by Biz Mackey.[37]

After Hilldale's World Series victory, Johnson traveled to Florida to play winter ball. Florida was one of several winter venues for ballplayers – both black and white. Whether players went to Cuba, Mexico, Florida, or California, the reason was the same: The job of ballplayers was to play ball and these locations provided additional venues in which to play. Negro League ballplayers often received better pay in the winter leagues because their regular ballclubs frequently struggled financially and could not afford to pay a high wage. In Florida the attraction was Palm Beach, where "[t]wo rival hotels, the Breakers and Poinciana, hired the best black professionals to wait on tables and entertain guests on the baseball diamond. The rivalry between the two hotels was intense. But it was the money-making opportunities that lured many of the players down there. The pay and tips were excellent."[38]

In 1926 Hilldale failed to match its three prior pennants and finished second to the Atlantic City Bacharach Giants. Atlantic City went on to play the Chicago American Giants in an epic World Series of their own. Although Johnson hit .316 that year, he suffered an injury during the season – he was hit in the head by a pitch – that affected his batting over the next couple of years. "After he was hit in the head by a pitch, Johnson's average slipped below .300 in 1927 and 1928, but he rebounded and hit .390 in 1929."[39]

The Eastern Colored League folded in midseason in 1928 when several of its teams collapsed financially. Hilldale played 64 games that year and finished with a record of 35-28-1. At the age of 28, Judy posted mediocre combined statistics for Hilldale and, later, a team of colored all-stars – a .242 batting average and .651 OPS in 219 at-bats. In 1929 Hilldale moved to the short-lived American Negro League masterminded by Cum Posey. The league consisted of five former ECL teams (the Bacharach Giants, the Baltimore Black Sox, the traveling Cuban Stars, Hilldale, and the Lincoln Giants) along with the Homestead Grays (who had been playing as an independent squad). The Black Sox won both halves of the season and were awarded the pennant.

Johnson mounted a career comeback of sorts in 1929. In 342 at-bats (mostly with Hilldale), he hit .365 with an OPS of .921 and 72 RBIs. At the end of the season, *Pittsburgh Courier* columnist W. Rollo Wilson wrote that "the best player in every respect on the club [Hilldale] was unassuming Judy Johnson, arrived at last as the best third baseman in Negro baseball. He was the most consistent and timely hitter for the Clan and he led the league in fielding his position and in the number of hits made." In fact, Wilson wrote, "the most valuable player in the [entire] baseball field I saw this summer was Judy Johnson of Hilldale. If you have ever seen him play and have marked his pep and ability, you can see why I chose him over all the rest."[40]

Johnson's superlative play and Hilldale's ascendancy were made for each other. "The key to success of the Hilldales during the 1920s rested with William 'Judy' Johnson," historian Heaphy asserted.[41] Neil Lanctot summarized the relationship, writing, "During the 1920s, a combination of a large black population, a strong team, and available home grounds enabled Philadelphia and Chicago to reign as the most consistently profitable venues in their regions."[42]

# THE 1935 PITTSBURGH CRAWFORDS

Johnson continued to play baseball in the winter, both in Florida and Cuba, as the money was simply too good to pass up. In all, Johnson played in Cuba during the 1926-27, 1927-28, 1928-29, and 1930-31 seasons. In 1926-27, Johnson played for the Almendares Alacranes (managed by Adolfo Luque), the winner of Cuba's Triangular Series. Johnson hit .374 in 115 at-bats. In 1927-28 he batted .333 in 32 games and 132 at-bats playing for the team named Cuba, which came in second to Habana, and he again played for Cuba in 1928-29 as the squad once more finished well behind Habana. His final appearance was in 1930 when Johnson's Almendarista team including Martin Dihigo, Pop Lloyd, Dick Lundy, and Clint Thomas came in first.[43]

In 1930, with the Depression's far-reaching impact affecting many black entrepreneurs and their Negro League teams, Cum Posey maintained the Homestead Grays as an independent squad. This approach contributed significantly to the Grays' financial stability. Homestead played games in and around Pittsburgh to keep traveling expenses down, and Posey made sure that the team garnered a reasonable portion of the gate when it played on the road.

Posey began to raid other teams that could not compete with the salaries he offered and, in 1930, assembled a powerhouse lineup. He signed Johnson and Oscar Charleston from Hilldale to strengthen a lineup that already had Vic Harris, Buck Ewing, and Smokey Joe Williams. Wilson, in the *Pittsburgh Courier*, lauded Johnson's signing, noting, "I don't think Johnson was ever fully appreciated by the Darby owners or fans."[44]

Historian Peterson wrote:

The Grays barnstormed their way through 1930. With no league in place, Negro League teams played each other on a catch-as-catch-can basis and filled their schedule against semipro teams. It was the aggressive road schedule that shaped Johnson's recollection of his year with the Grays: 'The Grays traveled all season long. Every day you were going, you'd go and ride over those hills. Every two hours you had to average a hundred miles. With nine men in the car!'[45]

Peterson characterized the Negro League ballplayer's season succinctly:

Clubs in the organized Negro leagues were not, strictly speaking, barnstormers, since they played a formal schedule with several series a year against other teams in the league. But more than half their 200-odd games a year (sometimes two-thirds) were outside the league; Negro clubs kept promoters around big cities busy booking them for their days off from league play, usually with white semi-pro teams in towns within driving distance of the city where they happened to be stopping for a day or two.[46]

And the term "driving distance" was liberally defined – as many as 200 miles to and from a venue.

Johnson reflected on playing three games every Sunday and admitted, "I said a lot of bad things before we had to play that first game. Everybody [had] their mouths hanging to the floor. But as soon as we put the uniform on, we were just a different team. We'd forget the last game we played, and we'd go out and win this one."[47]

Adding to the demands of the game in the early 1930s was the advent of night ball. Lighting created an evening time slot for games so that teams could attract more fans. The additional gate receipts contributed revenue but added another game to the daily grind. The lighting itself was uneven at best and posed risks for the players. Johnson recalled, "I couldn't see the outfielders out there. If the ball went above the lights, you'd have to watch it didn't hit you in the head."[48]

A vivid memory for Johnson was Josh Gibson's debut with the Grays that summer. Gibson had been playing since 1928 with a team called the Pittsburgh Crawford Giants, then styled a "neighborhood boys' team," that was the precursor to the

Pittsburgh Crawfords squad that Gus Greenlee quickly raised to heavyweight status through player acquisitions and aggressive scheduling. On July 25, the Kansas City Monarchs arrived in Pittsburgh to play the Grays at Forbes Field – a midsummer marquee event for the black community. The Monarchs came with their own lighting system so that the game could be played at night. Johnson recollected:

> We were in the clubhouse trying to discuss signals, because we had never played a night game. Buck Ewing was catching. When Buck got down to give the signal, why [Smokey Joe Williams] couldn't even see his hand. … Williams misunderstood the signal, and Ewing split his hand right down. My sub-catcher was in right field, he wouldn't come in to catch, he was afraid. Here we are, Forbes Field is packed. Josh Gibson was sitting in the stands, him and a bunch of boys who played sandlot baseball. I asked if he would catch. 'Yes sir, Mr. Johnson!' I had to hold up the game, let him go in the clubhouse and put on a suit.[49]

The Johnson/Gibson relationship was a special one. Gibson saw Judy (whom he called "Jing") as a mentor and would seek feedback after each game, talking shop with Judy to learn how to better his game.[50] In fact, Johnson's coaching skills had become widely appreciated; although Posey was listed as the Grays' manager that year, Johnson recollected that his role for Homestead was to be the manager on the field.

At the end of the season, the top two teams of the Eastern independent clubs were logical candidates for a playoff. Posey and John Keenan, owner of the New York Lincoln Giants, who were led by Pop Lloyd, organized an informal World Series. The two teams played 10 games, of which the Grays won six. Game Seven was famous for Gibson's mammoth home run. Johnson later reminisced that the ball "went out over the roof, over everything."[51] A hoped for series between the Grays and the St. Louis Stars, runaway winners of the Negro National League of Western teams, did not transpire.

In 1931 Johnson returned to Hilldale as a player-manager under new owner John Drew, who had purchased the team after the 1930 season. The *Pittsburgh Courier* offered more insight on Johnson's move. Staying in Pittsburgh "would have caused Johnson to lose a good all year-round job [in his Delaware home]. For this reason, it was indicated he decided to stay in the East."[52] The move backfired due to Hilldale's shaky financial condition at the height of the Depression. Hilldale's business model of controlling its own booking arrangements, rather than working with white booking agents to schedule games against white teams, was no longer sustainable. The team simply could not arrange enough games on its own against solvent opponents in front of decent crowds, which led to its financial demise in 1932.[53]

Players must have suspected that the end was near when, "[b]eginning on June 15th, the team stopped paying salaries and began to pay them according to a percentage plan. After deducting expenses and allocating a share to the club, the team dividing the remaining gate receipts or guarantee among the players."[54] Johnson and other Hilldale players objected and, when the team's finances worsened due to fewer bookings and reduced attendance, the team folded.

After Hilldale's collapse, Johnson joined the Crawfords for the remainder of the 1932 season. The *Pittsburgh Courier* celebrated the move, noting, "Judy Johnson has packed bag and baggage and gone to Pittsburgh to join the Crawfords."[55] Widely considered to be among the most talented Negro League teams ever, Pittsburgh fielded a formidable lineup.

That same 1932 season, Cum Posey founded the East-West League, a one-season venture that also collapsed in June. The league was the first to merge Eastern and Western clubs. Posey had taken a firm stance against Gus Greenlee's Crawfords because of Greenlee's raids of other teams' play-

# THE 1935 PITTSBURGH CRAWFORDS

ers and would not allow the Grays to join. The Crawfords finished third among independent clubs and booked a seven-game series against Casey Stengel's stars, another of the many series that Negro League teams played against white teams. Playing in York, Altoona, and Pittsburgh and wrapping up in Cleveland, the Crawfords won the series five games to two.[56]

In 1933 Greenlee spearheaded the new Negro National League. By then, the crosstown Grays were in a precarious financial plight and could not hang on to their players. The Crawfords lured away the Grays' Oscar Charleston and Josh Gibson. Charleston became manager, but Judy Johnson served as captain. That year witnessed the first East-West All-Star Game, an annual contest that was played until 1953; in some seasons, two all-star games were played. According to Lester, "Without a doubt, the East West All-Star Game held annually at Comiskey Park was Gus Greenlee's biggest contribution to the national pastime. The event became the most visible competition in black sports in America. Greenlee's influence was obvious in the inaugural contest, in which 7 of the 14 Eastern players were Crawfords."[57] Despite their presence, the team lost to Willie Foster and his Western mates, 11-7. Judy Johnson played in the inaugural game; he pinch-hit for Jud Wilson in the eighth inning and hit a single. Johnson did not play in the All-Star Game in 1934 or 1935, but he made one last appearance in 1936, his final season in the league. He was 1-for-2 and drove in a run in the East's 10-2 victory.[58]

From 1933 to 1936, the Crawfords were Negro National League champions every year except 1934. And even in that year, they had the best overall record while they finished second to the Philadelphia Stars and Chicago American Giants in the two separate halves of the season. Gus Greenlee's well-financed operation was able to attract and to retain the likes of Johnson, Gibson, Charleston, Jimmie Crutchfield, Cool Papa Bell, Sam Bankhead, Jud Wilson, Rap Dixon, Ted Page, Sam Streeter, Satchel Paige, Ted Radcliffe, and Willie Foster for many of those years. The 1935 Crawfords squad might have been the best team of all time in the Negro Leagues. They finished 10 games ahead of the Columbus Elite Giants, Philadelphia Stars, and New York Cubans as they won the first-half title, and then they defeated the second-half winners – the New York Cubans, who were managed by Martin Dihigo – in the NNL championship series, four games to three.

In early 1937, after 4½ years with the Crawfords, Johnson was the subject of trade rumors between the Crawfords and the Grays.[59] Greenlee faced pressure from local law enforcement on his numbers business that undercut his finances, so he proposed sending Johnson and Gibson to the Grays mainly for $2,500, "reportedly the largest sum involved in a player deal in black baseball to date."[60] Eventually the trade was consummated, as the *Pittsburgh Courier* reported, "The biggest deal in the history of Negro baseball was completed here [New York] Saturday morning when catcher Josh Gibson of the Pittsburgh Crawfords and third baseman Judy Johnson of the same club were sent to the Homestead Grays in exchange for catcher 'Pepper' Bassett, third baseman Spearman and $2,500 in cash."[61] According to Peterson, "Here is a measure of Negro baseball's finances. The game's greatest slugger – who was also the paramount drawing card (always excepting Satchel Paige) – and Negro baseball's most accomplished third baseman were to be traded for two journeymen players and $2,500."[62]

The trade made Johnson unhappy. Homestead's rigorous barnstorming schedule and the belief that he was a throw-in on the trade frustrated him. Newspaper reports recorded him in the Grays early-season lineup, but later he was conspicuously absent. He moved back east and played for the Philadelphia Red Caps of the Middle Atlantic League, but eventually he simply hung up his spikes.[63] Johnson said, "I could have played longer, but it was getting too rough."[64]

# Pride of Smoketown

*Judy Johnson, in the livery of the Homestead Grays, appears at the 1983 MLB All-Star Game. In 1975, Johnson had become on the sixth Negro League player to be inducted into the Hall of Fame.*

Johnson and his wife, Anita, had bought a house in Marshalltown, Delaware, that became their permanent home in retirement. In the years that followed, "Judy had a number of jobs in retirement from baseball. He was a supervisor at Continental Can Company. He and his brother bought and operated a variety store in Millside for a while. He drove a school bus for a while and worked at Mullins Department Store in security."[65]

However, his baseball days were not over. When Jackie Robinson broke the color barrier in 1947, the slow integration of African-Americans into the major-league game began. Some Negro League players made it to the majors, while others became involved as scouts. Johnson became a member of the latter group when the Athletics employed [him] ... to scout black prospects."[66] Johnson recalled, "I never dreamt it would happen, even in the late 1930s. I was just thrilled to see the day."[67]

Philadelphia Athletics owner-manager Connie Mack had become aware of Johnson in the 1920s when the Hilldale Daisies played in Philadelphia. Mack's appreciation for Johnson's talent in those years stayed with him. With the advent of integration, "Mack landed him his first job in the majors in 1952. Judy proudly became a scout, hired to scour local ballfields for major league prospects. In 1954 Judy became the first African American hired to coach in the majors, when he attended spring training to ease the transition of three black rookie players for the A's: first baseman Vic Power, pitcher Bob Trice, and [a third outfielder]."[68]

Johnson reminisced about several other promising players whom he encouraged the A's to sign, a list that included Hank Aaron, Larry Doby, and Minnie Miñoso. He claimed, "I could have gotten Hank Aaron for them for $3,500 when he was playing for the Indianapolis Clowns. I got my boss out of bed and told him I had a good prospect and he wouldn't cost too much, and he cussed me out for waking him up at one o'clock in the morning. He said, "Thirty-five hundred! That's too much money." Too much for a man like that! I could have gotten Larry Doby and Minnie Miñoso, too, and the A's would still be playing in Philadelphia, because that would be all the outfield they'd needed."[69]

The A's rejected his suggestions, but Johnson remained committed to the prospects he found. He confessed, "I wound up giving tips on all those players to scouts from other teams. I just wanted to make sure the kids got a chance."[70]

After working with the A's for several years, Johnson moved to the Milwaukee Braves as a regional scout. Among his finds was a young player named Bill Bruton, who not only eventually signed with the Braves, but also married Judy and Anita's niece/adopted daughter, Loretta.[71]

When John Quinn, the Braves' general manager, was hired by the Philadelphia Phillies in 1959, he asked Johnson to join him. Johnson remained with the Phillies as a scout and spring-training coach until 1974, when his health no longer allowed him to travel. While there, Johnson discovered another great talent: "I helped sign Richie Allen. I told our general manager, 'That's the best-looking prospect I have seen, please don't lose him,' and he went out and signed him."[72] Underscoring Johnson's natural talent for teaching, coaching, and managing was the role the Phillies asked him to play:

> Mr. Carpenter, the Phillies owner, liked me to go because I can help the Negro boys and also white boys. If a kid does something wrong, I've got to go through the motions and show him the right way. You can't just holler at him, you've got to show him how the ball is handled, and that's what my boss likes about me. I played a lot of baseball and I always tried to learn. I tell the kids baseball is like school and you get promoted if you learn.[73]

After his career Johnson, like many Negro League players, reflected on the quality of their game and what might have been. When asked if the Negro Leagues, in his view, were of major-league quality, Johnson replied, "Not day in and day out. But of course, you could have picked enough payers then to put a team in each major league – a whole colored team in each league and they would have been the same caliber as the other big-league teams. The Hilldale Club that played in the [Negro] World Series in 1924 would have belonged in the Triple A because there were a couple of positions where men would have had to be replaced. We had men in some positions that weren't major league caliber."[74]

When Johnson looked at the game of baseball through the prism of excellence alone, it was an enigma to him to figure out what kept major-league owners from signing African American players earlier. Johnson remembered, "I asked (Connie Mack) one day, I said, 'Mr. Mack, why didn't you ever take any of the colored boys into the Major Leagues?' He said, 'Well, Judy, if you want to know the truth, there were just too many of you to go in.' As much as to say, it would take too many jobs away from the other boys."[75]

Johnson realized that playing in the Negro Leagues was the only avenue he had, regardless of how much he believed he could have played and shined in the majors, and he asserted, "They were my happy days, and I don't regret one minute."[76]

Judy Johnson garnered the admiration and respect of many during his playing career. A superior hitter with a great batting eye, he was also considered a premier fielder; "William 'Judy' Johnson was the standard by which other third basemen were measured."[77]

According to Ted Page, Johnson was "a scientific player, he did everything with grace and poise. You talk about playing third base. Heck he was better than anybody I saw. ... He had a powerful, accurate arm. He could do anything: come in for a ball, cut it off at the line, or range way over toward the shortstop hole. He was really something."[78]

"Johnson 'was like a rock,' said ex-outfielder Jimmie Crutchfield, 'a steadying influence on the club. Had a great brain, could anticipate a play, knew what his opponents were going to do.' ... 'He had intelligence and finesse,' said Willie Wells, one of the game's best shortstops."[79]

Many of those who played alongside or against him in the Negro Leagues believed that Johnson would have been a great coach or manager in the majors, an opportunity whose time had not yet come for former Negro Leaguers. Ted Page said, "I credit the man who really helped Josh Gibson on foul balls as Judy Johnson. Johnson was one of the real smart ballplayers in my era. He really helped Josh become a great catcher."[80] Page further remarked, "He should have been in the major leagues 15-20 years as a coach. They talk about Negro managers. I always thought that Judy would have made a perfect major league manager."[81] Page lamented baseball's loss in not having him as a manager. "He had the ability to see the qualities, the faults, of ball players and have the correction for them."[82]

Johnson himself remarked, "I love to teach baseball and would rather do it than anything. I even coach a sandlot team here in Wilmington. It's like putting a seed in the ground, you like to watch it develop. As long as they're ballplayers, they're my kids. I love 'em all."[83]

In 1971, in conjunction with Commissioner Bowie Kuhn, the Hall of Fame formed its first Committee on the Negro Baseball Leagues. Monte Irvin chaired the committee whose purpose was to select Negro League players deserving of Hall of Fame induction. Johnson was one of 12 voting and ad hoc members who met to identify the players. After serving for four years, Johnson stepped down, after which the committee recommended his own induction in 1975. He became the sixth Negro League player selected to the Hall of Fame, after Paige (1971), Gibson (1972), Buck Leonard (1972), Irvin (1973), and Bell (1974). After him the committee named three more players, Charleston (1976), Lloyd (1976), and Dihigo (1977), before voting to disband in 1977.[84]

Unlike many of the Negro League players who were later inducted to the Hall of Fame, Johnson was able to accept his plaque with his wife, daughter, Loretta, and her husband, Bill Bruton, all present. On August 18, 1975, Commissioner Kuhn welcomed Johnson into the Hall alongside Ralph Kiner, Bucky Harris, Earl Averill, and Billy Herman.[85]

Johnson's speech, preserved in his Hall of Fame player file, was replete with "thank you's" to family, friends, fellow players, and the Phillies, and was punctuated by the story of his father's failed attempt to make him a boxer. To enter the Hall while alive and able to accept the award personally was the pinnacle for Johnson. As he continued to speak, "Judy couldn't contain his emotion as he made his acceptance speech at Cooperstown in 1975. He broke into tears, and his son-in-law Bill Bruton, a former Milwaukee Brave and Detroit Tiger center fielder, came out of the audience to console him. After a few moments, Judy returned to the microphone and finished his speech. His final words: "I am so grateful."[86]

## Sources

Seamheads is used as the database of record unless otherwise noted.

## Notes

1. John B. Holway, *Blackball Stars: Negro League Pioneers* (Westport, Connecticut: Meckler Books, 1988), 150.
2. Leslie A. Heaphy, *The Negro Leagues: 1869-1960* (Jefferson, North Carolina: McFarland & Company, 2003), 52.
3. James A. Riley, *The Biographical Encyclopedia of the Negro Baseball Leagues* (New York: Carroll & Graf Publishers, 1994), 444.
4. Riley, 444.
5. Ellen Rendle, *Judy Johnson: Delaware's Invisible Hero* (Wilmington, Delaware: Cedar Tree Press, Inc., 1994), 15.
6. Rendle, 16.
7. Kevin Kerrane and Rod Beaton, "Judy Johnson: Reminiscences by the Great Baseball Player," *Delaware Today*, May 1977: 32.
8. Kerrane and Beaton.
9. Kerrane and Beaton. The bracketed information about him working as a stevedore comes from Riley, 444.
10. Untitled document, Judy Johnson player file at the National Baseball Hall of Fame, 2.
11. Jim Bankes, *The Pittsburgh Crawfords* (Jefferson, North Carolina: McFarland & Company, 2003), 63.
12. Bankes, 64.
13. Holway, *Blackball Stars*, 153.
14. Holway, *Blackball Stars*, 153.
15. Holway, *Blackball Stars*, 153.
16. John B. Holway, unpublished player manuscript, Baseball Hall of Fame Player File, 2.
17. Riley, 302.
18. Mark Ribowsky, *A Complete History of the Negro Leagues: 1884-1955* (New York: Birch Lane Press, 1995), 96.
19. Kerrane and Beaton.
20. Ribowsky, 96.
21. Bankes, 64.
22. Monte Irvin with Phil Pepe, *Few and Chosen: Defining Negro Leagues Greatness* (Chicago: Triumph Books, 2007), 69.

# THE 1935 PITTSBURGH CRAWFORDS

23  Kerrane and Beaton.

24  Robert Peterson, *Only the Ball Was White* (New York: McGraw-Hill, 1984), 121.

25  Lawrence D. Hogan, *Shades of Glory: The Negro Leagues and the Story of African American Baseball* (Washington: National Geographic Society, 2006), 142.

26  Hogan, 144.

27  Peterson, 123.

28  Rendle, 32.

29  Seamheads.com. seamheads.com/NegroLgs/player.php?playerID=johns01jud, last accessed December 1, 2019. Note: All statistics and team records were taken from Seamheads.com unless otherwise indicated.

30  Neil Lanctot, *Fair Dealing and Clean Playing: The Hilldale Club and the Development of Black Professional Baseball, 1910-1932* (Syracuse, New York: Syracuse University Press, 2007), 102-106.

31  Holway, *Blackball Stars*, 161.

32  John Holway, *The Complete Book of Baseball's Negro Leagues: The Other Half of Baseball History* (Fern Park, Florida: Hastings House Publishers, 2001), 220-221.

33  Larry Lester, *Baseball's First Colored World Series: The 1924 Meeting of the Hilldale Giants and Kansas City Monarchs* (Jefferson, North Carolina: McFarland & Company, 2006), 8.

34  Lester, 36, 37.

35  "Judy Proves Hero in First Game in West," *Pittsburgh Courier*, October 18, 1924: 6.

36  Lester, 104-181.

37  Holway, *Complete Book*, 204-205.

38  Holway, unpublished manuscript, 15.

39  Irvin, 70. Seamheads shows his average as .365.

40  W. Rollo Wilson, "Sports Shots," *Pittsburgh Courier*, September 28, 1929: 16.

41  Heaphy, 62.

42  Neil Lanctot, *Negro League Baseball: The Rise and Ruin of a Black Institution* (Philadelphia: University of Pennsylvania Press, 2004), 93.

43  Jorge S. Figuererdo, *Cuban Baseball: A Statistical History 1878-1961* (Jefferson, North Carolina: McFarland & Company, 2003), 172-194. The 1930 Cuban League was an outlier; a contract dispute between the owners of the newly built La Tropical Stadium and the League teams shortened the season to games only in October and November.

44  W. Rollo Wilson, "Sports Shots," *Pittsburgh Courier*, April 5, 1930: 17.

45  Peterson, 142.

46  Peterson, 146.

47  Donn Rogosin, *Invisible Men: Life In Baseball's Negro Leagues* (New York: Atheneum, 1983), 75.

48  Hogan, 255.

49  John B. Holway, *Josh and Satch: The Life and Times of Josh Gibson and Satchel Paige* (New York: Carroll & Graf, 1992), 23.

50  Holway, *Josh and Satch*. 26.

51  Holway *Complete Book*, 267-269.

52  "Wilson to Play Third for Grays," *Pittsburgh Courier*, March 7, 1931: 14.

53  Lanctot, *Negro League Baseball*, 111.

54  Courtney Michelle Smith, *Ed Bolden and Black Baseball in Philadelphia* (Jefferson, North Carolina: McFarland & Company, 2017), 65.

55  W. Rollo Wilson, "Sports Shots," *Pittsburgh Courier*, July 2, 1932: 14.

56  Holway, *Complete Book*, 296-97.

57  Larry Lester, *Black Baseball's National Showcase: The East-West All-Star Game, 1933-1953* (Lincoln: University of Nebraska Press, 2001), 15.

58  Lester, *Black Baseball's National Showcase*, 91.

59  "Code of Organized Baseball to Govern National League," *Pittsburgh Courier*, January 30, 1937: 16.

60  Lanctot, *Negro League Baseball*, 61.

61  "Grays get Josh Gibson in Big Deal, Pay $2,500," *Pittsburgh Courier*, March 27, 1937: 16.

62  Peterson, 165-66.

63  "Philly Red Caps Meet Blacksox in Richmond, Va.," *Pittsburgh Courier*, July 24, 1937: 18.

64  Holway, unpublished manuscript, 7.

65  Rendle, 58.

66  Jules Tygiel, *Baseball's Great Experiment: Jackie Robinson and his Legacy* (New York: Random House, 1984), 292.

67  Rendle, 59.

68  Rendle, 59. The Rendle book cites Eddie Joost as the third player, but Joost was neither African American nor a rookie that year. It is believed the player Johnson meant was Joe Taylor, who played sparingly for the A's that season as a rookie outfielder.

69  Holway, unpublished manuscript, 8.

70  Rendle, 59.

71  Rendle, 60.

72  Holway, unpublished manuscript, 8.

73  Holway, unpublished manuscript, 8.

74  Peterson, 81.

75  Peterson, 173.

76  Rogosin, 66.

77  Arthur R. Ashe Jr., *A Hard Road to Glory: Baseball The African American Athlete in Baseball* (New York: Amistad Press, 1993), 28.

78  Irvin, 68.

79  Holway, *Blackball Stars*, 150.

80  Holway, *Josh and Satch*, 25-26.

81  Hogan, 228.

82  Holway, *Blackball Stars*, 164.

83  Holway, unpublished manuscript, 24.

84  Baseball Reference.com: baseball-reference.com/bullpen/Special_Committee_on_the_Negro_Leagues, last accessed December 3, 2019.

85  1975 Baseball Hall of Fame Induction Ceremony Transcript, Baseball Hall of Fame Player File, 2.

86  William Brashler, *Josh Gibson: A Life in the Negro Leagues* (New York, Harper and Row, 1978), 186.

# HARRY KINCANNON

## By Margaret M. Gripshover

In the 1920s, Harry Kincannon left the coalfields of southern West Virginia and headed north to Pittsburgh, where he developed into a right-handed curveball specialist in the city's sandlot leagues. He began his professional career in 1929 with the Pittsburgh Crawford Giants. Kincannon remained with the Crawfords organization through 1936, but did not make an appearance on the mound during the team's 1935 Negro League Championship Series against the New York Cubans. In 1937 he was signed by the New York Black Yankees and then spent the following year with the Washington Black Senators. Kincannon played his final season in the Negro Leagues with the short-lived 1939 Toledo Crawfords. After the Toledo team folded, Kincannon headed back home to West Virginia, where he spent the next 12 years as a pitcher and manager for a variety of successful semipro and amateur black baseball teams. When he wasn't in the dugout or on the mound, Kincannon was a coal miner, as was his father and all three of his brothers. These two legacies – coal and baseball – bookended Kincannon's life and served to both limit and expand his world.

*Pitcher Harry "Tin Can" Kincannon struggled during the 1935 season, but he had pitched well enough to represent the Crawfords as a member of the West team in the 1934 East-West All-Star classic.*

(Courtesy Noir-Tech Research, Inc.)

Kincannon's family roots trace back to Wythe County in southwestern Virginia, which borders the coalfields of southern West Virginia. Kincannon's grandparents were born into slavery in Wythe County. His paternal grandfather, Andrew Kincannon, worked as a furnace laborer in the Ivanhoe community, refining lead from local mines, a grueling job he held both before and after the Civil War.

Harry Kincannon was the eldest of 10 children born to Charles "Charlie" Kincannon Sr. and Arlena (also spelled as "Arlene" and "Arleana") Jones Kincannon. He was born on June 26, 1909, in Arlington, West Virginia, a coal-camp community in McDowell County, the southernmost county in the state.[1] During the decade in which Harry was born, McDowell County was experiencing a major economic and population boom. By 1910, McDowell had the highest percentage of black population of any West Virginia county.[2] The vast majority of African-Americans living in the county in 1910, including the Kincannons, came to work in the coal mines. Many were recruited by mine owners as a means to discourage unionization, or as strikebreakers where the unions had been established.[3] The town of Arlington was founded by the Arlington Coal & Coke Company, and when the coal was gone, so was Arlington. It ceased to function as a community by the early 1930s and today no longer appears on official West Virginia highway maps.[4]

Kincannon's genealogical background played a role in his life as a mixed-race man in the Jim Crow era. The 1910 Census classified Kincannon and his parents as "mulatto."[5] In 1942, when he registered for the World War II draft, he was described as a "negro" with "gray eyes" and a "light brown" complexion.[6] Based on his physical appearance, Kincannon was able to "pass" as white and test some of the racial boundaries of the era, including being served in "whites only" businesses.[7] For example, Kincannon, who was known for his good sense of humor, could enter a whites-only ice cream parlor without causing a stir, and enjoy his cone while he taunted his Negro League teammates who were denied entrance.[8] But just in case any given situation went awry, Kincannon kept a pistol in his pocket – a personal insurance policy that he carried throughout his life.[9]

By 1920, Kincannon's family moved to Northfork, a larger community just north of Arlington, where his father, Charlie, worked the dirty and dangerous job of a coal loader.[10] Around the time the family moved to Northfork, Charlie's uncle, Platfield "Platt" Kincannon, left Wythe County, Virginia, for Pittsburgh. Platt was born in Wythe County in 1898 and was 11 years younger than Charlie. Uncle Platt was probably the catalyst that inspired Harry Kincannon to move from Northfork to Pittsburgh. It is reasonable to assume that Platt was aware of his nephew's baseball talents and encouraged the young man to try his luck at pitching for one of the numerous semipro teams in the booming Pittsburgh area. It is highly probable that before leaving McDowell County, Kincannon was also a pitcher for one of the many coal-company-sponsored baseball teams that flourished in West Virginia in the early 1900s. According to historian William E. Akin, the "majority of West Virginia natives who reached the major leagues … did their apprenticeship in coalfield ball."[11]

Another factor that may have played a role in Kincannon's relocation to Pittsburgh was a desire to avoid the life of a coal miner, a career that left his father with permanent disabilities including a deformed pelvis and the shortening of his right leg.[12] At the time there were few other employment options for African-American men in the coalfields. Kincannon's foray into professional baseball in the 1920s and '30s afforded him an opportunity to temporarily postpone working in the mines. He did, however, work for coal companies before and after his days as a baseball player, as did all three of his brothers.

One of the challenges in documenting Kincannon's baseball career is the variety of ways in which his name appeared in newspapers. His name, or something similar to it, first appeared in box scores for semipro independent leagues in the Pittsburgh area in 1928, when he was about 18 years old.[13] From the beginning to the end of his career, Kincannon's name appeared in a variety of abbreviated forms and misspellings. This is not surprising given that the name is nine letters long and that box-score column space was limited. One popular option to shorten "Kincannon" was to drop the first syllable and go with just Canon or Cannon. When his last name was abbreviated in box scores, it was sometimes given as a jumble of random letters including Kcan, Kincn, Kincnn, and Kncn, to name just a few.

Another option used by newspapers to identify Kincannon was to tag him with a nickname. Assigning nicknames to athletes is a long-standing tradition and his last name allowed for some creative appellations. The most frequently used nicknames for Kincannon were various riffs on "tin can" including Tincan, Tincannon, and Tincanner. During the 1920s, when he played in Pittsburgh area sandlot leagues, "tin can" was part of the popular and sportswriting vernacular. For example, there were the tin-can tourists, a term that referred to an emerging demographic of sightseers who chose to drive their tin-can cars (Tin Lizzies) and formed vacation communities of tin-canners.[14] "Tincan" was also used in sports lingo. In boxing, it was used to describe a fighter who was retreating around the ring to "tincan to safety."[15] In horse racing, a tincan horse was one that won with ease.[16]

The first use of the nickname Tincan for Kincannon appeared in 1929 in a *Pittsburgh Press* account of the Twenty-fifth Ward Traders' 14-4 defeat of the Rinkeydinks in which "Tincan pitched a wonderful game, striking out 12 batters."[17] Later that year, he was also called Tincup.[18] By 1931, Tincannon was the most frequently used nickname for Kincannon but it largely disappeared by the mid-1930s.[19] Then, in 1935, he was tagged as Roy Tincannon in a photo taken with fellow Crawfords pitcher Bertrum Hunter.[20] This was not the only time Kincannon was mistakenly referred to as Roy. The origin of this name confusion is unknown, but it may have resulted from a conflation of the names of two Crawfords pitchers, Harry Kincannon and Roy Williams.

The first time something close to the correct spelling of Kincannon's last name appeared in a Pittsburgh sports page occurred on May 29, 1929, when it was reported that "Kincanon" tossed a one-hitter for the Traders, and defeated the Clayton nine, 2-1.[21] While the victory was notable enough to gain a few column inches in the *Pittsburgh Courier*, it was his batterymate was even more significant: his future Pittsburgh Crawfords teammate Josh Gibson, who likely was filling in for the Traders' regular catcher.[22] Gibson's moonlighting gig with the Traders may have played a role in Kincannon joining the Pittsburgh Crawford Giants just a few months later.

Kincannon continued to enjoy success with the Traders in the summer of 1929, including a winning effort against the Rinkeydinks in which he struck out 12 batters.[23] But by August he left the Traders and joined the Pittsburgh Crawford Colored Giants. "Tincup" won his first outing for the Crawford Giants when he held the Homestead Aces to four hits and led his new team to an 8-1 victory.[24] Kincannon had another successful start for the Crawfords on September 9, 1929. The *Pittsburgh Post-Gazette* reported, "The Crawfords defeated the Stowe Civics last night by a 4-1 score at Ammon field with Tincan and Roscoe staging an interesting pitching battle."[25] Kincannon pitched for Crawford Colored Giants in 1931 and picked up a few starts for the Moon Run nine of the Colored Panhandle League.[26] Although he moonlighted with other teams, the Crawfords were his main focus and, as the team improved, the *Courier* touted them as the "Pittsburgh district's second ranking colored team," a direct comparison with the more accomplished Homestead Grays.[27]

# Pride of Smoketown

Gus Greenlee purchased the Crawford Colored Giants in 1931 and Kincannon was among the players who remained with the team under its new ownership. Despite rumors that the team was about to be disbanded, the Crawfords took the field for a difficult 1931 season.[28] Financial uncertainty, fueled by a lack of games and silent turnstiles, brought into question the team's survival. For example, one game played at Ammon Field at the end of May, netted the Crawfords just $6 after they paid $15 for baseballs, $24 to the umpires, and $50 to compensate the visiting team.[29] Kincannon's season with the Crawfords had as many ups and downs as did the team's finances. He had two rough outings in August, but ended the 1931 season on a high note with a sterling four-hit, 20-0 win over Coraopolis at Ammon Field.[30]

If 1931 ended with a sense of optimism for Kincannon, then 1932 started off on the wrong foot – literally. While engaged in spring training at Hot Springs, Arkansas, Kincannon injured an ankle and was reduced to the role of spectator and equipment manager as his teammates took to the practice field.[31] He recovered in time to rejoin his team for a barnstorming tour that took the Crawfords from Arkansas to points west before heading back to Pennsylvania for the regular season.[32] Kincannon regained his pitching form on the road and "his curves were the talk of Omaha."[33] On July 17, 1932, he tossed a four-hitter against the Spiderwebs of Jamestown, New York.[34] By August he was described as a "young curve ball shark."[35] At the end of the season, he had accumulated a respectable record of 15 wins and eight losses.[36]

The Crawfords started 1933 with much optimism and enthusiasm for the newly formed National Association of Negro Baseball Clubs, chaired by Greenlee.[37] Kincannon was still viewed as a "youngster" and "showed perhaps more promise than any other twirler produced in this district for some time."[38] *Courier* columnist Charles "Ches" Washington lauded Kincannon for his "rare assortment of curves and twisters" and work ethic, and predicted that "with a bit more of the seasoning which he received last year [Kincannon] looks like a real comer."[39] Kincannon failed to meet expectations and finished the year with a record of just two wins against five losses.[40]

The 1934 season turned out to be Kincannon's best year with the Crawfords, but it didn't start out that way. Spring training came to abrupt end for him when he was "struck in the vital section with a batted ball" and was "forced to return home for treatment."[41] He recovered and finished the season with six wins and four losses in Negro League play, and made his only appearance in an East-West All-Star Game.[42] In the competition for the most popular Crawfords pitcher that year, Kincannon received 2,877 endorsements in the East All-Star balloting, second only to Leroy "Satchel" Paige, who garnered 3,913 votes by fans.[43]

The Crawfords' 1935 championship season began, as it had the year before, with spring training in Hot Springs. This time, however, Kincannon avoided any unpleasant injuries. Hopes were justifiably high in May as manager Oscar Charleston tagged "curve-baller" Kincannon as one of his pitching aces.[44] He rewarded his skipper's confidence by helping to sweep a doubleheader from the Nashville Elite Giants in May.[45] But after his sharp start to the season, Kincannon was relegated mainly to relief work for the bulk of the summer. His lack of success on the hill was reflected by the paucity of votes generated by his fans for the 1935 East-West All-Star lineup. As of late July, in the early balloting for the West All-Stars, Kincannon had garnered just 13 votes.[46] By early August, Kincannon had just 426 votes, far behind Leroy Matlock, the most popular Crawfords pitcher in the competition, with 3,843.[47]

Kincannon's last start of the 1935 Crawfords' regular season took place on September 9, when they played the New York Cubans in Paterson, New Jersey, before 4,000 fans, the largest regular-season attendance of the year.[48] It was not pretty. The New Yorkers "solved the fancy curve ball of Kincannon" and rang him up for 14 hits in a 9-3 setback.[49] It should be noted that although this particular game between the Crawfords and Cubans was thought by some to be the first game of the 1935 Negro League World Series, it was not.[50] Newspaper reporting on the Series was unanimous – the first game of the series was played on September 13 at the Dyckman Oval in New York. Kincannon did not take the mound for the Crawfords in the championship series.[51] Three days later he was mentioned as a possible starter when the Crawfords played the House of David in Altoona, Pennsylvania, as the team made its way back to Pittsburgh to continue the series against the Cubans.[52] The Crawfords trimmed the bearded House of David nine by a tidy score of 14-4, but Kincannon's name did not appear in the box score and teammate Sam Streeter picked up the win.[53]

It is not known why Kincannon did not play in the 1935 Negro League Championship Series. His disappearance from the Crawfords' roster in the postseason is puzzling. That same year he also failed to make the roster for the North-South game played in Memphis, Tennessee, in late September.[54] There were no reports that Kincannon was injured so it may have been simply a matter of his declining effectiveness. His lack of playing after early September could have been an indication of physical or off-field problems – or both.

Kincannon returned to the Crawfords' lineup in 1936. He was one of eight hurlers on the roster and had another uneven year.[55] His first start in a league game ended in a 5-0 loss to the Philadelphia Stars.[56] Four days later, he redeemed himself in a 12-4 rout of the House of David in Camden, New Jersey.[57] Kincannon was at the top of his game in early June when he led the Crawfords to a 9-4 victory over the Philadelphia Stars at Felton Field in Chester, Pennsylvania.[58] One of his best outings of 1936 season came on August 12, when his "fast balls and hooks" limited the Poughkeepsie All Stars to five hits and propelled the Crawfords to a 5-1 victory.[59] Kincannon also had a nifty 3-2 win at home against the local Dormont-Mt. Lebanon nine on August 28, but as with his triumph over Poughkeepsie, it was not against a Negro National League team.[60] By the end of August, Kincannon again was mainly relegated to relief duties. Increasingly, he walked more batters than he struck out. He was struggling with his control and his much-vaunted curveball was flattening out. During a game against the Washington Elite Giants in mid-August, in three innings of relief, Kincannon gave up five hits, walked one batter, and hit two batters.[61]

When the baseball season fired up in the spring of 1937, Kincannon found himself in an unusual situation. For the first time since he left West Virginia, he was not playing for a Pittsburgh-based team. His exit from western Pennsylvania was even the subject of a trivia question that appeared in the *Courier*:

"*Q. What twirler seems to have the widest-breaking curve ball?*

*A. Harry Kincannon, formerly of the Crawfords, now with the Grays.*"[62]

Actually, instead of a "trick question," the *Courier* provided its readers with a trick *answer*. Kincannon was not traded by the Craws to the Grays – he was acquired by the New York Black Yankees for the 1937 season. In fact, there are no records to indicate that Kincannon played for the Homestead Grays during his time in Pittsburgh.

Kincannon made a good first impression on the New York fans at the start of the 1937 season. He won one of his early outings for the Black Yankees by demonstrating his "speed artist" skills and by launching a triple of his own to drive in the winning run.[63] He followed up with a 5-4 victory in May against the Newark Eagles at Dexter Park in Queens, New York.[64] A few weeks later, however, he issued seven walks against three strikeouts in a loss to the Homestead Grays.[65] One game summary noted that his pitching against the Grays was especially "wild."[66] Things were no better in early July when Kincannon, working as the starter, was "pummeled" in a 14-3 loss to the Newark Eagles.[67] Kincannon's misfortunes continued in late July when his former team, the Crawfords, handed his Black Yankees a 15-8 loss in what was described as "one of the wildest and wooliest baseball games of the season.[68] At the end of the Black Yankees' season, Kincannon finished with a record of two wins and two losses in official Negro National League play.[69]

Kincannon began the 1938 season with a new team, the Washington Black Senators, a member of the Negro National League for just one year. They won only two of 21 official league games and finished 1938 in the basement with a dismal .095 winning percentage.[70] Washington also played the fewest games of all the Negro National League teams in 1938 and is considered to be one of the worst squads in Negro League history.[71] As a reflection of his minimal success on the mound and his team's dismal performance, Kincannon garnered a meager 214 votes in the 1938 East-West All-Star balloting.[72] His record for the entire season was one win and one loss, which doesn't sound impressive until one realizes that he was responsible for 50 percent of his team's victories. His year in Washington had its upsides and downsides: He had the worst ERA of his career, a beefy 5.75 in 20⅓ innings, but he batted an impressive .308, the highest BA of his Negro League career.[73]

After the Black Senators folded in August, Kincannon found a spot on the roster of the 1938 Atlantic City Bacharachs. The team was organized in 1916 as the Atlantic City Bacharach Giants from the remnants of the Duval Giants of Jacksonville, Florida.[74] They were a dominant African-American nine through the 1920s and briefly joined the Negro National League in late 1934 before devolving into an ad-hoc semipro outfit.[75] By the time they signed Kincannon, they were in a steep decline and four years away from being disbanded. Kincannon's brief association with the Bacharachs contributed little to his baseball résumé other than yet another variation on his first name. Describing a coming game against the semipro Brooklyn Bay Parkways, the sportswriter identified him as "Jack Kincannon, ex-Pittsburgh Crawford."[76]

Kincannon began 1939 with a new-old team, the Toledo Crawfords, and with another version of his name – "Dick Kincannon."[77] He signed on with what turned out to be the next to last incarnation of the Crawfords. The 1939 Toledo Crawfords started the year as members of the Negro National League but switched to the Negro American League in midseason. These Crawfords did have some faces familiar to Kincannon including manager Oscar Charleston, Spoon Carter, Jimmie Crutchfield, Bill Harvey, and Leroy Morney, but there weren't many high points for Kincannon or the Toledo Crawfords in 1939. They played fewer than 20 official league games, and spent most of the season barnstorming against local semipro and/or amateur nines.

After the season, Kincannon headed back home to West Virginia. His professional career was over, but he did not stop playing baseball. After the "Crawfords hit a financial skid and disbanded," Kincannon signed to play with the local semipro Slab Fork Indians, a team originally sponsored by a Raleigh County coal company.[78] He also worked in the coal mines in the Slab Fork community. By the time Kincannon arrived in Slab Fork, however, the golden era of company-sponsored baseball teams was over. Gone were the days when coal companies would "hire" a miner for his baseball skills rather than his potential to actually mine coal.[79] During the 1920s, professional nines regularly barnstormed throughout southern West Virginia, broadening their fan bases as well as scouting local talent. The Homestead Grays and other Negro League teams, including the Pittsburgh Crawfords, made regular stops in the region, crossing bats not only with African-American teams, but also with all-white squads.[80] It is possible that Kincannon interacted with some of these teams before moving to Pittsburgh and may help to explain how he got his start with the Crawfords.

Kincannon and the Slab Fork Indians played in the Tri-County Negro League in the coalfields of southern West Virginia. He was with the team off and on throughout the 1940s. In the summer of 1940 Kincannon enjoyed early successes with victories against other teams with coal company legacies, including the Winding Gulf Tigers and the New River Giants. He led his team to the Tri-County championship and was selected to play in an "All Star" game in which the region's top African-American players were pitted against the best players from the area's white teams. Kincannon played in these and other interracial contests throughout his career. Although one might assume these games were organized to exploit racial conflict, that was not necessarily the case. One former African-American baseball player who played in local coalfield leagues said that from his perspective, in games between blacks and whites, there were "no racial tensions. … We just played ball."[81] On October 16, 1940, just weeks after closing out his first season for the Slab Fork Indians, Kincannon registered for the US Army draft. In his draft documents, he was described as a 30-year-old unmarried and unemployed African-American man with gray eyes and black hair, standing 5-feet-11½, and weighing 172 pounds.[82]

Kincannon enjoyed his star turn as a pitcher for the Slab Fork Indians. Local newspapers frequently touted his professional baseball pedigree and noted that he was a "capable pitcher … and an especially consistent hitter."[83] In 1942 Kincannon also added "player-manager" to his baseball résumé.[84] While he was multitasking for Slab Fork, he also freelanced as a pitcher for other teams, including one of their main rivals, the Raleigh Clippers, who were the West Virginia Negro League champions in 1942.[85] Kincannon continued his fluid team allegiances through the early 1940s when many coalfield nines found themselves with thin rosters because of players lost to the military during World War II.[86] He did help the Clippers win the league championship in 1943, although his effectiveness was somewhat diminished after he was spiked in the right hand in early August.[87]

Kincannon came back strong for the Clippers in in the summer of 1944. The press described him as a "rubber-armed right-hander with a fast ball which comes down the alley looking like an aspirin tablet."[88] That year he was joined on the field by his younger brother Charles Kincannon Jr.[89] Charlie Jr. did some pitching but was better known as an outfielder. That year the brothers helped the Clippers repeat as league champions. The final game of 1944 for Harry was an exhibition tilt between the Clippers and a team of all-white "All-Stars" led by Johnny Gorsica, a pitcher for the Detroit Tigers.[90] Gorsica's All-Stars defeated the Clippers, 8-5, with Kincannon striking out seven and walking five batters in the losing effort.[91] Also on the field for the All-Stars was Harry Perkowski, a 22-year-old local favorite, who was two years away from being signed by the Cincinnati Reds.[92] The game was played at R.M.I. Field, a diamond that served as the focal point for coalfield baseball for decades.[93] But in a nod to declines in financial and fan support for local semipro baseball, each player on both teams was required to "bring his own bat."[94]

By 1945 it was apparent that Harry Kincannon was in the twilight of his pitching career. Even though he was spending more of his time as a skipper than as a star hurler, his services were still in demand. Early in the season, he forsook his Raleigh Clippers to sign as player-manager of the newly formed Beckley Indians.[95] Through the 1945 season, Kincannon split his time between the Clippers and the Indians. He had flashes of brilliance and at times his curveball was "breaking fast and his speedball [was] in there like a bullet."[96] Kincannon ended the year with the Clippers that relinquished their long-held title as the "Negro League" champions of West Virginia. The Clippers were plagued by bad weather and the lack of a home field. The league organization itself was falling apart and games were more likely to be scheduled on an ad-hoc basis.

Both Harry and Charlie Kincannon were on the field for the Clippers in 1946 – in the few games that were actually played. Coverage of Clippers games during the 1946 season was sparse at best, and fraught with omissions and errors at worst. But then again, Kincannon's season was nothing worthy of the record books. Harry supplemented his infrequent time on the mound with the Clippers with an occasional start for the rival Beckley Indians and the Mullens (West Virginia) Red Sox.[97] Charlie's participation with the Clippers may have been diminished by injuries he sustained during an altercation at a bar near Beckley in which he was stabbed in the head, back, and ribs.[98] (Another brother, Ray Kincannon, was also injured in the fray.[99]) But there was one bright spot in Harry's life that year involving a diamond, but happening off the field. In 1946 he married Dorothy Josephine Robertson in McDowell County. They remained married until his death in 1965, and together they raised five children.

Kincannon spent the summer of 1947 on the hill for the Clippers, with his brother Charlie doing his usual gardening in the outfield. That summer Kincannon tossed one of his finest games when he and the Clippers shut out the Gary (West Virginia) Miners, 2-0.[100] The victory was vintage Kincannon and his arm must have felt 10 years younger that day. He pitched a complete game, struck out nine, and walked just one batter.[101] The irony of this game was that Kincannon was not supposed to be the starting pitcher that day. That role was designated for Harold Hairston, but the "former Homestead Grays pitcher, didn't show up as expected to hurl for the Clippers ... but as it turned out he wasn't needed and Harry Kincannon, old standby of the Clipper mound staff, turned in a seven-hit shutout."[102] Hairston, like Kincannon, was a West Virginia native. He played for the Clippers before signing with the Homestead Grays, and was under contract with the Grays for the 1947 season.[103]

Kincannon signed up for the Slab Fork Indians in 1948. The only game in which he played that was reported in a local newspaper was a contest between the Slab Fork Indians and the Glen Rogers (West Virginia) Red Sox which "the Indians won 1 to 0 behind Kincannon."[104] Although no first name for the pitcher was provided, it is very likely that Slab Fork's starter that day was Harry Kincannon and not his brother, because in 1948 Charlie played for Glen Rogers.[105]

Harry and Charlie Kincannon were back with the Clippers in 1949 and things were looking up.[106] The Clippers had just built a new ballpark in Stanaford, four miles northeast of Beckley, and mapped out a schedule to include "top notch Negro teams ... as well as independent teams, white and colored."[107] The roster included 15 men who "worked in or around the mines" and all of whom, including Harry, were called upon to help with the construction of the new field.[108] The Clippers' booking manager, Grover Lewis, proclaimed that "the stage is set for Negro baseball to be bigger and better than before."[109] Throughout the season, Kincannon was used as a starter and in relief. In May he pitched an eight-hit shutout against the Hemphill (West Virginia) V-8's, striking out nine, and he hit a solo home run to lift the Clippers to a 4-0 win at their new home ballpark.[110] In June he pitched three scoreless innings in relief in a lopsided loss to the Homestead Grays.[111] Playing second base for the Grays that day was Josh Gibson Jr., son of the late Josh Gibson, one of Harry's former Crawfords teammates.[112] But the more things changed, the more they stayed the same – Kincannon's first name was incorrectly reported in local newspapers as Harold or Hal, a mistake that was repeated in future coverage.[113]

In the summer of 1949, at the advanced age of 40, Kincannon was still in command of the mound. By mid-July, he had a 3-0 record as a starting pitcher for the Clippers. The *Beckley*

# THE 1935 PITTSBURGH CRAWFORDS

*Post-Herald* proclaimed that Kincannon "has pitched a lot of fine ball games in his career, but other efforts were overshadowed by the stuff he produced yesterday at Clipper field," as it reported on his four-hitter against the Glen Rogers Red Sox.[114] In July Harry's role with the Clippers expanded to player-manager.[115] All in all, 1949 was not a bad year for the veteran hurler. He had one of his most successful post-Negro League seasons and for the first time in several years helped the Raleigh Clippers reclaim the "Negro championship of Southern West Virginia."[116] But despite his late surge, when the 1949 season came to a close, Kincannon's days as a starting pitcher for any team in any league were over.

In 1950 Kincannon served mainly as the Clippers' manager and made only sporadic appearances as a reliever. He admitted that despite having "performed creditably on the mound for the Clippers last season … that his days as an active player are nearing the finish."[117] He didn't "have the old zip on his fastball," but he could still come in as a reliever and "fool a lot of the present day hitters who swing from their heels."[118] His brother Charlie was the only Kincannon to see regular play for the Raleigh squad. Even though the Clippers took the championship title again that year, the highlight of the season was an exhibition game played in July between the Clippers and the Homestead Grays. Kincannon's former Crawfords teammate Satchel Paige was slated to start for the Clippers. Paige was touring the country as a "freelance" pitcher.[119] The spectacle was held at Watt Powell Park in Charleston, West Virginia, and was organized to benefit the city's recreation programs.[120] It was promoted as a reunion for Kincannon and Paige, who were roommates during their time with the Crawfords and "developed a strong friendship that lasted through the years."[121] If only Kincannon's team had been as reliable as his relationship with Paige. The Clippers were thrashed by the Grays, 11-1, thanks in part to the four errors committed by the Clippers during Paige's three-inning cameo on the

*Harry Kincannon, who became a West Virginia coal miner after his professional baseball pitching career ended, is pictured here in spring training with the 1935 Pittsburgh Crawfords in Hot Springs, Arkansas.*

(Courtesy of Robert D. Retort Enterprises)

mound.[122] No box score for the game was reported so it is unknown if either of the Kincannon brothers took the field.

For the last home game of the 1950 season, the Clippers slipped by the Eccles Admirals, an all-white team, 3-2.[123] Harry stayed in the dugout as the Clippers' manager while his brother Charlie was in his usual position in center field. And for this game, Kincannon had the hot corner covered by Sonny Watts of Beckley, a former Clippers star who had just finished his duties for the Birmingham Black Barons.[124] The victory may have been especially satisfying for Kincannon because the Admirals' starter, Harry Perkowski, who grew up in Eccles and later called Beckley his home, was now a pitcher for the Cincinnati Reds.[125]

Kincannon rejoined the Clippers bullpen in June for the 1951 season and ceded his managerial duties to Grover Lewis.[126] The year started on a cautiously optimistic note with Kincannon expected to draw on his professional pedigree to boost the team's image and bottom line. In the press, Kincannon was described as "a mound luminary in Negro baseball," who was "with the Pittsburgh Crawfords when Satch Paige came up as a rookie," and would be "used in relief roles until he gets in mid-season condition."[127] Kincannon did not, however, get into "condition" and made only infrequent appearances in relief during a mediocre year for the Clippers.

The 1952 baseball season began with the news that Kincannon was having recruiting problems. He found himself competing with the requirement that men between 18 and 26 register for the military draft.[128] Unfortunately for baseball rosters at every level, the US Army sought the same demographic for the Korean War effort as did baseball teams. In early April, in his call for tryouts, Kincannon lamented that "there is plenty of room for newcomers as age and the Selective Service draft have nullified the eligibility of many 1951 Clippers regulars."[129] By this time Kincannon was 42, which was too old for the Army. He did manage to cobble together a ragtag nine, but to no avail. By the end of August, the Clippers had accumulated a dismal record of five wins and 11 losses, and Kincannon retired from baseball.[130]

After 1952, Kincannon no longer played for the Clippers or any other competitive team in West Virginia. His brother Charlie, who for so many years had been with him on the ballfield, left the Beckley area and moved to Columbus, Ohio. Kincannon set his glove aside, put on his hard hat, and turned his full-time attention back to his family and to working in the mines. The 1950s and 1960s were difficult times for Harry's family. His life was disrupted by grief in 1955 when his father, Charles Kincannon Sr., died in Beckley at age 68. Three years later his mother died in Montgomery, West Virginia. Then, in the early 1960s, while working in a coal mine, Kincannon was seriously injured when a coal tram car ran over his foot twice and left him with a permanent disability.[131]

On October 21, 1965, Harry Kincannon died from pneumonia at age 56, three days after being admitted to the Beckley-Appalachian Regional Hospital. In his obituary, Kincannon was described only as a "retired miner," and there was no mention of his accomplishments in professional and amateur baseball.[132] His death certificate incorrectly states his age as 55, when in fact he had celebrated his 56th birthday a few months before his death. Also, it gave Kincannon's occupation as laborer under Aid to Dependent Children of the Unemployed, a work program developed as part of the federal War on Poverty program. Kincannon's qualification for the ADCU implied that he and his family had fallen on hard times and were living below the poverty line. Around the time he died, the average monthly wage for ADCU-employed men with five children was $211.[133]

Kincannon's wife, Dorothy Jones Smith, died in 1985. She was buried alongside Harry in the Greenwood Memorial Park cemetery in East Beckley. One of Harry's other survivors, his uncle Platt, the man who played a role in Kincannon's entry into the Pittsburgh baseball scene, died there in 1983. It is an appropriate coincidence that Platt is buried in the same Pittsburgh cemetery as August Wilson, the author of the Tony Award-winning play *Fences*, which is set in Pittsburgh in the 1950s and is centered on the themes of family tensions, racial prejudice, and baseball.[134] In some ways Kincannon had his own "fences" to conquer. He faced many racial barriers in his life, but was able to partially navigate around those Jim Crow-era impediments due to his mixed-race background, athletic prowess, and winning personality. He played with and against white players and white teams throughout his decades-long baseball career. Kincannon also found a way to stave off the ultimate obstacle – the limited lifespan of an athlete – and enjoyed success on the baseball diamond after age 40, years after many of his contemporaries had hung up their spikes. There was little he could do, however, to overcome crushing poverty in the coalfields, racism, and limits to his life after his playing days in the Negro Leagues were over, but he persisted and left a lasting mark on the Negro National Leagues as well as African American baseball in West Virginia.

## Sources

Seamheads.com was used for all Negro League statistics/team records.

## Acknowledgment

The author is deeply indebted to the family of Harry Kincannon Sr., especially Harry Kincannon Jr., Toni Lynn Kincannon, and Troy Thomas Robertson, who generously shared their memories with the author.

## Notes

1. US Selective Service, *Registrar's Report*, October 16, 1940.
2. Bureau of the Census, *Statistics for West Virginia* (Washington: Government Printing Office, 1913), 581.
3. William E. Akin, "West Virginia Coalfield Baseball, 1921-1941," in John B. Wiseman, ed., *Joy in Mudville: Essays on Baseball and American Life* (Jefferson, North Carolina: McFarland, 2009), 102.
4. West Virginia Department of Transportation, Official State Highway Map (Charleston: West Virginia Division of Highways, 2014).
5. US Census Bureau, *1910 Census of Population*.
6. US Army Selective Service Registration Card, World War II, October 16, 1940.
7. Personal correspondence with Harry Kincannon Jr., 2019.
8. Personal correspondence with Harry Kincannon Jr., 2019.
9. James A. Riley *The Biographical Encyclopedia of the Negro Baseball Leagues* (New York: Carroll & Graf Publishers, 1994), 464; Personal conversation with Harry Kincannon Jr., January 2020.
10. US Census Bureau, *1920 Census of Population*.
11. Akin, 98.
12. West Virginia Supreme Court of Appeals, "Proceeding Under the Workmen's Compensation Act by Charles Kincannon," February 10, 1930.
13. "Two More Victories Recorded for the Grays," *Pittsburgh Post-Gazette*, June 11, 1929: 19.
14. Kenneth L. Roberts, "The Sun-Hunters," *Saturday Evening Post*, April 15, 1922: 27, 55.
15. "Cedar-DeMarco Go Friday Should Be Genuine Thriller," *Pittsburgh Press*, February 18, 1929: 17.
16. "Slang of the Race Track," *Daily Racing Form* (Chicago), October 17, 1924: 17.
17. "Stop Rinkeydinks," *Pittsburgh Press*, June 12, 1929: 37.
18. "Crawfords Victor," *Pittsburgh Post-Gazette*, August 28, 1929: 21.
19. "May Start," *Pittsburgh Courier*, April 25, 1931: 15.
20. "Two Stellar Young Crawfords Hurlers," *Pittsburgh Courier*, May 4, 1935: 14.
21. "Kincanon Holds Clayton," *Pittsburgh Courier*, June 1, 1929: 16.
22. "Kincanon Holds Clayton."
23. "Stop Rinkeydinks."
24. "Crawfords Victor," *Pittsburgh Post-Gazette*, August 28, 1929: 21.
25. "Crawfords Win," *Pittsburgh Post-Gazette*, September 10, 1929: 21.
26. "Panhandle League," *National Labor Tribune* (Pittsburgh), June 9, 1930: 8.
27. "Crawford Giants of 1930 to Be Strong Aggregation," *Pittsburgh Courier*, February 22, 1930: 15.
28. "Crawfords to Have Strong Team," *Pittsburgh Courier*, March 28, 1931: 15.
29. C.E. Pendleton, "Public's Non-Support Makes Crawford's [sic] Future Dubious," *Pittsburgh Courier*, June 6, 1931: 14.
30. "Crawfords Easy Winner," *Pittsburgh Press*, August 30, 1931: 43.
31. "John L. Clark's Breezes from Arkansaw [sic]," *Atlanta Daily World*, March 20, 1932: 5.
32. "Crawfords Go to Texas from Spa," *Pittsburgh Courier*, April 2, 1932: 15.
33. "Crawfords Back, Set for Test," *Pittsburgh Courier*, April 30, 1932: 15.
34. "O.K. Kincannon," *Pittsburgh Courier*, July 23, 1932: 14.
35. "Rouseville Games with Crawfords Holds Interest," *News-Herald* (Franklin, Pennsylvania), August 26, 1932: 8.
36. Chester L. Washington Jr., "Sez Ches, New Ball League Clearing Decks for Action," *Pittsburgh Courier*, January 28, 1933: 13.
37. Washington.
38. Washington.
39. Washington.

40  Seamheads.com, "Harry Kincannon," seamheads.com/NegroLgs/player.php?playerID=kinca01har.

41  John L. Clark, "Wylie Avenue," *Pittsburgh Courier*, May 5, 1934: 6.

42  Seamheads.com, "Harry Kincannon," accessed online, seamheads.com/NegroLgs/player.php?playerID=kinca01har.

43  "Voting for East-West All Stars," *Pittsburgh Courier*, August 18, 1934: 15.

44  Paul Kurtz, "Negro Baseball Loop Ready to Play Ball," *Pittsburgh Press*, May 2, 1935: 33.

45  "Crawfords Win Two," *Pittsburgh Post-Gazette*, May 8, 1935: 20.

46  "How They Voted in the East-West Poll," *Pittsburgh Courier*, July 13, 1935: 15.

47  "Shifts Seen in Leaders as E-W Game Vote Spurts," *Pittsburgh Courier*, August 3, 1935: 14.

48  "Cubans Defeat Crawfords in Negro League National League Game," *Morning Call* (Paterson, New Jersey), September 9, 1935: 19.

49  "Cubans Defeat Crawfords in Negro League National League Game."

50  John B. Holway, *The Complete Book of Baseball's Negro Leagues* (Fern Park, Florida: Hastings House, 1998), 320.

51  seamheads.com/NegroLgs/team.php?yearID=1935&teamID=P-C&LGOrd=2&tab=pit.

52  Os Figard, "Colored Loop Title Seekers Battle Beards in Exhibition," *Altoona* (Pennsylvania) *Tribune*, September 16, 1935: 9.

53  "Crawfords Hand Beards 14-4 Lancing," *Altoona Tribune*, September 17, 1935: 6.

54  "Memphis Awaits the Big Tilt," *Pittsburgh Courier*, September 28, 1935: 14.

55  Paul Kurtz, "Exhibition Series Set for Champs," *Pittsburgh Press*, May 5, 1936: 29.

56  "Crawfords Blanked," *Pittsburgh Post-Gazette*, May 27, 1936: 21.

57  "Crawfords Ahead," *Pittsburgh Post-Gazette*, May 30, 1936: 15.

58  "Boldens Bow to Crawfords Here," *Delaware County Daily Times* (Chester, Pennsylvania), June 2, 1936: 10.

59  Drew Middleton, "Crawfords Defeat All Stars, 5 to 1, Behind Kincannon," *Poughkeepsie* (New York) *Eagle-News*, August 13, 1936: 8.

60  "Victory for Crawfords," *Pittsburgh Post-Gazette*, August 29, 1936: 15.

61  "Crawfords, Giants Battle to Draw," *Pittsburgh Sun-Telegraph*, August 16, 1936: 18.

62  Chester L. Washington Jr., "Sez Ches," *Pittsburgh Courier*, April 24, 1937: 16.

63  "The Sport Dial," *New York Age*, May 21, 1937: 8.

64  "Black Yankees Bow, 12-0; Win 5-4," *New York Daily News*, June 1, 1937: 64.

65  "Homestead Grays Beat Yanks, 6-2," *Pittsburgh Press*, June 20, 1937: 22.

66  "Homestead Grays Triumph Over the Black Yankees," *Paterson Morning Call*, June 21, 1937: 18.

67  "Eagles Beat Black Yankees Here by 14-3 Count," *Paterson News*, July 6, 1937: 47.

68  "Pittsburgh Crawfords Win in Game with Black Yankees," *Paterson Morning Call*, July 26, 1937: 18.

69  Seamheads.com, "Harry Kincannon," seamheads.com/NegroLgs/player.php?playerID=kinca01har.

70  Seamheads.com, "1937 Season," accessed online, seamheads.com/NegroLgs/year.php?yearID=1938.

71  Riley, 820.

72  "Thousands Vote as East-West Interest Mounts," *Pittsburgh Courier*, August 6, 1938: 16.

73  Seamheads.com, "Harry Kincannon, Batting," seamheads.com/NegroLgs/player.php?playerID=kinca01har&tab=bat.

74  James E. Overmyer, *Black Ball and the Boardwalk: The Bacharach Giants of Atlantic City, 1916-1929* (Jefferson, North Carolina: McFarland Publishers, 2018), 9.

75  Riley, 43.

76  "With the Semi-Pros," *Brooklyn Daily Eagle*, August 28, 1938: 33.

77  "Back [sic] Giants, 3-2; Play Two Today," *Chicago Tribune*, July 9, 1939: 27.

78  C.J. McQuade, "Needy's Notions," *Sunday Register* (Beckley, West Virginia), June 30, 1940: 10.

79  Akin, 100.

80  Akin, 102-103.

81  Akin, 105.

82  US Selective Service, *Registrar's Report*, October 16, 1940.

83  "Raleigh Clippers Meet Slab Fork Today," *Beckley Post-Herald*, July 4, 1942: 7.

84  "Slab Fork Has Perfect Record," *Beckley Post-Herald*, May 28, 1942: 6.

85  Roy Lee Harmon, "Speaking of Sports," *Beckley Post-Herald*, July 24, 1942: 10.

86  "Raleigh Clippers Beat Helen Team, 6 to 5," *Beckley Post-Herald*, May 3, 1943: 5.

87  Roy Lee Harmon, "Speaking of Sports," *Beckley Post-Herald*, August 10, 1943: 5.

# THE 1935 PITTSBURGH CRAWFORDS

88 "Clippers Will Meet Montcoal," *Beckley Post-Herald*, June 3, 1944: 5.

89 "Stars Beaten by Montcoal 6 to 4," *Beckley Post-Herald*, July 24, 1944: 5.

90 "Johnny Gorsica's All-Stars Face Raleigh Clippers Today," *Raleigh Register* (Beckley, West Virginia), October 15, 1944: 9.

91 Roy Lee Harmon, "Gorsica's Team Wins Contest," *Beckley Post-Herald*, October 16, 1944: 5.

92 Charles R. Lewis, "Perkowski Makes Hit with Cincy," *Beckley Post-Herald*, June 6, 1947: 10.

93 William E. Akin, 98.

94 "Johnny Gorsica's All-Stars Face Raleigh Clippers Today," *Raleigh Register*, October 15, 1944: 9.

95 "Indians Play Charleston," *Raleigh Register*, June 24, 1945: 6.

96 "Clippers and Indians Split," *Beckley Post-Herald*, July 4, 1945: 2.

97 "Negro Baseball Game at Ruby Field Today," *Raleigh Register*, June 2, 1946: 11.

98 "Knife Victim Reported Better," *Beckley Post-Herald*, January 21, 1946: 2.

99 "Knife Victim Reported Better."

100 "Clippers Humble Gary Miners, 2-0," *Beckley Post-Herald*, June 17, 1947: 5.

101 "Clippers Humble Gary Miners, 2-0."

102 "Clippers Shutout Gary Miners, 2-0," *Raleigh Register*, June 17, 1947: 6.

103 "Raleigh Clippers Play Jacksonville," *Charleston* (West Virginia) *Daily Mail*, June 28, 1947: 5.

104 "Sox, Indians Split," *Beckley Post-Herald*, August 23, 1948: 6.

105 "Red Sox Win Two," *Raleigh Register*, August 6, 1948: 8.

106 "Clippers Win Second in Row," *Raleigh Register*, May 9, 1949: 8.

107 "Ground Broken at Ball Park for Clippers," *Beckley Post-Herald*, March 22, 1949: 7.

108 "Ground Broken at Ball Park for Clippers."

109 "Raleigh Clippers Open Here Sunday," *Beckley Post-Herald*, April 29, 1949: 8.

110 "Clippers Get Shutout Win on Home Lot," *Beckley Post-Herald*, May 23, 1949: 6.

111 "Homestead Grays Clip Clippers, 11-3," *Raleigh Register*, June 27, 1949: 8.

112 "Homestead Grays Clip Clippers, 11-3."

113 "Clippers Lose 11-3 Contest to Homestead," *Beckley Post-Herald*, June 27, 1949: 8.

114 "Raleigh Clippers Shut Out Red Sox, 3-0," *Beckley Post-Herald*, June 29, 1949: 6.

115 "Clippers Top Virginians, Hosts to Gary," *Beckley Post-Herald*, July 4, 1949: 6.

116 "Perkowski to Hurl," *Beckley Post-Herald*, October 13, 1949: 12.

117 "Clippers Open Season with Bishop Outfit," *Beckley Post-Herald*, April 21, 1950: 12.

118 "A.L. Hardman, "Saturday Salad," *Charleston Gazette*, July 1, 1950: 5.

119 "Poor Support Hurts 'Satch' as Grays Win," *Charleston Gazette*, July 2, 1950: 16.

120 "Poor Support Hurts 'Satch' as Grays Win."

121 Hardman.

122 "Poor Support Hurts 'Satch' as Grays Win," *Charleston Gazette*, July 2, 1950: 16.

123 "Clippers Beat Admirals, 3-2," *Raleigh Register*, October 9, 1950: 6.

124 "Clippers-Admirals in Perkowski-Watts Day," *Raleigh Register*, October 8, 1950: 14.

125 "Clippers-Admirals in Perkowski-Watts Day."

126 "Clippers Play Black Cats Today," *Raleigh Register*, August 12, 1951: 6.

127 "Clippers Face Hemphill V-8 Here Sunday," *Beckley Post-Herald*, June 9, 1951: 6.

128 US Senate Committee on Armed Services, *Hearings Before the Preparedness Subcommittee on the Armed Services United States Senate Eighty-Second Congress First Session on S-1* (Washington: US Government Printing Office, 1951).

129 "Raleigh Clippers to Practice Today," *Beckley Post-Herald*, April 12, 1952: 6.

130 "Clippers Clash at Clipper Park," *Raleigh Register*, August 24, 1052: 11.

131 Personal conversation with Harry Kincannon Jr., January 2020.

132 "Harry Kincannon," *Raleigh Register*, October 21, 1965: 18.

133 US Congress Committee on Labor and Public Welfare, *Examination of the War on Poverty* (Washington: US Government Printing Office, 1967), 3066.

134 August Wilson, *Fences: With an Introduction by Lloyd Richards* (New York: Penguin/Random House, 1986).

# LEROY MATLOCK

## By Richard Bogovich

Fittingly, pitcher Leroy Matlock was called "the Black Carl Hubbell" in press releases promoting a 1937 barnstorming tour.[1] Hubbell, who entered the Hall of Fame in 1947, had completed a high-profile streak of 24 wins in a row earlier in 1937 for the pennant-winning New York Giants. Matlock, also a lefty, had 26 straight victories through early 1936, including an undefeated regular season for the Pittsburgh Crawfords in 1935.[2]

Leroy Matlock was born on March 12, 1907, in Moberly, Missouri,[3] to Pearl and Delia Matlock.[4] Delia already had two children, one named Clara and the other Otis Pitts.[5] By the 1920 census, Pearl's occupation was hod carrier, meaning he hauled either coal or bricks for a living.[6]

Before Leroy turned 13, he lost siblings repeatedly due to respiratory illnesses. In October 1910 his brother Alfred succumbed at the age of eight months. Four years later, Leroy's brother Lawrence was born and he lived well into adulthood. However, later in the decade, four more siblings died: In mid-1917, Clara, at the age of 17; their brother Hubert was 1½ when he died in March 1918; and, about a year later, Charles,

*Leroy Matlock was the ace of the 1935 Crawfords' pitching staff as he posted an 8-0 record and 1.52 ERA in NNL play and went 2-1 against the New York Cubans in the championship series.*

(Courtesy of Robert D. Retort Enterprises)

who was five weeks old. Lastly, in mid-1919 their 8-year-old brother Herman died.[7]

By the conclusion of this tragic span, the family at least had a support system close by, because they moved to the same block where Pearl's mother, Kate, owned a home for many years. The large family, headed by one of Leroy's great-uncles, Frank Matlock, also lived nearby.[8] The 1920 census indicated that Leroy attended school in the previous year.[9] That was Moberly's Lincoln School, which was for African-Americans only and combined elementary and high-school grades. According to the 1940 census, the eighth grade was the highest level that Leroy completed. Lawrence, who was seven years younger, graduated from high school in 1932.[10]

A racist incident in Moberly in late 1919 surely sent a shockwave through all the Lincoln school's families: A local mob tried to lynch four young African-American men, and though three escaped, the fourth was shot to death.[11] Moberly, which had a population of about 12,800, is in the "(north central) area of Missouri called little Dixie, because it was settled by migrants from the south before the Civil War," said best-selling author Malcolm Gladwell recently, adding, "There was a lot of slave owning in little Dixie compared with the rest of Missouri, a lot of racial hostility in that part of the state."[12] In early 1922, however, authorities were committed to preventing a similar outcome after a local white woman accused two young African-American men of burglary, in part by speaking positively of their character in newspaper articles despite arresting them. Also, when a mob did surge around the city jail, the local paper reported that "the entire police force worked to speed the two men to an unknown location via car." Authorities worked to clear the men in just three days. As a result, the police and newspapers immediately received praise for giving the suspects "the benefit of every reasonable doubt in protecting their lives," in a letter-to-the-editor by African-American minister W.B. Coleman, who lived across the street from the Matlocks and who would share a public moment with Leroy in 1931.[13]

The Matlock family was again immersed in sadness in April 1925 when Delia died at about 43. State death records indicate that the cause was heart disease. Leroy had turned 18 the previous month.

A turning point for Matlock as a ballplayer occurred by 1927: He and an older friend, Helbert Brown, recruited other young African-Americans to form the Moberly Eagles. Matlock was reportedly the winning pitcher in 27 of 32 games in their first season. Future East-West All-Star Jimmie Crutchfield became an Eagle in 1927, if not earlier.[14]

Matlock married Myra Etta Pulliam on May 20, 1927. She had an eight-year-old daughter, Delores Hill, from a previous marriage. In the 1930 census, the newlyweds and Delores were living with Myra's mother and stepfather. Leroy lived on that block for the rest of his years in Moberly.[15]

Details about Eagles games were sparse locally early on, but a friendly rivalry quickly developed with a white team in Browning, about 70 miles to the northwest. Matlock's pitching was praised more than once in the *Browning Leader-Record*'s lengthy accounts, such as in mid-1927 when it said he "had perfect control."[16] By mid-1928, Matlock's talent was forcing sportswriters regionally to pay attention, including to his batting; articles in Moberly that appeared two weeks apart each noted that he had produced three hits in the most recent game. His first headline may have been in early July, when he was borrowed by a team 35 miles to the south, the Columbia White Sox. A few weeks later a large ad in the Browning newspaper promoting a coming visit by the Eagles singled out Matlock.[17] In 1927-28 the Eagles reportedly lost just 11 games and won at least three times as many.[18]

When the Eagles opened the 1929 season in mid-April, Matlock was actually a member of the Columbia team, and 47-year-old newcomer

Bill Gatewood took over as Moberly's pitcher. By May 5 Matlock had rejoined the Eagles. With a game-winning hit from Crutchfield, Matlock earned a win against Jefferson City, 2-1. He struck out nine and was touched for only three hits.[19]

Matlock's return was temporary because Gatewood arranged a tryout with the St. Louis Stars of the Negro National League, and they signed Matlock as their seventh pitcher before the end of May. His new team featured future Hall of Famers Cool Papa Bell, Mule Suttles, and Willie Wells. During an interview in 1931, Matlock talked about his first game at length:

> You'd have thought I was poison, the way I was treated those first few weeks. To make it worse, I lost the very first game I pitched. Whenever I'd go sit down on the players bench, all the other fellows would get up and leave. They never spoke a word. While playing and at other times, the way they jeered and 'cussed out' the rookies was a caution. When I lost that first game and all the other players were treating me so bad, my wife got discouraged and wanted to come back to Moberly. But I said no, I was going to stay and make good. I wasn't going to leave until they made me. Well, I won the next game, and they kinda let up on the razzing, but I lost the next game and then they got just as bad.[20]

The *Moberly Monitor-Index* said Matlock's first game for St. Louis was a 17-3 complete-game win against the Cuban Stars on May 21, but the paper likely meant that it was his first start. He had pitched in a loss before that, which was presumably the debut he described in 1931 (assuming his teammates would not have tormented him for losing an exhibition game). On May 4, against the visiting Kansas City Monarchs, he relieved Roosevelt Davis with no outs in the second inning. The box score charged Davis with all four of the Monarchs' runs that inning and they never trailed, so Matlock was not the losing pitcher. Still, he may have allowed inherited runners to score and hurt his team further by giving up two runs in the fourth inning – the last frame he pitched – in a game that was ultimately decided by one run, 7-6. He more than made up for that mediocre performance in his start against the Cubans a week later, when he struck out eight, walked none, had a homer and two more hits, scored three runs, and stole a base. His hometown paper noted that his homer was "with two mates on bases."[21]

After his first three decisions, Matlock recalled winning four straight.[22] In the end, the Stars had the NNL's second-best record in 1929, though Matlock didn't pitch often. He returned to Moberly and the Eagles by mid-October, when he was dominant against a white team from the county to the north.[23]

About four weeks into the 1930 season, Matlock joined 4,000 fans to witness the first night game played in St. Louis, as the Monarchs brought their array of huge floodlights to town.[24] His personal high point may have been a 9-0 shutout of a new NNL team, the Nashville Elite Giants, on July 20.[25] In his second season he again was not used all that much, because the main change in the starting rotation was the addition of veteran pitcher Joe Strong.

St. Louis finished atop the NNL for the first half of 1930 and played the second-half titlist, the Detroit Stars, in a championship series. The most memorable moment for Matlock may have occurred in the second game on September 15. Strong started for St. Louis but yielded 10 runs over six innings, so Matlock finished the game. Not only was he effective on the mound, he also scored during a big rally in the seventh inning and, in the eighth, was the lead runner when St. Louis had the bases loaded with no outs and the potential tying run at bat. Suddenly, Detroit turned a line drive to third into a triple play, after which there was no more scoring.[26] Despite that demoralizing twist, St. Louis won the series, four games to three.[27]

## THE 1935 PITTSBURGH CRAWFORDS

Matlock continued to pitch with St. Louis in 1931. On August 4 the Stars played in Moberly, "before a record crowd," against the city's white team. "Just before play started Pitcher Matlock was presented with a leather traveling bag, the gift of Moberly friends," wrote the local newspaper. The aforementioned Rev. W.B. Coleman "made the presentation with a brief and very appropriate address." In action, the paper said, Matlock "proved himself a master slabman. Depending more on curves and a change of pace rather than burning speed, he pitched a careful, crafty and extremely effective game – so effective in fact that up to the ninth inning the local team had garnered but three singles on his delivery." The Stars prevailed, 12-1.[28] On September 3 the Stars visited Moberly again but played another NNL team, the Indianapolis ABCs. Matlock scattered nine hits and struck out nine batters as the Stars won, 6-1.[29]

The St. Louis Stars won both halves of the 1931 NNL season so there was no postseason championship series. Nevertheless, in early October they played home games of historical significance against a team of white major leaguers called Max Carey's All-Stars. St. Louis edged Carey's club, 10-8, on October 1, and Matlock started the game on October 2 against Bill Walker of the New York Giants, who had just won the National League's ERA title. The first four hitters Matlock faced were Lloyd Waner, Paul Waner, Babe Herman, and Bill Terry, all future Hall of Famers except Herman. They didn't score off Matlock until the sixth inning. In the meantime, Walker gave up seven runs in the first and 12 total in four innings. An obscure pitcher named Jess Doyle was then pressed into long relief. Matlock scored a run, had two hits, and was one of four Stars to homer that night. On his way to a complete-game victory before 5,000 fans, he scattered six hits and struck out seven. The final score was 18-1. Lloyd Waner had two of those hits and Terry, who scored his team's only run, had one.[30]

As far as is known, that was the final game ever played by the St. Louis Stars.[31] In the aforementioned interview, Matlock said they lost $14,000 during 1931 and did not re-form in 1932. He quickly received offers from the Homestead Grays and the Pittsburgh Crawford Giants. Though Matlock claimed a record of 19-1 during 1931, he still seemed "quiet, courteous and unassuming."[32] For at least the second consecutive offseason, he made extra money shining shoes at Moberly's White Palace Barber Shop. He modestly compared himself to the unlikely hero of the recent major-league World Series when he said, laughingly, "Like Pepper Martin, I played way over my head." The account of this conversation concluded with Matlock saying, "Do I like baseball? I'd rather play baseball than eat."[33]

In late March of 1932, Matlock's hometown paper said he had signed with Detroit of the new Negro East-West League. On April 2 he was scheduled to head for training camp in Parkersburg, West Virginia, and his wife was expected to join him at the start of the regular season. However, Detroit's first workout – which Matlock didn't attend – was about 75 miles to the south, in Charleston. Matlock had indeed been spending spring training in Parkersburg but with the Homestead Grays.[34]

According to early league statistics (which excluded runs), in Matlock's first 21 innings for the Homestead Grays, he started once and had a 2-0 record. He gave up 16 hits and 6 walks, which were offset by 12 strikeouts. Only nine other pitchers in the league had exceeded 10 strikeouts at that point. He was also among the league's batting leaders with a .444 average (4-for-9), including two doubles and four runs scored. Soon enough, he was in starting lineups at first base and in center field.[35]

After little more than a month, Matlock was squeezed out when the Detroit Wolves collapsed and the Grays absorbed them, thus overloading their roster. "The merging of the Wolves and Grays, two of the strongest teams in the circuit, will result in a wealth of baseball talent on the market for other clubs," wrote the *Chicago*

*Defender*. Matlock was among 13 players who were thus expected to "change uniforms," and by June 9 he was among seven players newly acquired by the Washington Pilots.[36]

One high point with his new team came on July 25, when he pitched in long relief against the Crawfords before more than 4,000 fans in Griffith Stadium during the first night game ever in the nation's capital. But the Great Depression had largely undercut the East-West League by that point, and the Pilots ceased to exist after 1932.[37]

In March 1933 the Crawfords expected Matlock to join them in Memphis for "a short training period."[38] He was indeed on Pittsburgh's Opening Day roster, and started their first official game in the new Negro National League as part of a doubleheader in Nashville on April 30. The Elite Giants led, 5-4, after five innings but Matlock held them scoreless the rest of the way as Pittsburgh scored three unanswered runs to win, 7-5.[39] On May 22 he pitched a gem against another NNL team, the Columbus Blue Birds, who managed just three hits in a 13-0 drubbing.[40] Over those early weeks, the Chicago American Giants faired just a little better and won the league's first-half title.[41]

Matlock had a particularly heartbreaking game against Chicago on July 24, in which he pitched all 15 innings. He gave up 14 hits and four walks but struck out 17 Giants. Chicago scored in only two innings, but Turkey Stearnes homered in both and the Crawfords lost, 4-3. "Never before has a twirler fought more brilliantly to stave off defeat before a home crowd," concluded the *Chicago Defender*.[42] Conversely, good news in August spoke to his overall success in 1933. In early voting for the first East-West All-Star Game, he was second only to teammate Satchel Paige among East pitchers. In the end, their totals slid to third and ninth, respectively, and Sam Streeter of the Crawfords won the right to start that historic contest.[43]

On September 30 the Crawfords and Nashville began a series to decide the second-half title, and Matlock drew the starting assignment at home. The contest was called after six innings on account of darkness, and the Crawfords prevailed, 4-3.[44] They soon won that series and then started the championship round against Chicago (the third franchise to complete the NNL schedule). After a Pittsburgh victory and tie, Chicago refused to play additional games in the East and thus forfeited the pennant to the Crawfords. Chicago had protested regular-season games against the Crawfords on several occasions, and at least once the two teams narrowly avoided a brawl.[45]

After the season Matlock figured in one of Judy Johnson's favorite stories (though when it has shown up in print, typically the time frame is vague).[46] At Cincinnati's Crosley Field on October 15, the Crawfords faced a team of white pros led by Jimmy Shevlin, a Cincinnati native who had played on the Reds in 1932 and 1934. At one point in the game, Leo Durocher reached third base and took a long leadoff. Time was called, and Johnson approached Matlock to warn, "If you don't watch out, that guy's gonna steal the cover right off the ball." He was confident Durocher heard the scolding. When Johnson returned to third, he muttered to Durocher, "Man, that's the dumbest pitcher we got." Johnson then whistled, which was a prearranged signal. Matlock threw a fastball and Durocher strayed farther toward home. Catcher Josh Gibson, while still in his crouch, fired the ball to Johnson as Durocher slid back to third. Durocher thought his foot beat the tag, so he barked after the umpire called him out, while Johnson laughed. "What the hell's so funny?" Durocher demanded, then realized he was standing on Johnson's foot and still hadn't touched the base itself. "He'd made a perfect hook slide right into my ankle," Johnson recalled.[47]

Matlock again spent the winter working for the White Palace Barber Shop. Around April 1, 1934, he and Jimmie Crutchfield left for spring training at New Orleans.[48] Matlock turned in another solid season in 1934 and finished 13th among East pitchers in all-star voting.[49] He won his final four decisions, and thus began his historic streak.[50] NNL secretary John L. Clark included two complete games by Matlock in a list of the season's closest contests: a 3-2 win over Philadelphia on May 30 and a 2-1 10-inning loss to Chicago on June 18.[51] Though the Crawfords had another very good season, Philadelphia and Chicago played in the postseason championship series.

In a game in southern Michigan on September 28, Matlock pitched for a white team, which was likely a first for him. On the previous day the Crawfords had lost a doubleheader to the Homestead Grays in Toledo, Ohio. For a semifinal game in a tournament about 60 miles to the northwest, a team from North Adams, Michigan, "imported a colored battery from Toledo" named Matlock and Gibson. The latter, presumably Josh, homered off a recent Toledo Mud Hen, Roy James. One of the first basemen for North Adams might have been the battery's manager, Oscar Charleston. Matlock hurled stifling shutout ball for eight innings but North Adams lost in 10.[52]

On October 21 Matlock and Crutchfield joined Moberly's Gatewood-Browns[53] to face a white team called the Salisbury-Dalton All-Stars. Matlock was opposite Chicago White Sox rookie hurler Vern Kennedy, who became a 20-game winner two years later. The two pitchers had actually squared off six years earlier, when Kennedy had played for the Browning nine. The visitors scored a run off Matlock in each of the first two innings, but he put his team on the board with a homer over the right-field fence in the bottom of the third, and Crutchfield tied the game in the seventh with a solo shot. Each team had two runs until the bottom of the 11th, when a "fluke" homer won it for Moberly and Matlock.[54] Earlier that year the ballpark itself had become a tribute to Matlock, Gatewood, and Crutchfield. The site had previously been called Collins' Park; however, in the wake of recent improvements at the site, someone came up with the clever idea of combining the second syllables of the trios' names to rename it Lockwood Field.[55]

For the 1935 season, superstar Satchel Paige jumped to a white semipro team in North Dakota, so pressure was on the pitchers remaining in the Crawfords' rotation.[56] Matlock pitched the second game of the regular season, which was the first game of a doubleheader, at home against the New York Cubans on May 12. He scattered five hits on the way to a 2-1 victory.[57] At home a week later, he pitched "brilliantly" during "a masterpiece" and was called "the Mighty Matlock" by the *Pittsburgh Courier* after hurling a four-hit shutout against the Chicago American Giants, 1-0.[58]

Numerous sources during and after the 1935 season indicated that Matlock was undefeated in league games, but he did lose the occasional (unofficial) exhibition game. After he lost on June 7 to the longtime semipro team the Bushwicks, one newspaper noted that "Matlock had been unbeaten this year in ten starts and was looked upon as invincible."[59] Nevertheless, the NNL secretary's office reported that on July 4 Matlock's record was 8-0.[60]

NNL data for the rest of July showed Matlock had only one start, which he completed and won, and pitched only 13 innings during that span.[61] One explanation is that on July 21, manager Charleston suspended Matlock, Davis, and Crutchfield indefinitely for "improper conduct off the playing field."[62] That didn't deter the *Courier* on July 27 from calling him "the super-man of the Crawford staff" whose "sterling" work had "caused Smoketown fans to forget Satchell[sic] and his 'fast ball.'"[63]

August brought better news, when Matlock finished second in all-star voting among West pitchers to Ray Brown of the Homestead Grays. As a result, on August 11 he was at Chicago's Comiskey Park, home of the White Sox. The game ended dramatically, after each side enjoyed four-run 10th innings before Suttles won it for the West with a three-run blast in the bottom of the 11th. Matlock's two innings of midgame toil were workmanlike. He retired the side in order in the sixth inning, after two defensive lapses led to a run for the East in his previous inning of work.⁶⁴ A week later Matlock and Brown squared off against each other in Cleveland, and each hurled a three-hitter as Pittsburgh prevailed, 1-0.⁶⁵

Several contemporaneous sources stated that Leroy Matlock finished the regular season in September still undefeated, and one specified that he went 15-0.⁶⁶ Much more recently, one scholar said his record was 18-0, while a prominent statistical website states it was 17-0. Whatever the most valid or correct total, Cool Papa Bell summed up Matlock's season nicely. "He didn't have great stuff, but he had outstanding control and the ability to spot his pitches," Bell recalled during an interview in 1984. "And nobody could scare him. In 1935, he just rolled past everybody."⁶⁷

That wasn't quite true during the championship series against the New York Cubans in September, because a sore arm kept Matlock from starting the first two games.⁶⁸ The Crawfords lost both, but in front of 7,000 fans in New York on September 15, Matlock shut out the Cubans, 3-0. Accounts of the two other games of the series in which he pitched are sketchy and inconsistent, but he apparently was the losing pitcher in the next game, on September 18, then won the sixth game in relief on September 20. The next day, the Crawfords completed their comeback to win the series and the pennant.⁶⁹

Matlock kept busy after September. On October 9 he started against a local team in Dayton, Ohio, that borrowed Dizzy Dean; after two innings, Dean was replaced on the mound by two other St. Louis Cardinals, Jim Winford and Mike Ryba. Matlock hit a two-run homer to left off Ryba in the fifth inning.⁷⁰ Four days later, before 20,000 fans at Yankee Stadium, Dean pitched the first game of a doubleheader between major leaguers and NNL players, but in the five-inning second game Matlock was opposite Bill Swift of the Pittsburgh Pirates and then Winford again, while Bob Garbark of the Cleveland Indians served as their catcher. Jimmy Ripple, a star of the 1936 World Series for the New York Giants, drove in the game's only run.⁷¹

On October 25 Matlock and the Crawfords faced a tougher major-league lineup in Mexico City, which was led by Jimmie Foxx and Rogers Hornsby. Matlock was lifted for a pinch-hitter in the middle of a ninth-inning rally and it ended with the Crawfords leading, 6-4. Foxx, however, homered with a man on in the bottom of that frame to tie the score, and the game ended that way after 11 innings.⁷²

Matlock and the Crawfords began the 1936 season by pounding the New York Cubans, 19-6, on May 9 in Paterson, New Jersey.⁷³ A week later, against the Philadelphia Stars, he was bailed out by a ninth-inning rally but apparently did not complete the game and was not the winning pitcher.⁷⁴ He did win at least two more games that month: On May 23 he hurled a complete game against the Washington Elite Giants and won, 3-1, and the next day, he was the winning pitcher in relief against the same team in an 11-inning contest that ended with a 10-8 score.⁷⁵

On May 30 Matlock started the first game of a doubleheader in Philadelphia, but the Crawfords also used two relievers. The Crawfords led after seven innings but the Stars won after putting up a five-run eighth inning. From an available box score, it is unclear who the losing pitcher was; for such reasons, it is difficult to determine with confidence when Matlock's winning streak ended in 1936. In June he also started games that he did not finish in at least two other losses.⁷⁶ In between those two games, he hurled a complete-game win on the road against the Newark Eagles; he had also been the starting pitcher roughly one week earlier in a home victory over Newark.⁷⁷

On August 8 Matlock and the Crawfords edged the New York Cubans, 4-3, at Paterson. At home on August 29 he defeated the Philadelphia Stars, and on September 12 he beat the Newark Eagles, 11-5.⁷⁸ The Crawfords surged to win the second half of the NNL season comfortably, and Matlock definitely contributed.⁷⁹ In the midst of that action, Matlock started the East-West All-Star Game before at least 24,000 fans in Comiskey Park on August 23. This time he was on the East squad, and he pitched three scoreless innings as the East won, 10-2. The *Chicago Defender* credited Matlock with being the winning pitcher.[80]

A few weeks later Matlock faced a powerful lineup drawn from several major-league teams. It was led by Hornsby and another Hall-of-Famer, Johnny Mize, and featured three other recent or future All-Stars in Harlond Clift, Gus Suhr, and Ival Goodman. They played a five-game series in Iowa and Colorado against a team of NNL All-Stars, and Matlock's start was on October 2 in Des Moines, Iowa, before 3,500 to 4,000 fans. Matlock gave up just four hits and the NNL nine won, 5-2. He saved another game with a scoreless frame, and in his 10 innings he struck out nine of Hornsby's players.[81]

In November Newark Eagles co-owner Abe Manley persuaded Matlock to play winter ball in Puerto Rico with several of the Eagles, including third baseman Ray Dandridge. Manley reportedly recruited several other Crawfords, including Paige, Gibson, and Crutchfield. According to passenger lists, Matlock reached San Juan on November 23, and departed the island on February 11 to return to New York.[82] In March at least three of those Crawfords – Gibson, Paige, and Matlock – were said to be holding out for higher pay. Crawfords owner Gus Greenlee accused Homestead Grays owner Cum Posey of trying to sign the holdouts.[83]

Posey did acquire Gibson for 1937, but Matlock remained with the Crawfords. His start on May 9, early in the regular season, was against Gibson and the Grays. Matlock exited before the Crawfords won in the 11th inning.[84]

Matlock remained with the Crawfords for only about another 10 days, because he and several teammates accepted attractive offers to play a short season in the Dominican Republic. Paige was among the first three players to jump their contracts, and he persuaded Cool Papa Bell to join him. In an interview many years later, Bell took credit for Matlock's decision as he recalled the Dominicans agreeing to his requirement that he, Matlock, and others receive $500 in Miami even before leaving the United States.[85]

Matlock pitched for the Ciudad Trujillo club that finished in first place with a record of 18-13. He won four games and lost once; the loss was apparently the one he experienced in the playoffs.[86] Matlock received $2,000 total, and the American players cost the Ciudad Trujillo club $30,000, including $2,800 paid to Gibson for just five weeks. At a concluding picnic in their honor, one Dominican congressman said Gibson, Bell, and Matlock seemed particularly sad to be leaving. Passenger lists indicate those three and a few teammates returned to New York together, via San Juan, in mid-July. Myra Matlock had not accompanied her husband to the Caribbean; the *Chicago Defender* happened to note that she and her daughter Delores were on a visit to the Windy City around Memorial Day.[87]

Matlock and Bell were among the players who barnstormed that summer under the name of the Negro All-Stars of the Dominican Republic.[88] They participated in the *Denver Post*'s annual semipro tournament, which included teams managed by Hornsby and Grover Cleveland Alexander. On August 1 Matlock shut out an Oklahoma team and on August 5 his team's win against Hornsby's drew a crowd of 10,000. The next day Matlock scattered four hits in a 17-1 drubbing of a Texas team. The finale, part of a doubleheader,[89] went past midnight and ended on August 10. Matlock defeated another Oklahoma team, 11-1, and also won a $1,000 bonus as the finale's winning pitcher. Nebraska sportswriter Walt Dobbins noted that the team as a whole collected $5,179 for its championship – in which it won seven of eight games – and he called Matlock "the outstanding tourney pitcher."[90]

From October through at least December, Matlock played under the leadership of Hall of Fame catcher Biz Mackey with the Philadelphia

Royal Colored Giants in the integrated California Winter League. Bell and Suttles were among Matlock's teammates. In five starts, Matlock completed two games and had a 3-1 record.[91] Perhaps most notably, he started and won the opener on October 10 in Los Angeles' White Sox Park. The second through sixth hitters in the opposing lineup were all future major leaguers. Matlock survived five innings of a 19-11 slugfest and was the winning pitcher.[92]

In March 1938 the NNL reinstated Matlock and the other players who had violated their contracts to play in the Dominican Republic, but each was to be penalized one month's salary. Matlock was thus a Crawford again. The *Pittsburgh Courier* signaled its pleasure by printing a photo of him with a caption that began, "Regarded by ball players as the smartest pitcher in the league… ."[93]

Matlock did not play much, or particularly well, during the 1938 season's first half. In June a newspaper reported that he had "been free from call due to an injured finger." Whatever its cause or extent, Matlock had a high point the next month during a start against the Philadelphia Stars in Cleveland. He pitched well, but the Craws came out on top, 5-4, because of his bat. He gave them their last two runs on a homer that was said to have flown 460 feet.[94]

Nevertheless, in early August, he was called one of "the year's biggest disappointments in baseball" by the *Courier's* Wendell Smith. "Matlock has been blasted by league teams with ease," Smith lamented in an article shortly before a game in front of 15,000 fans in New York that resulted in Matlock suffering a 9-1 defeat.[95]

Matlock's "last hurrah" with the Crawfords may have been on August 3, 1938, against the Bushwicks in New York. He outdueled future Hall of Famer Waite Hoyt (who had completed a 21-season major-league career earlier that year). Matlock held the Bushwicks scoreless through seven innings and the Craws won, 4-1.[96]

The NNL's regular season ended around September 5,[97] and a few days later the Crawfords began a playoff series with the Philadelphia Stars, while the Grays played Baltimore.[98] The Craws won the first two games, and Matlock started the third (the second game of a doubleheader) on September 10. Matlock shut out the Stars until the seventh inning, when he was the victim of a "called shot" homer by Curtis "Popeye" Harris. The score was 2-2 in the bottom of the ninth when a Philadelphia runner stole second on a call that the *Philadelphia Tribune*'s reporter said was "completely" wrong. That lead runner soon scored the winning run when Matlock attempted to pick off another runner only to find that his first baseman was daydreaming. That was likely his final start ever for the Crawfords. On September 13, with the best-of-five series tied at two wins apiece, the Crawfords jumped out to an early 8-0 lead. The Stars made it 8-3 after five innings and tied it in the next frame. Matlock was the Crawfords' second reliever in, or right after, that inning, and he was apparently the one who gave up four additional runs by the time it all ended in a 12-8 Philadelphia victory. As far as is known, that was the last game of 1938 for the Crawfords and for Matlock as well (at least against an NNL team).[99]

Furthermore, the game was the last ever for the franchise as a Pittsburgh club. Greenlee sold the team after the 1938 season, and the new ownership relocated the franchise to Toledo, Ohio, where it played the first half-season in the NNL before moving to the Negro American League.[100] The new Crawfords continued to be managed by Charleston, but Matlock was no longer on the roster.

Matlock spent the winter of 1938-1939 in Cuba, on the Santa Clara and "Cuba" teams. Dandridge was among familiar names on the latter, while Gibson played for Santa Clara. Matlock went 2-4 in eight games for Santa Clara and 4-4 in 10 games for Cuba.[101]

In the spring and summer of 1939 Matlock played in Venezuela's Maracaibo League, for the Vargas team and the Estrellas (Stars) Venezolanos.

Dandridge likewise played on both teams.[102] This time, at least, Myra Matlock spent some time abroad with her husband; a mid-1939 passenger list shows her traveling with two of Dandridge's relatives from La Guaira, Venezuela, back to New York.[103] Leroy Matlock arrived back in New York on November 1.

Shortly thereafter, it was announced that the New York Cubans, also known as the Cuban Stars, had signed Matlock for the 1940 season. As Greenlee was exiting the NNL, the Cubans were re-entering, and the NNL awarded the rights to Matlock to the Cuban Stars That motivated Cum Posey to use one of his regular columns in the *Pittsburgh Courier* to provide a profile of Matlock. Posey brought to light an overlooked aspect of Matlock's skill set when he called Matlock "exceptionally fast on the bases." In any event, there was a similar announcement about Matlock and the Cubans before the 1942 season, but that was one of his seasons in Mexico.[104] In fact, an article about the NNL's Opening Day in May of 1943 said Matlock would be "making his first appearance in the States in four years" after playing in Mexico,[105] but there is no currently available evidence that he played for the Cubans then either.

Instead, Matlock played for the Mexico Red Devils from 1940 through 1942, and his seasons are well documented. His won-lost records in 1940 and 1941 almost matched, at 15-10 and 15-9, respectively, and his four shutouts in 1941 led the league.[106]

After the 1940 season, government records indicate he re-entered the United States on November 6, and he soon completed a military draft registration card on which his approximate height was specified as 5-feet-11½ and his weight as 175 pounds. In mid-April 1941, he placed an ad in the Moberly paper seeking a passenger to help him drive to Mexico City that week; that may be the last confirmation of him residing in Moberly.[107]

Matlock returned to the United States after the 1941 season, at least briefly, for a 10-game barnstorming tour of Mexican League players, who also included Bell, Dandridge, and Willie Wells. Because some, if not all, of them had jumped contracts to play in Mexico, they could not play NNL or NAL teams. The Mexican League All-Stars team won all of its games.[108]

Pearl Matlock died on June 15, 1942, and it's uncertain whether Leroy made it back to Moberly for the funeral four days later. The local paper mentioned that his brother Lawrence was still living in Moberly but that Leroy was living in Mexico.[109] In any event, it may have merely been a coincidence that later in June he was again listed on the staff of the Cuban Stars.[110]

By July 1943, Matlock was back in the United States for good. He had taken a job at the Ordnance Steel Foundry plant in Bettendorf, Iowa, one of the Quad Cities. Not surprisingly, he was soon the ace of the plant's baseball entry in the six-team Davenport League.[111] Matlock likely chose to settle in the Quad Cities area because his brother Otis had married the former Ella Mae Brown in Davenport in mid-1942, and their brother Lawrence also lived there at that time.[112] Leroy also pitched there during 1944, including for the Eastern Iowa-Western Illinois (or simply Quad City) All-Stars. On July 23 he pitched them to victory over the semipro Chicago Brown Bombers, 8-1, in Davenport.[113]

In early September 1946, Myra Matlock filed for divorce from Leroy.[114] In the 1947 city directory for Rock Island, Illinois, one of the other Quad Cities, Leroy Matlock was listed as a factory worker for International Harvester. In 1949 he was signed to play about 400 miles to the northwest for Slayton, Minnesota, in the First Night League. Hall of Famer Hilton Smith of the Kansas City Monarchs was signed by a different team in the league and may have earned $1,000 per month.[115]

Around 1950 Matlock settled in St. Paul, Minnesota, and began to work for the Seeger Refrigerator Company, which merged with

Whirlpool in 1955. He continued to work there for the rest of his life.[116] Otis and Ella Mae had moved back to Moberly. She had taught at the Lincoln School for over 10 years,[117] but when the school board was compelled to integrate Moberly's public schools, it refused to retain any of Lincoln's teachers. In late 1955 Ella Mae was among eight teachers who initiated a historically significant lawsuit over that decision, though they didn't prevail.[118]

Leroy Matlock remarried on August 17, 1965, in his bride's hometown of Columbia, Missouri. His wife was the former Dorothy J. Booth, a widow. The 1940 census indicates that she had happened to be living in Moberly, across the street from Matlock's grandmother, Kate.[119] That census noted that she had completed two years of college and, in 1936, she had been assigned to teach adult-education classes in Moberly under the federal Works Progress Administration.[120]

However she and her new husband met, their marriage was brief because Leroy Matlock died unexpectedly on February 6, 1968, at the age of 60. His funeral was in St. Paul, and he is buried in that city. On the page facing the death announcement in his hometown paper, Dorothy, his brothers, and sister-in-law published a "card of thanks," especially for the "floral tributes to our loved ones, the sympathy cards, telegrams and other kindnesses."[121]

One way of judging a player's career is by how his peers rated him. Matlock was one of three pitchers on the all-time all-star team listed in 1944 by first baseman Dave "Showboat" Thomas, whose NNL career stretched from 1929 to 1946. More significantly, Matlock's longtime manager, Oscar Charleston, named him as one of the six pitchers on his all-time roster in 1950. In 1970 Hall of Famer Buck Leonard said Paige and Matlock were the two toughest pitchers he had ever faced.[122] In 1981 Judy Johnson rated him in a different way, by calling Matlock "a real gentleman."[123]

Matlock was also remembered meaningfully early in the new century. In 2001 the Pittsburgh Pirates created a permanent exhibit to honor the Crawfords and Homestead Grays. "Each time a baseball fan walks into the left field entrance at PNC Park, they'll see the names of 14 Negro League players and two owners emblazoned on eight fiberglass bats suspended above," noted a *New Pittsburgh Courier* reporter. One of those 14 names is Leroy Matlock.[124]

All in all, Matlock had a remarkable professional career with many high points. As ESPN's Tony McClean asserted, "[F]or a two-year period between 1935 and 1936, there may not have been a better pitcher than Leroy Matlock."[125] What's more, from 1931 to 1938 he faced down no fewer than nine white Hall of Famers. "Matlock was one of the most underrated pitchers in our league," concluded Cool Papa Bell.[126]

## Sources

Unless otherwise indicated, all Negro League statistics and team records have been taken from Seamheads.com.

## Notes

1. For examples of this short-lived nickname, see Jim Brahos, "Satchel Paige, Greatest of Colored Aces Here Tuesday," *Hammond* (Indiana) *Times*, September 3, 1937: 15, and "Sunday Game Will Decide Strength of David Hitters," *Daily Times* (Davenport, Iowa), September 10, 1937: 28. The nickname even made it into a headline: "'Black Carl Hubbell' Will Strut Stuff at Lexington," *Minneapolis Star*, September 8, 1937: 17. Matlock's hometown newspaper made a fuss when he was deemed "the equal of Carl Hubbell" in the *Denver Post*, which was not simply quoting a promotional press release. See "Moberly Negro Pitcher Praised," *Monitor-Index and Democrat* (Moberly, Missouri), August 12, 1937: 6.

2. Matlock won his final four games of 1934, went 17-0 in 1935, and started 1936 6-0 to extend his streak to "26," according to baseball-reference.com/bullpen/Leroy_Matlock, though the arithmetic actually works out to 27.

3. Leroy's birthplace and date of birth were specified on his 1940s military draft registration. His birthdate was also specified on a passenger list when he traveled to Puerto Rico in mid-1937.

4. Though the 1910 census indicated that Pearl Matlock and the former Delia Ganaway had been married for five years, they apparently didn't make it official until February 1, 1914,

# THE 1935 PITTSBURGH CRAWFORDS

in a ceremony performed by Rev. J.J. Miles. See "Granted Licenses," *Moberly Daily Monitor*, January 12, 1914: 1.

5. It's unknown whether Pearl and Delia had other children together before 1910 besides Leroy. If so, they presumably died before that census. Delia's life story before Leroy's birth is murky, but her death certificate revealed that her father's name was Oscar Holley, born in Missouri. Clara's surname on her death certificate was "Holly" and her father's name was Oliver Wright. Clues that this was in fact Delia's daughter include that the mother's maiden name was listed as "Dellie Holly" and the Informant was "Mrs Dellie Medlock." In fact, for some unknown reason the Matlock family's listing in the 1910 census used the surname Holley instead. Otis was about three years younger than Clara and four years older than Leroy. On Otis's marriage record in 1942 his father's name was entered as Lindsy Pitts. See Note 9 below regarding Delia's reported marriage before 1900 and regarding her mother. As of 2020 the State of Missouri makes statewide death records available online only back to 1910, so it is difficult to determine whether Delia had any children before that year besides Clara, Otis, and Leroy.

6. Even at the time of his death, more than two decades later, his occupation was the same. In the 1900 census, though, he was listed as a "coal hauler."

7. As mentioned in Note 5 above, the Matlock family's surname in the 1910 census was instead given as Holley, but more perplexing are the children's first names, except that Leroy was spelled correctly. The 10-year-old daughter was "Clarens" instead of Clara, and the oldest son was "Cleatus" instead of Otis. Oddest of all is that the baby boy of the family, whose age was either "2" months or "7" months, was listed as something that approximates "Demon." Still, because that census page was dated April 25, there is ample reason to believe that the newborn was Alfred, who was two months old in April of 1910, based on his death certificate. All five of these death certificates are accessible via s1.sos.mo.gov/Records/Archives/ArchivesMvc/ though Alfred's surname was entered as "Meadlock."

8. Pearl's father, Amos, had died by the 1900 census, and his mother, the former Kate or Katie Twyman, married a man named Kitchen in early 1904. From 1918 until at least 1925, Leroy and his nuclear family lived at 1019 Forrest Avenue (which today is the farthest west block of West End Place); Kate lived at 1047 from around the time of Leroy's birth until her death in 1941 at the age of 80.

9. Leroy was actually listed twice in the 1920 census, though as "Lela" in the entry with his parents. Just 15 days earlier, on January 2, Leroy (surname "Medlock") reportedly lived with his maternal grandmother, Lottie Ganaway. The household also included a second grandson, who, accounting for the census taker's penmanship, was likely Otis. Their grandmother, the former Lottie Herndon, married George Ganaway in 1892. However, in the 1900 census their household included Lottie's mother, George's 24-year-old son, George W., and his wife of two years, 19-year-old Delia Ganaway. This seems to indicate that Leroy Matlock's mother married her stepbrother (no blood relation) around 1898. Though her children's death certificates listed her maiden name as Holley, her own death certificate listed Lottie Ganaway as her mother, and Delia's maiden name was entered as Her[n]don rather than Holley on Otis's marital record. What's more, she was listed as Mrs. Delia Ganaway on her marriage license in 1914. It was apparently a different woman named Delia Holley who married a man named George Oney in Randolph County in 1894.

10. Lawrence Matlock completed high school, according to "Lincoln School to Graduate 31 Students Saturday," *Monitor-Index and Democrat*, May 19, 1932: 12.

11. This atrocity was covered coast to coast and beyond, and of course was big news across Missouri. For example, see "'Reds' and Blacks at Moberly," *St. Louis Post-Dispatch*, November 18, 1919: 24. Details were provided in "Mob Kills Negro Bandit Sunday," *Moberly Evening Democrat*, November 17, 1919: 1. For the aftermath, see "Lynching Victim May Have Been Killed by Police," *Dallas* (Texas) *Express*, December 20, 1919: 1.

12. Malcolm Gladwell, "Miss Buchanan's Period of Adjustment," *Revisionist History* season 2, episode 3, 2017. A transcript of this episode is available at blog.simonsays.ai/miss-buchanans-period-of-adjustment-revisionist-history-podcast-transcript-b4c65731f73c. Moberly's population history was provided by Steven E. Mitchell and Mary Aue Mitchell, *Survey Report: Moberly, Randolph County, Architectural/Historical Survey*, April 2007: 28, which is available at dnr.mo.gov/shpo/survey/RNAS001-R.pdf.

13. "Thrilling Story Told by Mrs. Oscar Oswalt," *Moberly Evening Democrat*, February 10, 1922: 1; "Dogs Did Not Trail Negroes," *Moberly Monitor-Index*, February 13, 1922: 1; W.B. Coleman, "People's Forum," *Moberly Evening Democrat*, February 14, 1922: 7. About a week later Mrs. Oswalt submitted a written statement asking that the two men not be prosecuted, and they were freed, with the prosecuting attorney issuing a stern warning against mob rule. See "2 Oswalt Case Negroes Freed," *Moberly Monitor-Index*, February 22, 1922: 1. It was ultimately reported that Mrs. Oswalt had been giving money to some other man, and as her fear grew that her husband suspected, she made up the entire story as a diversion. Her own children stated that she tied up them and herself. See *Biennial Report of the Missouri Negro Industrial Commission*, 1921-1922: 45.

14. Leo Branham, "Moberly Shoe Shiner Shines on the Baseball Diamond as One of Negro League Best Pitchers," *Moberly Monitor-Index*, December 9, 1931: 12. Brown's first name was spelled "Hilbert" in this interview with Matlock, which was a longer version of "Baseball Notes," *Chicago Defender*, November 21, 1931: 8. Crutchfield was the Eagles' center fielder and "Medlock" their right fielder in a rare early box score beneath "Moberly Defeated in Ninth Inning, 3-1," *Browning* (Missouri) *Leader-Record*, August 18, 1927: 1. In fact, this article also contained a full play-by-play of every inning. Anyone

wanting to research the Moberly Eagles and their successor, the Gatewood Browns, should keep in mind that there was a second man named Helbert Brown in Moberly until at least 1920, except that he was about five years younger and white.

15  The date of their marriage came from "Two Divorce Suits Filed in Circuit Court," *Moberly Monitor-Index and Democrat,* September 4, 1946: 9. Matlock's in-laws lived at 534 Winchester, and around 1938 he and Myra purchased a home two doors down, at 540. Like Forrest Avenue, mentioned in Note 8, Winchester eventually became a stretch of West End Place.

16  "A Large Crowd Attended Ball Game," *Browning Leader-Record*, July 28, 1927: 1. He was also praised in "Moberly Won the Ballgame Sunday," *Browning Leader-Record*, August 9, 1928: 1. In the latter article it was noted that the Eagles had played in Browning four times during 1927 and four more times during 1928 up to that point.

17  "Moberly Eagles Defeat Browning," *Monitor-Index and Democrat*, June 11, 1928: 2. "Moberly Eagles Lose to Slater," *Monitor-Index and Democrat*, June 25, 1928: 2. "'Lefty' Matlock Wins for Columbia," *Monitor-Index and Democrat*, July 5, 1928: 8. He arrived during the third inning and became the winning pitcher in the 14th when he singled and eventually scored to break a 2-2 tie. The large ad for an Eagles game was printed in the *Browning Leader-Record*, August 2, 1928: 8. Shortly before, it was reported that the Eagles had a record of 10 wins and four losses. See "Moberly Eagles Beat Columbia," *Monitor-Index and Democrat*, July 30, 1928: 2. They finished with a 16-6 record, according to "Eagles to Play Columbia Saturday," *Monitor-Index and Democrat*, April 10, 1929: 2.

18  "Eagles Play First Home Game Sunday with Mexico Team," *Monitor-Index and Democrat*, May 25, 1929: 6. The team's victory total for 1927 and 1928 combined looks like 88, but either digit could actually be a 3. This article implies that the team started in 1927 rather than 1926, contradicting Matlock's recollection in 1931, but it may be that the team did indeed form sometime during 1926 and was loosely organized until 1927.

19  "Eagles to Play Columbia Saturday," *Monitor-Index and Democrat*, April 10, 1929: 2. See also "Eagles to Play White Sox Tomorrow," *Monitor-Index and Democrat*, April 20, 1929: 6. Apparently rain kept the two teams from playing at all during April. Crutchfield, Matlock, and Gatewood were all mentioned in "Eagles Defeat Jefferson City," *Monitor-Index and Democrat*, May 6, 1929: 6.

20  Branham.

21  "Eagles Play First Home Game Sunday with Mexico Team," *Monitor-Index and Democrat*, May 25, 1929: 6. "St. Louis Stars Win Final Game of Series from Cubans, 17-3," *St. Louis Globe-Democrat*, May 22, 1929: 13. "St. Louis Stars and Kansas City Monarchs Split Twin Bill, 5-3, 7-6," *St. Louis Globe-Democrat*, May 15, 1929: 15. The box score specified that Matlock gave up two hits and two runs in two innings but other details indicate he pitched in the second, third, and fourth innings, including that he was lifted for a pinch-hitter in the bottom of the fourth. According to "National Negro Baseball League Standing," *Indianapolis Recorder*, June 8, 1929: 6, St. Louis had a record of 13-3 up to May 21. Their first loss was at the beginning of May to Detroit, and Matlock wasn't in the line score of their loss to the Monarchs on May 11. See "Monarchs Win, 12 to 3," *Kansas City Star*, May 12, 1929: 4B.

22  Branham. One of Matlock's early wins was a lopsided complete game on May 30; see "St. Louis Stars Trounce Memphis by 14-3 Score," *St. Louis Star*, May 31, 1929: 29. Afterward, Memphis pitcher Robert Poindexter thought teammate J.C. McHaskell was teasing him about the drubbing, and Poindexter shot him in the foot. This was news across the country. For a long account, see "Memphis Red Sox Hurler Shoots Teammate," *Pittsburgh Courier*, June 8, 1929: 1.

23  "Eagles Win 16th Victory of Season, Defeating LaPlata," *Monitor-Index and Democrat*, October 14, 1929: 6. Matlock pitched at least one other game for them that month, as reported in "Eagles Beat New Boston; Their 18th Victory This Year," *Monitor-Index and Democrat*, October 28, 1929: 9. The latter article mentioned Matlock, Gatewood, and Crutchfield in the same sentence.

24  Walter M. Smith, "Local Negro Club and Kansas City Play under Lights," *St. Louis Star*, May 20, 1930: 16.

25  "St. Louis Stars Sweep Series," *Chicago Defender*, July 26, 1930: 9. As of 2020 this shutout wasn't reflected in his 1930 statistics at seamheads.com/NegroLgs/player.php?playerID=matloo1ler or baseball-reference.com/register/player.fcgi?id=matlocoooler.

26  "Detroit Evens Series with St. Louis Stars," *St. Louis Globe-Democrat*, September 16, 1920: 19.

27  The series was supposed to be best of nine, not best of seven, but Mother Nature didn't cooperate, according to "Again Rain Halts Negro World Series Ball Game in Detroit," *St. Louis Post-Dispatch*, September 25, 1930: 19.

28  "St. Louis Stars Trounce Moberly," *Monitor-Index and Democrat*, August 5, 1931: 5.

29  "Stars Too Strong for Indianapolis," *Monitor-Index and Democrat*, September 4, 1931: 9.

30  "Stars Slam Walker and Trim Careyites," *St. Louis Globe-Democrat*, October 3, 1931: 7. At the bottom of the box score the line for Carey's All-Stars shows a zero in all nine innings, but the almost identical coverage in a nearby newspaper indicated that Matlock's shutout ended in the sixth. See "Colored Stars 18 to 1 Against Carey Players," *Belleville* (Illinois) *Daily News-Democrat*, October 3, 1931: 8. Both box scores excluded all pitching details and the like. Some of that information was provided in "St. Louis Beats All-Stars," *Chicago Defender*, October 10, 1931: 8. As of 2020, at baseball-reference.com/bullpen/Leroy_Matlock, the date of the game is incorrectly stated as October 8.

# THE 1935 PITTSBURGH CRAWFORDS

31 See Gary Ashwill, "St. Louis Stars, 1931," agatetype.typepad.com/agate_type/2019/07/st-louis-stars-1931.html. The Stars were supposed to face Bill Walker again in October but the rematch was rained out at least twice, according to "Dairies Will Try Again to Beat Roofers," *Belleville* (Illinois) *Daily News-Democrat*, October 24, 1931: 8.

32 Branham.

33 Branham. As of 2020, Matlock's Seamheads stats at seamheads.com/NegroLgs/player.php?playerID=matloo1er only confirm five wins in 1931. Of course, Matlock's count might have included exhibition games, such as against Carey's team. In any event, in the interview he also recalled that as a rookie in 1929 he compiled a record of 7-3, followed by 10-3 in 1930. His Seamheads totals for those two seasons aren't too far off, at 4-2 and 8-4, respectively.

34 "Matlock to Play with Detroit," *Monitor-Index and Democrat*, March 31, 1932: 6. "Detroit in Drills at Charleston," *Pittsburgh Courier*, April 9, 1932: section 2, 5. Chester L. Washington, "Sportively Speaking," *Pittsburgh Courier*, April 9, 1932: section 2, 5. (See also Washington's column on the same page one week later.) The Moberly paper was by no means alone in thinking he'd play with Detroit. See also "Wells, Suttles to Detroit: Creacy, Matlock, Redus also Join Dismukes' Wolverine Club," *Chicago Defender*, March 6, 1932: 8, and "Mule Suttles with Detroit," *Afro-American*, March 26, 1932: 15. The confusion is understandable, because Cum Posey owned both the Homestead Grays and the new Detroit franchise; see baseball-reference.com/bullpen/Detroit_Wolves.

35 "Lefty Grove Tiant Leads East-West Tossers With 3 Full Games, No Losses," *Atlanta Daily World*, May 23, 1932: 5. Chester L. Washington, "Crawfords Defeat Grays in Series," *Pittsburgh Courier*, June 4, 1932: section 2, 5. "Grays Batter Out 10-Inning Win from Sox," *Afro-American*, June 4, 1932: 14.

36 "Detroit and Grays Nines Consolidate," *Chicago Defender*, June 11, 1932: 8. "Pilots Get a Clouter," *Washington Evening Star*, June 9, 1932: D-1. Matlock's record at the time was reportedly 7-0, according to "Matlock Goes to Washington Club," *Monitor-Index and Democrat*, June 14, 1932: 6. If that count is even close to accurate, it seems unlikely that it refers only to regular-season games. Around that time the Grays had a record of 14-7, which would have meant Matlock won half of theirs. Standings accompanied "Trades Revive Interest in East-West League," *Philadelphia Tribune*, June 16, 1932: 11.

37 "Night Baseball Inaugurated in D.C. by Pilots," *New Journal and Guide* (Norfolk, Virginia), August 6, 1932: 13. Gary Ashwill, "Negro Leagues DB Update: 1932 East-West League, August 13, 2015, seamheads.com/2015/08/13/negro-leagues-db-update-1932-east-west-league/. For more on the dissolution of the East-West League, see Cum Posey, "Posey Answers Clark on League and Grays," *Pittsburgh Courier*, July 29, 1933: section 2, 5.

38 "Craws Sign Bell, Cooper, Hunter," *Pittsburgh Courier*, March 18, 1933: section 2, 5. "Detroit Team Out of Negro National Baseball League," *Philadelphia Tribune*, April 27, 1933: 11.

39 "Crawfords Win and Top League," *Chicago Defender*, May 6, 1933: 9. The box score states that he gave up 10 hits and a pair of walks. He helped his cause during a double play by snagging a heave from center field and throwing a runner out at third base.

40 "Crawfords Blank Birds," *Pittsburgh Post-Gazette*, May 23, 1933: 16.

41 "Chicago Wins First of Split Season Race," *Detroit Tribune*, July 15, 1933: 7. The conclusion of this article indicates that Sunday, July 9, was the start of the second half.

42 "Stearns [sic] Gets Two in Battle," *Chicago Defender*, July 29, 1933: 8. For the box score, see "A 15-Inning Midnite Tilt!" *Pittsburgh Courier*, July 29, 1933: section 2, 4. It identifies who Matlock walked and how many times he struck out each batsman.

43 "Want Rogan on Star Team," *Chicago Defender*, August 12, 1933: 8. "Leads Vote Parade of Eastern Pitchers," *Pittsburgh Courier*, September 9, 1933: section 2, 5. Only the top four pitchers were named to each All-Star roster.

44 "Crawfords Defeat Nashville in Opener," *Pittsburgh Sun-Telegraph*, October 1, 1933: part 2, 5. William G. Nunn, "Plucky Nashville Team Loses Three Thrillers to Craws," *Pittsburgh Courier*, October 7, 1933: section 2, 4.

45 "Baseball Moguls to Meet in Philly Next Month; Meeting of Owners Set for Feb. 10," *Pittsburgh Courier*, January 27, 1934: section 2, 5. See also John L. Clark, "Only Three Teams Finish National Baseball Race," *Afro-American*, October 7, 1933: 15. For a different interpretation on how the 1933 pennant race was decided, see Mark Ribowsky, *Josh Gibson: The Power and the Darkness* (Urbana, Illinois: University of Illinois Press, 2004), 121.

46 Shevlin formed his All-Professionals, aka All-Majors or All-Stars, from 1931 through 1936, but Durocher apparently played with them only in 1933, based on searching editions of the *Cincinnati Enquirer*. The Crawfords lost to Shevlin's team 6-1 on October 14, 1934, but Durocher wasn't in Shevlin's lineup published in a preview of the game that day See "Strong Teams," *Cincinnati Enquirer*, October 14, 1934: 30. Five days earlier Durocher had finished playing in the World Series with the Cardinals.

47 Lew Freedman, *African American Pioneers of Baseball: A Biographical Encyclopedia* (Westport, Connecticut: Greenwood Press, 2007), 21. "Curtains for Baseball; Shevlin's Pros to Battle Pittsburgh Crawfords Today," *Cincinnati Enquirer*, October 15, 1933: 33. For an example of Durocher specified as in Shevlin's lineup around that time – when they played the Chicago American Giants – see "Negroes to Be Opponents," *Cincinnati Enquirer*, October 5, 1933: 18. Durocher clearly remembered the play more than 20 years later

48. "Negro Baseball Stars Off Soon to Training Camp," *Moberly Monitor-Index and Democrat*, March 27, 1934: 5.

49. "Final Standing – The East," *Pittsburgh Courier*, August 25, 1934: section 2, 5.

50. See baseball-reference.com/bullpen/Leroy_Matlock. The 1934 East-West All-Star Game was played on August 26.

51. John L. Clark, "League Sec'y Recalls Close Ball Games During 1934," *Pittsburgh Courier*, September 29, 1934: section 2, 4.

52. "Adrian Has a Tiger Finish at Hillsdale," *Adrian* (Michigan) *Daily Telegram*, September 29, 1934: 5. This article refers to Adrian's starting pitcher as "Bill James" of the Toledo Mud Hens but records indicate that his first name was actually Roy. At least six other players in Adrian's starting lineup were also apparently minor leaguers at some point: Raymond Nebelung, Arthur Mason, Carl Huffman (Hoffman), Louie Batterson, Eddie Sobb(e), and most notably Harold Patchett, whose 15-year pro career included eight straight with San Diego of the Pacific Coast League. The doubleheader in Toledo on Thursday, September 27, was mentioned in "Grays Tackle Crawfords," *Pittsburgh Press-Gazette*, September 29, 1934: 14.

53. According to Gatewood's SABR biography by Bill Johnson, at sabr.org/node/54535, "The Moberly Eagles were re-dubbed the Gatewood Browns in late 1929," and that may have been implied in "Negro Baseball Club Reorganized," *Monitor-Index and Democrat*, May 1, 1934: 10. Still, the local paper apparently didn't use "Gatewood Browns" or some variation, before 1934. In fact, there were Browns and Eagles teams in Moberly simultaneously, at least briefly in 1944, according to "Browns to Play at Kirksville, Eagles Have Game Here," *Monitor-Index and Democrat*, June 23, 1934: 5. Their pitcher for that game was expected to be "Matlock, brother of Leroy Matlock who plays with the Pittsburgh Crawford Club," and that was presumably Lawrence rather than Otis Pitts. By that point Lawrence's team had played at least three games, according to "Eagles Will Play Richmond Tigers Here Sunday," *Monitor-Index and Democrat*, June 22, 1934: 5. Lawrence had pitched while still in high school, according to "Moberly Panthers Beat Madison, 9-2," *Monitor-Index and Democrat*, July 6, 1931: 7. Late that decade he was a pitcher for another local team, according to "Wheaties Ready to Play Ball," *Monitor-Index and Democrat*, May 13, 1939: 5. According to his draft registration card the next year, his height was 5-feet-9 and he weighed just 140 pounds.

54. "Browns Win, 3-2, in 11 Innings," *Monitor-Index and Democrat*, October 22, 1934: 8. There was considerable promotion for this game, including speculation that Matlock might not make it home in time, followed by a brief item when he did arrive. See "Browns to Play Salisbury-Dalton," *Monitor-Index and Democrat*, October 13, 1934: 10 and "Leroy Matlock Here," *Monitor-Index and Democrat*, October 16, 1934: 7. For an account of Matlock and Kennedy opposing one another some years earlier, see "Moberly Won the Ballgame Sunday," *Browning* (Missouri) *Leader-Record*, August 9, 1928: 1.

55. Goetze Jeter, "Around Town," *Monitor-Index and Democrat*, August 3, 1934: 4. The site's previous name was mentioned earlier in the season, but the new name not explained, in "Browns Defeat Jeff City; Play Fulton Next," *Monitor-Index and Democrat*, May 7, 1934: 5.

56. "Biggest Baseball Season in History Is Predicted for Bismarck," *Bismarck* (North Dakota) *Tribune*, April 13, 1935: 7. "Satchell[sic] Paige in Entanglement," *Negro Star* (Wichita, Kansas), April 26, 1935: 6.

57. "Craws-Cubans," *Pittsburgh Courier*, May 18, 1935: section 2, 5.

58. "Craws in 1st Place after Chi Series," *Pittsburgh Courier*, May 25, 1935: section 2, 4. Crutchfield helped considerably with a "most thrilling" one-handed catch of a fly in the right-field corner off the bat of Suttles. The article said Bankhead tripled and scored the game's only run on a single by Charleston, but the box score didn't credit Bankhead with any extra-base hit.

59. Wm. J. Granger, "Duffy's Great Pitching and Beazley's Bat Win for Bushwicks in Tenth," *Brooklyn* (New York) *Citizen*, June 8, 1935: 6. See also "Bushwicks Show Fighting Spirit, Win with Rally," *Brooklyn Times Union*, June 8, 1935: 2A. Matlock also lost an exhibition game, in relief, on August 22 to a white team in Madison, Wisconsin, according to Hank Casserly, "Blues Nip Crawfords 2-1 in Fast 10-Inning Battle," *Capital Times* (Madison, Wisconsin), August 23, 1935: 17. Matlock needn't have been embarrassed by the outcome, as the previous month the Chicago Cubs barely beat Madison's team. See Henry J. McCormick, "8,000 People See Cubs Nose Out Blues, 2-1," *Wisconsin State Journal* (Madison), July 13, 1935: 5.

60. "Matlock Tops League Pitchers," *Pittsburgh Courier*, July 20, 1935: section 2, 5.

61. "Josh Gibson Tops Hitters in Negro National League," *Chicago Defender*, September 7, 1935: 14. He finished a second game in relief.

62. "2 Managers Draw Suspensions after Rows with Umps," *Afro-American*, July 27, 1935: 21.

63. "Race for E-W Berths Hot as Voting Spurts," *Pittsburgh Courier*, July 27, 1935: section 2, 5. At that point, the Crawfords had played 11 NNL games in the second half, and had a middling 6-5 record. (Dubbing Matlock a "super-man" occurred about three years before the "Man of Steel" debuted in the pages of *Action Comics*.)

64. "'Dream Teams' of East, West Set for Big Game," *Pittsburgh Courier*, August 10, 1935: section 2, 4. Dan Burley, "Here's How the West Made History at Comiskey Park," *Chicago Defender*, August 17, 1935: 6. The latter is a batter-by-batter account of the entire game.

# THE 1935 PITTSBURGH CRAWFORDS

65 "Crawfords Cop 3 Out of 4 in Series with Homestead Grays," *Pittsburgh Courier*, August 24, 1935: section 2, 4.

66 Matlock "won all his league games this season," according to "Pittsburgh Crawfords Play Cubans Tonight," *Herald Statesman* (Yonkers, New York), September 13, 1935: 15. Similarly, he was "unbeaten this year," according to "Negro Baseball Teams to Play Contest Sunday," *New Orleans State*, October 9, 1935: 9. The NNL secretary mentioned the same more than a year later; see John L. Clark, "Fans Must Lend Aid to Help Baseball," *Pittsburgh Courier*, March 13, 1937: 16. Matlock had "a record of 15 wins and no losses last year," according to "Crawfords Held Back by Unfavorable Weather," *Pittsburgh Post-Gazette*, April 18, 1936: 16.

67 Jim Bankes, *The Pittsburgh Crawfords* (Jefferson, North Carolina: McFarland & Company Inc., 2001), 72. As pointed out in the first Note herein, Matlock won his final four games of 1934, went 17-0 in 1935, and started 1936 6-0 to extend his streak to 26, according to baseball-reference.com/bullpen/Leroy_Matlock. The Seamheads Negro Leagues Database's overall stats for 1935, at seamheads.com/NegroLgs/player.php?playerID=matloo1ler, show him with a loss but if one clicks on the "Show Individual Stints" button it indicates that his lone loss was during the postseason championship series. As of 2020 Seamheads' regular season data for Matlock excludes his NNL shutouts in May and August.

68 Bankes, 72.

69 Allan McMillan, "Pitt Crawfords Grab 3rd Game of Series," *Chicago Defender*, September 21, 1935: 13. This was an inning-by-inning account. Matlock didn't finish the fourth game, and if he gave up the run in the sixth inning that broke a 1-1 tie, he was the losing pitcher. No pitching data was in the box score that accompanied "Cubans Defeat Crawfords Again," *Pittsburgh Post-Gazette*, September 19, 1935: 18. Matlock was listed in the *Afro-American*'s box score for the sixth game, though it also identified Gibson and Crutchfield as pitchers and Harvey as a catcher; see "Crawfords Beat Cubans, 8 to 1, to Get First Pennant," *Afro-American*, September 28, 1935: 13. He also figured in the game's ninth-inning rally, according to "Crawfords Now League Champs," *New York Amsterdam News*, September 28, 1935: 12. Conversely, the *Philadelphia Tribune*'s box score for the sixth game didn't show Matlock at all; see "Crawfords Take 4 [of] 7, to Top Stars," *Philadelphia Tribune*, September 26, 1935: 10.

70 "Crawfords Win over Shroyers," *Dayton Herald*, October 10, 1935: 19.

71 "Major League Stars Score Twice, 3-0, 1-0," *New York Times*, October 14, 1935: 24.

72 "Local Ball Players Perform in Mexico," *Moberly Monitor-Index*, October 31, 1935: 6.

73 "Red-Hot Crawfords Go to Town and Smother New York Cubans, 19-6," *Paterson* (New Jersey) *Evening News*, May 11, 1936: 23.

74 "Crawfords Win, Even Series Here," *Pittsburgh Press*, May 17, 1936: section 2, 4. The box score shows Carter as a relief pitcher.

75 "Giants, Crawfords Trade Close Ones," *Washington Evening Star*, May 24, 1936: B-7. "D.C. Elites in Foldup to Pitt in Last Inning," *Chicago Defender*, May 30, 1936: 14.

76 "Crawfords Split with Philly Stars," *Pittsburgh Press*, May 31, 1936: section 2, 4; "Crawfords Lose to Elites, 10-4," *Pittsburgh Press*, June 7, 1936: section 2, 4; "Crawfords, Cubans Split," *Pittsburgh Post-Gazette*, June 29, 1936: 16.

77 "Crawfords Defeat Newark Eagles, 5-3," *Pittsburgh Press*, June 14, 1936: section 2, 4; "Crawfords, Newark Split," *Pittsburgh Post-Gazette*, June 22, 1936: 16.

78 See baseball-reference.com/bullpen/Leroy_Matlock about the final months of 1936, an assertion disproven by: "Pittsburgh Crawfords Defeat Cubans for Third Time, 4 to 3," *Paterson* (New Jersey) *Morning Call*, August 10, 1936: 21; "Crawfords Victors in Double Bill," *Pittsburgh Sun-Telegraph*, August 30, 1936: 20; "Grays Divide Games with Crawford Club," *Pittsburgh Post-Gazette*, September 8, 1936: 16; "Crawfords Win and Tie with Newark," *Pittsburgh Press*, September 13, 1936: section 2, 3.

79 The Crawfords clinched the NNL's second-half title around mid-September, and initially there was supposed to be a championship series with Washington. See "Crawfords Win Second Half," *New York Age*, September 26, 1936: 9. Right above this brief article is a table of NNL hitters with batting averages above .300 for July 11 through September 12, but the newspaper skimped on pitchers' stats. It named eight pitchers who were undefeated, and among pitchers with at least one loss, Matlock had the fifth-best winning percentage – though all of this information was presented without any numbers.

80 Franklin Penn, "West's Best No Match for Star Eastern Outfit," *Pittsburgh Courier*, August 29, 1936: section 2, 5. On the same page, see also William G. Nunn, "Satchell[sic] Paige Is Magnet At E-W Game; Players of Big League Calibre Perform" and Chester L. Washington's "Ches' Sez" column. The accompanying box said the second of the East's three pitchers, Bill Byrd, was the winning pitcher. Conversely, Matlock was deemed the winning pitcher in the box score that accompanied the account by Al Monroe, "East Wallops West 10-2," *Chicago Defender*, August 29, 1936: 13.

81 Everett Wadsworth, "Stars Nip Big Leagues' Best," *Chicago Defender*, October 10, 1936: 13. This account said Matlock was the "winner of twenty-four victories and no defeats this season," which may actually have been a reference to his winning streak from 1934 to that season. See also "Negro Hurler Stops Hornsby's All-Stars," *Omaha* (Nebraska) *World-Herald*, October 3, 1936: 9. Statistical totals for the series are available at seamheads.com/NegroLgs/year.php?yearID=1936&lgID=N-vM. For additional insights, see Timothy M. Gay, *Satch, Dizzy, and Rapid Robert: The Wild Saga of Interracial Baseball*

82   "Manley Sends Strong Team to Porto Rico," *New York Age*, December 5, 1936: 8.

83   "Crawfords and Grays in Exhibition Doubleheader at New Orleans April 25," *New York Age*, March 13, 1937: 8.

84   "Crawfords Nose Out Homestead Grays, 8-7," *Pittsburgh Post-Gazette*, May 20, 1937: 23. Matlock also faced Gibson in spring training, according to "Crawfords Lose Twice to Grays," *Pittsburgh Post-Gazette*, April 26, 1937: 20.

85   "Four More Players Desert Crawfords," *Pittsburgh Sun-Telegraph*, May 20, 1937: 25; James Bankes, *The Pittsburgh Crawfords: The Lives & Times of Black Baseball's Most Exciting Team!* (Dubuque, Iowa: William C. Brown Publishers, 1991), 128. For much more detail, see the compilation of Averell "Ace" Smith's impressive research at thepitcherandthedictator.com/. Bankes helped put Matlock's income in perspective on page 101 (of the first of his two books on the Crawfords): "When compared to the salaries of their major league contemporaries, the pay for blacks was indeed low, and a comparison with modern major league salaries becomes ridiculous. When compared to the earnings of most other black men, however, as well as most white men during the Depression, the compensation looms rather large."

86   William F. McNeil, *Black Baseball Out of Season: Pay for Play Outside of the Negro Leagues* (Jefferson, North Carolina: McFarland & Company Inc., 2007), 145-146. On page 145, Paige's record was listed as 7-2 prior to the final game of the playoffs, which he won, and on the next page McNeil wrote that Paige led all league pitchers that summer with a record of 8-2.

87   Lewis Dial, "The Sports Dial," *New York Age*, June 26, 1937: 8; Ollie Stewart, "San Domingo Club Pays $30,000 for Americans," *Afro-American*, July 24, 1937: 19; "Society," *Chicago Defender*, June 12, 1937: 6. Matlock was said to have gone 16-4 with the Dominican team, but if that's even close to accurate, it had to have included their subsequent barnstorming back in the States. See Wendell Smith, "If the Crawfords Hurlers Click," *Pittsburgh Courier*, April 23, 1938: 16.

88   At other times this team was called Trujillo's All-Stars and Satchel Paige's All-Stars, according to Mike Vago, "In 1937, a Dictator Assembled a Baseball Team for the Ages," March 25, 2018, avclub.com/in-1937-a-dictator-assembled-a-baseball-team-for-the-a-1823978045.

89   The winner of the tournament's final game was to receive $1,000, according to Larry Lester, *Black Baseball's National Showcase: The East-West All-Star Game, 1933-1953* (Lincoln: University of Nebraska Press, 2001), 100-101.

90   "Hornsby's Team Wins Over That of 'Old Pete,'" *Ada* (Oklahoma) *Evening News*, August 2, 1937: 8; "Matlock Stars as Outlaw '9' Batters Ofays," *Philadelphia Tribune*, August 12, 1937: 9; "Negro All-Stars Win Denver Post Semi-Pro Tourney," *Amarillo* (Texas) *Globe*, August 10, 1937: 7; Lester, 100-101; John Bentley, "I May Be Wrong," *Lincoln* (Nebraska) *Evening Journal*, August 11, 1937: 11. Bentley's column quoted Dobbins, who added that Satchel Paige lost the only tournament game in which he pitched, but he struck out 14 batters and scattered five hits in eight innings. See also Note 2 herein, about Matlock being called "the equal of Carl Hubbell" in the *Denver Post* itself.

91   McNeil, 185, 190.

92   McNeil, 188. The box score in the *Los Angeles Times* for a rematch on November 7 shows "Gomez" as the pitcher for the White Kings, and though McNeil says Lefty Gomez pitched for the White Kings that winter, the truth appears to be that Matlock was opposite Joe Gonzales of the 1937 Boston Red Sox, as noted by Harry Levette, "Watching the Scoreboard," *Chicago Defender*, November 20, 1937: 10.

93   "NNL Reinstates 'Jumpers'; New D.C. Club Is Admitted," *Afro-American*, March 12, 1938: 18. The photo of Matlock was in the *Pittsburgh Courier*, April 23, 1938: 16.

94   "Diamond Dope," *Afro-American*, June 25, 1938: 23. "Pittsburgh Crawfords Top Philly Stars 5-4," *Cleveland Call and Post*, July 14, 1938: 10.

95   Wendell Smith, "Smitty's Sport Spurts," *Pittsburgh Courier*, August 6, 1938: 16; "Nashville Beats Craws 9-1 Before 15,000 Fans," *Chicago Defender*, August 20, 1938: 10. In the latter article Mackey was the catcher for "Nashville," and the team was called the "Nashville Elite Giants making their home in Washington," in which case the team that pummeled Matlock was actually the Baltimore Elite Giants (who had been in Washington the previous season).

96   John Palmer, "Bushwicks Fail on the Fourth Try to Shake Pittsburgh Crawford Jinx," *Brooklyn Citizen*, August 4, 1938: 6.

97   Coverage of the Crawfords faded considerably in September, but one knowledgeable source said the NNL's regular season ended on Labor Day, which was Monday, September 5. See Cum Posey, "Posey's Points," *Pittsburgh Courier*, September 10, 1938: 17. However, the Craws and the Homestead Grays were scheduled to play a six-game series in four cities from September 3 through 6, according to "Grays and Crawfords Open Series Saturday," *Pittsburgh Post-Gazette*, September 2, 1938: 17. Results may not exist. It was reported that the final game was indeed played, in Welch, West Virginia, but neither the score nor even the winner was mentioned in "Homestead Grays Will Meet Locals Tonight, *Bluefield* (West Virginia) *Daily Telegraph*, September 7, 1938: 4.

98   "League Playoff Games Start Sept. 9," *Pittsburgh Courier*, September 3, 1938: 17.

99   "Stars Barely Escape Being Put Out of Loop Playoffs over Weekend," *Philadelphia Tribune*, September 15, 1938: 9. Harris's called shot received its own article on that page, under the headline, "Popeye's Feat Like 'The Babe.'" The final two games of the series were covered in "Stars Win 5th Game[,]

99  Will Play in Finals," September 15, 1938: 8. The *Tribune* said (twice) that the Crawfords' starting pitcher was named Davis, but both the Seamheads database and baseball-reference.com show that Roosevelt Davis's last season with the Craws was 1937.

100  For one overview of the end of the Greenlee era, see Doron Goldman, "1933-1962: The Business Meetings of Negro League Baseball" at sabr.org/research/negro-leagues-business-meetings-1933-1962.

101  See Jorge S. Figueredo, *Cuban Baseball: A Statistical History* (Jefferson, North Carolina: McFarland & Company Inc., 2003), 225-226, and McNeil, 47.

102  See the long list compiled by the Center for Negro League Baseball Research, at cnlbr.org/Portals/0/RL/Negro%20Leaguers%20in%20Venezuela.pdf. For some insights from Dandridge, see McNeil, 162.

103  One of the Dandridges was his baby daughter, Delores (or Dolores), and the other was 19-year-old Mary Dandridge. The latter was presumably Ray's wife, except that in the 1940 census her name was shown as Florence.

104  Examples of articles from 1942 that put Matlock on the Cubans' staff is "Cubans May Be Threat in NNL; Matlock And Morris Will Pitch," *New York Age*, April 25, 1942: 11, and "Cuban Stars, Equal of White Majors, Noted Baseball Scribes Say," *Atlanta Daily World*, April 15, 1942: 5. The latter said Matlock and the Cuban Stars beat the Brooklyn Dodgers in early 1942 in Havana. The Dodgers did lose three of five games to a team of Cuban all-stars in Havana during March of 1942, but the only pitcher on the Cuban team with a name similar to Matlock (winning or otherwise) was "Mayor," who beat the Dodgers 4-2 in the third game. That was longtime minor leaguer Agapito Mayor, according to "Hornet-Bound Cuban Handcuffs Bums, 4-2," *Charlotte* (North Carolina) *Observer*, March 8, 1942: section 2, 17.

105  "City Council Head to Throw Out First Ball at Stadium," *New York Amsterdam News*, May 8, 1943: 12. This article was printed in the *Pittsburgh Courier* on the same day.

106  His full stats for 1940 and 1941 are available at seamheads.com/NegroLgs/player.php?playerID=matloo1ler. See also Gerald F. Vaughn, "Mexico's Year of Josh Gibson," *The National Pastime*, Number 11 (SABR, 1992): 56. It was Vaughn who said Matlock's four shutouts led the league in 1941.

107  "Personal," *Moberly Monitor-Index and Democrat*, April 14, 1941: 7.

108  John Virtue, *South of the Color Barrier: How Jorge Pasquel and the Mexican League Pushed Baseball Toward Racial Integration* (Jefferson, North Carolina: McFarland & Company Inc., 2008), 99. For a photo of the team, see "Mexican League Players Visit Chicago," *Chicago Defender*, October 4, 1941: 22.

109  "Pearl Matlock Dies; Funeral Tomorrow," *Monitor-Index and Democrat*, June 18, 1942: 10; "Card of Thanks," *Monitor-Index and Democrat*, June 22, 1942: 3.

110  "Recreations Play Havana, Cuba, Stars Tonight in Attraction at Municipal Stadium Under Lights," *Kingston* (New York) *Daily Freeman*, June 26, 1942: 8.

111  "Rauschenberger Gives Only Three Hits as Indees Win Game 1 to 0," *Muscatine* (Iowa) *Journal and News-Tribune*, July 7, 1943: 8; "Leroy Matlock on Mound for Saturday Tilt," *Quad-City Times* (Davenport, Iowa), July 30, 1943: 13.

112  Lawrence Matlock signed Otis and Ella Mae's marriage certificate and listed a Davenport address. Leroy wasn't listed as the other witness; he was probably in Mexico. Otis and Ella Mae still lived in the Quad Cities in 1944, according to "Davenport," *Chicago Defender*, April 29, 1944: 17A.

113  "Local All-Stars Win Tussle from Chicago Negroes," *Moline* (Illinois) *Daily Dispatch*, July 24, 1944: 11. For another example of a game with the Quad City All-Stars, see "Seahawk Nine Whips All-Stars," *Waterloo* (Iowa) *Daily Courier*, May 15, 1944: 9. He also pitched for the Foundry. For example, see "Indees Lose to Blackhawks, 1 to 0, Then Defeat Foundry Club, 7 to 6," *Muscatine Journal and News-Tribune*, August 7, 1944: 5.

114  "Two Divorce Suits Filed in Circuit Court," *Monitor-Index and Democrat*, September 4, 1946: 9.

115  Armand Peterson and Tom Tomashek, *Town Ball: The Glory Days of Minnesota Amateur Baseball* (Minneapolis: University of Minnesota Press, 2006), 51. See also "Talkin' Baseball," *Marshall* (Minnesota) *Independent*, August 15, 2015, accessible at marshallindependent.com/news/local-news/2015/08/talkin-baseball/.

116  "Leroy Matlock, 60, Former Ball Player, Dies in Minnesota," *Monitor-Index & Evening Democrat*, March 8, 1968: 9. Matlock is listed in St. Paul city directories for 1950, 1955, and 1960. For insight into the significance of Seeger/Whirlpool in St. Paul, see "Seeger Co.'s Tenure Was Bittersweet for East Side, *St. Paul Pioneer Press*, twincities.com/2007/05/28/seeger-co-s-tenure-was-bittersweet-for-east-side/. This article was posted in 2007 but updated in 2015.

117  "93-Year-Old Man Steps Out – Daily," *Moberly Monitor Index and Evening Democrat*, January 6, 1973: 1.

118  "Former Teachers in Lincoln School File $32,000 Suit," *Moberly Monitor-Index*, November 26, 1955: 1. Malcolm Gladwell, "Miss Buchanan's Period of Adjustment," *Revisionist History*, season 2, episode 3, 2017. A transcript of this episode is available at blog.simonsays.ai/miss-buchanans-period-of-adjustment-revisionist-history-podcast-transcript-b4c65731f73c.

119  See Note 8.

120  "Adult Education Leaders Named," *Monitor-Index and Democrat*, January 25, 1936: "Adult Education Season Closes," *Monitor-Index and Democrat*, May 29, 1936: 4.

121  See Note 121. This obituary summed up his career as having been spent with "the St. Louis Stars, Pittsburgh (Pa.)

Crawfords, Kansas City Monarchs and Homestead Grays of Philadelphia, Pa." There is no known instance of Matlock having played with the Monarchs.

122 Dan Burley, "Confidentially Yours," *New York Amsterdam News*, May 27, 1944: 6-B. Chuck Davis, "Pupil Spanks Old Master in All Star Game," *Chicago Defender*, August 26, 1950: 17. Buck Leonard with John Holway, "A Gallery of Greats in Baseball's 'Other' League," *Washington Evening Star,* September 6, 1970: S-11. Leonard was consistent in this regard, because in 1938 he called Matlock *the* toughest, in "Buck Says Matlock Tough," *Pittsburgh Courier*, July 23, 1938: 16.

123 The interview is made available by the National Baseball Hall of Fame at collection.baseballhall.org/PASTIME/judy-johnson-oral-history-interview-1981-december-13-3.

124 Charles N. Brown, "Pirates Honor Negro Leaguers: Permanent PNC Park Exhibit Unveiled," *New Pittsburgh Courier*, July 18, 2001: A1.

125 Tony McClean, "Beyond Satchel: Part Two," June 11, 2005, at blackathlete.net/2005/06/beyond-satchel-part-two/.

126 Bankes, *The Pittsburgh Crawfords* (2001), 72.

# CLARENCE "SPOONY" PALM

## By Jon Henson

With both Josh Gibson and Bill Perkins, the 1935 Pittsburgh Crawfords were blessed in the receiving department. Any other catcher on the roster could not expect a lot of playing time. In April of '35, Clarence "Spoony" Palm was that additional catcher. An itinerant receiver who had played for eight different clubs since breaking onto the scene in 1927 with the Birmingham Black Barons, Palm had already served in the rotation that relieved Gibson (along with Perkins and Curtis Harris) in the second half of the 1934 campaign. He had made the spring-training trip to Hot Springs, Arkansas, playing in at least one game en route, on April 18, 1935, in New Orleans, where he hit two singles in a 5-4 victory over Memphis.[1] In late April, opportunity knocked. Abe and Effa Manley's Brooklyn Eagles were preparing for their NNL debut season, and they desperately needed experience behind the plate. Palm had proven his worth to the Craws as a reliable catcher with a strong bat and was "expected to furnish the back stop strength needed by the Brooklyn entry."[2] He started 32 games behind the plate for the Eagles' one season in the Borough and

*Catcher Clarence "Spoony" Palm, who had been a member of the 1934 Pittsburgh squad, spent spring training with the 1935 Crawfords but was assigned to the Brooklyn Eagles for the regular season.*

(Courtesy Noir-Tech Research, Inc.)

batted a respectable .285 (OPS .764) to help the team to a mediocre fifth-place finish with a record of 32–31.

When Brooklyn's season wrapped up in early October, Palm headed south and rejoined the Crawfords in Mexico City, where he provided a pinch-hit home run on October 25 in an 11-inning tie with the American All-Stars.[3] He may have played in more than this one late-season game with Pittsburgh; "Cum Posey's Pointed Paragraphs" reported in the December 21 *Pittsburgh Courier* that "'Spoony' Palm of the Brooklyn Eagles, came back, and caught the best ball he has caught since he left the Car Barn Park at St. Louis."[4] Palm's stint with the Crawfords was limited, but his career was extensive, starting in Birmingham in 1927 and finishing in New York with the Black Yankees in 1946, with seasons spent on the active rosters of at least a dozen franchises over that span. He also played several seasons in the Winter League in Puerto Rico, including the inaugural 1938-1939 campaign, and was among the group who absconded on their contracts in 1937 to play in dictator Rafael Trujillo's league in the Dominican Republic.[5]

Clarence Palm was born on October 27, 1907, in Georgetown, Texas, the youngest child of Will and Lula (Bonner) Palm.[6] Several well-regarded sources list Palm's place of birth as Clarendon, Arkansas, in October 1914, but this late birth year would have put him at age 13 when he made his big-league debut in Birmingham. Further research provides evidence that Palm himself listed his date of birth consistently as October 27, 1907, in Georgetown, Texas, when providing information for travel to and from the Caribbean for winter league play throughout the 1930s and '40s.[7]

The confusion stems from the fact that Clarence Palm often has been confused with Robert "Bob" Palm, who was indeed born in Arkansas in 1914 and who lived in St. Louis through much of his early life.[8] Bob Palm caught in at least one game for the St. Louis Stars in 1936, and then played with the semipro St. Louis Giants before signing a contract with Wilbur Hayes' Cleveland Buckeyes for the 1944 season.[9] By 1946 he was back in St. Louis managing the Giants.[10] Bob was the manager and catcher for the Brooklyn Brown Dodgers in Branch Rickey's United States League in 1946 when, as Giants manager, he insisted that if Brooklyn were to purchase the contract of Giants ace hurler Herbert "Doc" Bracken, "the whole club will have to go with him."[11] Bob Palm's death notice in the *St. Louis Post-Dispatch* of July 21, 1976, describes him as a "former catcher with the Cleveland Buckeyes and Brooklyn Brown Dodgers," and the Negro Leagues Database at seamheads.com lists Bob Palm as a cup of coffee with the Chicago American Giants in 1947.[12] Little additional information is available about catcher Bob Palm, and no sources suggest that he and Clarence are related or even knew one another. Clarence Palm's story is better documented, although it, too, retains its share of mystery.

Clarence is listed as two years old on the 1910 US Census in the household of Will (30) and Lula (28) Palm, and he was the youngest of five children. Besides Clarence, the family included Lenard (13), Lois (10), Eunace (8), and Edith (7). The family lived on Timber Street in Georgetown in an area known as the Ridge, just around the corner from Principal S.C. Marshall's Georgetown Colored School, which served the African American community through the elementary grades. On December 2, 1910, older brother Lenard died of typhoid fever.[13] Palm would have been too young to feel the full brunt of this loss, but certainly the experience marked the mood of the family in his early years. In 1916 his sister Lois became the first African American student to graduate from high school in Georgetown, completing her studies after Principal Marshall advocated for and received permission to teach secondary school courses in the city. The school was later known as Marshall High School in honor of its founder.[14] No records appear to have survived to indicate whether Clarence graduated, or even attended, the school as well, but with the circumstances of his family's proximity to the school and the celebrated achievements of his siblings, the likelihood exists that Clarence was enrolled here at least in his early childhood.

Younger brother William Arnett Palm was born in 1915 and studied sociology at the University of Kansas in the late 1930s before serving in World War II from 1942 to 1945.[15] In his later years, he recalled how Will and Lula Palm "placed great value on education, having seen first hand what ignorance could do to our people."[16] The pride the family took in Lois's achievement is evident in the description of her graduation ceremony as a "community celebration," held at the Wesley Chapel AME Church and attended by the whole community.[17] "Professor Marshall and the ministers from all the black churches made speeches, and Lois, as the only graduate, delivered both the valedictorian speech and the closing song."[18] By 1923 the secondary school's population and support had grown to the extent that a new facility was opened, a limestone building with five classrooms and a home economics room, situated on the corner of Timber and Second Streets. By the time Clarence would have been a student there in the mid-1920s, Marshall High School was well-established, and "students excelled in literary, athletic, and homemaking contests at county, district, and state levels. [Marshall alumna] Myrtle Stiner Tabor notes, '[We] won many medals and ribbons at these events, as well as in oratory, spelling, basketball, and football.'"[19] An athletic program at Marshall High School would have provided a budding young athlete such as Clarence Palm a perfect setting to hone his skills and attract the attention of scouts for area semipro clubs. But no records can be found to verify that Palm got his start at the school just blocks away from the family's home, which by then was located at 408 West Street in Georgetown.

Clarence's father, Will (Willie D.) Palm, was born on June 15, 1879, and worked as a butcher for many decades in the Williamson County, Texas, area. The 1920 and 1930 censuses list Will's occupation and disclose that he owned the family home on West Street outright. Every indication is that Will provided for his family a relatively comfortable standard of living with consistent employment in his trade. By 1910 at the latest, Will's father and Clarence's grandfather, Robert "Bob" Palm, was living with the family and was listed as "divorced" on the census. Bob was born in Mississippi (or possibly Arkansas) and brought to Texas in his youth, quite likely as a slave.[20] He found work in hotels and stayed in the area until his death in Georgetown in 1932.[21] Clarence's mother, Lula Bonner Palm, was born on August 28, 1880, in Georgetown to parents Emiline Williams of Texas and Marion Bonner of South Carolina.[22] She is listed in three decades of census data as a homemaker for her husband, six children, spouses of her children, and at least two grandchildren who lived with the family at one point or another throughout the 1910s, '20s, and '30s.[23] She died in Georgetown on July 8, 1946, a little more than a month before her 66th birthday. Her youngest son, Arnett, a resident of Parsons, Kansas, signed her death certificate.[24]

Little information has survived to document Clarence Palm's early life. Based on what is discoverable about the life and accomplishments of his parents and siblings, the best that can be offered is speculation. Even less clear is Palm's initiation into the ranks of local or regional baseball. With the loose, and often nonexistent, record-keeping that marks the era of black baseball, especially for teams and players not in the big leagues, answers to how, when, and where Clarence Palm broke into the baseball profession may never be forthcoming.[25] It is possible that Palm played for the Georgetown Black Tigers, an area team described as a chief regional rival for the Austin Black Senators of the Texas Colored League.[26] Perhaps Palm made the trip from Georgetown to nearby Austin to play for the Senators themselves, alongside Willie "El Diablo" Wells, the phenomenal shortstop and future Hall of Famer from Austin who was a contemporary of

Palm's and played with him on the St. Louis Stars championship squad in 1928.

The Texas Colored League, which ran from 1919 to 1926, included such teams as the Austin Black Senators, Dallas Black Giants, and Houston Black Buffaloes, and provided a talent pool for teams in the Negro Southern and National Leagues.[27] While no direct evidence of Palm's recruitment from this league to the Black Barons has surfaced, there is indication that a recruiting relationship existed between the leagues, and talent from Texas would often manifest in the big leagues. Will Patterson, a native of Houston and one-time manager of the Black Buffaloes, took the helm in Birmingham in 1925, and newspaper coverage of his ascent to the position as the Black Barons' manager describes the relationship between the two leagues. As the younger players contested the veterans for positions on the club, the *Birmingham News* reported on their origins: "A number of these newcomers are from the Texas League and some of them are expected to win berths on the local club."[28] Patterson's tenure with Birmingham was short-lived and occurred two seasons before Palm's matriculation to Alabama, but the connection between the two leagues described in 1925 lends credence to the speculation that an up-and-comer like Palm may have been spotted by scouts playing in the Lone Star State and brought up from there, along with many of his contemporaries, for the 1927 season.

Whatever the path that led the youthful catcher to Birmingham in the spring of 1927, one thing is certain: Clarence Palm burst onto the scene for the Black Barons seemingly out of nowhere. In April, as the Black Barons prepared at their spring-training facility in Gadsden, no mention of Palm is found in the press that reported on the progress of the squad and its probable roster.[29] Reuben Jones, a native Texan who had played for the Dallas Black Giants in the Texas Colored League and starred in the outfield for Birmingham from 1923 to 1925, had been selected as the new manager of the Black Barons in 1927 with their reentry into the NNL.[30] Previews of the preseason games in April list Poindexter Williams as the starting backstop, with William "Bobby" Robinson, typically a third baseman, cited as the alternate behind the plate.[31] Palm was not recognized in the papers even as a prospect this early in the season. However, with the lack of options in the receiving department, an opportunity existed for a second catcher to make the roster.

The draw of the Black Barons for Birmingham fans of baseball is evident in the preview writeup for the season opener at Rickwood Field on April 25. The press optimistically anticipated 20,000 fans to attend the inaugural homestand against the Cuban Stars (10,000 actually showed up), and the *Birmingham Reporter* described how local youth would be given permission to skip school in order to attend the game. Poindexter Williams is listed as the probable starter behind the plate for Birmingham with no other name identified as a potential receiver for ace hurler Sam Streeter.[32] The April 26 recap in the *Birmingham News* describes Clarence Palm's Negro National League debut. Apparently Williams batted once and left the game early, as Palm is listed with four at-bats. He knocked a triple and scored in the third inning, and he also reached base on a single in the ninth as Birmingham took the game from the Cubans, 5-4 in 10 innings. Palm was also involved in a double play with Roy Parnell from right field to home.[33] The effort was an auspicious entrance for the young catcher, but interestingly, Palm is referenced in this initial recap simply by his last name, with no description of his history or how he suddenly arrived on the scene.

By the end of the week, Palm had caught the attention of the beat writers at the *Birmingham Reporter* and was featured in a spread that covered the club's season prospects. An image of the 19-year-old ran with the caption "Clarence Palm: One of the star catchers on the Black Barons Club, who played in the opening game Monday [April 25]."[34] The youngster contributed somewhat inconsistently as a backstop early on, but he soon began to build a reputation as a power hitter. The following week vs. Cleveland, Palm was credited with a two-RBI double but also dropped a throw at home in the series-opening victory.[35] In the doubleheader that wrapped up this early series with Cleveland on May 5, Birmingham swept the day, and Palm's hitting ignited the scoring in the second game: "Dusky Palm broke up the second game with a home run in the first inning. He came back with a triple in the sixth that gave the Jonesmen their final run. Palm was the only player to bag two hits in the night cap."[36]

Palm continued regularly in the catching rotation, along with Poindexter Williams, and established a role for himself as an offensive contributor through May and June.[37] By the time Leroy "Satchel" Paige joined the Black Barons in late June, Palm was an integral member of the inconsistent Birmingham squad that was trying to right the ship in the first half of the season. Palm did not work in Paige's notorious first big outing with the Black Barons in St. Louis against the Stars. In that game at Stars Park on June 27, Satchel took the mound, throwing "hard, fast, and wild," ultimately tangling up Stars catcher Henry Williams in an errant pitch that forced him from the game. When replacement catcher Mitch Murray came up to bat in Williams' spot, Paige threw wild again; this time, the result was an injury to Murray's hand. Incensed at this apparent attack on the Stars' catchers, Murray advanced on Satchel, who quickly made his way toward the dugout. Murray flung his bat, which hit Paige on the hip. The "whole park was in an uproar," and the game was called off. The Black Barons were fortunate to take their leave without any additional physical harm.[38] In the game the next day, Palm hit two home runs to aid the 10-8 victory that broke up the Stars' 11-game win streak.[39]

Palm was mentioned, along with Roy Parnell, as a heavy hitter for Birmingham as the first half of the season came to a close.[40] By the end of August, Birmingham was leading the NNL in the second half of the season, boasting a 17-9 record even with a recent string of losses.[41] Despite a September slump, the club managed to win the second half, going 29-15, only to lose the pennant series to the Chicago American Giants in a four-game sweep.[42] Palm caught the final game, with starting pitcher Streeter getting pulled in favor of Paige after giving up four runs in the first inning. The Paige-Palm battery performed well for the duration, with Paige allowing only two more runs, but the Black Barons could not muster more than two tallies themselves and surrendered the flag to Chicago.[43] Notwithstanding the disappointment of this postseason sweep, Palm had a standout rookie season for Birmingham, playing in 57 games and hitting .282[44] with an .821 OPS. The young catcher with the powerful swing, just shy of his 20th birthday, was just getting started.

Palm claimed a spot on the roster in St. Louis for the 1928 season and stuck around the Mound City through 1929. Stars manager Candy Jim Taylor must have been eyeing a replacement for his aging and ailing catcher Mitchell Murray, the stalwart backstop who caused a ruckus with Paige in the previous season. Murray had signed with St. Louis in 1923 and had wielded a heavy bat through his first few seasons; he had remained reliable behind the plate, but his offensive contributions had fallen off considerably, and his average dropped from .315 to .259 from the 1926 to 1927 seasons. Perhaps Taylor's motivation to sign Clarence Palm away from the Black Barons was, in some way, the result of the bad blood that was made apparent on the day of the near-riot when Paige threw wild at the St. Louis receivers. It is also possible that the hand injury Murray received from Paige the previous June contributed to the veteran catcher's poor shape at the start of the 1928 season. Intentional or not, Taylor's signing of Palm to replace Murray served as some measure of revenge against a club whose ace pitcher had carelessly injured both of his receivers the previous season. In the 20-year-old Palm, Taylor would find youthful endurance and a heavy hitter who could generate runs alongside such greats as

James "Cool Papa" Bell, George "Mule" Suttles, and Willie "El Diablo" Wells. By May, Murray had been deactivated to "coach" and Palm had been signed. Soon after, Murray was released; he ultimately signed with Chicago. Palm shared receiving duties with veteran Henry Williams for the 1928 season, catching in 37 games (including four of the nine championship matches) and pinch-hitting in an additional eight. His offense trended upward, as he hit .319 (OPS .921) with seven home runs in league games in the sixth or seventh spot in support of the big sticks at the top of the order.

Palm and Williams were on the receiving end of some legendary pitching performances for St. Louis in 1928, as the staff included Ted Trent (19-3, 2.21 ERA), Logan "Slap" Hensley (10-4, 3.37), and Roosevelt "Rosey" Davis (8-0, 3.40). The exceptional batteries, along with the superlative batting up and down the order, propelled St. Louis to an easy title as champions of the first half of the season. Chicago, however, took the second-half banner to force a playoff for the pennant. Since the Eastern Colored League had folded earlier in the season, the winner of this championship playoff would be crowned 1928 Negro League champions. The teams split the first four games of the nine-game series, which were played in Chicago, and then headed to St. Louis for the remainder of the series. Palm and his manager, Taylor, hit back-to-back pinch-hit singles in an eighth-inning rally in Game One, with Palm ultimately scoring on Branch Russell's triple. These heroics were not enough for the win, however. In Game Four, Palm scored two runs in the key 5-3 victory for the Stars. Back in St. Louis, the teams traded victories, extending the series to the full nine games. The finale starred Wells, who dominated defensively and scored four runs off two home runs and a triple. The Stars had brought glory to St. Louis by knocking off the perennial champion Chicago club for their first Negro League title, and Clarence Palm had played a key role in the club's dominance throughout the season. In this climate of victory, Palm had found a home.

St. Louis began the 1929 season with great optimism, as the championship squad returned intact and added rookie southpaw Leroy Matlock. The Stars played great baseball in 1929, going 56-34-1 in league play. "Unfortunately for the Stars the Kansas City Monarchs played lights-out baseball all season long and fueled by a 34-6 (.850) record for the second half of the season, the Kansas City Monarchs easily won the Negro National League championship with a record of 62-17."[45] Palm had a breakout season in 1929, appearing in 65 games and batting .333 with an OPS of 1.038. He hit 16 home runs in league games, third-highest on the team behind Wells's 26 and Suttles' 18, while playing in 30 fewer games than the two future Hall of Famers. In an early-season series against the Black Barons at Rickwood Field, Palm went deep with back-to-back homers in the first game of a doubleheader on May 27, and then followed that feat with two homers in the rubber match the next day.[46] On June 6 the *St. Louis Post-Dispatch* opined that "'Devil' Wells, who features at short, 'Mule' Suttles at first base, and Palm, the hard-hitting catcher, are the outstanding players in the local aggregation."[47]

The Candy Jim Taylor era ended in St. Louis after the 1929 season, but many of the regulars stayed on with the Stars. Palm, however, was not one of them, as he signed with the Detroit Stars, for the 1930 and '31 seasons; he also returned to the Motor City in 1933. The 1930 census puts Palm back in Georgetown, where he was reportedly employed at the cottonseed oil mill in town. A question on the census asked whether the individual "was at work yesterday," to which the response "yes" was given for Clarence.[48] The census form is dated April 24, 1930. Whether Palm had actually returned to Georgetown during the offseason is unclear, but on April 27 he caught both games of a doubleheader loss in Chicago to the American Giants with Bingo DeMoss's Detroit Stars, going 1-for-4 at the plate in game one.[49] On May 6 he returned to St. Louis and delivered a pinch-hit home run in the ninth to defeat his former club, 7-6.[50]

Palm played in Detroit for two seasons and in 1930 helped lead the Stars to a second-half championship by way of a 24-game late-season win streak[51] that led to a showdown with his former teammates in St. Louis for the league pennant. This was Palm's third postseason series in his first four seasons. He caught every inning of all seven games for Detroit, committing three errors, with a passed ball, and allowing St. Louis four stolen bases. Batting fifth in the order, Palm contributed mightily, going 10-for-28 (.357) with four RBIs, three runs scored, two walks, one hit by pitch, and a pivotal home run. The shot came in Game Four in St. Louis, with the *Star and Times* declaring Palm "the hitting hero of the night, sending a homer over the wall" in the eighth inning, which was the difference in the 5-4 Detroit victory.[52] When the series moved back to Detroit, the St. Louis team won two of the three games played before heavy rains in the area washed out the remainder of the nine-game series.[53] St. Louis was declared the winner of the 1930 championship.

The 1931 season in the Negro National League was one of financial stress. Of the remaining clubs, Detroit finished a dismal fourth in the standings with a 25-33 record. Palm had another outstanding season as the primary catcher and hit .311 (OPS .786), with 50 hits in league games, and was second only to center fielder Turkey Stearnes in RBIs (32) and home runs (3). Despite the coming disarray of the league and the movement of franchises in this season, several exhibition games were played to thousands of fans of all races. In August Detroit faced off against the Regal Giants, a Triple-A outfit made up of former major- and minor-league white baseball stars, at Wigle Park in Windsor, Ontario, and embarrassed them 18-5 in nine innings. Palm hit a first-inning homer in the game, which the *Windsor Star* described as "one of the most uneven contests" in front of a crowd of 2,000 onlookers. "The Detroit Stars outclassed their opponents in every department of the game, hitting, fielding, and pitching, and might easily have piled up a dozen more runs had they felt inclined."[54]

As prolific a hitter as Palm appears to have been, he may have had some trouble with the breaking ball. An apocryphal tale from the early 1930s, reported by Dan Burley decades later in the *Chicago Daily Defender*, describes a memory from Harry Salmon, a batterymate of Palm's in Birmingham during his rookie season. Salmon explained that many Negro National League players would head to New Orleans during the winter to continue playing. He recalled a game in which the New Orleans Black Pelicans "had in their lineup, a catcher, one Clarence Palm, who used to backstop for the old Detroit Stars in the days of Hallie Harding and Grady Orange."[55] The team would attract "swarms of white fans" to Pelican Park, who would sit in a section separated from black fans by chicken wire, "so they wouldn't get black on 'em by rubbing up against Negroes." Burley relays Salmon's story:

> Well, as Harry used to tell it, Palm ... never could hit a curve ball and by the fifth inning, Salmon had fanned him twice. ... A big redneck white fellow was a personal fan of Palm and used to sit in the front row of the white folk's section behind the plate. ... Every time Palm got a hit, he'd throw a handful of 2 for $1 Productos [cigars] out to the hefty catcher and hollered encouragement at him on every opportunity. But watching Palm strike out was so disheartening that the white man was completely dejected and sat with bowed head as though in mourning as Palm swung futilely at Salmon's wicked and snaky curves. ... Finally, when the game entered the seventh inning and the Black Pelicans had two men on and none out and Palm was coming to bat, the white fellow suddenly jumped up, climbed over the fence, and marched up to the umpire. "Stop the game!" he ordered and then walked out to Salmon on

the mound. Pointing a fat finger under Tall Harry's nose, he hollered loud enough to be heard on Rampart street, "Look heah! Mah Nigra can't hit no curve balls an' by Gawd, don't you throw him no more of those curve balls, y'all heah me?" ... Harry, nervous and apprehensive, nodded as he got his instructions. ... Before the game ended, Palm had two home runs to his credit and a hatful of El Productos![56]

The chaos of the 1932 season in Negro League baseball was the start of Palm's true journeyman status. Homestead Grays owner Cumberland "Cum" Posey brought Spoony Palm on board as a replacement for Josh Gibson, who joined Gus Greenlee's Crawfords for a higher salary.[57] With the NNL disbanded, Posey's Homestead entry in his new East-West League initially included Palm leading the staff that caught for Smokey Joe Williams, George "Chippy" Britt, Leroy Matlock, and Columbus Vance.[58] The planned batteries with Palm as the lead receiver never really took shape, with Spoony catching 10 innings in two games, one of those a 5-4 preseason loss in late April to the Detroit Wolves (also owned by Posey).[59] By mid-May, Palm had parted ways with Posey and the fledgling (and soon-to-be defunct) East-West League and made his way to Chicago for a brief stint with Cole's American Giants.[60]

Spoony's stop in the Windy City was brief. The Negro Leagues Database at seamheads.com lists him catching in two games for Cole's squad and going a lackluster 1-for-9 at the plate. Within the first two weeks of his arrival, Clarence joined American Giants pitcher Luther "Vet" McDonald to journey north, signing a contract with the Crookston (Minnesota) Red Sox, an independent club that played in northern Minnesota and Canada. The Crookston club was made up mostly of white players, and the team's schedule included amateur teams from the area as far north as Winnipeg, but also tougher rivals in the likes of legendary hurler John Donaldson's All Stars as well as the Kansas City Monarchs.[61] Pitcher Chet Brewer, who had played the full 1931 schedule for Crookston, recalled his time there as "one of the most pleasurable experiences of his lifetime."[62] Brewer excelled on the team with a 10-1-1 record for the season and was lauded by the locals and received a key to the city in commendation of his heroic exploits on behalf of the town. The Crookston community was a welcoming one for black players, and Palm and McDonald must have found similar satisfaction as their performance on the field would indicate.

On May 23, 1932, Spoony and Vet McDonald starred in an evening-game victory for the Red Sox in Canada, with Palm going 4-for-5 at the plate with two triples in his first appearance.[63] On June 4 the *Chicago Defender* reported that the battery of McDonald and Palm, along with Spoony's offense, defeated Donaldson's stars, 10-2, in Crookston's home opener.[64] As early as mid-June, word of Palm's performance up north was spreading among his peers. The *Defender* reported the following in the National Edition on June 18:

> Clarence Palm, formerly of Detroit in the Negro National league and now catcher for the Crookston Red Sox, semipro baseball champions of the Northwest, is heading the Red Sox in batting.
>
> Palm has been at bat 52 times this season with 27 safe hits credited to him. Four of them were three-base clouts. His batting average is .519.
>
> Palm, who came to the club from Chicago for a tryout, was immediately proffered a contract. He has made a hit with the fans for his base stealing, his hook slide and his fleetness in covering the bags.
>
> The Crookston team, with Palm behind the rubber triangle, has trounced Winnipeg twice, defeated John Donaldson's Colored All-Stars two games, defeated Gilkerson's Union Giants, tied the House of David, 0-0,

in nine innings, conquered Fargo, Grafton and Neche N.D.[65]

Even Palm's baserunning was a standout for Crookston, but his offensive output solidified him as the star of the northern Minnesota outfit in 1932. He sustained his acumen with the timber through the season and newspapers continued to report on his hitting prowess through August.[66]

After Palm's season in Minnesota, his career took an even more nomadic turn, as he appeared on the rosters of eight distinct big-league clubs from 1933 to 1936. Palm returned to Hamtramck Stadium as a Detroit Star in May 1933, but this time, instead of Bingo DeMoss as his manager, he was reunited with Candy Jim Taylor, who was fresh in the Motor City by way of Indianapolis. As Gus Greenlee's new Negro National League took shape, Taylor's Indy entry showed signs in early May that it could not survive. As a result, the entire team was absorbed by Detroit, and Taylor resumed team leadership under the Stars' banner.[67] Immediately upon arrival, Taylor worked out a deal to sign Palm to anchor the receiving department for his otherwise youthful roster. The *Pittsburgh Courier* declared that "the addition of Palms [sic] has meant considerable hitting strength and confidence to the [Detroit] outfit."[68] Candy Jim's instincts about Palm were correct, as the 24-year-old catcher, still in his prime, was hitting .371 (13-for-35), with two doubles and two triples, by late June.[69] Despite Palm's numbers, Detroit had a dismal 13-20 record midway through the season and Taylor decided to walk away, taking the helm in Nashville for the second half. After Taylor's exit, Palm decided to abandon ship as well, and he joined Posey's Akron Grays, managed by Bingo DeMoss, for the remainder of 1933.[70] Palm hit well for Akron as the primary catcher in their short existence as a franchise, batting .267 (OPS .846) with a double, two triples, and a home run in nine games. In August, the Columbus Blue Birds merged with the Akron squad to form the Cleveland Giants, and Palm finished the season with this trimmed roster that represented the best of both former clubs. In at least one series with the Crawfords, in August, Palm may have played center field for Cleveland, a rare appearance up to this point in his career in a position other than behind the plate.[71]

In April 1934, Clarence was the barnstorming catcher with Juan Padrone's Cuban Giants, joining fellow receiver Mitch Murray, pitcher Logan "Slap" Hensley, and others in a nationwide tour, inviting all comers.[72] By June Palm had joined Posey's Homestead Grays to back up regular catcher Tex Burnett, and he also played a couple of games in right field to keep his bat active. Spoony's contribution to the club's success was minimal, as he achieved only three hits (one double) in 17 at-bats for a disappointing .176 average in seven games. On July 4 Homestead squared off in a doubleheader with Pittsburgh at Greenlee Field, with Satchel's shutout silencing the Grays' bats in the first game for a 4-0 Craws' victory before Homestead achieved the split with a 4-3 win in the second game.[73] Palm hit a single and double and scored a run in the Grays' win.[74] On July 14 the *Pittsburgh Courier* ran an image of Palm tagging Oscar Charleston out at home on a play in the first game, in which Charleston badly twisted his ankle.[75] On Sunday, July 15, Palm went hitless for the Grays vs. Baltimore in a game played in Columbus, Ohio.[76] By Saturday, July 21, Spoony was wearing a Crawfords uniform, and he smashed a triple in the first game and caught the second contest in a doubleheader sweep of the Bacharach Giants.[77] Palm fared better in the second half of the season with Pittsburgh and hit a respectable .250 (OPS .812) with a double, two triples, and a home run in just 11 games. He proved to be a dependable alternate to spell Gibson as the 1934 season wound down.

After Palm had been assigned by the Crawfords to the Brooklyn Eagles in April 1935, he played well for the Manleys immediately. On May 5 Palm caught for Leon Day and went 4-for-5 in the first game of a doubleheader sweep of the Newark Dodgers; he shared the offensive laurels with Clarence "Fats" Jenkins, a two-sport star from Harlem who also played for the Renaissance basketball team.[78] Even as Palm was beginning his ninth season of big-league play, he was considered the youth of the catching department in comparison to his rotation mate Tex Burnett, who at age 35 was nine years older. Palm's youthful experience was put to full use, as indicated by a road trip to Chicago in July. Burnett, who also played the hot corner on occasion, had injured his hand in June and was out. Twenty-three-year-old Leon Ruffin was scheduled to split catching duties with Palm on the road trip but presented with a split finger of his own, so Palm was required to catch four full games that included a Sunday doubleheader.[79] Despite the drama of manager Ben Taylor's summary dismissal by Abe Manley early in the season and the mediocre league finish, Palm played through the season for Brooklyn before rejoining the Crawfords for their late-season jaunt south of the border. The Manleys assembled a squad to play in Puerto Rico during the winter of 1936, where they faced off against the Cincinnati Reds and also won the winter league championship, taking home a trophy sponsored by the Bacardi rum company.[80] Palm does not appear in any news coverage for the Eagles in Puerto Rico that winter, which supports the assertion that he instead played in the Mexico City series with the Craws against a team of American all-stars. Oscar Charleston's anecdote featuring Palm and major-league pitcher George Pipgras, which he shared with Lewis Dial of the *New York Age* in September 1936, likely represents an encounter that took place during the 1935 postseason tour in Mexico.[81]

The draw of New York City was apparently enough to bring Spoony Palm back for the 1936 season. Fats Jenkins, who played for the Black Yankees for three seasons before his stint with the Eagles, rejoined the club for its first foray into the formal league structure, and Palm had come along as well, signing on to share catching duties with Yanks manager Bob Clarke.[82] Palm contributed offensively for owner Jim "Soldier Boy" Semler's Harlem outfit. In the Black Yankees' mostly cellar-dwelling existence in the NNL standings, 1936 proved to be one of their better seasons. Palm aided in this success, batting .351 (OPS .851), with a home run and six stolen bases. On Christmas Eve of that year, Palm took his maiden voyage to the Caribbean for winter ball, joining his fellow Black Yankees to follow the Manleys' lead with the Eagles, who had returned to the island to dominate the winter games. The press covered the Harlem team's departure widely, with some papers erroneously reporting their destination as Havana, while others correctly placed their port of call as San Juan.[83] This was the first of several excursions Palm took, over at least the next 13 years, to San Juan both to play as well as to manage in the island's fertile baseball community.

On February 11, 1937, Palm left San Juan for New York, along with Leroy Matlock, Henry McHenry, and other Negro League star pitchers and catchers to report for spring training.[84] In March, Palm is described as Clarke's alternate to catch Rosey Davis, Roy Williams, Bill Holland, and Barney Brown, as the rest of the Black Yankees returned from San Juan to prepare for Opening Day.[85] On April 24 the *Brooklyn Citizen* reported that Palm was expected to back up manager Clarke in catching recently signed pitcher John "Neck" Stanley in a preseason tilt with the semipro Brooklyn Bushwicks at Dexter Park in Queens the next day.[86]

What the sportswriters at the *Citizen* didn't know was that Palm had left town two days earlier, on April 22, to travel to Trujillo City in the Dominican Republic via San Juan. He sailed on the S.S. *Coamo* along with New York Cubans players Dave "Showboat" Thomas and Clyde Spearman.[87] This trio had followed the money of the Dominican dictator to bolster the talent in the country's league as he offered handsome salaries to Negro League players who were willing to make the jump to the island. Palm, Thomas, and Spearman did not play with Paige,

# THE 1935 PITTSBURGH CRAWFORDS

Gibson, Matlock, and Bell on the Ciudad Trujillo Dragones outfit designed to achieve glory for the sociopathic leader; instead, they joined the roster of the rival Aquilas Cibaenas that ultimately included such legends as Chet Brewer, Martin Dihigo, Red Parnell, and Luis Tiant Sr.[88] In the Dominican tournament that season, the Cibaenas Aquilas (Eagles) made a run in the finals against Paige and the Dragones squad, who were essentially given the ultimatum "win or else" in order to make a good showing for Trujillo. The Cibaenas club took the final game of the championship down to the wire with the Dragones, and Palm grounded out to short for the game's final out, as Paige and company dodged a bullet by eking out a victory for the dictator's chosen representatives on the diamond.[89] When the contract jumpers returned to the States at the conclusion of the Dominican tournament, they remained suspended by the NNL for the remainder of the season. The group, led by Paige and Martin Dihigo, formed a barnstorming troop that traveled the country under a variety of monikers, ultimately winning the renowned Denver Post Tournament for a nice payday.[90] Palm reportedly caught Satchel Paige on this all-star aggregation and presumably was also behind the plate for Matlock and Chet Brewer.[91]

Palm returned to the Black Yankees for the 1938 season and remained with the club until July of the following year, when he made the jump to the Philadelphia Stars. He remained with Philly through the 1942 season, save for a short stint late in 1941 with the Grays as an attempted replacement for Josh Gibson.[92] In 1943 Palm returned to Harlem as Tex Burnett tried to bolster a flagging Black Yankees roster that was suffering from depletion during the war years.[93] Continuing to shuttle back and forth between New York and Philadelphia, Palm signed again with the Stars for the 1944 campaign, anchoring Ed Bolden's catching department for the middling Pennsylvania entry.[94] He stayed in the City of Brotherly Love through June of 1945, when he again accepted an offer to return to the comforts of Harlem, where he finished out his career during the 1946 season with Semler's lowly squad. Over this latter period of Palm's career, he appeared in fewer games as the years rolled on, with only a smattering of extra-base hits, but still showed occasional flashes of brilliance at the bat. In June 1938 Palm was lauded as the home-run king of the Black Yankees and the talk of the winter league.[95] In 1940, for Philadelphia, Palm hit .321 but with no extra-base hits.

More noteworthy than his service for clubs in the NNL in the latter half of his career is Palm's success in Puerto Rico during the winter league's formative years. He was among the first imports from the Negro Leagues in the inaugural Puerto Rico Semi-Pro League of 1938-1939, along with Grays ace Raymond Brown, Jimmie Crutchfield, and Bill Perkins.[96] On October 29, 1938, Palm sailed from New York for San Juan.[97] On board with Clarence was Newark second baseman Dick Seay, who is not listed on a winter-league roster in this first season but had played several previous winters on the island. Palm signed on with the San Juan Senadores to form a battery with Brown.[98] Over the first two league seasons (1938-39 and 1939-40) the Brown-Palm battery racked up a 14-0 record.[99] For the 1940-41 season, both Brown and Palm signed with the Cangrejeros de Santurce (Santurce Crabbers), with Palm catching in place of Josh Gibson and Brown taking on pitching duties in lieu of Bill Byrd, who had contracted his services with the Caguas Criollos instead.[100] Palm had a record season for the Crabbers at the plate, joining the .400 hitters club as he went 65-for-159 for a .409 average.[101]

Palm's contract with Santurce, which is dated November 6, 1941, shows a weekly salary of $50 and a round-trip ticket to and from the island.[102] When Gibson returned to Puerto Rico from Mexico in late October, Palm was deactivated and took on the status of coach to make way for what would become Gibson's signature season on the island, when he batted .480 (59-for-123) to set the all-time league record.[103]

Soon after Gibson's return, Palm took over coaching duties for the Humacao team (recently moved to Arecibo because of financial problems). His new team posted a lackluster 5-9 record over the final 14 games of the season.[104] No travel records or teams statistics exist that put Palm in Puerto Rico in any capacity from 1943 through 1945. In the 1946-47 season, he came back to Santurce and managed the club to a fourth-place finish. He oversaw a Santurce squad that included Dick Seay as a coach as well as the Crabbers' debut of Monarchs slugger Willard "Sonny" Brown.[105] No sources list Palm as having any role in Puerto Rican baseball after this one managerial season, though passenger manifests for Pan Am flights show that he visited the island for three weeks in September 1949. Dick Seay made the flight from New York to San Juan with Palm on September 8, but he did not fly back with him on September 29.[106] Perhaps Palm was brought down for a consultation, or possibly another managerial position was in the works that did not pan out. Details of this apparently final excursion to Puerto Rico, as with much of his life, remain obscured.

For someone with a fairly well-documented playing career that lasted 19 years, remarkably little is known about Clarence Palm's personal life. He appears never to have registered for Social Security, he does not appear in any school records, and no records have surfaced to show that he fathered any children. No records can be located to describe how Clarence got the nickname Spoony.

Sometime between October 1938 and September 1939, Palm got married. On the passenger manifest for the trip to San Juan in his debut season for the Senators, he lists himself as single. When he returned for the following season in September 1939, Palm declared the status "married" in the travel paperwork. Neither a marriage certificate nor the name of the bride has materialized. Clarence Palm and "Wife Palm" appear in the 1940 census living in San Juan.[107] The first name of his wife is scrawled and illegible. Clarence's occupation is listed as "pelotero" (baseball player) for the San Juan club, and both he and his wife are misidentified as "blanco" (white) in the race column. His wife has no listed occupation. Palm continued to identify himself as married on all subsequent travel documents through the 1940s.

The few anecdotes of Palm that exist paint a picture of an affable man who seems to have taken things in stride. Outfielder Gene Benson, who played with him in Philadelphia and was with him in San Juan beginning in 1939, recalled his friend and teammate fondly: "Clarence Palm was one of the most comical men around.... He and I were great buddies. We would walk into [San Juan] together, check what was playing at the different movies. He would look up and see *Hoy*, so he said to me, 'Ben, you know, *Hoy* must be a heck of a picture. It's playing all over town.' But it was the coming attractions of today, it meant 'today.'"[108]

In an interview toward the end of his life, Newark Eagles' pitcher Max Manning reminisced about Palm's reluctance to deal with foul popups: "There was a catcher, 'Spoony' Palm, whose given name was Clarence. Spoony was funny. He didn't like foul pops. With the ball in the air, we'd yell, 'Better keep your mask on, Spoony!' He'd say, 'It's a tall one; someone better come get it.'"[109] By every account, Palm appears to have been the type of personality who liked to have fun and make his friends and colleagues chuckle. Perhaps this outlook on life was the origin of the nickname, since "spoony" can mean "silly" as well as "sentimental."

Whether out of professional convenience or a true affinity for the city, Palm continued to live in west Harlem from the time he settled there in the early 1940s until his death more than 30 years later. Palm's 1941 Puerto Rico Winter League contract lists his address on West

# THE 1935 PITTSBURGH CRAWFORDS

131st Street in Manhattan, and in 1942 he lived on Madison Avenue. Palm eventually resided at different addresses on 145th Street in Harlem, which is on the boundary between the Sugar Hill and Hamilton Heights neighborhoods. He is listed as living on 145th Street in city telephone directories throughout the 1950s, while otherwise he had managed to keep his name out of the press and public records.

Clarence "Spoony" Palm died on April 21, 1969, at his residence at 508 West 145th Street in Manhattan. Harlem's Benta Funeral Home handled his arrangements, but no information is available detailing cause of death or next of kin. Palm was interred in the Rosehill Cemetery in Linden, New Jersey, on April 25, 1969, 42 years to the day after his Negro National League debut with the Birmingham Black Barons.

## Acknowledgments

The author expresses thanks to Katherine Hooker, research and instruction librarian at the A. Frank Smith Jr. Library Center at Southwestern University, Georgetown, Texas, for her assistance in identifying sources for information on Palm's family. Gratitude is owed as well to Ruth Clusman, manager of the Rosehill and Rosedale Cemetery Association in Linden, New Jersey, for providing specifics to identify Clarence Palm's location of death, funeral location, and final resting place.

## Sources

All player statistics and team records, unless otherwise noted, are from the Negro Leagues database at seamheads.com.

## Notes

1. "Craws Win Two, Point for 4-Club Twin Bill," *Pittsburgh Courier*, April 20, 1935: A5.
2. "Pick-Ups from the Diamond." *Afro-American*, April 27, 1935: 21.
3. J.M. Campos, "Hornsby's Playing Astounds Mexicans," *The Sporting News*, October 31, 1935: 5.
4. "Cum Posey's Pointed Paragraphs," *Pittsburgh Courier*, December 21, 1935: 13.
5. Thomas Van Hyning, *Puerto Rico's Winter League* (Jefferson, North Carolina: McFarland & Company, 1995), 7.; "Raid National Assoc.," *Philadelphia Tribune*, April 29, 1937: 12.
6. Palm, "Williamson County Texas Births and Christenings, 1840-1981." Accessed October 23, 2019, ancestry.com. An official birth certificate remains elusive for Palm, but a registry of live births in Williamson County lists an entry recorded on October 28, 1907, for Will and Lula Palm giving birth to a son, no first name yet identified. On passenger manifests for trips to the Dominican Republic and Puerto Rico in the 1930s and '40s, Palm lists his birth date as October 27, so it's likely that the entry in the registry was recorded a day after his birth.
7. Passenger Manifest for S.S. *American Ponce* sailing from New York, New York, October 28, 1938, arriving at the port of San Juan November 3, 1938. Accessed November 1, 2019, ancestry.com.
8. US Census Bureau, Robert Palm in the 1930 Census, St. Louis, Missouri. Accessed October 17, 2019, ancestry.com.
9. "St. Louis Stars Split with Zulu Cannibals," *St. Louis Globe-Democrat*, July 5, 1936: 15. Only this one reference for Bob Palm playing with the Stars has surfaced. During or after the 1936 season, Bob played with the St. Louis Giants until he was signed, along with Doc Bracken, by Hayes for Cleveland's 1944 entry. The Cleveland paper published an image of Palm, Bracken, and Hayes taken as the contracts were executed. The Palm in the picture is decidedly not Clarence. See Morris Mills, "Wilbur Hayes Signs Crack Battery for New Buckeyes," *Cleveland Call and Post*, October 23, 1943: 10A.
10. "Monarchs Defeated 7 to 4 by Giants," *Chicago Defender*, June 8, 1946: 21B.
11. "Entire Club Purchased to Obtain Ace Pitcher," *Indianapolis Star*, June 4, 1946, 17. The conflation of Bob and Clarence Palm is understandable, as both were catchers who had spent time in St. Louis and later made appearances for New York teams. Larry Lester, in *Black Baseball in New York City* (Jefferson, North Carolina: MacFarland & Company, 2017), 134 and 136, mistakenly describes Clarence as a member, along with Bracken, of the Brooklyn Brown Dodgers in 1946, listing his place of birth as Clarendon, Arkansas, and attributing Bob's demand that the entire Giants' roster move to Brooklyn to Clarence. Dick Clark and Larry Lester, eds., *Negro Leagues Book* (Cleveland: Society for American Baseball Research, 1994), 118 and 134, lists Clarence on the roster both for the St. Louis Stars and the New York Black Yankees in 1936 and does not list Bob as a member of the 1944 Cleveland Buckeyes. However, reporting during the 1936 season shows Clarence consistently with the Black Yankees in 1936 as well as in 1946 when Bob was playing for St. Louis and Brooklyn respectively. See "1st Half Goes to Elites as Stars Get Off to Bad Start," *Philadelphia Tribune*, July 16, 1936: 13; *Cleveland Call and Post*, July 23, 1936: 2; "Black Yankees Battle Lloyd Here Tonight," *Chester* (Pennsylvania) *Times*, May 17, 1946: 16; "Brown Dodgers in 2 with Boston Blues," *Brooklyn Daily Eagle*, June 9, 1946: 25; "Top-Flight Negro Baseball Teams to Play Here June 17," *Daily Item* (Sunbury, Pennsylvania), June 12, 1946: 13; "Kaysee Monarchs Face Stars Mon.," *Philadelphia Tribune*, July 6, 1946: 10.

12  "Funeral Is Friday for Bob Palm," *St. Louis Post-Dispatch*, July 21, 1976: 10.

13  Lenard Palm, *Texas, Death Certificates, 1903-1982*. Accessed May 30, 2019, ancestry.com.

14  Brad Stratton, *Histories of Pride: Thirteen Pioneers Who Shaped Georgetown's African American Community* (Georgetown, Texas: City of Georgetown, 1998), 19.

15  US WWII Draft Cards Young Men, 1940-1947; US School Yearbooks, 1900-1999; US Department of Veterans Affairs BIRLS Death File, 1850-2010. Accessed December 7, 2019, ancestry.com.

16  Stratton, *Histories of Pride*, 19.

17  Stratton, 20.

18  Stratton, 20.

19  Stratton, 20.

20  Robert Palm, *Texas, Death Certificates, 1903-1982*. Accessed December 6, 2019, ancestry.com. Grandfather Robert Palm's age on the certificate of death is listed as "Bought [about?] 85," indicating he was likely born into slavery in Mississippi in the late 1840s.

21  Robert Palm, *Texas, Death Certificates*.

22  Lula Palm, *Texas Deaths, 1890-1976* Accessed December 5, 2019, familysearch.org.

23  US Census Bureau, Lula Palm in the 1910, 1920, and 1930 Censuses, Georgetown, Texas. Accessed December 5, 2019, ancestry.com.

24  Lula Palm, *Texas Deaths, 1890-1976*. Accessed December 5, 2019, familysearch.org.

25  Michael Chamy, "El Diablo – Willie Wells and the Lost History of Black Baseball in Austin," *Austin Chronicle*, July 4, 2003, austinchronicle.com/sports/2003-07-04/166641/.

26  "Austin Black Senators Play Georgetown Tigers Sunday at Lake Park," *Austin American-Statesman*, July 1, 1923: 5.

27  "Texas Colored League 1919-1926," Center for Negro Leagues Baseball Research. Retrieved October 23, 2019. cnlbr.org/Portals/0/Standings/Texas%20Colored%20League%20(1919-1926).pdf.

28  "Patterson Arrives to Direct Rushmen," *Birmingham News*, March 15, 1925: 28.

29  "Black Barons Lose to Chicago Giants," *Birmingham News*, April 16, 1927: 9; Oscar W. Adams, "What Negroes Are Doing," *Birmingham News*, April 17, 1927: 90; "Royal Giants to Play Here Monday," *Birmingham News*, April 17, 1927: 22.

30  Adams.

31  Adams.

32  "Baseball Monday, Black Barons to Face Cuban Stars, 20,000 to Attend," *Birmingham Reporter*, April 23, 1927: 1.

33  "Black Barons Win in Tenth from Cubans," *Birmingham News*, April 26, 1927: 18.

34  "Black Barons Defeat Cubans in Extra Inning Game," *Birmingham Reporter*, April 30. 1927: 3.

35  "Black Barons Defeat Hornets in First, 7-2," *Birmingham News*, May 3, 1927: 18.

36  "Black Barons Win Two from Dusky Hornets," *Birmingham News*, May 6, 1927: 26.

37  "Black Barons Win Again from Red Sox," *Birmingham News*, May 10, 1927: 16; "Black Barons Win and Lose," *Birmingham Reporter* May 14, 1927: 3; "Black Barons Drop Another from Giants," *Birmingham News*, May 17, 1927: 19; "Black Barons Drop First to Monarchs," *Birmingham News*, May 22, 1927: 22; "Black Barons Take Third from Monarchs," *Birmingham News*, May 24, 1927: 18; "Black Barons Lose Second to St. Louis Team," *Birmingham News*, June 10, 1927: 29; "Black Barons Take First on Road to Make 6 Straights," *Birmingham News*, June 12, 1927: 22.

38  "The Black Barons Must Wake Up," *Birmingham Reporter*, July 2, 1927: 3.

39  "Birmingham Team Beats Stars, 10 to 8," *St. Louis Post-Dispatch*, June 29, 1927: 21; "St. Louis Stars Blank Birmingham Black Barons 4–0, for 11th Victory in Row," *St. Louis Globe Democrat*, June 27, 1927: 16.

40  "Black Barons at Home Monday," *Birmingham Reporter*, July 9, 1927: 4.

41  "Black Barons," *Birmingham Reporter*, August 27, 1927: 7.

42  Clark and Lester, 160; "1927 in the Negro Leagues," Baseball-Reference. Accessed October 14, 2019. baseball-reference.com.

43  "Black Barons Lose Series," *Birmingham Reporter*, October 1, 1927: 7.

44  James A. Riley, *Biographical Encyclopedia of the Negro Baseball Leagues* (New York: Carroll & Graf, 1994), 600, reports that Palm's rookie batting average was .299.

45  Layton Revel and Luis Munoz, "Forgotten Heroes: James Allen 'Candy Jim' Taylor," (Center for Negro Leagues Baseball Research, 2013), 21. Retrieved May 30, 2019. cnlbr.org/Portals/0/Hero/Candy-Jim-Taylor.pdf.

46  "St. Louis Stars Split Double-Header with Birmingham, 17–7, 7–9," *St. Louis Globe-Democrat*, May 28, 1929: 22; "St. Louis Stars Win Over Birmingham Black Barons, 10–8," *St, Louis Globe-Democrat*, May 29, 1929: 13.

47  "St. Louis Stars to Open 5-Game Series in Chicago Saturday," *St. Louis Post-Dispatch*, June 6, 1929: 21.

48  US Census Bureau, Clarence Palm in the 1930 Census, Georgetown, Texas. Accessed October 30, 2019, ancestry.com.

49  "American Giants Win," *Chicago Tribune*, April 28, 1930: 23.

50  "Home Run in Ninth Gives Detroit Stars Victory Over St. Louis," *St. Louis Post-Dispatch*, May 7, 1930: 22.

# THE 1935 PITTSBURGH CRAWFORDS

51 "Cuban Stars Beat Detroit Nine Again," *Detroit Free Press*, August 19, 1930: 17.

52 "Detroit's Victory Over Stars Evens Series for Title," *St. Louis Star and Times*, September 18, 1930: 22.

53 "'Play-Off Championship' Series Summaries," Center for Negro Leagues Baseball Research. Retrieved October 11, 2019. cnlbr.org/Portals/0/RL/Negro%20League%20Play-Off%20Series%20(1930-1939).pdf.

54 "Winners Toy with Losers," *Windsor Star*, August 4, 1931: 15.

55 Dan Burley, "Down Yonder in New Orleans," *Chicago Daily Defender*, August 19, 1959: 22. Clarence Palm did share the field in Detroit with infielder Grady Orange in 1930 and possibly '31. Utilityman Hallie Harding, however, left the Stars for Kansas City in 1928.

56 Burley, "Down Yonder in New Orleans."

57 The 1932 season was the first of two times Posey turned to Palm as a replacement for Josh Gibson. In 1941 Palm would once again be called into service for the Grays when Gibson remained in Mexico. In both seasons, nine years apart, Spoony worked alongside longtime second-stringer Robert Gaston.

58 Chester L. Washington, "Sportively Speaking," *Pittsburgh Courier*, April 9, 1932: A5; "The Race Begins," *Pittsburgh Courier*, May 7, 1932: 14. Palm was listed in early April as having reported to Grays' spring training in West Virginia, and the *Courier* still saw him as the "lead catcher" for Homestead in early May. By mid-May, Palm had left Pittsburgh, likely en route to Chicago for a brief stint with Cole's American Giants.

59 Chester L. Washington, "Harris' Single Decides Opener," *Pittsburgh Courier*, April 23, 1932: 16.

60 Clark and Lester, 108; Phil Dixon with Patrick J. Hannigan, *The Negro Baseball Leagues: A Photographic History* (Mattituck, New York: Amereon House, 1992), 167. Clark and Lester show Palm on the CAG roster in 1932, while Dixon and Hannigan's book includes a team photo of the Chicago club dated 1931; cross-referencing the *Negro Leagues Book* with the players in the photo, including Palm and McDonald, it appears that this image is of the 1932 team. The Negro Leagues Database at seamheads.com lists Palm appearing in three games for Homestead and two for the American Giants in 1932. Riley's *Biographical Encyclopedia* places him on both rosters as well (600).

61 Revel and Munoz, "Forgotten Heroes: Chet Brewer," Center for Negro Leagues Baseball Research, 2014, 10. Retrieved November 3, 2019. cnlbr.org/Portals/0/Hero/Chet-Brewer.pdf.

62 Revel and Munoz, "Chet Brewer."

63 "Norwood and Tigers Turn Back Visitors," *Winnipeg Tribune*, May 25, 1932: 14.

64 "Ex-Giants Pitcher Beats Donaldsons," *Chicago Defender*, June 4, 1932: 9.

65 "Palm's Stick Work Is Talk of Pro Lots," *Chicago Defender*, June 17, 1932: 8.

66 "Local Baseball Team Trounced," *Winnipeg Tribune*, July 4, 1932: 14; "Crookston Reds Play on Monday," *Winnipeg Tribune*, July 29, 1932: 12; "Crookston Sweeps Ball Series from All-Stars," *Winnipeg Tribune*, August 2, 1932: 13; rookstonBeats Canucks," *Minneapolis Star*, August 2, 1932: 9; "Boosters Receive Their First Defeat on Northern Trip," *Daily Plainsman* (Huron, South Dakota), August 11, 1932: 9.

67 Revel and Munoz, "Candy Jim Taylor," 23.

68 John L. Clark, "Notes of the Negro National Association," *Pittsburgh Courier*, June 3, 1933: 15.

69 "'Texas' Burnett Leads Hitters, Summary Shows," *Pittsburgh Courier*, June 24, 1933: 14.

70 "Akron, Craws Clash Saturday," *Pittsburgh Courier*, July 29, 1933: A4.

71 "Craws, Cleveland Here Saturday," *Pittsburgh Courier*, August 19, 1933: A5.

72 "Cubans Touring U.S.," *Philadelphia Tribune*, April 19, 1934: 10.

73 Chester L. Washington, "Grays Win Second Holiday Tilt, 4-3," *Pittsburgh Courier*, July 7, 1934: 1.

74 "Grays, Crawfords Split Dual Bill," *Pittsburgh Post-Gazette*, July 5, 1934: 17.

75 "Part of Crowd; Oscar Out; No-Hit Hero; Gus Smile at Classic," *Pittsburgh Courier*, July 14, 1934: A5.

76 Dizzy Dismukes, "5 Homers Feature Grays-Sox Battle," *Pittsburgh Courier*, July 21, 1934: 15.

77 "Crawfords Beat Bacharach Twice," *Pittsburgh Press*, July 22, 1934: 14.

78 "Eagles Wallop Ball Hard, Beat Dodgers Twice," *Afro-American*, May 11, 1935: 21.

79 "Eagles Play at Home on Sunday," *New York Amsterdam News*, July 6, 1935: 15.

80 "Reds and Eagles Split Twin Bill," *Philadelphia Tribune*, March 5, 1936: 13; "Brooklyn Eagles Bacardi Trophy, 1936," National Baseball Hall of Fame. Accessed December 14, 2019. collection.baseballhall.org/PASTIME/brooklyn-eagles-bacardi-trophy-1936-0.

81 Lewis E. Dial, "The Sport Dial," *New York Age*, September 12, 1936: 9. Jeremy Beer, in his biography *Oscar Charleston: The Life and Legend of Baseball's Greatest Forgotten Player* (Lincoln: University of Nebraska Press, 2019), 263-264, highlights the story Oscar told on Palm, in which Clarence threatens the pitcher George Pipgras while in Mexico for throwing wild at him but defers to the white hurler once back in Texas. Pipgras, who had just finished his major-league career in '35, playing his final two seasons with the Boston Red Sox, had done so in lackluster fashion and would not have qualified as any type of "all-star" at this terminal stage

of his career. However, there's a strong possibility that he had joined this barnstorming campaign along with Rogers Hornsby and the rest as a swan song for what had been a remarkable 12-year career.

82  "Satchel Will Start Sunday with Yankees," *New York Amsterdam News*, April 25, 1936: 15.

83  "Black Yanks Invade Puerto Rican League," *New York Amsterdam News*, December 26, 1936: 14; "Black Yankees Journey to Warmer Climate," *New York Amsterdam News*, January 2, 1937: 15; "New York Black Yanks Sail for Havana, Cuba," *Baltimore Afro-American*, January 2, 1937: 22; "Black Yanks Embark for Havana," *Pittsburgh Courier*, January 9, 1937: 16; "Black Yanks Head for Puerto Rico," *Philadelphia Tribune*, December 31, 1936: 9.

84  Passenger Manifest for S.S. *San Jacinto* sailing from San Juan, P.R., February 11, 1937, arriving at the port of New York, February 18, 1937. Accessed October 20, 2019, ancestry.com.

85  "New York Black Yanks to Start with Youths," *Chicago Defender*, March 13, 1937: 15.

86  "Bushwicks Officially Open Season Playing Black Yanks for Two Games," *Brooklyn Citizen*, April 24, 1937: 6.

87  Passenger Manifest for SS *Coamo*, sailing from New York, April 22, 1937, to Trujillo City, D.R., via San Juan, P.R.; "Raid National Assoc.," *Philadelphia Tribune*, April 29, 1937: 12.

88  Revel and Munoz, "Forgotten Heroes: George 'Tubby' Scales," Center for Negro Leagues Baseball Research, 2015, 18. Retrieved December 3, 2019. cnlbr.org/Portals/0/Hero/309540%20Forgotten%20Heroes%20George%20Tubby%20Scales%20Single%20Pages.pdf.

89  Jonathan Blitzer, "Satchel Paige and the Championship for the Reelection of the General," *Atavist Magazine*, February 2016, magazine.atavist.com/satchel-paige-and-the-championship-for-the-reelection-of-the-general

90  Revel and Munoz, "George 'Tubby' Scales," 12.

91  Larry Lester, *Black Baseball in New York City* (Jefferson, North Carolina: McFarland & Company, 2017), 136.

92  "Battle for League at Yankee Stadium," *New York Age*, September 20, 1941: 11. Palm signed with Homestead in mid-season of 1941 and worked for them through the championship run in September. When Gibson returned at the end of the month, Palm was let go.

93  Dan Burley, "Confidentially Yours," *New York Amsterdam News*, July 24, 1943: 14.

94  Dan Burley, "Confidentially Yours," *New York Amsterdam News*, July 22, 1944: B6.

95  "Negro National Leaguers Will Play Here Today," *Paterson (New Jersey) Morning Call*, June 25, 1938: 22.

96  Van Hyning, *Puerto Rico's Winter League*, 7.

97  Passenger Manifest for S.S. *American "Ponce"* sailing from New York, October 29, 1938, arriving at the port of San Juan, P.R., November 3, 1938. Accessed October 20, 2019, ancestry.com.

98  Van Hyning, *Puerto Rico's Winter League*, 83.

99  Thomas E. Van Hyning, *The Santurce Crabbers: Sixty Seasons of Puerto Rican Winter League Baseball* (Jefferson, North Carolina: McFarland and Company, 1999), 12.

100  Van Hyning, *The Santurce Crabbers*, 12.

101  Van Hyning, *Puerto Rico's Winter League*, 248.

102  "1941 Clarence Palm Negro League Contract (.400 hitter)," Lelands Sports Memorabilia and Card Auctions. Accessed December 11, 2019. Lelands.com/bids/1941-clarence-palm-negro-league-contract--.400-hitter.

103  Van Hyning, *Puerto Rico's Winter League*, 247.

104  Ramon Luis Vazquez Collazo, "Historia de los Equipos de la Puerto Rico 'Baseball League.'" *Noticias Illescanos* (blog), November 13, 2008, illescanos.blogspot.com/2008/11/historia-de-los-equipos-de-la-puerto.html.

105  Van Hyning, *The Santurce Crabbers*, 26.

106  Passenger Manifests for Pan American Airways flights departing La Guardia Field, New York, September 8, 1949, arriving at San Juan P.R.; departing San Juan, P.R., September 29, 1949, arriving La Guardia Field. Accessed November 9, 2019, ancestry.com.

107  US Census Bureau, Clarence Palm in the 1940 Census, San Juan, P.R. Accessed November 8, 2019, familysearch.org.

108  Van Hyning, *Puerto Rico's Winter League*, 88.

109  "Manning: Memories Etched on Diamonds," *Philadelphia Inquirer*, July 17, 1994: 37.

# PAT PATTERSON

## By William H. Johnson

*Second baseman Andrew "Pat" Patterson, another formidable bat in the Crawfords line-up, hit .386/.414/.602 (1.016 OPS) in 1935 NNL league games. Eleven years later, he batted .308 for the Newark Eagles' championship team.* (Courtesy National Baseball Hall of Fame)

Andrew Lawrence Patterson was born on December 19, 1911, in Chicago.[1] Both of his parents died while he was extremely young, so the duty of raising the boy fell to his maternal grandparents.[2] Pat, as he became known, discovered athletics early on and augmented his classroom education as a multisport athlete at integrated Washington High School in East Chicago, Indiana, just across the state line from Chicago. There he starred in football, baseball, and basketball, as well as on the track oval.

After high school Patterson could have attended New York University to play football and baseball on scholarship, but he instead selected Wiley College in Marshall, Texas, just west of Shreveport, Louisiana, where he received a baseball scholarship and played all four sports as well. Patterson's choice to move from the Chicago area to staunchly segregated East Texas was not as odd a decision as it seems. According to Negro League historian Donn Rogosin, Patterson attended Wiley College "because of the cheap tuition and the chance to play serious baseball there. ...

## Pride of Smoketown

Patterson's decision was an indication of baseball's general preeminence at the time."[3]

By 1933, the 21-year-old Patterson was a player without a team, as the Great Depression forced Wiley to cancel the entire baseball program in order to save money. In the pre-NCAA days of institutional self-governance, the school did permit players to moonlight as professionals during the summer before returning in the fall. Patterson finagled a tryout with the independent Homestead Grays. After the tryout, he returned to college and graduated with a degree in education.[4]

The next year, 1934, the switch-hitting Patterson earned a spot with the still-independent Grays, and also played part of the season with the Cleveland Red Sox of the Negro National League. The team posted a 4-25 record before folding. Patterson, however, proved his mettle and enjoyed fan vote selection as the sole Cleveland representative in the annual East-West All Star Game in Chicago. There, in one of the "best pitching duels in East-West All Star game history," a game in which the sole run came in the top of the eighth inning when Jud Wilson drove in Cool Papa Bell, Patterson went 0-for-1 for the losing West squad as a late-game replacement for Sammy Hughes.[5]

In 1935, without a team but now with a professional reputation, Patterson caught on with Gus Greenlee's Pittsburgh Crawfords. There, playing alongside future Hall of Famers Josh Gibson, Oscar Charleston, Cool Papa Bell, and Judy Johnson on perhaps the finest Negro League team ever assembled, Patterson held his own. In the championship series against the New York Cubans, he was 7-for-27 at the plate, but his series highlight came in Game Six. With Pittsburgh trailing three games to two and with the game tied, 6-6, in the bottom of the ninth inning, Patterson doubled off Martin Dihigo and then scored on Judy Johnson's hit to win the game. The next day the Crawfords came all the way back in the series and won the title.

In 1935 Patterson left Pittsburgh in order to take up the nomadic baseball life with J.L. Wilkinson's Kansas City Monarchs. The statistics for the barnstorming teams of the day are notoriously unreliable, even more than normal league numbers, yet it is generally held that Patterson was one of the best hitters in the entire Midwest. He earned his second East-West Game bid, representing Kansas City in the August 23 game, and went 2-for-3 with a double, driving in a run in the West's 10-2 loss.[6]

The Monarchs often played against local white teams while on the road and, although conflict was rare during these interracial games, Patterson was involved in an unfortunate incident that presaged what black players would encounter once the integration of Organized Baseball began. In her history of the Monarchs franchise, Janet Bruce describes the incident involving Patterson:

> On a barnstorming tour in Texas, infielder Pat Patterson went up in the grandstand and punched a man because of his constant name-calling. Wilkinson fined Patterson $50. "He was right for fining me," Patterson recalled. "He explained to me, 'That's our policy – you just don't bite the hand that feeds you. Those people are coming out here and see you play ball.'" And for barnstorming black teams, the paying customer could say what he pleased.[7]

Patterson returned briefly to Negro League play, and Pittsburgh, in 1937, but like many of his contemporaries, he fell under the spell of the money bandied about by the Dominican Republic's dictator Rafael Trujillo and spent most of the season playing for Águilas Cibaeñas. After the Dominican season, Patterson returned to Kansas City for another round of barnstorming and joined the Monarchs in time for an exhibition slate against a team that featured Bob Feller, Lon Warneke, Mace Brown, and Johnny Mize. Patterson went 3-for-10 in the series, but the Monarchs lost three of the four games.[8]

Perhaps aware that he needed a more reliable livelihood should baseball not work out, Patterson began working in the offseason as a teacher and athletic coach at Jack Yates High School in his new home city of Houston, Texas.[9] As gifted Patterson was as an athlete, he was an even more talented and dedicated educator, and with the exception of three years in military service during World War II, he lived his life as an example to others of the area of the possible, even in a segregated America.

One example of Patterson's impact on black students in segregated Texas was his role in helping to shape the Prairie View Interscholastic League into a black sports league that would provide an organizational counterpart to the white schools' University Interscholastic League. Patterson created the organizational plan for highschool football, which he coached, and Yates principal William S. Holland met with E.B. Evans, the president of Prairie View A&M University, in the spring of 1939 in order to decide how to implement the plan the following year (1940).[10] Although the days of segregation were in the past, Patterson was honored as a member of the inaugural class of the Prairie View Interscholastic Coaches Hall of Fame in 1980.[11]

Patterson spent the 1938-39 baseball seasons in Pennsylvania, this time with the Philadelphia Stars. After a pedestrian 1938 season, he returned the East-West game in 1939. Two East-West games were played that season, and Patterson appeared in both. He started at third base in the first iteration, on August 6 at Comiskey Park, and had a hit and stole a base in four at-bats in a 4-2 loss. In the second game, played at Yankee Stadium on August 27, Patterson went 0-for-5 but drove in a run in a 10-2 East victory.[12]

Patterson's speed and ability to make contact at the plate, along with a touch of pop in his bat, were his most valuable baseball gifts, but he had intangibles as well. He "had good speed on the bases," was considered a solid fielder, and he always hustled. While he could play every position except pitcher or catcher, he will forever be considered one of the finest third basemen in the Negro Leagues in the late 1930s and the 1940s.[13]

*(Courtesy Noir-Tech Research, Inc.)*

Andrew "Pat" Patterson first made a name for himself as a champion on the baseball diamond. After his playing days, he became a Texas football coaching legend and champion at Houston's Yates High School.

At age 28, Patterson again left the United States, this time to play with manger Ernesto Carmona's Mexico City Diablos Rojos (Red Devils) in 1940 and 1941. He hit .341 with six home runs in 60 games in 1940, and improved to a .362 mark in 1941.[14] Patterson was part of a large contingent of Negro League players who spent the season south of the border, as stars like Cool Papa Bell, Josh Gibson, and Burniss Wright filled out Mexican rosters as well. During his time in Mexico, Patterson wed Gladys Inez Clowe, from Texas. He was such a popular player that Carmona "declared a team holiday and threw 'a lovely party,' according to Gladys Patterson. 'I'd never seen a roast pig before,' she confessed."[15] Their union produced twin sons, Andrew Jr. and Patrick, and thrived until Patterson's death in 1984.

With his bride on his arm, Patterson rejoined the Philadelphia Stars for the 1941 Negro League season, and was the team's regular third baseman. The following season, 1942, he was moved to second base and was again selected to represent the East in both East-West games that year. Over the two contests he walked twice, stole two bases, drove in a run and scored one.[16] Those proved to be the final East-West opportunities for Patterson. In six all-star games he posted four hits, including a double, drove in three runs, and stole four bases. That latter mark tied Patterson for the lead in stolen bases in East-West Games.[17]

With the nation at war, Patterson stepped away from baseball for three years. On December 5, 1942, he returned to Houston and enlisted in the Army Air Corps.[18] Although he had earned his degree at Wiley College, he started his military career at the lowest station in the hierarchy, that of private. His official position was Athletic Instructor[19] and he administered physical training at several bases in the United States. According to his family records, Patterson was awarded the American Theater Ribbon, the Good Conduct Medal, and the World War II Victory Medal.

After his release from active duty in 1945, Patterson returned to the classroom at Yates High School and mulled over the possibility of returning to the baseball diamond as well. Philadelphia still owed Patterson's contract, but there was ongoing friction between Patterson and the team's manager. Never one to miss an opportunity, Abe Manley traded for Patterson to take over third base on his Newark Eagles. "The only reason I can get Patterson," Manley told his wife, Effa, "is because he's not getting along with the manager. He's one of those outstanding players that Philly wouldn't think of giving up otherwise."[20] During the Eagles' 1946 championship season, Patterson helped fill out an infield that included Larry Doby and Monte Irvin. In the 1946 Negro League World Series, despite leaving before the Series concluded in order to return to his primary career as a high-school teacher and coach,[21] Patterson had six hits in 23 at-bats on the Eagles' march to the title.

Patterson turned 35 in 1947 and played for three teams: Newark, the New York Black Yankees, and the Homestead Grays. His successes in baseball were coming further apart, and the demands of his persona as teacher and role model for many of Houston's black teenagers were becoming more strident. Patterson finally chose to leave baseball, although he gave it one last go in 1949 when the Eagles relocated from Newark to Houston. After a season in which he hit only .217, he knew it was time to hang up his spikes for good.

As successful as Patterson had been as a professional baseball player, he was even better in his real profession. In 1950 he completed graduate work and earned a master's degree in education from what was then called the Texas State University for Negroes (now Texas Southern University). In the classroom he touched countless lives, and as a coach he directly influenced several future professional athletes, including Expos outfielder Steve Henderson and Washington Redskins defensive end Leroy Brown Jr.[22] Patterson continued to coach and teach at Jack Yates High School until 1967, and in 1982 became the first black coach ever named to the Texas High School Coaches Association Hall of Honor.[23] After leaving Jack Yates, Patterson worked for a time as a stadium consultant for Houston's Jeppesen (now Robertson) Stadium, and then in 1971 was appointed assistant athletic director for the Houston Independent School District.

According to his family, Patterson loved to travel with his wife, Gladys, especially after he retired from the school district, and he often said, "I just wanted to be remembered as someone who tried to help young men."[24] He exceeded that noble goal by a long measure. In the early 1980s Patterson endured a heart-valve replacement, and finally succumbed to complications from that procedure on May 16, 1984.[25] He is buried alongside Gladys, who died on February 18, 2004, at the Paradise South Cemetery in Pearland, Texas, a suburb of Houston.

# THE 1935 PITTSBURGH CRAWFORDS

Limiting Patterson's biography to only his athletic achievements would be underselling the man. He was a husband, a father, a citizen, an educator, and a role model. By coincidence, he was also a pretty darn good ballplayer.

## Notes

1. Biographical data form for a reunion banquet of Negro League players, filled out by Andrew Patterson (available in the Patterson family archives).
2. Family memory; myheritage.com/person-1000001_53176192_53176192/andrew-l-patterson-sr. Accessed January 2015.
3. Donn Rogosin, *Invisible Men: Life in Baseball's Negro Leagues* (Lincoln: University of Nebraska Press, 1983), 48.
4. Rogosin. 48.
5. Larry Lester, *Black Baseball's National Showcase: The East-West All-Star Game, 1933-1953* (Lincoln: University of Nebraska Press, 2001), 61.
6. Lester, 61.
7. Janet Bruce, *The Kansas City Monarchs: Champions of Black Baseball* (Lawrence: University Press of Kansas, 1985), 60-61.
8. John B. Holway, *The Complete Book of Baseball's Negro Leagues: The Other Half of Baseball History* (Fern Park, Florida: Hastings House Publishers, 2001), 349.
9. Family memory; myheritage.com/person-1000001_53176192_53176192/andrew-l-patterson-sr.
10. "History of the Prairie View Interscholastic League," pvilca.org/history.html, accessed December 29, 2018.
11. "History of the Prairie View Interscholastic League."
12. Lester, 88
13. James Riley, *The Biographical Encyclopedia of the Negro Baseball Leagues* (New York: Carroll and Graf, 1994), 608-609.
14. Pedro Treto Cisneros, *The Mexican League: Comprehensive Play Statistics 1937-2001* (Jefferson, North Carolina: McFarland, 2011), 214.
15. Rogosin, 172.
16. Lester, 88.
17. According to Lester, 448, Patterson tied for career East-West Game steals (4) with Henry Kimbro, Artie Wilson, and Sam Jethroe. Patterson required six games to reach the mark (compared with 10 games for Kimbro, and seven for Wilson and Jethroe).
18. Army Enlistment record, online: Ancestry.com.
19. Family memory; myheritage.com/person-1000001_53176192_53176192/andrew-l-patterson-sr.
20. James Overmyer, *Queen of the Negro Leagues: Effa Manley and the Newark Eagles* (Lanham, Maryland: Scarecrow Press, 1993), 198.
21. Neil Lanctot, *Negro League Baseball: The Rise and Ruin of a Black Institution* (Philadelphia: University of Pennsylvania Press, 2004), 164; Brent Kelly, *Voices from the Negro Leagues: Conversations with 52 Baseball Standouts from the Period 1924-1960* (Jefferson, North Carolina: McFarland, 2005), 347.
22. northdallasgazette.com/2014/09/11/former-nfl-player-looks-back-on-college-and-professional-career/ Accessed January 2015.
23. northdallasgazette.com/2014/09/11/former-nfl-player-looks-back-on-college-and-professional-career/ Accessed January 2015.
24. Family memory; myheritage.com/person-1000001_53176192_53176192/andrew-l-patterson-sr.
25. *Yates Times* (Jack Yates High School), September 7, 1984. Article part of digital archive supplied by Andrew Patterson (son) online at: myheritage.com/search-records?action=person&siteId=53176192&indId=1000001&origin=profile.

# BILL PERKINS

### By Bob LeMoine

"My catcher was George Perkins, who handled a pitcher like nobody's business," wrote Satchel Paige.[1] Bill Perkins, also known as William, George, and even Cy on occasion, was a catcher in the Negro Leagues for two decades and was the legendary Paige's favorite target behind the plate. When Paige was first notified of his induction into the Baseball Hall of Fame, he mentioned other Hall-worthy stars from the Negro Leagues. "Besides Josh Gibson, there was Frank Duncan, my catcher on the Monarchs, and another catcher, William Perkins of Birmingham, and outfielder Oscar Charleston, who were great, just to mention a few."[2] Perkins is not remembered as an all-time great in the Negro Leagues, possibly because Gibson was his teammate for several seasons so he was not even the greatest catcher on his own team. If circumstances had been different, the name Bill Perkins might be recognized today, but his endorsement by Paige, whom he followed from Birmingham to Cleveland to Pittsburgh and the Dominican Republic, is enough to confirm that Perkins was an excellent catcher.

*Bill "Cy" Perkins caught almost as many league games (38) as Josh Gibson (44) for the Crawfords in 1935 and more than held his own with a .328/.361/.540 slash line for the NNL champions.*

(Courtesy Noir-Tech Research, Inc.)

## THE 1935 PITTSBURGH CRAWFORDS

William George Perkins was born on January 26, 1906, in Dawson, in southwest Georgia, to Class and Lizzie (Dennison) Perkins. Class was a farmer, and William had two older sisters, Rosa and Susie. Grammar school was the highest education William received. Neither parent could read or write, according to the 1900 census.

Perkins first played baseball professionally in 1928. As the season opener approached, the *Birmingham Reporter* wrote that Birmingham Black Barons manager Poindexter Williams "has the find of the season in young Perkins, catcher, who receives, throws and bats with any catcher in this section of the country." The paper also mentioned Perkins's new batterymate, "Satchel, better known as Page [*sic*]."[3] It was the beginning of a historic relationship, and one has to wonder what Paige's career might have been without the presence of Perkins. "Finally he had a receiver who understood him," wrote Paige's biographer, Larry Tye. "The two shared a sense of swagger and humor, with the catcher supposedly emblazoning THOU SHALT NOT STEAL across his chest protector much as Satchel allegedly wrote FASTBALL on the sole of his elongated left shoe. Perkins knew how to extract the most from the temperamental pitcher."[4]

When the duo first met in Birmingham, Perkins asked what signs Paige wanted him to give. "There ain't any need for signs, I guess," Paige told him. "I don't take to them too good. Anyway, I'm the easiest guy in the world to catch. All you have to do is show me a glove and hold it still. I'll hit it. I could see George didn't believe me. Neither did any of the other Black Barons standing around, so I had them hold a couple of bats about six inches apart. I fired my fastball right through that space. From then on we went without signs. 'You sure think a lot of yourself' is all George would say."[5]

Perkins was also behind the plate for Poindexter's no-hitter against Chicago on June 27.[6] Birmingham finished in the middle of the pack in the NNL.

In 1929 Perkins was listed among returning Black Barons players, but was acquired in April by the Brooklyn Royal Giants, an independent black club. Ted Page remembered the encounter when Brooklyn played against a local team in Dawson, Georgia, Perkins's hometown. "Perkins was the idol of the town," Page recalled. "They had built a ball park for him out of old logs and broken-down doors. Everybody came to watch the ball games and the sheriff was the ticket taker. Well, we went down in spring training and saw him and wanted to take him back north, but the sheriff said, 'No, he has to stay here, we built a ball park for him. He said if we left town in the morning and his man – he didn't say 'man,' I'll let you guess what he said – if his man wasn't there, we better not be in Georgia. And we weren't. We hid Perkins under the bus and drove right past the sheriff sitting right in front of the store."[7]

Near the end of the season, Perkins was acquired by John Henry "Pop" Lloyd's Lincoln Giants of the Eastern Colored League.[8] In 1930 Perkins returned to Birmingham, a relief to the local fans as Perkins was "considered by many to be one of the best in the game today," wrote the *Birmingham Reporter*. "The owners made a master stroke when they obtained Perkins again, and one that pleases the fans, for Perkins was very popular with the fans here, because of his hard, earnest work and the ability to give the old pill a ride."[9] When Birmingham traveled to St. Louis for a series with the Stars, the *Chicago Defender* heaped praise on Perkins as "one of the greatest catchers in the South. This lad has been the sensation of the whole Birmingham team with the great way in which he holds down the backstopping position for his team. He can hit with the best of them, too."[10]

Perkins returned to Birmingham in 1931. Juan "Tetelo" Vargas of the barnstorming Cuban House of David club (a copycat of the Michigan-based team of the religious community in which men would not shave) stole six bases "each time beating perfect pegs from catcher Perkins," reported the *Philadelphia Tribune*.[11] Perkins did not stay long in Birmingham as he briefly returned to the Brooklyn Royal Giants, then was acquired by the Cleveland Cubs of the NNL, where he rejoined Paige.[12] Again on the move, the independent Pittsburgh Crawfords acquired the Paige-Perkins battery in June.[13] Perkins made immediate impressions. "Perkins attracted considerable attention with his work behind the plate here in the series with the Grays," wrote the *Pittsburgh Courier*. "His great throwing arm and a natural receiving stamps him as a real find."[14] The *Philadelphia Tribune* added later, "A genuine sensation is Perkins. He is a hustling little chatter box and an ace maskman in the bargain. Without a doubt Perkins is the most colorful performer seen here in recent years."[15] While he was a favorite of Paige, a 1932 article boasted of Perkins' work with another pitcher, Sam Streeter, saying, "[T]he pair formed the Crawfords' most dependable battery."[16]

Perkins and Paige returned to the Crawfords in 1932 and delighted Birmingham fans on a spring-training stop where they "have a large following of fans here," wrote the *Atlanta Daily World*.[17] The *Pittsburgh Courier* praised Perkins for adding "more zip and chatter to his topnotch program of last year. He is a sure shot backstop and continues to slam the old apple to the outer boundaries."[18] Perkins's first stint with the Crawfords was short-lived as he briefly played for the Cleveland Stars of the East-West League, then finished the season with the Homestead Grays, also of the EWL.[19] Perkins "is playing the game of his life with the Homesteaders," wrote the *Courier* in August. "'Perk' has led the team in home runs and hits during the past couple of weeks and is smashing the ball with a vengeance."[20] When the season concluded, Perkins joined the Monroe (Louisiana) Monarchs for a trip to Mexico.[21]

In 1933 Perkins returned to the Crawfords, who were now in the Negro National League. The *Chicago Defender* dubbed him "The Pride of the South," who was "the peppiest and surest receiver to bob up in recent years." Waiting in the wings, however, was the young catcher Josh Gibson, whom the paper called "the hardest hitter in baseball."[22] Reports from spring training must have given fans back in Pittsburgh visions of the Yankees' Murderers' Row as, in 10 games, Perkins slammed five home runs and Gibson three, prompting a *Courier* headline: "Crawfords May Have Best Club in History."[23] The Crawfords would need to deal with the "lively battle" of having two of the best catchers in all of Negro League baseball on the club.[24] The Crawfords' powerful lineup held true to predictions and when the *Courier* published statistics at the end of June, the Crawfords' four top hitters were Charleston (.450), Cool Papa Bell (.379) Gibson (.378), and Perkins (.344), with Charleston and Gibson slamming four home runs and Perkins four triples.[25] To get both bats into the lineup, player-manager Charleston would at times play either Perkins or Gibson in the outfield or first base while the other caught. The Crawfords were awarded the NNL championship.[26]

Despite being under contract with the Crawfords in 1934, Perkins held out much of the year and became manager of his hometown independent Birmingham Black Giants club.[27] Later, Perkins and Paige joined the House of David club in time for the *Denver Post*'s semipro tournament. Playing well for the House of David propelled fans to still vote in large numbers for Perkins for the East-West Game, the Negro Leagues' equivalent to the white All-Star Game.[28] Perkins played in the game as a reserve and Paige got the win in relief. The Crawfords failed to repeat as NNL champions.

The 1935 Crawfords returned with a vengeance, becoming what many consider one of the greatest Negro League teams of all time. In statistics published at the end of July, Perkins was credited with a .362 batting average.[29] The Crawfords won back-to-back championships in 1935-36.

Both Perkins and Paige created a stir when they jumped to the Dominican Republic team in the early part of 1937 in an apparent "raid" of Negro

League teams.³⁰ They both played for a club in Santo Domingo. Paige, Perkins, and others were barred from the NNL by President Gus Greenlee for these actions.³¹ The Santo Domingo club went on to win the Denver Post Tournament. In March of 1938, the "jumpers" were reinstated by the NNL and were penalized by losing one month's salary. Paige was returned to the Crawfords while Perkins was traded to the Philadelphia Stars.³² Perkins spent 1938-39 as the starting catcher for the Stars.

Early in the 1940 season, Perkins was signed by the Baltimore Elites "to bolster the backstop department, which has been manned chiefly by the youthful Roy Campanello [sic]," wrote Art Carter of the *Baltimore Afro-American*.³³ Perkins became the new mentor for the 18-year-old future Hall of Famer, Campanella taking over from the departed Biz Mackey. Although Perkins was in his 13th season, a columnist in the *New York Amsterdam News* was highly impressed with the veteran. With talk increasing of the national pastime needing to integrate, the writer felt that Perkins's skills had often been overlooked. He said Perkins exhibited "the same fire, dependability and showmanship he displayed when he caught Satchel's hottest offerings. Perkins has seldom been mentioned by the scribes in picking their players for possible candidates for the major leagues. Paige has. Paige may be slowing up. Perkins isn't."³⁴ Perkins was the starting catcher for the East in the East-West Game in August, his second appearance.³⁵

In the offseason Perkins was dealt to the New York Black Yankees, but he never played for the team; instead, he crossed the border and played for Mexico City. A July article mentioned Perkins batting .344 at the time.³⁶ Perkins also played for Mayaguez in Puerto Rico's Liga Semipro league until returning home to Birmingham to care for his ailing mother. Perkins apparently was out of baseball and remained in Birmingham until he was drafted into the US Army in the midst of World War II.³⁷

Perkins returned from military service in 1945 and played for the New York Black Yankees. He was released in the summer and signed on with the Philadelphia Stars. He spent 1947-1948, the final seasons in his 20-year career, with the Baltimore Elite Giants. In 1949 he was retired and back in Birmingham.³⁸

Perkins married Jessie Hatch, a schoolteacher originally from Alabama, in 1931. In 1934 their only child, William Jr., was born. The Perkinses ran a restaurant in Birmingham for a while.³⁹ Bill Perkins died on January 24, 1958, and was buried in Dawson, Georgia. "His death is believed to have resulted from a heart attack," his obituary reported. "He had walked home and entered the bathroom, where he dropped off dead, it was said. Mr. Perkins had not been in his usual health after coming home from World War II."⁴⁰ He and Jessie were divorced at the time of his death. "They were divorced about 1947 shortly after Mr. Perkins was honorably discharged from the Army," his obituary stated. "Mrs. Perkins is currently engaged in the café and hotel business."⁴¹

Perkins spent five offseasons playing in Cuba: Santa Clara (1935-36, 1936-37, 1937-38), Cuba (1938-39) and Cienfuegos (1940-41). Statistics supplied by the Ashland Collection through the Baseball Hall of Fame credit Perkins as a .288 hitter with nine home runs over that span. The Seamheads Negro League Database credits him with a career batting average of .267, but such incomplete records fail to tell much of a story of his career. As his obituary noted, "His name ranked along with Josh Gibson, Bizz [sic] Mackey and other luminaries of the mask and breastpad."⁴²

## Sources

Ancestry.com. US World War II Army Enlistment Records, 1938-1946.

Ancestry.com. US WWII Draft Cards Young Men, 1940-1947.

Baseball-reference.com.

Birmingham (Alabama) Public Library.

Cassidy Lent, A. Bartlett Giamatti Research Center, Baseball Hall of Fame.

# Pride of Smoketown

New York Passenger and Crew Lists, 1909, 1925-1957, database with images, FamilySearch.org

Seamheads Negro League Database

## Notes

1. LeRoy "Satchel" Paige and David Lipman, *Maybe I'll Pitch Forever: A Great Baseball Player Tells the Hilarious Story Behind the Legend* (New York: Doubleday & Company, 1962), 47.
2. Associated Press, "Baseball to Honor Black Players in the Hall of Fame," *Portsmouth (Ohio) Times*, February 4, 1971: 20.
3. "Black Barons Play Camp Benning Here Next Week," *Birmingham Reporter*, April 14, 1928: 7.
4. Larry Tye, *Satchel: The Life and Times of an American Legend* (New York: Random House, 2010), 46.
5. Paige and Lipman, 47-48.
6. "Poindexter Hurls No-Hit No-Run Game," *Chicago Defender*, July 7, 1928: 8.
7. John B. Holway, *Voices from the Great Black Baseball Leagues*, revised ed. (Mineola, New York: Dover Publications, 2010), 157.
8. "Royal Giants Heading East," *New York Amsterdam News*, April 17, 1929: 9; "St. Louis Stars to Play Lincoln Gts," *Chicago Defender*, September 28, 1929: 8.
9. "Black Barons Leave Tuesday for Training Camp," *Birmingham Reporter*, March 29, 1930: 7.
10. "Birmingham to Cross Bats with St. Louis," *Chicago Defender*, August 9, 1930: 8.
11. "10 Steals for Bearded Star as Mates Win," *Philadelphia Tribune*, May 7, 1931: 11.
12. "Brooklyn Royals Lose One, Then Tie," *Philadelphia Tribune*, May 14, 1931: 11; "Louisville Is Loser, 3 to 2, at Cleveland," *Chicago Defender*, June 20, 1931: 9; "Fix Upp [sic] Cleveland Park," *Chicago Defender*, May 16, 1931: 9.
13. "Crawfords Sign New Stars," *Pittsburgh Courier*, June 27, 1931: A5.
14. "Crawfords Sign New Stars."
15. "Diamond Dust," *Philadelphia Tribune*, August 20, 1931: 10.
16. "Catches 'Em," *News Journal and Guide* (Norfolk, Virginia), March 19, 1932: 12.
17. Wilson L. Driver, "Hits & Bits," *Atlanta Daily World*, April 10, 1932: 5.
18. "Crawfords Back, Set for Test," *Pittsburgh Courier*, April 30, 1932: A5.
19. "Cleveland and Grays Defeat Crawfords," *Baltimore Afro-American*, June 25, 1932: 14; "Works Hard," *Pittsburgh Courier*, July 9, 1932: A5.
20. "Perkins Setting Pace with Grays," *Pittsburgh Courier*, August 6, 1932: A4.
21. "Grays End Season with Win; Set Mark," *Pittsburgh Courier*, October 1, 1932: A4.
22. "Crawfords Out to Better 1932 Mark," *Chicago Defender*, April 15, 1933: 8.
23. "Crawfords May Have Best Club In History: Team Hits Stride on Invasion Of Dixie," *Pittsburgh Courier*, April 15, 1933: A4; "Crawfords Win Ten in South," *Baltimore Afro-American*, April 29, 1933: 16.
24. "Sez 'Chez,'" *Pittsburgh Courier*, April 29, 1933: A5.
25. "'Texas' Burnett Leads Hitters, Summary Shows," *Pittsburgh Courier*, June 24, 1933: A4.
26. The pennant was won in controversy. Gus Greenlee was both the owner of the Crawfords and the president of the NNL. One might thus argue that he had a conflict of interest. "Greenlee did not carry out plans for a playoff, though his decision was not made until the Crawfords had rallied to win the second-half title by sweeping a thrilling doubleheader against the Nashville Elite Giants on the last day of the season. ... When the Crawfords took the nightcap, Greenlee believed no more proof was needed to crown his boys as the league's first champions, which he declared them two months later. Gus left no room for Robert Cole, whose American Giants had won the first half, to challenge the decision; again, Greenlee's word was law. Besides, Gus had not formed this circuit to play a World Series, he did it to prove that black businessmen could make a profit in baseball, as that would be the most effective lever in prying open the majors' closed door." Mark Ribowsky, *A Complete History of the Negro Leagues 1884-1955* (New York: Birch Lane Press, 1995), 178.
27. "Deny Perkins Was Holding Out Over a Salary Dispute," *Chicago Defender*, April 7, 1934: 16.
28. The *Pittsburgh Courier* listed Perkins as receiving just under 5,000 votes, placing him fourth among East catchers and just under 500 votes fewer than first-place Gibson; "Final Standings – the East," *Pittsburgh Courier*, August 25, 1934: A5; "Perkins Will Return to the Crawfords' 9," *Chicago Defender*, August 11, 1934: 17.
29. "National Association Batting Averages," *Baltimore Afro-American*, July 20, 1935: 21.
30. "Paige Jumps Crawfords; Perkins Also Said to Have Skipped Loop; Both Believed with Semipro Nines in Canada," *Chicago Defender*, May 1, 1937: 13.
31. "Satchell Paige Will Be Barred from N.N. League," *News Journal and Guide* (Norfolk, Virginia), May 8, 1937: 18.
32. "NNL Reinstates 'Jumpers'; New D.C. Club Is Admitted," *Afro-American* (Baltimore), March 12, 1938: 18; "Player Deals Feature of N.N. League Meeting: Taylor, Paige to Craws," *Pittsburgh Courier*, March 12, 1938: 17.

# THE 1935 PITTSBURGH CRAWFORDS

33  Art Carter, "Elites Play Stars Twin Bill Sunday," *Baltimore Afro-American,* May 10, 1940: 23.

34  "Confidentially Yours, Daniel," *New York Amsterdam News,* June 1, 1940: 14.

35  Art Carter, "East Blanks West, 11-0, in Baseball's Big Classic," *Baltimore Afro-American,* August 24, 1940: 19.

36  "Elites and Yanks Swap Players," *Baltimore Afro-American,* January 11, 1941: 19; "Josh Gibson, Snook Wellmaker Among Negroes in Mexico," *Atlanta Daily World,* May 5, 1941: 5; "U.S. Ballplayers Muck up the Mexican Loop," *Philadelphia Tribune,* July 24, 1941: 9.

37  Dan Burley, "Terris MacDuffie, Pitching Star of Homestead Grays, Tells of Discrimination Against Negro Players in Cuba: White Minor League Stars Taking Over in Their Places," *New York Amsterdam Star-News,* January 17, 1942: 13; Emory O. Jackson, "Hits & Bits," *Atlanta Daily World,* August 7, 1942: 5; Perkins registered for the draft on October 16, 1940, with his current residence being listed as Los Angeles. His listed employer was Tom Wilson, president of the Negro National League. He was 5-feet-9 and 176 pounds. Military records show Perkins enlisting on July 31, 1942, at Fort Benning, Georgia.

38  Emory O. Jackson, "Hits & Bits," *Atlanta World Daily*, April 29, 1949: 7.

39  Brent Kelley, *The Negro Leagues Revisited: Conversations with 66 More Baseball Heroes* (Jefferson, North Carolina: McFarland, 2000), 183.

40  "William Perkins, Famed Baseball Catcher, Dies," *Birmingham World,* January 29, 1958: 6.

41  "William Perkins, Famed Baseball Catcher, Dies."

42  "William Perkins, Famed Baseball Catcher, Dies."

# SAM STREETER

## By Alan Cohen

In 1981 the Smithsonian Institution hosted an exhibition called "Black Baseball: Life in the Negro Leagues." A fair-sized crowd attended the exhibit when it opened on April 24 and Negro League stalwarts Buck O'Neil, Monte Irvin, Buck Leonard, and Judy Johnson were also on hand.

According to the *Washington Post*'s report about the exhibit's grand opening:

> At one of the Smithsonian display cases yesterday, a 10-year-old named Richie Stark looked puzzled at a baseball autographed in 1930 by Sam Streeter, a terrific lefthander for the Pittsburgh Crawfords, known as the best black baseball team money could buy. 'Who the heck was Sam Streeter?' he asked.[1]

Well, to be perfectly honest, Sam "Lefty" Streeter was not pitching for Crawfords in 1930, and Gus Greenlee did not start buying up players for the Crawfords until 1931. By the time he joined the Crawfords in 1931, Streeter, one of Greenlee's first acquisitions, was a 30-year-old veteran who had achieved fame with that other Pittsburgh dynasty, the Homestead Grays of Cumberland Posey.

He was a heck of a player. As Streeter himself recalled in 1971, "I think I pitched two or three no-hitters. I don't remember. They didn't keep records in those days. We just wanted to play. If they said, 'Sam, you pitch today,' I pitched. Never worried if I had enough rest."[2]

Sam Streeter was born in New Market, Alabama, about 120 miles north of Birmingham, on September 17, 1900, to Horace G. and Lula (McGuffey) Streeter. He had limited schooling and, per 1940 census data, received formal education only through the fourth grade. What his parents did to earn a living and more information in regard to his upbringing remain elusive.

The first notice of the 5-foot-7, 180-pound left-hander was in 1919 when he was pitching for Birmingham Industrial League teams. On June 23 he was hurling for Birmingham's Edgewater Cubs and defeated Montgomery, 12-2.[3] On July 1, pitching for the TCI Giants (also known as Ensley), he scattered five hits and hurled his first shutout as the team defeated Westfield, 5-0.[4] On July 9 he hurled his second shutout, defeating Chattanooga, 3-0.[5] He was on the mound for the first game of a doubleheader on September 8, nine days shy of his 19th birthday. He allowed four first-inning runs as his Ensley Steel Works Black Baron team lost to the ACIPCO Yellow Jackets, 6-2.[6]

In 1920 Streeter pitched for the Montgomery Gray Sox. His best performance of the early season was on June 7. The game at Birmingham's Rickwood Field went 17 innings, and he pitched a complete game, losing 3-2 on fielding lapses that led to Birmingham's run in the final inning.[7] Montgomery was in the Negro Southern League and in late June had a 24-11 record, second only to Knoxville. On July 22, in a nonleague game against the Chicago Black Sox, Montgomery won easily, 15-1. Streeter allowed only four hits and threw 20 consecutive strikes at one point.[8] On August 14 he spun a one-hitter as Montgomery defeated Birmingham 1-0.[9] The Gray Sox won the league pennant, but Streeter would play elsewhere the following season.

In 1921 the trail of Streeter's career is unclear. The then common practice of not including a player's first name in stories only confuses matters, as does the not-uncommon practice of players jumping from one team to another. One report had Streeter signed by Frank Perdue to play for the Birmingham Black Barons.[10] He didn't play for Birmingham. Another report has Streeter pitching for Mobile in a 7-5 loss to Birmingham on May 6, but there is no other mention of his being with Mobile. Streeter started the season with the Atlanta Black Crackers and was with the team through July 8. He signed with the Chicago American Giants of the Negro National League, and he first appeared with them on July 17, 1921, winning 11-2 against a team called the Magnets.[11] He spent the balance of the season with the American Giants.

In 1922 Streeter was on the move again, this time with the barnstorming Atlantic City Bacharach Giants team led by Dick Lundy. Statistics for the season are not readily available,

*Sam Streeter, who was already a 14-year veteran of the Negro Leagues, pitched to a 6-1 record in NNL games for the Crawfords in 1935.*

but it is known that on July 30 he pitched in both games of a doubleheader at home against the J&J Dobson team from Philadelphia. In the opener he scattered seven hits in a complete-game 4-3 win. In the nightcap, he relieved Joseph Wheeler in the ninth and saved a 3-2 win.[12]

On September 27, 1922, Streeter married Euzell Huguly, who had been born on July 9, 1902, in Georgia. It is not known how long they were together or if they had any children. Sometime after 1930, Streeter married again. He and his second wife, Myrtle, who was born on March 21, 1910, had a daughter named Mary Lou, who was 7 years old at the time of the 1940 census.

In 1923 Streeter joined the New York Lincoln Giants, a member of the Eastern Colored League that nevertheless played most of its games against nonleague opponents. On June 3 the bus stopped in Plainfield, New Jersey, and the opposition was provided by a team known as Recreation. Streeter started the game and was not scored upon in the first six innings. He weakened in the late innings as Recreation came back to tie the game, 6-6, in the ninth. In that inning Streeter surrendered a game-tying two-run homer to Hap Myers, who had played in the majors for parts of five seasons. After the homer, the frustrated Streeter removed himself from the mound and switched positions with right fielder Dave Brown. Brown stopped the bleeding, and the Giants won the game in the 11th inning when Robert Hudspeth tripled and came home on a single by Orville Singer.[13] On August 19, in one of his best performances of the season, Streeter shut out Brooklyn's Royal Giants, 5-0, allowing only three hits.[14]

In 1924 Streeter was with the Birmingham Black Barons and pitched for them through the early part of 1925. He was 14-6 in league play in 1924, when the team went 34-44, and he was 0-1 in early 1925. On May 25, 1925, he was signed by the Homestead Grays.[15] That day he defeated Braun's Knickerbockers, 12-4.[16] The Grays won 27 of their first 30 games with two losses and one tie, and Streeter contributed two wins to that total.[17]

By the time the bus stopped at Coshocton, Ohio, on June 18, the team was 42-3 and Streeter, who had a potent bat, was slated to play center field.[18] His second shutout of the season came on July 18 at Forbes Field against Bellevue. He scattered five hits and only one runner made it as far as second base.[19]

Lefty Streeter was not known for his blazing speed. He featured a curveball and at times could put a little extra on the ball. That little extra came courtesy of substances not necessarily allowed in baseball. On July 25, 1925, in Jeannette, Pennsylvania, he entered the game in relief of Smokey Joe Williams. A new ball had been put in play and Streeter, per his custom, had prepared the ball by rubbing it on the ground. The umpire took exception to this practice and threw Streeter out of the game. Shortstop Gerard Williams protested by throwing a new ball into the stands and was likewise asked to leave the premises. Jeannette won the game, 3-2.[20]

Jeannette was accused of using a ringer in the form of pitcher Louis "Red" Temple, who had gone to spring training with the Boston Red Sox in 1925, but had never pitched for them once the regular season had begun. In 1927 and 1928, Temple pitched with Jeannette in the Class-C Middle Atlantic League, going 18-10 in 1928. Grays player-manager Vic Harris protested so vigorously that he was ejected as well as Streeter and Gerard Williams. This gained the ire of William G. Nunn in the *Pittsburgh Courier* who called the game "a combination of football, volley ball, boxing (and) wrestling," and scolded the team for jeopardizing the outcome by losing three players via ejection.[21]

At Forbes Field on October 3, Streeter wrapped up his season with a 16-1 win over Homewood in the first game of a doubleheader. He allowed only five hits, struck out eight, and had four of his team's 20 hits.[22] According to the *Pittsburgh Courier*, the team won 125 of the 150 games it played in 1925, and wins on September 24 at

# THE 1935 PITTSBURGH CRAWFORDS

Finleyville and October 3 at Forbes Field brought Streeter's record to 23-5, an incredible feat since he had not joined the team until May and missed almost two weeks when he suffered a spike wound on August 25.[23]

Streeter was with the Grays through the end of the 1926 season. His teammate Oscar Owens reminisced in 1938, "That ... club had everything. Power ... speed ... and brains. That was the year we won 43 straight games, which I believe is some kind of record. We beat almost everything we came up against. They didn't come too big or too strong. All we wanted was a game with them and we never worried much about the outcome."[24]

The 1926 Grays were indeed a powerhouse. In a relief effort on May 15 against Bellevue (Pennsylvania), Streeter entered the game in the third inning with his team trailing by three runs. He pitched nine innings, allowing only three hits, as the Grays came back to tie the game. Darkness caused a halt to the proceedings with the game tied 3-3 after 11 innings.[25]

The team simply refused to lose. The Grays were undefeated in their first 47 games (43-0-4). On June 10 the streak was broken at Coshocton as Streeter suffered his first loss.[26] Through 64 games, the Grays were 57-3 with four ties.

On July 25 Homestead traveled to Cleveland to take on the Cleveland Elites of the Negro National League. With Streeter striking out eight, the Grays won 15-3.[27] According to the *Pittsburgh Courier*, the team's record by late August was 102-6 with six ties. At a dinner in August, team owner Cum Posey presented the players engraved gold baseballs in honor of their achievement.[28]

The Grays played relatively few games at their home ballpark in Homestead, Pennsylvania, outside Pittsburgh. They seemed to spend more time on the bus than at the ballpark. On August 28 the bus made a stop at Russell Field in Warren, Pennsylvania, where Streeter pitched a 7-0 shutout, scattering seven hits, to push his record to 24-3 as the Grays defeated the Warren Wreckers.[29] The team ended the season with 147 wins.

After the season the Grays were matched up against an American League all-star team. Streeter made a brief appearance in the game on October 3 when he took the mound in top of the 10th inning (replacing George Britt, who had been ejected) with the score tied and the bases loaded. Streeter, without ample opportunity to warm up, was ineffective and the American Leaguers wound up scoring five runs to win the game, 11-6. (Lefty Grove finished the game for the All-Stars and retired the Grays in the bottom of the 10th.)[30]

Although he had experienced great personal and team success with the Grays, Streeter returned to Birmingham in 1927. On May 3 he entered the game against the Cleveland Hornets with two out in the fifth inning after starter J. Burdine and reliever Fred Daniels allowed a pair of runs and left the bases loaded. After allowing a base-clearing triple to Orville Riggins that tied the game, Streeter retired the next 13 batters in order. The Barons came back to win the game, 7-5.[31] Three days later he shut out the Hornets on three hits, 4-0. The team's record at that point was 8-2, and they led the Negro National League. Among his teammates was a young Satchel Paige, who had started the season with Chattanooga. When the Black Barons completed a five-game series at St. Louis on June 29, Paige and Streeter combined to defeat the St. Louis Stars, 11-4.[32] Birmingham won the second-half championship with a 29-15 record but was swept in four games by the Chicago American Giants, winners of the first-half pennant, in the league championship. Available records indicate that Streeter was 14-12 and batted .381 in 1927.

Streeter and fellow pitcher Harry Salmon took the young Satchel under their collective wings. Years later, Streeter remembered, "See, he'd wind up and wouldn't watch his batter. He'd look around and when he'd come back, he didn't see *where* he was throwing it. I told him to kind of keep his eye on the plate, not to turn too far, to glance at the plate before he turned the ball loose. He got to the point where he had *good* control."[33]

## Pride of Smoketown

In 1928 Streeter was back with the Grays, and he got off to a good start with two early wins, the first of which came at home in an 11-1 win over the Eastern Ohio League All-Stars on May 12.[34] The Grays got off to another sensational start and won 26 of their first 27 games. They had an 18-game winning streak going when Streeter experienced misfortune as he had two years earlier. This time, he made an error at a key point and the Grays lost to New Castle to put an end to their winning streak.[35]

On Memorial Day, May 30, the Grays played three games. The morning was spent in Canton, Ohio, where they defeated the Canton Raven Oils. Streeter was given the ball in the second game and defeated Canton, 8-3. That evening, at Forbes Field, the Grays defeated Homewood and improved their record for the year to 37-3.[36] Streeter's record for the season was 6-1 at that point.

Streeter remained with the Grays in 1929, and the team became part of the six-team American Negro League, though the team still continued to barnstorm. In league competition, things were not easy as the Grays got off to only a 6-6 start and were in third place. They moved into contention in mid-June when they took four games in a row from Baltimore. Streeter posted a 5-2 win on June 13 and a 6-5 win in the second game on June 15. After defeating Hilldale in a doubleheader on June 23, the team was poised for a battle for the first-half championship, but fate stepped in the way. On June 25, the team was headed east when one of the team cars, driven by owner-manager Posey, went off the road. Pitcher Oscar Owens, second baseman Walter Cannady, and outfielder E.W. Graham were seriously injured.[37] The Grays pressed on. Streeter won a 6-3 game against Hilldale on June 29 in which he scattered nine hits and got support from Johnny Beckwith, who had three hits. With four games remaining in the first half, the Grays were 1½ games behind Baltimore and needed to win three of four games at Baltimore on June 30 and July 1 to capture the first-half championship. Baltimore swept the four games and the Grays slipped to third place. In the second half of the season, the Grays finished in fourth place with a 19-16 record.

The American Negro League only lasted for one season, and in 1930 Streeter was back with the Black Barons, who were in the Negro National League. Twice in August he defeated the Chicago American Giants at Birmingham's Rickwood Field. On August 5 he hurled a five-hitter in a 2-1 win.[38] On August 14 at Birmingham, the Black Barons swept a doubleheader from Chicago with Streeter winning the first game, 9-8. Birmingham concluded its season on Labor Day with a doubleheader sweep of the Nashville Elites. In the opener, Streeter won 4-2, pitching his way out of three jams, the last one in the eighth inning. In the second game, Satchel Paige pitched a 4-0 shutout.[39] The team finished the season at 46-48-2, the fifth best record in the league.[40]

In 1931 Streeter began the season with Cleveland and was among the first players signed by Gus Greenlee to play for the Pittsburgh Crawfords, joining the team on June 3.[41] A matchup with Streeter's former team, the Grays, took place on June 19 at Forbes Field and the Grays won, 9-0.[42] During the season, Greenlee openly raided other teams for talent, signing Grays outfielder Ambrose Reid and luring Satchel Paige away from Cleveland. The team barnstormed throughout the 1931 and 1932 seasons. One of the stops in 1932 was Dexter Park in Queens, New York, the home of the semipro Brooklyn Bushwicks. Streeter pitched the first game of a doubleheader against the Bushwicks, scattering four hits and winning 10-0.[43]

In 1933 the Crawfords joined the Negro National League and finished the first half in second place with a 20-8 record. Streeter's best performance of the season came at Birmingham's Rickwood Field when he hurled a two-hit masterpiece as the Crawfords defeated the Nashville Elites, 1-0, on July 17.[44] Streeter was selected to play in the first-ever East-West Game at Comiskey

Park, an all-star event that featured the best players in Negro baseball. He was the starting pitcher for the East and pitched into the sixth inning. He allowed a homer to former Birmingham teammate Mule Suttles in the fourth inning but still took a 5-4 lead into the sixth inning; however, a leadoff single by Willie Wells and a one-out double by Alex Radcliffe tied the score.[45] At that juncture Streeter left the game with the lead run on second base and Suttles due up at the plate. His mound replacement, Crawford teammate Bertrum Hunter, yielded a double to Suttles that put the West in front to stay as they won the game, 11-7. The Crawfords took the second-half NNL championship in a playoff with Nashville, but there was no postseason series between first-half champion Indianapolis and the Crawfords.

In 1934 Streeter returned to the Crawfords, and showed that he still could do the job in a whitewashing of the Philadelphia Stars on June 11. In a game at Harrisburg, Pennsylvania, all he needed was a solo homer by Vic Harris. The Crawfords won, 1-0, as Streeter scattered six hits.[46] Although the Crawfords had the best overall record, the league played a split season with Chicago winning the first half and the Philadelphia Stars the second half. The Stars won the championship in eight games. (There was one tie.)[47] The Crawfords' chance for the championship would come the next season.

In 1935 Streeter was part of the Crawfords team that won the first-half championship with a 26-6 record. On Memorial Day he pitched the first game of a doubleheader as the Crawfords defeated the Stars in Philadelphia, 11-4. The Crawfords swept the doubleheader and went on to sweep the next four games from Newark to separate themselves from the pack. Streeter was given the ball on July 4 and defeated the Homestead Grays in the first game of a doubleheader, 6-2. He scattered six hits and was given offensive support by Cool Papa Bell, who smashed a three-run homer.[48]

The Crawfords did their usual amount of barnstorming and on June 13, they were at Chester, Pennsylvania. Arriving late and missing a couple of stars due to a miscommunication, the team took the field with Streeter filling in at first base. In the third inning, Streeter hit a grand slam. That was all pitcher Rosey Davis needed as the Crawfords won 6-1.[49]

On August 21 Streeter defeated the Madison Blues in Madison, Wisconsin, 5-2. The Blues were kept off guard by Streeter's spitball, and the Crawfords pulled off a triple play in the first inning. The game was a vintage Crawfords effort. Cool Papa Bell led off the game with a double, stole third base, and came home on a single by Pat Patterson. Patterson then stole second and scored on a triple by Bill Perkins. An inning later, Bell's second double scored Chet Williams, and Sam Bankhead drove in Bell. The Crawfords' scoring was completed when Josh Gibson tripled in the third inning and scored on a groundout. Streeter scattered nine hits.[50]

Streeter opened the Negro National League Championship Series at New York's Dyckman Oval against the New York Cubans on September 13 and lost, 6-2, as the Cubans came from behind on two homers by Rap Dixon.[51] It was his only appearance in the Series. The Crawfords' first win in the Series was a 3-0 gem by Leroy Matlock at Dyckman Oval in Game Three. Down three games to one, the Crawfords came back to win the next three games, each by one run, to take the Series.

Streeter's last season with the Crawfords was the 1936 campaign. On May 10 they swept the Cubans in a doubleheader. In the opener Paige, with the help of homers by Josh Gibson and Oscar Charleston, won 8-4. Streeter pitched the second game and came away with a 6-5 win in which Gibson clouted two more homers. The *Pittsburgh Courier* wrote, "[L]ike the first, it was such a spectacular ballgame that almost every fan remained until the last strike was called on the last batter. Then they went home, as contented as the cows that give Carnation milk."[52]

In August things got a little muddled in the Negro National League. Streeter was named to a Negro League all-star team that won the annual *Denver Post* tournament on August 11. On the way back from Denver, the All-Stars faced the House of David in Des Moines, Iowa, on August 14. Satchel Paige started for the Negro All-Stars and left the game after homering in the second inning. Streeter took over and pitched the remainder of the game as his team won 19-0. Streeter struck out nine and allowed five hits to a version of the House of David team that was one of several teams using that name and bore little resemblance to the original House of David team.[53] While Streeter and the other Negro National League players were on a two-week barnstorming jaunt, the remaining players continued to play league games.

The Crawfords won the second-half NNL championship with a 20-9 record and played the Washington Elites for the league championship – or did they? In the confusing world of Negro League Baseball, Washington (also known as the Nashville Elite Giants) did not win the first-half championship until September 17, when they played a makeup game. What counted and what didn't in the postseason is not readily apparent. On September 21 Streeter started for the Crawfords in Game One of the playoff series and lost, 2-0. Doubles by Biz Mackey and Jim West accounted for Washington's runs.[54] There was no Game Two.

The appetite for a championship was still there and a best-of-three series was scheduled in Nashville, beginning with a doubleheader on September 27 and concluding with a single game, if necessary, the next day. The Crawfords won the first game, 9-8, and the Elites won the second, 2-1, to set up the Monday-night showdown. There is no record of that game ever having been played. In any case, Streeter had appeared in his last game as a professional player in the Negro Leagues.

Streeter pitched in Pittsburgh's South Hills League, a sandlot organization, in 1937, and on August 8, 1938, he was there when the Homestead Grays commemorated their 25th anniversary. After baseball, Streeter stayed in Pittsburgh and worked as a laborer at the Jones & Laughlin steel mill until he reached retirement age.[55] He died in Pittsburgh on August 15, 1985, at the age of 84, and was buried at Homewood Cemetery in Pittsburgh.[56]

## Sources

In addition to the sources shown in the Notes, the author used Baseball-Reference.com, Seamheads.com, Ancestry.com, and the following:

"Black Barons and Gray Sox to Play – Leading Negro Clubs to Furnish Labor Day Doubleheader." *Birmingham News*, September 5, 1920: Sports, 1.

Carter, Ulish. "Streeter Was a Class Pitcher and Man in the Negro Leagues," *Pittsburgh Courier*, November 23, 1974: 26.

Clark, Dick, and Larry Lester. *The Negro Leagues Book*, (Cleveland: Society for American Baseball Research, 1994).

Cowans, Russell J. "West Defeats East in Diamond Classic: Big Bats of West Hammer Three Eastern Pitchers Hard." *Detroit Tribune*, September 16, 1933: 7.

Holway, John. *The Complete Book of Baseball's Negro Leagues: The Other Half of Baseball History* (Fern Park, Florida: Hastings House Publishers, 2001).

Nunn, William D. "Modern Baseball's 'Miracle Team,'" *Baltimore Afro-American*, November 3, 1928: 12.

"Oscar Owens, Homestead Pitcher, Is in Class by Himself When It Comes to Hurling No-Hit Contests," *Warren* (Pennsylvania) *Tribune,* August 26, 1926: 7

Smith, Wendell. "Smitty's Sports Spurts," *Pittsburgh Courier*, August 13, 1938: 16.

## Notes

1. Jean M. White, "Ballpark Figures: The Other League," *Washington Post*, April 25, 1981: B1, B4.

2. Jerry Vondas, "Bucs Victory Stirs Memories for Former Grays Players," *Pittsburgh Press,* October 7, 1971: 42.

3. "Edgewater at Montgomery, June 23," *Birmingham News*, July 6, 1919: 23; "In the Baseball World: Edgewater at Montgomery, June 23," *Birmingham Reporter*, July 5, 1919: 8.

4. "Ensley Defeats Westfield," *Birmingham News*, July 6, 1919: 23; "Ensley TCI Giants Goose Egg Westfield, Holding Them to Five Scattered Hits," *Birmingham Reporter*, July 5, 1919: 8.

5. "In the Base Ball World: Streeter's Curves Puzzle the Chattanooga Giants," *Birmingham Reporter*, July 12, 1919: 8.

## THE 1935 PITTSBURGH CRAWFORDS

6 Walter S. Brown, "Yellow Jackets Take Game from Black Barons by Winning Twin Bill at Rickwood Park," *Birmingham Reporter*, September 13, 1919: 8; "Black Barons Are Given Double Loss," *Birmingham News*, September 9, 1919: 7. ACIPCO stands for American Cast Iron and Pipe Company.

7 "Black Barons Win Seventeen Inning Battle," *Birmingham News*, June 8, 1920: 8.

8 "Montgomery Sox Swamp Chicagoans," *Montgomery Advertiser*, July 23, 1920: 5.

9 "Black Barons Meet Third Straight Loss," *Birmingham News*, August 15, 1920: 4.

10 Zipp Newman, "Barons Tackle Alabama Squad in Tuscaloosa," *Birmingham News*, March 30, 1921: 14.

11 "Amer. Giants, 11; Magnets, 2," *Chicago Tribune*, July 18, 1921: 11.

12 "Bacharach Giants Win Both Games," *Philadelphia Inquirer*, July 31, 1922: 11.

13 "Lincoln Giants Go Eleven Innings to Beat Recreation 7-6," *Plainfield* (New Jersey) *Courier-News*, June 4, 1923: 12.

14 "Lincolns and Royal Giants Divide Double Header Last Sunday at Protectory Oval," *New York Age*, August 25, 1923: 6.

15 "Grays Sign Hurler," *Pittsburgh Gazette Times*, May 26, 1925: 12.

16 "Grays Down Knickers," *Pittsburgh Post*, May 26, 1925: 14.

17 "Streeter a Winner in Debut Here," *Pittsburgh Courier*, June 6, 1925: 12.

18 "Victorious Record Held by Visitors," *Coshocton* (Ohio) *Tribune*, June 18, 1925: 9.

19 William J. Pfarr, "Bellevue Blanked by Grays," *Pittsburgh Sunday Post*, July 19, 1925: 3-7.

20 "Homestead Grays Lose to Jeannette," *Pittsburgh Gazette Times*, July 26, 1925: 3-3.

21 William G. Nunn, "Diamond Dope: Getting the 'Bum's Rush' to the Showers," *Pittsburgh Courier*, August 1, 1925: 12.

22 "Homewood Loses Two to Grays," *Pittsburgh Gazette Times*, October 4, 1925: 3-4.

23 "Grays Twirling Staff, Turning 120 Victories Out of 144 Games, Takes Rank as 'Greatest Four' in Independent Circles," *Pittsburgh Courier*, September 26, 1925: 12.

24 Chester Washington Jr., "Sez Ches: Iron Man Back in Iron Town," *Pittsburgh Courier*, July 30, 1938: 16.

25 "Grays, Tied by Two Teams, Out for Independent Mark." *Pittsburgh Courier*, May 22, 1926: 14.

26 "Grays to Meet Coshocton Nine Saturday at Forbes Field," *Pittsburgh Courier*, May 7, 1927: Section 2: 4.

27 "Cleveland Beaten by Homestead Grays, 15-3," *Pittsburgh Courier*, July 31, 1926: 14.

28 William G. Nunn, "Diamond Dope," *Pittsburgh Courier*, August 21, 1926: 14.

29 "Homestead Lives Up to Advance Notices and Thrills Hundreds of Warren Fans Saturday Afternoon," *Warren* (Pennsylvania) *Tribune*, August 30, 1926: 6.

30 "Grays and American League Stars Split," *Pittsburgh Courier*, October 9, 1926: 15; "Big Leaguers Conquer Grays in Ten Frames," *Pittsburgh Post*, October 4, 1926: 11.

31 "Black Barons Beat Hornets in Second Tilt," *Birmingham News*, May 4, 1927: 13.

32 "Black Barons Beat St. Louis Stars in Series Final, 11-4," *St. Louis Daily Globe Democrat*, June 30, 1927: 10.

33 Larry Tye, *Satchel: The Life and Times of an American Legend* (New York: Random House, 2009), 44.

34 "Grays Decisive in Local Debut," *Pittsburgh Courier*, May 19, 1928: Section 2: 4.

35 "Grays Invade Ohio Thursday," *Pittsburgh Courier*, May 26, 1928: Section 2: 4.

36 "Generals to Clash with Homesteads; Nonskids at Home," *Akron Beacon Journal*, June 2, 1928: 23.

37 "Grays in Auto Wreck," *Pittsburgh Courier*, June 29, 1929: 1.

38 "Black Barons Win Again," *Birmingham Reporter*, August 9, 1930: 6.

39 "Black Barons Win Twin Bill from Elites," *Birmingham News*, September 2, 1930: 13.

40 The season record is according to seamheads.com, accessed February 2020.

41 "Streeter Now with Crawfords," *Pittsburgh Courier*, June 6, 1931: Section 2: 4.

42 "W. Foster Silences Crawfords," *Pittsburgh Courier*, June 27, 1931: Section 2: 4.

43 T. Jay Murphy, "Pattison Blanks Crawfords with Three Hits in Sunset Tilt; Visitors Take First," *Long Island Daily Press* (Queens, New York), September 26, 1932: 10.

44 William J. Moore, "Elites Win Series from Crawfords," *Birmingham Reporter*, July 22, 1933: 3.

45 Chester L. Washington, "'Mules' Suttles Scorching Homer Blazed West's 'Victory-Trail' in East-West Classic," *Pittsburgh Courier*, September 16, 1933: Sports-4.

46 "Streeter Blanks Stars," *Pittsburgh Post-Gazette*, June 12, 1934: 17.

47 Sources vary as to what Pittsburgh's overall record was in 1934, as well as who won the half-season titles. Seamheads.com says Philadelphia won the first half and Chicago won the second half, but several sources have it the other way around. According to contemporary sources and two books, Chicago won the first half and Philadelphia the second half. Books include John Holway, *The Complete Book of Baseball's Negro*

Leagues: The Other Half of Baseball History, 305, and Dick Clark and Larry Lester, eds., *The Negro Leagues Book*, 161. Newspapers showing standings are *Pittsburgh Press*, July 11, 1934: 26, and *Pittsburgh Courier*, September 8, 1934: 14 (second half). The overall record varies as well. Lester shows the record at 29-17, Holway shows it at 64-22; and Seamheads.com has it as 47-27-3 (in the league). Each shows that the Crawfords had the best overall record.

48   "Craws Win Four, Lose Two in Gray Feud," *Pittsburgh Courier*, July 13, 1935: 15.

49   "Pittsburgh Beats Chester; Cuban Stars Here This Evening," *Chester* (Pennsylvania) *Times*, June 14, 1935: 17.

50   Henry J. McCormick, "Crawfords Complete Triple Play, Beat Blues 5-2," *Wisconsin State Journal* (Madison), August 22, 1935: 11.

51   "Crawfords Lose to Cubans, 6-2," *Pittsburgh Post-Gazette*, September 14, 1935: 16.

52   Chester L. Washington, "Ches' Sez," *Pittsburgh Courier*, May 16, 1936: Section 2, 5.

53   Sec Taylor, "Paige Stars in Contest Here," *Des Moines Register*, August 15, 1936: 5, 7.

54   "Porter Pitches Three-Hit Ball to Give Elites 2-0 Victory over Craws in First game of Play-Off," *Pittsburgh Courier*, September 26, 1936: Section 2, 4.

55   John Holway, "Black All-Stars Celebrate Anniversary, Too," *Philadelphia Tribune*, July 5, 1983: 13.

56   Some sources indicate a death date six days earlier, on August 9, 1985.

# CHESTER WILLIAMS

## By Dave Wilkie

Over the years, the *Pittsburgh Courier*, one of the nation's leading African-American newspapers, used the following superlatives to describe Pittsburgh Crawfords infielder Chester Williams: Peppy, snappy, aggressive, hustling, scrappy, flashy. He was also referred to as sure-fielding, hard-hitting, a sparkplug, and even an inspired devil. From 1931 through the team's demise in 1938, Williams was a fixture, mostly at shortstop, and an instrumental cog in the finely tuned machine that was the Crawfords. For good measure, Williams also spent time with Smoketown's other Negro League powerhouse, the Homestead Grays, in 1932-33 and 1941-42.

Chester Arthur Williams was born on May 25, 1906, in Beaumont, Texas.[1] The identity of his parents and how and where he spent his childhood remain shrouded in mystery, but it appears likely that Williams's family must have moved to Lake Charles, Louisiana, when he was young and that he grew up there, since much of his life centered on that area.

Evidence of Williams appearing on a ball field pops up in 1929 with an independent team called the Shreveport Black Sports.[2] He may have also played for the Houston Black Buffaloes before beginning his Negro League career with the Chicago American Giants in 1930.[3] Williams played only a handful of games with the Giants before moving on to legendary manager and 32-year Negro League veteran Candy Jim Taylor's Memphis Red Sox. There, Williams showed that he belonged. In statistics found from 63 games in 1930, Williams batted .297 in 219 recorded at-bats. He followed Taylor to the Indianapolis ABCs for the 1931 season before finally settling in with Gus Greenlee's Pittsburgh Crawford Giants later in the year.

Pittsburgh racketeer, promoter, and baseball man Gus Greenlee's dream was to field a championship baseball team, and he began this quest in earnest in 1931. Williams was one of the first players he signed, along with Sam "Lefty" Streeter, Pistol Johnny Russell, Jimmie Crutchfield, and Bill Perkins. A late-season acquisition of Satchel Paige from the failing Cleveland Cubs for a paltry $250 had Greenlee's team headed in the right direction.[4] Interestingly, at one point during the

1931 season, Chester joined an all-Williams infield, playing alongside Bobby, Bucky, and Harry Williams.[5]

Cum Posey, the owner of the Homestead Grays, who also played in Pittsburgh, had an ongoing battle with Greenlee for local supremacy that resulted in many players moving back and forth between the Grays and the Crawfords.[6] Williams spent part of 1932 with the Crawfords, hitting .296 in limited action, but the bulk of his season had him as a member of the Homestead Grays. An early-season matchup against the New York Black Yankees shows the Grays' shortstop rapping out three hits, including a double and a triple, in a 2-1 victory. In another contest, played in late September, Williams managed four hits while leading off in the Grays' 10-0 drubbing of the Fort Wayne All-Stars.[7]

Williams started the 1933 campaign with the Homestead Grays and, in a May 25 matchup against the Pittsburgh Crawfords, he expressed his dissatisfaction with the way they had transferred him to the Grays the previous season. The *Pittsburgh Courier's* John L. Clark wrote of Williams's desire for revenge: "Chester has already served notice that the Decoration Day series, or any series with the Crawfords, for that matter, will find him at his best. That is saying something for the Texas star can play when he wants to."[8] Ironically, Williams found himself back with the Crawfords again by mid-July, but this time he stayed for a while, remaining a Crawford through the 1938 season.[9]

The 1933 Crawfords won a disputed Negro National League championship when Greenlee, president of the league at the time, declared them champs after the league failed to finish the second half of the season. The Chicago American Giants, winners of the first half, also laid claim to the title.[10] After adding four future Hall of Famers — Josh Gibson, Oscar Charleston, Cool Papa Bell, and Judy Johnson — to go along with returning members Satchel Paige, and the slick-fielding Williams, the Crawfords had built the foundation of one of the greatest teams in baseball history.

The 1934 season was a good one for the Crawfords. They finished 52-29-3, but they were unable to win either the first or second half of the season and thus were left out of the championship series. Williams had a stellar season as the starting shortstop, stroking .321 with 75 hits in 234 discovered at-bats. He played so well that he was voted to his first of four consecutive East-West All-Star Games.

Sportswriter Nat Trammell wrote of Williams and his exceptional fielding ability after a 1934 contest against the Philadelphia Stars:

> Williams turned in several beautiful fielding plays. He dived on his eyebrows to stop (Biz) Mackey's hit going across second base. Williams then somersaulted and threw perfect to (Leroy) Morney to force (Jud) Wilson at second and rob Mackey of a sure single, Williams again electrified the fans when he went back of (Oscar) Charleston to spear Chaney White's drive and tossed him out at first as well.[11]

The East-West All-Star Game was an extremely popular contest, first played the previous year, and its players were voted on by the fans and readers of the nation's leading African-American newspapers. Williams's first game was also his best as he smacked three hits and earned the batting honors of the day.[12]

Play-by-play announcer Lester Roberts described Williams's big day:

> Back to the action I now return you, with one out on the East and one player who stands at first base, Chester Williams, who hit a single that jumped past Mule Suttles' mitt.[13]

> Now Chester Williams is up next to face Foster and he singles just past first base on the first pitch, leaving no base free.[14]

## THE 1935 PITTSBURGH CRAWFORDS

… but that still leaves Williams holding the bat in the box with a count of two and two because that last pitch came in straight and true to serve up a strike, but now Foster sends a changeup to Williams as he swings on and bends past second base into shallow left field, putting Williams on base, and folks, he has a feel for the bat today because now he has three hits in the game from swinging so free.[15]

… the next pitch from Satch is one Parnell likes as he swings and shoots a groundball to Chester Williams at second, who flashes the leather by making the catch with a backhand grab to his right, then turns to make the tag on Suttles off base, but Williams isn't done – he spins and throws to first, and Charleston stretches to beat Parnell on the run. A great double play for outs two and three from Williams, who made it look so easy, ends the inning and ends the game, meaning today the East will be named champions of this East-West Classic in a game that was indeed a classic.[16]

Although Williams excelled on the field, he was known to spend his spare time with heavy drinkers, like Josh Gibson and Sam Bankhead, and would often find himself in off-the-field trouble.[17] He and catcher Curtis Harris were both suspended at one point during the 1934 season for "conduct unbecoming ball players and gentlemen," tainting what was otherwise a stellar season for Chester Williams.[18]

Williams joined teammates Cool Papa Bell and Satchel Paige in the integrated California Winter League for its 1934-1935 season, playing for Tom Wilson's Elite Giants. The Giants dismantled the competition with a 34-5-1 record. Williams got into seven games at second base and shined with a .483 average. He played sporadically in the league, but seemed to enjoy some success, last playing in the 1942-1943 season for the Royal Giants.[19]

*All-Star shortstop Chester Williams banged out two doubles and a triple in Game Seven of the NNL championship series as the Crawfords captured the title with an 8-7 victory over the New York Cubans.*

(Courtesy National Baseball Hall of Fame)

## Pride of Smoketown

The 1935 Pittsburgh Crawfords were a legendary team, sometimes compared to the 1927 New York Yankees, and finished the season 51-26-3, winning the NNL Championship Series in a nailbiter, four games to three over the New York Cubans. While Williams slumped to a .237 average during the regular season, he managed to come through when it most mattered in the final series. Williams pounded out three hits in the final game, two doubles and a triple, to help lead the Craws to an 8-7 Series-clinching victory.[20]

In 1936 Williams was voted to his third straight East-West All-Star Game, narrowly beating out future Hall of Famer Willie Wells for the starting nod at shortstop. Although he went 0-for-4 in the game, he did manage an RBI in his team's 10-2 walloping of the West.[21] *Pittsburgh Courier* city editor William G. Nunn praised Williams after the matchup: "We saw speed, dash and class. Oodles of it. We know that Chester Williams as he performed today is better than several major league shortstops."[22]

The 1936 Crawfords were once again crowned champions of the NNL, winning the first half of the season and having a far superior record than the second-half winner, the Washington Elite Giants, but no championship series was scheduled. Instead, a team of all-stars, including Crawford teammates Josh Gibson, Cool Papa Bell, Satchel Paige, Sam Streeter, and Chester Williams, played in the prestigious Denver Post Tournament. The All-Stars swept the seven-game competition and took home the $5,000 prize.[23]

The year 1937 began with Gus Greenlee proclaiming to the *Chicago Defender* that Williams "will be the nation's outstanding shortstop this season" and that he "wouldn't trade Chester for any two infielders in baseball."[24] But Williams and the Crawfords disappointed that season, mostly due to the trades of Gibson and Judy Johnson and the movement of players to the Dominican Republic. Players like Satchel Paige and Cool Papa Bell, fed up with low salaries and poor conditions, were happy to travel south of the border in search of much larger paychecks. Williams spent the bulk of the season with the Crawfords, but eventually took $1,000 to head south and play for dictator Rafael Trujillo's all-star team in the Dominican Republic.[25] Under extreme conditions and the threat of bodily harm, Ciudad Trujillo took the championship game and helped the dictator gain re-election. Williams played second base and chipped in with two RBIs in the final game.[26] Meanwhile, back home, the Crawfords finished dead last in the six-team Negro National League.

Once the defectors had returned stateside, Williams suited up for an exhibition game against a team called the Dominican Stars, made up mostly of the Trujillo team, which included Bell, Paige, and Sam Bankhead. On September 23 at the Polo Grounds in New York, young New York Cubans pitcher Johnny Taylor led the Negro National League All-Stars against Paige and his Dominican Stars. Taylor pitched the game of his life, hurling a no-hitter and defeating Paige, 2-0. Chester Williams received much of the credit in helping limit the Stars to no hits. *Pittsburgh Courier* writer John Clark described his sparkling play: "Chester Williams, brilliant sparkplug of the Pittsburgh Crawfords, was the shining star in the finest and sweetest fielding combinations ever to show in the Big City. Working with Hughes at second, the pair guarded and patrolled the infield like Texas Rangers rounding up horse thieves. Not a single pellet got past them."[27]

Always a popular player, Williams played in his fourth and final East-West All-Star Game in 1937 with the third most votes overall.[28] Strangely, he led all shortstops in voting in 1938 and came in second to Willie Wells in 1939, but not play in either game. He also showed up in the voting in 1941, but once again did not play.[29]

Unlike his teammates Bell and Paige, Williams returned to the Crawfords for the 1938 season to witness the end of the once-mighty franchise. Williams had a fine season, hitting .308, but his team finished in the middle of the pack. After two consecutive poor seasons, owner Gus Greenlee sold the team after the 1938 season and new owner Hank Rigney move the Crawfords to Toledo, Ohio.[30]

It is unknown when Williams and his wife, Nellie Laffnette, were married, but they welcomed their first child, Deloris Jean, into the world on June 8, 1938.[31] Deloris was followed by a second daughter, Chester Lee; a son, Leonard, who was born in March of 1943; daughter Patsy; and son Leroy Williams, who was named after Leroy "Satchel" Paige.[32]

Williams latched on with Philadelphia in 1939, hitting second and playing shortstop for the underachieving Stars.[33] He had been expected to join Oscar Charleston and the Crawfords in their move to Toledo, but instead decided to jump ship.[34] The 1939 season marked Williams's last productive Negro League campaign as he batted .338 for the Stars.

His time with Philadelphia was short-lived, and Williams spent the rest of 1939 through much of 1941 splitting his time between Cuba and Mexico. His two winter seasons in Cuba were almost identical. He hit .298 in 188 at-bats for Santa Clara in 1939-40 and .299 in 174 at-bats for Cienfuegos in the winter of 1940-41.[35] Williams also packed his glove and headed to Mexico to play for the 1940 Torreon team, for whom he tore the cover off the ball by cracking 107 hits in 311 at-bats for a .344 average. In his only foray into managing, Williams also skippered the 1940 Torreon team and led the club to a 45-41 record and a fifth-place finish. Hall of Famers Cool Papa Bell and Hilton Smith also played for Torreon that year. Williams returned to Torreon the following season, but he hit only .254 in 71 at-bats over 16 games.[36]

Hall of Fame third baseman Judy Johnson called Williams "a real holler guy" and Williams was known as a free spirit and someone who could get riled up easily. Two stories from his last two seasons in the Negro Leagues, when he again played for the Homestead Grays, show this side of him.[37] Just before the 1942 Negro World Series between the Grays and the Kansas City Monarchs, Satchel Paige told Williams, then playing shortstop for the Grays, that Monarchs owner J.L. Wilkinson would give all the profits from the Series to his players. Williams knew that Grays owner Cum Posey would never match this offer, and Paige had managed to upset Williams and get in every Grays player's head. Buck O'Neil commented, "These guys, they were stirred up. They were only getting a percentage of the money. That upset them. We had more to play for than they had to play for."[38] The Grays were swept in the Series, with Satchel Paige pitching in all four games for the victorious Monarchs.

A more humorous story was told by Memphis Red Sox lefty Verdell Mathis:

> I remember one time in Allentown, Pennsylvania, we were playing the Washington Homestead Grays – Josh Gibson, Buck Leonard, and those guys. They had a shortstop, a good one, named Chester Williams. He said, 'Come on in here, we're gonna run you to death.' I wasn't supposed to pitch that day, but Chester Williams kept 'woofin',' you know, kidding you, trying to get a rise out of you. I didn't like that. I didn't like no team to start woofin' about they were gonna do this or that. So our pitcher was warming up, and Chester Williams kept beefing and going on, so I got up off the bench, said, 'Give me that ball.' I went and took the ball away from Evans and warmed up four or five pitches. They got one run off me, and that was a home run Buck Leonard hit in the first inning. I wasn't quite warm. But by the bottom of the ninth, when the game was over, we beat 'em 7-1. Chester Williams cried all the way to the dressing room. He said, 'This just ain't fair. How can you do this?' I stopped him from woofin', though.[39]

After Chester Williams finished his Negro League career with two lackluster seasons for the powerhouse 1941 and 1942 Homestead Grays, he had a lifetime batting average of .285 and was compared favorably to New York Yankees shortstop Mark Koenig of Murderers' Row fame.[40] In 14 games against teams made up of white major leaguers, Williams had 17 hits in 52 at-bats for a .327 average.[41]

Chester Williams returned home to Lake Charles, Louisiana, after his playing days were through and was drafted into the Army on October 9, 1943. He was honorably discharged on August 8, 1944, after hurting his arm.[42] At the age of 46, Williams was shot and killed in a scuffle at his own establishment, the Cotton Club, in Lake Charles on Christmas Day in 1952. According to news accounts of the incident, Williams was shot five times with a .25-caliber pistol and died almost instantly from his wounds.[43] The man who shot him, Tom Scott, was taken to the hospital with ice-pick wounds inflicted by Williams in their scuffle. News accounts failed to report the further disposition of the case.[44] Williams was buried with a military headstone at Hi-Mount Cemetery in Lake Charles.[45]

The 5-foot-9, 180-pound, speedy, surehanded, dynamo certainly deserved a chance to play in the major leagues, but his career was over before the integration of the game began. It is certain that much of the storied Pittsburgh Crawfords' success from 1932 to 1936 can be attributed to Williams' presence in the middle of the team's infield.

## Acknowledgment

Frederick C. Bush, co-editor of this book, spoke briefly with Mrs. Chester Lee Moses, Chester Williams's second-born daughter, by phone on February 1, 2020, and then made contact with her daughter, Monique Jeffers. Bush's conversation with Mrs. Moses was brief, though a few family details now included in this biography emerged, because she was scheduled to visit her daughter in March and planned to bring additional information and photographs to be given to Bush at that time. As readers assuredly know, this turned out to be the time when the worldwide COVID-19 pandemic began to hit the United States full force. Bush was unsuccessful in making further contact during that time, and both this author and the editors fervently hope that Chester Lee Moses and Monique Jeffers fared well through the ordeal. We hope to reconnect with them to obtain additional information that would expand this biography for future printings of this book and/or the SABR Biography Project website.

## Sources

Unless otherwise noted, all statistics were taken from seamheads.com or baseballreference.com.

## Notes

1. Ancestry.com, US Headstone Applications for Military Veterans, 1925-1963. Chester Lee Moses, Williams's second daughter, confirmed that Williams was born in Beaumont, Texas, during a phone conversation with co-editor Frederick C. Bush on February 1, 2020.

2. Larry Lester and Wayne Stivers, *The Negro Leagues Book, Volume 2: The Players, 1862-1960* (Raytown, Missouri: NoirTech Research Inc., 2020), loc. 6926.

3. Ryan Whirty, "Lake Charles Link to Negro League History," *American Press* (Lake Charles, Louisiana), August 2, 2013. facebook.com/notes/negro-leagues-baseball-museum/lake-charles-link-to-negro-leagues-history/10151780555945236/.

4. Jim Bankes, *The Pittsburgh Crawfords* (Jefferson, North Carolina: McFarland & Company Inc., 2001), 21.

5. Baseballreference.com. baseball-reference.com/bullpen/Chester_Williams.

6. Bankes, 16.

7. *Pittsburgh Courier*, May 7, 1932: 15, and October 1, 1932: 14.

8. *Pittsburgh Courier*, May 27, 1933: 7.

9. *Pittsburgh Courier*, July 15, 1933: 14.

10. James A. Riley, *The Biographical Encyclopedia of the Negro Baseball Leagues* (New York: Carroll & Graf Publishers Inc., 1994), 629.

11. Phil Dixon and Patrick J. Hannigan, *The Negro Baseball Leagues: A Photographic History* (Mattituck, New York: Amereon House, 1992), 236.

12. *Pittsburgh Courier*, September 8, 1934. 15.

13. Chester R. Smith Jr., *Stars in the Shadows: The Negro League All-Star Game of 1934* (New York: Simon and Schuster, 2012) 59.

14. Smith, 14.

15. Smith, 15.

16. Smith, 16.

17. William Brashler, *Josh Gibson: A Life in the Negro Leagues* (Chicago: Ivan R. Dee, 2000), 68. See also Riley, 847.

18. Whirty.

19. William F. McNeil, *The California Winter Leagues* (Jefferson, North Carolina: McFarland & Company Inc., 2002), 171.

20. John Holway, *The Complete Book of Baseball's Negro Leagues: The Other Half of Baseball History* (Fern Park, Florida: Hastings House Publishers, 2001), 321.

21. Larry Lester, *Black Baseball's National Showcase: The East-West All-Star Game, 1933-1953* (Lincoln: University of Nebraska Press, 2001), 91-93.
22. Lester, 89.
23. Lester, 82-83.
24. *Chicago Defender*, April 10, 1937: 13.
25. Lester, 97.
26. Averell "Ace" Smith, *The Pitcher and the Dictator* (Lincoln: University of Nebraska Press, 2018), 114-115.
27. *Pittsburgh Courier*, September 25, 1937: 17.
28. Lester, 106.
29. Lester, 119, 139, 171.
30. Riley, 629.
31. Ancestry.com, US Social Security Applications and Claims Index, 1936-2007. Chester Lee Moses confirmed that her mother's maiden name was spelled Laffnette rather than any of the variations, such as Lafaynette, found in some census records.
32. *Pittsburgh Courier*, March 20, 1943: 9, mentioned Leonard's birth, though it did not provide his name. Chester Lee Moses provided the names and birth order of all of Chester and Nellie (Laffnette) Williams's children.
33. Riley, 847.
34. *Pittsburgh Courier*, April 22, 1939: 17.
35. Jorge S. Figueredo, *Who's Who in Cuban Baseball: 1878-1961* (Jefferson, North Carolina: McFarland & Company Inc., 2003), 385.
36. Pedro Treto Cisneros, *The Mexican League: Comprehensive Player Statistics, 1937-2001* (Jefferson, North Carolina: McFarland & Company Inc., 2002), 279.
37. Bankes, 68.
38. Brad Snyder, *Beyond the Shadow of the Senators: The Untold Story of the Homestead Grays and the Integration of Baseball* (New York: McGraw-Hill, 2003), 143.
39. John B. Holway, *Black Diamonds: Life in the Negro Leagues from the Men Who Lived It* (New York: Stadium Books, 1991), 149-150.
40. Bankes, 151.
41. Todd Peterson, *The Negro Leagues Were Major Leagues: Historians Reappraise Black Baseball* (Jefferson, North Carolina: McFarland & Company Inc., 2020), 242. Seamheads.com says that in six games against teams made up of white major leaguers, Williams had 5 hits in 17 at-bats for a .294 average.
42. Whirty.
43. "Five Pistol Shots Fatal to Negro," *Beaumont Journal*, December 26, 1952: 5.
44. "Ex-Baseball Great Slain," *Pittsburgh Courier*, January 10, 1953: 14.
45. Whirty.

# GUS GREENLEE

## By Brian McKenna

*Gus Greenlee was a numbers-game kingpin, philanthropist, and lover of sports. After he purchased the Pittsburgh Crawfords, he immediately turned the team into one of the Negro Leagues' premier squads.*

Gus Greenlee, famed owner of the Pittsburgh Crawfords, came from a family that valued education. His three brothers earned medical or law degrees, but Gus left college after a year and moved away from his family at age 19 to work in Pittsburgh. He soon purchased his own taxi and began running bootleg liquor out of it, along with Joe Tito, one of the owners of the Latrobe brewery. Within a few years he and Tito bought into an illegal lottery operation. Eventually, Greenlee became one of the leading numbers kings in the city and wielded a great deal of political power within the Hill District.

In the 1930s he entered the sports business, owning a stable of boxers and purchasing the semi-pro Pittsburgh Crawfords, a black baseball team. He built the club into one of the top squads in the Negro leagues. He also owned and operated one of the rare ballparks owned by a black club. Greenlee was the driving force behind the formation of the Negro National League in 1933 and ran it with a firm hand. By the end of the decade, he was in dire straits financially and facing legal troubles and was forced to disband

# THE 1935 PITTSBURGH CRAWFORDS

the club. The Crawfords were later reformed, but were shunned from membership in the existing leagues. Greenlee then organized the historically significant yet marginal United States Leagues.

William Augustus Greenlee was born on the day after Christmas in 1895 or perhaps 1896 in Marion, North Carolina, to Samuel R. and Julia R. Greenlee. Samuel supported the family as a brick and mason contractor, making a significant living. The couple had seven children, three girls and four boys. Gus was the oldest son and second child. Julia's father was locally a well-known white businessman. Julia's mother was African-American, thus Gus and his siblings were identified as mulatto in official government documents. Gus, a big man, had reddish-orange hair, and was nicknamed Big Red.

Gus dropped out during his second year of college and settled in the Hill District of Pittsburgh in 1916 at age 20. Shortly afterwards, he married a local woman named Helen. They had no children. Greenlee held a variety of job in his early years: he worked in a steel mill operating a steam drill, pushed a wheelbarrow for a construction company, shined shoes, toiled as a fireman and drove for an undertaker. He bought his own taxi cab. In October 1917 Greenlee enlisted in the army, and soon landed in the 367th Infantry Regiment, 153rd Depot Brigade as a machine gunner. Greenlee saw combat at Verdun and was later injured, hit with shrapnel in the left leg, at St. Mihiel, France and discharged in March 1919.

Returning to Pittsburgh, Greenlee began working with the white Tito (a silent partner) to sell whiskey out of his taxi to speakeasies, also transporting liquor throughout the area. Prohibition made this profitable and soon the partners opened the Paramount Club on Wylie Avenue. It was closed down after a police raid in 1922, but reopened in 1924 with its own orchestra. That club was closed down again amid charges that Caucasian women were "running wild" at the establishment. Greenlee opened once again and also operated a musical booking agency out of the establishment.

Greenlee also owned the Workingmen's Pool Hall on Fullerton Street, the Sunset Café and the famous Crawford Grill at 1401 Wylie Avenue. The Grill, nearly a block long, became a hotspot of Hill District, known as "Little Harlem." The third floor, Club Crawford, was a semi-private VIP section where the top Jazz performers of the day entertained. Over the years, Louis Armstrong, Dizzy Gillespie, Ella Fitzgerald, Stanley Turrentine, Count Basie, Duke Ellington, Cab Calloway, Billy Eckstein, Lena Horne, Bill Robinson and Miles Davis performed for Greenlee's audiences. The club became a hangout for both black and white entertainers and sportsmen. Steelers' owner Art Rooney was a friend of Greenlee's and a frequent visitor at the Grill. Lena Horne's father Teddy was one of Greenlee's right-hand men in his numbers business.

About 1926, Greenlee, William "Woogie" Harris and Tito purchased an illegal lottery business. The group proved quite adept at their new trade, spreading their business throughout Pittsburgh and Allegheny County. At their height they administered close to one hundred individual clearing houses where bets were placed and money changed hands. It's estimated that as much as $25,000 was being made on a daily basis. Greenlee also operated evening dice games.

To protect himself against local police and authorities, Greenlee allied with several Republican politicians. In fact, Greenlee ran the Third Ward Voters' League. Black voters supported his candidates en masse. The numbers business flourished during the 1920s and '30s. Clients would pick three numbers with the winners defined by the final digits of that day's New York Stock Exchange volume index or some other measure. For as little as a penny, one could receive a payout between five or six dollars. The odds were in the bank's favor, as the actual odds against winning were 999 to 1. Greenlee was not above manipulating the numbers further in his favor if circumstances warranted. By 1933, he owned two hotels, several nightclubs and other enterprises including the Pittsburgh Crawford baseball club.

Like most numbers kings, especially in African-American neighborhoods, Greenlee was considered a community benefactor by many in his day. He was respected and admired for his charitable contributions and holiday giveaways to Hill District residents. The clearinghouses were the banks of the black community, since African Americans were typically shunned by white bankers. In essence, Greenlee was the Hill District's leading banker and was named local Businessman of the Year in 1948. He was known to help many with rent, college expenses, and medical care and even with more basic needs such as food and heating. He even operated a soup line during the Depression. His Christmas parties were hailed by hundreds in Western Pennsylvania and into Virginia and Ohio as the finest galas of the year. Greenlee also supported local hospitals, the NAACP and provided the start-up capital for many local entrepreneurs. Furthermore, he was one of the leading employers of African-Americans in the area, providing income for hundreds of individuals and their families.

In the 1930s Greenlee began showing an interest in sports promoting, particularly baseball and boxing. He became the manager and promoter for a stable of black boxers, including John Henry Lewis, who joined up with Greenlee in May 1935 and became light heavyweight champion on Halloween night 1935 in St. Louis.

The Homestead Grays were the dominant black baseball attraction in Pittsburgh. In 1931, in fact, the Grays purportedly finished 136-10, dominating all competition. Back in 1925 a group of neighborhood boys, one of which was Charles Harris, Woogie's brother, from the local McKelvey School had formed what became known as the Crawford Colored Giants. The name stemmed from their sponsor in a 1926 tournament, the Crawford Bath House, a municipal recreation center.

In 1930 at the behest of the Crawford players Greenlee purchased the semi-pro club, soon after Josh Gibson had jumped the club to join Cum Posey's Grays. Greenlee put the players on salary and charged into the baseball arena. He coaxed Atlantic City Bacharachs shortstop Bobby Williams to manage the Crawfords and recruit and build a winner. Pretty soon, Williams added Lefty Streeter, Jimmie Crutchfield, Chester Williams, Pistol Russell and, most dramatically, Satchel Paige. By 1932, Greenlee purchased a new Mack bus for the men and further fortified the lineup by raiding other clubs for Josh Gibson, Judy Johnson, Cool Papa Bell, William Bell, Rap Dixon, Ted Radcliffe, and Oscar Charleston, who was named player-manager.

In 1932 Greenlee purchased a plot of land from the Entress Brick Company and opened the first ballpark built for a black team, which he named Greenlee Field. The concrete and steel structure sat about 7,500 at an estimated cost of $100,000, half of which was financed out of Greenlee's pocket. He added lights to the field the following year. The park officially opened on April 29, 1932 with about 4,000 in attendance. The Crawfords played the New York Black Yankees. Paige pitched for Pittsburgh while New York sent Jesse Hubbard to the mound. Paige struck out ten and allowed only six hits; however, Hubbard topped that, giving up only three hits. The Yankees won 1-0. The Crawfords drew an impressive 69,000 fans to Greenlee Field that season, but still lost an estimated $15,000 due to the heavy expenditures.

The Crawfords tried to join the East-West League in 1932 but were rebuffed by league operator Cum Posey, with whom Greenlee would continue to feud throughout his time in black baseball. After the EWL disbanded, Greenlee set out to establish a new league, one on solid financial footing. This would be no easy task during the Depression. Thus, the National Negro Association, later called the Negro National League, was formed before the 1933 season. Greenlee served as the league's chairman, or president. He also helped form and organize the highly successful East-West All-Star Game that year which in time would become the showcase of black baseball. With no place else to go, Posey's Grays sought admission into Greenlee's Negro National League. Greenlee permitted the Grays to join but promptly expelled them after they raided the Detroit Stars' roster.

Mindful of the Depression and failures of the East-West League, the NNL set a few cost-conscience guidelines. First, rosters were limited to sixteen until June and to 14 thereafter. Second, a salary cap was imposed at $1,600 monthly; he insisted that salaries be kept down. The league also decided not to guarantee visiting clubs a minimum percentage of the gate. During the early to mid-1930s the Pittsburgh Crawfords fielded some of the best clubs in Negro league history with Gibson, Paige, Charleston, Bell, and Johnson filling the marquee. Noticing this, dictator Rafael Trujillo of the Dominican Republic plucked eight of the Crawfords' best players in early 1937. With that, Greenlee found it difficult to make payroll and the team eventually collapsed.

With further Trujillo raids and the poor American economy, the Negro National League suffered severe losses in 1937 and '38. Greenlee was also spending an increasing amount of time with his boxers. As a result, league owners, particularly Posey and Abe and Effa Manley of the Newark Eagles, became disgruntled with Greenlee's leadership and pushed for his removal from office.

Greenlee suffered other financial setbacks as well. In December 1938 Greenlee Field, badly in need of repairs, was claimed by the city via eminent domain and later demolished for a housing project. Competitors also made their way into the Pittsburgh numbers business. In January 1939 Greenlee's brother Marcus was killed in an auto accident and, the following day, John Henry Lewis was knocked out in the first round after moving up in class to fight heavyweight champ Joe Louis. In June Lewis was stripped of his Light Heavyweight title and his career was over after it was discovered that he suffered from partial blindness. Under pressure financially and by league owners, Greenlee resigned as president of the NNL in February 1939 and disbanded the Crawfords in April.

By the following year, Greenlee was looking to get back into the baseball business. He placed an open call for ballplayers and established a new semi-pro Crawford club. He made repeated efforts to gain admittance to the Negro National League and the Negro American League. Each time he was turned away. He was rebuffed for a variety of reasons, foremost among them the opposition of Cum Posey. Many were also turned off by Greenlee's autocratic reign as NNL president. A big man, 6'2" and 230 lbs., he was often pushy and overbearing. Moreover, there was speculation that Greenlee was involved in a game-fixing scheme against the Brooklyn Bushwicks in 1936. Finally, Greenlee had left the NNL on a sour note. He verbally attacked the other owners and left behind numerous debts and bounced checks.

Recovering financially by 1944, Greenlee tried once again to get back into black baseball. He soon realized that the established leagues didn't welcome his return; hence, he took steps to upset their balance. First, he raided the Homestead Grays, Chicago American Giants, and Baltimore Black Sox for players for his independent squad. He also stirred up the players, telling them that they were being treated unfairly. Of note, he riled up the all-star players just prior to the East-West Classic. Negro league officials were furious when all the eastern players demanded $200 for their participation.

In 1945 Greenlee started the United States League, headquartered out of his nightclub. Former player and Cleveland lawyer John Shackelford became the league's president. The league, which lasted into a second season, situated franchises in Pittsburgh, Brooklyn, Chicago, Boston, Detroit, Cleveland and Philadelphia. In May 1945 Branch Rickey threw his support behind the league in a very public manner, calling a press conference. He offered Ebbets Field and all the 22 ballparks controlled by the Brooklyn Dodgers organization to the USL. The Hilldale club was shifted to Brooklyn, renamed the Brown Dodgers and managed by Oscar Charleston. Rickey would later tell Jackie Robinson that the Brooklyn Dodgers pumped $30,000 into the USL. The USL lacked top talent though and never approached the quality of the other black leagues. Of historical significance, the United States League provided a cover for Rickey to scout and otherwise delve into black baseball, one result of which was the signing of Jackie Robinson in August 1945.

Throughout his time in baseball, Greenlee faced legal difficulties. He was charged, later dismissed, in connection to election fraud in a race in the 3rd Ward in 1931. In December 1932 he was indicted, not for the first time, in connection with his illegal lottery business. He was eventually sued by the government for failure to pay income taxes and for tax fraud. Creditors were also looming.

Greenlee suffered a heart attack in July 1946, just 50 years old. In 1950 he became quite ill, spending six months in the Veterans Hospital at Aspinwall, Pennsylvania. The next year his nightclub burned down, never to be rebuilt. Gus Greenlee died at home after suffering a stroke on July 7, 1952. He was interred at Allegheny Cemetery in Pittsburgh in the same section as Josh Gibson. His widow died in August 1958.

## Sources

Alleghenycemetery.com, Ancestry.com, *New York Times*, *Pittsburgh Courier*, Riverofsteel.com, and:Holway, John. *The Complete Book of Baseball's Negro Leagues: The Other Half of Baseball History* (Fern Park, Florida: Hastings House Publishers, 2001).

Ingham, John N. and Lynne B. Feldman. *African-American Business Leaders* (Westport, Connecticut: Greenwood Press, 1994).

Riley, James A. *The Biographical Encyclopedia of the Negro Baseball Leagues* (New York: Carroll and Graf Publishers, 1994).

Ruck, Rob. *Sandlot Seasons: Sport in Black Pittsburgh* (Champaign, Illinois: University of Illinois Press, 1993).

# ROY WILLIAM SPARROW

## By Margaret M. Gripshover

*Roy Sparrow helped to inaugurate the annual East-West All-Star classic in 1933. Ironically, he joined the New York Cubans in 1935 and saw his new employer's team lose to his former employer's squad, the Crawfords.*

(Courtesy Noir-Tech Research, Inc.)

Roy Sparrow was a likable hustler, huckster, and self-promoter who throughout his life appeared to be in perpetual motion. While living in Pittsburgh, Sparrow juggled multiple occupations. He was a shoe salesman, worked for two newspapers, and developed a reputation for local sports promotions. He was a determined, albeit unsuccessful, entrepreneur who opened and closed a billiard parlor, a miniature-golf course, two cafes, and a bakery. Sparrow's involvement in professional baseball started with the Pittsburgh Crawfords. He served as a promoter for three Negro National League teams and is often credited with idea for the first East-West Classic all-star game and for the "four-team doubleheader" series format. Sparrow got his start in Negro League baseball under the tutelage of Gus Greenlee and until 1935 was the main publicity man for the Crawfords. Sparrow reinvented himself numerous times, but his association with Alejandro "Alex" Pompez, the numbers racketeer and owner of the New York Cubans, precipitated his ultimate fall from grace. He recovered only to experience disappointment once more with the abysmal and short-lived 1939 Washington Black Senators, which turned out to be his final professional association with any Negro National League team.

## Pride of Smoketown

Roy William Sparrow was born on February 2, 1900, in Indian Rock, Virginia, to Lucian H. and Lillie (Howe) Sparrow. Indian Rock was a small community on the James River in Botetourt County, in west-central Virginia. Sparrow descended from a long line of Virginia-born freedmen whose trade of choice on his father's side of the family was coopering – making wooden barrels. Roy was the eldest of four children. By 1910 he and his family moved to Alexandria, a Washington suburb, where his father worked primarily as a cooper for the Portner Brewery, but also as a fireman shoveling coal into a steam locomotive.[1] In 1915 Roy's life was turned upside down by the deaths within two months of both of his parents from tuberculosis, which was at the time the leading cause of death in Virginia and the United States.[2] Long life expectancies were not in the cards for Roy or his siblings. All four of the Sparrow children died before their 50th birthdays.

Sparrow was a 14-year-old orphan when he was thrust into the working world. During World War I he was employed as a porter in the dining room of the US Naval Base Hospital in Nitro, West Virginia.[3] His Army registration documents described him as stout, medium in height, with blue eyes and brown hair.[4] After a stint in the explosives industry in Nitro, he found his way to Pittsburgh, where some of his relatives had settled as early as 1917.[5] By the early 1920s, Roy was living in Homestead, a steel-mill community near Pittsburgh, where he worked for the Carter Shoe Company. Within two years, he rose from the lowly position of porter to assistant manager.[6] About a year after his promotion, the Carter Shoe Company went bankrupt,[7] but Roy didn't miss a step. He formed a partnership and reopened the store under a new name, the Almar Boot Shop.[8] It was during these early years as a salesman that Sparrow honed his promotional skills and curried favor with local newspapermen who were willing to publish his advertising copy as "news." For example, while he was with Carter Shoes, the *Pittsburgh Courier* ran a story about Roy's meteoric rise thanks to his "enviable record" as a salesman.[9] There was no byline on the *Courier* feature, but there is no doubt as to the author – it was Roy Sparrow.

Sparrow's participation in any one of Pittsburgh's many sports leagues was most likely limited to the sidelines, although it is possible that he did play on some local teams in the 1920s. On occasion a player named Sparrow appeared on the roster for local football, basketball, and baseball teams. But since no first names were included in the brief game summaries, it is difficult to determine if it was really Roy. He may have been the defensive lineman identified as Sparrow on the Pittsburgh Courier Collegians football squad, the "Negro champions of Western Pennsylvania," in 1924.[10] The florid reporting on the Collegians' games in the *Courier* points to Roy being involved with the team.[11] He was linked to local basketball leagues, was with the Carter Shoe Five for several years, and in 1927 was named as the coach of the Pittsburgh Courier Big 5.[12] As for baseball, Sparrow's name cropped up a few times in the late 1920s and early 1930s, mainly with the Crawfords, but any evidence to suggest that he actually played baseball is inconclusive. Sparrow's physique and talents were better suited to promoting the game rather than playing it.

In the late 1920s, as Sparrow was becoming more involved with the Crawfords, his life was as frenetic as it was complicated. In 1928, while he contributed sports stories and theater reviews for the *Courier*, he opened the Cloverdale Sandwich Shop on Wylie Avenue in the Hill District.[13] The *Courier* story about the shop trumpeted that place as the "newest lunch sensation in the upper Hill District."[14] But apparently it was not sensational enough. The Cloverdale closed within months. In 1929 Sparrow was hired as a traveling salesman by the *Pittsburgh Sun-Telegraph* to market the newspaper to "race readers" in cities in western Pennsylvania.[15] That same year, with partner Lewis Harrington, he opened Lew-Roy Billiards, on Wylie Avenue.[16] But this was no ordinary billiard parlor. It was advertised as the "Hilltops Most Beautiful Resort," a place with laundry services, a newsstand, and the "daintiest luncheon in town."[17] Lew-Roy Billiards failed within a year.

Details about Roy Sparrow's personal life as an adult are sparse and, at best, opaque. The only evidence to indicate that he was ever married comes via Pittsburgh city directory listings. In 1929, Roy and Teresa Sparrow lived on Barnett Way in the Middle Hill neighborhood.[18] His marriage can be counted among his many failed partnerships and was dissolved by 1930. In 1930, his "wife" claimed she was a "widow," even though Roy was still very much alive.[19] When she married Sparrow, she was the widow of Alphonso DeLouvpre and had a teenage son. By describing herself as a widow in 1930, Teresa was shading the truth. At the time, it was not uncommon for a divorcee to hide the shame of a failed marriage with the veil of widowhood. After divorcing Roy, she not only reclaimed her widowhood, but also her identity as Teresa DeLouvpre, the name she used until her death in 1975. Although Sparrow never remarried after his union with Teresa was dissolved, his death certificate stated his marital status as "widowed."[20]

In the early 1930s, the newly single Sparrow combined his flair for entrepreneurship and promotion with his passion for sports. For example, he used the *Courier* to advertise a baseball game between the Pittsburgh Crawford Giants and the Stowe Civics that was being staged to benefit a local orphanage.[21] Likewise, the *Courier* announced Sparrow's opening of Madam Queen's, an indoor miniature-golf course in the Hill District that featured "an alluring layout" including a "Fresh Air Taxi" flivver."[22] Madam Queen's was a curious choice as a name for Roy's business: she was a character in the "Amos 'n' Andy" cartoon strip – an African-American woman who was also a bigamist – and the object of editorial scorn by the *Courier*.[23] The Fresh Air Taxi was also a reference to the racially inflammatory comic strip.[24] The golf course didn't last a year and Sparrow was back in the shoe business as the "new floor manager" of Mack's Shoe Store on Wylie Avenue.[25]

By the summer of 1932, Sparrow was hitting his showmanship stride. A shoe salesman, Sparrow took credit for the "well-shod feet" of Gus Greenlee and William "Woogie" Harris, a well-known denizen of the Crawford Grill. Like Greenlee, Harris was a successful numbers game runner.[26] More importantly, Sparrow devised a splashy promotion for a game between the Crawfords and the Baltimore Black Sox that featured "long distance throwing, accurate throwing by catchers, accurate throwing by outfielders, fungo hitting, and a one hundred yard dash."[27] He boasted that Satchel Paige would challenge a Black Sox player to a "special backward race around the bases."[28] One of the stated intentions of the event was to "give fans an opportunity" to witness the high level of talent on display in the Negro leagues, which was equal to that of white players.[29] The dash and baserunning contests were won by the "rabbit-like Ted Page, fleet Crawford outfielder."[30] Pittsburgh's Josh Gibson won the long-distance throwing challenge and Baltimore's Robert "Bob" Clarke took the catchers' accuracy event.[31] In the end, Paige did not participate. He complained of a sore ankle and begged out.[32] Although Sparrow's special promotion for the Crawfords game does not appear to have been repeated that year, it does shed some insight on how his innovative thinking influenced the creation of the East-West Classic and his four-team doubleheaders.

Of all Roy Sparrow's accomplishments, he is most closely tied to the origin of the Negro League East-West Classic All-Star Game, which debuted at Chicago's Comiskey Park in the late summer of 1933. But before he basked in the glowing reviews of the East-West game, Sparrow's year got off to a rocky start. In early 1933, he and a partner opened the Grenada Grill on Watt Street in the Hill District. They invested heavily in the venture by "extensively remodeling the interior."[33] Like his failed indoor miniature-golf course, the Grenada turned out to be subpar. By mid-June it had closed and Sparrow was looking for his next opportunity.[34] Two weeks later, on July 6, 1933, the National and American Leagues staged their first All-Star game, at Comiskey Park in Chicago. Plans for a similar contest for Negro League teams had yet to be put to paper. That was about to change and Sparrow was ready to get in the game.

On September 10, 1933, about 25,000 fans braved the soggy weather to witness the debut of the Negro League East-West Classic, in which the West defeated the East, 11-7.[35] How did the game, which evolved into the most popular and profitable promotion in Negro baseball history, come to fruition in such a short period of time? The answer usually points to Roy Sparrow. Larry Lester asserts that the spectacle was the "brainchild" of Sparrow and Bill Nunn of the *Courier*, and that these two men then took the concept to Greenlee, after a meeting earlier that evening with Cum Posey of the Homestead Grays failed to yield a commitment.[36] Alan Cohen credits Sparrow, Nunn, and Greenlee as originators of the East-West Game, as well as King Cole, Fay Young of the *Chicago Defender*, and Chester L. Washington and John L. Clark of the *Courier*.[37] In 1939 Washington acknowledged Sparrow's role in the birth of the East-West game and claimed Sparrow laid "much of the ground floor work" and "paved the way" for the long-term success of the event.[38] Mark Whitaker, in his book, *Smoketown*, states that "Roy Sparrow, black stringer for the *Sun-Telegraph*, had been floating the idea of a black all-star game for some time."[39]

Should Sparrow be granted sole authorship for the East-West Classic? That is difficult to determine, because there was very little in the way of contemporaneous reporting on the evolution of the game. Nearly all of the accountings of its origin came years after it was first played, and long after most of the actors had left the scene. Such was the case in 1942, when Posey claimed that the concept of an "all-star Colored" game was a "pet idea of Roy Sparrow," and that the original vision was for the game to be held at Yankee Stadium as a benefit for the New York Milk Fund Day.[40] Posey said that the Milk Fund idea was dropped in favor of a North-South game.[41] However, those plans were also scuttled and replaced with the East-West format after Sparrow and Nunn met with Greenlee who, according to Posey, "was a bitter rival of everything and persons connected to the Homestead Grays."[42] Certainly there was no love lost between Posey and Greenlee. Posey's recollections of the meetings do ring true, however, when compared with other versions of the events. Posey further credits Sparrow with traveling to Chicago and handling promotion of the game, and acknowledged Nunn's effective use of the *Courier* to gin up interest in the event.[43]

By all accounts, Sparrow's efforts to promote the first East-West Classic were successful, despite the rainy weather – something that even he, the great "champion ballyhoo artist," could not control.[44] He worked with all media outlets to spread the good word about the event, but later found himself doing public-relations damage control when some "insidious propaganda" in "Eastern newspapers" groused that the Classic would be nothing more than a "Chicago-Crawford affair."[45] Sparrow did receive accolades for scoring a major publicity coup when he arranged for a radio interview with Oscar Charleston and Willie Foster on Chicago's WGN.[46] Roy definitely set the stage for the future success of the game. But after the novelty of the Classic died down and the Crawfords' 1933 season ended, Sparrow went back to the reality of making ends meet in the Hill District.

As in previous years, Sparrow cobbled together a string of jobs to pay the bills in 1934. He worked for the *Sun-Telegraph*, sold shoes, and assisted Greenlee with the Crawfords. Sparrow handled the publicity for the 1934 East-West Game, but he found himself becoming marginalized by the growing shadow of other publicity hawks, including Abe Saperstein, owner of the Harlem

Globetrotters.[47] The 1934 Classic was Sparrow's last direct association with the event. Meanwhile, Greenlee and others were laying the groundwork for him to move to New York, where columnist Romeo L. Dougherty was touting Sparrow as Greenlee's "highly efficient" secretary, "a man of good and rare judgment, a fiend for figures and a lightning calculator."[48] Dougherty piled it on by crediting Sparrow with the success of a recent series between the Crawfords and the Black Yankees.[49] There is no doubt that Greenlee and Dougherty were greasing the skids for Sparrow to assume the role of business secretary for Alex Pompez's New York Cubans. Sure enough, in the spring of 1935, the *Courier* reported that "Roy Sparrow, well-known local publicity man, left last week with Alexander Pompez," and "will take charge of Pompez's new ball park [Dyckman Oval] in New York City."[50]

And so it came to pass that Roy Sparrow departed Pittsburgh to handle promotions for the New York Cubans, the very team that the Crawfords defeated in the 1935 Negro National League championship series. When Sparrow left Greenlee's employ to join up with Pompez, he was essentially traded from one larger-than-life numbers game runner to another. Sparrow swapped the Hill for Harlem, and in the process his professional life was forever changed —not necessarily for the better.

One of Sparrow's main responsibilities with the Cubans was to stage profitable exhibition games including his trademark four-team doubleheaders. By all accounts, he succeeded in that task. One such event in late September 1935, however, drew more derision than praise. At the center of the controversy was Satchel Paige. Sparrow and Greenlee had assured New York fans that Paige would pitch for the Kansas City Monarchs in a tilt with the Chicago American Giants in Yankee Stadium, but Paige was a no-show.[51] Cum Posey pounced on this opportunity to castigate both Greenlee and Sparrow for "advertising players to appear at various games when they know positively that these players will not appear," and called out Paige for what Posey considered to be extortion in the form of demanding "three hundred and fifty dollars in advance."[52] A week later, Sparrow was ridiculed again, this time about an exhibition game he staged between Babe Ruth's "All Stars" and the Cubans. Joe Bostic of the *New York Age* mocked what he referred to as the "Pompez Production Co., Inc.," which featured the Cubans playing a "bunch of guys named 'Jim' masquerading as All-Stars."[53] Bostic ended his review with a flourish by adding, "Then came the Babe's most profitable maneuver of the day, his little tete-a-tete with Roy Sparrow and the collection of his share of the day's take."[54]

The storm clouds that eventually engulfed and destroyed Sparrow's baseball career began to gather in the spring of 1936, when infighting within the Negro Leagues began to take its toll on their most profitable enterprise, the East-West Classic. Greenlee dropped out and shifted his focus to the management of light-heavyweight boxing champion John Henry Lewis.[55] Eastern interests set forth a proposal to move the Classic to Yankee Stadium in July and then stage a four-team doubleheader there in August.[56] Critics were outraged by the lack of cooperation within the executive ranks and geographical divisions and charged that the league was violating its own bylaws in failing to share profits from these special events.[57] Sparrow was right in the middle of it all. After the dust settled, the 1936 East-West Game remained in Chicago, but Sparrow's plans for a four-team series in New York moved forward.[58] Sparrow sold more than 20,000 tickets for the series and, at least for the owners of the four teams, it appeared to be a lucrative venture.[59]

In January 1937, Chester L. Washington published a list of suggested new-year resolutions for various sports celebrities, including Roy Sparrow.[60] Washington suggested that Sparrow should "do a bigger and better job of baseball ballyhooing and publicizing the crack New York Cubans."[61] As it turned out, Sparrow would have been better advised to lay low and avoid the spotlight. Three months later, while he was representing the Cubans at the Negro National League meeting in New York, the police arrived to question Sparrow as to the whereabouts of his boss, Alex Pompez, who had vanished.[62] Suddenly Sparrow found himself at the center of a sensational criminal investigation. Pompez's association with Dutch Schultz, a fellow numbers game magnate, placed him in the crosshairs of Federal Special Prosecutor Thomas E. Dewey and the Internal Revenue Service.[63] When first questioned, Sparrow claimed that he knew nothing of Pompez's disappearance.[64] But after telephone lines at Dyckman Oval were tapped, Sparrow's conversations with Pompez led the police to Mexico City, where Pompez was arrested.[65] Pompez's escape from New York garnered front-page headlines and generated endless speculation as to how he had eluded the authorities. The press theorized that Pompez had escaped through a secret passage in his office and had flown to Mexico in his private plane, stocked with "bullet-proof vests" and a team of bodyguards comprised of "a dozen desperadoes."[66] After the wiretap placed in him legal peril, Sparrow was spirited off to the Tombs – the Manhattan jail – and held on a $25,000 bond.[67] Sparrow's friends back in Pittsburgh were bewildered and complained that "[t]hey can't put Roy Sparrow in jail – and in New York, too."[68] To add insult to injury, the *Courier* chided, "Bet you wish you were home Roy. ... [Y]ou know country folks should stay away from the big town."[69] A short time later, he was released from custody and went back to work in hopes of salvaging the Cubans' 1937 season, but his efforts were in vain. They were locked out of the second-half schedule and were suspended from the Negro National League.[70] While Pompez was in Mexico fighting extradition, the Cubans temporarily disbanded, Dyckman Oval was turned over to the Black Yankees, and Sparrow was out of a job.[71] As for Pompez, he eventually returned to the United States but famously avoided prison by turning state's evidence against his fellow racketeers.[72] Pompez regained a degree of respectability after his return to New York. He remodeled the Cubans into a minor-league operation and created a pathway for Latin and African American baseball players to sign with the major-league teams.[73] Pompez was posthumously inducted to the National Baseball Hall of Fame in 2006.[74]

After being set adrift in New York as a result of Pompez's misdeeds, Sparrow spent the next three years in a tenuous relationship with baseball. His friends in the press tried to keep his name in the papers, including one fantastical account by *New York Daily News* columnist Jimmy Powers about how Sparrow claimed to have discovered Josh Gibson.[75] This story appears to have been based on conversations between Sparrow and Powers and had not previously been published in a Pittsburgh newspaper. According to Powers, Sparrow was a "coach" for the 1928 Pittsburgh Junior Crawfords when, as he drove down a road, "a baseball came flying over an incline and smacked into the radiator."[76] While inspecting the damage to his truck, he "spied a diamond 500 feet away," where one boy [Josh Gibson], who was "particularly shamefaced ... was carrying a bat at big as a wagon tongue."[77] Sparrow supposedly offered Josh a contract with the Crawfords and with that, Gibson was summarily "shanghaied on the spot."[78] Even the mildest of skeptics would have a hard time swallowing this event. For example, how could he have determined that Gibson was "shamefaced" from 500 feet away? But the main problem with this story is that it does not square with other accounts of how Gibson was scouted and signed. Bill Johnson's excellent biography of Gibson points to Crawfords manager Harold "Hooks" Tinker, not Sparrow, as the one who signed Gibson to a Crawfords contract in 1927.[79] If Sparrow had recruited Gibson in such a "made for Hollywood" fashion, it would have been sensationalized in the baseball-centric *Courier* when it was alleged to have happened, but it was not.

# THE 1935 PITTSBURGH CRAWFORDS

Only years – decades – after Gibson joined the Crawfords did Sparrow's version of events come to light, and only in New York-based newspapers.

After his disastrous year in New York, Sparrow tried to get back on his horse and ride out the 1938 baseball season on the backs of the newly minted Washington Black Senators. He was hired as the team's business manager, but he didn't have much to manage. The Black Senators were rated as one of the worst nines ever to participate in the Negro National League, and the team folded before the end of the season.[80] But for Sparrow, there was at least one familiar face from Pittsburgh on the squad – pitcher Harry Kincannon, who played for the Crawfords when Sparrow was with the club. The Black Senators won no more than two league games and Kincannon was responsible for one of those victories.

With the collapse of the Black Senators, Sparrow retreated to New York City but was unable to find employment when baseball resumed in the spring of 1939. He was, however, present for the staging of the second of two East-West Classics that were held that year. The first was at Comiskey Park and the second was played at Yankee Stadium. The exact nature of Sparrow's responsibilities is unclear, but that didn't stop his friends in the press from doing their best to amplify Sparrow's importance to the game, if only to recall his past glories. Chester L. Washington of the *Courier* and Alvin "Al" Moses of the Associated Negro Press devoted considerable space in their columns to lauding his previous contributions to the Classic, presenting him as an indefatigable force of nature.[81] They claimed that had it not been for his media and promotional mastery, there would never have been an East-West game.[82] Moses admonished his followers not to "make the mistake of pinning the medal for best public relations men in baseball on anyone who fails to answer to the name of Roy Sparrow or Frank Forbes."[83]

All of this well-intentioned puffery did little to improve Sparrow's career. According to the 1940 Census, he was unemployed and received no cash income for all of 1939.[84] For Sparrow, who was used to rubbing elbows with the elite and powerful, his state of poverty must have been a humbling experience. He shared an apartment in New York with a cousin and three others. Roy was fortunate to have relatives to take him in, but clearly he was without financial resources or professional prospects. As one indication as to how far off the baseball radar he had fallen, a subscriber to the *Atlanta Daily World* sent in this question: "What has happened to Roy Sparrow, the 'Forgotten Man,' who staged all the important games between National Negro league clubs?"[85] Perhaps by 1940, his "fifteen minutes of fame" were up.

Destitution and irrelevance were not, however, the sorts of barriers that Sparrow was willing to abide. In March 1940 he was spotted in Chicago at a joint meeting of the Negro National League and Negro American League that was called to discuss strategies to combat the "South American promoters" who were signing away the leagues' top players.[86] Sparrow's presence was noted, but schmoozing with his former associates did nothing to enhance his state of unemployment. Al Moses continued to do his best to keep his friend's name in the papers and in his column for the Associated Negro Press, proclaiming that "Roy Sparrow and Frank Forbes are two of the best front executive men in Negro baseball, and we'd like to see them receive the sort of money for their services, the job they perform, calls for."[87] Moses' plea was answered – but not to Sparrow's benefit. It was Forbes, not Sparrow, who got the job of promoting Negro League games at Yankee Stadium, while Sparrow, it was reported, was "ousted from this post in the Chicago meeting."[88]

And with that, the door on Roy Sparrow's baseball career closed for good. He left New York and returned to friendlier confines in Pittsburgh, where he resumed his entrepreneurial adventures by opening yet another short-lived business, a bakery in the Hill District.[89] His allies at the

*Courier*, however, continued to tout Sparrow as the greatest thing since sliced bread and urged baseball executives to give their friend a second look. Wendell Smith called upon Tom Wilson, president of the Negro National League, to hire Sparrow to take over publicity duties for the 1941 season.[90] Smith boasted:

> I have in mind a gentleman who could sell snowballs to an Eskimo. He can also sell Negro League baseball if given the opportunity. He is Roy Sparrow, who played an all important part in selling four-team doubleheaders to New York fandom, and was once Alex Pompez's first lieutenant with the Cuban Stars [sic]. Of course there are many who claim credit for selling the four-team bills to New York fans but this Mr. Sparrow, boys and girls, is the guy who put it over. He concocted some of the most ingenious ideas ever used to sell baseball.[91]

Smith wrapped up his sales pitch by asking if "Tom Wilson knows someone better for this proposed job than Roy Sparrow. … He's got the greatest since Barnum!"[92] Smith played up Sparrow's New York connections, asserting that he was known from "the Bowery to the very top of Fifth Avenue's exclusive penthouses," but in the same breath downplayed Sparrow's association with Pompez and any unsavory connections to numbers racketeers.[93] But as columnist Dan Burley noted later, while Sparrow was well-liked, "he did have a few professional enemies."[94]

When spring training began in 1942, more than three years had passed since Sparrow had played an active role with the Negro National League. He was back in Pittsburgh working for the *Courier*, hustling for advertising sales. On Valentine's Day in 1942, he registered for the World War II draft.[95] Sparrow was not called to serve. His work on the home front consisted of drumming up advertising revenue for the *Courier* and on occasion sharing a pithy comment or two for columnist Lucius Jones's "The Sports Roundup."[96] The week before he registered for the draft, Sparrow was considering a different kind of draft – an advertising campaign in the *Courier* for the Pabst Brewing Company that was hoping to expand its African-American consumer base.[97]

In late May 1943, about three months after having his photo taken with the Pabst representatives, Sparrow was in Presbyterian Hospital in Pittsburgh being treated for heart failure.[98] Lucius Jones may have had lifting Sparrow's spirits in mind when he reminded readers that Sparrow was "one of Negro baseball's most successful promoters," and "popularized three and four-team double-headers between colored pro nines in white major league ball parks."[99] But Sparrow's condition did not improve and by mid-June he was described as a "shut-in."[100] He was readmitted to the hospital and died there on July 31, 1943, at 5:30 A.M., from cardiac failure and complications from hypertension.[101] The informant who signed his death certificate was a cousin with whom he lived after his return to Pittsburgh.

The night before Roy Sparrow died, sports editor Wendell Smith was finishing his column for the Saturday edition of the *Courier*. The East-West Classic was to be played in Chicago on Sunday. Smith devoted his entire column to the history and significance of the game and to Sparrow:

> Roy Sparrow, the super-salesman, the man who 'sold' the idea and had a dream that is now a $300,000 reality, is fast to a bed in a Pittsburgh hospital fighting for his life. I am no sentimentalist, but I'm wondering if in the midst of all this drama, during the course of this great spectacle, just a moment can't be allowed to pay homage to Roy Sparrow. I'm wondering if President Wilson and Martin, and the other officials of the classic, won't take the time to look back eleven years and remember the contribution that Roy Sparrow made. If they will, I'm sure they'll allow us to stand together Sunday. … all 50,000 of us … for a moment in silence

as a tribute to a grand guy, whose dream and ingenuity has made all of this possible. This one humane gesture, and expression of appreciation, may save a man's life![102]

Per Smith's request, there was indeed a moment of silence offered up for Sparrow at the East-West Classic. By then it was a mourning moment rather than a hopeful one. At the conclusion of the fifth inning, a reported 51,723 fans, the largest attendance in the game's history, paid tribute.[103] Two days later, on August 3, 1933, Roy Sparrow was laid to rest in Allegheny Cemetery in Pittsburgh. Two other Crawfords notables are also buried in Allegheny Cemetery, Josh Gibson and Gus Greenlee.

Smith's first column after Sparrow's death was a passionate and personal tribute to his late friend:

> Drape the flag of baseball at half-mast … Another of the game's illustrious pioneers has been called out by the Great Umpire! Roy Sparrow, friend of a million or more, and promoter extraordinary, is dead!

At the end of his eulogy, Smith added this sentiment:

> It's too bad we had to wait so long to give Roy the pat on the back he deserved. It's too bad we didn't give him the credit due a long time ago. But that's life, I guess. We usually wait until it's all over before we realize our error. Look how we treated Abe Lincoln and some of the others. It would have been nice if Roy could have been here for this record-breaking promotion today. If he could have been here long enough to have seen this tremendous crowd. … I know he would have been thrilled beyond all expression. He would have been the happiest man in this ball park.[104]

When Roy Sparrow died in the summer of 1943, he had no wife or children to mourn his loss or tell his story. He left nothing in the way of a material estate to provide evidence of his legacy. Most of what has been written about Sparrow has been told through the gauzy memories of others and through his own spin on the truth. His accomplishments in baseball, both real and imagined, were made possible by the deep pockets of the rich and the near-empty pockets of the poor who funded the gambling operations of his most notable bosses, Gus Greenlee and Alex Pompez. When Greenlee shipped Sparrow off to New York to promote the Cubans for Pompez, it was the beginning of the end of Sparrow's career. His greatest sphere of influence was the Hill District, not Harlem. At heart, he was a salesman, a hustler and huckster. If someone gave him an idea, he would run with it and make it better. Can Sparrow be definitively credited with the idea for the East-West Classic, and four-team doubleheaders – two of the most profitable ventures ever produced by the Negro Leagues? The conflicting archival evidence makes one wish that instant replay had existed in 1933 because we may never know. But there is no doubt that Roy Sparrow was a key player in turning two of the most exciting and lucrative double-marketing-plays in Negro League history.

## Acknowledgment

The author wishes to thank Rich Bogovich and Alan Cohen for generously sharing their respective research materials on Roy Sparrow.

## Notes

1. Commonwealth of Virginia Certificate of Death, Lucien Sparrow, November 9, 1915; US Census Bureau, *Census of Population*, 1910.
2. Krystyn R. Moon, *A Brief History of Public Health in Alexandria and Alexandria's Public Health Department* (Fredericksburg, Virginia: University of Mary Washington, 2014), 22.
3. US Army Registration Card and Registrar's Report, "Roy William Sparrow," September 6, 1918.
4. US Army Registration Card and Registrar's Report, "Roy William Sparrow."
5. *R.L. Polk's Pittsburgh City Directory* (Pittsburgh: R.L. Polk & Co. Publishers, 1917), 2326.
6. "Assistant Manager in Carter Shoe Store," *Pittsburgh Courier*, May 31, 1924: 5.

# Pride of Smoketown

7   "Legal Notices," *Pittsburgh Daily Post*, May 28, 1925: 21.

8   "New Shoe Store to Be Opened in Homestead Next Saturday," *Pittsburgh Courier*, December 6, 1924: 5.

9   "Assistant Manager in Carter Shoe Store."

10  "Courier Collegians Claim Independent State Title," *Pittsburgh Courier*, December 13, 1924: 7.

11  "Courier Collegians Lose Hard-Fought Game," *Pittsburgh Courier*, October 25, 1924: 7.

12  Shelkie, "Cage Capers," *Pittsburgh Courier*, January 29, 1927: 18.

13  "Satisfied Patrons Promoting Success of Sandwich Shop," *Pittsburgh Courier*, September 15, 1928: 11.

14  "Satisfied Patrons Promoting Success of Sandwich Shop."

15  "Local Circulation Man Returns from Successful Tour," *Pittsburgh Courier*, March 22, 1930: 17.

16  "Lew-Roy Billiards," *Pittsburgh Courier*, December 7, 1929: 11.

17  "Lew-Roy Billiards."

18  *R.L. Polk's Pittsburgh City Directory* (Pittsburgh: R L. Polk & Co. Publishers, 1929), 2083.

19  US Census Bureau, 1930 Census of Population.

20  Commonwealth of Pennsylvania, Department of Health, Bureau of Vital Statistics Certificate of Death, "Mr. Roy Sparrow," July 31, 1943.

21  "Thrills Promised in Crawford Benefit Tilt," *Pittsburgh Courier*, July 19, 1930: 14.

22  "Plan Golf Tourney on Unique New Course," *Pittsburgh Courier*, October 18, 1930: 14.

23  Holloway, "After Two Years of Reckless Driving," *Pittsburgh Courier*, May 16, 1931: 11.

24  Holloway, "After Two Years of Reckless Driving."

25  "Mack's Shoe Store Ranks as Finest in the Hill District," *Pittsburgh Courier*, September 12, 1931: 5.

26  "Mack's Plan Greatest Shoe Sale in History," *Pittsburgh Courier*, June 11, 1932: 19.

27  "Big Field Day Here Saturday," *Pittsburgh Courier*, July 30, 1932: 14.

28  "Big Field Day Here Saturday."

29  "Big Field Day Here Saturday."

30  "Arm of Josh, Legs of Ted Hits of Meet," *Pittsburgh Courier*, August 6, 1932: 15.

31  "Arm of Josh, Legs of Ted Hits of Meet."

32  "Arm of Josh, Legs of Ted Hits of Meet."

33  John L. Clarke, "Wylie Avenue," *Pittsburgh Courier*, June 3, 1933: 6.

34  Clarke.

35  Chester L. Washington, "'Mules' Suttles Scorching Homer Blazed West's 'Victory Trail' in East-West Classic," *Pittsburgh Courier*, September 16, 1933: 14.

36  Larry Lester, *Black Baseball's Showcase: The East-West All-Star Game, 1933-1953* (Lincoln: University of Nebraska Press, 2001), 21-22.

37  Alan Cohen, "Negro Baseball at Comiskey Park: The East West Game (1933-1960): An All-Star Legacy," Gregory H. Wolf, ed., *The Baseball Palace of the World: Comiskey Park* (Phoenix: SABR, 2019), 19-26.

38  Chester L. Washington Jr., "Sez Ches," *Pittsburgh Courier*, September 9, 1939: 16.

39  Mark Whitaker, *Smoketown: The Untold Story of the Other Great Black Renaissance* (New York: Simon & Schuster, 2018), 111.

40  Cum Posey, "Posey's Points," *Pittsburgh Courier*, August 15, 1942: 16.

41  "Posey's Points."

42  "Posey's Points."

43  "Posey's Points."

44  John L. Clarke, "Wylie Avenue," *Pittsburgh Courier*, April 1, 1933: 7.

45  William G. Nunn, "WGN Sports Broadcast Talks," *Pittsburgh Courier*, September 16, 1933: 15.

46  Nunn.

47  Chester L. Washington, "Sez Ches," *Pittsburgh Courier*, September 15, 1934: 15.

48  Romeo L. Dougherty, "Sports," *New York Age*, September 29, 1934: 10.

49  Dougherty.

50  Harry Beale, "Local Sports Slants," *Pittsburgh Courier*, May 25, 1935: 18.

51  "Paige Coming with Kans. City Monarchs," *New York Amsterdam News*, October 5, 1935: 12.

52  Cum Posey, "Pointed Paragraphs," *Pittsburgh Courier*, December 28, 1935: 15.

53  Joe Bostic, "Latins Hand Babe Ruth and his Team Lacing," *New York Amsterdam News*, October 5, 1935: 12.

54  Bostic.

55  John L. Clark, "Big Internal Baseball War Looms," *Chicago Defender*, November 7, 1936: 15.

56  "American Giants Fired by League, *New York Amsterdam News*, May 23, 1936: 14.

57  W.R. Wilson, "National Sports Shots," *Pittsburgh Courier*, August 8, 1936: 16.

## THE 1935 PITTSBURGH CRAWFORDS

58 "Four-Game Double Is on Diamond Fan Fare," *New York Amsterdam News*, August 15, 1936: 15.

59 "Black Yankees Triumph," *New York Times*, August 17, 1936: 10; "Cuban Hurler Falls Before Vet of Yanks," *New York Amsterdam News*, August 22, 1936: 14.

60 Chester L. Washington, "Sez Ches," *Pittsburgh Courier*, January 2, 1937: 14.

61 Washington, "Sez Ches."

62 Ken Jessamy, "Things and Stuff," *New York Amsterdam News*, March 27, 1937: 16.

63 "Phone Call Traps Pompez," *New York Amsterdam News*, April 3, 1937: 1, 23.

64 "Phone Call Traps Pompez."

65 "Phone Call Traps Pompez."

66 "Phone Call Traps Pompez."

67 "Pompez Took in $34,000 Daily!," *Pittsburgh Courier*, April 10, 1937: 1.

68 "Talk O' Town," *Pittsburgh Courier*, April 10, 1937: 9.

69 "Talk O' Town."

70 Lewis Dial, "The Sports Dial," *New York Age*, June 26, 1937: 8.

71 "Black Yanks Take Over Dyckman Oval; Cuban Team Is Disbanded," *New York Age*, April 17, 1937: 8.

72 James A. Riley, *The Biographical Encyclopedia of the Negro Baseball Leagues* (New York: Carroll & Graf Publishers Inc., 1994), 633, 634.

73 Riley, 634.

74 "Alex Pompez," accessed online at: baseballhall.org/hall-of-famers/pompez-alex.

75 Jimmy Powers, "The Power House," *New York Daily News*, August 27, 1939: 75.

76 Powers.

77 Powers.

78 Powers.

79 Bill Johnson, "Josh Gibson," accessed online: sabr.org/bioproj/person/df02083c.

80 Riley, 820.

81 Chester L. Washington, "Sez Ches," *Pittsburgh Courier*, September 9, 1939: 6; Al Moses, "Beatin' the Gun," *Indianapolis Recorder*, September 19, 1939: 11.

82 Al Moses, "Beatin' the Gun," *Indianapolis Recorder*, September 19, 1939: 11.

83 Moses, "Beatin' the Gun," *Indianapolis Recorder*, October 14, 1939: 16.

84 US Census Bureau, 1940 Census of Population.

85 Lucius Jones and Al Moses, "Slants on Sports," *Atlanta Daily World,* April 23, 1940: 5.

86 Daniel, "Baseball Magnates Try to Hold Players," *New York Amsterdam News*, March 2, 1940: 19.

87 Alvin Moses, "Beatin' the Gun," *Indianapolis Recorder*, June 8, 1940: 16.

88 "Newark Still League Club," *New York Amsterdam News*, March 8, 1941: 19.

89 Wendell Smith, "Smitty's Sport Shorts," *Pittsburgh Courier*, January 18, 1941: 17.

90 Wendell Smith, "Smitty's Sport Shorts," *Pittsburgh Courier*, February 22, 1941: 17.

91 Wendell Smith, "Smitty's Sport Shorts": 17.

92 Wendell Smith, "Smitty's Sport Shorts": 17.

93 Wendell Smith, "Smitty's Sport Shorts": 17.

94 Dan Burley, "Confidentially Yours," *New York Amsterdam News*, August 14, 1943: 15.

95 US Army World War II Draft Registration Card, "Roy William Sparrow," February 14, 1942.

96 Lucius Jones, "The Sports Roundup," *Pittsburgh Courier*, April 24, 1943: 19.

97 "Pabst Representative Maps District Sales Campaign," *Pittsburgh Courier*, February 6, 1943: 23.

98 Wendell Smith, "Smitty's Sports Spurts," *Pittsburgh Courier*, May 29, 1943: 18.

99 Lucius Jones, "The Sports Roundup," *Pittsburgh Courier*, May 29, 1943: 19.

100 Toki Schalk, "Toki Types," *Pittsburgh Courier*, June 19, 1943: 10.

101 Commonwealth of Pennsylvania, Department of Health, Bureau of Vital Statistics Certificate of Death, "Mr. Roy Sparrow," July 31, 1943.

102 Wendell Smith, "Smitty's Sports Shorts," *Pittsburgh Courier*, July 31, 1943: 19.

103 "Roy Sparrow Dies in Pa.," *Baltimore Afro-American,* August 7, 1943: 23.

104 Wendell Smith, "Smitty's Sport Shorts," *Pittsburgh Courier*, August 7, 1943: 19.

# GREENLEE FIELD

## By Jeb Stewart

In 1931 the United States economy was drowning in the sea of the Great Depression, which brought nearly every industry in the nation to a standstill. The ripple effects of the crisis hit Pittsburgh's black community particularly hard as thousands were out of work and unable to meet financial commitments.[1] So, it was remarkable when William "Gus" Greenlee, a benevolent racketeer, built a baseball park on Bedford Avenue in Pittsburgh's Hill District to serve as the home of the Pittsburgh Crawfords. Greenlee Field was truly a Depression-era facility during its short life, which ended abruptly when it was torn down in 1938. The fate of the park, the Crawfords, and Gus Greenlee's involvement in the Negro Leagues were intertwined during this period.

Gus Greenlee grew up in North Carolina. His three brothers went into the medical and legal professions, while Greenlee was a college dropout who found his calling in the underworld.[2] His first documented crime occurred in 1916, when he hopped a freight car from North Carolina to Pittsburgh.[3] He drove a taxi and became a bootlegger during Prohibition. Eventually Greenlee became a powerful figure in the numbers and loan-shark rackets in the Hill District.[4] He ran his empire out of the Crawford Grill on Wylie Avenue and made a fortune, reportedly earning up to $25,000 in a single day.[5] Surely Greenlee must have realized he needed to find legitimate investments. Owning a professional baseball club and constructing a ballpark presented him with an easy opportunity to launder money from his criminal enterprises.[6]

*Pittsburgh Courier* columnist John L. Clark helped organize the Crawfords to represent the Crawford Recreation Center in the mid-1920s.[7] He promoted the players and worked tirelessly to raise money to buy equipment. Clark soon became friends with Greenlee. Using the power of his column, he became Greenlee's "part-time publicist."[8] It was a natural marriage of personal and financial interests when Clark persuaded Greenlee to become the Crawfords' benefactor in 1930.[9]

After acquiring a principal ownership stake in the Crawfords, Greenlee provided baseball uniforms and a $10,000 bus for travel.[10] He decided

## THE 1935 PITTSBURGH CRAWFORDS

*Greenlee Field, located in the 2500 block of Bedford Avenue, had its official opening on April 29, 1932, when the Crawfords hosted the New York Black Yankees and lost a tough 1-0 game.*

to not just compete, but dominate Negro League baseball, much to the ire of Homestead Grays owner Cum Posey. During his relatively short tenure as owner, Greenlee assembled a Who's Who of black baseball's best players and future Hall of Famers, which included at various times: Satchel Paige, Josh Gibson, Oscar Charleston, Judy Johnson, Cool Papa Bell, Bill Foster, and Jud Wilson.

According to Clark, who added the titles of Crawfords publicity director and secretary to his duties as a columnist,[11] Greenlee quickly became disenchanted with having to rent facilities for home games. Many ballparks were inadequate, and others were simply expensive, including Forbes Field.[12] At Forbes, the players suffered the further indignity of not being allowed to use the clubhouse.[13] Greenlee solved these problems by building his own ballpark. He knew that putting it in the Hill District would help the Crawfords build a following among residents of the area.[14] Creating a fanbase was a critical step in competing against Posey's established Grays in what sportswriters were already describing as a "baseball war."[15]

In 1931 Greenlee found an ideal parcel of land on Bedford Avenue, where the Entress Brick Company had its operations. He was opportunistic in his choice; the company was in financial distress, which saved him money on the acquisition. Clark recalled:

"Greenlee began negotiations with Dr. Toms, principal stockholder of the Entress Brick and owner of the land. Zoning restrictions were modified, and the project approved by Lincoln cemetery, situated on the west and the Municipal hospital on the east. The corporation was set up, with Dr. Toms, president; Joe Tito, treasurer, and Robert F. Lane, secretary. W.A. Greenlee, owning 25 per cent of the stock, held no office. The operating company was known as the Bedford Land Company."[16]

A black architect, Louis Arnett Stuart Bellinger, designed Greenlee Field,[17] which made it one of the few baseball parks designed and constructed by African-Americans for a Negro league team. The reported cost of construction was $100,000, which was an exorbitant sum to spend on an entertainment venue during the Depression.[18] Grandstand seats were originally priced at 50 cents, while access to the bleachers cost 35 cents.[19]

Greenlee located the park "in the 2500 block [of] Bedford Avenue between Junilla and Watt Streets," with an enclosure around the field.[20] The capacity of the concrete and steel grandstand was initially reported as 5,000. Additional bleachers were placed between right and center field, which may have seated an additional 1,000 patrons;[21] later reports suggested between 7,000 and 7,500 fans could attend baseball games.[22] As a boxing arena, 10,000 seats accommodated spectators.[23] By November, the ballpark became a true multisport facility, which could expand to 15,000 for football.[24] In December 1933, Greenlee Field also served an important civic role in the community as the site of protests against the trial of the falsely accused Scottsboro Boys.[25]

The interior was modest but included dugouts for both sides. A brick veneer extended along the interior of the grandstand from the third-base side to the edge of right field.[26] Although there were restrooms for fans,[27] other aspects were spartan. There was no roof over the stands, so spectators experienced the same elements as the players;[28] while there may have been some seats with backs, aerial photographs suggest most of the available seats were bleachers. The clubhouses were located under the first-base stands, and the Crawfords' offices were incorporated as a two-story building beneath the home-plate stands facing Bedford Avenue.[29]

The *Pittsburgh Press* reported the planned outfield dimensions as 375 feet in left field, 345 in right, and a massive 500 feet to dead center. Geri Strecker's *The Rise and Fall of Greenlee Field:* *Biography of a Ballpark* is the gold standard of its history.[30] Strecker left no stone unturned in her comprehensive research. Using aerial photographs, she calculated the actual distance of the fences as 342 in left, 338 in right, and 410 in center, which was similar to Shea Stadium's outfield.[31] Using the same method, it appears the backstop was approximately 55 to 60 feet from home plate. The photos show about 25 feet of foul territory on the first-base side, which narrowed to roughly 15 feet down the right-field line.

In right field, a row of trees stood between the bleachers, which were pressed against an eroding hill, and the Municipal Hospital, perched above the field and its meandering wooden fence. Just over the left- and center-field fences was a steep hill, which stretched several hundred feet down. Beyond the third-base stands, the foul territory was much larger and probably measured up to 60 feet from the baseline to an unkempt hill, and another 30 feet from there to the exterior fence, which marked the boundary with Lincoln Cemetery.

The most recognizable aspect of Greenlee Field was the exterior brick façade, which began at the Crawfords offices and "extended the full length of Bedford Avenue between Junilla and Watt Street."[32] In the Crawfords' most famous photograph, the players are kneeling in front of their bus, with the façade in the background. A ticket window appears on the left of the picture next to three archways where fans entered. A sign in the photograph advertised a championship boxing match between Charlie Massera and John Henry Lewis, whom Greenlee managed.

While excitement was building for the opening, the Crawfords held their 1932 spring training in Hot Springs, Arkansas, and then played exhibition games across the Midwest and South on their way home.[33] The Sports Fans of Pittsburgh announced a dance and reception at Princess Hall, along with a parade, as part of the official dedication on April 29.[34] The Crawfords unofficially opened the ballpark on April 28 by thumping a local amateur team, the Vandergrift Baseball Club, 11-0.[35]

The next day Greenlee Field officially opened with 4,000 fans reportedly in attendance. Chester L. Washington was sufficiently impressed by the opening to feature it in his *Sportively Speaking* column, writing:

> All the color, glamour and picturesqueness that usually attends the opening of a big league ball park was in evidence as Goodsen's New York Black Yankees helped the popular Pittsburgh Crawfords dedicate the attractive new Greenlee Park here Friday. Photos of both teams were taken ... the band played ... an impressive dedicatory speech was made by attorney R.L. Vann, during which the spectators stood to pay homage to Gus Greenlee, builder of the park. ... [B]oth teams paraded to deep center field, led by Charley Stewart, Mr. Vann and the band, where the American flag and the Crawford pennant were raised to zephyr-like breezes. ... Attorney Vann strode to the plate and dramatically pitched out the first ball ... the electrified radio amplifiers announced the batteries – and the game was on.[36]

After the pregame festivities, player-manager Oscar Charleston gave Satchel Paige the honor of starting against the Black Yankees.[37] Had Josh Gibson started at catcher, the duo arguably would have formed the greatest battery ever to open a stadium. However, Bill Perkins got the start behind the plate and Gibson played in left field.[38] The Black Yankees countered with Jesse Hubbard, a tall right-hander from Texas, who had pitched in the Negro leagues since 1919.

For eight innings, Hubbard and Paige dueled; Paige struck out 10 and allowed six hits, while Hubbard allowed three hits, and the game remained scoreless.[39] In the top of the ninth, the Black Yankees finally scratched out a run. With one out, Orville Riggins singled and Ted Page's fielder's-choice grounder forced him at second. Page stole second and advanced to third on Perkins's throwing error. A bloop single by Thomas[40] brought Page home and the Black Yankees led 1-0.[41] In the bottom of the ninth, the Crawfords made two quick outs, and Josh Gibson was Pittsburgh's last hope: "The mighty Gibson sent a terrific clout to deep center field that looked for an instant like an extra base hit, but the fleet footed Thomas was away with the crack of the bat and gathered in the speeding pellet and the first pitchers' battle was over."[42]

Despite the Opening Day loss, the Crawfords bounced back and played well as an associate member of the East-West League. The highlight of the campaign undoubtedly occurred on July 15 at Greenlee Field. With Ted "Double Duty" Radcliffe behind the plate, Satchel Paige threw a no-hitter against the Black Yankees.[43] Remarkably, Paige overcame seven errors by his fielders in the 6-0 win.

In August the Crawfords hosted their first night game, against the House of David.[44] By September, the always innovative Greenlee made the lights permanent several years before major-league ballparks did the same.[45] The lights proved useful that month when the Crawfords and Grays experimented by starting a game at midnight on a Monday to circumvent Pittsburgh's ban on Sunday baseball.[46] Paige later recalled that the crowd "jammed the park" that night.[47]

Historian Jim Bankes credited the Crawfords with 99 wins in 1932, which seems improbable and likely included barnstorming games. Both Seamheads.com and the Center for Negro League Baseball Research calculate a record of 32-26.[48] After completing their regular schedule, the Crawfords played exhibition contests against major-league all-stars. Pittsburgh defeated Casey Stengel's National League All-Stars, 11-2, in York, Pennsylvania.[49] The next day, the All-Stars got their revenge, winning 20-8, as Hack Wilson homered twice at Greenlee Field.[50]

Greenlee's baseball operations lost between $15,000 and $16,000 in 1932, most likely because of construction costs, generous salaries for his players relative to other franchises, and ticket sales reported at only 69,229.[51] Football, boxing, and soccer accounted for an additional 50,164 patrons for a total attendance of 119,384 from April 1932 to April 1933.[52] Clark blamed the Depression and miserable conditions for spectators as a partial explanation for modest fan support at games. He contended that attendance dwindled in June as the summer turned hot because of the cost-cutting measure of leaving the grandstand uncovered. Clark also asserted that the black community grew disenchanted with practically every stadium job – concessions, groundskeeping, ticket sales, etc. – going to whites, who lived outside of the neighborhood.[53]

Greenlee remained undeterred in his efforts to promote baseball in the Hill District. In 1933 he formed a new Negro National League and installed himself as president.[54] Meanwhile, his club, which already included a star-studded lineup of Paige, Gibson, Charleston, and Judy Johnson, added fleet-footed outfielder, Cool Papa Bell.[55] Bell loved playing on the Crawfords' home field and later recalled, "[i]t was beautiful. It had lots of grass and you almost felt like you were playing in a major league park. ... The best thing for me was the outfield. It gave me lots of room to run."[56] Depending on the source, the Crawfords finished 1933 either with a record of 40-21, tied for first with the Chicago American Giants,[57] or 38-17 and a second-place finish behind Chicago.[58] After winning a playoff series against the Nashville Elite Giants, instead of playing Chicago, Greenlee exercised his league office power and declared the Crawfords pennant winners.[59]

Greenlee's presidency of the NNL irritated other owners, who called for a commissioner to be appointed because of Greenlee's obvious conflict of interest.[60] Posey's Grays left the league in the middle of the 1933 campaign. Posey claimed he did so voluntarily because Greenlee demanded that owners share 5 percent of gate receipts with the league.[61] However, Clark claimed the Grays withdrew from the league before members could vote on his franchise's expulsion for signing players already under contract with the Detroit Stars.[62]

Prohibition officially ended on December 5, 1933, which was surely damaging to Greenlee's criminal empire. However, as Clark reported, Greenlee had a contingency plan and mitigated his losses. His nearby Crawford Grill was the first local establishment with an alcohol license. The Grill was quickly "jammed and packed [with customers] – buying – the hard stuff at 15 cents per drink and high-test beer at 10 cents a glass."[63]

In the spring of 1934, Greenlee Field's grandstand remained uncovered, which left the structure unfinished. To the stockholders of the Bedford Land Company, Greenlee proposed adding an awning-style roof, but they declined his request.[64] On the field, the Crawfords were 47-27, but finished second in the NNL behind the Philadelphia Stars.[65] The Crawfords played a home schedule of 25 games.[66] Even the rival Grays occasionally played home games there.[67] Once again Paige provided the highlight of the Crawfords' season. On July 4 he struck out 17 Grays as he threw his second no-hitter at Greenlee Field.[68] This time Gibson was his catcher in the 4-0 victory over Homestead before a reported audience of 10,000.[69]

Paige was one of the most popular Crawfords. Throughout the spring of 1935, area newspapers published accounts of his whereabouts and were hopeful about his return to the Crawfords.[70] However, because of a contract dispute he never reported; he pitched in Bismarck, North Dakota, for the semiprofessional Churchills. Even without its star pitcher, Pittsburgh dominated the first half of the NNL and cruised to a record of 50-23, or 42-15, depending on the source.[71]

Pittsburgh then faced the second-half champion, the New York Cubans, in the NNL championship series. Oscar Charleston's Crawfords defeated Martin Dihigo's Cubans in an exciting seven-game series, taking the finale 8-7.[72] Two series games were played at Greenlee Field. On

September 18, Dihigo threw a complete game and the Cubans won Game Four easily, 6-1.[73] The victory gave New York a three-games-to-one advantage in the series. With the Crawfords facing elimination, Bell began the comeback in Game Five by scoring the winning run on an errant throw in the ninth inning by Frank Blake, as Pittsburgh won, 3-2.[74]

After a summer as a baseball expatriate, Paige returned to the Crawfords in April 1936.[75] Greenlee had not given up on putting a roof over his grandstand. However, with uncooperative stockholders unwilling to underwrite the project, he needed to find another way to raise money.

To increase revenues, he offered season tickets. According to the *Pittsburgh Courier*, "[t]he season pass answers a demand by fans since the club was organized in 1932 and will sell for $8.00, admit the holder to a grandstand seat to any game played at Greenlee Field by the Crawfords, whether opposed by a league or independent club."[76] In addition, during the first half, Greenlee promoted a drawing for a 1936 Ford sedan with the winning ticket to be announced on July 4.[77] The Crawfords swept an Independence Day doubleheader from Homestead; the *Pittsburgh Courier* did not report who won the car.[78] The promotions failed to raise the funds needed to cover Greenlee Field's grandstand. Years later, Buck Leonard always recalled fans broiling in the hot afternoon sun at the park.[79]

With a record of 48-33, the Crawfords again raced to the stop of the NNL standings.[80] They were scheduled to face the Washington Elite Giants in a playoff series at Nashville's Sulphur Dell.[81] On September 28, 1936, the *Tennessean* reported the series was tied at one game apiece.[82] For reasons that remain unclear, the owners aborted the series; the Center for Negro League Baseball Research has concluded that "the Pittsburgh Crawfords clearly had the best team over the course of the entire season."[83] Nonetheless, Gus Greenlee's fortunes soon took a downward turn.

In March 1937 Greenlee had financial setbacks in his numbers business.[84] Because he needed money, he dealt Gibson and Johnson to Posey's Grays for Lloyd "Pepper" Bassett, Henry Spearman, and cash.[85] Despite the trade, the Crawfords returning players should have made them competitive in the NNL. However, later that spring, Dominican Republic dictator Rafael Trujillo signed eight of the Crawfords to big contracts. Paige, Bell, Leroy Matlock, Pat Patterson, Harry Williams, Sam Bankhead, Spoon Carter, and Bill Perkins jumped to Trujillo's San Domingo Stars. An angry Gus Greenlee lodged a complaint with US State Department, which proved fruitless.[86] To add insult to injury, the Stars actually played the New York Cubans in an exhibition game at Greenlee Field that September.[87] Charleston, who was now 40, remained one of the few holdovers; however, Pittsburgh sank to a distant sixth in the NNL with a record of 18-35.[88]

The following spring, in an apparent cost-cutting measure, the Crawfords stayed in Pittsburgh for spring training.[89] They improved their record to 22-21 and finished in fourth place in the NNL.[90] However, the summer of 1938 held no reprieve for Greenlee or his ballpark. On July 23, the *Pittsburgh Courier* reported that the Federal Housing Administration had allocated money to construct three housing projects in Pittsburgh. The Pittsburgh Housing Authority selected Greenlee Field as the site for one project and offered $50,000 for the property.[91] The news story suggested that if the stockholders turned down the sale, the Housing Authority would take the parcel by eminent domain.[92]

Clark reported that the Authority actually offered $60,000 as its opening bid, but it eventually paid the shareholders only $38,000 for the property.[93] That fall, the Authority began making payments for properties in the Hill district to construct "Bedford Dwellings."[94] The Crawfords played their final game at Greenlee Field on September 3, 1938, against the Grays.[95] Although a box score has not been located, one week later, the *Courier* mentioned that the Grays had beaten the Crawfords 13 straight times.[96] The last sporting contests at the field appear to have been a softball game between boxer Joe Louis's Detroit Brown Bombers and local all-stars,[97] and a soccer tournament.[98]

Wendell Smith lamented the end of the brief era, writing, "Greenlee Field, home of the Pittsburgh Crawfords, once the best Negro League ball park in the country, looks like a graveyard now."[99] Soon after his summation, classified advertisements for Greenlee's lights and steel beams appeared in the *Pittsburgh Press*.[100] Workers officially began tearing down the grandstand and the offices in December.[101] Although Posey expressed some sadness at losing Greenlee Field, he candidly admitted it had "been a financial stumbling block in the path of the Grays since 1932."[102]

In February 1939 Greenlee skipped the annual winter meeting of the NNL; the members treated his absence as a resignation of his presidency.[103] Later that spring, he also resigned as the president of the Crawfords.[104] In his letter to the board, he cited the loss of his ballpark as a tipping point in his decision:

> Greenlee Field has passed into history, and we have no home grounds that we can control. We can no longer plan for the day when improved industrial conditions will appear and make more profitable athletic activity in this section – from which activity our own organization would share in these profits. The stinted support given to Greenlee Field when it was considered one of the best diamonds in the organized circuit, is taken as an indication by me that a positive loss must be arranged for in Pittsburgh this year.[105]

Greenlee sold the franchise to Hank Rigney, who moved the Crawfords to Toledo, Ohio, where the club switched to the Negro American League in 1939.[106] After moving to Indianapolis the next year, the Crawfords wound up their operations after the 1940 NAL season. Greenlee died on July 7, 1952. In his obituary, the *Pittsburgh Courier* cited his ballpark as marking the beginning of "an era of diamond lore which eventually gave Negro players recognition in white organized baseball."[107]

In his epitaph for the park, John Clark documented Greenlee's financial losses in providing a venue that black fans could proudly call their own. In an oft-cited passage, he bitterly closed: "Greenlee Field joins the list of banks, industries and other enterprises which should not be again attempted in this city for the next 100 years."[108]

On July 17, 2009, the State of Pennsylvania unveiled a historical marker in the Hill District forever memorializing the ballpark's place in the history of the Negro Leagues and Pittsburgh.[109] Thanks to Geri Strecker's meticulous research, the marker was properly located "directly where Greenlee Field's arched entry gates had been."[110] The marker reads:

> **GREENLEE FIELD**
>
> "Located here from 1932 to 1938, this was the first African American owned stadium in the Negro Leagues. Home of Gus Greenlee's Pittsburgh Crawfords baseball team, 1935 Negro League champs. Players included Hall of Famers Satchel Paige, Josh Gibson, and Cool Papa Bell."

There has been debate over where Greenlee Field fits within the realm of baseball parks built for black clubs, and whether it really was the first of its kind. In "A Historical Look at the Pittsburgh Crawfords and the Impact on Black Baseball on American Society," Richard L. Gilmore Jr. cites the Hill District's Central Park as an earlier example.[111] According to baseball historian Gary Ashwill, Tate Field in Cleveland was a black-owned ballpark that predated Greenlee Field.[112] Ashwill argues that Greenlee's ballpark was actually the final attempt at true autonomy by a Negro league owner, writing:

> It also strikes me that Greenlee Field is misunderstood if it's thought to be a

pioneering enterprise, the 'first' of anything. In fact the Crawfords' ballpark was actually a backwards-looking enterprise, an attempted revival of the golden age of the Negro leagues in the 1920s. With the collapse of Rube Foster's NNL and the Eastern Colored League, black teams in the 1930s turned more and more to barnstorming, and instead of building their own parks they rented major and minor league venues. Greenlee Field was not the first of its kind, but the last. Its demolition in 1938 marked the end of a particular dream of black self-sufficiency, and served as a harbinger of the age of integration that was to follow.[113]

By 1955, as the Negro leagues were winding down, columnist Marion Jackson opined that "[t]he decline of Negro baseball is due to the failure of clubs to own their ball parks."[114] Thus, Greenlee Field should not just be remembered as the home of arguably the most successful team in the history of black baseball, but also within a much broader historical context of independent black-owned businesses.

## Acknowledgments

The author wishes thank Cassidy Lent, a reference librarian at the National Baseball Hall of Fame and Museum, who provided him with Geri Strecker's excellent article on the history of Greenlee Field. Strecker's research was so exhaustive that the author resisted the temptation to read the article until the first draft of this chapter was complete. Longtime SABR member William J. Plott was helpful in discussing Marion Jackson's 1955 column about the decline of the Negro leagues. Finally, the author is grateful to members of the Historical Negro League Baseball Site on Facebook, who helped to identify other baseball parks that were owned by Negro league clubs.

## Notes

1. phmc.state.pa.us/portal/communities/documents/1865-1945/great-depression.html.
2. Mark Whitaker, *Smoketown: The Untold Story of the Other Great Black Renaissance* (New York: Simon & Schuster, 2018), 91; Brian McKenna, "Gus Greenlee," SABR BioProject: sabr.org/bioproj/person/fabd8400.
3. Jeremy Beer, *Oscar Charleston: The Life and Legend of Baseball's Greatest Forgotten Player* (Lincoln: University of Nebraska Press, 2019), 225; John N. Ingham and Lynne B. Feldman, *African-American Business Leaders: A Biographical Dictionary* (Westport, Connecticut: Greenwood Press 1994), 297.
4. Monte Irvin, *Few and Chosen Negro Leagues: Defining Negro Leagues Greatness* (Chicago: Triumph Books, 2007), 172; Leslie A. Heaphy, *The Negro Leagues: 1869-1960* (Jefferson, North Carolina: McFarland & Company, 2003), 103.
5. Whitaker, 94; McKenna.
6. Whitaker, 99-100; Heaphy, 228; Brian Carroll, "To Pittsburgh from Chicago: A Changing of the Guard in Black Baseball and the Black Press in the 1930s," *Black Ball*, Vol 2. No. 2, 2009: 92.
7. Lewis Dial, "The Sports Dial," *New York Age*, September 3, 1932: 6.
8. Whitaker, 97.
9. Dial, 6; Whitaker, 99; Richard L. Gilmore Jr., "A Historical Look at the Pittsburgh Crawfords and the Impact of Black Baseball on American Society," *The Sloping Halls Review*, 1996: 67.
10. Gilmore, 67.
11. Dial, 6.
12. John L. Clark, "The Rise and Fall of Greenlee Field," *Pittsburgh Courier*, December 10, 1938: 17; Phil Dixon, *The Negro Baseball Leagues: A Photographic History* (New York: Amereon Ltd. 1992), 156. Chris Fullerton's book, *Every Other Sunday* (Birmingham, Alabama: R. Boozer Press, 1999), 67-68, delves into the issue of the availability of Rickwood Field for the Birmingham Black Barons, when the Birmingham Barons (the primary tenant) were on the road. Without their own ballpark, the Black Barons traveled so much, they rarely played games in Birmingham. Fullerton, 65.
13. Dixon, 156; Geri Strecker, "The Rise and Fall of Greenlee Field: Biography of a Ballpark," *Black Ball*, Vol. 2, Number 2, Fall 2009: 37-67.
14. Clark, "The Rise and Fall of Greenlee Field," 17.
15. William G. Nunn, "Sport Talks," *Pittsburgh Courier*, December 26, 1931: 14.
16. Nunn, "Sport Talks."
17. Strecker: 40.
18. Paul A.R. Kurtz, "Crawfords, Black Yanks Vie Tonight," *Pittsburgh Press*, April 29, 1932: 41; Clark, "The Rise and Fall of Greenlee Field": 17.
19. "Crawfords Cut Prices for All Baseball Games," *Chicago Defender*, July 16, 1932: 8. Getting to the ballpark was also economical for fans who were not within walking distance. On November 19, 1932, the *Pittsburgh Courier* published a public

service article entitled, "How to Reach the Greenlee Field With Only One Car Token."

20. "Oscar Charleston to Lead Crawford Club this Year," *Pittsburgh Press*, February 14, 1932: 18.

21. "Gus Greenlee and the Crawfords," *Pittsburgh Post-Gazette*, August 11, 2006: C-7.

22. Clark, "The Rise and Fall of Greenlee Field": 17; Jennifer Kaye, "Let's Learn from the Past (Greenlee Field)," *Pittsburgh Post-Gazette*, February 15, 2007: 53; McKenna.

23. "Gleanings from Greenlee Field," *Pittsburgh Courier*, June 11, 1932: A4.

24. "Ticket Rush On for Pittsburgh Grid Classic," *Pittsburgh Courier*, November 19, 1932: 1. The Pittsburgh Pirates professional football team, who were later renamed the Rooneys and finally the Steelers, used Greenlee Field for workouts. "Local Pros Drill for Cincinnati Fray," *Pittsburgh Sun-Telegraph*, October 6, 1933: 43; "Pro Eleven Faces Cuts, Says Coach," *Pittsburgh Press*, August 23, 1936: 20.

25. John L. Clark, "Wylie Avenue," *Pittsburgh Courier*, December 9, 1933: 2.

26. The wall, and other aspects of Greenlee Field can be seen by searching the Charles "Teenie" Harris collection at Pittsburgh's Carnegie Museum of Art. collection.cmoa.org/.

27. "Oscar Charleston to Lead Crawford Club This Year," *Pittsburgh Press*, February 14, 1932: 18.

28. Clark, "The Rise and Fall of Greenlee Field": 17; Art Rust Jr., "Walter 'Buck' Leonard: Fence buster: Black League's Lou Gehrig," *New York Amsterdam News*, May 26, 1979: 72.

29. "Oscar Charleston to Lead Crawford Club this Year."

30. Strecker: 37-62.

31. Strecker: 47.

32. Strecker: 44. Strecker discovered in her research that "[t]he facade used locally kilned red brick with simple corbelling along the top of the two-story section and along the lower section between the arched entrances and the two exit gates." Strecker, 47. However, no source has confirmed whether Greenlee and the Bedford Land Company utilized bricks from the now defunct Entress Brick Company, but this would have been a local decision, which would have saved material costs.

33. "Crawfords Work Out at Hot Spring[*sic*]," *Pittsburgh Courier*, March 19, 1932: 15; John L. Clark, "I Believe You Should Know: Following the Crawfords," *Pittsburgh Courier*, April 9, 1932: 14; "Crawfords Back, Set for Test," *Pittsburgh Courier*, April 30, 1932: 15.

34. "Plan Dance to Honor Crawfords," *Pittsburgh Courier*, April 9, 1932: 15; "Crawfords Reception Next Week," April 23, 1932: 5; "Crawford Club Opens Tonight," *Pittsburgh Post-Gazette*, April 29, 1932.

35. "Crawford Club Opens Tonight"; Paul A.R. Kurtz, "Carl Jordan to Play with Geisler Nine," *Pittsburgh Press*, April 28, 1932: 27.

36. Chester L. Washington, "Sportively Speaking," *Pittsburgh Courier*, May 7, 1932: 15.

37. "Expect Record Crowd at Park," *Pittsburgh Courier*, April 30, 1932: 15.

38. "Hubbard Pitches Three-Hit Game to Beat Page, 1 to 0," *Pittsburgh Courier*, May 7, 1932: 15. According to Strecker, Gibson was "recovering from an appendicitis operation he had undergone in Hot Springs." Strecker, 54.

39. "Crawfords Defeated in Opening Game," *Pittsburgh Press*, April 30, 1932: 9.

40. It is unclear whether Dave Thomas or Clint Thomas delivered the winning hit for New York. Both played for the Black Yankees in 1932, but only one "Thomas" appeared in the box score for the opener. Bankes cited Clint Thomas with making the final catch in center, so it appears he also got the winning hit. Jim Bankes, *Pittsburgh Crawfords* (North Carolina: McFarland & Co., Inc., 2001), 24.

41. "Hubbard Pitches Three-Hit Game."

42. "Hubbard Pitches Three-Hit Game."

43. "New York Yanks Win Series from Crawfords," *Pittsburgh Courier*, July 16, 1932: A5; "Paige Twirls No-Hit Win Over Black Yanks," *Chicago Defender*, July 16, 1932: 8.

44. "Night Hero," *Pittsburgh Courier*, August 20, 1932: A5.

45. "Greenlee Field Installs Lights," *Pittsburgh Courier*, September 10, 1932: A5; Strecker: 49.

46. "Crawfords, Grays Play at Midnight," *Chicago Defender*, September 10, 1932: 9; "Greenlee Field Introduces The Midnight Game," *Norfolk* (Virginia) *Journal and Guide*, September 17, 1932: 13.

47. Al Abrams, "Sidelights on Sports, *Pittsburgh Post-Gazette*, December 22, 1964: 20.

48. seamheads.com/NegroLgs/organization.php?franchID=PC; cnlbr.org/Portals/0/Standings/East-West%20League%20(1932)%202019-10.pdf.

49. "National League Downed by Crawfords," *Evening News* (Harrisburg, Pennsylvania), September 28, 1932: 12.

50. "Major All-Stars Beat Crawfords by 20 to 8," *Pittsburgh Post-Gazette*, September 29, 1932: 16.

51. McKenna; Dixon, 158; "Greenlee Field Preparing for Opener on May 6," *Pittsburgh Courier*, April 15, 1933: A4.

52. "Greenlee Field Preparing for Opener."

53. Clark, "The Rise and Fall of Greenlee Field": 17.

54. "Eastern Owners Meet New League Head, Boom Seen," *Pittsburgh Courier*, March 11, 1933: 14.

55. "Craws Sign Bell, Cooper, Hunter," *Pittsburgh Courier*, March 18, 1933: 15.

56. "Greenlee Field Site Earns Place in History," *Pittsburgh Post-Gazette*, July 17, 2009: 31.

# THE 1935 PITTSBURGH CRAWFORDS

57  seamheads.com/NegroLgs/year.php?yearID=1933&lgID=NN2.

58  cnlbr.org/Portals/0/Standings/Negro%20National%20League%20(1920-1948)%202019-10.pdf.

59  cnlbr.org/Portals/0/Standings/Negro%20National%20League%20(1920-1948)%202019-10.pdf.

60  "No Owner Should Be Prexy, Says Wilson," *Afro-American*, August 5, 1933: 20.

61  Cum Posey, "Posey Reveals Why Grays Left Nat'l Ass'n," *Pittsburgh Courier*, July 8, 1933: A4.

62  John L. Clark, "Baseball's Future Lies in Organization," *Pittsburgh Courier*, July 22, 1933: 15.

63  John L. Clark, "Wylie Avenue," *Pittsburgh Courier*, December 9, 1933: 2.

64  Clark, "The Rise and Fall of Greenlee Field," 17. Strecker suggests that once Greenlee Field got lights the roof was no longer a necessity. Strecker, 55-54. However, most baseball games would have still be played in the daytime during this era and the roof would have also kept fans dry during rain delays.

65  seamheads.com/NegroLgs/team.php?yearID=1934&teamID=PC.

66  "Free Ford, Season Passes Offered at Greenlee Field," *Pittsburgh Courier*, May 9, 1936: A4.

67  Chester L. Williams, "Grays Blast Birmingham Barons' Victory Hopes by 9-2 Score," *Pittsburgh Courier*, June 30, 1994: A5; Robert Peterson, "Josh Gibson Was the Equal of Babe Ruth, But …," *New York Times*, April 11, 1971: SM12. By 1938 Greenlee Field presented Cum Posey with a Hobson's choice. Fans of the Grays did not attend games at Greenlee Field. However, he also did not want to alienate residents "who honestly believe that the Grays should play all of their homes games at Greenlee Field because of the money put in it by colored investment." Posey's curious solution to the dilemma was to play home games outside of Pittsburgh. "Posey's Points," *Pittsburgh Courier*, June 4, 1938: 17.

68  William G. Nunn, "Paige Hurls No-Hit Classic," *Pittsburgh Courier*, July 7, 1934: 1.

69  William G. Nunn, "Paige Hurls No-Hit Classic." By 1954, the reported attendance for the game had grown to 13,000. "Sports Slice," *Pittsburgh Courier*, January 16, 1954: 15. Paige's teammate Harold Tinker later remembered, "when Satchel pitched, there was nowhere to put all the people anyway." Clara Herron, "Lost Pittsburgh," *Pittsburgh-Post Gazette*, December 25, 1990: 35.

70  "Pirates Beat Semi-Pro Team in First, 3 To 1," *Pittsburgh Post-Gazette*, March 11, 1935, 15; "Cum Posey's Pointed Paragraphs," *Pittsburgh Courier*, May 4, 1935: 14; "Cubans Meet Crawfords," *Pittsburgh Sun-Telegraph*, May 11, 1935: 9.

71  seamheads.com/NegroLgs/year.php?yearID=1935&lgID=NN2&tab=standings; cnlbr.org/Portals/0/Standings/Negro%20National%20League%20(1920-1948)%202019-10.pdf.

72  "Crawfords Snare Negro Loop Crown," *Philadelphia Inquirer*, September 22, 1935: 44; "Crawfords Take 4 to 7, to Top Stars," *Philadelphia Tribune*, September 26, 1935: 10; "Grid Circus Now in Town," *Pittsburgh Courier*, September 28, 1935: 14; "Thousands See Defeat of Cubans and Stars," *New York Amsterdam News*, September 28, 1935: 12.

73  "Cubans Defeat Crawfords Again," *Pittsburgh Post-Gazette*, September 19, 1935: 18.

74  "Crawfords Beat Cubans by 3 To 2," *Pittsburgh Post-Gazette*, September 20, 1935: 18.

75  "Satchell Paige Returns to Crawfords," *Pittsburgh Courier*, April 25, 1936: A4; Chester L. Washington, "Satchell's Back in Town," *Pittsburgh Courier*, May 9, 1936: 14.

76  "Free Ford, Season Passes Offered at Greenlee Field."

77  "Free Ford, Season Passes Offered at Greenlee Field."

78  "Crawfords Take Two from the Grays," *Pittsburgh Courier*, July 5, 1936: 16.

79  A.J. Carr, "At Age of 40, Leonard Belted 42 Homers," *The Sporting News*, March 4, 1972: 24; Art Rust Jr., "Walter 'Buck' Leonard: Fence Buster: Black League's Lou Gehrig," *New Amsterdam News*, May 26, 1979: 72.

80  seamheads.com/NegroLgs/year.php?yearID=1936&lgID=NN2.

81  "Negro Club Will Play Pittsburgh," *Tennessean* (Nashville), September 23, 1936: 10; "Elite Giants Slight Favorite to Defeat Crawfords," *Tennessean*, September 27, 1936: 9.

82  "Crawford Split Two with Giants," *Tennessean*, September 28, 1936: 8.

83  cnlbr.org/Portals/0/RL/Negro%20League%20Play-Off%20Series%20(1930-1939).pdf.

84  Robert Peterson, "Josh Gibson Was the Equal of Babe Ruth, But …"

85  "Grays, Crawfords in Player Trade," *Pittsburgh-Sun Telegraph*, March 24, 1937: 26.

86  Richard J. Lamb, "Gus 'Whereas-es' Diplomats into Action Over Foreign 'Raid' on Negro Ball Team," *Pittsburgh Press*, June 20, 1937: 2.

87  "Former Crawford Stars Play Here," *Pittsburgh Courier*, September 4, 1937: 10.

88  seamheads.com/NegroLgs/year.php?yearID=1937&lgID=NN2.

89  "Crawford Nine Trains Here," *Pittsburgh Sun-Telegraph*, April 7, 1938.

90  seamheads.com/NegroLgs/year.php?yearID=1938.

91  "Greenlee Field," *Pittsburgh Courier*, July 23, 1938: 6.

92  "Greenlee Field."

93  Clark, "The Rise and Fall of Greenlee Field": 17.

94  "Hill District Dweller Paid $2,000 in Slum Cleanup," *Pittsburgh Courier*, September 9, 1938: 36; "City's Housing

Fund Total Now Close to $18,500,000," *Pittsburgh Sun-Telegraph,* October 10, 1938: 8.

95 "Craws Battle Grays in Holiday Series," *Pittsburgh Courier,* September 3, 1938: 17.

96 Wendell Smith, "Smitty's Sport Spurts," *Pittsburgh Courier,* September 10, 1938: 17. Strecker cited September 3 as the date of the final scheduled home game but reached no conclusions as to who won. Strecker: 61-62. To further complicate the issue, the following spring a columnist wrote, "in the final series with the Homestead Greys [*sic*], the Crawfords won four out of five." Jerry Liska (Associated Press), "Press Passes," *Fremont (Ohio) News-Messenger,* April 28, 1939: 12.

97 "All-Star Mushball Tryouts Arranged," *Pittsburgh Press,* September 5, 1938: 14.

98 Harry Fairfield, "Keystone League Teams Collide Today at Greenlee," *Pittsburgh Press,* October 30, 1938: 23.

99 Smith.

100 "Dismantling Greenlee Baseball Field" (Lights), *Pittsburgh Press,* November 20, 1938: 50; "Dismantling Greenlee Baseball Field" (Steel Beams), *Pittsburgh Press,* December 4, 1938: 31.

101 Clark, "The Rise and Fall of Greenlee Field": 17.

102 Cum Posey, "Posey's Points," *Pittsburgh Courier,* December 10, 1938: 17.

103 "Baseball League to Be Headed By Wilson; Gus Greenlee Absent," *New York Age,* February 15, 1939: 8.

104 "Crawfords' President Resigns," *Chicago Defender,* April 8, 1939: 8; "Future of Craws Still in Doubt," *Pittsburgh Courier,* April 8, 1939: 17.

105 "Crawfords' President Resigns."

106 Heaphy, 89.

107 William G. Nunn Sr., "Sports, Political Figure Dies Quietly at Home," *Pittsburgh Courier,* July 12, 1952: 1.

108 Clark, "The Rise and Fall of Greenlee Field": 17 (quoted in Whitaker, 121); Rob Ruck, *Sandlot Seasons: Sport in Black Pittsburgh* (Urbana, Illinois: University of Illinois Press, 1987), 164.

109 "Greenlee Field Remembered," *Pittsburgh Post-Gazette,* July 18, 2009: 10.

110 Strecker: 67 n. 83.

111 Gilmore: 67-68.

112 Gary Ashwill, "Louis Bellinger and Central Baseball Park," February 26, 2012, accessed at agatetype.typepad.com/agate_type/greenlee-field/.

113 Ashwill.

114 Marion Jackson, "Black Barons, K.C. Monarchs Owned by Tom Baird, Sid Lyne," *Alabama Tribune* (Montgomery), April 22, 1955: 6; William J. Plott, *Black Baseball's Last Team Standing: The Birmingham Black Barons, 1919-1962* (Jefferson, North Carolina: McFarland & Company, Inc., 2019), 232.

# A NOTE ON ADDITIONAL PLAYERS WHO SOMETIMES APPEAR ON PITTSBURGH'S 1935 ROSTER

## By Frederick C. Bush

Any attempt to research the Negro Leagues is apt to result in the discovery of long-buried treasures on some occasions and utter frustration on others. Press coverage of the leagues was inconsistent, and players often moved from one team to another, whether by sale, by trade, or by jumping their contracts. In an effort to provide the most comprehensive picture possible of the 1935 Pittsburgh Crawfords, it is necessary to address players who do not have a feature biography included in the current volume. These individuals spent very little time or, in one instance, no time at all with the 1935 Crawfords, and little is known about most of their lives and careers.

What is known about these players' participation, or lack thereof, on Pittsburgh's 1935 championship squad is as follows:

**W. Breen** is such a mystery that neither his first name nor his position is known. An April 12, 1935, article in the Wichita, Kansas, *Negro Star* named him as a player who began spring training with the Crawfords in Hot Springs, Arkansas.[1] Breen must not have lasted long; he does not appear in a team photo taken at Hot Springs. James Riley lists a player named Breen (with no first name) as a first baseman with the 1928 Philadelphia Tigers, but there is no evidence that W. Breen was the same player.

**Alfred Carter**, an outfielder and utility infielder, is listed as a member of the Crawfords in Riley's *Biographical Encyclopedia* and in *The Negro Leagues Book*. Carter also was named in the April 12 *Negro Star* article,[2] but no further evidence of his participation on the team, beyond an apparently brief stint in spring training, has been found.

**Charlie Cook**, a pitcher, is identified merely as **C. Cook** in the *Negro Star* article about the Crawfords who reported for spring training in Hot Springs;[3] he is listed with the first name "Charlie" in *The Negro Leagues Book*. No evidence of his participation in any games has been uncovered.

**Robert "Bob" Harris** is credited with a lone pinch-hitting appearance for the 1935 Crawfords in Riley's *Biographical Encyclopedia* and is also listed on the Crawfords' roster in *The Negro Leagues Book*. It is possible that the plate appearance in question may actually have been made by Curtis Harris. The alternative explanation is that Robert Harris may have been a one-game fill-in player.

**Norman "Jelly" Jackson**, a shortstop, is listed on the 1935 Crawfords' roster in *The Negro Leagues Book*; however, all other sources list Jackson only as a member of the crosstown Homestead Grays that year. An April 5 article in the *Negro Star* named Jackson as one of the Grays players who reported for spring training in Rocky Mount, North Carolina, and box scores from various points in the season show him to have been with Homestead as well.[4] Since both the Crawfords and Grays were Pittsburgh teams, and, since Jelly Taylor was briefly with the Crawfords, it is possible that a news article may have mixed up the two players and reported incorrect information.

**Olan "Jelly" Taylor**, a first baseman and catcher, is yet another of the players named in the April 12 *Negro Star* article about the Crawfords' spring-training roster.[5] He also appears in the photo taken at Hot Springs. However, he was named as a new member of the Cincinnati Tigers in an April 19 *Cincinnati Enquirer* article.[6] Game articles and box scores show Taylor to have been Cincinnati's first baseman throughout the 1935 season.[7]

**Irving "Lefty" Vincent**, a pitcher, had spent part of the 1934 season with the Crawfords and was named as one of the players who reported to spring training in both the *Chicago Defender* and *Negro Star* articles.[8] On May 22, the *Bismarck Tribune* announced that Vincent had been signed by Neil Churchill's integrated semipro ballclub in North Dakota. The *Tribune* article claimed that Vincent "[a]lready this spring has hurled several games for the Pittsburgh Crawfords of the National Colored League.'"[9] No game article or box score to support the *Tribune's* claim have been discovered, but it is entirely possible that Vincent pitched in exhibition games for the Crawfords before leaving the team to join the Bismarck squad.

The players listed above appear in various major sources about the Negro Leagues. However, the fact that players were sometimes "borrowed" for a single game is demonstrated by an August 12, 1935, article in the *Brooklyn Daily Eagle* that was discovered by SABR member Alan Cohen, one of the authors who contributed his work to the current volume.[10] The box scores from an August 11 doubleheader against the semipro Brooklyn Bay Parkways list the following players in the Crawfords' lineup that day:

**A. Cooper** in center field. This was probably **Anthony "Ant" Cooper,** who had played for the Crawfords in 1933 and who can be found listed on the roster of the 1935 Bacharach Giants in *The Negro Leagues Book*.

**W. Cooper** in left field. This player's first name remains unknown, but he too is listed as a member of the 1935 Bacharach Giants in *The Negro Leagues Book*. Whether or not he was related to Anthony Cooper is also unknown.

**Gillispie** [sic] in right field. This was most likely **Henry Gillespie**, a pitcher and outfielder, who had played for numerous teams in both the Philadelphia and New York areas. Most sources indicate that the 1934 season was Gillespie's last year to play in the Negro Leagues, but he certainly could have been available to fill in for one game on an emergency basis.

**Lackey** at third base. This had to be **Obie Lackey,** who also had played for the Crawfords in 1933 and who was a member of the Philadelphia Stars in 1935. No other player with the last name Lackey has been documented as having played in the Negro Leagues.

The *Daily Eagle's* report of the two games made no mention of the whereabouts of the Crawfords' missing regulars; thus, it remains a

# THE 1935 PITTSBURGH CRAWFORDS

mystery as to why these "borrowed" players had to be used for this August 10 doubleheader.

## Sources

Clark, Dick, and Larry Lester. *The Negro Leagues Book* (Cleveland: Society for American Baseball Research, 1994).

Riley, James A. *The Biographical Encyclopedia of the Negro Baseball Leagues* (New York: Carroll & Graf Publishers, Inc., 1994).

Seamheads.com.

## Notes

1 "Training Camp News," *Negro Star* (Wichita, Kansas), April 12, 1935: 3.
2 "Training Camp News."
3 "Training Camp News."
4 "Grays Arrive for Spring Training," *Negro Star*, April 5, 1935: 6; "Jerseys Divide with Bacharachs – Grays Display Class," *Jersey Journal* (Jersey City, New Jersey), June 24, 1935: 17, 22.
5 "Training Camp News."
6 "New Players to Show When Tigers Meet Louisville at Crosley Field Sunday," *Cincinnati Enquirer*, April 19, 1935: 18.
7 "Amateur Baseball"; "Tigers to be Rivals of Nashville Tomorrow – Visitors Boast Strong Outfit," *Cincinnati Enquirer*, August 7, 1935: 12.
8 "Training Camp News"; "Craws, Grays in Big Trade/Detroit Also Enters Market and Comes Up with New Aces," *Chicago Defender*, March 23, 1935: 16.
9 "Lefty Vincent Is Added to Mound Staff of Locals," *Bismarck Tribune*, May 22, 1935: 7.
10 "Bay Parkways Get Even Break," *Brooklyn Daily Eagle*, August 12, 1935: 8.

# SPRING TRAINING FOR THE 1935 PITTSBURGH CRAWFORDS

## By Mark Blaeuer

Baseball spring training had a long run in Hot Springs, Arkansas, from 1886, when the Chicago White Stockings came to town, to 1955, when the Detroit Stars prepared there for their season. Within this timeframe, individual players also traveled to Hot Springs to take thermal baths in the 4,400-year-old spring water that emerges every day on one hillside at an average of 143 degrees Fahrenheit. The water is, of course, cooled to a safe temperature for use in the tubs. These spa baths – and related activities, like Swedish-style massage and trail hiking in Hot Springs Reservation[1] brought millions of health-seekers to the Ouachita Mountains of southwest Arkansas. A host of physicians, in Hot Springs and elsewhere, prescribed a three-week bathing course for a variety of ailments. Consequently, ballplayers were only engaging in what the general public had done for at least two centuries. While modern science holds a more limited view of the mineral water's reputed medicinal power, the baths can still be obtained there today.[2] Teams and individual players could choose from dozens of hotels, some of which provided the baths. Other bathhouses operated without sleeping accommodations, including the famous Bathhouse Row in what is now the national park adjoining the city of Hot Springs. These hotels and bathhouses, however, were racially segregated during the Jim Crow era.[3] Integration of facilities was assured in 1963 after "two national officers of the National Association for the Advancement of Colored People tested the Buckstaff Bathhouse for nondiscrimination on March 28."[4]

A number of ballparks were built for visiting and local teams. At the height of the spring-training phenomenon in Hot Springs, circa 1911, one might have encountered "about 200 major league players of national importance [practicing] at the Spa" in a single vernal season, not to mention minor leaguers.[5] Never to be outdone, African-American aggregations began to visit Hot Springs for games by at least the 1890s. Their players were enticed into the federally regulated bathhouses by 1920, and Negro Leagues teams were conducting spring training in the tourist destination by at

# THE 1935 PITTSBURGH CRAWFORDS

*The Pittsburgh Crawfords, pictured here in April 1935, were one of many teams – both black and white – that trained in Hot Springs, Arkansas.*

(Courtesy National Baseball Hall of Fame)

least 1927, when the Kansas City Monarchs and Memphis Red Sox trained there. The Monarchs returned in 1928 and stayed at the Woodmen of Union Hotel. In 1930 and 1931 the Homestead Grays set up camp at the Spa City, and in 1932 the Crawfords followed suit.[6]

Dick Lundy sent his Newark Dodgers to train at Rocky Mount, North Carolina, in 1935, but he himself went first to Hot Springs. An April 6 newspaper article revealed that he "left last Thursday for Hot Springs, Ark., where he will take the baths. While at Hot Springs, Lundy will train with the Pittsburgh Crawfords, who are doing their spring training at this noted health resort. … He will also look over a few promising youngsters, who are at Hot Springs. …"[7]

On April 12, 1935, a Wichita newspaper, the *Negro Star*, reported, with a Hot Springs dateline: "The Pittsburgh Crawfords blew into town this week to establish their spring training camp. Gus Greenlee, owner of the Crawfords, declares that the Crawfords will be right in the hottest part of the race for the Negro National League flag. Here with the Crawfords are: Satchell [*sic*] Paige, Betrum [*sic*] Hunter, William Bell, Sam Streeter, H. Kincannon, Roosevelt Davis, Alfred Carter, Wm. Harvey, Carl Howard, C. Cook, J. Johnson, C. Williams, Bond, M. Charleston, J. Crutchfield, S. Bankhead, T. Gibson, H.G. Perkins, Taylor, J. Bell, L. Palm, Curtis Harris, Paterson, Vincent and W. Breen."[8] The list in the April 12 paper seems to have been largely copied from the March 23 edition of the *Pittsburgh Courier*, and is not an eyewitness record of the team members who were in Hot Springs at that juncture.

The *Pittsburgh Courier* of April 13 carried text and photos of players at Hot Springs. Featured was an image of the Crawfords players standing in a line at a location here, with captions – "Left to right: Bond, Crutchfield, Hunter, Howard, Streeter, Davis, Palm, Bankhead, Perkins, Bell, Kincannon, Judy Johnson, Matlock, Taylor, Carter, Gibson, Schofield and Charleston. Kneeling, Trainer Whitten [*sic*];" a picture of club owner Gus Greenlee, in team uniform, with Josh Gibson and Crawfords bus driver Mack Hart; plus a photo of non-Crawford players Kenneth "Ping" Gardner (perhaps hoping to restart his career, he appears to be wearing a Crawfords jersey), Biz Mackey, and Dick Lundy, who were training there independent of their own teams.[9] The "Ches Sez" column on the same page states, "And Gus sends word from the famous Spa that the Craws are taking baths regularly and that the sunny Hot Springs atmosphere is sure to put the boys in great shape for the hard National Association grind."[10]

The April 27 *Chicago Defender* also reported that "[t]he Crawfords are in training at Hot Springs." A team photo taken by a *Defender* photographer that spring indicates that the team members "(left to right) are: front row: Bond, Howard, Hunter, Streeter, Kincannon, Davis; middle: J. Bell, Bankhead, Charleston, Palm, Crutchfield, Carter, Perkins; top: Taylor, Johnson, Matlock, Schofield, Gibson, Whitten [*sic*]."[11] More complete IDs for these men, sometimes with nicknames, can be found in numerous sources.[12] The team makeup in the *Defender* photo caption matches that accompanying the April 13 *Courier* image but differs from the *Negro Star* list by the absence of Paige, Cook, Harris, Paterson, Williams, William Bell, Vincent, and Breen, and the inclusion of Matlock and Schofield. Schofield was "'Lefty' Schofield, another promising young portsider."[13] Paige never showed up in the spa town that April. One newspaper reported he was "A.W.O.L. at the 'Craws' training camp in Hot Springs," despite being under contract to the Crawfords. Paige never did join the Crawfords in 1935 and spent most of the season playing for a semipro team in Bismarck, North Dakota.[14]

It seems fair to speculate that Cook, Harris, Paterson, Williams, William Bell, Vincent, and Breen were also absent from Hot Springs during the Crawfords' 1935 training session, as no record of their presence here that year – other than the suspect *Negro Star* piece – was found. Of course, some of these players may have joined the Crawford contingent after the photographs were taken, or they simply may have missed the photo sessions despite being in Hot Springs.

Both the *Courier* and *Defender* photos appear to have been taken at what was originally christened Fogel Field, when it was built in Hot Springs for the 1912 Philadelphia Phillies (a team then owned by Horace Fogel). This diamond was located behind a pair of recreational attractions, the Alligator Farm and the Leap the Dips roller-coaster, both on Whittington Avenue. Presumably, Fogel Field (or Older Field, as it was sometimes called during the 1930s) was where the Crawfords trained, since nearby Ban Johnson Field at Whittington Park, directly across Whittington Avenue, would have been temporarily occupied by the minor-league Milwaukee Brewers, who trained in Hot Springs that year until April 13, as well as the St. Paul Saints, who worked out until April 11.[15]

Where the 1935 Crawfords quartered while in Hot Springs has not been pinpointed. Several African-American hotels were operating here, including two – the Pythian and the Woodmen of Union – that also offered thermal baths with spring water piped from the national park.[16] One might suspect that they stayed at the Woodmen of Union, based on this observation about the team's 1932 visit: "John L. Clark, traveling with the [Crawfords], praised not only the mineral water, but also the Woodmen of the Union Hospital and its doctors."[17] On the other hand, a 1991 newspaper article conveyed the reminiscences of 80-year-old Jimmie Crutchfield about Hot Springs in 1932: "On any given day, the same guy might wind up pitching and catching and driving the bus. The players slept most nights on makeshift beds in a bath house. If a white team showed up to claim the hardscrabble diamond that morning, [Crutchfield] and the rest of the Pittsburgh Crawfords were driven out of town and training began with a 5-mile walk through the Arkansas hills back into Hot Springs. The bills were picked up by a numbers runner back in Pittsburgh. 'And that,' he recalled, 'was when things were good. We used to eat on 65 cents a day, and the luckier ones had a few dollars in their pockets left over from working in the offseason,' Crutchfield said. 'We knew the (white) big leaguers had it better, but we definitely loved what we had. ...'"[18] As for their manager, Oscar Charleston: "'We had only 10 days down there, but Oscar, he was one of those hard-driving guys from the old school,' Crutchfield said. 'And he got us ready to play.'"[19] We do not know whether the Crawfords' 1935 sleeping accommodations in Hot Springs resembled those Crutchfield described in 1932, but owner W.A. "Gus" Greenlee enjoyed sufficient wealth to pay for actual beds.[20]

Hot Springs offered cheap rooms to visitors of modest means, yet all but two of the African-American hotels lacked the very desirable thermal spring water. At that time, the Pythian and the Woodmen of Union would have represented the best available lodging. Both were located on Malvern Avenue, the town's "Black Broadway," and could boast of having their own bathhouses – and associated businesses. The WOU Building, for example, contained a 2,500-seat auditorium, a 100-bed hospital, a training school for nurses, a bank, and other services for patrons in the African-American community.[21]

The Pythian Hotel operated between 1914 and 1974; the structure has since been demolished. The Woodmen of Union was built in 1923, became the National Baptist Hotel in 1950, and closed in 1982.[22] After lying vacant for many years, the National Baptist was rehabilitated for "low-income elderly housing."[23]

It appears that the 1935 Crawfords arrived at Hot Springs in early April to train for the coming season and that they departed by bus in time for barnstorming games in Memphis, Tennessee, on April 13 and 14. These were the first of numerous exhibition contests in which the Craws participated on their route back to Pittsburgh.

Their first home game of the season was against the New York Cubans on May 11 at Greenlee Field in Pittsburgh, and they defeated the Cubans, 6-5. The Craws' training foray through the South was officially over.[24]

The 1935 Pittsburgh Crawfords were neither the first nor the last team from the Negro Leagues to hold spring training drills in Hot Springs, but they may have been the most formidable. Their presence added luster to the town's unique history, a heritage that is now recounted along the Hot Springs, Arkansas, Historic Baseball Trail.[25]

## Notes

1. The Hot Springs Reservation was a resource reserve created by Congress and President Andrew Jackson in 1832, to protect the hot springs and surrounding acreage. It was renamed Hot Springs National Park in 1921.

2. Don Duren, *Boiling Out at the Springs: A History of Major League Baseball Spring Training at Hot Springs, Arkansas* (Dallas: Hodge Printing Company, 2006); "Curry New Pilot of Black Barons," *Pittsburgh Courier*, April 9, 1955: 23; "Hot Springs Geology," nps.gov/hosp/learn/nature/hotsprings.htm; Sharon Shugart, "Hot Springs National Park," in Isabel Burton Anthony, ed., *Garland County, Arkansas: Our History and Heritage* (Hot Springs: Garland County Historical Society and Melting Pot Genealogical Society, 2009), 345-356.

3. "African Americans and the Hot Springs Baths," nps.gov/hosp/learn/historyculture/upload/african_americans.pdf.

4. Sharon Shugart, *When Did It Happen? A Chronology of Events at the Hot Springs of Arkansas* (Hot Springs, Arkansas: Eastern National, 2009), 58.

5. Duren, 326.

6. Dave Wyatt, "Rube Foster, as I Knew Him," *Pittsburgh Courier*, December 27, 1930: 14; "Rube Foster and Johnson in South," *Chicago Defender*, December 18, 1920: 6; "Negro National League Preparing for Spring Practice," *Pittsburgh Courier*, February 12, 1927: 16; "Hot Springs, Arkansas, Is Picked as Training Camp for Kansas City Monarchs," *Chicago Defender*, February 11, 1928: 9; "Grays Leave Spa for La.," *Pittsburgh Courier*, March 29, 1930: 15; "Grays Show Fine Form at Springs," *Pittsburgh Courier*, April 4, 1931: 14; "Crawford Vanguard Off for Hot Springs; Josh Gibson, Radcliffe Depart," *Pittsburgh Courier*, February 20, 1932: 15.

7. "Newark Dodgers Off for Spring Camp; Look Great," *Chicago Defender*, April 6, 1935: 16.

8. "Training Camp News," *Negro Star* (Wichita, Kansas), April 12, 1935: 3.

9. "'Gus' at the Spa – Crawfords Conditioning at Hot Springs – 'Bizz,' Lundy," *Pittsburgh Courier*, April 13, 1935: 16.

10. "Process of a Sports Editor Cleaning Up His Desk," *Pittsburgh Courier*, April 13, 1935: 16.

11. "League Clubs in Training in Southern Camps," *Chicago Defender*, April 27, 1935: 17.

12. E.g. Phil Dixon with Patrick J. Hannigan, *The Negro Baseball Leagues: A Photographic History* (Mattituck, New York: Amereon Ltd., 1992), 161. "Whitten" is identified as trainer Hood Witter.

13. "Crawfords Set to Make Strong Bid for League Championship," *New York Age*, April 27, 1935: 5.

14. "Report or Be Barred from Ass'n, Warn Paige," *Pittsburgh Courier*, April 6, 1935: 15.

15. Duren, 16; "Brewers Break Camp," *Akron Beacon Journal*, April 13, 1935: 18; "Saints Break Camp," *Indianapolis News*, April 11, 1935: 4.

16. "African Americans and the Hot Springs Baths."

17. Thomas Aiello, *The Kings of Casino Park: Black Baseball in the Lost Season of 1932* (Tuscaloosa: University of Alabama Press, 2011), 60.

18. Jim Litke, "Negro Leagues Full of Drawbacks, Fun," *Indiana (Pennsylvania) Gazette.* March 1, 1991: 15.

19. Litke.

20. James A. Riley, *The Biographical Encyclopedia of the Negro Baseball Leagues* (New York: Carroll & Graf Publishers, 2002), 339.

21. "Hotels," *Polk's Hot Springs City Directory* (Kansas City and Detroit: R.L. Polk & Co., 1935), 494. Black-owned businesses were denoted by the symbol "(c)" in this volume, and included the Crittenden Hotel at 314 Cottage and the Hotel Johannah at 338 Garden; *Garland County, Arkansas: Our History and Heritage*, 148.

22. "African Americans and the Hot Springs Baths."

23. "Woodmen of the Union Building, Arkansas," nps.gov/articles/woodmen-of-the-union-ar.htm.

24. "Crawfords Win Home Opener," *Pittsburgh Press*, May 12, 1935: 17.

25. hotspringsbaseballtrail.com.

# 1935 PITTSBURGH CRAWFORDS TIMELINE

## By Bill Nowlin

*Crawfords See Big Year In Baseball*

Chicago Defender, May 4, 1935: 11.

### SPRING TRAINING

The Crawfords trained at Hot Springs, Arkansas. Team owner Gus Greenlee said the 1935 team was going to be "right in the hottest part of the race for the Negro National League race."[1] The list of those who started spring training was given as: Satchell Paige, Betrum Hunter, William Bell, Sam Streeter, H. Kincannon, Roosevelt Davis, Alfred Carter, Wm. Harvey, C. Williams, Bond, M. Charleston, J. Crutchfield, S. Bankhead, T. Gibson, H.G. Perkins, J. Bell, L. Palm, Curtis Harris, Paterson, Vincent and W. Breen."[2] As a glance at the list makes clear, a number of those present at the start do not appear to have ultimately made the team, or – as was the case with Paige – found other places to play.

Biz Mackey and Dick Lundy trained with the Crawfords at Hot Springs. There is a photograph of them in the April 13, 1935 *Pittsburgh Courier*. Work on this timeline helped inspire a separate article "1935 Pittsburgh Crawfords: Spring Training in the Sunny South."

April 7, 1935: This day's *Arkansas Gazette* had one sentence under the headline "Negro Nines Meet." It read: "The Memphis Red Sox and Pittsburgh Crawfords, semi-professional Negro baseball clubs, meet at Cox Park at 2 this afternoon." Presumably to play a baseball game, but one of which we can find no other trace.

### APRIL 12, 1935:
### PITTSBURGH CRAWFORDS 5,
### MEMPHIS RED SOX 4,
### AT NEW ORLEANS, LOUISIANA

Bond had three singles, with Chester Williams and Clarence Palm both getting a pair of singles.

Four pitchers got some work: Schofield, Howard, Kincannon, and Carter. Palm had been with the Crawfords in 1935, but during the 1935 regular season he seems to have primarily played for the Brooklyn Eagles and then may have joined the Crawfords again for their postseason exhibition tour.

**APRIL 13, 1935:**
**PITTSBURGH CRAWFORDS 10,**
**MEMPHIS RED SOX 3,**
**AT NEW ORLEANS, LOUISIANA**

Matlock started but Hunter was the winning pitcher. Apparently the Craws put together a "bat bombardment" in the fifth inning.[3]

**CRAWS WIN 2. POINT FOR 4-CLUB TWIN BILL**

*Pittsburgh Courier*, April 20, 1935: A5.

**APRIL 15, 1935:**
**PITTSBURGH CRAWFORDS 12,**
**FISHER MONARCHS 3,**
**AT CLARKSDALE, MISSISSIPPI**

We're guessing this game took place on the 15th, but we can't say for sure. The *New York Amsterdam News* story describing the game in its April 27 issue was datelined April 25 from Clarksdale. It reported: "Another big day at bat for the Pittsburgh Crawfords here Monday resulted in a 12 to 3 victory over the Fisher Monarchs." The April 27 *Chicago Defender* ran the same story.

**'CRAWS' TAKE CLARKSDALE**

Continue Southern Invasion, Overwhelming the Fisher Monarchs by 12-3

*New York Amsterdam News*, April 27, 1935: 11.

The Monday preceding April 27 was, of course, April 22 – but we see (below) that the Crawfords played in Monroe, Louisiana, that day.

**APRIL 16, 1935:**
**PITTSBURGH CRAWFORDS 16,**
**GREENWOOD ALL-STARS 0,**
**AT GREENWOOD, MISSISSIPPI**

On April 16 the Crawfords traveled to Greenwood, Mississippi, and played a 3:00 P.M. game against the Greenwood All-Stars, with Bert Hunter throwing a one-hitter while the Pittsburghers scored 16 runs on 19 hits. Cool Papa Bell had six hits, including a triple.[4]

**APRIL 17, 1935:**
**PINEY WOODS GIANT COLLEGIANS 4,**
**PITTSBURGH CRAWFORDS 2,**
**AT LEAGUE PARK, JACKSON, MISSISSIPPI**

The first game was scheduled for 3:00 P.M. Choice seats were priced at 28 cents, with box seats "as long as they last" for 38 cents. The *Jackson Clarion-Ledger* advised that there were "special seats for white patrons."[5]

**APRIL 18, 1935:**
**PITTSBURGH CRAWFORDS 8,**
**PINEY WOODS GIANT COLLEGIANS 2,**
**AT JACKSON, MISSISSIPPI**

No further details have yet been located regarding the April 17 game. The score for the April 18 game comes from the *Baltimore Afro-American*.[6] The *Pittsburgh Sun-Telegraph* offered two sentences about the game on the 18th, from which we learn that Josh Gibson caught Leroy Matlock and Harry Kincannon, who combined to allow the Collegians six hits. The Crawfords had eight base hits.[7]

**APRIL 19, 1935:**
**PITTSBURGH CRAWFORDS 7,**
**ALCORN COLLEGE 0,**
**AT ALCORN COLLEGE, ALCORN, MISSISSIPPI**

Bert Hunter, Spoon Carter, and Leroy Matlock each worked in turn on the mound. Josh Gibson caught the game.⁸ Unfortunately, we lack further details about the game and inquiries at the college in 2020 turned up no information.

**APRIL 21, 1935:**
**MONROE MONARCHS 9,**
**PITTSBURGH CRAWFORDS 8,**
**AT CASINO PARK, MONROE, LOUISIANA**

Hayward Jackson filed a story from Monroe on May 10 describing this Easter Sunday game and another couple the Monarchs played against the St. Louis Blues the following Sunday and Monday. "Before three thousand howling fans the Monarchs staged one of the most dramatic climaxes ever seen here to come from behind and score six runs in the ninth inning of Easter Sunday's fracas with the strong Pittsburgh Crawfords and down the Easterners 9-8."⁹

According to the article in the *Defender*, the Crawfords scored all eight of their runs over the first three innings, driving starter Barney Morris from the game; Hilton Smith "rushed to the rescue." Bert Hunter pitched for Pittsburgh. He allowed two runs in the first inning. In the ninth, after a leadoff single and a base on balls, Smith hit a three-run home run over the wall in right field. A triple, an error by Charleston, a walk, and a bases-clearing double down the right-field line won the game.

All well and good, but the *Pittsburgh Post-Gazette* published a very brief two-sentence summary and line score. Hunter is not shown as pitching; Carter and Matlock are the pitchers shown. And the line score shows the Monroe team not scoring at all until they put over two runs in the bottom of the sixth. They scored once in the eighth, and then won the game with six runs in the ninth inning.¹⁰ These are significant discrepancies, but at least both papers agreed on the score. Regretfully, inquiries directed to Monroe turned up nothing.

**APRIL 22, 1935:**
**PITTSBURGH CRAWFORDS 8,**
**MONROE MONARCHS 2,**
**AT CASINO PARK, MONROE, LOUISIANA**

The April 23 *Monroe News-Star* ran a story on the April 22 game headlined "Crawfords Beat Monarchs to Even Two-Game Series." In the April 22 game, the "effective hurling" of Pittsburgh's Sam Streeter held Monroe to two runs, while the Crawfords got two runs in the third inning on two singles and an error by the Monroe first baseman. The Monarchs got one back on two doubles in the fourth. Barney Morris pitched pretty well for the Monarchs. (Only Cool Papa Bell had an extra-base hit, a double.) But two more errors in the sixth inning combined with that double and three singles to give the Craws a total of five unearned runs in the game. In the eighth, the Craws scored their eighth run when Bell walked, stole second, then stole third, and finally scored on an infield out. Monroe got its second run in the bottom of the eighth on an error and two successive singles. The final was 8-2, Crawfords.

**APRIL 23, 1935:**
**PITTSBURGH CRAWFORDS 8,**
**ACME GIANTS 4,**
**AT SHREVEPORT, LOUISIANA**

There were 28 base hits in the game, 16 of them by the Crawfords and 12 of them garnered by the Acme Giants off Harry Kincannon. The Giants committed four errors to the Crawfords' one. The Craws scored often, but never in big bunches – one run each in the first, fourth, fifth, and sixth, and two in the third and the seventh. The Acme team scored once to tie the game in

> BASEBALL
> CASINO AMUSEMENT PARK
> Special Engagement
> PITTSBURGH CRAWFORDS
> vs.
> MONROE MONARCHS
> SUNDAY, APRIL 21—3:00 P. M.
> MONDAY, APRIL 22—3:30 P. M.
> Same Low Admission

Newspaper advertisements for April 21 and 22 games. *Monroe Morning World* (Monroe, Louisiana, April 21, 1935: 12.

the first inning, then rallied for three runs in the bottom of the eighth to make things a little more respectable. Kincannon pitched for Pittsburgh.[11]

### April 24, 1935:
### Pittsburgh Crawfords 15,
### Acme Giants 1,
### at Alexandria, Louisiana

The day after their game at Shreveport, the teams ventured to Alexandria for a Wednesday game. This one was lopsided, in part thanks to Leroy Matlock pitching for Pittsburgh. Pitching to Perkins, he allowed just six hits. The game was close through three innings, 1-0 in favor of the Crawfords. They added another run in the fourth, then four in the first, five in the seventh, and a final four in the top of the ninth. The only run the Acme Giants scored came in the bottom of the ninth.

### April 25, 1935:
### Pittsburgh Crawfords 3,
### Louisiana Stars 2,
### at Donaldsonville, Louisiana

One sentence in the April 26 *Pittsburgh Press* reported the score.[12] Likewise, the *Chicago Defender*, but the *Defender* article provided at least some minimal details: "Hunter was the victor in the hard-fought game Thursday, defeating Wade, star Louisiana hurler, holding the Dixie club to 5 hits."[13] The *Post-Gazette* said "O. Hunter" was the pitcher, and that he had struck out 14. Gibson homered. The line score shows only two runs for each team, which clearly doesn't match the score, but the *Sun-Telegraph*'s line score showed a third run (one of two in the seventh inning).[14]

### April 26, 1935:
### Pittsburgh Crawfords 12,
### Louisiana Stars 3,
### at Donaldsonville, Louisiana

There were purportedly to be three games played in Donaldsonville – on the 25th, 26th, and

## CRAWFORDS COP TWO FROM LOUISIANA STARS

*Chicago Defender*, May 4, 1935: 9.

27th. The only other one we could find was reported in the April 27 *Pittsburgh Post-Gazette*. It is datelined April 25, but we are guessing that it was actually reporting the game on the 26th.[15] Josh Gibson tripled and homered. The Crawfords collected 20 base hits in all, scoring at least one run in every inning by the eighth. The May 4 *Chicago Defender* said that both Carter and W. Bell worked in the game, caught by Gibson.

If there was a game on the 27th, we have not yet located it. The Ascension Parish Library in Donaldson was unable to find trace of any of the games played there.

### April 28, 1935:
### Pittsburgh Crawfords 6,
### New York Cubans 4,
### at New Orleans, Louisiana

The Crawfords beat the New York Cubans 6-4 in a "hard-fought game played before a good-sized crowd" at New Orleans.[16]

### April 29, 1935:

## CRAWS BEAT CUBANS, 6-4

*Pittsburgh Courier*, May 4, 1935: A3.

### Pittsburgh Crawfords
### vs. Hercules Tigers,
### at Hercules Park, Hattiesburg, Mississippi

SABR researcher Rich Bogovich turned up a brief note in the *Hattiesburg American* that announced a 3:30 P.M. game on Monday, April 29. The Tigers were "a negro team sponsored by the Hercules Powder company." A program designed to make the day a memorable one: "An added attraction will be a 'red hot' negro jazz band direct from Harlem to play all the latest tunes."[17] Memorable it may have been, but we were unable to find any information about the game or the performance.

### April 30, 1935:
### Pittsburgh Crawfords 7,
### Black Cats (of Laurel) 3,
### at Laurel, Mississippi

A two-sentence note in the *Pittsburgh Post-Gazette* informed readers that the Crawfords beat the Black Cats, 7-3.[18] Harry Kincannon pitched and Bill Perkins caught. Kincannon and Bankhead each had two doubles in the game. The Craws scored four runs in the top of the third inning and added single runs in the fifth, sixth, and seventh. The Black Cats chipped away at the 7-0 lead with two in the bottom of the seventh and a final run in the bottom of the ninth. The Craws got 15 hits and played error-free ball. The Black Cats collected seven hits and made one error. The team (formerly known as the Big M Black Cats) had disbanded in 1935 but was reorganized for 1935 "through the generosity of white business men and colored friends."[19]

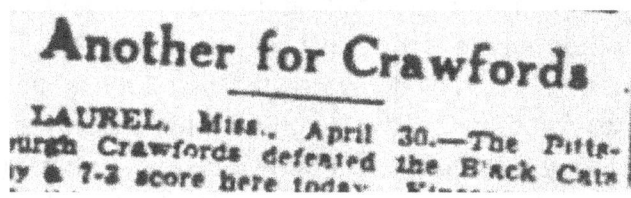

*Pittsburgh Post-Gazette*, May 1, 1935: 20.

### May 1, 1935:
### against the New York Cubans
### at Jackson

The April 30 *Clarion-Ledger* announced the game and noted that "[a] large crowd of the local colored folk are expected to attend."[20] Again, special seats were being reserved for white patrons, but even the Mississippi Department of Archives and History was unable to find any trace of the fate of the game – was it played? Was it canceled? We don't know.

### May 2, 1935:
### Pittsburgh Crawfords 8,
### Meridian Giants 3,
### at Meridian, Mississippi

A *Pittsburgh Courier* story datelined May 9 reported the Crawfords in Meridian, Mississippi, beating the Meridian Giants, 8-3, behind the six-hit pitching of Ernest "Spoon" Carter. The Crawfords outhit Meridian, 14-6. There were no errors.

Were the datelines accurate? Was this the Meridian game originally scheduled (against the New York Cubans) for May 2? The dateline of a number of articles in different newspapers leads to confusion. Peggy Gripshover turned up a copy of the May 11, 1935, *Indianapolis Recorder*. That issue had two articles datelined the same day as the newspaper – May 11. Both stories appear on page 12. One story announced the opening of the Crawfords season that day in Pittsburgh, and the other also reported on the game in Meridian (with a May 11 dateline).

Rick Bush located an article in the *Pittsburgh Post-Gazette* of May 3, which fully agreed with the *Courier*. Carter pitched (Perkins caught), and gave up six hits, while the Crawfords collected 14 hits, winning 8-3.

### ON THE BRINK

Saturday, May 4, was the scheduled Opening Day for the Negro National League season. As the regular season was about to get underway, the *Pittsburgh Courier* was hopeful that Satchel Paige would soon return to the fold. On May 4 Cum Posey's column in the paper read, in part, "Pittsburgh Crawfords have made changes, which will find a rejuvenated pitching staff and new men at shortstop and in the outfield. There is no doubt, Satchel Paige will soon return to the club, but without Paige the club is evenly balanced and contain some of the best players in colored baseball. Bond, Bankhead, Harvey, Carter are new men this season."[21]

Games had been scheduled for May 5 and May 6 in Nashville between Jim Taylor's Detroit Elite Giants and the Crawfords. Both games were rained out. A doubleheader was played on May 7.

**MAY 7, 1935:**
**PITTSBURGH CRAWFORDS 8,**
**DETROIT ELITE GIANTS 5 (FIRST GAME),**
**AT WILSON PARK, NASHVILLE, TENNESSEE**

Harry Kincannon and William Bell pitched the first game, giving up 11 hits and five runs. Josh Gibson caught. Detroit scored first, in the first, but just one run. In the top of both the second and third, the Crawfords scored a pair. Detroit scored again in the bottom of the third, and it was 4-2. Pittsburgh made a point, pushing three runs across in the top of the fourth. The Giants matched that with three of their own in the bottom of the fifth, narrowing the game to 7-5. The only other scoring came when Pittsburgh scored once in the eighth. Detroit used three pitchers, Thompson, Porter, and Byrd. Together, they gave up 14 hits.

## Crawfords Win Two

*Pittsburgh Post-Gazette*, May 8, 1935: 20.

**MAY 7, 1935:**
**PITTSBURGH CRAWFORDS 3,**
**DETROIT ELITE GIANTS 1 (SECOND GAME),**
**AT WILSON PARK, NASHVILLE, TENNESSEE**

The second game was a seven-inning game, with many fewer base hits. Pittsburgh scored three runs on seven hits; Detroit got just the one run off Hunter, on four hits. The Crawfords scored twice in the second and once in the third, while Detroit's only run was scored in the sixth.

Note: Taylor's Detroit Elite Giants were unable to find a home field on which to play in Detroit, so the team moved to Columbus, Ohio.

**MAY 8, 1935:**
**COLUMBUS ELITE GIANTS 6,**
**PITTSBURGH CRAWFORDS 2,**
**AT BOWLING GREEN, KENTUCKY**

Columbus scored once in the bottom of the first, saw the Crawfords take a 2-1 lead in the top of the second but then put another one on the board to draw even, 2-2. The Giants scored four times in the bottom of the third inning, and then neither team put across another run for the rest of the game. Columbus outhit the Crawfords, eight hits to six. There were no errors.

A May 9 game was scheduled at Crosley Field against the Cincinnati Tigers, but it was rained out.[22]

## THE REGULAR SEASON

**MAY 11, 1935:**
**PITTSBURGH CRAWFORDS 6,**
**NEW YORK CUBANS 5,**
**AT GREENLEE FIELD**

The first home game for the Crawfords was held on Saturday afternoon, May 11, at 3:30 P.M. The *Pittsburgh Courier* said the Crawfords were expected to be a "strong, hustling club, with a powerful pitching staff, and an outfield and an infield which will be hard to surpass in Negro baseball."[23] The scores of the first four games proved that the two teams couldn't be more closely matched – the first two games were won by one-run margins and the next two ended up as ties.

A week later, the *Courier* added the observation: "This year's Crawford outfit seems to have that 'something' which will make them the most dangerous contenders to league-honors."[24]

Starting for Pittsburgh was William Bell. Cocaina Garcia started for Alex Pompez's New York Cubans but was quickly replaced by Johnny Taylor.

The festive Opening Day featured martial music from the Kay Community House Marching Club and Drum and Bugle Corps, and a

# THE 1935 PITTSBURGH CRAWFORDS

ceremonial first pitch by Special Assistant to the U.S. Attorney General Robert L. Vann.

The Cubans outhit the Crawfords, 11 to 6. The Cubans scored two runs in the top of the first inning, but the Crawfords quickly came back with three of their own, thanks to a three-run home run by manager-first baseman Oscar Charleston that "cleared the distant right-field fence by many feet."[25] Three batters, three runs scored, and Taylor was brought in to relieve Garcia.

The Crawfords scored two more runs in the bottom of the second inning and added a sixth run in the bottom of the fourth. The Cubans had scored another run in the top of the third. The 6-3 lead the Crawfords built up held up, when the Cubans scored twice more in the top of the fifth. From that point on, neither team scored. The final was 6-5. Left fielder Sam Bankhead doubled for Pittsburgh, as did three of the Cubans. Three Crawfords each had two hits: Charleston, Bankhead, and Cool Papa Bell. Bell scored three of the six Pittsburgh runs.

Johnny Davis relieved William Bell at the end of the game and gave up a pinch-double to Havana-born Anastasio Santaella. With just the one-run lead, the game was well-contested until the final out.

The *Pittsburgh Press* provided the uniform numbers of the 10 Crawfords who played in the game:

8 – J. Bell, cf
7 – Bankhead, lf
12 - C. Harris, 1B
11 - Gibson, c
5 – J. Johnson, 3B
4 – C. Williams, 2B
9 – Crutchfield, rf
6 – Bond, ss
14 – Hunter, p
15 – Kincannon, p

## MAY 12, 1935:
### PITTSBURGH CRAWFORDS 2, NEW YORK CUBANS 1 (FIRST GAME), AT GREENLEE FIELD

The Crawfords hosted a Sunday afternoon 2:00 P.M. doubleheader at Greenlee Field.

Left-hander Leroy Matlock started the first game for Pittsburgh and pitched a complete game, holding the Cubans to five hits, and beating them, 2-1. He walked just one and struck out four. Pitching for the Cubans was their catcher, Heliodoro Diaz. Diaz had been a starter for the Cuban Stars in 1932 and 1933, but in 1935 he ended up catching in 14 games while pitching just this one. He pitched quite well, as is evident in the score, a complete game allowing just eight hits and two walks. The Craws got to him for two triples, though, by Cool Papa Bell and Judy Johnson. Neither team scored until the bottom of the sixth, when Pittsburgh got one on Bankhead's single, a sacrifice by Charleston, and a base hit by Judy Johnson. The Cubans scored their run in the top of the seventh, and the Crawfords got their go-ahead run in the bottom of the seventh when Bond singled to right field, took second base on an infield out, and then scored with ease on Bell's triple to left field.

## MAY 12, 1935:
### PITTSBURGH CRAWFORDS 4, NEW YORK CUBANS 4 (TIE) (SECOND GAME), AT GREENLEE FIELD

Most newspapers gave more complete coverage to the first game of doubleheaders, and the *Courier*'s coverage was no different in its May 18 edition. Sunday's second game was scheduled as a seven-inning game, but with the score tied 4-4 after nine, both teams played two more innings before calling it due to darkness.

The Cubans started Luis "Lefty" Tiant, replacing him with Neck Stanley near the end of the game. The Crawfords started Bert Hunter; Sam Streeter relieved, followed by Roosevelt Davis. Both teams scored a pair of runs in the first inning.

The Crawfords scored two more in the bottom of the second. The Cubans got one back in the top of the third, and tied the game for good with another run in the top of the seventh, when Tiant "lashed a single through the box to score [Martin] Dihigo."[26] New York used 17 players, and had nine hits; Pittsburgh had six hits. The Cubans almost took the lead in the ninth. With two outs, Dihigo was on third base and Javier Perez on first. Cando Lopez hit the ball hard between first and second – but it struck Perez just as Dihigo was crossing the plate, ending the inning.

**MAY 13, 1935:**
**PITTSBURGH CRAWFORDS 3,**
**NEW YORK CUBANS 3 (TIE),**
**AT GREENLEE FIELD**

Monday's game was a 6:00 P.M. twilight game. It too ended in a tie, this time by the score of 3-3. Kincannon and Dihigo were the starting pitchers. We see a bit of a see-saw affair. The New York Cubans scored first, in the top of the first. Pittsburgh waited until the second inning, scoring one run to tie. In the top of the third, the Cubans restored their one-run advantage. The Crawfords tied it, 2-2, in the fifth. Both teams scored a run in the seventh inning, the Cubans taking the lead, but then Cool Papa doubled, took third on a groundout, and scored the tying run when Oscar Charleston hit a fly ball to deep center. The game was called after nine innings on account of darkness. The Craws outhit the Cubans, eight hits to seven. Dihigo had two of the Cubans' base hits, but both Stanley and Fernandez pitched in the game, too, while the Crawfords saw both Bill Harvey and Spoon Carter follow Kincannon in pitching for Pittsburgh.[27]

**MAY 14, 1935:**
**NEW YORK CUBANS 7,**
**PITTSBURGH CRAWFORDS 3,**
**AT BEAVER FALLS, PENNSYLVANIA**

The Cubans won this one in what the *Post-Gazette* called "an interesting game."[28] Each team had one triple (Judy Johnson for Pittsburgh, Martin Dihigo for the New York team) and each team had two doubles. The Cubans had a dozen hits while the Crawfords had 10, three of them singles by Chester Williams. It was 4-0 after five innings. In the sixth, the Cubans scored three more runs and the Crawfords scored two. Pittsburgh got one run in the ninth. Crawfords pitchers were Streeter, Carter, and William Bell.

## Crawfords Tripped

*Pittsburgh Post-Gazette*, May 15, 1935.

**MAY 15, 1935:**
**PITTSBURGH CRAWFORDS 4,**
**NEW YORK CUBANS 3,**
**AT JACKSON, MISSISSIPPI**

A brief couple of sentences in the *Mississippi Weekly* of May 18 informed us that over 1,000 spectators came out to see the game. Even though the "New York Cubs" (as they were called) lost, the paper said, Pittsburgh "did not give as good a show for themselves as the New Yorkers. But the game was good and tight. And no doubt the winning team was the best after all."[29]

May 16, 1935: The *Pittsburgh Press* reported that the Crawfords were to play the Swissvalers at the Switch and Signal Grounds that evening. (Swissvale is an Allegheny County borough about six miles east of Pittsburgh.) Inquiries to Swissvale and neighboring communities in the county have not turned up any account of a game.

**MAY 17, 1935:**
**PITTSBURGH CRAWFORDS 6,**
**HOUSE OF DAVID 2,**
**AT GREENLEE FIELD**

There was more than one House of David team during its heyday. The "Eastern group of the House of David" played the Crawfords in a 6:00 P.M. game at Greenlee Field. Kincannon pitched, giving up seven hits but also walking six. Josh Gibson hit a home run and Bankhead doubled. O'Grady of the House of David stuck out six Crawfords.[30]

## CRAWS, HOUSE OF DAVIDS

*Pittsburgh Courier,* May 18, 1935: A5.

**MAY 18, 1935:**
**CHICAGO AMERICAN GIANTS 7,**
**PITTSBURGH CRAWFORDS 4,**
**AT GREENLEE FIELD**

Davis started for Pittsburgh "but ran into a batting attack in the fourth inning, which netted the Chicagoans three runs. He was relieved by Streeter."[31] Mule Suttles homered and Double Duty Radcliffe had two doubles. Josh Gibson had two singles, but otherwise the Crawfords were simply outmatched. The winning pitcher was Chicago right-hander William McKinley "Willie" Cornelius.

**MAY 19, 1935:**
**PITTSBURGH CRAWFORDS 1,**
**CHICAGO AMERICAN GIANTS 0 (FIRST GAME),**
**AT GREENLEE FIELD**

The Craws got quick revenge on the Chicagoans, taking both halves of the Sunday doubleheader by very different scores – one run in the first game and 14 in the second. Leroy Matlock threw a complete-game four-hit shutout in the first game, two of them by Radcliffe. The only run of the game was scored in the bottom of the sixth inning. Left fielder Sam Bankhead tripled and scored moments later when Oscar Charleston singled him home. Jimmie Crutchfield got three of the Crawfords' eight hits – two singles and a double. The "sterling" right fielder helped out Matlock with "one of the most thrilling one hand catches of a fly ball ever seen in Greenlee Field … when he ran to the extreme right hand corner of the lot and speared 'Mule' Suttles wallop."[32] The game story said the triple was Bankhead's but the accompanying box score shows J. Bell (Cool Papa) with the triple. The *Chicago Defender* box score had Bankhead with a three-base hit, and not Bell, and the game story said it was Gibson and not Charleston who singled him home, but the box score shows Gibson 0-for-4 and Charleston 2-for-3.[33]

**MAY 19, 1935:**
**PITTSBURGH CRAWFORDS 14,**
**CHICAGO AMERICAN GIANTS 7 (SECOND GAME),**
**AT GREENLEE FIELD**

Josh Gibson hit a three-run homer in the first inning and Bill Perkins hit one in the fourth. Both homers were impressive, "two of the longest hits ever recorded in Greenlee Field baseball history." Gibson "poled a high, wide and handsome homer over the deep right field fence which bounded up onto the hospital grounds. The other long-distance clout was made by Perkins, Crawford catcher, which also cleared the mid-right field stands and bounded back into a remote corner of the park."[34] The *Chicago Defender* explained that this game ended after seven innings due to a Sunday 6:00 P.M. closing law.

## GIANTS AND CRAWFORDS SPLIT FOUR GAMES WIN TWIN BILL

*Chicago Defender,* May 25, 1935: 14.

**MAY 20, 1935:**
**CHICAGO AMERICAN GIANTS 15,**
**PITTSBURGH CRAWFORDS 7,**
**AT GREENLEE FIELD**

Chicago achieved a two-two split of its four-game visit to Greenlee Field, slugging for 15 runs off five Crawfords pitchers: W. Bell, Carter, Davis, Kincannon, and Hunter. Cornelius and Thomas pitched for Chicago.

Regarding this same game, however, the May 25 issue of the *Chicago Defender* provided a two-sentence summary of the game under the headline GIANTS WIN as follows: "The Giants won Monday's final by a score of 3 to 2 to regain the lead. Cornelius again started and was opposed by Kincannon." In fact, the score in the final inning was 3-2 and it may be that a simple error was made by the writer glancing at the wrong column in the line score.

The May 21 *Pittsburgh Post-Gazette* published a box score and a couple of lines on the game. It appears to simply be a coincidence that the tables had been turned from a 14-7 win one day to a 15-7 loss the next. The box score shows Chicago outhitting Pittsburgh 18-8, off that array of pitchers. For Chicago, Double Duty Radcliffe had four hits and both Jack Marshall and Turkey Stearnes had three. Judy Johnson and Jimmie Crutchfield each had a pair of hits for the Crawfords. It was a seven-inning game.

**MAY 21, 1935:**
**CHICAGO AMERICAN GIANTS 8,**
**PITTSBURGH CRAWFORDS 1,**
**AT ISLAND PARK, HARRISBURG, PENNSYLVANIA**

An estimated 600 fans turned out to watch the Pittsburgh Crawfords (as home team) take on the Chicago Americans for a night game on May 21. Ernest Carter started for the Craws and Melvin "Putt" Powell for Chicago. Chicago scored one run in the top of the first, then five more in the top of the sixth. David "Bill" Harvey replaced Carter for the final three innings, and two more runs scored in the top of the seventh. The only run Pittsburgh scored came in the bottom of the ninth, on a double by Harvey and a triple by Cool Papa Bell. It was far too little to do more than deprive Powell of a shutout. In the sixth inning, Mule Suttles hit a three-run homer; and he and first baseman Steel Arm Davis homered back-to-back for Chicago, part of the five-run sixth inning. Jimmie Crutchfield had the only other extra-base hit of the game, a double.

**MAY 22, 1935:**
**PITTSBURGH CRAWFORDS 10,**
**CHICAGO AMERICAN GIANTS 3,**
**AT EAGLE PARK, YORK, PENNSYLVANIA**

A similarly same-size crowd as at Harrisburg turned out to watch the two teams contend again, for an 8:15 P.M. game under the floodlights at Eagle Park. Sam Streeter struck out 12 and walked only one. Brown of the Giants and Josh Gibson of the Crawfords each hit home runs. Gibson was 3-for-4 with three RBIs. Bankhead drove in two. The game took 2:05 to play. Pittsburgh outhit Chicago, 15-8. The Craws scored once in the second and twice in the third and, after Chicago scored once in the top of the fifth, came back with two more in the bottom of the fifth and another four in the sixth. Chicago had single runs in the seventh and eighth, and Pittsburgh punctuated the game with a final 10th run in the bottom of the eighth. Both the game story and the box score in the *York Gazette and Daily* showed the Crawfords' pitcher as "Struler."[35]

An article in the *Bismarck* (North Dakota) *Tribune* reported that Crawfords pitcher Lefty Vincent would be joining forces with Satchel Paige and playing with Bismarck beginning on May 23.[36]

**MAY 23, 1935:**
**PITTSBURGH CRAWFORDS 2,**
**NEW YORK CUBANS 0,**
**AT HAGERSTOWN, MARYLAND**

The Crawfords were due to play the New York Cubans at 8:30 P.M. in Hagerstown. Tickets were 40 cents. William Bell pitched brilliantly, a one-hitter. The only details we were able to find regarding the game were two sentences in the *Pittsburgh Post-Gazette*: "The Crawfords defeated the Cuban Stars, 2 to 0, here tonight when Bell held the Islanders to one hit. Josh Gibson hit another home run."[37] There was no box score or line score. Attendance was apparently something like 1,300-1,500 people.

May 24, 1935: The May 18 *Pittsburgh Courier* announced a game for the 24th in Pittsburgh between the Crawfords and the House of David ("one of the greatest aggregations of bearded stars ever assembled"). The game, the *Courier* said, "promises to be a sizzler." It appears that the game was not held. See next entry.

**MAY 24, 1935:**
**PITTSBURGH CRAWFORDS 4,**
**PHILADELPHIA STARS 4,**
**AT BEAVER FALLS, PENNSYLVANIA**

It was back to Beaver Falls for a game against "the Easterners."[38] Kincannon pitched for the Crawfords, who scored twice in the second and twice in the eighth. The Easterners scored twice in the fourth and added single runs in the eighth and ninth. The box score in the *Post-Gazette* shows an unusual number of players switching positions. It shows Harvey pitching, as well as Kincannon, but also a third pitcher named "Cannor." It shows "Harrisn" playing center field and "Pt'r'n" playing second base and third base. The *Sun-Telegraph* had only a line score, but that also included Cannor.

**MAY 25, 1935:**
**PITTSBURGH CRAWFORDS 10,**
**PHILADELPHIA STARS 4,**
**AT GREENLEE FIELD**

Carter pitched and held the Stars to six hits. Both teams scored twice in the first inning. The Stars got two more in the top of the third, while the Craws put up just one run to counter. But in the bottom of the fifth inning, the home team exploded for six runs, driving starter Rocky Ellis from the mound and putting the game away. Pittsburgh second baseman Pat Patterson doubled twice and tripled in what was reported as his first game in a Crawfords uniform.[39]

**MAY 26, 1935:**
**PITTSBURGH CRAWFORDS 4,**
**PHILADELPHIA STARS 2 (FIRST GAME),**
**AT GREENLEE FIELD**

The Crawfords swept a doubleheader from Philadelphia. Matlock doled out six hits in the 1-hour 48-minute game. One was a homer by Dick Seay. The Stars scored once in the first and once in the fourth, while the Craws put nothing on the board until they scored once in the sixth and again

## Crawfords Whip Philly Stars; Keep Loop Lead

*Chicago Defender*, June 1, 1935: 14.

– to tie it – in the seventh. Two eighth-inning runs meant they didn't have to bat in the bottom of the ninth. Oscar Charleston homered, Bill Perkins tripled, and Josh Gibson hit two doubles. Patterson, in his second Crawfords game, suffered a deep cut over his eye when a groundball took a sharp hop and struck him.

**MAY 26, 1935:**
**PITTSBURGH CRAWFORDS 2,**
**PHILADELPHIA STARS 1 (SECOND GAME),**
**AT GREENLEE FIELD**

The margin was even tighter in the second game. Roosevelt Davis pitched for the Crawfords. Neither team scored until Pittsburgh put up two runs in the bottom of the sixth. The Stars got one in the top of the seventh, and that was it. Judy Johnson tripled and sacrificed twice. Pittsburgh outhit Philadelphia, nine to seven.

**MAY 27, 1935:**
**PITTSBURGH CRAWFORDS 6,**
**PHILADELPHIA STARS 2,**
**AT GREENLEE FIELD**

The night game at Greenlee Field saw William Bell start for the Crawfords, later in the game replaced by Bill Harvey. The Pittsburgh pitchers gave up 12 hits, but the visiting Stars scored only twice – once in the seventh and once in the eighth. Right-hander Webster McDonald pitched a complete game for the Stars, giving up just seven hits but seeing the Craws score two runs in each of three consecutive innings – the second, third, and fourth. Crutchfield had two of the hits, and so did Harvey.

As of May 27, the Crawfords were in first place with a 9-3 record per the standings in the June 1 *Baltimore Afro-American*.

> **NIGHT BASEBALL GAME**
> Tuesday Evening, May 28, Eagles Park, York, Pa., — 8:15 P. M.
> Famous Pittsburgh Crawfords vs. Phila. Stars (World's Champions)
> Regularly scheduled Negro National league game
>
> Bleachers ........25c
> Grandstand ....... 40c
> Get buses at Center Square
> Auspices of Old Timer's A. A.

Newspaper advertisement for May 28 game against the Stars. *York Daily Record* (York, Pennsylvania), May 28, 1935: 10

Greenlee Field didn't host another Crawfords game until June 30.

### May 28, 1935:
### Philadelphia Stars 9,
### Pittsburgh Crawfords 0,
### at Eagle Park, York, Pennsylvania

The 8:15 P.M. game was sponsored by the Old Timers A.A. and York's *Gazette and Daily* advised readers, "Arrangements have been made for bus service from Continental square direct to the ball park, every ten minutes after 7 o'clock."[40] Lefty Holmes of the Philadelphia Stars was masterful, shutting out the Crawfords on a two-hitter. Only Bankhead (shown in the box score as B.Head, lf) and J.Bell, 3b (Cool Papa) managed hits for the Crawfords. William Bell pitched for Pittsburgh. The game was a real pitchers' duel through the first five, though, with the Stars scoring just one run in the second inning. Bell struck out nine in the game, but saw the Stars put across five runs in the top of the sixth. Holmes, on the other hand, "fanned only two but had the Crawfords batters tapping weakly to his fielders."[41]

May 29, 1935 – Did the planned game at Harrisburg's Island Park Field between the Crawfords and the Chicago American Giants take place on this date? It had been announced on page 20 in the May 25 *Afro-American,* but after numerous attempts, we have not been able to locate information about the game, played, postponed, or canceled.

### May 30, 1935:
### Pittsburgh Crawfords 11,
### Philadelphia Stars 4 (first game),
### at PRR YMCA Field, 44th & Parkside, Philadelphia

A lot of two-run innings won the game for Pittsburgh. In the morning game of a doubleheader, the Crawfords scored two runs each in the first, third, fifth, sixth, and ninth innings, and one run in the eighth. Bell, Charleston, and Harris each had three base hits, and Perkins had four. Even though they only outhit the Stars by two hits, 17 to 15, they put across the runs. Philadelphia scored only single runs in the sixth and the seventh, and then a pair in the bottom of the ninth. Sam Streeter pitched for Pittsburgh and despite the large number of hits allowed, he kept most of the runs from scoring – the "Stars had men left on base in every inning."[42]

### May 30, 1935:
### Pittsburgh Crawfords 9,
### Philadelphia Stars 3 (second game),
### at Passon Field, 48th and Spruce Streets, Philadelphia

The two Memorial Day games reportedly drew nearly 7,000 fans. In the afternoon game, the two teams shifted to another park, at 48th and Spruce Streets. The park was filled to more than capacity with the crowd overflowing onto the field, requiring that ground rules be implemented. Hunter pitched for the Crawfords and Slim Jones for the Stars. It was 3-2 in Pittsburgh's favor until the sixth, when Judy Johnson drove a hard hit at Jones, who stopped it with his bare hand and had to leave the game. The Crawfords got a fourth run in that inning, then added two in the seventh and three more in the eighth.[43]

# THE 1935 PITTSBURGH CRAWFORDS

May 31, 1935: The Crawfords were expected to play the Philadelphia Stars in Phillipsburg, Pennsylvania, on this Friday night at 9:00 P.M. So said a story in the May 29 *Morning Call* of Allentown, Pennsylvania.

JUNE 1, 1935:
PITTSBURGH CRAWFORDS 11,
NEWARK DODGERS 3,
AT OLLEMAR PARK, IRVINGTON, NEW JERSEY

Roosevelt Davis pitched for the Craws and Bob Evans for the Newark Dodgers. Davis struck out six Dodgers, but gave up two home runs to first baseman Jim Starks. All told, however, the Dodgers scored only three runs on five hits. Davis himself drove in three of Pittsburgh's 11 runs, on a bases-loaded double in the four-run fifth inning. The Crawfords already held a 6-2 lead at the time, so they were all insurance runs.

JUNE 2, 1935:
PITTSBURGH CRAWFORDS 15,
NEWARK DODGERS 3 (GAME ONE),
AT OLLEMAR PARK, IRVINGTON, NEW JERSEY

The Crawfords pretty much overwhelmed the Newark team with 15 runs on 13 hits, against three runs on six hits. Two of the six were by Ray Dandridge. Matlock was on the mound for Pittsburgh. Josh Gibson had three hits, with Harris and Williams each collecting two. The game was called after seven innings, perhaps reflecting something like a mercy rule in order to allow a little more time to get in the second game.

JUNE 2, 1935:
PITTSBURGH CRAWFORDS 7,
NEWARK DODGERS 5 (GAME TWO),
AT OLLEMAR PARK, IRVINGTON, NEW JERSEY

The *Indianapolis Recorder* said the score was 8-5, but the line score in the *Newark Star-Eagle* shows an eight-inning game with a 7-5 final score.[44] The Dodgers scored one run in the bottom of the second, matched by one Crawfords run in the top of the fourth. The Craws added four more runs in the fifth, with Newark scoring once in the bottom of the inning. The seventh inning saw Pittsburgh score twice more, to take a 7-2 lead. Perkins was Pittsburgh's leading batter, going 3-for-4. The Dodgers put three runs across in the bottom of the seventh, narrowing the gap to 7-5. Neither team scored in the eighth and final frame.

JUNE 3, 1935:
PITTSBURGH CRAWFORDS 7,
NEWARK DODGERS 6,
AT NEW BRUNSWICK HIGH SCHOOL STADIUM,
NEW BRUNSWICK, NEW JERSEY

*Gibson's Prodigious Homer Paves Way For Crawfords Victory Over Dodgers*

*Central New Jersey Home News* (New Brunswick, New Jersey), June 4, 1935: 12.

The 6:15 P.M. game was won by Bert Hunter, who worked the first six innings, relieved by Harry Kincannon. The Dodgers scored first, with one run in the second. In the top of the fourth inning, Josh Gibson homered, "a prodigious 400 foot drive that cleared the left center-field fence with plenty to spare."[45] It was the first home run over the newly-erected fence at the high-school stadium. Curtis Harris had singled and was on first base; the two-run homer gave the Craws the lead. Newark tied it up with one run in the fourth and took a 5-2 lead with three more in the sixth, but Pittsburgh got four more runs in the top of the seventh. The seventh run, the one that proved the game-winner, came when Cool Papa Bell singled, stole second, took third base on an overthrow, and scored on a wild pitch by Newark's Bun Hayes. The Dodgers out-hit the Crawfords, 14 to 10, but went down to defeat for the ninth consecutive league game. About 500 fans watched the game.

**CRAWS SWEEP NEWARK SERIES, INCREASE LEAD**

*Pittsburgh Courier*, June 8, 1935.

**JUNE 5, 1935:**
**CAMDEN GIANTS 5,**
**PITTSBURGH CRAWFORDS 4,**
**AT BROADWAY AND EVERETT STREET, CAMDEN, NEW JERSEY**

About 2,500 fans turned out and saw the Camden Giants beat the Crawfords, overcoming a 3-0 lead that the Pittsburghers had built up with two in the first and one in the third. Sam Bankhead did something he doesn't seem to have done in a league game – he pitched, striking out four. But he and Roosevelt Davis gave up 11 hits, and Bankhead walked three. They saw Camden score two runs in the bottom of the third and three more in the seventh, all scored after there were two outs. Judy Johnson had three of the Crawfords' eight base hits.

**JUNE 6, 1935:**
**PITTSBURGH CRAWFORDS 8,**
**POCONO CLUB 5,**
**AT STROUDSBURG, PENNSYLVANIA**

Spoon Carter pitched for Pittsburgh against the semipro Pocono Club. The game was a fairly close one, and could well have gone the other way when the Pocono team loaded the bases with nobody out in the bottom of the ninth inning. Carter struck out three batters.

**JUNE 7, 1935:**
**BROOKLYN BUSHWICKS 6,**
**PITTSBURGH CRAWFORDS 5 (10 INNINGS),**
**AT DEXTER PARK, QUEENS, NEW YORK**

the *Brooklyn Daily Eagle* of June 6 announced that the Crawfords would be playing the Bushwicks at Dexter Park on the night of June 7. The *New York Amsterdam News* of June 15 referred to "the humiliation handed to the Pittsburgh Crawfords at Dexter Park."[46] But no score was reported. It took a little digging, but both the *Brooklyn Citizen* and the *Brooklyn Times Union* provided considerable detail. Was any 6-5 score really a humiliation?

Lefty Leroy Matlock started for the Craws. He had 10 starts so far and hadn't yet been beaten.[47] The Crawfords scored once in the second, then three more in the fourth. In the top of the fifth, Harris singled and Josh Gibson tripled to right-center and the Crawfords had a 5-1 lead, but Bushwicks pitcher Jim Duffy struck out the next three batters. The Craws never scored again. Duffy whiffed 12 in the game and walked none; Matlock struck out seven and walked one. The Bushwicks tied it with four in the bottom of the sixth. Had the Crawfords turned a double play faster in the bottom of the 10th, the game would have gone on, but the ball hit to Jimmy Williams at shortstop was just too slow and the winning run came in from third.

On June 8 the Bushwicks were due to host Buck Lai's All-Star Chinese-Hawaiian team at Dexter Park.

A game planned for June 9 between the Farmers and the Crawfords was rained out.

As of June 10, the Crawfords were 15-3 in league play, per the June 15 *Baltimore Afro American*.

The June 10 edition of the *Long Island Press* announced a game for that evening between the Crawfords and the Long Island Athletics, to be played at 9:00 P.M. at Jericho Recreational Park.

**JUNE 11, 1935:**
**PITTSBURGH CRAWFORDS 9,**
**SPRINGFIELD GREYS 1,**
**AT SHERWOOD OVAL, SPRINGFIELD GARDENS, QUEENS, NEW YORK**

The June 12 *Brooklyn Daily Eagle* reported on a game in neighboring borough Queens. The semipro Greys scored first, in the bottom of the second. The Crawfords tied it up with one run

## Crawfords Conquer Springfield Greys

*Brooklyn Daily Eagle*, June 12, 1935: 21.

in the top of the fourth. Carter was pitching for the Greys, with Josh Gibson catching. The game remained tied, 1-1, through six innings. In the top of the seventh, however, the Craws cut loose and scored eight runs – which pretty much put the game away.

**JUNE 13, 1935:**
**PITTSBURGH CRAWFORDS 7,**
**CHESTER 1,**
**AT FELTON FIELD, CHESTER, PENNSYLVANIA**

The Crawfords pulled into town as late as 6:20 P.M., arriving from Philadelphia, but drawing 3,500 fans. When they did arrive, "they were without the services of two stars due to a misunderstanding with their eastern booking agent."[48] If the *Chester Times* box score is any indication, the two missing may have been Charleston and Gibson. Streeter played first base. Popeye Harris caught Johnny Davis, and the battery pulled off a six-hitter. The Chester team was a white semipro team. Chester scored first, one run in the first, in part due to an error by Hunter. A close play at first base, a bunt single, and a walk loaded the bases in the top of the third. Then Streeter hit a grand slam over the right-center field fence.

"From then on it was all Pittsburgh. Roosevelt Davis, the cunning spitball artist, held the locals in the palm of his hand." He struck out 13 opponents and allowed just six hits. The Crawfords added single runs (both unearned) in the seventh and ninth.

Eastern booking agent? We're not sure what that means. Might it have been that Charleston and Gibson read the *Philadelphia Tribune* that morning and thought they were supposed to go to PRR Field in Philadelphia? The *Tribune* ran a story saying the Crawfords would play a "special game" against the Philadelphia League All Stars at PRR Field that night.[49]

**JUNE 15, 1935:**
**PITTSBURGH CRAWFORDS 6,**
**PHILADELPHIA STARS 5 (FIRST GAME),**
**AT PRR YMCA FIELD, 44TH & PARKSIDE, PHILADELPHIA**

Almost 4,000 fans came out to see the doubleheader between the Stars and Crawfords. The Crawfords were losing the first game, 5-3, but thanks to a "rousing rally" in the ninth won the game, 6-5. Charleston had three hits, while Crutchfield, Patterson, and Matlock each had two.[50]

**JUNE 15, 1935:**
**PITTSBURGH CRAWFORDS 6,**
**PHILADELPHIA STARS 5 (SECOND GAME),**
**AT PRR YMCA FIELD, 44TH & PARKSIDE, PHILADELPHIA**

The second game's score was the same as the first. This one was a Carter vs. Carter battle, Paul Carter pitching for the Phils and Spoon Carter pitching for the Craws. Once more the Stars were out in front, holding a 2-0 lead through six innings. Pittsburgh scored four runs in the top of the seventh, only to see Philadelphia re-establish the lead with three runs in the bottom of the seventh. The Crawfords scored once in the eighth and once in the ninth, first to tie the game and then to take the lead. Crutchfield and Patterson each had a pair of hits.

# CRAWS COP TWO TILTS BY SCORES OF 6 TO 5

*Pittsburgh Courier*, June 22, 1935: A5.

**June 16, 1935: Brooklyn Bushwicks 7, Pittsburgh Crawfords 0 (first game), at Dexter Park, Queens, New York**

The semipro Bushwicks gave the Crawfords a tough time in 1935, none tougher than shutting them out in the first game of the June 16 doubleheader. The Bushwicks were 22-4 at this point in their season and the shutout was their third of the week. Charley Perkins pitched for the Bushwicks. Bankhead and Johnson doubled for Pittsburgh; Johnson had two hits, as did Patterson, but the Crawfords as a whole mustered only seven hits – and no runs. Streeter, Kincannon, and Harris pitched for Pittsburgh.

**June 16, 1935: Pittsburgh Crawfords 8, Brooklyn Bushwicks 1 (second game), at Dexter Park, Queens, New York**

In the second game, the Craws turned the tables, Johnny Davis limited the Bushwicks to seven hits and one sixth-inning run, striking out eight. The Crawfords scored one in the fourth and three runs each in the fifth and sixth innings, with one more in the eighth. Four Bushwicks errors did little to help their cause. Gibson doubled and Crutchfield tripled. Judy Johnson had three of the Craws' 11 hits, while Crutchfield and Patterson each had a pair.

**June 16, 1935: Penn Red Caps 9, Pittsburgh Crawfords 6, at Freeport Stadium, Freeport, Long Island, New York**

Apparently playing a doubleheader wasn't enough, so after the second game at Dexter Park, the Crawfords hustled to Freeport, Long Island, to play a team nicknamed the Porters, a successful semipro team that had already beaten the Chicago American Giants, Brooklyn Eagles, and New York Black Yankees.[51] The 8:45 P.M. game had Harvey pitching for Pittsburgh; he gave up 17 hits. The Crawfords had nine hits, three of them by Sam Bankhead. The Nassau newspaper had a full box score; the *Brooklyn Daily Eagle* story had Harris pitching as well as Harvey, but had only a line score.

**June 17, 1935: Pittsburgh Crawfords 6, Philadelphia Stars 0, at Felton Field, Chester, Pennsylvania**

With "an immense crowd" on hand, thunderstorms halted the game with two outs in the bottom of the fifth. The Crawfords were the home team, however, and the 6-0 lead held, making it nine of 10 games the Craws had won from the Stars at this point in the season.[52]

June 19, 1935: A preview in the June 17 *Washington Evening Star* said the Crawfords were to play the Chicago American Giants in an 8:15 P.M. game at Griffith Stadium. The June 20 *Evening Star* had four pages of sports coverage but did not mention this game, nor did the June 18 or 19 issues list it as a coming attraction.

**June 20, 1935: Pittsburgh Crawfords 13, West Phillies 6, at Passon Field, Philadelphia**

Two thousand fans came out to a night game and saw the Crawfords beat the West Phillies, starting with five runs in the first inning, two in the second, and one in the third. Harvey pitched for the Craws.

The game may have been one that filled a sudden hole in the schedule. The June 19 *Daily Mail* of Hagerstown, Maryland, reported that a game between the Crawfords and the Chicago American Giants for "tomorrow night at the stadium has been called off due to the great damage caused at the stadium."[53] A major storm had blown down sections of the fence around Municipal Stadium "and the powerful arc lights used for lighting during night baseball games were broken."[54]

June 21, 1935: The *Brooklyn Daily Eagle* of June 19 said the Crawfords would play the Bay

# THE 1935 PITTSBURGH CRAWFORDS

> **BASEBALL'S SENSATION!**
> **PITTSBURGH CRAWFORDS**
> — VERSUS —
> **CHICAGO AMERICAN GIANTS**
> PROFESSIONAL BASEBALL GAME!
> STADIUM — THURS. NITE, JUNE 20
> Game at 8:15    Admission 40c
> NOTE: Extreme Left Section Grand Stand, Also Open Stand Reserved for Colored Patrons.

Newspaper advertisement for game that appears not to have occurred. *Daily Mail* (Hagerstown, Maryland), July 18, 1935: 4.

Ridge Baseball Club on Friday night, the 21st, at Bay Ridge Oval.

**JUNE 22, 1935:**
**NEW YORK CUBANS 6,**
**PITTSBURGH CRAWFORDS 2,**
**AT BELMAR, NEW JERSEY**

Bert Hunter pitched for Pittsburgh this afternoon. Martin Dihigo's two-run home run in the seventh inning gave the Cubans a come-from-behind 3-2 lead, one they built on for the 6-2 final score. The Crawfords outhit the Cubans, seven to six, but Hunter walked five and the Craws made three errors.

**JUNE 23, 1935:**
**PITTSBURGH CRAWFORDS 7,**
**NEW YORK CUBANS 1 (FIRST GAME),**
**AT DYCKMAN OVAL IN MANHATTAN**

The Craws swept the Sunday doubleheader from the Cubans, racking up a total of 17 runs to 1. Matlock pitched the first game for the Crawfords; Lefty Tiant started for the Cubans. The Cubans scored their lone run in the bottom of the fifth, on a home run by first baseman Lazaro Salazar. Tiant seemed to be cruising, but the Crawfords suddenly scored four runs off him in the top of the eighth inning, driving him from the game. Bankhead had three hits and Gibson had four. Eight thousand fans saw the games.

**JUNE 23, 1935:**
**PITTSBURGH CRAWFORDS 10,**
**NEW YORK CUBANS 0 (SECOND GAME),**
**AT DYCKMAN OVAL, MANHATTAN**

Davis shut out the Cubans in the second game, allowing eight hits (all singles). The Crawfords scored in every other inning throughout the game – three in the first, two in the third, two in the fifth, two in the seventh, and a final 10th run in the top of the ninth. Bill Perkins hit two home runs. Gibson, Bankhead, and Charleston all hit doubles.

June 25, 1935: The June 20 *New York Daily News* contained a one-sentence notice: "The Cedarhurst, Nassau, baseball team will meet the Pittsburgh Crawfords June 25 at the village park, in a twilight contest."[55] The Peninsula Public Library in nearby Lawrence said it was too small to retain local newspapers dating back that far. No other inquiries bore fruit. We have yet to determine whether this game ever occurred.

**JUNE 26, 1935:**
**PITTSBURGH CRAWFORDS 9,**
**SPRINGFIELDS 3,**
**AT RECREATION PARK, QUEENS, NEW YORK**

The Springfields were one of a few white semipro teams that played the Crawfords in these times. Sam Streeter pitched and Harris caught. Crutchfield had four of the 10 Crawford hits. The Crawfords scored first, three runs in the top of the third, adding two each in the sixth and seventh, and single runs in the eighth and ninth.

A night game planned for June 27 against the Union City Bengals was rained out.

That same night, Gus Greenlee was in New York City for the Joe Louis-Primo Carnera heavyweight boxing match, and was robbed of $300 cash plus some tickets to the bout. A shot was fired, but he was not hit.

**JUNE 29, 1935:**
**PITTSBURGH CRAWFORDS 6,**
**NEWARK DODGERS 1 (FIRST GAME),**
**AT PRR YMCA FIELD, 44TH & PARKSIDE,**
**PHILADELPHIA**

The Crawfords and Dodgers played back-to-back doubleheaders on Saturday and Sunday, June 29 and 30, the Saturday games in Philadelphia and the Sunday games in Pittsburgh. The bottom of the order came through for the Craws in the first game Saturday, with the 6-7-8-9 batters each getting two hits: Pat Patterson, Chester Williams, Curtis Harris, and the pitcher, Bill Harvey. Newark got on the board first with its one run in the top of the fourth. Pittsburgh scored three in the bottom of the fourth, adding two more in the seventh and one in the eighth. Harvey held the Dodgers to seven hits.

**JUNE 29, 1935:**
**NEWARK DODGERS 7,**
**PITTSBURGH CRAWFORDS 6 (SECOND GAME),**
**AT PRR YMCA FIELD, 44TH & PARKSIDE, PHILADELPHIA**

The Crawfords jumped on Newark starter Bob Evans early, scoring two runs in the first inning and four in the second. Evans clearly settled down, completing the game without giving up another run. He saw his team battle back and overcome the Crawfords with solo runs in the fourth and fifth and then a big five-run sixth inning to take the lead. Spoon Carter started for the Crawfords, relieved by Bert Hunter.

**JUNE 30, 1935:**
**NEWARK DODGERS 12,**
**PITTSBURGH CRAWFORDS 5 (FIRST GAME),**
**AT GREENLEE FIELD**

The Crawfords returned home to Greenlee Field for the first time in more than a month.

The Dodgers batters picked up where they'd left off Saturday, scoring runs almost at will — or so it may have seemed. They scored two in the second, two in the third, one in the seventh, three in the eighth, and three in the ninth. The Crawfords didn't score at all for the first four innings, then scored one run per inning in each of the final five innings.

**JUNE 30, 1935:**
**PITTSBURGH CRAWFORDS 9,**
**NEWARK DODGERS 1 (SECOND GAME),**
**AT GREENLEE FIELD**

Matlock pitched the second game and "added to his unbeaten record" by holding the Dodgers to one second-inning run and three hits, in a seven-inning second game that saw the two teams split the two doubleheaders. The Crawfords scored two runs in the second, three runs in the third, and four in the fifth inning.

July 2, 1935: The Crawfords were scheduled to play a game against the Petrolia Refiners ballclub of the Northwestern Pennsylvania League, at Petrolia. – *News-Herald* (Franklin, Pennsylvania), June 29. As with a number of these announced games, we have been unable to determine whether the game was played.

The July 4 *Springfield* (Massachusetts) *Republican* wrote that Connie Rector of the New York Black Yankees had "recently hurled the Yankees to a 6 to 4 win over the Pittsburgh Crawfords."[56]

The July 5 *Chester Times* (page 15) says the Camden Giants handed the Pittsburgh Crawfords a double defeat. When did this occur? It may have been two different games on different dates. Camden did win on June 5, and the *Jersey Journal* of July 27 (more than three weeks after he *Chester Times* story) reported that the Giants "defeated the Crawfords, 7-5, in the only game the teams have played this season."[57] There's more than one mystery here.

**CRAWFORDS CINCH FIRST HALF CHAMPIONSHIP**

*New York Amsterdam News*, July 13, 1935: 14.

**JULY 4, 1935:**
**PITTSBURGH CRAWFORDS 6,**
**HOMESTEAD GRAYS 2 (FIRST GAME),**
**AT GREENLEE FIELD**

The Crawfords hosted Homestead on the Fourth of July, in the first game of the year between the two teams. The first game was set for a 10:30 A.M. start, with the second planned for 2 P.M. The Grays scored once in the first inning and once in the second. The Craws got one back in the third, added two in the sixth, and another three in the bottom of the seventh. Streeter pitched a complete game, allowing six hits. Pittsburgh had seven hits, including two each by Cool Papa Bell and Sam Bankhead. Bell hit a three-run homer, which either occurred in the sixth (per the game story) or the seventh (per the accompanying line score). There was a great deal of action at first base; Charleston recorded 17 putouts.

JULY 4, 1935:
PITTSBURGH CRAWFORDS 8,
HOMESTEAD GRAYS 6 (SECOND GAME),
AT GREENLEE FIELD

The second game was not one of Matlock's best, but he still got the win. After 3½ innings, the Grays held a 4-0 lead, but the Crawfords scored two runs in the bottom of the fourth, with three in the sixth, and then a decisive four more in the seventh. That provides a 9-6 win. At least, that's what was reported on page 21 in the *Baltimore Afro-American* of July 13. What is apparently another edition of the same paper shows only two runs scored in the sixth, for an 8-6 score. Because line scores in the *Pittsburgh Post-Gazette* and the *Courier* present the same line score as 8-6, we decided to go with majority rule in this case, simply noting that there are many possibilities, including that one just copied from another – and even that all four newspapers could have been incorrect. There doesn't seem to be any dispute as to which team won. The Grays appear to have outhit the Craws, 11-10, but committed four errors to the Crawfords' two.

JULY 5, 1935:
PITTSBURGH CRAWFORDS 11,
HOMESTEAD GRAYS 1,
AT GREENLEE FIELD

Spoon Carter pitched for the Crawfords, and 39-year-old left-hander Ralph Mellix for Homestead. Mellix bore the loss, the victim of "poor support" by his teammates.[58] No further information was provided in the *Courier* article – just one sentence and not even a line score. Despite this game being played right in Pittsburgh, we are left without more information.

JULY 6, 1935:
HOMESTEAD GRAYS 18,
PITTSBURGH CRAWFORDS 5 (FIRST GAME),
AT GREENLEE FIELD

In something of a reversal from the July 4 game, it was the Crawfords who were spotted four runs. They led 4-0 after four innings. The Grays got two runs in the fifth, but the Craws added three more runs in the sixth. The 7-2 lead did not hold, though. Homestead scored seven runs in the seventh, to take the lead, then added six more in the eighth, and another three in the top of the ninth. Maybe. Again, there is a discrepancy. In this case, the *Pittsburgh Courier* presents the line score as 18-7, but when adding up runs scored in the accompanying box score, one finds only five, one each by five different Crawfords. We could split the difference and go with 6, but decided to follow the lead of Gary Ashwill at Seamheads and elect to believe the box score (and accompanying game story) over the line score. The *Baltimore Afro-American* also lists the score as 18-5. An arbitrary choice, admittedly. Either way, this was a skunking.

The July 5 *Pittsburgh Press* said the two games were to be played in different cities – the first game at 3:30 at Greenlee Field and the second one just three hours later at McKeesport, some 16 or 17 miles away.

JULY 6, 1935:
PITTSBURGH CRAWFORDS 3,
HOMESTEAD GRAYS 3 (TIE) (SECOND GAME),
AT CYCLER PARK, MCKEESPORT, PENNSYLVANIA

The second game at McKeesport was to be a seven-inning benefit game for McKeesport Hospital.[59] The result was a 3-3 tie. No other information and no box score has been located.

**July 7, 1935:**
**Pittsburgh Crawfords 14,**
**Homestead Grays 2 (first game),**
**at Island Park, Harrisburg, Pennsylvania**

About 1,500 fans turned out to the Island for a Sunday afternoon doubleheader, seeing a lopsided first game and then a second game in which one big inning made all the difference. Rosey Davis limited the Grays to nine hits and two runs with a complete-game 14-2 win in the opener, Homestead getting one run in the top of the fourth and the other in the top of the ninth. Davis was 3-for-4 at the plate. Shortstop Chester Williams had three hits, too.

The Crawfords built their total in bursts – three runs in the third, five more in the fourth, and six in the bottom of the seventh. They wore through four Grays pitchers, collecting 15 hits in all. The only three extra-base hits were doubles by Gibson, Johnson, and Bankhead. Papa Bell and Bankhead each led with three RBIs. Both Homestead runs were driven in by third baseman Jimmy Binder.

**July 7, 1935:**
**Homestead Grays 8,**
**Pittsburgh Crawfords 3 (second game),**
**at Island Park, Harrisburg, Pennsylvania**

The Grays got the best of the Crawfords in the second game, which lasted six innings, curtailed by the 6:00 P.M. Sunday curfew in effect. Homestead was the home team in the second game. Harry Kincannon started for Pittsburgh but didn't make it out of the second inning. Both teams scored once in the first inning, but the Grays put the game away with seven runs in the bottom of the second inning. Spoon Carter took over for Kincannon. Catcher Bill Perkins made two of Pittsburgh's four errors, though he was 3-for-3 at the plate. Pittsburgh scored two runs in the top of the sixth before the game was called. Ray Brown got the complete-game win, apparently without striking out a single batter. Both teams had seven hits, but clearly the Grays made the most of theirs, as well as taking advantage of the Crawfords' miscues.

A third game on July 7? Was there a third game, perhaps one of those 9:00 P.M. night games, in Baltimore? The July 6 *Pittsburgh Press* previewed the 2:00 P.M. doubleheader at Harrisburg, but also said the doubleheader would be followed by a night game at Bugle Field in Baltimore. With a 6:00 P.M. curfew in Harrisburg, it is possible – even given the roads in 1935 – to have traveled the 78 or so miles to Baltimore in time for a 9:00 P.M. game. We have yet to find a report on a Baltimore game.

**July 8, 1935:**
**Pittsburgh Crawfords 6,**
**Homestead Grays 4,**
**at Griffith Stadium, Washington**

A magnifying glass helped provide the following information (the story is printed in full here): "A steady downpour of rain failed to stop the Pittsburgh Crawfords – Homestead Grays base ball game last night at Griffith Stadium and the Crawfords pounded out a 6-4 victory before 2,500 fans."[60]

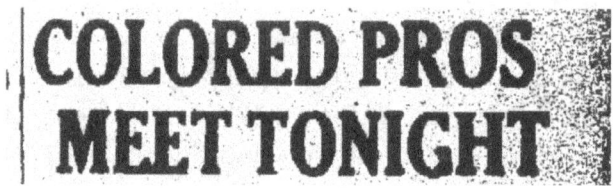

*Hagerstown Daily Mail*, July 9, 1935: 9.

**July 9, 1935:**
**Pittsburgh Crawfords 4,**
**Homestead Grays 1,**
**at City Stadium, Hagerstown, Maryland**

This game had a big buildup in the local press for two days running. On July 8 the *Hagerstown Morning Herald* wrote that the game was a league contest, adding, "Both these clubs are Pittsburgh products and the rivalry is at fever pitch." The article ended, "Sports fans have a real treat in store for tomorrow night."[61] On the morning of the game, the *Hagerstown Daily Mail* offered

## THE 1935 PITTSBURGH CRAWFORDS

**CRAWFORDS WINNERS**

The Pittsburgh Crawfords, leaders in the colored National League, gained a 4 to 1 victory over the Homestead Grays of Pittsburgh last night on the Stadium grounds before a fairly large gathering of fans. Play was fast and of the best and promoters have announced that another game will be staged at the Stadium next week.

*Hagerstown Daily Mail,* July 10, 1935: 4.

a subhead: "Real Battle in Store for Fans." The game was set for 8:15 P.M., and the newspaper said, "[F]ans are in for a real treat, as both teams are 'out for blood.'"[62] All well and good, but what really happened? The sum total of the coverage of the actual game was in the *Daily Mail*. The newspaper devoted a total of two sentences to the game. It provided the score, declared that it was played "before a fairly large gathering of fans," and added "play was fast and of the best."[63] The *Morning Herald* appears not to have even mentioned the game. It would be nice to have more information.

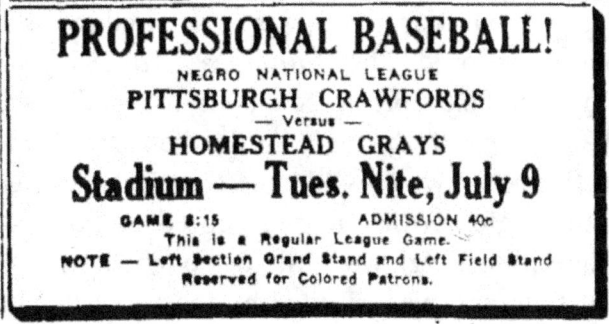

Newspaper advertisement for game against the Grays. *Daily Mail* (Hagerstown, Maryland), July 8, 1935: 8.

**JULY 11, 1935:**
**PITTSBURGH CRAWFORDS 10,**
**HOMESTEAD GRAYS 5,**
**AT CRICKET FIELD, ALTOONA, PENNSYLVANIA**

The Crawfords were designated the home team as they took on the Grays at Cricket Field in Altoona on a very hot day. The park was packed. The Crawfords scored early and often, building up an 8-0 lead over the first four innings while Bert Hunter kept the Grays hitless. The Craws got to the usually reliable Ray Brown, who was far from his best; he walked six batters. The Craws scored one run each in the first (on Jimmie Crutchfield's leadoff homer "over the right field stands," per the July 12 *Altoona Mirror*), second, and fourth innings, and five runs in the third. The final score was 10-5, with five Crawfords each boasting a pair of RBIs: Crutchfield, Bell, Johnson, Williams, and Hunter. By game's end the Grays had outhit the Craws, 12-10, but five of the Crawfords' hits were for extra bases and the final score reflected a big difference in the runs department.

**JULY 12, 1935:**
**BELMAR BRAVES 5,**
**PITTSBURGH CRAWFORDS 3,**
**AT MEMORIAL FIELD, BELMAR, NEW JERSEY**

The Braves were a "white team" which started the game understaffed, but then came from behind and won. The Braves were no-hit for the first four innings, while the Crawfords built up a 3-0 lead. We're not sure what the full story was, but the *New York Amsterdam News* reported: "The game was complicated by the breakdown of the Victory Bridge over Raritan Bay, between Perth and South Amboy, which held up the three basemen of the Belmar team. They arrived in time to get to the game at the fifth inning and turned defeat into victory."[64] Bankhead and Harris drove in all three Crawfords runs on home runs, a two-run homer in the first and a solo home run in the fourth.

## Crawfords Capture Flag for First Half

*Baltimore Afro American,* July 13, 1935: 20.

Schrieber, the Belmar pitcher, homered in the fifth inning to start the scoring. Belmar tied the game with three runs in the fifth, and scored two more runs in the seventh.

Why were the Crawfords playing so many games at other venues? Joe Sephus wrote in the *Cumberland* (Maryland) *Evening Times* that even though the Crawfords were the first-half champions of the league's Eastern Division, they were "having financial troubles. ... Failing to draw at home, the Crawfords and Homestead Grays have been playing some of their games on neutral fields at Hagerstown, Altoona, and elsewhere."[65] Perhaps this explains the absence of games at Greenlee Field for more than one full month, from May 27 to June 30. There were other activities at Greenlee, including midget auto racing.[66]

In the July 11 *Philadelphia Tribune*, the question was raised –after the NNL second-half schedule was released – why were no games planned between the Crawfords and the Philadelphia Stars?[67]

The *Baltimore Afro-American* assessed the season's first half by writing, "It is conceded in all quarters that the loop is better balanced this year." Regarding the Crawfords' capture of the flag for the first half, the newspaper wrote that the team, "deprived of the services of baseball's most spectacular right-hander, Satchell Paige[sic], has developed into one of the best defensive teams ever assembled. Pitching has been uniformly good and every man on the roster is a starting moundsmen[sic]."[68]

**JULY 13, 1935:**
**PITTSBURGH CRAWFORDS 7,**
**BROOKLYN EAGLES 3 (FIRST GAME),**
**AT EBBETS FIELD, BROOKLYN**

The Crawfords and Eagles played back-to-back doubleheaders on Saturday and Sunday, July 13 and 14, at Brooklyn's Ebbets Field. Each twin bill was split, with the visitors taking the first game both days and the home team winning the second. Davis was no slouch as a hitter, as well as being a fine pitcher, and he and Josh Gibson each had three hits in the first game, while Bankhead had two.

**JULY 13, 1935:**
**BROOKLYN EAGLES 4,**
**PITTSBURGH CRAWFORDS 3 (SECOND GAME),**
**AT EBBETS FIELD, BROOKLYN**

Bob Harvey gave up only five hits, but an error in the sixth (or seventh) inning led to three Eagles runs and a lead they did not relinquish. The Eagles scored first, with one run the second inning. Pittsburgh then scored two in the fourth and one in the first, taking a 3-1 lead. The *Afro-American* box score showed the three-run inning as the sixth.

## Matlock Stars As Craws And Brooklyn Split Two

*Chicago Defender*, July 20, 1935: 13.

**JULY 14, 1935:**
**PITTSBURGH CRAWFORDS 5,**
**BROOKLYN EAGLES 3 (FIRST GAME),**
**AT EBBETS FIELD, BROOKLYN**

The *Courier* story and box score said the score was 5-3, but four Eagles were each credited with one run scored. The *Baltimore Afro-American* story and box score agreed it was 5-3, and so did the *Brooklyn Daily Eagle*. As did the *Times Union* of Brooklyn, which – like the *Courier* – showed four Eagles with one run scored apiece. No matter; Pittsburgh won. Matlock pitched, striking out four, and was credited by the *Courier* with "masterful twirling." Josh Gibson homered – one of his two hits. Patterson had a pair and Bankhead collected three hits, two of them doubles.[69] The victory brought Matlock's season record to 8-0.[70] The *Afro-American* box score showed the Craws scoring twice in the first and adding single runs in the sixth, eighth, and ninth, staving off the Eagles, who rallied late with one in the seventh and two in the ninth.

# THE 1935 PITTSBURGH CRAWFORDS

**July 14, 1935:**
**Brooklyn Eagles 12,**
**Pittsburgh Crawfords 6 (second game),**
**at Ebbets Field, Brooklyn**

The Eagles piled up runs in every inning but the sixth and eighth, easily winning the most lopsided of the four games. Hunter, Harvey, and Carter all pitched for the Crawfords, but the Eagles were relentless. Harris was 3-for-4 with a home run for Pittsburgh. Cannonball Jackman pitched a complete game for Brooklyn.

**July 16, 1935:**
**Chester 5,**
**Pittsburgh Crawfords 1,**
**at Chester, Pennsylvania**

"One of Few Times Famous Pitt Team Bows to White Club" – so read the subhead in the next day's *Chester Times*. The story began: "Lefty Vann's Chester team attained their greatest achievement of the year last night on their home lot when they defeated the crack Pittsburgh Crawfords by the score of 5 to 1. The victory was due largely to Babe Mitchell's flawless pitching."[71] Mitchell allowed only four base hits. He set down the first nine batters in order. Mitchell struck out eight and walked one. Oscar Charleston said it was some of the best pitching he had faced. Carter was the losing pitcher. "The whole Chester team had a night on," said the *Times*. The only run the Crawfords scored was in the top of the ninth. Reading the game account, it sounded as though Bell – who had singled and moved up to second on a walk to Charleston – tagged up and scored from second base on a fly ball to deep left field.

**July 17, 1935:**
**Pittsburgh Crawfords 8,**
**Passon 0,**
**at Passon Field, 49th and Spruce Streets, Philadelphia**

Leroy Matlock shut out Passon, 8-0, under the lights. He struck out eight and allowed six hits. Third baseman Harris had three hits for the Craws. Gibson and Perkins each had a pair. The Crawfords had 13 hits in all, with at least one hit from everyone in the lineup. For some reason, the *Inquirer* gave Matlock the first name Jess.

**July 18, 1935:**
**Pittsburgh Crawfords 10,**
**Philadelphia Stars 4,**
**at Sixth and Jeffrey St., Chester, Pennsylvania**

The July 18 *Chester Times* referred to "the Crawfords smarting under the defeat at the hands of the Chester team Tuesday night …" Bill Harvey took the mound for the Crawfords. He gave up two runs in the bottom of the first inning, but the Crawfords scored three runs in the third, two runs in the fourth, and two more runs in the fifth. The Stars came back with two more in the bottom of the fifth, but the Craws added three more runs later in the game. Gibson, Bankhead, and Patterson each had two hits for Pittsburgh.

## PITTSBURGH TOPS GIANTS IN 3 GAMES

*Chicago Defender,* July 27, 1935: 13,

**July 19, 1935:**
**Chicago American Giants 11,**
**Pittsburgh Crawfords 4,**
**at Biddle Field, Carlisle, Pennsylvania**

There was a regular league game scheduled and advertised at the Stadium in Hagerstown between the Crawfords and the Chicago American Giants, but neither team turned up. Instead, they played a game in Carlisle, Pennsylvania. Proceeds from the 4:00 P.M. game were to be shared with four organizations sponsoring a street fair in Carlisle.[72]

The *Hagerstown Daily Mail* wrote, "Fans who paid out good dough [to see the Giants-Crawfords game in Hagerstown] were still plenty hot today in more ways than one for being left holding the bag for more than an hour. The two negro outfits put up the excuse their bus broke down but later it was learned they had played a ten-inning game at Carlisle. The question now is did Carlisle … fans witness an actual league game or merely an exhibition."[73]

Although the *Daily Mail* raised the question afterward, Carlisle's newspaper, *The Sentinel*, had announced the Carlisle game beforehand, proclaiming it "a regular National Negro League tilt."[74]

The Carlisle game was played at Biddle Field on the Dickinson College campus. Kincannon was hit hard by the Giants, finding himself behind 9-0 after three innings. He'd given up four runs in the second and five in the third. Carter replaced Kincannon before the third inning was done. Cool Papa Bell had four base hits – two singles, a double, and a triple. It was 9-0 for Chicago through the first seven innings. The Crawfords exploded for five hits and scored three times in the eighth, and added one more run in the ninth.

Newspaper advertisement for the July 19 game. *Daily Mail* (Hagerstown, Maryland), July 17, 1935: 4.

The game was not a 10-inning game. The *Sentinel*, Carlisle's newspaper, incorrectly reported that the two teams had played the night before in Hagerstown and planned to head for Pittsburgh, to play a game on the 20th.[75]

**JULY 20, 1935:**
**PITTSBURGH CRAWFORDS 12,**
**CHICAGO AMERICAN GIANTS 8,**
**AT GREENLEE FIELD**

Both Josh Gibson and Sam Bankhead homered in this game. Sam Streeter got the win, Hunter taking over later in the game. There was quite a bit of scoring, as the line score indicates:
Chicago    1 1 0 0 0 3 2 1 0 - 8
Crawfords  3 1 1 3 0 1 3 0 x - 12
The final score was 12-8.[76] Bankhead and Gibson each had three hits, and both saw one of them go for a home run. Charleston and Williams each had a pair of hits. Streeter struck out seven.

**JULY 21, 1935:**
**PITTSBURGH CRAWFORDS 17,**
**CHICAGO AMERICAN GIANTS 2 (FIRST GAME),**
**AT LEAGUE PARK, CLEVELAND**

Nearly 8,000 fans flocked to League Park to see the Crawfords play the Chicagoans in a doubleheader. Pittsburgh was deemed the home team for both games. Had these fans wanted to see a lot of runs, they picked the right day – the Crawfords scored 29 times. Davis pitched the first game and he was hit pretty hard – for 16 hits – but gave up only two runs, both in the fourth. Josh Gibson had three hits, including a double and a home run. Cool Papa Bell had three singles and a double.

**JULY 21, 1935:**
**PITTSBURGH CRAWFORDS 12,**
**CHICAGO AMERICAN GIANTS 8 (SECOND GAME),**
**AT LEAGUE PARK, CLEVELAND, OHIO**

The Giants may have thought they had something going when they scored four runs off Hunter in the top of the first inning. And they did – but the Crawfords quickly burst their bubble by scoring six runs in the bottom of the inning. They added four runs in the third. In the fifth inning, Chicago once again put up a "4." Pittsburgh scored once in the fifth and once in the sixth. It was a seven-inning game, with the Crawfords not needing to bat in the bottom of the seventh. Bell had two more hits in this game, for six hits in the doubleheader.

The doubleheader had been billed as a benefit for the Jesse Owens Educational Fund.[77]

Effective July 21, manager Oscar Charleston suspended three players "for improper conduct of the playing field." The players were Leroy Matlock, Roosevelt Davis, and Jimmie Crutchfield.[78]

**JULY 22, 1935:**
**CHICAGO AMERICAN GIANTS 9,**
**PITTSBURGH CRAWFORDS 7,**
**AT GREENLEE FIELD**

The two teams matched each other, run for run, in every inning but the fifth:
Chicago    1 1 0 0 2 4 0 0 1 - 9
Crawfords  1 1 0 0 0 4 0 0 1 - 7

Come the end of the game, that pair of runs the Giants put across was the margin of victory. Kincannon, Carter, and Harvey all pitched for the Crawfords. Everyone in the Crawfords lineup save the pitchers had at least one base hit. Josh Gibson and Judy Johnson each had three, while Bell, Patterson, and Harris each had two hits. In what the *Post-Gazette* called "a free hitting league game," the Crawfords collected 16 hits and Chicago had 13.[79]

## CRAWFORDS WIN TWO FROM ELITE GIANTS

*New York Amsterdam News*, August 2, 1935: 12.

**JULY 23, 1935:**
**PITTSBURGH CRAWFORDS 17,**
**ELECTRICAL DEPARTMENT 7,**
**AT WEIR-COVE PARK, STEUBENVILLE, OHIO**

The *Steubenville Herald-Star* reported that the Crawfords would be playing a 5:00 P.M. exhibition game at Weir-Cove Park that evening against the Electrical Department baseball team of the Weirton Steel League. The game drew 3,500 spectators. Carl Howard pitched for Pittsburgh. Three pitchers worked for the Electrics. The Craws scored two runs in the first inning, seven in the second, and six runs in the eighth. Patterson had two home runs. The Electrics did manage 12 hits off Howard, and scored four runs in the seventh inning.

**JULY 26, 1935:**
**PITTSBURGH CRAWFORDS 9,**
**ANDERSON INDIANS 5,**
**AT ANDERSON, INDIANA**

Johnny Twigg, the "ace hurler" of Anderson's Indians, was "invincible" for all but two innings of this night's game. "But in those two innings, he was bombarded and the Pittsburghers won, 9 to 5."[80] Gibson caught three Crawfords pitchers: Howard, Harvey, and Harris, and he homered. The Indians committed four errors. The two big innings saw the Craws score five in the third, and four in the ninth.

**JULY 27, 1935:**
**PITTSBURGH CRAWFORDS 10,**
**COLUMBUS ELITE GIANTS 2,**
**AT NEIL PARK, COLUMBUS, OHIO**

The Columbus ballclub (described sometimes as the Columbus-Nashville Elite Giants) was apparently without its usual shortstop, second baseman, and first-string catcher, so the depleted lineup didn't fare too well against the visiting Crawfords in a Saturday night game played under newly installed lighting. Hunter struck out 14 of the Giants and allowed just six hits. Josh Gibson had three hits – a single, a double, and a home run. Johnson also doubled, and Charleston tripled.

**JULY 28, 1935:**
**PITTSBURGH CRAWFORDS 12,**
**COLUMBUS ELITE GIANTS 3,**
**AT NEIL PARK, COLUMBUS, OHIO**

## Pride of Smoketown

There was to be a 2 P.M. Sunday doubleheader but only the first game was played, and it lasted only six innings before a downpour brought the proceedings to a close. Things were clearly not going Columbus's way. Patterson hit a solo home run in the first inning. The Crawfords scored three more in the second, knocking starter Jim Willis out of the game. Bill Harvey allowed the Giants just five hits. No box score of the game could be located.

**JULY 29, 1935:**
**COLUMBUS ELITE GIANTS 7,**
**PITTSBURGH CRAWFORDS 4,**
**AT NEIL PARK, COLUMBUS, OHIO**

The 7-4 score is verified by the *Columbus Evening Dispatch* of the following day, but no other details of the game were provided.

**JULY 30, 1935:**
**MINGO INDIANS 3,**
**PITTSBURGH CRAWFORDS 0,**
**LOCATION UNCERTAIN.**

The Crawfords were held to five hits by Lefty Vitas of the semipro Mingo Indians, who threw a 3-0 shutout. The August 3 *Steubenville Herald Star* suggests this was a game in very late July, hence probably this one, and probably in Steubenville.

July 31, 1935: the Crawfords were reportedly planning to play the Crafton Church League All-Stars at the Crafton High School field in a 6:30 P.M. game.[81] Crafton is an Allegheny County borough near Pittsburgh. Inquiries to libraries in the area failed to turn up any information.

**AUGUST 1, 1935:**
**COLUMBUS ELITE GIANTS 7,**
**PITTSBURGH CRAWFORDS 5 (12 INNINGS),**
**AT LEAGUE PARK, AKRON, OHIO**

This game drew 1,500 fans and they got their money's worth – 12 innings. The Crawfords scored once in the first inning and once in the sixth. With Johnny Davis on the mound, they looked to have the game reasonably well under control.

The Akron newspaper referred to the team as the Nashville Elite Giants. Gary Ashwill explains, "Newspapers often still referred to them as the Nashville Elite Giants for years, and sometimes (usually in the spring) they returned to Nashville to play games."[82] The Elite Giants scored three times in the top of the seventh, though, and briefly held the lead – until the Craws scored themselves, to tilt it the other way. In the top of the ninth, the Giants tied it up. Harvey took over pitching for Pittsburgh at some point. Both teams scored in the 10th. Finally, in the top of the 12th, the Giants scored two more runs on a leadoff walk and back-to-back doubles. The Crawfords failed to match the pair of runs and lost the game, 7-5. Jim Willis itched all nine innings for the Giants. Pittsburgh outhit the Giants, 15-10, with Bell collecting three singles and a double.

**AUGUST 3, 1935:**
**EAST ORANGE BASEBALL CLUB 4,**
**PITTSBURGH CRAWFORDS 0,**
**AT EAST ORANGE, NEW JERSEY**

The Crawfords were whitewashed – shut out. The opposition was the East Orange Baseball Club, a "white team" that outhit the Crawfords by just one hit, 11 to 10, but won the game 4-0. They scored once in the first, once in the fourth, and twice in the seventh. The "Smokytowners" scored not at all.[83]

August 4, 1935: Back on June 22, a brief note on page 2 of the *Cleveland Gazette* said that O.W. Singer was promoting a game between the Homestead Grays and Pittsburgh Crawfords "at the Stadium, August 4, in honor of Jesse Owens."

**AUGUST 5, 1935:**
**PITTSBURGH CRAWFORDS 7,**
**CHESTER 3,**
**AT CHESTER, PENNSYLVANIA**

Chester had apparently beaten the Crawfords at a game we haven't turned up yet. "Known as the greatest Negro club in baseball the boys from the Smoky City aren't used to taking a licking from white semi-pro clubs, but that is just what happened to them in their last appearance here in town."84 So the Crawfords were primed. And the August 6 *Chester Times* wrote, "It became evident in the very warm-up drill that the Crawfords were out to give the locals an unmerciful lacing if possible." In winning the game, the *Times* wrote, "They revenged the setback handed them on their last Chester appearance."

Kincannon pitched for Pittsburgh. Cocoa Bell (known as Cool Papa Bell today) doubled to lead off. He stole third and then scored on an infield groundout. The fourth man up in the first inning, Josh Gibson ("the Big Bertha of colored baseball") greeted Chip Bennett's pitch with a "human dynamo and it sailed far, wide and handsome over the railroad tracks."85 Gibson's next time up was when he led off in the third inning. He hit another homer almost to the same location in left-center field, this one landing on the concrete base of a tower on the tracks. They were "two of the longest drives ever witnessed in Delaware County." Bell had four hits in the game – three doubles and a triple. Oscar Charleston had three hits and impressed the *Times* sportswriter with his baserunning. "The lumbering Charleston, long past his prime, picked up his 355 pounds and sprinted down the third base line on Juliano's wind-up to make a clean steal of home."86 With all the offense, it's surprising the Crawfords didn't score a lot more runs than they did.

**August 7, 1935:**
**Pittsburgh Crawfords 11,**
**Brooklyn Bushwicks 1,**
**at Dexter Park, Queens, New York**

The *Brooklyn Daily Eagle* said this was the fourth meeting between the two teams in 1935, and with this win for the Pittsburghers, each team could boast of two. Roosevelt Davis held the Bushwicks to five hits and one second-inning run, which came in on an error. Gibson had two doubles and Patterson had a triple. The other 12 Crawfords hits were all singles. The Craws did all their scoring early: 2 1 3 5 – and then neither team scored for the rest of the game. The game attracted a reported 7,200 fans.87

**August 8, 1935:**
**Pittsburgh Crawfords 3,**
**Homestead Grays 2,**
**at PRR YMCA Field, 44th & Parkside,**
**Philadelphia**

Hits and runs were relatively few, but the Crawfords had both Streeter and Matlock pitch, and two catchers as well – Perkins and Gibson. Homestead scored one run in the top of the first and another in the top of the second. The Crawfords put up their first run in the bottom of the sixth. Josh Gibson, pinch-hitting in the seventh inning, tripled and gave his team the 3-2 lead. Ray Brown worked the whole game for the Grays, allowing just four hits. The Streeter/Matlock ombo allowed the Grays six – three of them by first baseman Buck Leonard.

**August 9, 1935:**
**Homestead Grays 11,**
**Pittsburgh Crawfords 2,**
**at Griffith Stadium, Washington**

The Homestead Grays were in the cellar, but they trounced the first-half champion Crawfords this night in Washington. Center fielder (and switch-hitter) Jerry Benjamin was the star of the game (and the only one to get his name in the *Evening Star*. Benjamin hit a single, a double, and a triple, and scored four of Homestead's 11 runs.88

**August 11, 1935:**
**Bay Parkways 10,**
**Pittsburgh Crawfords 2 (first game);**
**Pittsburgh Crawfords 14,**
**Bay Parkways 0 (second game),**
**at Erasmus Field, Brooklyn**

The Crawfords traded lopsided games in Brooklyn as the home field of the semipro Bay Parkways team. In the first game, Roosevelt Davis was hammered for 10 runs on 14 hits (including five doubles and two home runs), the Parkways scoring four in the first, one in the second, and three in the third. Right-hander George Smith held the Crawfords to just six hits and two runs; Perkins had two of the Craws' hits.

The second game saw the Crawfords feast while Sam Streeter held the semipros to six hits. Pittsburgh scored once in the first, eight runs in the second, and a 10th run in the third. The Craws added a pair in the eighth and a pair in the ninth. Bankhead collected three doubles and Perkins two.

The Crawfords were shorthanded. Oscar Charleston and Judy Johnson had gone to Chicago to play in the East-West Al-Star Game. Davis played first base in the second game. Streeter played part of the first game at first base.

The Crawfords apparently added some pickup players: W. Cooper played left field in both games and A. Cooper played center. "Gillispie" played right, and Lackey played third base. The games drew a reported 3,000 spectators.[89]

August 13, 1935: the Philadelphia Stars and Crawfords were to play an 8:15 P.M. game at Griffith Stadium, but the game was rained out.

### August 14, 1935:
### Philadelphia Stars 8,
### Pittsburgh Crawfords 2,
### at Griffith Stadium, Washington

Right-hander Laymon Yokely of the Stars was the star of this game, holding the Crawfords to just two runs. Pepper Bassett led the offense for the Stars, with two singles and a double. The brief four sentences covering the game named none of the Crawfords, and there was no line score so we don't know who pitched for them. We do know that there was a flurry of activity at the end of the game: "When the Crawfords rallied in the night Yokely cooled off things with two strikeouts."[90]

Net receipts from the game were less than they should have been. The *Evening Star* reported that "Wendell F. Pierson, representing the Pittsburgh Crawford base ball team, was checking receipts from a game at Griffith Stadium last night when a prowler snatched $173 in bills from a counter and fled."[91]

August 15, 1935: The morning's *Washington Post* reported "the fastest infield in colored professional baseball is that of the Pittsburgh Crawfords, playing Philadelphia here tonight."[92]

This may have been a makeup of the August 13 rainout – but was this game ever played? It was right in the nation's capital, but we cannot answer the question.

### August 17, 1935:
### Homestead Grays 5,
### Pittsburgh Crawfords 4,
### at Greenlee Field

It was Strong against Hunter. Matlock entered the game as a pinch-runner for Hunter, but then it was Streeter who took over pitching duties in the eighth. It was just an eight-inning game, ended early due to darkness. All the scoring occurred in the first six innings. The Grays scored twice and the Crawfords once in the second inning. Each team added a run in the third. In the fifth the Crawfords tied it, with two runs to the Grays' one. The Grays took a 5-4 lead in the sixth and that remained the score at the end. The Grays outhit the Craws eight to seven, and five of the hits were doubled. Bankhead had three of Pittsburgh's seven hits, one of them a double.

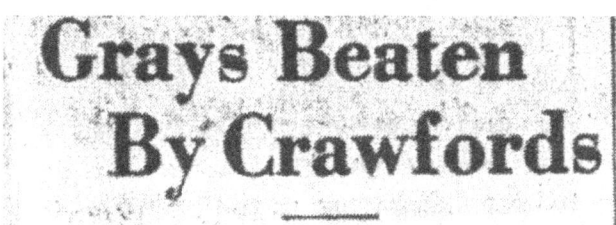

Unidentified newspaper.

### August 18, 1935:
### Pittsburgh Crawfords 10,
### Homestead Grays 6 (first game),
### at Cleveland Stadium, Cleveland

The first game saw Homestead's Vic Harris touch up Johnny Davis for a homer, a triple, and a double, but Davis otherwise handled the Grays satisfactorily. Though he gave up six runs, the Craws scored 10 off Willie Gisentaner and Tom Parker. A reported 5,800 fans watched the game.

**AUGUST 18, 1935:**
**PITTSBURGH CRAWFORDS 1,**
**HOMESTEAD GRAYS 0 (SECOND GAME),**
**AT CLEVELAND STADIUM, CLEVELAND**

The *Pittsburgh Courier* declared the second game a "classic – one of the finest baseball exhibitions ever witnessed here … a masterful pitcher's battle between [Ray] Brown of the Grays and Matlock of the Crawfords, each twirler allowing but 3 hits apiece."[93] It was the third hit for the Crawfords that won the planned seven-inning game. Tied after seven, they played the eighth and that's when the Crawfords won it "on a hit by Perkins, a walk, fielder's choice and Carlyle's [Matt Carlisle] wild throw trying to nip Perkins at the plate."[94]

**AUGUST 19, 1935:**
**PITTSBURGH CRAWFORDS 9,**
**HOMESTEAD GRAYS 3,**
**AT LEAGUE PARK, AKRON, OHIO**

The Crawfords were back in Akron (see August 1), and this game drew maybe 1,000 more fans – a reported 2,500.[95] As with the August 1 game, they collected 15 hits. The Grays jumped on Sam Streeter for three runs in the top of the first inning. Before the inning was over, Spoon Carter had come on in relief to stop the onslaught. He secured the third out, and then pitched the rest of the game, without giving up a run. The Craws went to work in the second, scoring twice when Gibson and Charleston both singled, with Williams doubling both baserunners home. Pat Patterson homered over the right-field fence to tie things up in the bottom of the third. Charleston singled again in the fourth and scored on three errors. He took second when Buck Leonard misplayed the throw in from right field. Backing up the play, the catcher, Robert Gaston, threw the ball wildly into left field and Charleston chugged nto third base. When Vic Harris threw the ball wildly toward home plate, Charleston scored.

The Crawfords scored three more runs in the seventh inning. Williams and Gibson were each 3-for-4. One of Gibson's hits was a home run.

**AUGUST 21, 1935:**
**PITTSBURGH CRAWFORDS 5,**
**MADISON BLUES 2,**
**AT BREESE STEVENS FIELD, MADISON, WISCONSIN**

The highlight of this game was a triple play. Sam Streeter pitched for Pittsburgh; Bill Goff started for the Blues. The Crawfords scored twice in the first, twice in the second, and once in the third, and then took the rest of the night off as far as offense goes. The Blues scored single runs in the sixth and eighth. Perkins and Gibson both tripled for Pittsburgh; Perkins had two RBIs. In the bottom of the first, the Blues' leadoff batter, Joe Hady, reached base on a bad throw by Curtis "Moochy" Harris, playing third base. Art Bramhall singled to left. Hady stopped at second. The second baseman, Ray Gaffke, "hit a sizzling liner to Harris, and the runners were off at the crack of the bat; Harris speared the drive, threw to Patterson to double Hady, and Patterson shot the ball to Josh Gibson to catch Bramhall."[96]

The Crawfords may have been practicing their baserunning; they "hustled every minute and ran the bases like mad men."[97] They stole five bases but also got caught five times.

**AUGUST 22, 1935:**
**MADISON BLUES 2,**
**PITTSBURGH CRAWFORDS 1 (10 INNINGS),**
**AT BREESE STEVENS FIELD, MADISON, WISCONSIN**

The excitement of the previous evening brought out 2,250 fans to watch a rematch of the two teams. There was no triple play, but it was a well-fought battle that ran to 10 innings and saw the home team prevail. Blues starter Alvin "Butch" Krueger allowed just nine scattered hits. Only in the eighth inning was there more than one base hit. Leading off the bottom of the 10th, he singled, ran to third on Hady's double, and scored the winning run on a fly ball by Bramhall.

Hady had a triple and a double, in addition to his second double that put Krueger on third. And in the top of the 10th, he made a spectacular running catch that saved at least one and maybe two runs. Bankhead had singled to lead off the 10th and taken second on Patterson's sacrifice. Gibson was walked intentionally. Perkins came to the plate and hit the ball over Hady's head to deep left-center. Hady caught it running toward the outfield fence and threw back in.

The Crawfords got their one run in the sixth. Madison got theirs in the seventh, off the starter, Kincannon. The Craws pitcher almost cost himself the game. After giving up the run, when he was pulled for a reliever, rather than hand the ball over, he "threw it over the grandstand in a pettish gesture."[98] A Blues runner ran across the plate, claiming Kincannon had thereby put the ball in play. Umpire Slim Lewis waved him back to third base.

The August 24 *Pittsburgh Courier*, reflecting a story written before publication date, said the Crawfords were going to play in Gary on the 23rd. Did they? Inquiries to Gary libraries and historical societies turned up nothing.

### August 24, 1935:
### Pittsburgh Crawfords 11,
### Chicago American Giants 8 (19 innings),
### at Cole's 39th Street Park, Chicago

The longest game of the season took 19 innings to conclude. It took 3 hours and 30 minutes to play. Harvey started, relieved by Kincannon and then the ultimate winning pitcher, Hunter.

## CRAWFORDS WIN FROM GIANTS IN 19TH, 11 TO 8

*Chicago Daily Tribune*, August 25, 1935.

Chicago scored one run in the bottom of the first. Pittsburgh tied it in the second, but the Giants quickly put up three more runs. In the top of the third, the Craws scored three times, to even the score once again, 4-4. For the third time, Chicago took the lead, adding two runs in the fifth and another in the sixth. They held the 7-4 lead until the top of the ninth. The Crawfords tied the game for the third time, sending it into extra innings. In the 11th inning, Pittsburgh scored once, but now it was Chicago's turn to tie it up, and they did. Neither team scored for the next seven innings, but in the 19th the Crawfords scored three runs, and Hunter held the Giants at bay.

The Crawfords scored 21 hits to Chicago's 13. All but one of the game's 10 extra-base hits were off the bats of Pittsburgh batters. So were both sacrifices, and three of the five stolen bases. Cool Papa Bell had six hits – five singles and a double.

### August 25, 1935:
### Chicago American Giants 10,
### Pittsburgh Crawfords 9 (first game),
### at Cole's Park, Chicago

The first game on Sunday was another high-scoring, close game, but almost all the scoring was done in the first five innings. The Giants held a 10-8 lead after five, allowing just one final Crawfords run in the ninth. To date, researchers have been unable to turn up a box score.

### August 25, 1935:
### Pittsburgh Crawfords 7,
### Chicago American Giants 5 (second game),
### at Cole's Park, Chicago

In the words of the *Afro-American*, "the mighty Matlock of the Craws took the Giants in hand in the second game."[99] He pitched a game and held down the run total, with eight scattered hits. The Giants didn't score at all for the first five innings but then started accumulating runs as the game wore on.

# THE 1935 PITTSBURGH CRAWFORDS

AUGUST 27, 1935:
PITTSBURGH CRAWFORDS 17,
CHICAGO AMERICAN GIANTS 2,
AT BORCHERT FIELD, MILWAUKEE

The *Milwaukee Sentinel* was a little harsh on the Giants, writing that the team "cocky as Maxie Baer at his best because of three previous high class showings here, went down to inglorious defeat before the Pittsburgh Crawfords at Borchert Field last night in a National Negro league game."[100] Mule Suttles and Turkey Stearnes were both out with injuries, but it was the pitcher, Bancy Thomas, who suffered the most, left in the entire game while giving up 17 runs on 21 hits. Spoon Carter pitched for Pittsburgh, allowing nine hits and only solo runs in the second and third innings. The Crawfords had started things off with a bang, an explosion of six runs in the top of the first. They put up five more in the third. Everyone in the Crawfords lineup had multiple base hits except Judy Johnson, who had just one, and Oscar Charleston, who had none at all. Patterson added five hits to his season total.

AUGUST 28, 1935:
PITTSBURGH CRAWFORDS 8,
CHICAGO AMERICAN GIANTS 3,
AT BORCHERT FIELD, MILWAUKEE

It was Ladies' Night and Sam Streeter pitched a superb game, a one-hitter through the first eight innings. Chicago had scored one run in the first, but no more. Patterson and Gibson homered for the Crawfords, who piled up runs one or two at a time, scoring in five different innings. In the bottom of the ninth, Streeter weakened and gave up two solo home runs. It was still a three-hitter, and the Crawfords won with ease.

AUGUST 29, 1935:
PITTSBURGH CRAWFORDS 10,
POSTUMS 4,
AT ALUMNI FIELD, DOWAGIAC, MICHIGAN

This game was held as part of a "homecoming celebration" in Dowagiac and more than 2,000 fans turned out for a Thursday afternoon game.[101] The Postums were a semipro team from Battle Creek, and they put up a decent fight against the Crawfords. Carroll Grimm, manager of the Postums, pitched the full game. The Crawfords scored once in the top of the first inning on Bell's walk and stolen base, and then a double by Patterson. Kincannon started for Pittsburgh, but was knocked out of the box in the bottom of the second when the Postums (dubbed the "Cereals" in one newspaper) scored four runs off him. Johnny Davis took over and pitched the rest of the game.

The Crawfords got one back in the third and added three more to take the lead for good in the top of the fourth. With the score 5-4 after eight innings, the Crawfords cut loose with five runs in the top of the ninth to put the game away for good. Each team made four errors. Cool Papa Bell starred on offense, 3-for-4 with two doubles. He scored three runs. Patterson, Charleston, and Harris each had a pair of hits.

AUGUST 30, 1935:
PITTSBURGH CRAWFORDS 5,
CHICKY GIANTS 3,
AT RAMONA ATHLETIC PARK, GRAND RAPIDS, MICHIGAN

The Friday night game was scheduled to begin at 5:30. Advance notices of the game in the *Grand Rapids Press* said the game was the first the Crawfords had ever played in the state of Michigan other than in Detroit. The game itself was a 5-3 win, a game "marked by brilliant fielding."[102] Carl Howard and Harry Kincannon pitched for the Crawfords.

AUGUST 31, 1935:
PITTSBURGH CRAWFORDS 11,
HOMESTEAD GRAYS 9,
AT SANDLOTTERS FIELD, DETROIT

Patterson homered in the first inning and the Crawfords scored three times. In the second inning, they knocked Homestead's starter, Joe Strong, out of the game. It was a "game marred by errors."[103] Pitching for the Crawfords, said the *Baltimore Afro-American*, was Williams – presumably shortstop Chester Williams.

# PITTSBURGH CRAWFORD 9 NIPS GRAYS

*Chicago Defender,* September 7, 1935: 15.

**SEPTEMBER 1, 1935:**
**HOMESTEAD GRAYS 10,**
**PITTSBURGH CRAWFORDS 9,**
**AT OFFERMANN STADIUM, BUFFALO, NEW YORK**

Offermann Stadium was the home ballpark for the International League's Buffalo Bisons. The *Buffalo Courier-Express* promoted the 3:00 P.M. game, declaring, "Fans and followers of colored baseball have been clamoring for an opportunity to see such a meeting in or near this vicinity for a long time."[104] The *Buffalo Evening News* said it was a regular league game, originally scheduled to be played in Pittsburgh "but transferred here to satisfy the demands of local fans."[105] Despite the buildup, none of the Buffalo newspapers appear to have provided any report on the actual game, which the close score suggests must have held some excitement. SABR member Brian M. Frank says that the day after the game, September 2, was Labor Day and neither the *Buffalo News* nor the *Buffalo Times* published that day. The *Courier-Express* did, but didn't mention the game.

**SEPTEMBER 2, 1935:**
**HOMESTEAD GRAYS 8,**
**PITTSBURGH CRAWFORDS 7 (FIRST GAME),**
**AT GREENLEE FIELD**

The Crawfords scored twice in the first and the Grays got one, then they tied the game with a run in the bottom of the third. The Grays then took the lead, adding two in the fourth, one in the sixth, and three in the seventh. Davis, Hunter, and Kincannon were the Craws pitchers. The Crawfords put a scare in the Grays, racking up four runs in the eighth and coming within a run of tying the game in the ninth, but falling a run short.

**SEPTEMBER 2, 1935:**
**PITTSBURGH CRAWFORDS 7,**
**HOMESTEAD GRAYS 3 (SECOND GAME),**
**AT GREENLEE FIELD**

Matlock pitched and the Crawfords earned a split in the doubleheader. He allowed six hits, while the Crawfords collected a dozen. The Grays scored once in the top of the first; the Crawfords matched that in the bottom of the inning. The Grays topped that with two runs in the second, and the Crawfords fought back with five runs in the bottom of the second. They added a seventh run in the fourth inning, and did not bat in the bottom of the seventh, when the second game concluded.

September 4, 1935: "Colored Nines Clash" – according to the *Cleveland Plain Dealer*, the Grays and Crawfords were to play a 9 P.M. game in Cleveland, with a girls' softball game at 8. It is conceivable this was the game planned for September 5, and the newspaper was mistaken. The next day's *Plain Dealer* said the game was to be *that* evening, but that the Grays would be playing "the Nashville Elites instead of the Pittsburgh Crawfords."[106]

**SEPTEMBER 5, 1935:**
**HOMESTEAD GRAYS VS.**
**PITTSBURGH CRAWFORDS,**
**AT CLEVELAND STADIUM (GAME CANCELED).**

The game was planned for Thursday night, September 5. The advertisement for the game in the August 25 *Cleveland Call and Post* offered readers a number of good reasons to attend the game. Not only were these two first-rate Negro League teams, but before the main game started at 9 P.M., there was a "Girls' Game" planned at

## THE 1935 PITTSBURGH CRAWFORDS

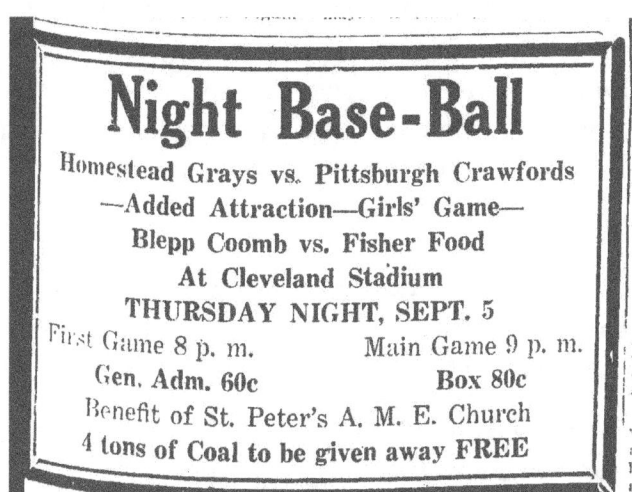

*Cleveland Call and Post,* August 29, 1935: 7.

8. The two teams were Blepp Coomb vs. Fisher Food. The evening itself was a benefit for St. Peter's A.M.E. Church. Most enticing of all, however, was the featured element: "4 tons of Coal to be given away FREE."

The Crawfords didn't show. "When game time arrived the Nashville Elites walked out upon the field instead of the Craws. Why the substitution?" That was the question posed in the September 12 *Call and Post* by writer Bill Finger.[107] The "Greenlee clan" canceled, Finger wrote, and Cum Posey of the Grays invited the Nashville team to come up from Philadelphia and play. Gus Greenlee was "said to have threatened to throw Nashville out of the league if they played the game. Finally he gave permission to them."

Finger explained: "Cum was in the Crawford Grill in Smokytown Tuesday night." The rest of the paragraph lacks a starting quotation mark but it appears to be a lengthy comment from Cum Posey. "In walked Gus. He told me the game in Cleveland was off. I thought he was only joking, so waited until morning when Gus again reiterated his statement of the previous evening that he wouldn't play in Cleveland. So I called Nashville in Philly. Gus claimed that Jackson, our business manager, had insulted him. Now Jackson worked for Greenlee at one time. He recently sued Gus for back pay. So Gus said that he wouldn't ever play the Grays until we got rid of Sonny. After I got Nashville to come here he was willing to go through with the game. But I couldn't turn down Tom Wilson's club after getting them on short notice." Six more paragraphs follow, with details that are difficult to decipher nearly a century later. It ended with the following: "It certainly wasn't the sporting thing to assist in creating troubles for a rival promoter."

### SEPTEMBER 7, 1935:
### NEW YORK CUBANS 9,
### PITTSBURGH CRAWFORDS 3 (FIRST GAME),
### AT HINCHLIFFE CITY STADIUM, PATERSON, NEW JERSEY

Kincannon had a rough time of it, while the Cubans' Frank Blake allowed only four hits and struck out nine. One of the hits was a solo home run by Josh Gibson. Charleston had two hits. The Cubans collected 13 base hits; Blake himself had two doubles. Martin Dihigo had a triple and drove in three runs. First baseman Lazaro Salazar tripled and was also credited with three runs batted in. More than 4,000 fans took in the game at Paterson, played in 2½ hours.

### SEPTEMBER 7, 1935:
### PHILADELPHIA STARS 5,
### PITTSBURGH CRAWFORDS 3 (SECOND GAME),
### AT PRR YMCA FIELD, 44TH & PARKSIDE, PHILADELPHIA

Playing under the floodlights, Bill Harvey was hammered for four runs in the bottom of the first inning. Judd Wilson drove in two runs with a double and Jack Dunn drove in another two runs with another double. The four runs were enough to win the night game.[108]

There were two games reported as having occurred, but we question what really happened. The September 7 *Cleveland Gazette* said on its front page that the Crawfords and Grays "met in an exhibition game at the stadium on Wednesday night." That would make it September 4, the Wednesday. The past tense was used, but no score was reported. For something to appear on the front page of the paper, one wonders if an "e" was dropped, and the article intended to preview a September 11 game, that the two teams would "meet in an exhibition game at the stadium on Wednesday night."

Then there was the 18-word story in the *Pittsburgh Sun-Telegraph* on September 8, which read: "The original Crawfords scored an easy victory over the Kay Club yesterday. The score as 19 to 0."[109] No more details were provided. The reference to the "original Crawfords" may have been an old-timers team. Rich Bogovich explains: "In 1934 there was a team called the Old Crawfords, which was briefly called the Original Crawfords in 1932." He quotes a 1934 article in the *Courier*: "The original Crawford fans will have a chance to see their favorite players in action at Greenlee Field on Sunday, June 24th at 3 p.m., when the Old Crawfords meet the Homewood Club of the City League in a game which promises to be a thriller. The old Crawfords include Neal Harris, 'Showboat' Joe Ware, Kimbo, the giant pitcher; Claude Johnson, Charles Hughes, Bill Pope, Mellix, Rollan, the Talbert brothers and other stars. Don't miss seeing them in action."[110]

**SEPTEMBER 8, 1935:**
**PITTSBURGH CRAWFORDS 12,**
**BROOKLYN EAGLES 3,**
**AT EBBETS FIELD, BROOKLYN**

The Crispus Attucks Community Council held a charity doubleheader featuring the Crawfords, the Brooklyn Eagles, the Philadelphia Stars, and the New York Cubans at Ebbets Field. The Cubans and Stars played the first game, a 2-2 tie, and the Crawfords and Eagles played in the second.

Twelve runs on 15 hits off three Eagles pitchers helped the Crawfords (and Leroy Matlock, with a complete-game effort) win with ease, the Craws scoring eight runs in the seventh and eighth innings. Brooklyn scored three runs on eight hits. The Eagles committed two errors. Matlock and Judy Johnson both doubled; the "mighty Matlock" (*Courier*) had three hits. Crutchfield tripled. About 7,000 to 8,000 fans took in the game.

The *Philadelphia Tribune* wrote, "The devastating machine that the Pittsburgh Crawfords are so proud of moved its powerful way across the diamond and when the game was over the Brooklyn Eagles were just a small spot in the sod."[111]

**THE PLAYOFFS**

See the separate article on the 1935 playoffs by Rich Puerzer.

Other games:

**SEPTEMBER 10, 1935:**
**BELMAR BRAVES 1,**
**PITTSBURGH CRAWFORDS 0 (11 INNINGS),**
**AT MEMORIAL FIELD, BELMAR, NEW JERSEY**

For the second time in 1935, the Belmar Braves beat the Crawfords. (See July 12.) The Crawfords collected eight base hits but didn't ever score. Belmar had only two hits, but the second one won the game. With a runner on base in the bottom of the 11th inning, Belmar's Bill Arlington doubled and won the game. We do not know who pitched for the Crawfords.[112]

**SEPTEMBER 11, 1935: PITTSBURGH CRAWFORDS 12, ALCYON PARK 7, AT ALCYON PARK, PITMAN, NEW JERSEY**

The Alcyon Park team scored three runs in the first inning and three more in the second. Then Harvey buckled down, allowing just one seventh-inning run. He allowed six hits in the game. The Crawfords were blanked in only the second and fourth innings. The runs added up, with four runs in the top of the seventh producing the most runs in a given inning. The Craws had 21 base hits. Bankhead had four. Harris, Patterson, Johnson, and Williams each had three.

**SEPTEMBER 11, 1935:**
**BROOKLYN BUSHWICKS 3,**
**PITTSBURGH CRAWFORDS 1,**
**AT DEXTER PARK, QUEENS, NEW YORK**

Was this night game played on the same day as the game at Alcyon Park? Yes, it was an "arc-light tilt."[113] The *New York Daily News* reported on September 12 that "Dazzy Vance's fastball was responsible for another Bushwick victory last night as the Pittsburgh Crawfords, first half negro league winners, were beaten, 3 to 1, at Dexter Park. Vance, toiling for the first three innings, yielded only one hit and struck out four."[114]

### September 14, 1935:
### New York Cubans 4,
### Pittsburgh Crawfords 0,
### at PRR YMCA Field, 44th & Parkside, Philadelphia

Only the fourth time the Crawfords were shut out, it was at the hands of left-hander John Wesley "Neck" Stanley, who struck out five and allowed only four hits but surprisingly walked nine. Roosevelt Davis didn't walk any. He struck out three, but he allowed 11 hits. The scoring came with three runs in the fifth and one in the sixth. Roy Spearman's three-run homer accounted for the fifth-inning runs. The game drew about 2,000, attendance depressed a bit by "lowering skies."[115] It was an unusual game in that four umpires worked, rather than the more usual two. The *Afro-American* commented, "The game was delayed by more than thirty-five minutes because three of the umpires were reported not to know what park was to house the battle. The fourth ump, Bert Gholston, was in the park an hour before the zero hour, however." Patterson, Perkins Gibson, and Bankhead each had a hit for the Crawfords, none for extra bases.

### September 16:
### Pittsburgh Crawfords 14,
### House of David 4,
### at Cricket Field, Altoona, Pennsylvania

The 8:00 P.M. benefit game saw "a good crowd on hand" as the Crawfords "completely slaughtered" the Whiskers, 14-4. The *Altoona Tribune* said "[T]here was practically nothing to thegame but the all around hitting and playing of the Pittsburg crew. They scored at will and accumulated 23 hits including nine doubles."[116] It was also noted that "the pepper game drew much applause." The eight-run fourth inning was the big one for the Craws. Johnson and Patterson each drove in four runs. Patterson was 5-for-6 at the plate. Streeter worked the full game, allowing eight hits.

### September 22, 1935:
### Pittsburgh Crawfords 12,
### Philadelphia Stars 2,
### at Yankee Stadium, the Bronx

More than 15,000 fans flocked into Yankee Stadium, many expecting to see Satchel Paige pitch for the Crawfords. Gus Greenlee explained, reported the *New York Age*, that Paige had "stopped off in Chicago enroute east and while there was offered $500 to pitch for the Kansas City Monarchs on Sunday. This caused him to forget all about his agreement."[117] They still saw a dominant Crawfords team. Carter pitched for Pittsburgh, giving up two runs on 10 hits. The Crawfords had all the triples and home runs in the game: Chester Williams hit two homers; Perkins and Patterson each hit one, while Gibson, Perkins, and Bankhead each tripled.

### September 23, 1935:
### Pittsburgh Crawfords 6,
### New York Cubans 4,
### at Dyckman Oval, Manhattan

The Crawfords last league game of the season. After the game Gus Greenlee gave his championship team a banquet.

### September 26, 1935:
### Pittsburgh Crawfords 4,
### Alcyon Park 1,
### at Pitman, New Jersey

The night game was the last of the season for the Alcyon Park team. Hunter pitched for the

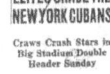

*New York Amsterdam News*, September 28, 1935: 13.

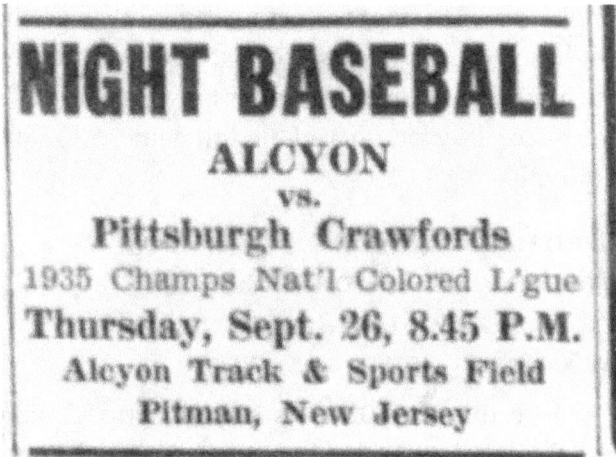

Newspaper ad before game against Alcyon. *Daily Journal* (Vineland, New Jersey). September 25, 1935: 12.

Crawfords and allowed seven hits and one second-inning run. The run evened the game at 1-1, Pittsburgh having scored in the top of the first. In the top of the fourth, Bankhead walked and Johnson singled. Then Hunter tripled, driving them both in. He scored when Williams hit the ball to the third baseman, who committed an error. From that point on, the game was without further scoring.

### September 27, 1935:
### Bushwicks 3,
### Pittsburgh Crawfords 0,
### at Dexter Park, Queens, New York

The Crawfords were the cream of the crop in 1935 – "rulers of the Negro baseball domain" – yet, wrote the *New York Amsterdam News*, "there is always a smudge on their escutcheon which reads – Bushwicks four victories and two defeats in the 1935 series with the champions."[118] Pitching for the Bushwicks was Jimmy Pattison, who had pitched for Toronto in the International League during the regular season. He shut out the Crawfords despite the Craws outhitting the Bushwicks, 11 hits to 4. Roosevelt Davis and Josh Gibson each had three hits. One of Gibson's hits went 400 feet, but he was held to a triple and did not score. Pitcher Matlock played first base. The Bushwicks scored once in the first and two in the third. Pattison struck out seven Crawfords;

Pittsburgh left 11 men on base. The game was played in a crisp 1:30.

### October 4:

There might have been a postseason game in Charleston, West Virginia, on this date, but we've not been able to confirm that.

### October 6, 1935:

The *Plain Dealer* of Cleveland announced a doubleheader involving "four of the greatest colored baseball teams in the country" meeting at 1:30 that afternoon at League Park. The Crawfords were to play the Nashville Elites, and the Philadelphia Stars were to play the Brooklyn Eagles. We have yet to find information about the games.

### October 9, 1935:
### Pittsburgh Crawfords 5, Dayton
### Shroyers 2 (10 innings),
### at Duck's Park, Dayton, Ohio

This game featured three St. Louis Cardinals helping out the locals. Dizzy Dean was one of them. The other two were Mike Ryba and Jim Winford, both pitchers in the Cardinals farm system who had been brought up from Columbus after the American Association season was over. Three thousand fans came to the game. The *Canton Repository* informs us that "Dean pitched two innings and then played the remainder of the game in the outfield."[119] Dean struck out four, and then played right field.

Neither team scored for four innings. The Crawfords scored twice in the top of fifth, on starting pitcher Leroy Matlock's two-run homer (off Ryba) which exited the park over the left-field wall. The 2-0 lead was matched by two runs by the Shroyers in the bottom of the sixth. Ryba had begun the game as catcher, and finished it at first base.

Dean came up with the bases loaded in the bottom of the seventh, but grounded into an inning-ending double play. The game remained tied, 2-2, after nine innings. In both the eighth and ninth the Shroyers got runners as far as third base, but did not score. In the top of the 10th the Crawfords got two men on base and Cotton Williams doubled them both in, then scored himself on Josh Gibson's single.

October 13, 1935: The October 9 *New Orleans Item* announced a game at Heinemann Park on Sunday the 13th between the Crawfords and a "picked team of Negro ball players."

**October 15, 1935:**
**Pittsburgh Crawfords 4,**
**Monroe Monarchs 4**
**(tie, 12 innings),**
**at Casino Park, Monroe, Louisiana**

A Tuesday afternoon game resulted in a 4-4 tie, and players from both teams "almost mobbed the umpire because he called the game on account of darkness."[120] After they acceded to the umpire's decision, the two managers, Frank Johnson of the Monarchs and Oscar Charleston of the Crawfords, "engaged in a heated verbal battle" and they decided to play another game on October 16, declaring that they would play that one to the finish, regardless of how dark it might become. The Crawfords had been scheduled to play a game in Austin, Texas on the 16th, but Charleston reportedly said, "Hang the Austin game. We stay here and finish this mess up. We'll either make 'em or break 'em."[121]

**October 16, 1935:**

Was there a game in Monroe? Did the Crawfords turn up in Austin at some point on their way to Mexico? The next day's *Monroe News-Star* has no mention of either team engaging in a game of any sort. The *Austin Statesman* provides no information.

**October 20, 1935:**

The October 17 *Houston Chronicle* announced two games to be played starting at 2:30 P.M. on Sunday, October 20, at Houston's West End Park between the Crawfords and the Texas Centennials, "champions of the Negro Dixie League." The games were said to be part of a series that would also feature games in Austin and Dallas.

Somewhat upping the ante, the October 18 *Chronicle* billed this as the "Negro World Series."

The October 20 paper said that Satchel Paige would pitch for the Crawfords and that "half of the grandstand will be reserved for white fans." The brief article also listed "Gosh Gibson" as among the Pittsburgh players. Despite the extreme unlikelihood of Paige and the Crawfords working together after the rupture of their relationship earlier in 1935, the notion of this being a "Negro World Series" also seemed fanciful.

One gathers that at least one game of some sort was played. The November 3 *Houston Chronicle*, while announcing a West End Park game that afternoon between the Texas Centennials and Parnell's Negro All-Stars, said, "The Centennials are managed by Chuffie Alexander and are champions of the South, losing only to the Crawfords."[122] If nothing else, this suggests that the Crawfords did play the Centennials, for at least one game.

To end their year, the Crawfords ventured south of the border, to Mexico.

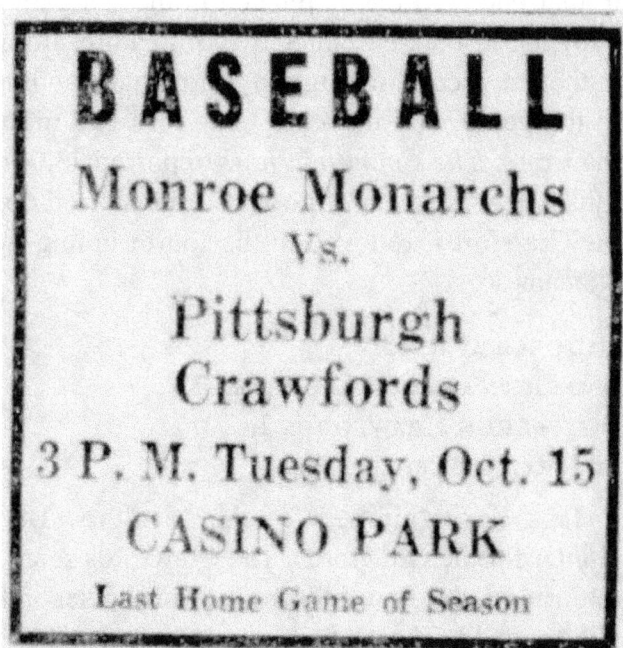

Newspaper advertisement before game in Monroe. *Monroe News-Star* (Monroe, Louisiana). October 14, 1935: 5.

They met up with a team of ballplayers from the American League in Mexico City for a three-game series.

After the major-league baseball season, Earl Mack and a group of American Leaguers (including Rogers Hornsby) traveled to Mexico and played a number of games in locales such as Nuevo Laredo, Puebla, Pachuca, Veracruz, and Mexico City. Among Mack's players were Jimmie Foxx, Ted Lyons, Earl Whitehill, Roger Cramer, Charlie Berry, Eric McNair, Pinky Higgins, Vernon Kennedy, Jack Knott, and Red Kress.

### October 25, 1935:
### American League All-Stars 6, Pittsburgh Crawfords 6
### (11 innings), at Mexico City

On October 25, the All-Stars took on the Pittsburgh Crawfords. J.M. Campos wrote up the game for *The Sporting News*. His account:

"[T]he All-Stars came back on October 25, to stage a thrilling 6 to 6 11-inning tie with the Pittsburgh Crawfords, before 10,000 excited fans. Earl Whitehill and Leroy Matlock, the colored team's pitching ace, staged a duel until the ninth inning, when the Crawfords scored four runs, thanks to a pinch home run by Palm, who batted for Matlock, to take a two-run lead. Jimmy Foxx of the All-Stars, however, tied it up in their half, driving in two runs with a circuit clout.

"Both teams then went scoreless until the eleventh when, with the bases full, Foxx again came to bat, with one out. He sent a terrific smash over third base. Johnson got hold of it, dropped it and picked it up again. McNair chased home and Johnson threw to the catcher, who touched home, but not the runner. However, it was claimed that Johnson stepped on third, while making the throw, and that the force had been removed. There was plenty of argument, but the decision stood and the next out ended the inning and the game, the umpires calling quits on account of darkness, but the arguments continued far into the night."[123] The All-Stars had scored first, with one run in the bottom of the first. The Crawfords tied it with one in the top of the second, then took a 2-1 lead with another run in the top of the third. The All-Stars regained the lead, 3-2, with a run in the bottom of the third, and added another run in the bottom of the seventh. So it stood until the ninth when, as Sr. Campos described, the Craws scored four times and the All-Stars came by with two.

Johnny Davis took over pitching duties for Matlock after the Palm pinch hit. RBIs in the game were by Gibson, Charleston, Bankhead, and Palm (2) for the Crawfords, and Foxx (3), Cramer (2), and Higgins for the All-Stars. The Palm in question was almost certainly Clarence Palm, who had been a Crawford for part of 1934 and was with them in April 1935.

### October 26, 1935:
### American League All-Stars 11, Pittsburgh Crawfords 1,
### at Mexico City

It was a three-game series between the Crawfords and the All-Stars. The All-Stars prevailed in the second and third games, 11-1 and 7-2. Hornsby homered in each game. So did Cramer in the second game; Heinie Manush had four hits in that one. Ted Lyons pitched in the 11-1 game, allowing just six base hits, two of them resulting in the one second-inning run. Harris had two hits in the game, and no other Crawford had more than one. *The Sporting News* reported 13,000 fans at the game.[124] Spoon Carter started for the Crawfords, relieved in the fourth inning by Kincannon.

### October 27, 1935:
### American League All-Stars 7, Pittsburgh Crawfords 2,
### at Mexico City

Jack Knott pitched for the All-Stars, Bert Hunter for the Crawfords. The Crawfords scored one run in the first and one run in the second. Gibson and Bell each had one run batted in. With the score tied, 2-2, Hornsby came up to bat in the third inning with two baserunners on. He hammered the ball "so far that two outfielders chasing the ball were not able to catch up with it before he crossed the plate." The All-Stars padded the resulting 5-2 lead with two more runs later in the game.

The *Pittsburgh Courier* had almost no coverage of the trip, save for one sentence reporting that the All-Stars had won two of the three games, and then this remark in its December 14 edition: "Pittsburgh Crawfords have returned from Mexico. The boys all report a fine trip."[125]

A week later, looking back on the season, Posey wrote, "Let's give a little credit to some of the boys who have been in baseball a long time, for their work in 1935. Oscar Charleston of Pittsburgh Crawfords, over whom there was some question in 1934 concerning his managerial ability, led the Crawfords to the championship with a team which on paper was the weakest they have had since 1931. Charleston's hitting, fielding and all around playing was one of the features of the Crawford team in 1935."[126]

### Acknowledgments

Thanks to Gary Ashwill of Seamheads, who responded to all my requests for information and helped locate quite a few games that were proving difficult to pin down. After the article seemed nearly complete, Rich Bogovich supplied several dozen clippings, many of which were ones I had not previously seen. Rick Bush came up with a score of helpful newspaper clippings. Thanks also to Ted Knorr for the *Harrisburg Telegraph*.

Thanks for research assistance to Colleen Alles of the Grand Rapids Public Library; Nathan Bierma; Matt Blaeuer; Rich Bogovich; Michael Broe; Thomas Brubaker; Rick Bush; Alan Cohen; Brian M. Frank; Greg Gajus; Kay Gray, Dowagiac District Library; Peggy Gripshover; Bill McMahon; Lora D. Peppers (Ouachita Parish Public Library, Monroe, Louisiana); Roger Parmelee; Bob Savitt; Blake W. Sherry.

### Notes

1 "Training Camp News," *The Negro Star*, April 12, 1935.
2 "Training Camp News." All spellings of names are as they were in the newspaper article.
3 "Craws Top Memphis, to Play in Orleans," *Pittsburgh Courier*, April 20, 1935: 17.
4 "Hunter Hurls 1-Hit Game, 'Cool Papa' Gets 6 Hits as Craws Win," *Pittsburgh Courier*, April 20, 1935: 17.
5 "Piney Woods to Play Pitt Team," *Jackson Clarion-Ledger*, April 15, 1935: 5.
6 "Collegians Win and Lose with Crawfords," *Baltimore Afro-American*, May 11, 1935: 20.
7 "Crawfords Victors Over College Nine," *Pittsburgh Sun-Telegraph*, April 19, 1935: 33.
8 "Craws Win and Lose One," *Pittsburgh Courier*, April 27, 1935: 17.
9 Hayward Jackson, "Monroe Monarchs Show Class in Early Games," *Chicago Defender*, May 11, 1935: 14.
10 "Crawfords Lose One," *Pittsburgh Post-Gazette*, April 22, 1935: 18.
11 "Crawfords Beat Acme," *Pittsburgh Post-Gazette*, April 24, 1935: 17.
12 "Crawfords Winners," *Pittsburgh Press*, April 26, 1935: 48.
13 "Crawfords Cop Two from Louisiana Stars," *Chicago Defender*, May 4, 1935: 9.
14 "Crawfords Ahead," *Pittsburgh Post-Gazette*, April 26, 1935: 21; "Crawfords Win," *Pittsburgh Sun-Telegraph*, April 26, 1935: 36.
15 "Crawfords Beat Louisiana," *Pittsburgh Post-Gazette*, April 27, 1935: 17.
16 "Craws Beat Cubans, 6-4," *Pittsburgh Courier*, May 4, 1935: 13.
17 "Orchestra Will Jazz Up Ball Game," *Hattiesburg American*, April 26, 1935.
18 "Another for Crawfords," *Pittsburgh Post-Gazette*, May 1, 1935.
19 "Laurel Black Cats Warm Up at Greenwood," *Laurel (Mississippi) Leader*, April 13, 1935: 7. The *Courier* reported the Pittsburgh pitcher as "Roy Kincannon." See "Craws Claw Cats," *Pittsburgh Courier*, May 4, 1935: 15.
20 "Negro Ball Clubs Clash Tomorrow," *Jackson (Mississippi) Clarion-Ledger*, April 30, 1935.
21 "Cum Posey's Pointed Paragraphs," *Pittsburgh Courier*, May 4, 1935: 14.
22 "Tigers Rained Out," *Cincinnati Enquirer*, May 10, 1935: 35.
23 "Cubans, Craws Vie Saturday," *Pittsburgh Courier*, May 11, 1935: 15.
24 "Crawfords Win 2, Tie Pair in Series with N.Y.," *Pittsburgh Courier*, May 18, 1935: 14.
25 "Crawfords Win 2, Tie Pair in Series with N.Y."
26 "Crawfords Win 2, Tie Pair in Series with N.Y."
27 "Crawfords in Tie," *Pittsburgh Sun-Telegraph*, May 14, 1935: 26.
28 "Crawfords Tripped," *Pittsburgh Post-Gazette*, May 15, 1935: 19.

29  *Mississippi Weekly*, May 18, 1935: 4.

30  "Chicago Faces Crawfords," *Pittsburgh Sun-Telegraph*, May 18, 1935: 10.

31  "Craws in First Place After Chi Series," *Pittsburgh Courier*, May 25, 1935: 16.

32  "Craws in First Place After Chi Series."

33  "Giants and Crawfords Split Four Games," *Chicago Defender*, May 25, 1935: 14.

34  "Giants and Crawfords Split Four Games."

35  "Pittsburgh Beats Chicago Giants, 10-3," *Gazette and Daily* (York, Pennsylvania), May 23, 1935: 10.

36  "Lefty Vincent Is Added to Mound Staff of Locals," *Bismarck* (North Dakota) *Tribune*, May 22, 1935: 6.

37  "Hurls One-Hit Game," *Pittsburgh Post-Gazette*, May 24, 1935: 19.

38  *Pittsburgh Sun-Telegraph*, May 25, 1935: 10.

39  "Crawfords Win 3 from Philly; Lead League," *Baltimore Afro American*, June 1, 1935: 21.

40  "Crack Colored Teams Play at Eagle Park," *Gazette and Daily* (York, Pennsylvania), May 28, 1935: 10.

41  "Philadelphia All-Stars Shut Out Pittsburg Crawfords, 9-0," *Gazette and Daily* (York, Pennsylvania), May 29, 1935: 10.

42  "Craws Have Easy Time with Stars," *Philadelphia Tribune*, June 6, 1935: 10.

43  "Crawfords Take Two from Phila. Stars," *Philadelphia Inquirer*, May 31, 1935: 19.

44  "Newark Dodgers Lose 2 More Games," *Newark Star-Eagle*, June 3, 1935: 20.

45  "Gibson's Prodigious Homer Paves Way for Crawfords Victory Over Dodgers," *Daily Home News* (New Brunswick, New Jersey), June 4, 1935: 12.

46  "Dexters Hope to Cop Tilts," *New York Amsterdam News*, June 15, 1935: 15.

47  So reported the *Citizen*. "Duffy's Great Pitching and Beazley's Bat Win for Bushwicks in Tenth," *Brooklyn Citizen*, June 8, 1935: 6. Thanks to Gary Ashwill for the Brooklyn clippings.

48  "Streeter's Home Run with 3 on Beats Chester," *Chester* (Pennsylvania) *Times*, June 14, 1935: 17.

49  "Pittsburgh Crawfords Meet All-Stars Tonight," *Philadelphia Tribune*, June 13, 1935: 11.

50  "Craws Cop Two Tilts by Scores of 6 to 5," *Pittsburgh Courier*, June 22, 1935: 15.

51  "Crawfords Drop Decision to Caps," *Nassau Daily Review*, June 17, 1935: 11.

52  "Crawfords Top Bolden's Stars," *Chester Times*, June 18, 1935: 13.

53  "Pro Baseball Game Is Off," *Daily Mail* (Hagerstown, Maryland), June 19, 1935: 9.

54  "Survey Shows Storm Damage Not So Heavy," *Daily Mail*, June 19, 1935: 1, 12.

55  "Slate Ball Game," *New York Daily News*, June 20, 1935: 73.

56  "Rector and Spearman Black Yankee Stars," *Springfield* (Massachusetts) *Republican,* July 4, 1935: 10.

57  *Jersey Journal* (Jersey City), July 27, 1935: 9.

58  "Craws Win 4, Lose 2, Tie 1 in Gray Feud," *Pittsburgh Courier,* July 13, 1935: 15.

59  "Grays and Crawfords to Meet Twice Today," *Pittsburgh Post-Gazette,* July 6, 1935: 14.

60  "2,500 See Game in Rain," *Evening Star* (Washington), July 9, 1935: 14.

61  "Colored Nines Set for Battle," *Hagerstown* (Maryland) *Morning Herald,* July 8, 1935: 7.

62  "Colored Pros Meet Tonight," *Hagerstown Daily Mail,* July 9, 1935: 9.

63  "Crawfords Winners," *Hagerstown Daily Mail,* July 10, 1935: 4.

64  "Crawfords Lost to Belmar Braves 5 to 3," *New York Amsterdam News,* July 20, 1935: 15.

65  "Joe Sephus' Cullings," *Cumberland* (Maryland) *Evening Times,* July 22, 1935: 4.

66  See a mention of midget auto racing on page 17 or the July 17 *Post-Gazette.*

67  "What! No Craws Games for Stars?" *Philadelphia Tribune,* July 11, 1935: 9.

68  "Crawfords Capture Flag for First Half," *Baltimore Afro-American,* July 13, 1935: 21.

69  "Crawfords Divide Two Twin Bills with Brooklyn," *Pittsburgh Courier,* July 20, 1935: 15.

70  "Matlock Tops League Pitchers," *Pittsburgh Courier,* July 20, 1935: 15.

71  "Negroes Can't Find 'Babe' Mitchell's Tosses; Lose, 5-1," *Chester Times,* July 17, 1935: 11.

72  "Fan of Edge for Colored Tilt," *The Sentinel* (Carlisle, Pennsylvania), July 17, 1935: 4.

73  "Sports of Sorts," *Hagerstown Daily Mail,* July 20, 1935: 7.

74  "Colored Teams Here Tomorrow," *The Sentinel* July 18, 1935: 4.

75  "Crawfords Bow to Giants, 11 to 4," *The Sentinel* July 20, 1935: 4.

76  "Crawfords Beat Chicago Giants," *Pittsburgh Sun-Telegraph,* July 21, 1935: 15.

77  "Crawfords Home," *Pittsburgh Press,* July 17, 1935: 24.

# THE 1935 PITTSBURGH CRAWFORDS

78 "Matlock Benched for Misconduct," *Pittsburgh Courier*, July 27, 1935: 15.

79 "Crawfords Beaten," *Pittsburgh Post-Gazette*, July 23, 1935: 20.

80 "Pittsburgh Nine Wins at Anderson," *Indianapolis Times*, July 27, 1935: 10.

81 "Crawfords at Crafton," *Pittsburgh Post-Gazette*, July 31, 1935: 20.

82 Email from Gary Ashwill, February 26, 2019.

83 "Crawfords Are Whitewashed," *New York Amsterdam News*, August 10, 1935: 15.

84 "Locals Split Even in Games with Davids and Italians," *Chester Times*, August 5, 1935: 10.

85 All quotations regarding this game come from "Chester Loses to Pittsburgh Crawfords in Slugfest, 7 to 3," *Chester Times*, August 6, 1935: 10.

86 "Chester Loses to Pittsburgh Crawfords in Slugfest, 7 to 3."

87 Wm. J. Granger, "Pittsburg Crawfords Hand Bad Beating to Bushwicks to Even Up Series at 2 Wins Apiece," *Brooklyn Citizen*, August 8, 1935: 6.

88 "Grays Win Night Tilt," *Evening Star* (Washington), August 10, 1935: A11.

89 "Bay Parkways Get Even Break," *Brooklyn Daily Eagle*, August 12, 1935: 8. Rick Bush figures "Gillispie" was Henry Gillespie, whose Negro League career had finished the year before, and Lackey was probably Obie Lackey, who had been with the Crawfords in 1933 and with the Philadelphia Stars in 1935. A. Cooper was probably Anthony Cooper, who had also been with the Crawfords in 1933. W. Cooper's first name is not known but Clark and Lester show him with the Bacharach Giants in 1935.

90 "Philly Stars on Top," *Evening Star* (Washington), August 15, 1935: 52.

91 "Robbers Get Cash and Clothing Here," *Evening Star* (Washington), August 15, 1935: 33.

92 "Post Mortems," *Washington Post*, August 15, 1935: 22.

93 "Crawfords Cop 3 Out of 4 in Series with Homestead Grays," *Pittsburgh Courier*, August 24, 1935: 14.

94 "Crawfords Win Over Grays Nine," *Pittsburgh Press*, August 19, 1935: 20.

95 The *Akron Beacon-Journal* reported 2,500, but the *Times-Press* reported 2,000. Oddly, both box scores reflect a 7-3 game. The *Times-Press* game account, however, says the Crawfords scored twice in the eighth (which would make it 9-3), on three hits, an error, and a wild pitch.

96 Henry J. McCormick, "Crawfords Complete Triple Play, Beat Blues, 5-2," *Wisconsin State Journal* (Madison), August 22, 1935.

97 "Crawfords Complete Triple Play, Beat Blues, 5-2."

98 Henry J. McCormick, "Blues Shade Crawfords in 10 innings, 2-1," *Wisconsin State Journal,* August 23, 1935.

99 "Craws Win in 19 Innings, 11-8, from Chicago Giants," *Baltimore Afro-American,* August 31, 1935: 20.

100 "Crawfords Tip Giants, 17 to 2," *Milwaukee Sentinel*, August 28, 1935.

101 "Pittsburgh Crawfords Collect 13 Hits to Beat Postums 10 to 4," *Dowagiac* (Michigan) *Daily News*, August 30, 1935.

102 *Grand Rapids* (Michigan) *Press*, August 31, 1935.

103 "Craws Trounce Grays in Detroit," *Baltimore Afro-American*, September 7, 1935: 20.

104 "Negro Teams Meet," *Buffalo Courier-Express*, August 29, 1935: 17.

105 "Crawfords to Play Grays Tomorrow in League Contest," *Buffalo Evening News,* August 31, 1935: 6.

106 "Grays Play Nashville," *Cleveland Plain Dealer,* September 5, 1935: 17. The article from the day before was "Crawfords Play Grays," *Cleveland Plain Dealer*, September 4, 1935: 15.

107 "Passing in Review," *Cleveland Call and Post*, September 12, 1935: 7.

108 "Stars Clip Crawfords 5-3," *Philadelphia Tribune*, September 12, 1935: 11.

109 "Easy for Crawfords," *Pittsburgh Sun-Telegraph*, September 8, 1935: 18.

110 "Old Crawfords Meet Homewood in Sunday Tilt," *Pittsburgh Courier*, June 23, 1934: section 2, 5.

111 "10,000 Watch Cubans Tie Stars in N.Y.," *Philadelphia Tribune*, September 12, 1935: 11.

112 "Braves Outhit, 8-2, Beat Crawfords, 1-0," *Daily Record* (Long Branch, New Jersey), September 11, 1935: 7.

113 "Dexters Top Pittsburgh Crawfords, 3 to 1," *Long Island* (New York) *Daily Press*, September 12, 1935: 16.

114 "Vance Hurls Bushwicks to 'Nother Win," *New York Daily News*, September 12, 1935.

115 "Cubans Win Two from Crawfords," *Baltimore Afro-American,* September 21, 1935: 21.

116 Os Figard, "Crawfords Hand Beards 14-4 Lacing," *Altoona Tribune*, September 17, 1935: 6.

117 "Satchel Paige Disappoints Ball Fans," *New York Age*, September 28, 1935: 8.

118 "Bushwicks Scalp Fast Crawfords and Cubans," *New York Amsterdam News*, October 5, 1935: 13.

119 "Card Twirlers Lose Fray to Pittsburgh Crawfords," *Repository* (Canton, Ohio), October 10, 1935. Dean's major- and minor-league records show no evidence he ever played any position other than pitcher in pro ball.

120 "Monarchs in Tie with Pittsburgh," *Monroe (Louisiana) News-Star*, October 16, 1935: 6.

121 "Monarchs in Tie with Pittsburgh."

122 "Negro Nines Play at West End Park," *Houston Chronicle*, November 3, 1935: 16.

123 J.M. Campos, "Hornsby's Playing Astounds Mexicans," *The Sporting News*, October 31, 1935: 5.

124 "A.L.'s All-Stars Settle an Argument in Mexico," *The Sporting News*, November 7, 1935: 8.

125 "Cum Posey's Pointed Paragraphs," *Pittsburgh Courier*, December 14, 1935: 15.

126 "Cum Posey's Pointed Paragraphs," *Pittsburgh Courier*, December 21, 1935: 13.

# MULE SUTTLES LEADS WEST TO 11-INNING VICTORY IN THIRD ANNUAL ALL-STAR CLASSIC
## AUGUST 11, 1935: WEST 11, EAST 8, AT COMISKEY PARK, CHICAGO

*By Frederick C. Bush*

The annual Negro League East-West All-Star Classic, played at Chicago's Comiskey Park, originated in 1933, with the West team triumphing, 11-7. After the East had answered in kind with a 1-0 win in 1934, interest in the annual game – which soon would become the highlight of every season – increased greatly in 1935. The *New York Amsterdam News* reported, "It is revealed that over 150,000 persons in eighteen states made choices on complete teams and individual players" and that "[a]lready plans have been announced from many cities in these different states to form excursion parties and motorcars. 'Air' parties are expected from New York, Pittsburgh, St. Louis, Kansas City, and Memphis, Tenn."[1] The number of fans in attendance on August 11, 1935, totaled 25,000 and they witnessed an extra-inning duel that provided the greatest all-star excitement yet.

Paul "Country Jake" Stephens led off the game for the East against the West's starting hurler, Ray Brown.[2] Stephens stroked a single to center and advanced to second when one of Brown's pitches got past catcher Josh Gibson. George Giles reached first safely when shortstop Willie Wells bobbled his grounder for an error, and Stephens advanced to third. Martin Dihigo followed with a hit to center that drove in Stephens with the first run of the game; Dihigo advanced to second on the play when center fielder James "Cool Papa" Bell had trouble corralling the ball and was charged with the West's second error of the afternoon.[3] Jud Wilson and Alejandro Oms were retired on grounders, but Giles scored on Oms' ball. Brown retired Raleigh "Biz" Mackey for the third out, but the West was already in a 2-0 hole. East starter

Slim Jones took the hill and allowed only a harmless single to number-two batter Sammy Hughes.

Brown fared better in the second inning. Although he allowed consecutive one-out singles to Dick Seay and Jones, he retired the next two batters to keep the East from increasing its lead. The West's George "Mule" Suttles drew a walk to lead off the bottom of the inning; he advanced to second on Oscar Charleston's grounder and took third when Stephens fumbled a knock by Alec Radcliffe. Jones escaped his jam when third baseman Jud Wilson "speared [Jimmie] Crutchfield's grasscutter and stepped on third to double Suttles, unassisted."[4]

Neither team scored in the third inning, but the top of the frame was notable for right fielder Crutchfield's leaping, barehanded catch that robbed Mackey of an extra-base hit, a play so extraordinary that the *Pittsburgh Courier* asserted it "will go down in history the greatest fielding play of all East-West games."[5] Crutchfield, whom the *Courier* labeled "a 147-pound package of grit, speed, and ability," had been the hero of the 1934 East-West game, as he had saved the East's 1-0 win "when he made a perfect throw to home plate to catch Mule Suttles trying to score from third base on a fly hit to right field."[6]

In the top of the fourth, Jones mashed a homer that made it a 3-0 game. Although the game was far from over, the press noted that Jones, "elongated southpaw 'ace' of the Philly Stars, 'stole' the show in the early innings."[7] Leon Day took over the mound from Jones in the bottom of the inning and surrendered a leadoff double by Gibson and a walk to Suttles. After Charleston lined out, Gibson attempted to steal third and was gunned down by Mackey. Radcliffe hit what would have been an RBI single had Gibson still been on second, and Radcliffe was retired on Crutchfield's fielder's choice.

Leroy Matlock came on to pitch for the West in the top of the fifth and was let down by his defense. Third baseman Radcliffe rifled Dihigo's one-out grounder to Charleston at first, but the first sacker dropped the ball. Dihigo stole second and, went to third when Gibson's throw sailed into the outfield. Wilson then singled to drive in Dihigo with the East's fourth run of the game before Matlock retired the next two hitters. Matlock then made the West's first out in the bottom of the frame; he was one of two strikeout victims as Day kept the West off the scoreboard.

After Matlock set the East down in order, two freak plays took place in the bottom of the sixth. Wells, the first batter, hit a pop foul that bounced out of catcher Mackey's mitt but landed right in third baseman Wilson's glove for the out. The next unusual play was frightening rather than funny. Center fielder Dihigo was running full bore after a smoking Gibson liner and crashed into the outfield wall. The ball bounced back into center field as Gibson pulled into second base while Dihigo lay unconscious on the field. At once, "The entire playing cast rushed out to the side of the stricken player. The crowd sat in stunned silence as doctors, photographers and newspapermen ran to where Dihigo lay."[8] In an age without concussion protocols, Dihigo "recovered and continued in the game."[9]

Once play resumed, Matlock intentionally walked Suttles to pitch to Charleston, but the strategy backfired when second baseman Seay made a fielding error on Charleston's grounder that loaded the bases. Radcliffe's single to center scored Gibson and Suttles and advanced Charleston to third; Charleston scored on the play when Dihigo, who likely was still woozy, "threw the ball on the ground in front of him."[10] Day retired two pinch-hitters – Turkey Stearnes (for Crutchfield) and Buck Leonard (for Matlock) – to preserve the East's 4-3 lead.

The West tied the game in the bottom of seventh. Bell led off with a single, went to second on Hughes's sacrifice, and advanced to third on Chester Williams's grounder. Suddenly, the game became a comedy of errors. Gibson lofted a ball down the third-base line that left fielder Fats Jenkins and third baseman Wilson both chased as

# THE 1935 PITTSBURGH CRAWFORDS

the wind carried it to the outfield, while Gibson stood and watched – a play for which, one reporter asserted, he should have "won the booby prize" – while the ball fell between the two fielders for a hit.[11] Mackey retrieved the ball and threw to Seay at second where Gibson would have been out had Seay not dropped the ball. Suttles, in his first opportunity to give the West the lead, struck out to end the inning.

All was quiet in the eighth and ninth innings but the bats exploded in the 10th. Bob Griffith now was pitching for the West and he loaded the bases by allowing singles by Wilson and Oms and a walk to Mackey. Shortstop Williams committed an error on Jenkins' grounder that allowed Wilson to score. Ray Dandridge drove in Oms with a base hit and, after pitcher Luis Tiant whiffed, Stephens' single scored Oms and kept the bases jammed with runners. Jenkins scored on Giles' grounder and Dihigo walked to keep the pressure on Griffith. However, Dandridge wandered too far off base and was tagged out by Griffith in a rundown between third and home. Still, all the East had to do was to hold on to a four-run lead to win the game.

That turned to be too tall an order as the West scored four runs of its own in the bottom of the inning. Tiant followed his mound opponent Griffith's lead by allowing the first three batters – Williams (walk), Gibson (single), and Suttles (walk) – to reach base. Dihigo was brought in from center field to pitch in relief. The first batter he faced, Felton Snow, pinch-hitting for Griffith, singled to drive in Williams and Gibson. Suttles scored next on a fielder's choice by Radcliffe that forced Snow at second. Radcliffe advanced to third on a single by Stearnes and scored on a fly ball by Leonard. Mackey caught Stearnes at second on the play, with Stephens applying the tag, but the game was tied once more, 8-8.

After an uneventful top of the 11th inning, Dihigo remained on the mound for the East. He walked Bell, the leadoff batter, who went to

*Hall of Famer George "Mule" Suttles, the Chicago American Giants' powerful left fielder, led the West team, which included six Crawfords players, to victory with a 10th-inning homer in the third annual East-West All-Star Classic.*

second on Hughes's sacrifice. Williams tried to reach base via a bit of chicanery as he tried to sell the home-plate umpire on the idea that he had been hit on the hand by one of Dihigo's pitches. No amount of arguing worked and Williams ended up being called out on strikes.

At this point, Dihigo intentionally walked Gibson, who led all players with four hits in the game, to face Suttles with two men on base and two outs. Suttles had been walked four times and had struck out once, but this time the "Donkey Bludgeon Wielder" launched a homer over the center-field wall and "sent 22,000 fans on the way screaming in the wake of an 11-8 victory for the Western All-Stars in the third annual intersectional baseball classic at Comiskey Park Sunday afternoon."[12]

# Pride of Smoketown

## Notes

1. "Voters Send Diamond Aces to Chicago for Classic Contest," *New York Amsterdam News*, August 10, 1935: 11.

2. Most news articles and the game box score spell Stephens's name as "Stevens"; however, the correct spelling is with "ph" rather than "v."

3. As exciting as the competition turned out to be, it was marred somewhat by copious errors as each team made five miscues.

4. Dan Burley, "Here's How the West Made History at Comiskey Park," *Chicago Defender*, August 17, 1935: 6. Burley's article also provided the majority of the play-by-play description included in the present article.

5. William G. Nunn with Frank Young, "Mule Suttles 'Steals' East-West Classic Again; Drives Ball 475 Feet for Eleventh Inning Homer to Break Deadlock; West Cops Most Colorful Game in History of Series," *Pittsburgh Courier*, August 17, 1935: 15. It should be noted that the headline misstated the distance of Suttles' homer; it traveled 375 feet, not 475.

6. Nunn with Young.

7. Nunn with Young.

8. Burley.

9. Burley.

10. Burley.

11. Burley.

12. Al Monroe, "Suttles' Home Run Wins for West, 11-8, *Chicago Defender*, August 17, 1935: 6. It should be noted that Monroe gave the attendance as 22,000; all other sources gave the 25,000 attendance figure.

# PAIGE TAKES THE MONEY BUT NOT THE MOUND
## SEPTEMBER 22, 1935: PITTSBURGH CRAWFORDS 12, PHILADELPHIA STARS 2, AT YANKEE STADIUM

### By Mark S. Sternman

Although the 1935 Pittsburgh Crawfords had performed remarkably well during the regular season and postseason even without ace Satchel Paige, who had gone 13-3 with a 1.54 ERA for Pittsburgh in 1934, the tall, slender hurler was already a legend who still ranked among the best players in the Negro Leagues. However, Philadelphia's Slim Jones had bested Paige the previous season, as the young southpaw went 20-4 with a 1.24 ERA for the 1934 Stars. The two hooked up after the season in a game that, a historian said, "would become known as 'The Greatest Negro League Game Ever,'" adding, "Over 30,000 fans watched Slim sling a six-inning perfect game to lead Satch's squad 1-0. Oscar Charleston broke it up in the seventh and … Pittsburgh … pushed across a run to tie. Slim and Satch dueled mightily, trading strikeouts until the heart-pounding nail biter was called by nightfall in the tenth."[1]

Paige got married less than seven weeks after the game, and Pittsburgh owner Gus Greenlee gave his hurler an unusual wedding present: "With his guests expecting a wedding toast, the Crawfords' owner threw a curve. 'Satchel won't be leaving us, don't worry about that.' Gus announced, arm around his star. 'I got a new contract here for him.' Satchel and Gus sat down and signed right there, as they had agreed beforehand."[2]

Paige did not fulfill the first year of his contract, opting instead to play semipro ball in North Dakota. Greenlee "was so miffed that he had Paige barred from the league for 1935. ... Chester Williams wrote a tentative, premature obituary in the *Pittsburgh Courier*: 'The champ of today may be the chump of tomorrow. So it may be with Paige. The league helped to make him and now the league may be the medium to break him.'"[3]

Hard feelings notwithstanding, the Crawfords took the title without Paige, and Greenlee sought to re-create the magical matchup of 1934 by having his squad take on Philadelphia again on September 22, 1935. A *New York Amsterdam News* article touted the highly anticipated matchup by declaring, "Satchel Paige vs. Slim Jones! This is the attractive centerpiece of the big four-team Negro National League double-header slated Sunday at the Yankee Stadium as the Pittsburgh Crawfords and Philadelphia Stars, arch foes in colored baseball, come to grips in the featured game."[4] The first game, an afterthought in light of the premier second-game matchup, pitted the Nashville Elite Giants against the New York Cubans.[5] Greenlee paid Paige the handsome sum of $350 to pitch, but Satchel did not show for the game that took place just two days after the Crawfords had topped the New York Cubans in the seventh game of the 1935 Negro National League Championship Series.

Paige's failure to appear was not entirely unusual for a player whom the *Amsterdam News* termed "as eccentric and talented as the late Rube Waddell,"[6] but Satchel's absence obviously made the sequel far less satisfying than the original. The fact was that "a crowd of more than 15,000 fans were disappointed at Yankee Stadium Sunday … when Satchel Paige, star pitcher, failed to appear as advertised and when 'Slim' Jones, who last year beat Paige in a pitching duel, was knocked out after only one inning on the mound."[7] Greenlee informed the press that Paige had stopped in Chicago en route to the Empire State for the big doubleheader and had been offered $500 to pitch for the Kansas City Monarchs on September 22. Typical for Paige, the higher dollar amount "caused him to forget all about his agreement to appear in New York."[8]

Pittsburgh had survived without Paige all season and did so again in the exhibition game against the Stars. In fact, "The Crawfords, with their new world crown posing jauntily askew on their kingly brows, put on an exhibition of sheer pulverizing power that left the crowd and the Philadelphia Stars as well completely stunned and thoroughly convinced that they were the boys who REALLY deserve to reside in the thrown [sic] room of Negro baseball."[9]

Earnest "Spoon" Carter took the mound for the Crawfords and went the distance as Pittsburgh pounded its intrastate rivals, 12-2. With a 4-5 record and a 5.88 ERA, Jones had slipped severely from his star turn in 1934 and surrendered four runs in his lone inning of work. Relievers Webster McDonald, the ace of the 1935 Stars with an 8-4 record and a 4.30 ERA, and Rocky Ellis fared no better than Jones. Any notion that the game would be as competitive as the previous year's contest vanished quickly. "From the moment that 'Cool Papa' Bell opened the game with a blistering double to deep left field, the Pittsburgh power attack kept up a steady bombardment," and the Crawfords scored in each of the first five innings to build a 12-1 lead.[10]

The Crawfords outhit the Stars, 20 to 10, and belted four home runs. Pat Patterson and Bill Perkins smacked one home run apiece while "[s]hortstopper [Chester] Williams hit two of the round-trippers. Every one of the Crawfords managed to get himself at least one safe hit. Young Addie Ward, Quaker City centerfielder, scored both of the Stars' runs."[11]

Pittsburgh had again shown that it could win easily without Paige, but bad publicity resulted from the star hurler's no-show. On October 5 the *Amsterdam News* reported that "a number of fans [are] all het up over the non-appearance of Satchel Paige" for the Jones rematch. "[M]any fans remarked that they would not have been present had they known that Paige would not be on hand."[12]

*Daily Mirror* columnist Dan Parker asserted, "Promoters of the colored baseball games at Yankee Stadium last week advertised Satchel Paige as one of the players, though they knew he was playing in Chicago that day. This cheap gag is used on other large cities, too. It surprises me that Satchel doesn't sue for damages."[13] Given that

Greenlee had wired money to Paige as payment for his September 22 appearance, the *Amsterdam News* countered, "From what could be gleaned on this end of the unfortunate affair it would seem that Satchel is the one who is surprised that he isn't being sued."[14]

Whether the greater sum of $500 offered by the Monarchs was the sole reason why Paige got paid but did not play remains lost to history. Perhaps his resentment had built up and resulted in his seeking payback for Greenlee's season-long ban. Or perhaps Paige just did not feel like coming to New York on this particular day. Negro League players, even stars, rarely got the last word, but Paige later explained his general outlook in his autobiography, stating, "Before I went with the Monarchs, I hadn't thought anything about jumping contracts when I felt like it. I guess I never cared much about anything except myself. It'd made guys like Abe Saperstein … and Gus Greenlee and Candy Jim Taylor and lots others mad at me because of that."[15]

### Acknowledgment

The author thanks Rick Bush for his helpful edits and additions.

### Notes

1. Jack Morelli, *Heroes of the Negro Leagues* (New York: Abrams Books, 2007), 120. Paige struck out 12 in the tie. Jeremy Beer, *Oscar Charleston* (Lincoln: University of Nebraska Press, 2019), 243.
2. Larry Tye, *Satchel* (New York: Random House, 2009), 75.
3. Robert Peterson, *Only the Ball Was White* (New York: McGraw-Hill, 1984), 134.
4. "Yankee Stadium Diamond Games Season's Most Attractive: Mound Aces Set for Big Battles," *New York Amsterdam News*, September 21, 1935: 13.
5. The opening game of the doubleheader ended up as the better game of the day with Nashville surviving a ninth-inning rally by the Cubans to hold on to a 4-3 victory.
6. "Yankee Stadium Diamond Games Season's Most Attractive: Mound Aces Set for Big Battles."
7. William E. Clark, "15,000 Fans See 4-Team Series at Yankee Stadium Sunday; Crawford and Elite Gts, Win," *New York Age*, September 28, 1935.
8. Clark.
9. Joe Bostic, "Thousands See Defeats of Cubans and Stars," *New York Amsterdam News*, September 28, 1935: 12.
10. Bostic.
11. Bostic. This game may have represented Ward's best effort with the Stars. Given that he would turn 26 less than two months after this game, Ward does not retrospectively appear particularly young in baseball terms. The Seamheads database lists Ward's first name as Willie; Addie comes from his middle name (Addison). According to the database, Ward played in only one regular-season game for Philadelphia during which he scored a single run. See seamheads.com/NegroLgs/player.php?playerID=ward-01wil (accessed October 18, 2019).
12. Artie La Mar, "Fans All Het Up Over Non-Appearance of Paige at the Yankee Stadium Games Here," *New York Amsterdam News,* October 5, 1935: 13.
13. La Mar.
14. La Mar.
15. LeRoy (Satchel) Paige as told to David Lipman, *Maybe I'll Pitch Forever* (Lincoln: Bison Books, 1993), 141.

# THE 1935 NEGRO NATIONAL LEAGUE CHAMPIONSHIP SERIES:
## PITTSBURGH CRAWFORDS VS. NEW YORK CUBANS

### By Richard J. Puerzer

The Pittsburgh Crawfords faced the New York Cubans in the 1935 Negro National League Championship Series. The Crawfords finished the season with the best overall record in the league, and had won the first half of the season with a 24-6 record.[1] After a weak first half, the Cubans played excellent ball and captured the second-half title, which earned them the right to play against the Crawfords in the best-of-seven series for the league championship. During the regular season, the two teams had played each other eight times. The Crawfords had dominated in those games, winning five and losing only one, with two games ending in ties.[2]

The Cubans were an excellent ballclub. Under the ownership of Alex Pompez, the team was playing its first season as a member of this second incarnation of the Negro National League, which was now in its third year. Pompez's roster was populated primarily by Latinos, including players from Puerto Rico, Mexico, the Dominican Republic, and Cuba. Their best player was their manager, Martin Dihigo, a Cuban who was an extremely versatile player, even for his time. Dihigo was a great offensive player, who usually played the outfield and third base, and he was also an outstanding pitcher. Alejandro Oms was another tremendous player as was Rap Dixon, who joined the Cubans through a trade from the Brooklyn Eagles about halfway through the 1935 season. Perhaps the greatest strength of the Cubans was their pitching staff, which featured Schoolboy Johnny Taylor, who at 19 years old was playing in his first season. The staff had two other excellent pitchers, veteran left-hander Neck Stanley and fellow southpaw Luis Tiant Sr.

There was strong interest in the series as demonstrated by the coverage in both the black and white press. However, especially in the black newspapers, there was considerably more coverage of the coming Joe Louis/Max Baer fight for boxing's heavyweight championship, which was

# THE 1935 PITTSBURGH CRAWFORDS

to take place on September 24 at Yankee Stadium. The newspapers featured cover stories and full pages of articles regarding Louis's training and preparation for the fight. Regardless, fans of black baseball who attended the games in New York, Pittsburgh, or Philadelphia witnessed one of the greatest postseason series in baseball history.

**GAME ONE**
**FRIDAY, SEPTEMBER 13, 1935**
**DYCKMAN OVAL, NEW YORK CITY**
**NEW YORK CUBANS 6,**
**PITTSBURGH CRAWFORDS 2**

The opening game of the Championship Series was played on Friday night, September 13, at Dyckman Oval in New York City, the home park of the Cubans. About 7,500 attended the game. The umpires for the entire series were John Craig, Judy Gans, Bert Gholston, and Mo Harris. Craig and Gholston were reputed to be among the best umpires in the league, and Gans and Harris were former players. The pitching matchup featured Frank Blake for the Cubans and Sam Streeter for the Crawfords. There is no question that the Cubans prevailed in the game, 6-2. It is unusual that, although the final score was reported the same everywhere, the game stories and line scores reported by the *New York Age* and the *Pittsburgh Post-Gazette* differ significantly. The *Post-Gazette* reported that the Cubans came from behind to win, powered by a pair of two-run home runs by Rap Dixon. It also reported that the Cubans committed three errors in the game. In addition to recounting a different game story, the *New York Age* provided a box score for the game. The box score showed Dixon with two hits but no runs scored. It indicated that the only extra-base hit in the game was a double by the Cubans' first baseman, Dave "Showboat" Thomas. Given that the *Age* was the paper local to where the game was played, and the specificity provided by the box score, it is deemed the more reliable source. Additionally, a very brief story in the *New York Daily News* stated that "Rap Dixon starred for New York, getting two safeties," thus corroborating the *New York Age* story. Regardless of the specifics of the game, the Cubans were able to take the first game of the series behind timely hitting and the pitching of Frank Blake, who pitched a complete game and scattered six hits.[3]

|  |  |  |  |  |  |  |  |  |  | R | H | E |
|---|---|---|---|---|---|---|---|---|---|---|---|---|
| Crawfords | 0 | 0 | 0 | 0 | 2 | 0 | 0 | 0 | 0 | 2 | 6 | 1 |
| Cubans | 2 | 0 | 4 | 0 | 0 | 1 | 0 | 0 | x | 6 | 5 | 2 |

**GAME TWO**
**SATURDAY, SEPTEMBER 14, 1935**
**44TH AND PARKSIDE, PHILADELPHIA**
**NEW YORK CUBANS 4,**
**PITTSBURGH CRAWFORDS 0**

Game Two of the Championship Series was played at the 44th and Parkside ballpark in Philadelphia starting at 4:30 P.M. The Cubans were the home team for the game at the neutral site. The attendance was estimated to be about 2,000, the size of the crowd held back by threatening weather. The game was delayed for 35 minutes because three of the four umpires did not know where it was to be played. Once the game began, Cubans starter Neck Stanley faced off against Roosevelt Davis for the Crawfords. Game stories provided few details, aside from the dominant pitching of Stanley, who held the Crawfords to four singles while striking out six and walking three in a complete-game effort. The Cubans hit Crawfords hurler Davis hard, scoring four runs on 11 hits. Despite the multitude of hits, Davis allowed runs only in the fifth and sixth innings and pitched a complete game. Clyde Spearman was the hitting star for the Cubans, blasting a home run in the fifth and driving in three of the four Cubans runs.[4] The surprising Cubans now led the series 2-0.

|  |  |  |  |  |  |  |  |  |  | R | H | E |
|---|---|---|---|---|---|---|---|---|---|---|---|---|
| Crawfords | 0 | 0 | 0 | 0 | 0 | 0 | 0 | 0 | 0 | 0 | 4 | 0 |
| Cubans | 0 | 0 | 0 | 0 | 3 | 1 | 0 | 0 | x | 4 | 11 | 1 |

# Pride of Smoketown

**GAME THREE**
**SUNDAY, SEPTEMBER 15, 1935**
**DYCKMAN OVAL, NEW YORK CITY**
**PITTSBURGH CRAWFORDS 3,**
**NEW YORK CUBANS 0**

The third game of the Championship Series was played Sunday afternoon, September 25, back at Dyckman Oval. The pitching matchup featured the teams' best starters, Leroy Matlock for the Crawfords and Johnnie Taylor for the Cubans. Matlock was probably the best pitcher in the Negro National League in 1935 and had won all eight league games he started while sporting an ERA of 1.52. Schoolboy Johnnie Taylor had pitched more league innings than anyone on the Cubans' staff. An estimated 5,000 fans made their way to the Sunday afternoon game, including a delegation of 200 people from Pittsburgh. In the top of the first inning, the Crawfords scored with two outs when Pat Patterson singled and scored on Josh Gibson's triple. The Crawfords picked up another run in the fifth when Cool Papa Bell tripled to the left-field bleachers and scored as the relay throw was juggled in the infield. In the sixth, Oscar Charleston walloped a home run over the center-field wall to make the score 3-0. Matlock scattered six hits and two walks while striking out nine.[5] The Cubans now led the series two games to one.

|           |   |   |   |   |   |   |   |   |   | R | H | E |
|-----------|---|---|---|---|---|---|---|---|---|---|---|---|
| Crawfords | 1 | 0 | 0 | 0 | 1 | 1 | 0 | 0 | 0 | 3 | 8 | 1 |
| Cubans    | 0 | 0 | 0 | 0 | 0 | 0 | 0 | 0 | 0 | 0 | 6 | 2 |

**GAME FOUR**
**TUESDAY, SEPTEMBER 17, 1935**
**GREENLEE FIELD, PITTSBURGH**
**NEW YORK CUBANS 6,**
**PITTSBURGH CRAWFORDS 1**

Game Four of the series was played on Tuesday afternoon, September 17, at Greenlee Field in Pittsburgh, the home park of the Crawfords. Dihigo named himself the Cubans' starter and faced Matlock, who was pitching on only one day's rest for the Crawfords. Pittsburgh scored first when, in the second inning, Josh Gibson singled and was knocked home. Matlock kept the Cubans' bats quiet until the fifth inning, when he gave up the tying run. He surrendered the lead when he allowed another Cubans tally in the sixth. Matlock was chased from the game in the eighth inning when the Cubans scored four runs, and was relieved by Ernest "Spoon" Carter. Although a box score for the game was published, neither it nor the game stories provided many details regarding the play-by-play. Clyde Spearman and Lazaro Salazar were reported to have hit home runs, although it is unclear in which inning(s) they were hit. It was clear that the star of the game was Dihigo, who pitched effectively and held the Crawfords to one run. The Cubans now led the series three games to one, which put them on the verge of taking the series from the mighty Crawfords.[6]

|           |   |   |   |   |   |   |   |   |   | R | H  | E |
|-----------|---|---|---|---|---|---|---|---|---|---|----|---|
| Crawfords | 0 | 0 | 0 | 0 | 1 | 1 | 0 | 4 | 0 | 6 | 11 | ? |
| Cubans    | 0 | 1 | 0 | 0 | 0 | 0 | 0 | 0 | 0 | 1 | 7  | ? |

**GAME FIVE**
**WEDNESDAY, SEPTEMBER 18, 1935**
**GREENLEE FIELD, PITTSBURGH**
**PITTSBURGH CRAWFORDS 3,**
**NEW YORK CUBANS 2**

The fifth game of the series was played in the afternoon on Wednesday, September 18, again at Greenlee Field. Frank Blake, who got the win in Game One for the Cubans, went up against Rosey Davis for the Crawfords. Jimmie Crutchfield scored in the first inning to give the Crawfords the early lead, and he scored again in the third inning. Davis pitched well for the Crawfords, and kept the Cubans scoreless until the sixth, when Lazaro Salazar scored. The Crawfords held their tight lead until the top of the ninth, when Cocaina Garcia, pinch-hitting for Cubans catcher Frank Duncan, lofted a home run to tie the game. In the bottom of the ninth, Davis singled and Cool Papa Bell ran for him. Bell took second on a ground-

# THE 1935 PITTSBURGH CRAWFORDS

out by Crutchfield. Chester Williams bunted back to the pitcher. As Bell ran for third, Blake uncorked a wild throw to Dihigo at the hot corner that allowed Bell to score the winning run. The Crawfords had survived to play another day. The Cubans now led three games to two.[7]

|           |   |   |   |   |   |   |   |   |   | R | H | E |
|-----------|---|---|---|---|---|---|---|---|---|---|---|---|
| Crawfords | 0 | 0 | 0 | 0 | 0 | 1 | 0 | 0 | 1 | 2 | 8 | 2 |
| Cubans    | 1 | 0 | 1 | 0 | 0 | 0 | 0 | 0 | 1 | 3 | 8 | 0 |

## GAME SIX
**THURSDAY, SEPTEMBER 19, 1935**
**44TH AND PARKSIDE, PHILADELPHIA**
**PITTSBURGH CRAWFORDS 7,**
**NEW YORK CUBANS 6**

For Game Six of the Championship Series, the teams traveled back to Philadelphia where they played on Thursday night, September 19. The Crawfords played as the home team. Bert Hunter made his first appearance in the series as he started the game for Pittsburgh. The Cubans' moundsman was Neck Stanley, who had pitched masterfully in Game Two. This time neither Stanley nor Hunter was terribly sharp. For the first six innings, the game went back and forth. The Cubans took the lead in the first, the Crawfords scored twice in the second, and the Cubans tied the game in the top of the fourth. Schoolboy Johnny Taylor relieved Stanley and gave up a run in the bottom of the fifth. The Cubans answered again with a run in the top of the sixth. In the seventh inning the Cubans scored twice more to knock Hunter out of the game. Bill Harvey, who also was making his first appearance for the Crawfords in the series, came in and got out of the seventh inning. After the Crawfords went down quietly in their half of the seventh, the Cubans scored again in the top of the eighth to build a three-run lead and drive Harvey to the bench. Leroy Matlock completed the inning unscathed and held the Cubans in check in the top of the ninth.

The Crawfords were behind 6-3 and were on the verge of losing the series when they came to bat in the bottom of the ninth. Rather than going down quietly, they put together one of the most improbable playoff rallies in baseball's history. Dihigo, who had pitched brilliantly in Game Four, put himself on the mound to attempt to close out the game. He retired Cool Papa Bell for the first out but then allowed Chester Williams to reach base. After Bill Perkins made the Crawfords' second out, the Cubans were still up by three runs and needed just one more out to win the Series. Josh Gibson stepped to the plate and singled; Williams advanced to second on the hit. Oscar Charleston became the man of the moment as he drove a game-tying home run over the left-field fence. Dihigo gave up a double to the next batter, Pat Patterson. Judy Johnson, who was 0-for-10 in the series thus far, entered the game as a pinch-hitter and battled against Dihigo. After working a full count, Johnson fouled off three straight pitches and then smacked the ball down the first-base line. Cubans first baseman Showboat Thomas was able to get his glove on the ball, but he was unable to make a play as Patterson scampered around third base and scored the winning run. The Crawfords had scored four runs with two outs to win the game and extend the series to a seventh game.[8]

|           |   |   |   |   |   |   |   |   |   | R | H  | E |
|-----------|---|---|---|---|---|---|---|---|---|---|----|---|
| Crawfords | 1 | 0 | 0 | 1 | 0 | 1 | 2 | 1 | 0 | 6 | 10 | ? |
| Cubans    | 0 | 2 | 0 | 0 | 1 | 0 | 0 | 0 | 4 | 7 | 13 | ? |

## GAME SEVEN
**FRIDAY, SEPTEMBER 20, 1935**
**44TH AND PARKSIDE, PHILADELPHIA**
**PITTSBURGH CRAWFORDS 8,**
**NEW YORK CUBANS 7**

The seventh and deciding game of the 1935 Negro National League Championship Series was played under the lights on Friday night, September 20, in Philadelphia. The Cubans were the home team. Bill Harvey, who had pitched poorly in relief the previous day, got the start for the pitching-depleted Crawfords while Luis Tiant Sr., in his first Series appearance, started for the Cubans. The Crawfords struck first when they scored two runs in the second inning on consecutive singles by Josh Gibson, Pat Patterson, Curtis Harris, and Sam Bankhead. The Cubans took the lead in the third on a three-run home run by Rap Dixon. In the Crawfords half of the fifth, Bankhead and Chester Williams scored and Pittsburgh retook the lead. It was short-lived, however: The Cubans tallied a run in the bottom of the fifth when Correa doubled and was driven home by Rap Dixon's single. Rosey Davis relieved Harvey, his third appearance in the Series. In a back-and-forth game, Pittsburgh reclaimed the advantage in the seventh as Bankhead singled, stole second, and scored on Chester Williams's single. Schoolboy Taylor relieved Tiant to start the eighth inning and gave up back-to-back home runs by Josh Gibson and Oscar Charleston; Charleston's blast was his third home run of the series. Then Bankhead walked, took second on a wild pitch, and scored his third run of the game on an infield error to give the Crawfords an 8-4 lead. The Cubans did not give up, however, and rallied to get one run closer when Rap Dixon scored in the bottom of the eighth. The Cubans were game to the end and went down swinging when their rally in the ninth fell just short. Thomas led off the inning with a single and with two out Clyde Spearman hit a two-run homer to bring the Cubans within one run, but both the game and series ended when Alejandro Oms grounded out to the pitcher.

The Pittsburgh Crawfords had come back from a three-games-to-one deficit to defeat the New York Cubans in a tremendously competitive series.[9]

|  |  |  |  |  |  |  |  |  |  | R | H | E |
|---|---|---|---|---|---|---|---|---|---|---|---|---|
| Crawfords | 0 | 2 | 0 | 0 | 2 | 0 | 1 | 3 | 0 | 8 | 11 | 0 |
| Cubans | 0 | 0 | 3 | 0 | 1 | 0 | 0 | 1 | 2 | 7 | 9 | 3 |

**SERIES POSTSCRIPT**

The stars of the series for the Cubans were Rap Dixon with eight hits and a slash line of .421/.500/.579; Clyde Spearman, who hit three home runs; and Frank Blake, who threw two complete games and posted an ERA of 1.59. Future Hall of Famer Martin Dihigo was perhaps the goat of the series: He surrendered the lead in the sixth game and struggled defensively as well. He was reported to have resigned as manager after the series, but he was back at the helm of the Cubans for the 1936 season.

The Crawfords were led by 38-year-old player-manager Oscar Charleston, who hit three home runs, including huge homers in Games Six and Seven. Josh Gibson collected 11 hits in the series and posted a slash line of .355/.355/.516. Leroy Matlock struck out 16 batters in 17⅓ innings as both a starter and reliever.

On Sunday, September 22, the two teams played in a four-team doubleheader at Yankee Stadium, with the Crawfords besting the Philadelphia Stars 12-2 and the Cubans falling to the Nashville Elite Giants, 4-3. The games drew a reported 27,000 fans, significantly more than in any of the Championship Series games, and all the more impressive because the previous day the New York Giants hosted the Brooklyn Dodgers for a doubleheader at the Polo Grounds and drew only a reported 12,000 fans.

A few weeks later, several of the players from the Crawfords, Cubans, and other teams traveled together and played under the banner of the Pittsburgh Crawfords. This barnstorming version of the Crawfords played against a team of major-league players led by Dizzy Dean in various locations throughout the country. The team of Negro League players generally outperformed the major leaguers.[10]

### Sources

Burgos, Adrian Jr. *Cuban Star: How One Negro-League Owner Changed the Face of Baseball* (New York: Hill and Wang, 2011).

Clark, Dick, and Larry Lester, eds. *The Negro Leagues Book* (Cleveland: Society for American Baseball Research, 1994).

Riley, James A. *The Biographical Encyclopedia of the Negro Baseball Leagues* (New York: Carroll & Graf Publishers, Inc., 1994).

seamheads.com

# THE 1935 PITTSBURGH CRAWFORDS

## Notes

1. "Craws Win First Half," *Afro-American*, July 13, 1935: 20.

2. "World Series Opens in N.Y. Saturday," *Chicago Defender*, September 14, 1935: 15.

3. For Game One: "N.Y. Cubans Lead Crawfords in Colored World Series; Finals in Pittsburgh This Thursday," *New York Age*, September 21, 1935: 8. (This article covers Games One and Three); "Cubans Defeat Pittsburgh, 6 to 2," *New York Daily News,* September 14, 1935; "Crawfords Lose to Cubans, 6 to 2," *Pittsburgh Post-Gazette*, September 14, 1935: 17.

4. For Game Two: "Cubans Win Two from Crawfords," *Afro-American*, September 21, 1935: 21; "Crawfords Given 4 to 0 Shutout," *Pittsburgh Press*, September 15, 1935: 18; "Crawfords Lose to Cubans Again," *Pittsburgh Sun-Telegraph*, September 15, 1935: 21.

5. For Game Three: William E. Clark, "N.Y. Cubans Lead Crawfords in Colored World Series; Finals in Pittsburgh This Thursday," *New York Age*, September 21, 1935: 8. (This article covers Games One and Three); Joe Bostick, "Craws Stop New York Cubans 3-0," *New York Amsterdam News*, September 21, 1935: 13; Allan McMillan, "Pitt Crawfords Grab 3rd Game of Series," *Chicago Defender*, September 21, 1935: 13.

6. For Game Four: "Cubans Defeat Crawfords Again," *Pittsburgh Post-Gazette*, September 19, 1935: 18; "Cubans Cop Wednesday's Game; Play Thursday," *Pittsburgh Courier*, September 21, 1935: A4.

7. For Game Five: "Crawfords Beat Cubans by 3 to 2," *Pittsburgh Post-Gazette*, September 20, 1935: 18.

8. For Game Six: "Crawfords Rally and Beat Cubans," *Philadelphia Inquirer*, September 21, 1935: 17; "Crawfords Beat Cubans, 8 to 7, to Get First Pennant," *Afro-American*, September 28, 1935: 11. (This article covers Games Six and Seven); "Crawfords Now League Champs," *New York Amsterdam News*, September 28, 1935: 12. (This article covers Games Six and Seven.)

9. For Game Seven: "Crawfords Snare Negro Loop Crown," *Philadelphia Inquirer*, September 22, 1935, 44; "Crawfords Win Negro Title, 8-7," *Pittsburgh Press*, September 22, 1935: 18; "Crawfords Beat Cubans, 8 to 7, to Get First Pennant," *Afro-American*, September 28, 1935: 11. (This article covers Games Six and Seven); "Crawfords Now League Champs," *New York Amsterdam News*, September 28, 1935: 12. (This article covers Games Six and Seven.)

10. Timothy M. Gay, *Satch, Dizzy, & Rapid Robert* (New York: Simon and Schuster, 2010), 125-130.

# GUS GREENLEE AND THE CRAWFORD GRILLS

## By Leslie Heaphy

*Gus Greenlee's Crawford Grill was the place to be for black ballplayers, musicians, and other celebrities who wanted to enjoy the nightlife in Pittsburgh.*

(Courtesy Center for Negro League Baseball Research)

Baseball and music have a long history together. Many songs, such as "Take Me Out to the Ball Game" or "Talkin' Baseball," have been written specifically about the game. The National Anthem is played prior to every game, and music has long been played for fans throughout the game. In modern times, walk-up music for every batter has been added, and relief pitchers, especially closers, have chosen a signature song to announce their entrance into a game.

Historically, black baseball teams had a strong connection to their communities and jazz music. Bill "Bojangles" Robinson owned his own ballclub in addition to being a performer. Kansas City immediately comes to mind when one thinks of the jazz scene – especially with the Negro Leagues Baseball Museum and American Jazz Museum now being located next door to each other – but another city with those same strong connections is Pittsburgh. The connecting figure was not a performer but an owner, Gus Greenlee, who not only owned the famous Pittsburgh Crawfords but also opened three Crawford Grills in Pittsburgh's

# THE 1935 PITTSBURGH CRAWFORDS

*Gus Greenlee's Crawford Grill was the place to see and to be seen for African American athletes and entertainers in Pittsburgh for many years.*

Hill District. At the Grill, ballplayers and musicians hung out together, creating an entertainment community for themselves and anyone who came out to listen. The story of Greenlee, the Grills, and the Crawfords is not often told, but is a part of the history of the city and the team. Greenlee's importance to the music scene, as well as the local baseball scene, cannot be overlooked.

Gus Greenlee was born in 1897 in Marion, North Carolina. He moved north to Pittsburgh in 1916 to look for work. Greenlee ended up serving in France during World War I and, when he came back to Pittsburgh, had saved enough money to be able to buy a cab. Not only did he provide rides, but he sold alcohol from the cab during Prohibition. The added income allowed Greenlee the chance to buy his first club, The Collins Inn, which he renamed the Paramount. Greenlee used the Paramount as a place for gathering, introducing jazz musicians such as Edna Lewis, and as a front for his numbers game. Greenlee became the king of the hill and was the go-to source for loans, mortgages, college funds, placing simple bets, and so much more.[1]

Greenlee added to his growing economic empire by becoming a sports promoter, primarily for boxers. His premier boxer was light heavyweight champion John Henry Lewis. He also became the owner of the Pittsburgh Crawfords, a semipro team known as the Crawford Colored Giants at the time Greenlee purchased the franchise. He entered the Crawfords into the Negro Leagues in 1932 and the team won championships in 1935 and 1936. To help promote the team, he paid for the construction of Greenlee Field, which opened in 1933 at an approximate cost of $100,000. The park could seat up to 7,500 and was also used for boxing and college football when the Crawfords were not in town. Greenlee was also the architect of the annual East-West classic at Chicago's Comiskey Park, which began in 1933, the same year as the first major-league All-Star Game, and helped to put the Negro Leagues on the map by becoming an annual showcase for its biggest stars.[2]

In addition to his sports activities, Greenlee made his mark on the community and the music world when he opened the first Crawford Grill in 1931. His success led to the opening of a second Grill in 1943 as well as a third grill that operated for a short period in 1948. Each of his clubs opened in a different section of the Hill District, following some of the changes that occurred in the city as its people and businesses adapted to the Great Depression and World War II.

Crawford Grill No. 1 operated from 1931 to 1951/52 when a fire forced the club to close. The building then had to be torn down because of the damage and cost of repairs. Crawford Grill No. 2 kept its doors open from 1943 to 2002; two decades later there were efforts to try to reopen the Grill as a historic landmark. The third grill operated only seven years, from 1948 to 1955, and never gained the popularity of the first two. Two reasons might account for the shorter life span. The Hill District changed after World War II: People continued to move in and out of the area as soldiers came home and took advantage of the GI Bill. The bigger concern was the building's location on the outer edge of the Hill District. The first two Grills were more accessible because they were located in the heart of the community along Wylie Avenue in the lower Hill District. Each section of the Hill District had its own identity, but the people all shared strong connections to the business community due to segregation. They supported what they had so they did not need to leave to find the products needed.[3]

All of Greenlee's ventures benefited from the presence of the *Pittsburgh Courier* in the Hill District (operated 1910-66). The *Courier* writers helped promote and advertise businesses in their weekly columns. For example, John Clark had a column titled "Wylie Avenue" in which one could read all about the happenings at every business on that main thoroughfare. Lee Matthews' column "Swingin' among the Musicians," informed everyone as to who was playing where each night of the week.[4]

Crawford Grill No. 1 began life as the Leader House. When Greenlee bought the club it already had a reputation in the jazz community; the Louis Deppe band played there. Deppe not only played at the Leader House but his band toured Ohio and West Virginia. Greenlee renamed it when he purchased and opened his new club in 1931. It became the meeting place for Crawford players after games and on offnights. On any given night, local folks could stop by and they might see Satchel Paige hanging out with band leader Billy Eckstine or pianist Mary Lou Williams. The Grill had three floors and took up an entire city block. The main music area had a revolving stage, perfect for small combos, with a glass-topped bar. The third floor housed "Club Crawford," which was reserved for insiders only. Those given entrance might be there for a special music performance or sports betting, a theme night, or even the numbers game at higher stakes. Greenlee invited all the Negro League owners to the Grill for their business meeting in January 1934.[5]

Greenlee and William "Woogie" Harris were two of many individuals involved in the numbers game – the local street lottery – in Pittsburgh. At one point Greenlee was estimated to be making $20,000 to 25,000 a day from his numbers racket. A person could place a bet for as little as a penny and make $5 if his three digits hit that day. The small amount required to place a bet made the game accessible to all. Greenlee was the go-to person in the Hill District because he always paid out while some other numbers racketeers had reputations for stiffing their clients. Greenlee had a reputation for helping those who were in need in the Hill District, and his generosity benefited him, too, as it made his clubs all the more popular as gathering places. There might have been better music elsewhere in the city, but the Grills were always the place to hang out and meet people.[6]

Over the years many famous musicians passed through the Grills and several local sensations got their start there. Big-band members came late at night to join the jam sessions with the locals, and cast members from local theaters came out after their shows. Nationally known jazz musicians regularly stayed in Pittsburgh for weeklong gigs because of the vast array of venues where they could play. Greenlee's Grills were part of a large scene that included such places as the Savoy Ballroom, the Pythian Temple, the Bambola Social Club, and the Hurricane Club. The Roosevelt Theater brought in some of the biggest names such as Dizzy Gillespie, Louis Armstrong, and Ray Brown.[7] In the early years Greenlee liked to bring in musicians from New York City, such as Jean Daniels and Jack Spruce and his septet, to create a vibrant and busy club scene. Nelson Harrison, a jazz musician, had this to say about the Grill: "The Crawford Grill didn't pay [hardly] any money. It was just the place to play … [but] everybody who was anybody was in your audience."[8] For a period at Grill No. 1, Greenlee even brought in a New York City chef and redecorated so the place so that it looked like a Spanish hacienda, which gave it a unique feel compared with all the other clubs people could frequent. Later, Grill No. 2 shifted to smaller combos and solo artists, such as Ted Birch and Bobby Dummit, as the music scene moved away from big bands.[9]

Gus Greenlee, promoter of a light heavyweight boxer and owner of a championship baseball team, brought national fame to his community. As owner of a café, a pool hall, a music booking agency and the Crawford Grill, Greenlee was integral to the music scene, giving many young musicians their start. Additionally, as one of the most respected numbers runners, he really was the King of the Hill. Though the Grills may no longer be around, they are still a part of the history of Pittsburgh.

## Notes

[1] *Pittsburgh Courier*, July 8, 1933: 70; James Bankes, *The Pittsburgh Crawfords: The Life and Times of Black Baseball's Most Exciting Team* (Dubuque, Iowa: William C. Brown, 1991).

[2] David M. Brown, "Crawfords' Owner Sinner and Saint," *Pittsburgh Tribune Review*, February 10, 2008.

[3] Colter Harper, *"The Crossroads of the World": A Social and Cultural History of Jazz in Pittsburgh's Hill District, 1920-1970* (MA Thesis, Duquesne University, 2001), 43.

[4] Harper, 50-51.

[5] Greenlee obituary, *The Sporting News*, July 23, 1952: 30; Harper, 65, 103.

[6] Harper, 92-94; Michael Santa Maria, "King of the Hill," *American Visions*, June 1991: 21-24.

[7] Pittsburgh Music History, sites.google.com/site/pittsburghmusichistory/pittsburgh-music-story/jazz/hill-district; Harper, 117.

[8] "Crawford Grill Hosted Jazz Legends," *Pittsburgh Post-Gazette*, February 12, 2003.

[9] Harper, 100-101, 105; Ron Ieraci, "The Crawford Grill – A Pittsburgh Jazz Legend," *Old Mon Music*, November 29, 2008, oldmonmusic.blogspot.com/2008/11/crawford-grill.html.

# GUS GREENLEE AND THE EAST-WEST ALL-STAR GAME:
## ORIGINS AND CONFLICT (1932-1944)

*By Duke Goldman*

**INTRODUCTION**

"Since the August Day in 1933, when 'King' Cole of Chicago, Gus Greenlee of Pittsburgh, and Tom Wilson of Nashville, saw a dream, which originated in the minds of Roy Sparrow and Dave Hawkins, come true, the East-West game has grown by leaps and bounds until it now rivals the annual National versus American League All-Star Game."[1]

The above quote, which appeared in the August 26, 1939, edition of the *New York Amsterdam News*, provides a simplified version of how the annual signature event of the Negro Leagues, the East-West (E-W) All-Star Game, came to be. In this account, Pittsburgh Crawfords owner and Negro League head honcho William A. "Gus" Greenlee was one of several individuals who played a role in the creation of an all-star game that rivaled, and sometimes surpassed (in attendance and, arguably, importance), that of the major leagues.

There are many conflicting versions of the birth of the "big idea"[2] of the Negro Leagues that need to be sorted to separate fact from fiction. Like many stories of conception, in baseball and elsewhere, the E-W Game truly had many "fathers." Greenlee, though, was undoubtedly the most influential of the many creators – and developers – of the E-W Game. His control of the game's presentation and revenue distribution was a source of contention from the first such contest in 1933 through the sixth edition in 1938. Greenlee's Pittsburgh Crawfords withdrew from the Negro Leagues in 1939, but his involvement in battles over the distribution of its proceeds again became an issue in 1944, when Greenlee encouraged Negro League players to threaten a strike in order to obtain "reasonable" compensation from Negro League owners.

# THE 1935 PITTSBURGH CRAWFORDS

Greenlee was the driving force behind the establishment of the second Negro National League (NNL) in 1933. He became the first chairman of the 1933 edition of the NNL and was credited with "spreading the word in various cities of the new league's advent."[3] Before that, Greenlee had started out his involvement in Black baseball by purchasing the semipro Pittsburgh Crawford Giants in 1930. In 1932 he built Greenlee Field, one of very few ballparks owned and operated by a Black franchise, and competed in the 1932-only East-West League, which was the brainchild of Greenlee's Pittsburgh-area counterpart, Cumberland "Cum" Posey, who owned the Homestead Grays, a longtime NNL rival of the Crawfords.

Prior to 1933, when the major leagues and the Negro Leagues each played their first league All-Star Games, teams of stars occasionally were formed. In the major leagues, an assemblage of stars from seven teams played the Cleveland Indians on July 24, 1911, as a benefit game for Hall of Fame Indians pitcher Addie Joss's widow after Joss died at age 31 of tubercular meningitis early that year. Throughout the first half of the twentieth century, teams of Black and White players were pitted against each other, usually (but not always) in the baseball offseason; according to eminent Black-baseball historian John Holway, the Black teams won 269 of those contests, lost 172, and tied one.[4]

In 1932 an example of a White team playing a Black team occurred in early October when Greenlee's Pittsburgh Crawfords played a series of games at Greenlee Field against "the National League All-Stars, featuring some of the best players of the leading teams of the National League this season."[5] According to the *Pittsburgh Courier*, "Casey Stengle (*sic*), formerly of the New York Giants is handling the club and is anxious for a win over the Greenlee outfit."[6] As it turned out, "[D]espite the big bats of Hack Wilson, English, Todd, and the strong arms of Larry French, Swift, Parmalee and the rest" the Pittsburgh Crawfords won the series, five games to two.[7]

In the 1930s, the Crawfords themselves were a bit of an all-star assemblage. At various times they featured future Hall of Famers Leroy "Satchel" Paige, Josh Gibson, James "Cool Papa " Bell, Oscar Charleston, and William "Judy" Johnson, along with legendary Black stars Herbert "Rap" Dixon, Jimmie Crutchfield, Elander "Vic" Harris, and 1933 E-W All-Star Game East squad starting pitcher Sam Streeter. Not surprisingly, then, when the first E-W contest was played, 12 of the 17 players named to the East squad played for the Crawfords.[8]

## WHOSE "BRAINCHILD" WAS IT?

According to Robert Peterson in *Only the Ball Was White*,

> Gus Greenlee fathered the East-West game, promoting the first one in 1933 in cooperation with Robert A. Cole of the Chicago American Giants. The idea for the game came from Roy Sparrow, one of Greenlee's employees, who dreamed it up in 1932, the year before the first major league all-star game, which played in Chicago under the auspices of the *Chicago Tribune*. Greenlee handled the promotion and took ten percent of the East-west game receipts until he had a falling out with the other owners and resigned the presidency of the [Negro] National League in 1939.[9]

As has become apparent in the interim, Peterson's seminal work is incomplete both in its characterization and timing of Sparrow's "idea" as well as Greenlee's compensation for his role in developing and promoting the game.

Where, then, did Robert Peterson find evidence to conclude that Roy Sparrow had first conceived of the East-West Game in 1932? The answer to this query can be found in the Black press. Several noted columnists, some of whom were participants in the NNL's operations, wrote stories in the 1940s that presented their version of the origin of the E-W Game. In 1941, then- *Pittsburgh Courier* managing editor William G. Nunn wrote:

> The writer has followed the East-West classic from a stormy wintry night in 1933 until the present. He was present at the birth of the idea, along with W.A. "Gus" Greenlee, whose fertile and imaginative brain furnished the "key." ... Roy Sparrow, who first conceived the idea and passed it along to Greenlee: John L. Clark, former Secretary of the Negro National League; 'See' Posey, now with the Homestead Grays and Ches Washington, Sports Editor of this paper.

### TOOK A GAMBLE

> We have followed the growth of the Greenlee-Sparrow 'dreamchild.' We know that in 1933 it was Greenlee, Tom Wilson, now president of the N.N.L.; R.A. Cole, now head of the Metropolitan Burial Association and Hall, present boss of the Chicago American Giants, who backed and went along with the idea.

> "We know that these men gambled" (*sic*) and won for Negro baseball. And we can't forget that the idea could have grown out of the game which Dave Hawkins staged in Cleveland in 1932.[10]

Nunn could forget the year that Dave Hawkins staged a game in Cleveland – Hawkins' "One Big Day" was held in 1933, not 1932. Perhaps Nunn also was "forgetting" when the discussion he purportedly engaged in happened.

It is not only Nunn who stated that the original idea for the E-W Game came from Roy Sparrow. Randy Dixon, who usually wrote for the *Philadelphia Tribune* but in this instance appeared in the *Courier*, mentioned that Nunn "sat in the conference that gave birth to the East-West Idea" and then added parenthetically "(although Roy Sparrow spouted the thought from his fertile and active conk)."[11] Perhaps Dixon may have been taking the word of Nunn, whose above statement was published two weeks before Dixon gave credit to Sparrow, adding that Nunn "rates as the most hep newsman in the profession. He knows all the questions and answers all the answers."[12]

But there were at least three other voices that add support to the contention that Roy Sparrow "planted the seed" for the E-W Game, then saw it developed by Gus Greenlee and others – none other than Greenlee's bitter rival Cum Posey, noted Black sportswriter Wendell Smith, and, in an earlier version, American Negro Press sportswriter Alvin Moses.

It is Posey's version of the E-W Game's conception that has been sourced by two of the most esteemed historians of the institution of Negro League Baseball (Neil Lanctot) and of the history of the East-West Game from 1933 to 1953 (Larry Lester). Lester, in his book *Black Baseball's National Showcase*, asserted that "[t]he East-West All-Star game was the brainchild of writers Roy Sparrow of the *Pittsburgh Sun-Telegraph* and Bill Nunn of the *Pittsburgh Courier*."[13] Both Lester and Lanctot referenced Cum Posey's column "Posey's Points" of August 15, 1942, as their primary source for crediting Sparrow with the idea of a contest between Negro League stars of the East and West.[14]

On the eve of the 10th E-W game in 1942, Posey published his version of how the game came to be, suggesting that other versions did not tell the entire genesis of the game: "The idea was born at a conference in Loendi club, Pittsburgh. The writer of the column had invited Roy Sparrow ... and Bill Nunn ... to talk over the possibility of having two All-Star Colored Teams feature the Annual New York Milk Fund Day at Yankee Stadium. *This idea was a pet idea of Roy Sparrow.*" (emphasis added)[15]

Posey went on to say that, after some discussion, the three decided on a North-South contest at Yankee Stadium, but Nunn and Sparrow shared this idea with Gus Greenlee on the same July 1933 night of the Loendi club meeting. According to Posey, Greenlee, his "bitter rival," persuaded Sparrow and Nunn to adopt Greenlee's version of this idea, transforming it into an East-West rather than a North-South contest and playing it in Chicago's Comiskey Park, where the first major-league All-Star Game had just been held, rather than in New York City.[16]

Two years prior to the conception stories of Nunn, Dixon, and Posey, Alvin Moses had described the birth of the E-W idea happening on Wylie Avenue in Pittsburgh on a "mid-summer afternoon in 1933. Roy [Sparrow] is chatting chiefly about baseball with the then Negro National League president, Tom Wilson, Rufus Jackson, and Gus Greenlee. The conversation centered around 'why shouldn't colored players at least be permitted to show their wares to colored and white fans alike in parks like Comiskey Field [sic], Chicago, or Forbes Field, Pittsburgh?' At the time, Sparrow was writing for a leading white newspaper and in a key position to broach the idea."[17] Moses went on to describe how Sparrow convinced key individuals in the White community of Chicago to come aboard and support the event.[18]

Finally, Wendell Smith's 1943 version places Sparrow on the scene in the winter of 1932: "The idea for this extravaganza was conceived here in Pittsburgh in the winter of 1932. It was not an idea of any particular individual, but it took Roy Sparrow, now critically ill in a local hospital, to 'sell' the idea to Gus Greenlee, who was the 'angel' of the promotion. Sparrow, Cum Posey, Greenlee, and William G. Nunn, now managing editor of the *Pittsburgh Courier*, first saw the possibilities of the 'dream game.'"[19] It seems likely that Robert Peterson drew upon influential African-American sportswriter Wendell Smith's account in dating Sparrow's initial role in the E-W Game's conception to 1932.[20]

So how did Dave Hawkins enter the discussion? Hawkins promoted a doubleheader match called "One Big Day" that was played on Sunday, July 23, 1933, between the Chicago American Giants and the Pittsburgh Crawfords in Cleveland's League Park, which was used by the Cleveland Indians for their home games in part of 1932 and again in 1934 but not in 1933.[21] Hawkins was a Cleveland-based promoter, but he was bedridden in North Carolina when One Big Day was actually staged.[22] Although Bill Nunn was in fact one year off when he stated that Hawkins's promotion occurred in 1932, one can speculate that he remembered wrongly because it seems odd for such a game to be a catalyst for the first E-W Game being played – July 23, 1933, being virtually the same time that the inaugural E-W contest was announced in the Black press. Nevertheless, several commentators have given Hawkins partial credit for "birthing" the idea of the E-W Game, and part of the reason is likely that they were aware of Hawkins promoting his Cleveland doubleheader well before the E-W Game was declared in the Black press. In W. Rollo Wilson's *Pittsburgh Courier* column of August 5, 1933, he described the genesis of Hawkins's promotion as being a desire to "sell Negro baseball to white newspapers and white fans."[23] According to Wilson, in the winter of 1933 Hawkins first tried to get White broadcasters and writers interested in the "proposition of admitting Negroes to the ranks of Organized Baseball." Shortly thereafter, Hawkins tried to get Negro League baseball scores announced on broadcasts once the NNL was formed that year. When Hawkins got no cooperation in this effort from league officials, he turned to promoting a "big game" (which became a doubleheader), a promotion that involved gaining "buy-in" from the Indians and city officials along with the Cleveland dailies. He then negotiated the park fees and the share of receipts for the competing teams, as well as the ultimate choice of the Crawfords and the Giants as the protagonists, as there had been a time when the New York Black Yankees rather than the Giants were being considered.[24]

In the end, the Crawfords swept a doubleheader from the American Giants, 8-1 in the first game and 13-12 in 12 innings in the second contest. In the first game, Giants pitcher Sam Streeter bested Willie Foster, giving up only four hits and one run, compared with 14 hits allowed by Foster. These same two pitchers would start the first E-W Game seven weeks later. In the second game, Josh Gibson hit for the cycle, tying the game at 12-12 in the ninth inning with a home run, before Cool Papa Bell drove in Jimmie Crutchfield with the 13th and deciding run with a "crashing single."[25] Attendance was approximately 7,000, "one of the biggest turnouts in the history of Negro baseball and one of the most enthusiastic and appreciative crowds ever to witness a struggle between two of America's best diamond aggregations."[26] Hawkins himself could not attend the game, as he was laid up in a veterans hospital in North Carolina, but he sent a telegram that was read out to the crowd, which included "many of Cleveland's civic and political celebrities. …"[27]

Hawkins continued to lend his talents to promoting future E-W games, most notably writing a folksy letter in 1934 that was printed in the *Pittsburgh Courier* in a column by NNL league secretary John Clark; in the column, Hawkins provided his suggestions of "pitchers for the koming klouters ALL-Star Baseball Klassic."[28]

In sum, the genesis of what became the annual signature event of Negro League history included several motivating factors. First, there were contests between Black and White baseball stars, and perhaps undeveloped ideas like those of Roy Sparrow prior to 1933. Second, the intense competition being developed in this first season of the second NNL stimulated Dave Hawkins to successfully promote the "One Big Day" doubleheader between the American Giants and the Crawfords, which became a prototype for the first E-W Game. Contemporaneous with Hawkins's planning of his Cleveland doubleheader, *Chicago Defender* columnist Doyle Clivelle wrote that Giants owner Cole and Crawfords owner Greenlee "'Should Sell' That Foster-Page [sic] [Chicago American Giants pitcher Willie Foster and Pittsburgh Crawfords pitcher Satchel Paige] Diamond Feud" by "printing the things Foster and Page are supposed to have said to each other the last time they met on the field" and thereby build a big rivalry.[29] Finally, the major-league All-Star Game played in Chicago on July 6, 1933, likely gave rise to meetings that Posey claimed to have had with Roy Sparrow and Bill Nunn and to a "call to action" for Gus Greenlee to stage a Chicago version of "One Big Day" that pitted East teams against West teams. In fact, the first E-W Game, on September 10, 1933, was primarily played by Eastern players drawn from the Crawfords against Western players drawn from the American Giants. And though Satchel Paige did not pitch in the 1933 E-W Game, he faced off against Willie Foster in the final three innings of the 1934 contest, won by the East, 1-0.

## 1933 – FROM ARCH WARD'S MAJOR LEAGUE CLASSIC TO GUS GREENLEE'S INAUGURAL EAST-WEST CLASSIC

*Chicago Tribune* sportswriter Arch Ward conceived of the first major-league All-Star Game, held on July 6, 1933, at Chicago's Comiskey Park in connection with the 1933 World's Fair. The American League stars defeated the National League, 4-2, in a game that featured a two-run homer by Babe Ruth. Eighteen years earlier, sportswriter and *Baseball Magazine* editor F.C. Lane had been hit by an inspiration: Stars of the two leagues ought to play a seven-game series against each other the week of July 4, which would be the "grand opera of baseball" and "might readily be staged in midseason, where it would serve not only as the grand scenic display of the year, but stimulate greater interest in the pennant race.[30] According to Lew Freedman, "[C]ertainly Ward was aware of the merits of Lane's suggestions."[31] Undoubtedly, Gus Greenlee and others were aware of the excitement attendant to the playing of a contest between teams of star players, and articles in the Black press indicate as much.

Ches Washington, in his "Sez" *Courier* column of June 17, 1933, wrote that "several prominent business men" were considering "the bringing together of the major league's super greats and the Negro League's most brilliant stars for the biggest battle of baseballdom" – and that this attraction would be connected to the Chicago World Fair.[32] Washington went on to say that "[T]he idea is somewhat in keeping with the nation-wide poll to select All-Star major leaguers who will clash at the Fair. ..."[33] It makes sense that one of those businessmen would have been Greenlee, who was not only the owner of one of the powers of the newly established NNL but was also the league's chairman. Despite Washington's view that "the rivalry and interest would be at a much higher pitch for a mixed or inter-racial diamond clash than in a contest where there is no color line," the NNL instead moved on to develop an all-star contest within the Negro Leagues.[34] On July 22, 1933, a *Pittsburgh Courier* piece headlined "Here's Posey's Idea of an All-East, All-West Team" listed Cum Posey's roster choices "if the East could meet the West in an All-star colored baseball game."[35] It was not until July 29, 1933, that the Black press first announced the playing of an all-Black, all-star baseball contest:

> The 'dream game' of Negro baseball is going to be staged! Late advices from the offices of the Negro National Association indicate that two crack teams, to be selected by popular vote, will play in a big colored classic at Comiskey Park in Chicago on September 10.[36]

There is little more than speculation as to whether or not Posey had already gotten wind of Greenlee's supposed co-opting of Posey, Sparrow, and Nunn's North-South conception when Posey was quoted with his player choices for East and West teams. We do not know for sure when Greenlee, American Giants owner Robert Cole, future NNL President and Elite Giants owner Tom Wilson, Sparrow, and Nunn began the process of negotiating for a game date at Comiskey Park and developing a method of promoting the first E-W contest, but it must have begun before the end of July of 1933.

Sportswriter Rollo Wilson provided the most insight into Greenlee's preeminent role in successfully staging the 1933 E-W game. Wilson was not only a columnist for the *Pittsburgh Courier*, but in 1934 he was named the NNL commissioner, a salaried position (which was not a given in Black baseball of the Depression era), in which his chief responsibility was to arbitrate legal disputes, a job for which his chief qualification was his perceived impartiality.[37] Less than one month after the first E-W Game, Wilson's regular column, "Sports Shots," positively depicted the role of Greenlee in being "that rare type of sportsman – one who will spend his money in the game and send more good dollars after the ones which have gone beyond recall."[38] As Wilson recounted Greenlee's seminal role in forming the second incarnation of the NNL, he wrote that Greenlee "conceived the idea of an East-West game, the players to be selected by the vote of the fans and he had to put $2,500 on the line weeks before the date of the game. All that he has received for his efforts has been ill-advised criticism ... even from the very men who accepted his money to pay their personal bills."[39] Eleven years later, Wilson wrote another column about Greenlee's trailblazing role in Black baseball in which he referred to Greenlee as "the father of the East-West game and it was his money which guaranteed the owners of the White Sox park that they would get their excessive rental."[40]

Whether or not Rollo Wilson was impartial when it came to Gus Greenlee, he made three important points in his columns regarding Gus's organizing role in the inaugural E-W Game: Greenlee was really the game's creator, he bankrolled the contest, and he was criticized heavily for the game's execution. In 1951, as Greenlee's life was winding down due to a lengthy illness, Wendell Smith summed up Greenlee's contribution as follows: "He launched the first game, invested his own money, and eventually made it an affair of national significance."[41] In his seminal book *Negro League Baseball*, Neil Lanctot concluded that "it was reportedly Greenlee who took the greatest risk by paying $2,500 in advance for the exorbitant rental of Comiskey Park" for the first E-W contest.[42] While it is not clear whether Greenlee ended up paying the entire fee out of his own pocket, Wilson did make it clear that Greenlee fronted the money to reserve the park.

Wilson's counterpart, John Clark, was another person who participated in some fashion in the organization of the E-W Game. Clark was not only a regular columnist for the *Pittsburgh Courier*, but he was also a front-office employee of the Crawfords and Greenlee as he was the NNL secretary. One could presume that Clark, as both a league and Crawfords official, would have had an informed idea of whose money was spent and who shared in the proceeds. It was Clark who reported that "all expense of promoting the game will be borne by three club owners, namely W.A. Greenlee, R.A. Cole, and Tom Wilson."[43] Later in the column, Clark stated that the 1933 "East-West experiment, which cost over $5,000 before the park gates were opened on September 10," garnered a net profit of less than $400 to each of the three owners.[44] While Clark was describing the 1934 game's promotional expenses in this column when he named the three owners, it is easy to conclude from a careful reading of the rest of his column that those three owners also shared in the 1933 expenses. Does Clark's reporting of an equal division of the profits mean that Chicago American Giants owner Cole and Nashville Elites owner Wilson partly reimbursed Greenlee for his payment of the expensive Comiskey Park rental? According to Greenlee:

Tom Wilson, R.A. Cole and myself took the first gamble in 1933. That year we couldn't get anyone to go in with us. The game drew 12,000 people.

The next year, the three of us promoted the game, giving the league ten percent. We paid all expenses. …

We gave the league the East-West game, after we struggled and sacrificed to put it over. When no one had any faith in the idea, it was perfectly all right for us to gamble with our money' …[45]

While it is uncertain whether or not Greenlee's "gamble" included his payment in full of the park rental, it is known approximately how much revenue the first E-W Game generated. The *Courier* reported in 1941 that $9,500 was received from fans attending the game.[46]

For Greenlee, his partners Cole and Wilson, and his media assistants Nunn of the *Courier* and Sparrow of the *Pittsburgh Sun-Gazette*, August and September 1933 were a very busy time. Sparrow in particular was very busy promoting the game, as he "not only barraged 55 black weeklies with news of the upcoming game, but also contacted 90 white newspapers."[47] And there was more. Sparrow engaged Norman Ross, who interested "big name movie stars and executives" while he "personally conducted fifty-one broadcasts" and "placed the East-West directly in the lap of Chicago World's Fair officials who went for it, hook, line and sinker."[48] Meanwhile, various prominent Black newspapers, including most notably the *Chicago Defender* and the *Pittsburgh Courier*, were printing ballots for the fans to vote on who should participate. The *Courier* reported on August 12, 1933,

The almost phenomenal response on the part of fans and followers of Negro baseball is evidenced by the heavy voting which marked the first few days of the contest to select the nation's best players to represent the East and the West in the Comiskey Park battle.[49]

Both the *Defender* and *Courier* reported that the game would be a doubleheader. The *Defender* stated that the first game would be the official game, and the *Courier* reported, "[I]n case of a split victory in the doubleheader, the third game will be played in an Eastern city which will be designated later."[50]

In the end, only a single game was played on September 10, 1933, with the West squad defeating the East, 11-7. Although the game was well attended,[51] it was preceded by much "ugly talk" regarding the methods of choosing players and the game's receipts going "into the pockets of the promoters."[52] *Philadelphia Tribune* sports editor Randy Dixon, a notable (but also humorous) scolder of Negro League owners, described the game as "basically a commendable idea" but one suffused with "promotorial [sic] greed" resulting in an "over-commercialized stench" which was intended to make money for the backers rather than providing a true test of the playing abilities of Eastern vs. Western players.[53] After the contest, Cum Posey perceived the first E-W Game as "not a true estimate of the strength between East and West" which he believed would have been better as a Crawfords-American Giants game, but he also said that "the promoters ... put up all the money and deserved all the profits."[54] Posey later developed a different opinion about the handling of East-West revenue by Greenlee and his partners.

## 1934-1938 – GREENLEE AND HIS PARTNERS CHALLENGED – AND EXTOLLED – WHILE THE GAME BECOMES AN INSTITUTION

### 1934 – THERE WILL BE A SECOND E-W GAME – AND THERE WILL BE CONFLICTS

At the end of the 1933 NNL season, Rollo Wilson, not yet the commissioner of the NNL but an informed observer of league operations, portrayed Greenlee as essentially the savior of a fledgling operation: "[O]ne thing and another conspired to stop the circuit but Greenlee and his bankroll shifted clubs, cities and players and kept the thing going somehow or other."[55] After describing how Greenlee funded the first E-W contest with little help from his fellow owners, Wilson quoted Greenlee as "visioning a new and a better league" and concluded that "knowing Gus, I am optimistic about 1934."

Looking backward, one can easily conclude that having another All-Star event was a sure thing. Nevertheless, it was not until early July of 1934 that an "[O]fficial announcement was made ... that this 'game of games'... will be staged again this year."[56] *Amsterdam News* columnist Romeo Dougherty asserted, "[T]he game this year has the approval of league officials and the club owners. ... They realize that the East-West games, if continued, will perpetuate Negro baseball, and through Negro baseball will perpetuate the league. It's the greatest bit of 'good-will' advertising ever engineered, and the games will be permanent."[57] Implied in Dougherty's pronouncements is that many in the Negro League hierarchy were not so supportive of the E-W Game in the previous year. Negro League owners and officials now realized how crucial the E-W Game was to the successful promotion of Black baseball and the Negro Leagues.

For Greenlee, the general enthusiasm for staging a successful all-star contest in Black baseball by no means meant that criticism of his promotional methods, the competitive structure of the game, and especially the financial arrangements he and his partners Cole and Wilson were making would abate. Chief among the critics were Frank A. "Fay" Young and Cum Posey, but other negative voices also weighed in. From Young's perspective, the selection process was flawed in 1933, such that star players like Newt Allen, Bullet Rogan, and Chet Brewer of the Kansas City Monarchs were not selected for the game even though they had gained substantial support in fan balloting.[58] Young also questioned why no entity such as a "home for disabled Negro ballplayers or some worthwhile Negro charity" had yet to be designated as a beneficiary of the game.[59] In addition, Young saw no purpose in having an East vs. West contest when there was no Eastern or Western circuit in the NNL. Young proposed that the Negro League game model itself after the American Association, which had the league's leading club play an all-star team.[60] Instead, what was being offered was "an East vs. West game in which the votes of the public are ignored ... that is for the benefit of two promoters and their two dependent sports editors."[61] While Young did not name any names, columnist Ed Harris, in writing a year-end review of the 1934 season, noted that Cum Posey had accused Gus Greenlee, Robert Coles, and Ed Bolden (owner of the Philadelphia Stars) of dominating the NNL, and specifically, that the balloting for the E-W contest was "dominated by these men," an accusation that was confirmed in that both squads were largely populated by players from their three teams.[62] Meanwhile, Lewis Dial wrote in the *New York Age* that a lot of "unsavory criticism" was being leveled at the 1934 E-W Game, and noted that Cum Posey had issued a press release announcing that his Homestead Grays would not participate in the game, as they had in 1933, because the voting was "a fake."[63] Dial then derided the sponsors of the 1933 game for failing to report on its financial outcome, while being "parsimonious with its tickets among sun-down scribes, but very generous to the white brethren."[64]

John Clark had answers for all these criticisms. He editorialized that critics like Young and others, though "exercising a right as members of the fourth estate," were criticizing "everything in general but nothing in particular" while the three game sponsors, Greenlee, Wilson, and Cole, were again bearing all expenses for the game and this time would "donate ten per cent of the gross receipts to the Negro National League."[65] Clark indicated that Greenlee and his partners were giving the public what it wanted and gambling their own money on the venture, while the critics were "those who have a chronic inclination to oppose anything which they do not conceive or develop."[66] Clark detailed all the efforts of 1933 to reach out to newsmen, to advertise, and to operate openly to deliver a product worth watching by the general public. He also specified a careful approach, run by NNL personnel and endorsed by Commissioner Wilson, to make the 1934 game an even bigger success.[67]

Clark was not only one of those league personnel, but also an employee of Gus Greenlee, so his defense of Greenlee, Cole, and Wilson's methods may have been less than objective. However, he was far from alone in his praise of the staging of the 1934 E-W game. Sportswriters Ches Washington, Romeo Dougherty, Dan Burley, and Nat Trammell all offered praise for the handling of the event, and much of it specifically lauded Greenlee's efforts. Washington praised Greenlee, Wilson and Coles as "pioneers and advocates of a New Era – all men who were willing to put up their own money and take a chance" and who succeeded in drawing 25,000 fans to the 1934 East-West Game and a similar turnout to a four-team doubleheader at Yankee Stadium.[68]

Dougherty was even more fulsome in his praise of Greenlee, describing him as "one of the big men behind the staging of the East-West game. … Greenlee saw the possibilities last season after the first game … and decided if people are given the things they want in a big way they are only too glad to come out and patronize a real show or a real baseball game."[69] In another column devoted especially to depicting the 1934 Yankee Stadium doubleheader that Greenlee and his staff staged, Dougherty extolled Greenlee as "the man who could turn the attention of so many thousands of people towards a Negro ballgame … a man capable of Herculean efforts" and someone who "gathered unto himself a handful of men with hearts and hands determined. … In his systematic way of doing things, Mr. Greenlee chose and appointed each man of his promoting organization to a post to which he thought him best adapted."[70]

Dan Burley was quoted extensively by Dougherty in a November 24, 1934, *New York Amsterdam News* column headlined, "What Negro Business Men Could Do if They Only Have Foresight." According to Dougherty, Burley had a "style of voicing opinions this writer has held in the past, to say nothing of the present" and, in this case, Burley was in enthusiastic agreement with Dougherty about Greenlee's successful role in staging the 1934 East-West Game.[71] In a paragraph captioned "**Greenlee Did It**" (bold in original) Burley is quoted as follows:

> "I have established as an undisputable fact that Gus Greenlee and others decided that an All-Star game could be arranged and played in a major league park and attract a crowd. This theory is established through published reports and the testimony of eye-witnesses at Chicago on September 26. ...
>
> "You know, of course, the results and the emphatic boost that colored baseball gained therefrom. Heroes, born under the hot sun of that sultry afternoon, bathed in the favor of the multitude. Such men as, as they so quaintly term them, Satchel Paige, Willie Wells, Willie Foster, and a fellow named Mule Suttles."

Nat Trammell, who wrote for the short-lived *Colored Baseball & Sports Monthly,* which made its debut in September 1934 and called itself "The Only Publication of Its Kind in the World,"[72] later wrote a piece on the 1934 game entitled "Baseball Classic – East vs. West." He waxed eloquent as he described the game as "one of those classics where you must draw upon your aesthetic appreciation to fully digest its beauty."[73] Not only did Trammell credit Greenlee, Coles, and Wilson as "co-workers of this gigantic plan," which he called "the greatest event that could be put over by anyone for the benefit of promoting interest in Colored baseball," but he also implicitly gave the lion's share of the credit for the game's success to Greenlee, as he wrote that "(I)t is a source of joy to us to learn of the success of the East-West game. Mr. Greenlee is a real business man and a baseball promoter."[74]

The 1934 East-West game was a pitcher's duel, with the East prevailing, 1-0, when Cool Papa Bell walked, stole second, and was driven home on a bloop hit by Jud "Boojum" Wilson. Satchel Paige pitched four scoreless frames to close out the game and earned the win for the East, with Willie Foster giving up one run in three innings to take the loss.[75] John Clark's January 5, 1935, *Pittsburgh Courier* column reviewed the 1934 season and summed up Greenlee's successful promotion of the 1934 game thusly:

> The game went on, and 20,000 people agreed that it was one of the greatest shows ever staged on a baseball diamond. ...
>
> The National Association [NNL] benefitted to the extent of almost $1,000 from this game – a fact which proved to be a very good reply to critics of the classic. ...
>
> It was [Greenlee's] determination which inspired his organization to carry on the East-West promotion when critics speeded up their ammunition, and fired away at their targets.[76]

## 1935 – GREENLEE AND POSEY SPAR OVER E-W GAME PROFIT DISTRIBUTION

At the start of 1935, the NNL partially adopted Romeo Dougherty's suggestion that it add two Eastern teams and form an Eastern and Western baseball association, with Gus Greenlee as president of the Eastern association, leading to a series at season's end between the Eastern and Western champions.[77] At the January 12, 1935, NNL meeting, the league voted to admit the Brooklyn

Eagles and the New York Cubans and to give the Homestead Grays, previously an NNL associate member, a full league membership, which meant that eight teams now competed in the NNL; there were four teams in the East and four teams in the West, with Homestead and Pittsburgh considered to be Western outfits.[78] Gus Greenlee continued as league president, but at the March 1935 league meeting, Commissioner Rollo Wilson was replaced by Ferdinand Q. Wilson.[79]

> At the January 1935 meeting, it was reported that baseball officials "conceded 1934 to be a "best year" for colored baseball, and pointed to the East-West Game and the two exhibition doubleheaders in New York as highlights of the season."[80] President Greenlee, though, "reminded his colleagues that 'in spite of the success of last year we have not arrived.'"[81] The league passed five resolutions, including the following: "That the East-West game be repeated this year, with almost all profits going to the association's treasury. (Last year only ten percent of net went to the association.)[82]

> This resolution, as well as John Clark's assertion that same month that almost $1,000 had been realized by the league treasury from the 1934 E-W game, indicated that Clark had erred earlier when he said that 10 percent of gross receipts would be contributed to the league treasury from the 1934 game. Whether the *Pittsburgh Courier's* 1941 report that the 1934 E-W Game took in $14,000 in receipts or its 1947 reporting of $20,000 in East-West receipts was accurate, the less than $1,000 contribution did not amount to 10 percent of gross receipts.[83]

In July 1935 the NNL announced that the league treasury would receive "50 percent of the proceeds" from the 1935 E-W Game, with Greenlee, Cole, and Wilson "sacrificing their share for the purpose of setting up a fund to meet future emergencies affecting players and owners." This, of course begs the question of what was happening to the other 50 percent that was not earmarked for the league treasury.

Cum Posey's initial reaction to this declaration was very positive (for Posey, that is). He suggested that the pointed criticism he and Frank Young had leveled at Greenlee, Cole, and Wilson for benefiting themselves when they promoted the 1933 game was effective, leading to players and owners "working in harmony this season to put this game over in a 'big way.' Mr. Greenlee and Mr. Cole have sacrificed personal profit to strengthen the coffers of the league. ..."[84] Clearly, Posey was accepting the word of the three E-W sponsors that they would not directly profit from their promotional efforts.

The game itself was played on August 11, 1935, and resulted in an 11-8 slugfest won by the West squad in the 11th inning on a two-out, three-run homer by the powerful Mule Suttles before another turnout of 25,000 fans.[85] Apparently, though, at least some of the players were disgruntled, as they were paid only $5 to participate in the game. An article by "Arbiter" in the August 24, 1935, *Baltimore Afro-American* reported that Greenlee had been willing to give the players $10 each, but other owners wanted to give them nothing. Commissioner Morton prevailed by suggesting $5 as a compromise, but Arbiter reported that players responded with "howls of protest" with one player throwing "his five dollars back on the table with a blasphemous opinion of the procedure."[86] The article went on to report that "the league did not promote the game, but was supposed to get 50 percent of the profits," with one unnamed owner who was behind on his payroll to be "the chief beneficiary of the game, *aside from the promoters, Greenlee, Cole and Wilson* (emphasis added)."[87]

However, that wasn't all the trouble that was brewing in the NNL. In an August 29, 1935, *Philadelphia Tribune* column headlined "Double, Double, Toil and Troubles Baseball Association Kettle Bubbles," columnist Ed Harris avowed that the $5 payment to the players was "chicken feed considering the magnitude and the importance of the spectacle; questioned the validity of the player voting counts, noting that two players received the exact same number of votes; reported that Gus Greenlee was "reaching the limit of his financial resources" and gave as evidence for this assertion that the bus that was to take Crawfords players to the E-W Game had been attached for the non-payment of a debt; and noted that "a goodly portion of the [E-W game revenues] was to go to the Association [NNL] treasury but at present such a settlement has not been made."[88]

Not surprisingly, Greenlee felt compelled to respond to these charges in his own newspaper column. He identified himself as the "developer of the idea and principal promoter" of the East-West Game.[89] He then wrote:

> I have never taken 'all the profits.' R.A. Cole, Tom T. Wilson shared in 1933 and 1934, and this year 50 per cent of the net receipts went to the league treasury. Having never promoted a game of this kind, few of the owners have any idea of the detail and expense involved. It only follows, however, that since they do not understand, they would oppose.[90]

Greenlee addressed the players' gripes about nominal payment for participation in the E-W Game and asserted that most of the players had not made a fuss. He made no mention of the alleged voting irregularities and did not directly address Harris's claim that the Crawfords were in financial trouble. He did, however, mention his investment of substantial money, with significant losses, since 1932 in the Crawfords' ballpark and operations as well as in league operations, and charged that "only a few of my associates" shared his vision that all the owners needed to make sacrifices to develop and maintain the viability of the NNL.[91]

One of the most prominent owners who did not share Greenlee's vision was Cum Posey. Posey was so incensed that he wrote columns in 1935, 1936, and 1937 in which he vented his spleen at Greenlee and his associates for not living up to their promises regarding the distribution of the game's proceeds. On November 30, 1935, "Cum Posey's Pointed Paragraphs" ended thusly:

> The writer's criticism of the financial settlement of the [1935 E-W] game rests on the resolution passed wherein the promoters and the league were each to receive half of the net receipts. Had this been lived up to, the league would have received all the money as it was the league's money that 'promoted' the game.[92]

Here, Posey did not name names, but his readership knew that this was directed especially at Gus Greenlee. Posey was much more direct and detailed in his criticisms nearly a year later. In his November 7, 1936, column "Posey's Points," he started out by saying, "[T]o think about the East-West game of 1935 is a headache."[93] He then proceeded to give the reader a headache as he stated that "[T]he plain facts about that game are: The league treasury furnished every cent for promotion. … The expenses were padded so strong that only $1,700.00 [94] were cleared. If the league should rejoice because they got $850 out of a $14,000.00 promotion … then the league is only made up of two clubs and a secretary, as they are the only ones who profited." Posey's explanation was as clear as mud, but he did say directly that Robert Cole and Gus Greenlee "should have given the league all the money cleared."[95]

Finally, Posey revisited – and revamped – his critique of Greenlee and his associates in a September 25, 1937, *Pittsburgh Courier* article headlined, "Posey Scores Gus on Setup for All-Star 9."[96] Now, Posey added more depth to his charges against Greenlee, stating that the night of the 1935 game, it was decided that the four Western clubs (Homestead Grays, Pittsburgh Crawfords, Chicago American Giants, and Nashville/Columbus Elite Giants) would share in the East-West Game profits, leaving the four Eastern clubs to share in the coming Yankee

Stadium doubleheader proceeds. Posey did not say if he had participated in this decision, but he stated that Robert Cole later announced that they "would deposit half of the net receipts to the league's credit, the other half he and Mr. Greenlee decided to keep."⁹⁷

It is entirely possible that, at the time of the 1935 game, Greenlee, Cole, and Wilson had only intended to sacrifice their share of the 50 percent of the profits earmarked for the league. As the "money men" and promoters of the 1933 and 1934 contest, it seems likely that Greenlee, Cole, and Wilson thought they still deserved compensation for their pioneering efforts, even if they were not solely responsible for the promotion of the 1935 game. It is possible that Greenlee's financial troubles led him to change his mind about sacrificing all compensation, but the league plainly stated that only half of the profits were to go into the league treasury, which left the other half for someone else. Posey's 1937 broadside suggested that the three promoters had an obligation to share that half with the other Western teams, but they chose to keep it for themselves, and, according to Posey, "the only way any other club could get any of it would be through a judge's order, and no other club did get it."⁹⁸ Posey's charge is further supported by an article in the August 20, 1936, *Philadelphia Tribune*, which stated that "last year fifty per cent, was the league's share, but owners were displeased because the remaining profits were not pro-rated among them."⁹⁹

Posey also asserted that Greenlee, Cole, and Wilson did not spend their own money on promotions for the 1935 E-W Game. Though Greenlee said in September 1935 that the other owners had no idea of the expense involved in promotion, that does not necessarily mean that he and his partners paid out of their own pockets; it could well have been a justification of their expense reports, since Posey in his 1936 article seems to have suggested that Greenlee and his cohort were exaggerating their expenses and thereby were pocketing money that should have been deemed profits. Arbiter's 1935 article stated that the league did not promote the game, but he did not say that the league did not pay for those promotions. On the other hand, in an "exclusive interview" Greenlee gave to the *Pittsburgh Courier* in late August of 1936, he was quoted as follows: "Last year, the N.N. League [NNL] promoted the game, getting fifty-fifty [*sic*] per cent."¹⁰⁰

There is no doubt that Greenlee invested his own money in the 1933 and 1934 E-W Games and that he seemed to expect compensation for his investments, whether in the past only or continuing, as well as for his efforts and those of his sponsorship teams. Posey seemed to feel that he and other owners were not consulted about the decision-making process for disbursing profits; however, Greenlee felt that he had every right to make those decisions because of his role in developing and institutionalizing the E-W Game.

## 1936 – A DISGRUNTLED GREENLEE RELINQUISHES CONTROL OVER THE E-W GAME, THEN "SAVES" IT FOR CHICAGO.

In the aftermath of the 1935 game, Greenlee had his own grievances against the other league owners. He resented all the criticisms he faced about his role as "developer of the idea and principal promoter" of the East-West Game, as he felt that "[B]eneath the criticisms which are going the rounds is the vilest meanest kind of ingratitude."¹⁰¹ Greenlee referenced "drastic moves now being planned" by other owners to take over league and East-West Game organization, saying that "Up to this time I have been a congenial fellow. But if these rumors are to develop into factual realities, you will see a fighting Greenlee, equipped with everything needed to win – and I will call the meeting, name the place and date."¹⁰²

In early May of 1936, Greenlee again wrote to air his grievances with the talk of the other "colored baseball men, especially members of the Negro National League, that I have wasted money on Satchell[*sic*] Paige."¹⁰³ Greenlee indicated that he had "no regrets for a single dollar I have spent on Satchell Paige. He is worth it. He is a part of my baseball gamble."[104] In discussing Paige, Greenlee reviewed the E-W games and Yankee Stadium doubleheaders he had principally staged in 1933 and 1934, saying that "[I]n all of these games I invested money. Advertising, park forfeits, transportation and the different items which go with promotions of this kind. … My friends in the East … can see no value in my pioneering work. …"[105] Notably, Greenlee did not mention any 1935 expenditures that he undertook; rather, his complaints suggest he felt strongly that, having taken enormous monetary gambles and having succeeded in establishing the East-West and Yankee Stadium games, he deserved a separate share of the profits from these events in 1935 and perhaps going forward.

Greenlee felt that "after its [E-W Game] success had been assured, we were sorta shunted aside. …"[106] He refused to serve on the NNL committee appointed to promote the 1936 East-West Game and, since he had already resigned the position of chairman of the NNL in January of 1936, it seemed that he was dramatically scaling back his participation in Negro League operations.[107] As it turned out, Greenlee ended up being principally involved in the staging of the 1936 game, as the three appointed members of that committee – Newark Eagles co-owner Abe Manley, Roy Sparrow, and NNL Commissioner Ferdinand Morton – first decided to hold the East-West Game in New York in July and then, "[F]or some unexplained reason, the official committee made no attempt to promote the East-West game. …"[108] Up to the plate stepped Greenlee, along with Tom Wilson, new Chicago American Giants owner H.G. Hall, and Kansas City Monarchs owner J.L. Wilkinson. Greenlee disagreed with "the action in deserting Chicago" and, when he discovered that the game would not be staged in New York, he "decided to go through with the game, because we wanted to keep faith with the public as well as revitalize the sport and perpetuate the game. And so, the game will be held in Chicago, where it has been held for the last six years."[109]

On August 23, 1936, before 26,000 spectators at Comiskey Park, the East routed the West, 10-2, on a 14-hit barrage that included three hits and a stolen base by Cool Papa Bell.[110] But the game, "featuring players from only four teams, lacked the all-star quality of previous years."[111] Naturally, those four teams were Greenlee's Pittsburgh Crawfords, Wilson's now-Washington Elite Giants, Hall's Chicago American Giants, and Wilkinson's Kansas City Monarchs. The Crawfords players were switched over to the East and played alongside the representatives of the Elite Giants, while the Chicago and Kansas City players represented two Western franchises that were independent of the NNL in 1936.[112] Although the fourth annual E-W Game was still a success, five of its teams – the Homestead Grays, Philadelphia Stars, Newark Eagles, New York Cubans, and the New York Black Yankees, who became an NNL member for the season's second half – were not a part of the contest and, according to league secretary John Clark, the league treasury received no money from the game.[113]

Clark provided explanations for the failure of the Manley-Sparrow-Morton triumvirate to carry out their plans for a New York E-W game, while also questioning the "motives behind the proposal" by Greenlee, et al. in taking over the contest.[114] Manley, Sparrow, and Morton were going to give all the game's profits to the league, but those three lacked the "finances, prestige and harmony" that Greenlee and his partners wielded.[115] Nonetheless, Clark thought that the league still should have received a percentage of the game's profits. Instead, Wilkinson received a fixed percentage, and apparently the other three promoters split the rest of the profits. In the final analysis, according to Clark, "[I]f the Negro National league is to continue it must have a treasury balance. This balance can only be piled up by earnings from games of this type."[116]

## 1937 - GREENLEE'S PARTICIPATION WANES

In 1937 Gus Greenlee returned to the presidency of the NNL, but his involvement in the E-W Game diminished, as other leaguewide and personal financial problems intervened. In March 1937 Greenlee traded the great Josh Gibson and star third baseman Judy Johnson to his bitter rival, Cum Posey's Homestead Grays, in exchange for the considerably lesser talents of catcher Pepper Bassett and third baseman Henry Spearman. The deal was an exchange of talent at two positions, but was considerably augmented by the $2,500 sent to the Crawfords. It was a signal that Greenlee was in dire need of funds.[117]

Three major developments occurred in 1937, one of which had some promises but also challenges for the future viability of the NNL, while the other two were threats to its successful continuation. A rival league, the Negro American League, was founded in 1937 with Major R.R. Jackson named president, and eight teams from the Midwest joining. An incipient rivalry between the two leagues meant that there were ongoing disputes about teams from one league raiding those of the other, along with other periodic conflicts, but there was also a clear-cut delineation between East and West that could only enhance the competitiveness and prestige of the E-W Game. On the downside, the New York Cubans suspended operations in 1937 as team owner Alex Pompez left the country to avoid being arrested for his involvement in New York's numbers rackets. Also, Dominican Republic dictator Rafael Trujillo successfully raided the Negro Leagues, signing a total of 18 players, mostly from the Cubans and the Crawfords, and including such luminaries as Satchel Paige, Cool Papa Bell, and player-manager Martin Dihigo.[118]

Greenlee decreed that no players who left for the Dominican Republic would be allowed to play in the East-West Game even if they returned in time. He had concerns that new faces would therefore have to be introduced to the contest, ut his concerns were alleviated when "20,000 frenzied fans paid to see the new faces take part in the East-West Game on August 8, and thereby demonstrated their confidence in Negro baseball and Greenlee's promotions."[119] The game was won by the East, 7-2, with Buck Leonard driving in the first two runs on a home run in the second inning.[120]

Once again, though, Posey and Greenlee butted heads over the proceeds, with Newark Eagles co-owner Effa Manley playing a supporting role in the drama. According to Posey, Manley refused to allow her players to participate in the 1937 E-W Game unless NAL President Jackson made sure that all the NNL clubs got their share of the proceeds, which she secured and then gave to the other NNL clubs. Posey also charged that she uncovered an agreement between Jackson and Greenlee that guaranteed Greenlee 10 percent of the game's receipts rather than "the 10 percent from the East which was legally his."[121] Of course, Greenlee had a different version of this encounter and claimed that Effa Manley "threatened to keep the ballplayers of all the clubs she represented out of the game unless all the monies were turned over to her. ... Of course this was not done (ellipsis in original)."[122] Furthermore, Greenlee stated that he asked all the clubs whether they wanted the E-W Game proceeds due them put into the league treasury or split among them and asserted that they all, "with the exception of Greenlee's Crawfords, voted for the 'split.' This only goes to show that these owners do not have the good of the League at heart because the League owes plenty of bills right now."[123]

## GREENLEE'S FINAL CLASSIC

West Beats East in Classic Thriller, 5 to 4"

Thirty thousand fans, bordering on hysteria, all did a 'Susie Q' Sunday afternoon at Comiskey Park in the home third of the sixth annual East versus West classic when Neil Robinson (Memphis Red Sox) slammed what should have been a single (or perhaps a double) to center field and Sam

Bankhead (Pittsburgh Crawfords) let the ball go through him for a home run inside of the park – and away went the ball game."[124]

The last East-West All-Star Game that directly involved Gus Greenlee was played on August 21, 1938. Greenlee had remained the NNL president, but he eventually resigned from his position and withdrew the Crawfords from the NNL in early 1939.[125] To the end of his involvement, Greenlee would trumpet the success of the East-West All-Star classic and, even without his participation, the game continued to be played annually in Chicago for 22 more seasons.[126] Also to the end of his involvement, Greenlee and his fellow owners were "haggling over disposition of profits."[127] The September 3, 1938, edition of the *Chicago Defender* reported that Greenlee, "who voted 10 per cent for originating the idea [of the E-W Game] … donated, presented or gave $600 to a Negro American League official. What was it for? Also for the good of baseball why isn't a report published as to where all the money goes."[128]

Perhaps Greenlee already knew that he would soon withdraw from the league at the time of the 1938 E-W Game, because he seemed to be giving valedictory speeches to the press about his role in its conception and its glorious future. In the August 6, 1938, *Defender*, Greenlee was quoted thusly: "… [T]he profit angle with me, Tom Wilson, and R.A. Cole, the men who first gambled with the idea, was secondary. What we set out to do, was put aside one day of glory for the players. … In presenting these players to the public, we replied to the demands which loyal fans had been making. … The manner in which the classic has been supported each year, bears me out in this claim."[129] Once more, in the September 3, 1938, *Defender*, he was quoted as follows: "'As for the game itself, that has been a real success as was proven in the game held in Chicago last Sunday. Thirty thousand fans were present despite a Pittsburgh-Cubs doubleheader, which is proof of success. … The game in Chicago, Greenlee explained, will never be moved. 'That contest is an institution now.'"[130]

## CONCLUSION

Gus Greenlee made one final appearance on the scene of the East-West Game. In mid-1944 he applied for an associate membership for his revived Pittsburgh Crawfords. The league declined his application, although Cum Posey later said that the league approved Greenlee for an associate membership but not in Pittsburgh.[131] Greenlee was not going to take this lying down, so he decided to sign away several players from each league by offering them much higher salaries than they were currently making, and also suggest that the players chosen for the East-West game go on strike if they were not offered more money.[132] According to the *Amsterdam News*, "[T]he men with whom Greenlee was associated … are mostly against him and are fighting him tooth and nail to prevent his return to the baseball picture."[133]

The players did not strike, as they got what Greenlee suggested they ask for, which was $200 apiece from NNL President Wilson and $100 plus expenses from NAL President J.B. Martin.[134] Greenlee, who was "[a]lways known for his square-shooting with players and his willingness to help them," said that "league club owners are getting 'greasy with money.'" while "the ballplayers are still getting as low as $40 a week playing in many cases three games in one day.…"[135]

Gus Greenlee died in 1952 after a long illness. One of his most important legacies is his prominent role in developing and organizing the East-West All-Star Game. In his autobiography, *I Was Right on Time*, Buck O'Neil said:

> Let me tell you a little bit about the East-West game, because for a black ballplayer and for black baseball fans, that was something special. … That was the greatest idea Gus ever had, because it made black people feel involved in baseball like they'd never been before. While the big leagues left the choice of players up to the sportswriters, Gus left it up to the fans.[136]

# Pride of Smoketown

## Notes

1. *New York Amsterdam News*, August 26, 1939.
2. The concept of the "big idea" is a well-known principle of advertising. Simply put, a groundbreaking creative slogan, execution, or principle can become a signature of a company's brand, thereby aiding and enhancing its promotional efforts. See, e.g., David Ogilvy, *Ogilvy on Advertising* (New York: Vintage Books, 1985). The E-W Game was arguably, therefore, the key element of the identity of the Negro Leagues from its inception in 1933 onward.
3. Duke Goldman, "1933-1962: The Business Meetings of Negro League Baseball," *Baseball's Business: The Winter Meetings Volume 2 1958-2016* (Phoenix: Society for American Baseball Research, 2017), 393; *Pittsburgh Courier*, March 4, 1933. Greenlee was variously referred to as the chairman of the NNL and the NNL president.
4. John Holway, *Voices from the Great Black Baseball Leagues* (New York: Da Capo Press, rev. ed. 1992), xviii-xix.
5. *Pittsburgh Courier*, October 1, 1932.
6. *Pittsburgh Courier*, October 1, 1932.
7. *Pittsburgh Courier*, October 8, 1932.
8. Larry Lester, *Black Baseball's National Showcase* (Lincoln: University of Nebraska Press, 2001), 29.
9. Robert Peterson, *Only the Ball Was White* (New York: Random House Value Publishing, Inc., 1970), 100.
10. *Pittsburgh Courier*, July 26, 1941.
11. *Pittsburgh Courier*, August 9, 1941.
12. *Pittsburgh Courier*, August 9, 1941.
13. Lester, 21.
14. Lester, 484 n. 1 (1933); Neil Lanctot, *Negro League Baseball* (Philadelphia: University of Pennsylvania Press, 2004), 404 n. 34.
15. "Posey's Points," *Pittsburgh Courier*, August 15, 1942.
16. "Posey's Points," *Pittsburgh Courier*, August 15, 1942.
17. Alvin Moses, "Beating the Gun," *Baltimore Afro-American*, September 9, 1939.
18. Moses.
19. *Pittsburgh Courier*, July 31, 1943.
20. Peterson's seminal work lacked footnotes, so there is no direct evidence of the source material he used for delineating the role of Roy Sparrow in the E-W Game's creation. It may also be possible that Posey's 1942 account suggesting that in July 1933 Sparrow related a "pet idea" that Greenlee then turned into the E-W Game bolstered Peterson's statement that Sparrow's inspiration occurred prior to 1933.
21. Philip J. Lowry, *Green Cathedrals* (New York: Walker & Company, updated ed. 2006), 73.
22. *Pittsburgh Courier*, July 29, 1933,
23. *Pittsburgh Courier*, August 5, 1933.
24. *Pittsburgh Courier*, August 5, 1933.
25. *Pittsburgh Courier*, July 29, 1933.
26. "Sez 'Ches,'" *Pittsburgh Courier*, July 29, 1933.
27. *Pittsburgh Courier*, July 29, 1933.
28. *Cleveland Call and Post*, August 18, 1934.
29. *Chicago Defender*, June 17, 1933.
30. F.C. Lane, "An All-Star Baseball Game for a Greater Championship," *Baseball Magazine*, July 1915, as quoted in Lew Freedman, *The Day All the Stars Came Out* (Jefferson, North Carolina: McFarland & Company Inc. 2010), 11.
31. Freedman, *Stars*, 12.
32. "Sez 'Ches,'" *Pittsburgh Courier*, June 17, 1933.
33. "Sez 'Ches,'" *Pittsburgh Courier*, June 17, 1933.
34. "Sez 'Ches,'" *Pittsburgh Courier*, June 17, 1933.
35. *Pittsburgh Courier*, July 22, 1933. Posey placed 1933 Homestead Grays players like Vic Harris and Jimmy Binder and 1933 Pittsburgh Crawfords players like Josh Gibson and Oscar Charleston on the West squad. In the actual game, Harris, Gibson, Charleston, and other Crawfords and Grays players played for the East team.
36. *Pittsburgh Courier*, July 29, 1933.
37. Lanctot, 33-34.
38. "Sports Shots," *Pittsburgh Courier*, October 7, 1933.
39. "Sports Shots," *Pittsburgh Courier*, October 7, 1933
40. *Philadelphia Tribune*, March 11, 1944.
41. *Pittsburgh Courier*, August 11, 1951.
42. Lanctot, 23.
43. *New York Amsterdam News*, July 28, 1934.
44. *New York Amsterdam News*, July 28, 1934.
45. *Pittsburgh Courier*, August 1, 1936.
46. *Pittsburgh Courier*, July 26, 1941, July 26, 1947. In both 1941 and 1947, the *Courier* published a box listing attendance and receipts for each E-W Game to date. In 1947 the *Courier* reported the same $9,500 figure as receipts in 1933 but, for example, adjusted upward the amount of receipts for the 1934 game to $20,000 from a $14,000 figure reported in 1941.
47. Lanctot, 23. Note that Lanctot seems to be deducing this effort from John Clark's July 28 *Amsterdam News* column, in which Clark stated that "(S)ports writers of 55 weeklies, 90 dailies were notified, and invited to comment and criticize." Clark does not mention Sparrow's name, but he was clearly heading the promotional activities for the first E-W Game. Black

# THE 1935 PITTSBURGH CRAWFORDS

newspapers generally published weekly and White newspapers daily.

48 *Baltimore Afro-American*, September 9, 1939. Columnist Alvin Moses also reported that all the activity engendered by Sparrow and others he involved in his promotions led to "ninety-one press items all dealing with Roy Sparrow's brainchild."

49 "Fans Rally to East-West Baseball Poll," *Pittsburgh Courier*, August 12, 1933.

50 *Chicago Defender*, August 5, 1933; *Pittsburgh Courier*, August 12, 1933.

51 Attendance was reported as 11,000 in the July 26, 1941, *Pittsburgh Courier*, 12,000 in Lanctot, 23, and 19,568 in Lester, 37, citing *Kansas City Call*, September 14, 1933. All three figures exceed the approximately 7,000 fans who turned out in Cleveland on July 23 to witness the "One Fine Day" doubleheader promoted by Dave Hawkins that featured the Crawfords and American Giants, from whom the majority of the East and West squad players were drawn.

52 *Baltimore Afro-American*, September 9, 1933 (ugly talk); *Philadelphia Tribune*, September 7, 1933 (receipts).

53 *Philadelphia Tribune*, September 7, 1933.

54 *Pittsburgh Courier*, September 30, 1933.

55 "Sports Shots," *Pittsburgh Courier*, October 7, 1933.

56 *New York Amsterdam News*, July 7, 1934.

57 *New York Amsterdam News*, July 7, 1934.

58 *New York Amsterdam News*, July 21, 1934. According to Lester, 37, 41, in 1933 Newt Allen got the most votes of any second baseman, while Chet Brewer ranked sixth in pitching votes and Bullet Rogan was seventh in the outfield. Right behind Rogan in eighth place was Sam Bankhead, who was one of only two starting players for the West squad who did not play for the Chicago American Giants – the other being shortstop Leroy Morney of the Cleveland Giants.

59 *New York Amsterdam News*, July 21, 1934.

60 *Baltimore Afro-American*, July 28, 1934.

61 Frank Young, *New York Amsterdam* News, July 21, 1934.

62 *Philadelphia Tribune*, September 13, 1934.

63 *New York Age*, August 4, 1934. Left fielder Vic Harris of Homestead started the 1933 game and pitcher George Britt relieved.

64 *New York Age*, August 4, 1934.

65 *New York Amsterdam News*, July 28, 1934.

66 *New York Amsterdam News*, July 28, 1934.

67 *New York Amsterdam News*, July 28, 1934.

68 "Sez Ches," *Pittsburgh Courier*, September 15, 1934.

69 *New York Amsterdam News*, September 8, 1934.

70 *New York Amsterdam News*, September 9, 1934.

71 *New York Amsterdam News*, November 24, 1934.

72 *Colored Baseball & Sports Monthly*, Vol. 1, No. 1, September 1934. East-West Game file, Hall of Fame Library, Cooperstown, New York

73 Undated article, East-West Game file, Hall of Fame Library, Cooperstown, New York. The article has a handwritten notation underneath stating "Copied from Jimmie Crutchfield's scrapbook."

74 Undated article, East-West Game file, Hall of Fame Library, Cooperstown, New York.

75 Lester, 59, 61, citing *Pittsburgh Courier*, September 1, 1934.

76 *Pittsburgh Courier*, January 5, 1935.

77 *New York Amsterdam News*, October 20, 1934.

78 An associate member paid a smaller franchise fee than a full member and was included in the league schedule but not the final standings, and therefore could not play in any postseason games. See Goldman, *Baseball's Business,* 391. In the 1935 E-W game, representatives of the Homestead Grays and Pittsburgh Crawfords played for the West team, whereas in the previous two games, they played on the East team. Lester, 37, 61, 78.

79 Goldman, *Baseball's Business*, 401.

80 *Baltimore Afro-American*, January 19, 1935.

81 *Baltimore Afro-American*, January 19, 1935.

82 *Baltimore Afro-American*, January 19, 1935.

83 *Pittsburgh Courier*, January 5, 1935 (almost $1,000); *Baltimore Afro-American,* July 28, 1934 (gross receipts*); Pittsburgh Courier*, July 26, 1941 (1934 E-W receipts reported as $14,000); *Pittsburgh Courier*, July 26, 1941 (1934 E-W receipts reported as $20,000).

84 *Cleveland Call and Post*, July 25, 1935.

85 Lester, 79.

86 *Baltimore Afro-American*, August 24, 1935.

87 *Baltimore Afro-American*, August 24, 1935.

88 *Philadelphia Tribune*, August 29, 1935.

89 *Chicago Defender*, September 14, 1935.

90 *Chicago Defender*, September 14, 1935.

91 *Chicago Defender*, September 14, 1935.

92 "Cum Posey's Pointed Paragraphs," *Pittsburgh Courier*, November 30, 1935.

93 "Posey's Points," *Pittsburgh Courier*, November 7, 1936.

94 "Posey's Points," *Pittsburgh Courier*, November 7, 1936.

95 "Posey's Points," *Pittsburgh Courier*, November 7, 1936.

96 *Pittsburgh Courier*, September 25, 1937.

97 *Pittsburgh Courier*, September 25, 1937.

98 *Pittsburgh Courier*, September 25, 1937.

99 *Philadelphia Tribune*, August 20, 1936.

100 *Pittsburgh Courier*, August 1, 1936.

101 *Chicago Defender*, September 14, 1935.

102 *Chicago Defender*, September 14, 1935.

103 *Chicago Defender*, May 9, 1936.

104 *Chicago Defender*, May 9, 1936.

105 *Chicago Defender*, May 9, 1936.

106 *Pittsburgh Courier*, August 1, 1936

107 *New York Amsterdam News*, May 23, 1936 (Greenlee declines E-W committee membership); Goldman, *Baseball's Business*, 402, citing *Chicago Defender*, January 18, 1936 (Greenlee resigning as chair of NNL)

108 *Chicago Defender*, November 7, 1936.

109 *Pittsburgh Courier*, August 1, 1936.

110 Lester, 91-92.

111 Lanctot, 54.

112 Lanctot, 54. (Western teams independent); Lester, 91 (Crawfords representing East).

113 Goldman, *Baseball's Business*, 403 (1936 NNL teams); *Chicago Defender*, November 7, 1936 (no money to league treasury).

114 Goldman, *Baseball's Business*, 403; *Chicago Defender*, November 7, 1936.

115 Goldman, *Baseball's Business*, 403; *Chicago Defender*, November 7, 1936.

116 Goldman, *Baseball's Business*, 403; *Chicago Defender*, November 7, 1936.

117 Goldman, *Baseball's Business*, 404.

118 Goldman, *Baseball's Business*, 402-404.

119 *Pittsburgh Courier*, August 21, 1937. Note that Lester, 105, reported an attendance of 25,000 for the 1937 contest.

120 Lester, 103, citing *Pittsburgh Courier*, August 14, 1937.

121 *Pittsburgh Courier*, September 25, 1937.

122 *Pittsburgh Courier*, September 18, 1937.

123 *Pittsburgh Courier*, September 18, 1937.

124 Lester, 112, citing *Chicago Defender*, August 27, 1938.

125 Goldman, *Baseball's Business*, 407-408; *Pittsburgh Courier*, February 25, 1939.

126 In 1961, the E-W Game was finally played in Yankee Stadium, and the last E-W Game was played in Kansas City on August 26, 1962. See Goldman, *Baseball's Business*, 446.

127 Lester, 112, citing *Chicago Defender*, August 6, 1938.

128 *Chicago Defender*, September 3, 1938.

129 Lester, 112, citing *Chicago Defender*, August 6, 1938.

130 *Chicago Defender, September 3, 1938.*

131 Goldman, *Baseball's Business*, 422.

132 *New York Amsterdam News*, September 2, 1944.

133 *New York Amsterdam News*, September 2, 1944.

134 Lester, 225.

135 *New York Amsterdam News*, September 2, 1944.

136 Buck O'Neil, *I Was Right on Time* (New York: Simon & Schuster, 1997), 121.

# WHERE WAS SATCHEL IN 1935?
## PAIGE AND GREENLEE FEUDED AS CRAWFORDS RULED THE NNL

### By Frederick C. Bush

As the 1935 baseball season approached, Pittsburgh Crawfords owner Gus Greenlee had every reason to be optimistic about his team's chances to win the Negro National League championship. Although the 1934 squad had finished in second place in both halves of the season, it still posted a 47-27-3 record in league play, and the returning roster was the most imposing in all of Negro baseball.[1] The Crawfords had four future Hall of Famers in James "Cool Papa" Bell, Oscar Charleston, Josh Gibson, and Judy Johnson along with stalwarts like Sam Bankhead, Jimmie Crutchfield, Roosevelt Davis, Leroy Matlock, and Andrew "Pat" Patterson. Greenlee also anticipated the return of a fifth future Hall of Famer in the person of Satchel Paige, who had led the 1934 Crawfords' pitching staff with a 13-3 record, 152 strikeouts in 145⅔ innings pitched, and a minuscule 1.54 ERA. In fact, Greenlee had gone to great lengths to ensure that Paige would come back, but he found out – as did so many other owners over the course of Satchel's career – that nothing was certain where the lanky hurler was concerned. As it turned out, bad blood between Greenlee and Paige led to each man having to fend for himself

*1934 Crawfords pitchers (L-R) Satchel Paige, Leroy Matlock, William Bell, Harry Kincannon, Sam Streeter, and Bertrum Hunter were expected to return in 1935, but Paige held out and Bell joined the Brooklyn Eagles in midseason.*

(Courtesy of Center for Negro League Baseball Research)

and resulted in the most unusual circumstance of both emerging as champions.

The animosity between Paige and Greenlee that kept the pitcher from donning a Crawfords uniform in 1935 had its origins, oddly enough, in Paige's marriage to Janet Howard, who was a waitress at Greenlee's Crawford Grill. The couple tied the knot on October 26, 1934, with tap dancer Bill "Bojangles" Robinson as Satchel's best man, and Greenlee threw a lavish wedding reception at the Grill afterward. Greenlee had an ulterior motive behind his generous gesture: he used the occasion to announce that Paige would be signing a new two-year contract to return to the Crawfords. In his autobiography, Paige stated that he had agreed beforehand to this move and recalled, "While they still were yelling and cheering, Gus and I sat down and signed the contract."[2] Paige and his bride went on their honeymoon to California, where Satchel played for Tom Wilson's Nashville Elite Giants during the California Winter League season.

The Elite Giants team, which in addition to Paige also included fellow Hall of Famers Cool Papa Bell, Turkey Stearnes, Mule Suttles, and Willie Wells, dominated the California Winter League with a 34-5-1 record and won the pennant for the 1934-35 season. Though Paige arrived in the Golden State after the campaign had started, he was still the center of attention whenever and wherever he pitched, and he compiled a perfect 8-0 record in league play with 104 strikeouts in 69 innings pitched.[3]

Although Greenlee had paid most of Paige's wedding expenses and also had funded the honeymoon, and Paige was earning money for his winter league play, all was not well financially for Satchel. The spendthrift Paige observed, "After that honeymoon, I started noticing a powerful lightness in my hip pocket. Married life was a mighty expensive thing and those paychecks of mine weren't going as far as they used to."[4] His solution was to hit Greenlee up for a raise, even though he had not yet done anything to earn the money he had coming to him on his new Crawfords contract.

Paige's meeting with Greenlee did not go as he had expected it would. In his account of their summit, Paige wrote, "[G]us was mad or something like that. He turned me down flat. ... All he said was something like 'don't forget those games we got coming up next week.'"[5] Satchel could not have cared less about "those games," and he remembered, "I was so mad I went home and started throwing clothes into a suitcase"[6] and told Janet that they were leaving Pittsburgh. According to Paige, a few days later he called Neil Churchill, a car dealer and semipro baseball team owner-manager, and received an offer to return to Churchill's integrated squad in Bismarck, North Dakota. Paige had pitched for Churchill in 1933, had spurned him in 1934 – as he was now doing to Greenlee – and took his new wife with him to Bismarck for the 1935 season.

Greenlee was irate at Paige's departure. He called Churchill and warned him "that he'd carve him to pieces if he ever got within knife-slashing distance, a threat that had to make Churchill glad for every inch of the 1,124 miles between Pittsburgh, Pennsylvania, and Bismarck, North Dakota."[7] Instead of traveling west to commit murder, Greenlee first tried to unload Paige's contract since he still considered the pitcher to be his property. A February 9 article in the *Chicago Defender* reported that Paige "is the most sought after ball player in the land today, or he was, until Gus announced the salary his star was receiving" and his fellow team owners pointed out that they "cannot afford to pay such salaries and continue to operate."[8]

Paige arrived in Bismarck on March 24 to prepare for spring training with Churchill's team. Soon thereafter, in mid-April, Greenlee revealed what he had decided to do about his impasse with Paige over the pitcher's services. The *Chicago Defender* summarized the state of affairs in one succinct paragraph:

W.A. Greenlee announces that Satchell [sic] Paige has been assigned to Ray L. Dean, western promoter for one year. It is believed that the sensational righthander is being disciplined and will be required to perform for the House of David. A clause prohibiting his appearance or service in games against league clubs has been inserted.[9]

Paige had helped the House of David squad win the Denver Post Tournament in 1934, but he had no intention of returning to the team, and he was unconcerned about being banned from playing for, or against, NNL teams.

There was as much sparring in the press over Paige's contract-jumping as there was between Satchel and Greenlee. *Pittsburgh Courier* columnist Chester Washington heartily approved of Greenlee's banishment of his ace pitcher, writing, "Heroes come and heroes go. The champ of today may be the 'chump' of tomorrow. So it may be with Paige. The league helped to make him and now the League may be the medium to break him."[10]

*Chicago Defender* columnist Al Monroe, on the other hand, was in the pro-Satchel camp and wrote of Paige's motivation: "(Paige knows that) big pay can be asked only while you are at the top after which the club owners set the figures, which you either take or leave." Monroe made an apt comparison as he wrote, "Babe Ruth, you will remember, employed the greatest part of each spring training period arguing over what he was to receive for playing during the regular season and usually got what he asked for," and he asserted, "Say what you will or may, there is little doubt but that Satchel Paige is the Babe Ruth of Race baseball."[11]

While most of the press focused on Paige, Homestead Grays owner Cum Posey made the astute observation that, although he still expected Satchel to return to Pittsburgh for the 1935 season, "without Paige the [Crawfords] club is evenly balanced and contain [sic] some of the best players in colored baseball."[12]

On April 24, the *Bismarck Tribune* announced that Churchill's squad would open the season against Jamestown on May 5.[13] Greenlee's threats, reassignment of Paige to the House of David, and NNL ban notwithstanding, it was a foregone conclusion that Paige would start for Bismarck on Opening Day. As Satchel later recalled, "I didn't do anything about the noises Gus was making. ... Those Negro league owners were just spiting themselves, I figured. ... There was plenty of green floating in and I was getting my share of it, but Gus and his pals weren't."[14]

Surprisingly, Satchel lost Bismarck's opener, 2-1, in spite of holding Jamestown to five hits and striking out 10 batters.[15] It would be one of his few setbacks in all of 1935. Paige also still was able to test his mettle against some of the best players the Negro Leagues had to offer, because Greenlee's NNL ban did not preclude him from playing against NAL teams. On June 6 Bismarck faced the Kansas City Monarchs in Winnipeg, Manitoba, and Paige dueled with Chet Brewer in an instant classic. The press raved that "Paige struck out 17 batters. Brewer, of Kansas, also a colored boy, struck out 13, making the amazing total of 30 strikeouts in one game. The score, incidentally, was 0-0."[16]

Meanwhile, Paige was still being used as a drawing card for Crawfords games. On June 13 the *Delaware County Daily Times,* in a preview article for the Pittsburgh nine's game against a semipro team from Chester, Pennsylvania, wrote, "Paige may not pitch the entire game tonight, but the Crawford management has assured Vann that he will work part of the contest."[17] Two days later, the same newspaper had to explain, "The reason Satchel Paige didn't show with the Crawfords against Vann's team is because the lanky pitcher is in North Dakota. He is still the Crawfords' property in the Negro League."[18] The tactic of tempting fans to attend Crawfords games in hopes of catching a glimpse of Paige ended up backfiring tremendously on Greenlee in late September.

By early July, Paige sported a 16-2 record for Bismarck,[19] while the Crawfords were headed toward the first-half NNL title. Soon, voting was underway for the Negro Leagues' third annual East-West All-Star Game, at Chicago's Comiskey Park on August 11. The *Pittsburgh Courier* reported that Crawfords pitcher Leroy Matlock "is having his greatest year, and has caused Smoketown [Pittsburgh] fans to forget Satchell [sic] and his 'fast ball,'" but it added, "That Satchell has not been forgotten altogether, however, is manifested by the votes which show he still has prestige."[20] Paige may have hoped that he would be allowed to participate in the East-West game; however, as the *Chicago Defender* noted, "[t]he moguls refused to gamble on the big fellow. And as a result Paige must now sit back and watch [other pitchers] grab off the glory that was once his."[21]

As the season progressed, Churchill continued to add Negro Leaguers to his Bismarck squad, and the formidable team now included Hilton Smith, Ted "Double Duty" Radcliffe, Barney Morris, Quincy Troupe (who had not yet added the second 'p' to his last name), and Red Haley. Bismarck participated in three tournaments in Manitoba, and invariably faced the Devil's Lake, North Dakota, team for each title. They lost the Brandon Tournament in July, but won both the Portage La Prairie and Virden Tournaments in early August.[22]

It seemed that the only thing that might have stopped Bismarck's domination of its opponents that season would have been for something to sideline Paige, which almost happened. Quincy Trouppe recounted the anecdote in his autobiography:

> Coming back from a little trip to Winnipeg, Canada, in my car, Satchel began to ride me. ... As I was driving along, engrossed in his joking, I missed a curve sign. ... We skidded into a ditch on the side of the road and bounced back onto the road into the other bend of the 'S' curve. When we made it through that, I stopped the car.
>
> Barney Morris opened the door on his side in the back and fell out, rolling into the ditch, yelling, 'Oh! Oh! Lord!'
>
> I bolted out of the driver's seat, ran around back, and slid into the ditch beside Barney. ... I knelt beside him, anxious ... he was convulsed with laughter. ... 'Hey, what's wrong with you?' I asked.
>
> He pointed toward the front door of the car where Satchel was just emerging, and roared anew. 'Oh, Lord! I've never seen anything like that – that big man getting down on the floor rolling into a ball. Man, what a sight!' He was enjoying every minute of it. ...
>
> Satchel came to the ditch, too, and told Barney, 'Look, I don't know what you're laughing about, but whatever it is, it ain't funny!' Then Satch gave me the full measure of his steady gaze. 'Look heah, Troupe, if you can't drive this jalopy no better than this, you better let me take over.'"[23]

With Haley driving the rest of the way, the foursome made it back to Bismarck in good order, and the team continued to roll over all opponents. After the squad's regular-season finale on August 11, the *Bismarck Tribune* rhapsodized:

> With an overture of five home runs in the first inning opening a riotous grand opera of extra-base hits and a profusion of singles, Bismarck's mightiest baseball team sang its swan song for the season to home fans Sunday afternoon by crushing the Twin City Colored Giants, 21 to 6.
>
> The booster game victory was Bismarck's 12th in a row and its 66th for the season thus far against 14 losses and four ties."[24]

In light of the romp, Paige was up to some old shenanigans, as the *Tribune* also noted, "The

# THE 1935 PITTSBURGH CRAWFORDS

*Satchel Paige (back row, center) spent most of 1935 pitching in Bismarck, North Dakota, for car dealer Neil Churchill's integrated semipro team, which also won the first National Baseball Congress tournament held in Wichita, Kansas.*

(Courtesy Robert D. Retort Enterprises)

game ended with only Bismarck's battery on the field, lanky Satchel Paige in the box and Barney Morris behind the plate. This unusual calling in of the fielders gave the visitors one more home run and two more runs than they rightfully earned."[25]

Churchill had been seeking stiffer competition for his squad that also would provide greener financial pastures. The annual Denver Post Tournament, which took place in early August, would have been the logical choice over the minor Canadian tourneys, but racism and segregation had reared their ugly heads once again and prevented the Bismarck team's participation in Colorado. Paige and catcher Bill Perkins had helped to lead the House of David to the 1934 championship in Denver. As a result, in 1935 the tournament's organizers "banned a colored pitcher from performing on either a white or a mixed ball club," although one all-black team would be allowed to participate.[26] *New York Age* columnist Lewis E. Dial reported, "In the meet last year an American Legion team had a Negro on its roster and one southern club refused to play that team" and then stated in no uncertain terms, "The powers that be ruled against the crackers, but this year they have tried to safeguard the dough for the white boys by issuing such an asinine ruling."[27]

As good fortune had it, however, Raymond Harry "Hap" Dumont had formed the National Baseball Congress of semipro teams in 1934 and wanted to start a tournament in his hometown of Wichita, Kansas, that would bring together teams from around the country and which would rival the *Denver Post's* contest. Dumont needed a drawing card and Churchill had just the right one in Paige. Fortunately, there was sufficient cash for the endeavor since "[i]t cost Hap Dumont $1,000 to get Churchill to bring his team and his crowd-pleasing pitcher to Wichita."[28]

Everyone – Dumont, Churchill, and the fans – got their money's worth as Bismarck continued its season-long domination in the NBC Tournament. Before the championship game, the *Bismarck Tribune* recapped how the local nine had fared to that point: "Bismarck turned back the Monroe, La., Monarchs, 6-4; beat the favored Wichita Watermen, 8-4; defeated the Denver Fuelers [the winners of that year's Denver Post Tournament], 4-1; trounced Shelby, 7-1; conquered Duncan, 3-1 and walloped Omaha, 15-6."29 The title game was a rematch against the Duncan (Oklahoma) team that Bismarck – with Paige making his fourth start – won, 5-2, to capture the inaugural NBC championship.

The *Bismarck Tribune* extolled Paige's performance after he had thoroughly dominated the field, and reported, "The ebony hurler struck out 66 batters, allowed only 29 hits, and issued five bases on balls during the five games he was on the slab for Bismarck" [Paige had relieved Chet Brewer in the game against Wichita].30 The team played several post-tournament exhibition games that included another tilt against the Kansas City Monarchs in which Paige this time "whiffed 16 batters despite a cold, damp day" in an 8-4 Bismarck triumph on September 4.31 One week later, it was reported that "Satchel Paige, dubbed by sports writers as the 'Dizzy' Dean of the Negro pitching world ... joined the Kansas City Monarchs for a winter tour of the south."32

Greenlee no doubt had taken notice of all the publicity Paige had generated for Bismarck, the NBC Tournament, and now the K.C. Monarchs, and he set aside his grudge toward Paige for the sake of his own profit. He offered Satchel $350 to pitch for the Crawfords in a four-team doubleheader at Yankee Stadium on September 22, which turned out to be exactly one day after the Crawfords won the NNL championship series over the New York Cubans, four games to three.

Greenlee put the word out and, on September 18, the news was trumpeted that "'Satchel' Paige, the greatest pitcher in colored baseball, will oppose his old rival, Slim Jones, on the mound in the Pittsburgh Crawfords-Philadelphia Stars battle ... next Sunday afternoon."33 Three days later, the *Chicago Defender* reported, "All eyes this Sunday will be focused on Comiskey Park where it is expected fifteen thousand fans will gather to see the great Satchel Paige with the Kansas City Monarchs versus the American Giants in a game which will go a long way towards deciding the Western championship[,]" and also noted that Paige had been "signed by the Monarchs for this important series."34 As great as Paige was, even he could not be in two different places at the same time.

On September 22 Satchel was in Chicago, where he pitched five innings of shutout ball for the Monarchs before ceding the mound to Chet Brewer in a 7-1 loss to the American Giants. Farther east, in New York, "A crowd of more than 15,000 fans were disappointed at Yankee Stadium ... when Satchel Paige, star pitcher, failed to appear as advertised and when 'Slim' Jones, who last year beat Paige in a pitching duel, was knocked out after only one inning on the mound."35 As they had done all season long in 1935, the Crawfords fared just fine without Paige and beat the Stars, 12-2, but the fans and the New York press were not pleased.

The *New York Amsterdam News*, in particular, felt embarrassed that it had unintentionally misled fans by reporting that Paige would pitch at Yankee Stadium on September 22. Artie La Mar wrote, "The sporting editor of the *Amsterdam News* has been in a position to know that the promoters had good reason to believe that Paige would show up but the fans did not know that."36 La Mar addressed accusations that harkened back to false claims that Paige would pitch for the Crawfords, such as the one made on June 13 in Chester, Pennsylvania: "In speaking of the affair Dan Parker said in the Mirror: 'Promoters of the colored baseball games at the Yankee Stadium last week advertised Satchel Paige as one of the players, though they knew he was playing in Chicago that day. This cheap gag is used on other large cities, too. It surprises me that Satchel doesn't sue for damages.'"37 According to La Mar, however, there was a witness, R.L. Dougherty, who "said he has seen money wired to Paige by Greenlee, therefore it should be easy for Greenlee to give his side of the case" and asserted that, due to this eyewitness testimony, "From what could be gleaned on this end of the unfortunate affair it would seem that Satchel is the one who is surprised that he isn't being sued."[38]

The problem was that Greenlee had told a somewhat different story. After Paige's no-show, he told the press that "the western star stopped off in Chicago enroute east and while there was offered $500 to pitch for the Kansas City Monarchs on Sunday. This causing him to forget all about his agreement to appear in New York …"[39] Since the exact date of the alleged Greenlee-Paige agreement was never reported, it remains a mystery as to who was telling the truth. Given Paige's propensity to follow the money, it is possible that Greenlee had contacted him about the Yankee Stadium game before Satchel's signing with the Monarchs; in this scenario, Paige reneged on the deal by failing to show up in New York. On the other hand, Dan Parker may have been correct, and Greenlee may have lied about Paige pitching for the Crawfords; if that was the case, it is likely that Greenlee assumed that his offer would be sufficient enticement for Satchel to rejoin the team for one game. When Paige failed to show up, Greenlee had to do damage control and invent a story to cover for his blunder. The bottom line, as the *Amsterdam News* stated, was that "[n]o matter who is right in the premises there are a number of fans all het up over the non-appearance of Satchel Paige in the line-up of the Pittsburgh Crawfords. …"[40]

One person who was not "all het up" was Satchel Paige, who tended simply to ignore controversy and negative press because he knew that his pitching prowess would always lure back both owners and fans. He simply continued to pitch for the Monarchs in the early fall. On October 6 in Kansas City, Paige "hurled a three-hit ball game … but it wasn't enough to beat the touring exhibition team headed by Dizzy and Paul Dean and Mike Ryba. The exhibition team won, 1-0."[41]

Shortly thereafter, Paige finished 1935 in the same circuit where he had started it, the California Winter League. A November 23 headline in the *Chicago Defender* read, "Satchel Paige Stars in California Winter Loop," and the article reported on Paige's latest feats.[42] On November 16, Paige had hurled five innings for Tom Wilson's Elite Giants in which he had allowed Pirrone's All Stars only two hits and struck out seven before giving way to Bob "School Boy" Griffith, who finished a 7-0 shutout victory.

In the yearlong battle of wills between Greenlee and Paige, both were fortunate to emerge with team championships. However, Paige ended up as the ultimate victor because he had the talent and the drawing power that Greenlee needed. After Paige once again ruled the California Winter League to the tune of a 13-0 record[43] and pitched successfully against exhibition teams of major-league all-stars, there was talk about Paige being signed to a major-league team. Paige himself realized that, at that point in time in America, it was empty talk, but he figured that it nonetheless was the reason why Greenlee conceded defeat prior to the 1936 NNL season.

In his autobiography, Paige recounted how quickly the two made up:

> 'We've lifted the ban on you,' he told me. 'When can you rejoin the team?'
>
> 'I'll have to do some thinkin' on that,' I told him.
>
> I didn't have to do as much thinking as I thought. Janet jumped me real quick about it when I told her.[44]

Somewhat grudgingly, Satchel acceded to his wife's wishes: "I got ahold of Gus and told him I was coming back."[45]

In 1936 Gus Greenlee and Satchel Paige became champions together as Paige pitched to an 8-2 record for the Crawfords, who captured their second consecutive NNL title.

# Pride of Smoketown

## Sources

Unless otherwise indicated, Seamheads.com has been used as the source for all Negro League statistics, team records, and championship series.

## Notes

1. The first-half champion Philadelphia Stars won the 1934 NNL title by defeating the second-half champion Chicago American Giants in the NNL championship series by four games to three, with an additional game ending in a tie.
2. Leroy (Satchel) Paige, as told to David Lipman, *Maybe I'll Pitch Forever* (Lincoln: University of Nebraska Press, 1993), 86. (Originally published by Doubleday & Company in 1962).
3. William F. McNeil, *The California Winter League: America's First Integrated Professional Baseball League* (Jefferson, North Carolina: McFarland & Company, Inc., 2002), 171.
4. Paige, 86.
5. Paige, 87.
6. Paige, 87.
7. Tom Dunkel, *Color Blind: The Forgotten Team That Broke Baseball's Color Line* (New York: Atlantic Monthly Press, 2013), 129.
8. "Everybody Wants Satchel Paige, Nobody His Salary," *Chicago Defender*, February 9, 1935: 16.
9. "Paige's Contract to the House of Davids," *Chicago Defender*, April 27, 1935: 17.
10. Chester Washington, "Sez Ches: Contracts or 'Scraps of Paper'?" *Pittsburgh Courier*, April 20, 1935: 16.
11. Al Monroe, "Speaking of Sports," *Chicago Defender*, April 13, 1935: 16.
12. "Cum Posey's Pointed Paragraphs," *Pittsburgh Courier*, May 4, 1935: 14.
13. "Capital City Team to Make '35 Debut Against Jamestown," *Bismarck Tribune*, April 24, 1935: 8.
14. Paige, 96.
15. "Capital City Team Makes Home Debut Against Jamestown Sunday," *Bismarck Tribune*, May 11, 1935: 6.
16. "Paige Whiffs 17 Monarchs," *Regina* (Saskatchewan) *Leader-Post* June 8, 1935: 17.
17. "Famous Negro Team Here with All Star Line-up," *Delaware County Daily Times* (Chester, Pennsylvania), June 13, 1935: 19.
18. "Sports Shorts," *Delaware County Daily Times*, June 15, 1935: 10.
19. "Red Sox to Start Starr or Brady in Inter-City Contest," *Bismarck Tribune*, July 6, 1935: 6.
20. "Race for E-W Berths Hot as Voting Spurts/Outfield and Infield Races Grow Hectic," *Pittsburgh Courier*, July 27, 1935: 15.
21. "Satchel Paige's Aim Out," *Chicago Defender*, August 3, 1935: 14.
22. "Devil's Lake Noses Out Bismarck, 2-1, to Win Brandon Tournament," *Bismarck Tribune*, July 18, 1935: 8; "Bismarck Blanks Devil's Lake in Canadian Tourney Finals," *Bismarck Tribune*, August 6, 1935: 6; "Capital City Team Wins 2nd Manitoba Tournament Crown," *Bismarck Tribune*, August 9, 1935: 10.
23. Quincy Trouppe, *20 Years Too Soon: Prelude to Major-League Integrated Baseball* (St. Louis: Missouri Historical Society, 1995), 53-54.
24. "Bismarck Overwhelms Twin City Giants in Final Home Game, 21-6," *Bismarck Tribune*, August 12, 1935: 6.
25. "Bismarck Overwhelms Twin City Giants."
26. Lewis E. Dial, "The Sports Dial," *New York Age*, May 11, 1935: 5.
27. Dial.
28. Dunkel. 185.
29. "Capital City Nine, Undefeated in Six Starts, Is Favored," *Bismarck Tribune*, August 27, 1935: 6.
30. "Great Negro Athlete Pitches Bismarck to Title," *Bismarck Tribune*, August 28, 1935: 6. Official NBC records show that Paige recorded 60 strikeouts; although the number is six fewer than the *Tribune* reported, it is a record for most strikeouts by a pitcher in the tournament that still stood as of 2019. See nbc-baseball.com/about-us-2/history/.
31. "Bismarck Defeats Monarchs, 8 to 4," *Bismarck Tribune*, September 5, 1935: 8.
32. "City Fetes Manager of Bismarck's U.S. Semi-Professional Champions," *Bismarck Tribune*, September 11, 1935: 6.
33. "Paige Versus Jones at Stadium Sunday," *New York Daily News*, September 18, 1935: 120.
34. "Satchel Paige to Hurl for Kansas City Against Giants," *Chicago Defender*, September 21, 1935: 13.
35. William E. Clark, "15,000 Fans See 4-Team Series at Yankee Stadium Sunday; Crawfords and Elite Gts. Win," *New York Age*, September 28, 1935: 8.
36. Artie La Mar, "Fans All Het Up Over Non-Appearance of Paige at the Yankee Stadium Games Here," *New York Amsterdam News*, October 5, 1935: 13.
37. La Mar.
38. La Mar.
39. Clark, 8.
40. La Mar.

## THE 1935 PITTSBURGH CRAWFORDS

41 "Dizzy's Team Wins, 1-0: Satchel Paige Yields Three Hits," *Moberly* (Missouri) *Monitor-Index*, October 7, 1935: 5.

42 James Newton, "Satchel Paige Stars in California Winter Loop," *Chicago Defender*, November 23, 1935: 14.

43 McNeil, 179.

44 Paige, 109.

45 Paige, 110.

# KINGS OF THE HILL:
## THE STORY OF THE PITTSBURGH CRAWFORDS

### By Jeremy Beer

The Pittsburgh Crawfords franchise, one of the most famous in the history of black baseball, was started in 1926 by a group of youths connected to one of Pittsburgh's neighborhood recreation clubs. For five years the Crawford Giants, as they were first known, labored in relative obscurity as an amateur or semipro outfit. Things changed dramatically when a wealthy local gangster named William A. "Gus" Greenlee decided the team provided the perfect vehicle for burnishing his reputation, laundering a little money, and having a lot of fun.[1]

Greenlee had become involved with the Crawfords around the time of the team's founding by donating money for the boys' uniforms. Over the next few years he focused less on baseball than on building his numbers empire. In that effort he was spectacularly successful. Building on lessons learned from running liquor as a taxi driver in the years following World War I, and leveraging the opportunities offered by the speakeasy he owned, by late 1931 Greenlee had become both Pittsburgh's undisputed Numbers King and one of its most charismatic and recognizable figures. Alternately charming or ruthless, as circumstances warranted, Greenlee flashed as his calling cards expensive suits (silk preferred), expensive cars (usually a Lincoln convertible), and beautiful women (obtained and discarded with equal ease). The illegal numbers lottery made such indulgences financially feasible. Greenlee probably raked in between $20,000 and $25,000 per day during the height of his seemingly Depression-proof business in the mid-1930s.[2]

Yet, although the numbers lottery was profitable, the cash it generated was problematic. That seems to be one of the reasons Greenlee decided in 1931 to increase his investment in the Crawfords significantly. Since its formation in 1926, the Craws had gradually separated themselves from Pittsburgh's other black sandlot teams. The team's collection of impressive talent had included outfielder Jimmie Crutchfield, pitcher Sam Streeter, and, most notably, a catcher named Josh Gibson, who began playing with the team in 1928 as a side gig to his work in the steel mills. Gibson had

## THE 1935 PITTSBURGH CRAWFORDS

*(L to R) Leroy Matlock, Oscar Charleston, boxer John Henry Lewis (who was promoted by Crawfords owner Gus Greenlee), Satchel Paige, and Josh Gibson pose in front of the team bus at Greenlee Field in Pittsburgh.*

been plucked away from the Crawfords by the Homestead Grays – then Pittsburgh's highest-level and only fully professional Negro Leagues team – in 1930. In June 1931, after Greenlee had decided to assert team control, the Crawfords replaced him with a catcher from Cleveland named Bill Perkins. Perkins was joined by an intriguing pitcher by the name of Satchell (yes, spelled at first with two l's) Paige.[3]

Earlier during that 1931 season Streeter and the Craws had been crushed by the Homestead Grays, 9-0. But when the Crawfords met the Grays in McKeesport, Pennsylvania, on August 1, things were different. The Grays had just clawed back from a five-run deficit to tie the score at seven when a tall, long-limbed, rail-thin young man strolled slowly to the mound to relieve Craws starter Harry Kincannon. Paige's fastball was like nothing the Grays, or anyone, had ever seen. He held Posey's dangerous lineup at bay, and the Craws won, 10-7.[4] It was a proof-of-concept game for Greenlee and his rising club.

The next year, 1932, Greenlee began to push in all his chips. First, he finished construction on the Crawfords' very own ballpark in Pittsburgh's Hill district, an area called home by tens of thousands of black Pittsburghers. Despite its lack of a covered grandstand – an omission that would soon be lamented – the community marveled at the new red-brick, $100,000 Greenlee Field, which seated 7,500 and included showers and dressing rooms for both the home and visiting teams – an important amenity, given that Negro Leagues teams were not allowed to use those facilities at the Pirates' Forbes Field, their usual venue for big games. That Greenlee had managed to build his new ballpark in the midst of the Great Depression was widely considered an incredible feat, and it increased his prestige substantially.

Second, Greenlee succeeded in hiring as the Crawfords' new manager the man who was considered the greatest all-around player in Negro Leagues history and still was considered the black game's best gate attraction: Oscar Charleston, who had burst onto the scene in 1915; had carved out a legendary career with the Indianapolis ABCs, Harrisburg Giants, and Hilldale Daisies (among other clubs); and, for the previous two years had played first base for the Grays.[5] This was a coup, as Charleston was not only popular but was well-connected and widely respected. Within days of his hiring, Charleston had obtained commitments from Paige, Streeter, Kincannon, Roy Williams, Ted "Double Duty" Radcliffe, Bobby Williams, and Jimmie Crutchfield to join the club (Williams and Radcliffe had been Oscar's teammates on the 1931 Grays). A short time later, Josh Gibson, Rev Cannady (perhaps the best hitter in black baseball in 1931), and Rap Dixon signed on as well.

Third, Greenlee, never one to take half-measures, invested heavily not just in facilities and players, but in amenities as well. The team now traveled in a new, comparatively luxurious Mack bus with the words "Pittsburgh Crawfords Baseball Team" emblazoned along its side. The team's equipment was first rate, as Al Monroe of the *Chicago Defender* once noted. "[I]n comparison with many another club [Greenlee's equipment] rates with the major leagues. Carrying no more than fifteen men Gus has supplied his club with more than two bats per player and then, they tell me, an order was placed for a dozen more. Now, if you don't think that an exception, then stop and have a talk with some of the players on other teams," wrote Monroe.[6] Furthermore, as of 1933, team members could hang out with pride at their owner's new Crawford Grill. With its diverse clientele and celebrity acts, the Grill quickly became the most popular spot on the Hill district's main thoroughfare, Wylie Avenue. Virtually every Negro Leaguer who came through the city hung out there. The Depression made life difficult for everyone, not least the nation's African-Americans, but at the Grill, as on the diamond, it was damn good to be a Crawford.

Fourth and finally, in 1933 Greenlee rebooted the Negro National League and cast himself in the Rube Foster founding-father role. The new NNL enjoyed more than its share of controversies and financial challenges, but for 16 years Greenlee's league provided a measure of stability and structure for players and fans. From 1933 through 1936, it was the only major black baseball league in existence.

The history of the Crawfords can be neatly divided into two phases: the major period of 1932-36, marked by black baseball championships, legendary contests, and the rise of Paige and Gibson, especially, to superstardom; and the minor period of 1937-40, marked by financial struggle, decay, and Oscar Charleston's poignant attempt to keep the club afloat. (We will ignore here the very brief period, in 1945-46, during which the Crawfords were revived by Greenlee as part of the new and short-lived United States League.)

The 1932 version of the Crawfords, sometimes said to be one of the finest teams ever assembled, was in truth something of a disappointment. Although they featured five future Hall of Famers in Paige, Gibson, Charleston, Judy Johnson, and Jud Wilson (the latter two joined the team in midseason), and although the supporting cast included above-average to excellent players in Dixon, Cannady, and Ted Page, the 1932 Crawfords somehow lost their season series with the Homestead Grays. At the time, the team was reported as having put together an overall record of 99-36, but as usual that record included games against scores of semipro and minor-league-level teams. As best we can now tell, the Craws finished 32-26-1 against top black competition.[7]

That was an entirely unexpected outcome. But any expressions of disappointment were largely muted thanks to the development of Paige and Gibson. By midsummer 1932, Charleston, who was at first the team's biggest star, had been forced to share the spotlight with Satchel and Josh. In an eight-game late-June series versus the Grays, Paige and Gibson were the Craws most praised by the Pittsburgh press, and, on July 16 at Greenlee Field, Paige won more esteem by hurling a no-hitter against the Black Yankees. By the end of the season, it was the amazingly powerful Gibson, rather than Charleston, who was being called "the black Babe Ruth." The 1932 Crawfords kept careful hitting records, and Gibson's achievement, in just 490 at-bats, of 114 runs, 186 hits, 45 doubles, 16 triples, 34 homers, a .380 batting average, a .417 on-base percentage, and a .745 slugging percentage heralded the arrival of the black game's newest star. Or rather, one of them, for Paige managed the stunning feat (for the time) of striking out more than a man per inning on his way to an ERA of 2.46.[8]

In 1933 the speedy James "Cool Papa" Bell replaced Rap Dixon in center field. With Bell leading off, Page hitting second, Charleston batting third, Gibson manning the cleanup spot, and Johnson protecting him in the five hole, four Hall of Famers filled the 1933 lineup's top five slots – and the one non-Hall of Famer, Page, would that year post a 138 OPS+ against top competition. (The 33-year-old Johnson, in truth, was slipping; he would post a mere 72 OPS+ for the year.) Led by Charleston, a super-fast outfield, the game's hardest hitter in Gibson, and its hardest-throwing pitcher in Paige, the Crawfords rolled through the season's first two months like the elite club they were. As of June 24, they reportedly led the league with an 18-7 record, due in large part to Oscar's .450 batting average in 60 official at-bats. Bell was hitting .379, Gibson .378, and Perkins .344. Nevertheless, the Chicago American Giants – which featured four future Hall of Famers of their own in Turkey Stearnes, Mule Suttles, Willie Wells, and Willie Foster – claimed the new NNL's first-half pennant.

After the first East-West All-Star Game – another successful Greenlee innovation – was played in Chicago's Comiskey Park on July 6, 1933, the Crawfords picked up the intensity. On September 30 and October 1, the club played the Nashville Elite Giants in a three-game series that would decide the second-half pennant, with the winner to play the American Giants for the league championship. The Crawfords needed to win only one of these contests. After losing the first at Greenlee Field, Charleston sent Paige to the mound for the first game of the next day's doubleheader. The Craws took a 4-2 lead into the bottom of the ninth, but the Elites managed to scratch across the tying runs off Paige before Leroy Matlock relieved him and ended the threat. Finally, in the top of the 12th, Cool Papa Bell hit a screaming liner to deep center and flew around the bases for an inside-the-park home run. Matlock closed the door in the bottom of the frame.

And then ... there was no championship series after all – or at least none that was completed.[9] The Craws and American Giants met in Cleveland on October 8, 1933, and played to a 7-7 tie. But for the series' second game, in Wheeling, West Virginia, only seven American Giants players showed up. The game was played anyway – and predictably won by the Crawfords. That was enough for the remaining American Giants, who refused to go on to Pittsburgh for the series' scheduled third game. Thus was the 1933 NNL championship forfeited to the Crawfords in most anticlimactic fashion.

With Vic Harris supplanting Ted Page in the two hole, the 1934 Crawfords boasted an even better first four in their lineup – Bell, Harris, Charleston, Gibson – than they had in 1933. The pitching depth was strong, too, with Paige leading a staff that still featured the underrated Leroy

Matlock, Sam Streeter, Harry Kincannon, and Bert Hunter. By the end of the year, Paige separated himself from this pack forever; however, in early 1934, it wasn't yet clear that he was the staff's sure ace.

Paige's importance to the club didn't stop Greenlee from loaning him to the House of David to play in the *Denver Post* baseball tournament in the middle of the season.[10] Thanks to Paige's absence and injuries to Charleston and Judy Johnson, the Crawfords again finished behind the American Giants for the NNL's first-half flag. Getting Paige back for the second-half chase was not enough to lift the Crawfords to that flag, either, which was taken by the Philadelphia Stars. The Craws' 47-27-3 total record in 1934 was the second-best in the league, but it was not good enough in either half to put them in line for a championship. The months of September and October nevertheless contained two of the most memorable series of games the Pittsburgh Crawfords ever played.

The first consisted of a string of doubleheaders in which Paige continued to blossom into a full-blown superstar.[11] On Sunday, September 9, the Crawfords participated in a four-team doubleheader at Yankee Stadium. Battling the Philadelphia Stars in the second game of the day, in front of a raucous crowd estimated to be between 25,000 and 30,000, the Craws were no-hit by Slim Jones for six innings before Oscar Charleston broke through with a single in the seventh. They failed to score, but with Paige holding the Stars to a single run, the Crawfords tied the game in the eighth. Then, in the bottom of the ninth, the Stars loaded the bases against Satchel with one out. Paige struck out the next two men he faced – his 11th and 12th strikeout victims of the day – to preserve the tie before the game was called because of darkness. Bill "Bojangles" Robinson memorialized the duel by giving both Paige and Jones travel bags embossed with the words "the greatest game ever played."[12]

The Crawfords returned to Yankee Stadium on Sunday, September 30. This time 35,000 fans showed up to watch Paige again battle Slim Jones and the Stars. Once again, Paige got the best of Jones, fanning 18 Stars to lead the Crawfords to a 3-1 victory. There was no doubt who the Crawfords' – and black baseball's – biggest star was now. Satchel Paige had come into his own.

Never one to allow himself to be saddled by the burden of team expectations, Paige decided in spring 1935 to forsake the Crawfords and the two-year contract he had signed with Greenlee in favor of Bismarck, North Dakota, where a white auto dealer named Neil Churchill, who had lured Paige to the high plains in 1933, had once again offered him a handsome amount to pitch for his semipro club. With Vic Harris and Ted Page also departing the Craws, Charleston a year older at 38, and a fast-declining Judy Johnson now 35, the 1935 club did not project to be nearly as powerful as previous year's squads. Expectations, on the outside, were for the team to be good, but no longer the juggernaut it once was.

Led by Josh Gibson, who was still just 23 (and who had allegedly hit 69 home runs in 1934), and pitchers Bertrum Hunter and Harry Kincannon, the team got off to a fast start. It was greatly aided when, in June, another 23-year-old, Andrew "Pat" Patterson, came on board to take over second base. After the Crawfords beat the Homestead Grays in both ends of a July 4 doubleheader in Pittsburgh, before a crowd of 12,000, their 24-6 record was good enough to claim the first-half pennant.

Things didn't go as well in the second half. The team surely missed Paige, although Matlock was brilliant in his stead, posting a 1.52 ERA, and the rest of the staff was solid. But the main problem was the degradation of Charleston's game. Far from serving as a powerful complement to the young Gibson, Charleston hit just .271 and slugged only .387 over the year, offensive numbers that lagged far behind those posted by Gibson, Bell, Patterson, and outfielder Sam Bankhead. As a result, the second-half NNL flag was taken by the New York Cubans, who were

# THE 1935 PITTSBURGH CRAWFORDS

led by Cubans Alejandro Oms and Martin Dihigo, the latter of whom also managed the squad. The Cubans' second-half victory set up a Crawfords-Cubans NNL championship series.

In their level of organization, publicity, and generated interest, black-baseball World Series never managed to live up to those staged by the majors. As the 1933 championship debacle demonstrates, the leagues themselves simply didn't command enough respect for pennants to be viewed with awe, and the owners never stuck with one model long enough for fans to become invested. The 1935 series was no exception to the rule. The seven-game series started at New York's Dyckman Oval on Friday, September 13.[13] It bounced to 44th and Parkside in Philadelphia the next day, then back to Dyckman Oval on Sunday the 15th, before finally getting to the Crawfords' home city for Games Four and Five on the 17th and 18th. The schedule was so confusing that three of the four umpires went to the wrong ballpark for Game Two, and the crowds were of only middling size. The players, nevertheless, were fully engaged. Legitimate blackball World Series were rare enough that for them to win one really meant something. Plus, there was some real money on the line.

The Cubans landed the series' first punches, winning the first two games, 6-2 and 4-0. Matlock came back to blank the Cubans 3-0 in the third contest, in which Charleston homered, but he was too gassed to stave off Dihigo in Game Four, losing 6-1 at Greenlee Field. Down three to one in the series, the Crawfords were on the verge of elimination.

The next day, Roosevelt Davis and Cool Papa Bell willed the Crawfords to victory. Davis pitched a brilliant complete game but unfortunately gave up a tying pinch-hit home run in the top of the ninth. Bell then came to the rescue. In the bottom of the inning, his aggressive baserunning led to a wild throw to third. He scampered home to give the Craws a 3-2 victory, narrowing their series deficit to the same margin.

The following night, play resumed in Philadelphia. Charleston started Bert Hunter, but the best he, Bill Harvey, and Matlock could do was to hold the Cubans to six runs. The Crawfords found themselves down 6-3 as the game headed into the bottom of the ninth. Dihigo then made a fateful mistake. Instead of letting his splendid rookie pitcher Schoolboy Johnny Taylor try to close things out, he took the mound himself. It was a defensible decision, given that Dihigo had that year posted a virtually identical ERA to Taylor's (2.70 and 2.78, respectively). But with Taylor pitching well, it was probably unnecessary. Dihigo allowed light-hitting shortstop Chester Williams to reach base. Then Gibson got aboard. There were two outs, and the Craws were still down three, when Oscar Charleston stepped into the left-side batter's box.

The field at 44th and Parkside had been the site of some of Oscar's most memorable moments. But he was nearly 39 now, overweight, and had just struggled through his worst offensive season. Dihigo, at 30, was in his prime. He still had a three-run lead. And all he needed was one out. The odds against Charleston winning this battle were so long that Cubans owner Alex Pompez and team business manager Frank Forbes were already counting out the winners' share of the money in the clubhouse. As they counted, they heard the crowd erupt. Charleston had timed a Dihigo offering and sent it sailing over the center-field wall for a game-tying three-run blast. Forbes, disgusted, threw a bundle of $500 across the room.[14] Soon thereafter, the Crawfords' Pat Patterson doubled, and, when pinch-hitter Judy Johnson knocked him in with a single, the Craws had completed one of the most dramatic big-game comebacks the Negro Leagues had ever seen.

The next night, September 20, the Crawfords were nursing a 5-4 lead on the same diamond in the top of the eighth when Josh and Oscar struck again, hitting back-to-back home runs. Dihigo made an error that allowed another run to score, and the Craws held off a furious Cubans rally in the bottom of the ninth to complete a thrilling 8-7 win. This time there would be no doubt about it. The Crawfords – sans Satchel Paige – were the 1935 NNL champs.

Some days later, when the Craws returned to Pittsburgh, Greenlee feted them with a victory feast at the Crawford Grill. Pittsburgh Steelers owner Art Rooney, Bojangles Robinson, and the singing Mills Brothers, who were such big fans of the team that they had their own Craws uniforms and sometimes worked out with the club before games, were all there.[15] It was a huge, happy affair, and Judy Johnson thought Gus took all the more satisfaction in the championship because it had been achieved without Satchel.[16] That was probably true of not just Greenlee, but everyone.

It was nevertheless a pleasant surprise when, on April 21, 1936, Paige reported to the Crawfords' spring-training camp in Pittsburgh. Having pitched in the California Winter League over the winter, Satchel was already in midseason form, as he demonstrated convincingly enough when he threw a no-hitter in an exhibition game vs. the Akron Grays on May 3. By this time, Paige was transcendently popular, and his presence redounded to everyone's benefit on the field and at the gate, even when one accounted for his exasperating habits – like failing to show up for games, for example. As *Pittsburgh Courier* columnist Chester Washington wrote on May 9, throughout the East black baseball fans were now "Crawford-crazy," and the return of Paige, "a natural showman ... as spectacular as a circus and as colorful as a rainbow," would only make the team more popular.[17]

A balanced Washington Elite Giants club edged the Crawfords and the Philadelphia Stars for the NNL's first-half flag in 1936, in part because – outside of Gibson and first baseman Johnny Washington (whom Charleston had allowed to replace himself as the usual starter at the position) – none of the Craws had a particularly good offensive season. Judy Johnson was now a shell of himself, and new acquisition Dick Seay, although a wizard at second base, barely hit his weight. But the Crawfords started the second half hot and never took their foot off the gas. In late July they were 8-2, and as of mid-August they remained in first with a 13-6 record; ultimately, they would win the flag with a 19-8 mark.[18] By that point, however, the NNL was fraying at the seams, and a championship had come to mean little to both the players and the fans. On September 21 the Elite Giants won the first game of the NNL title series in Philadelphia, but numerous Crawfords stars were absent.[19] They were off barnstorming in the West, figuring that the money they could earn on the road was worth more than the crown of a league that commanded little prestige. No other series games were played; as a result, the NNL had no official champion in 1936. Reconstructed records show that the Crawfords, at 48-33-2, had the league's best record against top competition.

With Paige, Gibson, and several other players still in their primes, the Crawfords appeared poised to remain one of black baseball's most dominant teams for years to come. But in spring 1937 everything changed.

First, Greenlee's luck ran out. He reportedly suffered a big hit in the numbers game and suddenly was short of cash.[20] When Gibson held out for more money, the Crawfords traded him (and the broken-down Judy Johnson, who immediately retired) to the Grays for catcher Pepper Bassett (and, perhaps most importantly, $2,500 in cash). Greenlee may have had little choice, but this must nevertheless be considered of baseball's most disastrous trades. Think Brock-for-Broglio, but much, much worse.

Next, Greenlee encountered competition from a most unlikely source: a tinpot tyrant from the Caribbean named Rafael Trujillo.

The Crawfords were training in New Orleans in April when a Dominican man named Dr. José Enrique Aybar, along with a few associates, cornered Satchel Paige on the street. Aybar was on a recruiting trip.[21] His task was to find the best players possible for the Dragones de Ciudad Trujillo,

# THE 1935 PITTSBURGH CRAWFORDS

*The Pittsburgh Crawfords franchise was a rarity in the Negro Leagues in that the team had its own stadium, Greenlee Field. The Crawfords played at the venue from 1932 through 1938.*

a baseball team representing the Dominican Republic's capital city, recently renamed for the megalomaniacal dictator who had taken control of the nation a few years earlier. Trujillo had made ample funds available to Aybar – not so ample that he could lure white players away from the major leagues, but plenty to turn the head of a Negro Leaguer like Paige. Once Aybar, brandishing a pistol (in Paige's telling), had Satchel's attention, he offered the astounding sum of $30,000 for Paige and eight of his teammates to come play in the island nation. From that amount Satchel could take whatever he thought was his fair share. Much stronger men than Satch would have been unable to resist such an offer. Paige accepted and began to recruit his fellow Crawfords.

News that Paige and others had jumped or were thinking about jumping had already reached Greenlee and Charleston when, on or about Friday, May 8, two Trujillo men showed up in Pittsburgh looking for yet more players. Ernest "Spoon" Carter was among those who agreed to go. But the next day he had second thoughts and decided to confer with his wife and Charleston. Charleston reported the conversation to Greenlee, who, after fruitlessly threatening legal action, pivoted to plan B, which was to try to work out an arrangement with the men representing Trujillo. He may have wanted to sell a couple of players in exchange for a deal that would prevent any further tampering. Indeed, he reached out to his fellow owners with a proposal that would require

*The formidable starting outfield of the 1935 Pittsburgh Crawfords: (L-R) Sam Bankhead, left field; James "Cool Papa" Bell, center field; and Jimmie Crutchfield, right field*

the Dominicans to deal directly with league headquarters if they wished to acquire anyone. Alas, seeing that the Crawfords were the only team that was really going to be decimated by the raids, Greenlee's fellow owners reacted coolly to his idea. They could hardly have done anything to prevent the raids in any case.

By the beginning weeks of the 1937 NNL season, the Crawfords had been destroyed. They had lost nine men to Trujillo, including stalwarts like Paige, Leroy Matlock, Cool Papa Bell, and Sam Bankhead. The only experienced pitcher remaining was journeyman Barney Morris. Suddenly, Oscar Charleston was forced to scramble to put together a credible club. For half the season, the Craws surprised and impressed with their gutty, heads-up play. Bassett acquitted himself particularly well. But neither his emergence nor the no-name Crawfords' grittiness was enough to keep the club afloat in the competitive NNL. By the beginning of August, the Craws had slid back to fifth place. That is the position in which they would end. The 1937 Crawfords posted an abysmal 18-35-1 record against major black teams.

Paige, Bell, and the rest of the "outlaw" players who had been lured to the Dominican in spring 1937 returned stateside in late July and, by the beginning of the following season, were restored to the NNL owners' good graces. But when Satchel held out for more money the following spring, Greenlee reluctantly agreed to trade him for Schoolboy Johnny Taylor. Meanwhile, Charleston tried to put together a quality team that could actually compete for a pennant. Things were so bad that open tryouts were held during spring training. By the time the season started, the Crawfords did not look like a very promising group. The team featured some solid veterans in Matlock, Sam Bankhead, and infielders Harry Williams and Chester Williams, as well as some rising talents in Johnny Washington, Pepper Bassett, Schoolboy Johnny Taylor, new outfielder Gene Benson, and new third baseman Bus Clarkson, but it lacked elite talent.[22] For much of the season the club overachieved, even managing to put together an impressive 13-7 record as of June 25. Alas, in July, things unraveled, thanks in part to a six-game series sweep suffered at the hands of the Grays. It didn't help that, according to one columnist, Taylor was "doing most of his pitching in night clubs."[23]

The Crawfords still finished the 1938 season with an impressive 24-16 record, good for fourth place in the league and just 4½ games out of first.[24] They were even supposed to play in a four-team playoff with the Homestead Grays, Philadelphia Stars, and Baltimore Elite Giants that was to serve as a new kind of NNL championship series. But the Grays refused to participate, and the series never came off. Its failure was a fitting symbol of the Negro National League's persistent dysfunction.

Overall, from 1932 through 1938 the Crawfords went 299-218-14 versus major Negro Leagues teams; the club's winning percentage in 1932-36, before it was busted up by Trujillo's raid, was a robust .617. The 1938 season was the last the Crawfords would play with Pittsburgh as their home base – or with Greenlee as their owner. By 1939, Greenlee's finances were in bad shape.[25] He could not even properly maintain Greenlee Field, which in any case was dismantled to make way for a New Deal housing project. In mid-April, Greenlee sold the Crawfords to a group of Ohio businessmen.[26] Their first move was to sign Charleston as the rechristened *Toledo* Crawfords' manager. The legendary Oscar, they figured, would help draw fans. But the Craws' new owners had another, even bigger card to play: one of their number was none other than the dazzling star of the 1936 Berlin Olympics: Jesse Owens.

The Toledo group was not well-heeled. Years later, the daughter of the lead investor, promoter Hank Rigney, estimated that her father and Owens had both probably invested no more than $50 in the venture.[27] With little margin to spare and the Depression refusing to lift, the Crawfords' new owners were betting in part on their promotional abilities, in part on Charleston's appeal to black baseball fans, and in much larger part on the extraordinarily popular Owens's ability to attract both black and white fans who would otherwise rarely, if ever, come to a baseball game.

By spring 1939, Owens was 25 and had a wife and three children. He had been scrambling for several years to capitalize on the fame he had won at the 1936 Berlin Olympics. For a brief while, Jesse had made good money as a celebrity spokesman (most notably for 1936 Republican presidential nominee Alf Landon), but as he spent freely and supported family members and old friends generously, his funds had rapidly diminished. In summer 1938 he had invested much of his remaining savings in a dry-cleaning company on Cleveland's east side, but the business failed to turn a profit. In the meantime, the Internal Revenue Service had put a lien on his home for failure to pay income taxes. The result was that, in May 1939 – shortly after he helped purchase the Crawfords – Owens filed for bankruptcy. The Toledo Crawfords' new co-owner had no head for business.[28]

Owens was, however, entirely willing to race for money, and that was what the Crawfords needed more than anything else. For the next two years, the usual Crawfords program called for Owens to put on a running exhibition between games, if a doubleheader had been scheduled, or after the game, if not. Usually Owens raced other players and fans. Sometimes he raced motorcycles or even horses. Although he ran frequently on muddy fields or a bum ankle, and almost always after enduring the grueling rigors of Negro Leagues travel, Owens usually emerged victorious, and he always earned the gaping crowd's admiration.[29]

Later, in his memoirs, Owens looked back at this period as a degrading and humiliating way to have had to make a living, not recording the name of the team he traveled with (and co-owned) or that of anyone else with whom he partnered in the baseball world.[30] Whether any of the Crawfords thought Owens's role a degrading one is unknown, but it is certain that they were still trying to win. Alas, despite having decent talent on the roster in the form of Schoolboy Johnny Taylor, Harry Kincannon, Johnny Wright, Bus Clarkson, and Jimmie Crutchfield, the 1939 Crawfords, thanks to their new position well west of the NNL's other clubs, couldn't even get many league games. At the end of the NNL's first half, the Craws, sporting a record of 4-5-1, withdrew from the circuit. The next day they were accepted as members of the more geographically appropriate Negro American League, in which they finished the season with an 8-11-1 mark.

The next year, 1940, Charleston bought a stake in the Crawfords himself, and he persuaded his partners to split the team's 1940 home games between Toledo and Indianapolis.[31] Charleston spent the spring looking under every rock in the South and Southwest for undiscovered talent. In Atlanta he scored a huge find in a tall, skinny, raw country boy named Connie Johnson, whom he would help develop into a pitcher who would play professionally for more than 20 years, including five seasons in the majors.[32] Nevertheless, the 1940 Crawfords were less competitive than ever. Owens stayed with the team all season, continuing to race between or after both home and away games, leading clinics, often speaking for a few minutes to the fans, and generally lending his championship aura to the Crawfords' operation. Auras, alas, can only do so much. The Craws finished in last place in the 1940 Negro American League with a 6-17 record.

The once-mighty Crawfords had reached the end of their journey. After the 1940 season the club broke up, never to play as a major Negro League team again. Eight years later, the end came for the Negro National League as a whole, thanks to the beginning of a new chapter for African American baseball players. It was a chapter that came too late for most of the ex-Crawfords, but they could take some solace from the knowledge that their own persistence, toughness, and excellence had helped make it possible.

## Sources

All statistics and records given in this article come from Seamheads.com, the best source of statistics for the Negro Leagues. Note that the Seamheads database is continually being added to and refined, so that some of the numbers given here may shift as time goes on.

## Notes

1. A fuller account of the Crawfords' early years can be found in Rob Ruck, *Sandlot Seasons: Sport in Black Pittsburgh* (Urbana: University of Illinois Press, 1987).

2. Biographical information on Greenlee can be found in Ruck, *Sandlot Seasons*; James Bankes, *The Pittsburgh Crawfords: The Lives and Times of Black Baseball's Most Exciting Team* (Dubuque, Iowa: William C. Brown, 1991); and Mark Whitaker, *Smoketown: The Untold Story of the Other Great Black Renaissance* (New York: Simon and Schuster, 2018).

3. "Crawfords Sign New Stars," *Pittsburgh Courier*, June 27, 1931: 15.

4. "Paige Stops Grays as Crawfords Cop, 10 to 7," *Pittsburgh Courier*, August 8, 1931: 15.

5. "Charleston Is Elected Captain," *Philadelphia Tribune*, January 28, 1932: 11.

6. Al Monroe, "Speaking of Sports," *Chicago Defender*, May 19, 1934: 16.

7. This record comes from Seamheads.com, accessed December 15, 2019. Ruck, *Sandlot Seasons*, 157, is the source for the 99-36 claim.

8. For Gibson and other Crawfords hitter statistics from 1932, see "Sez 'Ches,'" *Pittsburgh Courier*, January 21, 1933: 15; the statistics reported there were clearly not solely compiled against major competition. Paige's statistics are taken from Seamheads.com, accessed December 15, 2019, and therefore include only games versus top-tier teams.

# THE 1935 PITTSBURGH CRAWFORDS

9   The elements of the story may be found in the *Pittsburgh Courier*, October 14, 1933: 14, and "Baseball Moguls to Meet in Philly Next Month," *Pittsburgh Courier*, January 27, 1934: 15.

10  For this story, and for much else on Paige, see Larry Tye, *Satchel: The Life and Times of an American Legend* (New York: Random House, 2009), 89-90. See also "Satchel Paige Hurls Bearded Nine to Title," *Indianapolis Recorder*, August 25, 1934: 7.

11  Timothy Gay, *Satch, Dizzy, and Rapid Robert: The Wild Saga of Interracial Baseball before Jackie Robinson* (New York: Simon and Schuster, 2010), 75.

12  Gay, 76.

13  Rich Puerzer has sifted through the inconsistent media coverage to provide a coherent account of this series. "The 1935 Playoff Series: The New York Cubans vs. the Pittsburgh Crawfords," presentation delivered at SABR's Jerry Malloy Negro League Conference, Pittsburgh, August 7, 2015.

14  Forbes told John Holway this story. See John B. Holway, *Black Giants* (Springfield, Virginia: Lord Fairfax Press, 2010), 5-6, and John B. Holway, *Josh and Satch: The Life and Times of Josh Gibson and Satchel Paige* (Westport, Connecticut: Meckler Books, 1988), 82. Forbes, however, is an unreliable source for the game's details (and for much else).

15  Bankes, 85.

16  Bankes, 73.

17  Chester L. Washington, "Sez Ches," *Pittsburgh Courier*, May 9, 1936: 14.

18  The Crawfords became involved in a brief controversy near the end of the 1936 season when columnist Dan Parker of the *New York Daily Mirror* charged them with throwing a game against the white semipro Brooklyn Bushwicks. (Gibson dropped a popup when the Bushwicks had the bases loaded in the bottom of the ninth; to anyone who knew Josh's troubles with pop flies there was nothing fishy in that at all, but Parker was apparently not clued in.) Commissioner Kenesaw Mountain Landis, overstepping his authority per usual, was said to have even interviewed members of the Crawfords about the affair. In the end, Parker retracted his claim. See Donn Rogosin, *Invisible Men: Life in Baseball's Negro Leagues* (New York: Atheneum, 1983), 114-15.

19  W. Rollo Wilson, "National Sport Shots," *Pittsburgh Courier*, September 26, 1936: A5.

20  Buck Leonard with James A. Riley, *Buck Leonard: The Black Lou Gehrig: An Autobiography* (New York: Carroll and Graf, 1995), 79.

21  Tye, *Satchel*, has the best discussion of this affair. See 110-16. Other details are taken from newspaper accounts.

22  The 1938 contract between Taylor and the Crawfords called for him to be paid $400 per month between May 15 and October 1. It was signed by Taylor, Greenlee, and Charleston (as witness). The four-page document disproves the notion that Negro Leagues players did not have formal contracts. See sports.ha.com/itm/baseball/1938-39-pittsburgh-crawfords-negro-league-player-s-contract-for-johnny-schoolboy-taylor-signed-by-oscar-charleston/a/7100-80064.s?ic4=GalleryView-Thumbnail-071515.

23  Wendell Smith, "Smitty's Sport Spurts," *Pittsburgh Courier*, July 16, 1938: 16.

24  This record comes from the Center for Negro League Baseball Research. See cnlbr.org/Portals/0/Standings/Negro%20National%20League%20(1920-1948)%202016-08.pdf. Seamheads has the Crawfords at 22–22–1.

25  "Sammy Bankhead Will Play with Toledoans," *New York Amsterdam News*, April 22, 1939: 19.

26  "Oscar Charleston to Manage Strong Toledo Nine in NNL," *Pittsburgh Courier*, April 22, 1939: 17; Cum Posey, "Posey's Points," *Pittsburgh Courier*, April 22, 1939: 17.

27  John Wagner, "Swayne Field Was Full of History," *Toledo Blade*, October 5, 2001. See toledoblade.com/Mud-Hens/2001/10/05/Swayne-Field-was-full-of-history.html.

28  I take this biographical information about Owens largely from William J. Baker, *Jesse Owens: An American Life* (New York: The Free Press, 1986).

29  For a more extensive account of Owens's time with the Crawfords, see Jeremy Beer, *Oscar Charleston: The Life and Legend of Baseball's Greatest Forgotten Player* (Lincoln: University of Nebraska Press, 2019). Two representative articles about Owens's racing are "Doubleheader and Jesse Owens at Park Monday," *Lima* (Ohio) *News*, June 4, 1939: 15, and "Jesse Owens Dazzles Louisville People," *Atlanta Daily World*, September 8, 1939: 5.

30  See Jesse Owens with Paul G. Neimark, *Blackthink: My Life as Black Man and White Man* (New York: William Morrow, 1970), 49-50; Jesse Owens with Paul G. Neimark, *I Have Changed* (New York: William Morrow, 1972), 71; and Baker, *Jesse Owens*, 143.

31  "Toledo Crawfords Here Sun., May 26 at Stadium," *Indianapolis Recorder*, May 18, 1940: 14.

32  See Johnson's account of coming to play for the Crawfords in Brent Kelley, *The Negro Leagues Revisited: Conversations with 66 More Baseball Heroes* (Jefferson, North Carolina: McFarland, 2000), 114-16.

# CONTRIBUTORS

**Jeremy Beer** is the author of *Oscar Charleston: The Life and Legend of Baseball's Greatest Forgotten Player*, winner of the CASEY Award and SABR's Seymour Medal. His writing on baseball and other topics has appeared in the *Washington Post*, the *Utne Reader*, the *Washington Examiner*, *National Review*, and *Baseball Research Journal*, among other venues. Beer is the principal partner at American Philanthropic, LLC. He and his wife live in Phoenix, Arizona.

**Mark Blaeuer** has since 2011 been a research team member for the Hot Springs, Arkansas, Historic Baseball Trail, along with Mike Dugan, Don Duren, Bill Jenkinson, and Tim Reid. Steve Arrison, CEO of Visit Hot Springs, headed and funded this project as well as the annual Hot Springs Baseball Weekend event. Mark got his BA from Illinois College and his MA from the University of Arkansas. He is a member of the Garland County Historical Society (Liz Robbins, executive director).

**Richard Bogovich** is the author of *Kid Nichols: A Biography of the Hall of Fame Pitcher* and *The Who: A Who's Who,* both published by McFarland & Co. He has contributed to such SABR books as *The Newark Eagles Take Flight: The Story of the 1946 Negro League Champions* and *Bittersweet Goodbye: The Black Barons, the Grays, and the 1948 Negro League World Series*. He works for the Wendland Utz law firm in Rochester, Minnesota.

**Frederick C. Rick Bush** joined SABR in March 2014. Since that time he has written articles for numerous SABR books as well as the BioProject and Games Project websites. In addition to co-editing the current volume, he has served in the same capacity for the books *Bittersweet Goodbye: The Black Barons, the Grays, and the 1948 Negro League World Series* and *The Newark Eagles Take Flight: The Story of the 1946 Negro League Champions*. Rick lives with his wife, Michelle, their three sons, Michael, Andrew, and Daniel, and their Border collie mix, Bailey, in the greater Houston area. He is in his 16th year of teaching English at Wharton County Junior College's satellite campus in Sugar Land.

Since 1993, not a day has passed on which **Matt Clever** did not watch, read about, or dream about baseball. Growing up in eastern Pennsylvania, his heart was captured that summer by an unforgettable Phillies squad that came up just short in October. Matt is an Air Force veteran who now works as a land surveyor, and also part-time as a scorekeeper at the Phillies' Double-A affiliate in Reading, Pennsylvania.

# THE 1935 PITTSBURGH CRAWFORDS

**Alan Cohen** has been a SABR member since 2010. He serves as vice president-treasurer of the Connecticut Smoky Joe Wood Chapter and is datacaster (MiLB First Pitch stringer) for the Hartford Yard Goats, the Double-A affiliate of the Colorado Rockies. His biographies, game stories, and essays have appeared in more than 40 SABR publications. Since his first *Baseball Research Journal* article appeared in 2013, Alan has continued to expand his research into the Hearst Sandlot Classic (1946-1965), which launched the careers of 88 major leaguers. He has four children and eight grandchildren and resides in Connecticut with wife Frances, their cats, Morty, Ava, and Zoe, and their dog, Buddy.

**Duke Goldman** has been a SABR member for approximately half of its existence. A member of the Negro Leagues Committee, Duke has published several articles on the Negro Leagues and baseball integration, including SABR-McFarland award winners "The Double Victory Campaign and the Campaign to Integrate Baseball" and "1933-1962: The Business Meetings of Negro League Baseball." Duke was also awarded the Robert Peterson Recognition Award for his *Black Ball Journal* articles and other SABR publications. A native of the Bronx now living in Northampton, Massachusetts, he calls a Yankees loss, Red Sox win, and Mets win a trifecta.

**Margaret M. "Peggy" Gripshover** is a professor of geography at Western Kentucky University. She earned her Ph.D. in geography at the University of Tennessee and her MS and BS degrees in geography from Marshall University. She has been a SABR member since 2006 and combines her love of baseball with her geographic research on race, ethnicity, urbanization, horse racing, and cultural landscapes. Peggy has published articles in the *Baseball Research Journal*, contributed a chapter to *Northsiders: Essays on the History and Culture of the Chicago Cubs*, edited by Gerald R. Wood and Andy Hazucha (McFarland, 2008), and a chapter in *Bittersweet Goodbye: The Black Barons, the Grays, and the 1948 Negro League World Series* (SABR, 2017), and two chapters in *The Newark Eagles Take Flight: The Story of the 1946 Negro League Champions* (SABR, 2019). She is a native of Cincinnati and lifelong Reds fan. She lives in Bowling Green, Kentucky, with her husband, Thomas L. Bell, and their Australian Shepherd, Bella.

**Leslie Heaphy** is an associate professor of history at Kent State University, Stark, chair of the WIBC for SABR, and author/editor of numerous books and articles about women's baseball and the Negro Leagues.

**Jon Henson** celebrated his first anniversary as a SABR member in February 2020 and is grateful for this first opportunity to contribute to a SABR book. He is the president and historian for the Providence Grays Historic Base Ball Club in Rhode Island, a vintage team that travels the Northeast from April through October to bring the old game to life as it was played in the mid- to late 1800s. Jon is a writer and editor for the elevator industry's national educational program and teaches writing at Roger Williams University. He and his family reside in Tiverton, Rhode Island.

**Paul Hofmann**, a SABR member since 2002, is the associate vice president for international affairs at Sacramento State University and a frequent contributor to SABR publications. Paul is a native of Detroit and a lifelong Detroit Tigers fan. He currently resides in Folsom, California.

**Jay Hurd** is a librarian and museum educator. A member of the Society for American Baseball Research for more than 20 years, he is a contributor to the SABR Baseball Biography Project, and presents on baseball-related topics including the Negro Leagues, baseball literature for children and young adults, women in baseball, and baseball and the Blue Laws. Currently, he is studying baseball in Rhode Island, with a focus on baseball in the town of Bristol. A longtime fan of the Boston Red Sox, Jay relocated from Medford, Massachusetts, to Bristol, Rhode Island, in 2016.

## Pride of Smoketown

**William H. "Bill" Johnson** is the author of a full-length biography, *Hal Trosky: A Baseball Biography* (McFarland & Co., 2017), along with more than two dozen essays for the Society for American Baseball Research's BioProject. He retired from the US Navy in 2006 after a 24-year career in naval aviation. He has presented papers at several baseball-history conferences. He graduated from the University of California (Berkeley) with a degree in rhetoric, and has subsequently earned a master of arts in military history from Norwich University and a masters in aeronautical science from Embry-Riddle Aeronautical University. He currently teaches unmanned aviation at Embry-Riddle.

**Thomas E. Kern** was born and raised in Southwest Pennsylvania. Listening to the mellifluous voices of Bob Prince and Jim Woods, how could one not become a lifelong Pirates fan? Tom has been a SABR member dating back to the mid-1980s. He now lives in Washington, DC, and sees the Nationals and Orioles as often as possible. With a love and appreciation for Negro League baseball, Tom wrote a SABR biography of Leon Day after having met him at a baseball card show in the early 1990s. He has since written a number of Negro League bios for the SABR BioProject. Tom's day job is in the field of transportation technology.

**Kevin Larkin** retired after 24 years as a police officer in his hometown of Great Barrington, Massachusetts. He has always been a baseball fan and has been going to minor-league and major-league baseball games since he was 5 years old. He has authored two books on baseball: *Baseball in the Bay State (*a history of baseball in the Commonwealth of Massachusetts) and *Gehrig: Game by Game* (an account of all of the major-league baseball games played by his hero, Lou Gehrig). He also co-authored *Baseball in the Berkshires: A County's Common Bond* along with James Tom Daly, James Overmyer, and Larry Moore. The book details a history of baseball in Berkshire County, where Larkin grew up. He has authored numerous articles for SABR and also recently had published on Legends on Deck a list of who Larkin thinks are the top 100 Black Baseball/Negro League baseball players. Black Baseball and the Negro Leagues are a subject he really enjoys. Researching and learning about this great game are what drives him and he loves researching, reading, and writing about the game's history. He does fact-checking and hyperlinking for SABR, as well as writing biographies and game accounts, and is living the dream of writing and researching about the great sport of baseball.

**Bob LeMoine** grew up in Maine and has lived and died with the Red Sox for most of his life. He joined SABR in 2013 and has contributed to several SABR book projects. Having a love for both history and baseball, he usually contributes to most SABR book projects. Bob lives in Rochester, New Hampshire, and works as a high-school librarian and adjunct professor.

**Len Levin,** a retired newspaper editor in New England, is currently the grammarian and editor for the Rhode Island Supreme Court. He also is the copyeditor for many SABR publications, including this one.

**Brian McKenna** has been a member of SABR since 1991. He lives in Baltimore and works as a retail manager. He has written nearly 60 biographies for SABR's BioProject.

**Bill Nowlin** still remembers with embarrassment a few years from his earliest teenage years when the Boston Red Sox lacked an African-American ballplayer on the team. Times have changed for the better, but there is always work to be done. He has been a member of SABR for more than 20 years and has been active with SABR's publications. This is the third book looking at aspects of Negro League history that he has co-edited with Rick Bush.

**Tim Odzer** has been fascinated by the Negro Leagues ever since he pulled a Cool Papa Bell card from a Topps pack in 2001. Tim joined SABR in 2011; since then, he has written articles for the BioProject and Games Project. Tim is a 2015 graduate of Duke University and a 2019 graduate of the University of Chicago Law School. He currently resides in Monroe, Louisiana, and works as a law clerk for a federal judge.

**Richard J. Puerzer** is an associate professor and chairperson of the Department of Engineering at Hofstra University. He has contributed to several SABR books, including *When Pops Led the Family: The 1979 Pittsburgh Pirates* (2016); *Bittersweet Goodbye: The Black Barons, The Grays, and the 1948 Negro League World Series* (2017); *Moments of Joy and Heartbreak: 66 Significant Episodes in the History of the Pittsburgh Pirates* (2018); and *The Newark Eagles Take Flight: The Story of the 1946 Negro League Champions* (2019). His writing on baseball has also appeared in: *Nine: A Journal of Baseball History and Culture, Black Ball, The National Pastime, The Cooperstown Symposium on Baseball and American Culture* proceedings, *Zisk*, and *Spitball*.

**Carl Riechers** retired from United Parcel Service in 2012 after 35 years of service. With more free time, he became a SABR member that same year. Born and raised in the suburbs of St. Louis, he became a big fan of the Cardinals. He and his wife, Janet, have three children and he is the proud grandpa of two.

**Wes Singletary** is the author of three books: *The Right Time: John Henry "Pop" Lloyd and Black Baseball*, 2011; *Al Lopez: The Life of Baseball's El Senor*, 1999; and *Florida's First Big League Baseball Players: A Narrative History*, 2006. He has also published numerous articles in *Nine, Blackball,* and other historical journals. Wes has a Ph.D. in history from the Florida State University, and continues to teach locally at Lawton Chiles High School and Tallahassee Community College. He is married to the former Toni Zarate and they have two children, Patricia and Nelson. A proud native of Tampa, Wes resides with his family in Tallahassee, where he coaches the five-time state American Legion baseball champions, Tallahassee Post 13.

A fan of the Negro League baseball ever since he read *Only the Ball Was White* by Robert Peterson, **Mark S. Sternman** also contributed to the SABR book on the 1946 Newark Eagles.

**Jeb Stewart** is a lawyer in Birmingham, Alabama, who enjoys taking his sons (Nolan and Ryan) and his wife, Stephanie, to the Rickwood Classic each year. He has been a SABR member since 2012 and is co-president of the Rickwood Field SABR Chapter. He is an executive committee member on the Board of the Friends of Rickwood Field and is a regular contributor to the *Rickwood Times*. He has written several biographies for SABR's Baseball Biography Project.

**Dave Wilkie** is an upper elementary teacher at the Montessori School of the Mahoning Valley in Youngstown, Ohio. He grew up in Western Canada idolizing the San Francisco Giants and Willie McCovey. He has written SABR biographies on Negro League greats Sam Bankhead, Johnny Davis, Chester Williams, and Cool Papa Bell. His obsession with Negro League baseball and its players can be traced to a 1983 mail-order purchase of the book *The All-Time All-Stars of Black Baseball*, by SABR member James A. Riley. He plans to continue writing biographies on these forgotten legends with the hopes of publishing his own book some day.

# Friends of SABR

You can become a Friend of SABR by giving as little as $10 per month or by making a one-time gift of $1,000 or more. When you do so, you will be inducted into a community of passionate baseball fans dedicated to supporting SABR's work.

Friends of SABR receive the following benefits:
- ✓ Annual Friends of SABR Commemorative Lapel Pin
- ✓ Recognition in This Week in SABR, SABR.org, and the SABR Annual Report
- ✓ Access to the SABR Annual Convention VIP donor event
- ✓ Invitations to exclusive Friends of SABR events

**SABR On-Deck Circle - $10/month, $30/month, $50/month**
Get in the SABR On-Deck Circle, and help SABR become the essential community for the world of baseball. Your support will build capacity around all things SABR, including publications, website content, podcast development, and community growth.

A monthly gift is deducted from your bank account or charged to a credit card until you tell us to stop. No more email, mail, or phone reminders.

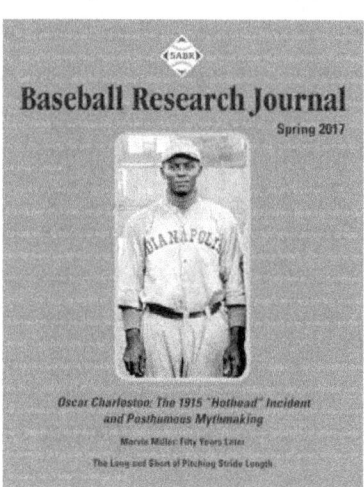
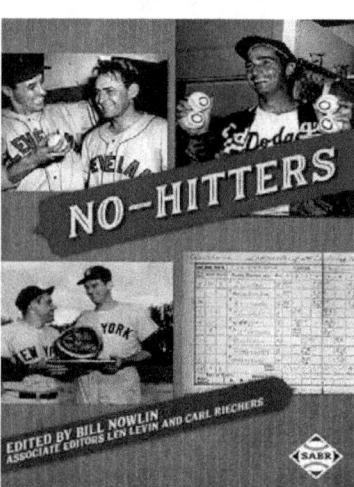

---

## Join the SABR On-Deck Circle

Payment Info: _____ Visa _____ Mastercard    ○ $10/month

Name on Card: _____    ○ $30/month

Card #: _____    ○ $50/month

Exp. Date: _____ Security Code: _____    ○ Other amount _____

Signature: _____

**Go to sabr.org/donate to make your gift online**

# Society for American Baseball Research

Cronkite School at ASU
555 N. Central Ave. #416, Phoenix, AZ 85004
602.496.1460 (phone)
SABR.org

## Become a SABR member today!

If you're interested in baseball — writing about it, reading about it, talking about it — there's a place for you in the Society for American Baseball Research.

SABR memberships are available on annual, multi-year, or monthly subscription basis. Annual and monthly subscription memberships auto-renew for your convenience. Young Professional memberships are for ages 30 and under. Senior memberships are for ages 65 and older. Student memberships are available to currently enrolled middle/high school or full-time college/university students. Monthly subscription members receive SABR publications electronically and are eligible for SABR event discounts after 12 months.

Here's a list of some of the key benefits you'll receive as a SABR member:

- Receive two editions (spring and fall) of the *Baseball Research Journal*, our flagship publication
- Receive expanded e-book edition of *The National Pastime*, our annual convention journal
- 8-10 new e-books published by the SABR Digital Library, all FREE to members
- "This Week in SABR" e-newsletter, sent to members every Friday
- Join dozens of research committees, from Statistical Analysis to Women in Baseball.
- Join one of 70+ regional chapters in the U.S., Canada, Latin America, and abroad
- Participate in online discussion groups
- Ask and answer baseball research questions on the SABR-L e-mail listserv
- Complete archives of *The Sporting News* dating back to 1886 and other research resources
- Promote your research in "This Week in SABR"
- Diamond Dollars Case Competition
- Yoseloff Scholarships
- Discounts on SABR national conferences, including the SABR National Convention, the SABR Analytics Conference, Jerry Malloy Negro League Conference, Frederick Ivor-Campbell 19th Century Conference, and the Arizona Fall League Experience
- Publish your research in peer-reviewed SABR journals
- Collaborate with SABR researchers and experts
- Contribute to Baseball Biography Project or the SABR Games Project
- List your new book in the SABR Bookshelf
- Lead a SABR research committee or chapter
- Networking opportunities at SABR Analytics Conference
- Meet baseball authors and historians at SABR events and chapter meetings
- 50% discounts on paperback versions of SABR e-books
- Discounts with other partners in the baseball community
- SABR research awards

We hope you'll join the most passionate international community of baseball fans at SABR! Check us out online at SABR.org/join.

---

## SABR MEMBERSHIP FORM

|          | Standard | Senior  | Young Pro. | Student |
|----------|----------|---------|------------|---------|
| Annual:  | ❏ $65    | ❏ $45   | ❏ $45      | ❏ $25   |
| 3 Year:  | ❏ $175   | ❏ $129  | ❏ $129     |         |
| 5 Year:  | ❏ $249   |         |            |         |
| Monthly: | ❏ $6.95  | ❏ $4.95 | ❏ $4.95    |         |

*(International members wishing to be mailed the Baseball Research Journal should add $10/yr for Canada/Mexico or $19/yr for overseas locations.)*

### Participate in Our Donor Program!

Support the preservation of baseball research. Designate your gift toward:
❏ General Fund ❏ Endowment Fund ❏ Research Resources ❏ _____
❏ I want to maximize the impact of my gift; do not send any donor premiums
❏ I would like this gift to remain anonymous.

Note: Any donation not designated will be placed in the General Fund.
SABR is a 501 (c)(3) not-for-profit organization & donations are tax-deductible to the extent allowed by law.

Name _____

E-mail* _____

Address _____

City _____ ST ____ ZIP _____

Phone _____ Birthday _____

* Your e-mail address on file ensures you will receive the most recent SABR news.

**Dues** $_____
**Donation** $_____
**Amount Enclosed** $_____

Do you work for a matching grant corporation? Call (602) 496-1460 for details.

*If you wish to pay by credit card, please contact the SABR office at (602) 496-1460 or sign up securely online at SABR.org/join. We accept Visa, Mastercard & Discover.*

Do you wish to receive the *Baseball Research Journal* electronically? ❏ Yes ❏ No
Our e-books are available in PDF, Kindle, or EPUB (iBooks, iPad, Nook) formats.

**Mail to: SABR, Cronkite School at ASU, 555 N. Central Ave. #416, Phoenix, AZ 85004**

# SABR BioProject Team Books

In 2002, the Society for American Baseball Research launched an effort to write and publish biographies of every player, manager, and individual who has made a contribution to baseball. Over the past decade, the BioProject Committee has produced over 6,000 biographical articles. Many have been part of efforts to create theme- or team-oriented books, spearheaded by chapters or other committees of SABR.

*The 1986 Boston Red Sox:*
*There Was More Than Game Six*
One of a two-book series on the rivals that met in the 1986 World Series, the Boston Red Sox and the New York Mets, including biographies of every player, coach, broadcaster, and other important figures in the top organizations in baseball that year. .
**Edited by Leslie Heaphy and Bill Nowlin**
**$19.95 paperback (ISBN 978-1-943816-19-4)**
**$9.99 ebook (ISBN 978-1-943816-18-7)**
8.5"X11", 420 pages, over 200 photos

*The 1986 New York Mets:*
*There Was More Than Game Six*
The other book in the "rivalry" set from the 1986 World Series. This book re-tells the story of that year's classic World Series and this is the story of each of the players, coaches, managers, and broadcasters, their lives in baseball and the way the 1986 season fit into their lives.
**Edited by Leslie Heaphy and Bill Nowlin**
**$19.95 paperback (ISBN 978-1-943816-13-2)**
**$9.99 ebook (ISBN 978-1-943816-12-5)**
8.5"X11", 392 pages, over 100 photos

*Scandal on the South Side:*
*The 1919 Chicago White Sox*
The Black Sox Scandal isn't the only story worth telling about the 1919 Chicago White Sox. The team roster included three future Hall of Famers, a 20-year-old spitballer who would win 300 games in the minors, and even a batboy who later became a celebrity with the "Murderers' Row" New York Yankees. All of their stories are included in Scandal on the South Side with a timeline of the 1919 season.
**Edited by Jacob Pomrenke**
**$19.95 paperback (ISBN 978-1-933599-95-3)**
**$9.99 ebook (ISBN 978-1-933599-94-6)**
8.5"x11", 324 pages, 55 historic photos

*Winning on the North Side*
*The 1929 Chicago Cubs*
Celebrate the 1929 Chicago Cubs, one of the most exciting teams in baseball history. Future Hall of Famers Hack Wilson, '29 NL MVP Rogers Hornsby, and Kiki Cuyler, along with Riggs Stephenson formed one of the most potent quartets in baseball history. The magical season came to an ignominious end in the World Series and helped craft the future "lovable loser" image of the team.
**Edited by Gregory H. Wolf**
**$19.95 paperback (ISBN 978-1-933599-89-2)**
**$9.99 ebook (ISBN 978-1-933599-88-5)**
8.5"x11", 314 pages, 59 photos

*Detroit the Unconquerable:*
*The 1935 World Champion Tigers*
Biographies of every player, coach, and broadcaster involved with the 1935 World Champion Detroit Tigers baseball team, written by members of the Society for American Baseball Research. Also includes a season in review and other articles about the 1935 team. Hank Greenberg, Mickey Cochrane, Charlie Gehringer, Schoolboy Rowe, and more.
**Edited by Scott Ferkovich**
**$19.95 paperback (ISBN 9978-1-933599-78-6)**
**$9.99 ebook (ISBN 978-1-933599-79-3)**
8.5"X11", 230 pages, 52 photos

*The Team That Time Won't Forget:*
*The 1951 New York Giants*
Because of Bobby Thomson's dramatic "Shot Heard 'Round the World" in the bottom of the ninth of the decisive playoff game against the Brooklyn Dodgers, the team will forever be in baseball public's consciousness. Includes a foreword by Giants outfielder Monte Irvin.
**Edited by Bill Nowlin and C. Paul Rogers III**
**$19.95 paperback (ISBN 978-1-933599-99-1)**
**$9.99 ebook (ISBN 978-1-933599-98-4)**
8.5"X11", 282 pages, 47 photos

*A Pennant for the Twin Cities:*
*The 1965 Minnesota Twins*
This volume celebrates the 1965 Minnesota Twins, who captured the American League pennant in just their fifth season in the Twin Cities. Led by an All-Star cast, from Harmon Killebrew, Tony Oliva, Zoilo Versalles, and Mudcat Grant to Bob Allison, Jim Kaat, Earl Battey, and Jim Perry, the Twins won 102 games, but bowed to the Los Angeles Dodgers and Sandy Koufax in Game Seven
**Edited by Gregory H. Wolf**
**$19.95 paperback (ISBN 978-1-943816-09-5)**
**$9.99 ebook (ISBN 978-1-943816-08-8)**
8.5"X11", 405 pages, over 80 photos

*Mustaches and Mayhem: Charlie O's Three Time Champions:*
*The Oakland Athletics: 1972-74*
The Oakland Athletics captured major league baseball's crown each year from 1972 through 1974. Led by future Hall of Famers Reggie Jackson, Catfish Hunter and Rollie Fingers, the Athletics were a largely homegrown group who came of age together. Biographies of every player, coach, manager, and broadcaster (and mascot) from 1972 through 1974 are included, along with season recaps.
**Edited by Chip Greene**
**$29.95 paperback (ISBN 978-1-943816-07-1)**
**$9.99 ebook (ISBN 978-1-943816-06-4)**
8.5"X11", 600 pages, almost 100 photos

*SABR Members can purchase each book at a significant discount (often 50% off) and receive the ebook edtions free as a member benefit. Each book is available in a trade paperback edition as well as ebooks suitable for reading on a home computer or Nook, Kindle, or iPad/tablet.*
*To learn more about becoming a member of SABR, visit the website: sabr.org/join*

# The SABR Digital Library

The Society for American Baseball Research, the top baseball research organization in the world, disseminates some of the best in baseball history, analysis, and biography through our publishing programs. The SABR Digital Library contains a mix of books old and new, and focuses on a tandem program of paperback and ebook publication, making these materials widely available for both on digital devices and as traditional printed books.

## Greatest Games Books

*TIGERS BY THE TALE:*
*GREAT GAMES AT MICHIGAN AND TRUMBULL*
For over 100 years, Michigan and Trumbull was the scene of some of the most exciting baseball ever. This book portrays 50 classic games at the corner, spanning the earliest days of Bennett Park until Tiger Stadium's final closing act. From Ty Cobb to Mickey Cochrane, Hank Greenberg to Al Kaline, and Willie Horton to Alan Trammell.
**Edited by Scott Ferkovich**
**$12.95 paperback (ISBN 978-1-943816-21-7)**
**$6.99 ebook (ISBN 978-1-943816-20-0)**
**8.5"x11", 160 pages, 22 photos**

*FROM THE BRAVES TO THE BREWERS: GREAT GAMES AND HISTORY AT MILWAUKEE'S COUNTY STADIUM*
The National Pastime provides in-depth articles focused on the geographic region where the national SABR convention is taking place annually. The SABR 45 convention took place in Chicago, and here are 45 articles on baseball in and around the bat-and-ball crazed Windy City: 25 that appeared in the souvenir book of the convention plus another 20 articles available in ebook only.
**Edited by Gregory H. Wolf**
**$19.95 paperback (ISBN 978-1-943816-23-1)**
**$9.99 ebook (ISBN 978-1-943816-22-4)**
**8.5"X11", 290 pages, 58 photos**

*BRAVES FIELD:*
*MEMORABLE MOMENTS AT BOSTON'S LOST DIAMOND*
From its opening on August 18, 1915, to the sudden departure of the Boston Braves to Milwaukee before the 1953 baseball season, Braves Field was home to Boston's National League baseball club and also hosted many other events: from NFL football to championship boxing. The most memorable moments to occur in Braves Field history are portrayed here.
**Edited by Bill Nowlin and Bob Brady**
**$19.95 paperback (ISBN 978-1-933599-93-9)**
**$9.99 ebook (ISBN 978-1-933599-92-2)**
**8.5"X11", 282 pages, 182 photos**

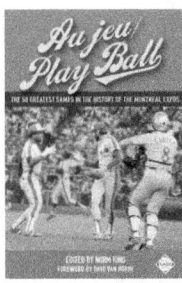

*AU JEU/PLAY BALL: THE 50 GREATEST GAMES IN THE HISTORY OF THE MONTREAL EXPOS*
The 50 greatest games in Montreal Expos history. The games described here recount the exploits of the many great players who wore Expos uniforms over the years—Bill Stoneman, Gary Carter, Andre Dawson, Steve Rogers, Pedro Martinez, from the earliest days of the franchise, to the glory years of 1979-1981, the what-might-have-been years of the early 1990s, and the sad, final days.and others.
**Edited by Norm King**
**$12.95 paperback (ISBN 978-1-943816-15-6)**
**$5.99 ebook (ISBN978-1-943816-14-9)**
**8.5"x11", 162 pages, 50 photos**

## Original SABR Research

*CALLING THE GAME:*
*BASEBALL BROADCASTING FROM 1920 TO THE PRESENT*
An exhaustive, meticulously researched history of bringing the national pastime out of the ballparks and into living rooms via the airwaves. Every play-by-play announcer, color commentator, and ex-ballplayer, every broadcast deal, radio station, and TV network. Plus a foreword by "Voice of the Chicago Cubs" Pat Hughes, and an afterword by Jacques Doucet, the "Voice of the Montreal Expos" 1972-2004.
**by Stuart Shea**
**$24.95 paperback (ISBN 978-1-933599-40-3)**
**$9.99 ebook (ISBN 978-1-933599-41-0)**
**7"X10", 712 pages, 40 photos**

## BioProject Books

*WHO'S ON FIRST:*
*REPLACEMENT PLAYERS IN WORLD WAR II*
During World War II, 533 players made the major league debuts. More than 60% of the players in the 1941 Opening Day lineups departed for the service and were replaced by first-times and oldsters. Hod Lisenbee was 46. POW Bert Shepard had an artificial leg, and Pete Gray had only one arm. The 1944 St. Louis Browns had 13 players classified 4-F. These are their stories.
**Edited by Marc Z Aaron and Bill Nowlin**
**$19.95 paperback (ISBN 978-1-933599-91-5)**
**$9.99 ebook (ISBN 978-1-933599-90-8)**
**8.5"X11", 422 pages, 67 photos**

*VAN LINGLE MUNGO:*
*THE MAN, THE SONG, THE PLAYERS*
40 baseball players with intriguing names have been named in renditions of Dave Frishberg's classic 1969 song, Van Lingle Mungo. This book presents biographies of all 40 players and additional information about one of the greatest baseball novelty songs of all time.
**Edited by Bill Nowlin**
**$19.95 paperback (ISBN 978-1-933599-76-2)**
**$9.99 ebook (ISBN 978-1-933599-77-9)**
**8.5"X11", 278 pages, 46 photos**

*NUCLEAR POWERED BASEBALL*
Nuclear Powered Baseball tells the stories of each player—past and present—featured in the classic Simpsons episode "Homer at the Bat." Wade Boggs, Ken Griffey Jr., Ozzie Smith, Nap Lajoie, Don Mattingly, and many more. We've also included a few very entertaining takes on the now-famous episode from prominent baseball writers Jonah Keri, Joe Posnanski, Erik Malinowski, and Bradley Woodrum.
**Edited by Emily Hawks and Bill Nowlin**
**$19.95 paperback (ISBN 978-1-943816-11-8)**
**$9.99 ebook (ISBN 978-1-943816-10-1)**
**8.5"X11", 250 pages**

*SABR Members can purchase each book at a significant discount (often 50% off) and receive the ebook edtions free as a member benefit. Each book is available in a trade paperback edition as well as ebooks suitable for reading on a home computer or Nook, Kindle, or iPad/tablet.*
*To learn more about becoming a member of SABR, visit the website: sabr.org/join*

# SABR BioProject Books

In 2002, the Society for American Baseball Research launched an effort to write and publish biographies of every player, manager, and individual who has made a contribution to baseball. Over the past decade, the BioProject Committee has produced over 2,200 biographical articles. Many have been part of efforts to create theme- or team-oriented books, spearheaded by chapters or other committees of SABR.

### THE YEAR OF THE BLUE SNOW:
### THE 1964 PHILADELPHIA PHILLIES
Catcher Gus Triandos dubbed the Philadelphia Phillies' 1964 season "the year of the blue snow," a rare thing that happens once in a great while. This book sheds light on lingering questions about the 1964 season—but any book about a team is really about the players. This work offers life stories of all the players and others (managers, coaches, owners, and broadcasters) associated with this star-crossed team, as well as essays of analysis and history.
**Edited by Mel Marmer and Bill Nowlin**
**$19.95 paperback (ISBN 978-1-933599-51-9)**
**$9.99 ebook (ISBN 978-1-933599-52-6)**
**8.5"X11", 356 PAGES, over 70 photos**

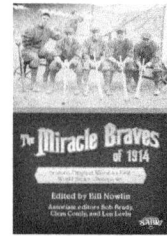

### THE MIRACLE BRAVES OF 1914
### BOSTON'S ORIGINAL WORST-TO-FIRST CHAMPIONS
Long before the Red Sox "Impossible Dream" season, Boston's now nearly forgotten "other" team, the 1914 Boston Braves, performed a baseball "miracle" that resounds to this very day. The "Miracle Braves" were Boston's first "worst-to-first" winners of the World Series. Refusing to throw in the towel at the midseason mark, George Stallings engineered a remarkable second-half climb in the standings all the way to first place.
**Edited by Bill Nowlin**
**$19.95 paperback (ISBN 978-1-933599-69-4)**
**$9.99 ebook (ISBN 978-1-933599-70-0)**
**8.5"X11", 392 PAGES, over 100 photos**

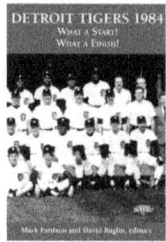

### DETROIT TIGERS 1984:
### WHAT A START! WHAT A FINISH!
The 1984 Detroit tigers roared out of the gate, winning their first nine games of the season and compiling an eye-popping 35-5 record after the campaign's first 40 games—still the best start ever for any team in major league history. This book brings together biographical profiles of every Tiger from that magical season, plus those of field management, top executives, the broadcasters—even venerable Tiger Stadium and the city itself.
**Edited by Mark Pattison and David Raglin**
**$19.95 paperback (ISBN 978-1-933599-44-1)**
**$9.99 ebook (ISBN 978-1-933599-45-8)**
**8.5"x11", 250 pages (Over 230,000 words!)**

### THAR'S JOY IN BRAVELAND!
### THE 1957 MILWAUKEE BRAVES
Few teams in baseball history have captured the hearts of their fans like the Milwaukee Braves of the 1950s. During the Braves' 13-year tenure in Milwaukee (1953-1965), they had a winning record every season, won two consecutive NL pennants (1957 and 1958), lost two more in the final week of the season (1956 and 1959), and set big-league attendance records along the way.
**Edited by Gregory H. Wolf**
**$19.95 paperback (ISBN 978-1-933599-71-7)**
**$9.99 ebook (ISBN 978-1-933599-72-4)**
**8.5"x11", 330 pages, over 60 photos**

### SWEET '60: THE 1960 PITTSBURGH PIRATES
A portrait of the 1960 team which pulled off one of the biggest upsets of the last 60 years. When Bill Mazeroski's home run left the park to win in Game Seven of the World Series, beating the New York Yankees, David had toppled Goliath. It was a blow that awakened a generation, one that millions of people saw on television, one of TV's first iconic World Series moments.
**Edited by Clifton Blue Parker and Bill Nowlin**
**$19.95 paperback (ISBN 978-1-933599-48-9)**
**$9.99 ebook (ISBN 978-1-933599-49-6)**
**8.5"X11", 340 pages, 75 photos**

### NEW CENTURY, NEW TEAM:
### THE 1901 BOSTON AMERICANS
The team now known as the Boston Red Sox played its first season in 1901. Boston had a well-established National League team, but the American League went head-to-head with the N.L. in Chicago, Philadelphia, and Boston. Chicago won the American League pennant and Boston finished second, only four games behind.
**Edited by Bill Nowlin**
**$19.95 paperback (ISBN 978-1-933599-58-8)**
**$9.99 ebook (ISBN 978-1-933599-59-5)**
**8.5"X11", 268 pages, over 125 photos**

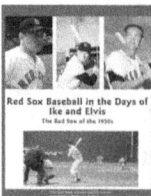

### RED SOX BASEBALL IN THE DAYS OF IKE AND ELVIS: THE RED SOX OF THE 1950S
Although the Red Sox spent most of the 1950s far out of contention, the team was filled with fascinating players who captured the heart of their fans. In *Red Sox Baseball*, members of SABR present 46 biographies on players such as Ted Williams and Pumpsie Green as well as season-by-season recaps.
**Edited by Mark Armour and Bill Nowlin**
**$19.95 paperback (ISBN 978-1-933599-24-3)**
**$9.99 ebook (ISBN 978-1-933599-34-2)**
**8.5"X11", 372 PAGES, over 100 photos**

### CAN HE PLAY?
### A LOOK AT BASEBALL SCOUTS AND THEIR PROFESSION
They dig through tons of coal to find a single diamond. Here in the world of scouts, we meet the "King of Weeds," a Ph.D. we call "Baseball's Renaissance Man," a husband-and-wife team, pioneering Latin scouts, and a Japanese-American interned during World War II who became a successful scout—and many, many more.
**Edited by Jim Sandoval and Bill Nowlin**
**$19.95 paperback (ISBN 978-1-933599-23-6)**
**$9.99 ebook (ISBN 978-1-933599-25-0)**
**8.5"X11", 200 PAGES, over 100 photos**

*SABR Members can purchase each book at a significant discount (often 50% off) and receive the ebook editions free as a member benefit. Each book is available in a trade paperback edition as well as ebooks suitable for reading on a home computer or Nook, Kindle, or iPad/tablet.*
*To learn more about becoming a member of SABR, visit the website: sabr.org/join*

www.ingramcontent.com/pod-product-compliance
Lightning Source LLC
Chambersburg PA
CBHW081152070526
44583CB00021B/2803